iOS

Apprentice

Sixth Edition

By Fahim Farook & Matthijs Hollemans

iOS Apprentice, Sixth Edition

Fahim Farook & Matthijs Hollemans. Copyright ©2017 Razeware LLC.

Notice of Rights

Notice of Liability

Trademarks

License

ISBN: 978-1-942878-39-1

About the team

(Author) Matthijs Hollemans is a mystic who lives at the top of a mountain where he spends all of his days and nights coding up awesome apps. Actually he lives below sea level in the Netherlands and is pretty down-to-earth but he does spend too much time in Xcode. Check out his website at www.matthijshollemans.com.

(Author) Fahim Farook is a developer with over 25 years of experience in developing in over a dozen different languages. Fahim's current focus is on mobile development with over 80 iOS apps and a few Android apps under his belt. He has lived in Sri Lanka, USA, Saudi Arabia, New Zealand, Singapore, Malaysia, France, and the UAE and enjoys science fiction and fantasy novels, TV shows, and movies. You can follow Fahim on Twitter at @FahimFarook.

(Editor) Chris Belanger is the Book Team Lead and Lead Editor for raywenderlich.com. He was a developer for nearly 20 years in various fields from e-health to aerial surveillance to industrial controls. If there are words to wrangle or a paragraph to ponder, he's on the case. When he kicks back, you can usually find Chris with guitar in hand, looking for the nearest beach. Twitter: @crispytwit.

About the cover

Striped dolphins live to about 55-60 years of age, can travel in pods numbering in the thousands and can dive to depths of 700 m to feed on fish, cephalopods and crustaceans. Baby dolphins don't sleep for a full a month after they're born. That puts two or three sleepless nights spent debugging code into perspective, doesn't it?

Table of Contents:

Section 1: Getting Started

This section introduces you to the first of the four apps you'll build over the course of this book - *Bull's Eye*.

As you progress through building the Bull's Eye app, the section will teach you how to think like a programmer and how to plan your programming tasks. In addition, you'll also learn how to use Xcode, Interface Builder and even the basics of coding for iOS.

While some of the concepts in this section might seem a bit basic, please do not skip this section if you are new to iOS development - you will learn some fundamentals which act as the building blocks for what you learn later.

Chapter 1: Introduction

Hi, welcome to *The iOS Apprentice: Beginning iOS Development with Swift, Sixth Edition*, the swiftest way (pardon the pun) to iOS development mastery!

In this book you'll learn how to make your own iPhone and iPad apps using Apple's Swift 4.0 programming language (and Xcode 9), by building four interesting iOS apps.

The apps you'll be making in The iOS Apprentice

Everybody likes games, right? So, you'll start by building a simple but fun iPhone game named *Bull's Eye*. It will teach you the basics of iPhone programming, and the other apps will build on what you learn there.

Taken together, the four apps you'll build cover everything you need to know to make your own apps. By the end of the book you'll be experienced enough to turn your ideas into real apps that you can put on the App Store!

Even if you've never programmed before or if you're new to iOS, you should be able to follow along with the step-by-step instructions and understand how these apps are made. Each chapter has a ton of illustrations to prevent you from getting lost. Not everything might make sense right away, but hang in there and all will become clear in time.

Writing your own iOS apps is a lot of fun, but it's also hard work. If you have the imagination and perseverance, there is no limit to what you can make your apps do. It is my sincere belief that this book can turn you from a complete newbie into an accomplished iOS developer, but you do have to put in the time and effort. By writing this book, I've done my part. The rest is up to you…

About this book

The iOS Apprentice will help you become an excellent iOS developer, but only if you let it. Here are some tips that will help you get the most out of this book.

Learn through repetition

You're going to make several apps in this book. Even though the apps will start out quite simple, you may find the instructions hard to follow at first – especially if you've never done any computer programming before – because I will be introducing a lot of new concepts.

It's OK if you don't understand everything right away, as long as you get the general idea. As you proceed through the book, you'll go over many of these concepts again and again until they solidify in your mind.

Follow the instructions yourself

It is important that you not just read the instructions but also actually **follow them**. Open Xcode, type in the source code fragments, and run the app in the Simulator. This helps you to see how the app gets built step by step.

Even better, play around with the code and with the Xcode settings. Feel free to modify any part of the app and see what the results are - make a small change to the code and see how it affects the entire app. Experiment and learn! Don't worry about breaking stuff – that's half the fun. You can always find your way back to the beginning. But better still, you might even learn something from simply breaking the code and learning how to fix it.

Don't panic – bugs happen!

You will run into problems, guaranteed. Your programs will have strange bugs that will leave you stumped. Trust me, I've been programming for 30 years and that still happens to me too. We're only humans and our brains have a limited capacity to deal with complex programming problems. In this book, I will give you tools for your mental toolbox that will allow you to find your way out of any hole you have dug for yourself.

Understanding beats copy-pasting

Too many people attempt to write iOS apps by blindly copy-pasting code that they find on blogs and other websites, without really knowing what that code does or how it should fit into their program.

There is nothing wrong with looking on the web for solutions – I do it all the time – but I want to give you the tools and knowledge to understand what you're doing and why. That way you'll learn quicker and write better programs.

This is hands-on practical advice, not a bunch of dry theory (although we can't avoid *some* theory). You are going to build real apps right from the start and I'll explain how everything works along the way, with lots of pictures that illustrate what is going on.

I will do my best to make it clear how everything fits together, why we do things a certain way, and what the alternatives are.

Do the exercises

I will also ask you to do some thinking of your own – yes, there are exercises! It's in your best interest to actually do these exercises. There is a big difference between knowing the path and walking the path… And the only way to learn programming is to do it.

I encourage you to not just do the exercises but also to play with the code you'll be writing. Experiment, make changes, try to add new features. Software is a complex piece of machinery and to find out how it works you sometimes have to put some spokes in the wheels and take the whole thing apart. That's how you learn!

Have fun!

Last but not least, remember to have fun! Step by step you will build up your understanding of programming while making fun apps. By the end of this book you'll have learned the essentials of Swift and the iOS development kit. More importantly, you should have a pretty good idea of how everything goes together and how to think like a programmer.

It is my aim that by the time you reach the end of the book you will have learned enough to stand on your own two feet as a developer. I am confident that eventually you'll be able to write any iOS app you want as long as you get those basics down. You still may have a lot to learn, but when you're through with *The iOS Apprentice*, you can do without the training wheels.

Who this book is for

This book is great whether you are completely new to programming, or whether you come from a different programming background and are looking to learn iOS development.

If you're a complete beginner, don't worry – this book doesn't assume you know anything about programming or making apps. Of course, if you do have programming experience, that helps. Swift is a new programming language but in many ways it's similar to other popular languages such as PHP, C#, or JavaScript.

If you've tried iOS development before with the old language, Objective-C, then its low-level nature and strange syntax may have put you off. Well, there's good news: now that we have a modern language in Swift, iOS development has become a lot easier to pick up.

It is not my aim with this book to teach you all the ins and outs of iOS development. The iOS SDK (Software Development Kit) is huge and there is no way we can cover everything. Fortunately, we don't need to. You just need to master the essential building blocks of Swift and the iOS SDK. Once you understand these fundamentals, you can easily find out by yourself how the other parts of the SDK work and learn the rest on your own terms.

The most important thing I'll be teaching you, is how to think like a programmer. That will help you approach any programming task, whether it's a game, a utility, a mobile app that uses web service, or anything else you can imagine.

As a programmer you'll often have to think your way through difficult computational problems and find creative solutions. By methodically analyzing these problems you will be able to solve them, no matter how complex. Once you possess this valuable skill, you can program anything!

iOS 11 and better only

The code in this book is aimed exclusively at iOS version 11 and later. Each new release of iOS is such a big departure from the previous one that it just doesn't make sense anymore to keep developing for older devices and iOS versions. Things move fast in the world of mobile computing!

The majority of iPhone, iPod touch, and iPad users are pretty quick to upgrade to the latest version of iOS anyway, so you don't need to be too worried that you're leaving potential users behind.

Owners of older devices, such as the iPhone 4S, iPhone 5, or the first iPads, may be stuck with older iOS versions but this is only a tiny portion of the market. The cost of supporting these older iOS versions for your apps is usually greater than the handful of extra customers it brings you.

It's ultimately up to you to decide whether it's worth making your app available to users with older devices, but my recommendation is that you focus your efforts where they matter most. Apple as a company always relentlessly looks towards the future – if you want to play in Apple's backyard, it's wise to follow their lead. So back to the future it is!

What you need

It's a lot of fun to develop for the iPhone and iPad, but like most hobbies (or businesses!) it will cost some money. Of course, once you get good at it and build an awesome app, you'll have the potential to make that money back many times.

You will have to invest in the following:

iPhone, iPad, or iPod touch. I'm assuming that you have at least one of these. iOS 11 runs on the following devices: iPhone 5s or newer, iPad 5th generation or newer, iPad mini 2 or newer, 6th generation iPod touch - basically any device which has a 64-bit processor. With iOS 11, Apple dropped support for 32-bit processors and apps. If you have an older device, then this is a good time to think about getting an upgrade. But don't worry if you don't have a suitable device: you can do most of your testing on the Simulator.

> **Note:** Even though I mostly talk about the iPhone in this book, everything I say applies equally to the iPad and iPod touch. Aside from small hardware differences, they all use iOS and you program them in exactly the same way. You should also

be able to run the apps from this book on your iPad or iPod touch without problems.

Mac computer with an Intel processor. Any Mac that you've bought in the last few years will do, even a Mac mini or MacBook Air. It needs to have at least macOS 10.12.4 Sierra. Xcode, the development environment for iOS apps, is a memory-hungry tool. So, having 4 GB of RAM in your Mac is no luxury. You might be able to get by with less, but do yourself a favor and upgrade your Mac. The more RAM, the better. A smart developer invests in good tools!

With some workarounds it is possible to develop iOS apps on Windows or a Linux machine, or a regular PC that has macOS installed (a so-called "Hackintosh"), but you'll save yourself a lot of hassle by just getting a Mac.

If you can't afford to buy the latest model, then consider getting a second-hand Mac from eBay. Just make sure it meets the minimum requirements (Intel CPU, preferably more than 2 GB RAM). Should you happen to buy a machine that has an older version of OS X (10.11 El Capitan or earlier), you can upgrade to the latest version of macOS from the online Mac App Store for free.

Apple Developer Program account. You can download all the development tools for free and you can try out your apps on your own iPhone, iPad, or iPod touch while you're developing, so you don't have to join the Apple Developer Program just yet. But to submit finished apps to the App Store you will have to enroll in the paid developer program. This will cost you $99 per year.

See developer.apple.com/programs/ for more info.

Xcode

The first order of business is to download and install Xcode and the iOS SDK.

Xcode is the development tool for iOS apps. It has a text editor where you'll type in your source code and it has a visual editor for designing your app's user interface.

Xcode transforms the source code that you write into an executable app and launches it in the Simulator or on your iPhone. Because no app is bug-free, Xcode also has a debugger that helps you find defects in your code (unfortunately, it won't automatically fix them for you, that's still something you have to do yourself).

You can download Xcode for free from the Mac App Store (apple.co/2wzi1L9). This requires at least an up-to-date version of macOS Sierra (10.12.4), so if you're still running an older version of macOS, you'll first have to upgrade to the latest version of macOS (also available for free from the Mac App Store). Get ready for a big download, as the full Xcode package is about 5 GB.

Important: You may already have a version of Xcode on your system that came pre-installed with your version of macOS. That version could be hopelessly outdated, so don't use it. Apple puts out new releases on a regular basis and you are encouraged to always develop with the latest Xcode and the latest available SDK on the latest version of macOS.

I wrote this revision of this book with **Xcode version 9** and the **iOS 11** SDK on macOS Sierra (10.12.6). By the time you're reading this, the version numbers might have gone up again. I will do my best to keep the PDF versions of the book up-to-date with new releases of the development tools and iOS versions but don't panic if the screenshots don't correspond 100% to what you see on your screen. In most cases, the differences will be minor.

Many older books and blog posts (anything before 2010) talk about Xcode 3, which is radically different from Xcode 9. More recent material may mention Xcode versions 4, 5, 6, 7, or 8, which at first glance are similar to Xcode 9 but differ in many of the details. So if you're reading an article and you see a picture of Xcode that looks different from yours, they might be talking about an older version. You may still be able to get something out of those articles, as the programming examples are still valid. It's just Xcode that is slightly different.

What's ahead: an overview

The iOS Apprentice is spread across four apps, moving from beginning to intermediate topics. For each app, you will build it from start to finish, from scratch! Let's take a look at what's ahead.

App 1: Bull's Eye

You'll start off by building a game called *Bull's Eye*. You'll learn how to use Xcode, Interface Builder, and Swift in an easy to understand manner.

App 2: Checklists

For your next app, you'll create your own to-do list app. You'll learn about the fundamental design patterns that all iOS apps use, and about table views, navigation controllers, and delegates. Now you're making apps for real!

App 3: MyLocations

For your third app, you'll develop a location-aware app that lets you keep a list of spots that you find interesting. In the process, you'll learn about Core Location, Core Data, Map Kit, and much more!

App 4: StoreSearch

Mobile apps often need to talk to web services and that's what you'll do in you final app. You'll make a stylish app that lets you search for products on the iTunes store using HTTP requests and JSON.

Let's get started and turn you into a real iOS developer!

The language of the computer

The iPhone may pretend that it's a phone but it's really a pretty advanced computer that also happens to have the ability to make phone calls.

Like any computer, the iPhone works with ones and zeros. When you write software to run on the iPhone, you somehow have to translate the ideas in your head into those ones and zeros that the computer can understand.

Fortunately, you don't have to write any ones and zeros yourself. That would be a bit too much to ask of the human brain. On the other hand, everyday English is not precise enough to use for programming computers.

So, you will use an intermediary language, Swift, that is a little bit like English so it's reasonably straightforward for us humans to understand, while at the same time it can be easily translated into something the computer can understand as well.

This is an approximation of the language that the computer speaks:

```
Ltmp96:
        .cfi_def_cfa_register %ebp
        pushl   %esi
        subl    $36, %esp
Ltmp97:
        .cfi_offset %esi, -12
        calll   L7$pb
L7$pb:
        popl    %eax
        movl    16(%ebp), %ecx
        movl    12(%ebp), %edx
        movl    8(%ebp), %esi
        movl    %esi, -8(%ebp)
        movl    %edx, -12(%ebp)
        movl    %ecx, (%esp)
        movl    %eax, -24(%ebp)
        calll   _objc_retain
        movl    %eax, -16(%ebp)
        .loc    1 161 2 prologue_end
```

Actually, what the computer sees is this:

```
0001100101001111010010001100111110010100
0010100010011110101101100111101101101001
0101000111001111101011101100001110001100
1001000001110001010011010011110011001100111
```

The movl and calll instructions are just there to make things more readable for humans. I don't know about you, but for me it's still hard to make much sense out of it.

It certainly is possible to write programs in that arcane language – that is what people used to do in the old days when computers cost a few million bucks apiece and took up a whole room – but I'd rather write programs that look like this:

```swift
func handleMusicEvent(command: Int, noteNumber: Int, velocity:
Int) {

  if command == NoteOn && velocity != 0 {
    playNote(noteNumber + transpose, velocityCurve[velocity] /
127)

  } else if command == NoteOff ||
            (command == NoteOn && velocity == 0) {
    stopNote(noteNumber + transpose, velocityCurve[velocity] /
127)

  } else if command == ControlChange {
    if noteNumber == 64 {
      damperPedal(velocity)
    }
  }
}
```

The above code snippet is from a sound synthesizer program. It looks like something that almost makes sense. Even if you've never programmed before, you can sort of figure out what's going on. It's almost English.

Swift is a hot new language that combines traditional object-oriented programming with aspects of functional programming. Fortunately, Swift has many things in common with other popular programming languages, so if you're already familiar with C#, Python, Ruby, or JavaScript you'll feel right at home with Swift.

Swift is not the only option for making apps. Until recently, iOS apps were programmed in Objective-C, which is an object-oriented extension of the tried-and-true C language. Because of its heritage, Objective-C has some rough edges and is not really up to the demands of modern developers. That's why Apple created a new language.

Objective-C will still be around for a while but it's obvious that the future of iOS development is Swift. All the cool kids are using it already.

C++ is another language that adds object-oriented programming to C. It is very powerful but as a beginning programmer you probably want to stay away from it. I only mention it because C++ can also be used to write iOS apps, and there is an unholy marriage of C++ and Objective-C named Objective-C++ that you may come across from time to time.

I could have started *The iOS Apprentice* with an in-depth exploration of the features of Swift, but you'd probably fall asleep halfway. So instead, I will explain the language as we go along, very briefly at first but more in-depth later.

In the beginning, the general concepts – what is a variable, what is an object, how do you call a method, and so on – are more important than the details. Slowly but surely, all the arcane secrets of the Swift language will be revealed to you!

Are you ready to begin writing your first iOS app?

Book source code and forums

You can get the source code for the book here:

www.raywenderlich.com/store/ios-apprentice/source-code

We've also set up an official forum for the book at forums.raywenderlich.com.

This is a great place to ask any questions you have about the book or about making iOS apps in general, or to submit any errata you may find.

Digital editions

We also have PDF and ePub digital editions of this book available, which can be handy if you want a soft copy to take with you, or you want to quickly search for a specific term within the book.

Buying the digital edition of the book also has a few extra benefits: free updates each time we update the book, access to older versions of the book, and you can download the digital editions from anywhere, at anytime.

Visit the book store page here:

• https://store.raywenderlich.com/products/ios-apprentice.

And since you purchased the print version of this book, you're eligible to upgrade to the digital edition at a significant discount!

Simply email support@razeware.com with your receipt for the physical copy and we'll get you set up with the discounted digital edition of the book.

Chapter 2: The One-Button App

There's an old Chinese proverb that "A journey of a thousand miles begins with a single step." You are about to take that first step on your journey to iOS developer mastery. And you will take that first step by creating the *Bull's Eye* game.

This chapter covers the following:

- **The Bull's Eye game:** An introduction to the first app you'll make.

- **The one-button app:** Creating a simple one-button app where the button can take an action based on a tap on the button.

- **The anatomy of an app:** A brief explanation as to the inner-workings of an app.

The Bull's Eye game

This is what the *Bull's Eye* game will look like when you're finished:

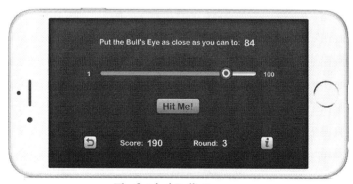

The finished Bull's Eye game

The objective of the game is to put the bull's eye, which is on a slider that goes from 1 to 100, as close to a randomly chosen target value as you can. In the screenshot above, the aim is to put the bull's eye at 84. Because you can't see the current value of the slider, you'll have to "eyeball" it.

When you're confident of your estimate, you press the "Hit Me!" button and a popup, also known as an alert, will tell you what your score is:

An alert popup shows the score

The closer to the target value you are, the more points you score. After you dismiss the alert popup by pressing the OK button, a new round begins with a new random target. The game repeats until the player presses the "Start Over" button (the curly arrow in the bottom-left corner), which resets the score to 0.

This game probably won't make you an instant millionaire on the App Store, but even future millionaires have to start somewhere!

Make a programming to-do list

Exercise: Now that you've seen what the game will look like and what the gameplay rules are, make a list of all the things that you think you'll need to do in order to build this game. It's OK if you draw a blank, but give it a shot anyway.

I'll give you an example:

The app needs to put the "Hit Me!" button on the screen and show an alert popup when the user presses it.

Try to think of other things the app needs to do – it doesn't matter if you don't actually know how to accomplish these tasks. The first step is to figure out *what* you need to do; *how* to do these things is not important yet.

Once you know what you want, you can also figure out how to do it, even if you have to ask someone or look it up. But the "what" comes first. (You'd be surprised at how many people start writing code without a clear idea of what they're actually trying to achieve. No wonder they get stuck!)

Whenever I start working on a new app, I first make a list of all the different pieces of functionality I think the app will need. This becomes my programming to-do list. Having a list that breaks up a design into several smaller steps is a great way to deal with the complexity of a project.

You may have a cool idea for an app but when you sit down to write the program the whole thing can seem overwhelming. There is so much to do… and where to begin? By cutting up the workload into small steps you make the project less daunting – you can always find a step that is simple and small enough to make a good starting point and take it from there.

It's no big deal if this exercise is giving you difficulty. You're new to all of this! As your understanding grows of how software and the development process works, it will become easier to identify the different parts that make up a design, and to split it into manageable pieces.

This is what I came up with. I simply took the gameplay description and cut it into very small chunks:

- Put a button on the screen and label it "Hit Me!"

- When the player presses the Hit Me button the app has to show an alert popup to inform the player how well they did. Somehow you have to calculate the score and put that into this alert.

- Put text on the screen, such as the "Score:" and "Round:" labels. Some of this text changes over time, for example the score, which increases when the player scores points.

- Put a slider on the screen and make it go between the values 1 and 100.

- Read the value of the slider after the user presses the Hit Me button.

- Generate a random number at the start of each round and display it on the screen. This is the target value.

- Compare the value of the slider to that random number and calculate a score based on how far off the player is. You show this score in the alert popup.

- Put the Start Over button on the screen. Make it reset the score and put the player back into the first round.

- Put the app in landscape orientation.

- Make it look pretty. :]

I might have missed a thing or two, but this looks like a decent list to start with. Even for a game as basic as this, there are quite a few things you need to do. Making apps is fun, but it's definitely a lot of work too!

The one-button app

Let's start at the top of the list and make an extremely simple first version of the game that just displays a single button. When you press the button, the app pops up an alert message. That's all you are going to do for now. Once you have this working, you can build the rest of the game on this foundation.

The app will look like this:

The app contains a single button (left) that shows an alert when pressed (right)

Time to start coding! I'm assuming you have downloaded and installed the latest version of the SDK and the development tools at this point.

In this book, you'll be working with **Xcode 9.0** or better. Newer versions of Xcode may also work but anything older than version 9.0 probably would be a no-go.

Because Swift is a very new language, it tends to change between versions of Xcode. If your Xcode is too old – or too new! – then not all of the code in this book may work properly. (For this same reason you're advised not to use beta versions of Xcode, only the official one from the Mac App Store.)

Create a new project

➤ Launch Xcode. If you have trouble locating the Xcode application, you can find it in the folder **/Applications/Xcode** or in your Launchpad. Because I use Xcode all the time, I placed its icon in my dock for easy access.

Xcode shows the "Welcome to Xcode" window when it starts:

Xcode bids you welcome

➤ Choose **Create a new Xcode project**. The main Xcode window appears with an assistant that lets you choose a template:

Choosing the template for the new project

Xcode has bundled templates for a variety of application styles. Xcode will make a pre-configured project for you based on the template you choose. The new project will already include some of the source files you need. These templates are handy because they can save you a lot of typing. They are ready-made starting points.

➤ Select **Single View Application** and press **Next**.

This opens a screen where you can enter options for the new app.

Configuring the new project

➤ Fill out these options as follows:

• Product Name: **BullsEye**. If you want to use proper English, you can name the project Bull's Eye instead of BullsEye, but it's best to avoid spaces and other special characters in project names.

• Team: If you already are a member of the Apple Developer Program, this will show your team name. For now, it's best to leave this setting alone; we'll get back to this later on.

• Organization Name: Fill in your own name here or the name of your company.

• Organization Identifier: Mine says "com.razeware". That is the identifier I use for my apps. As is customary, it is my domain name written in reverse. You should use your own identifier here. Pick something that is unique to you, either the domain name of your website (but backwards) or simply your own name. You can always change this later.

• Language: **Swift**

Make sure the three options at the bottom – Use Core Data, Include Unit Tests, and Include UI Tests – are *not* selected. You won't be using those in this project.

➤ Press **Next**. Now Xcode will ask where to save your project:

Choosing where to save the project

➤ Choose a location for the project files, for example the Desktop or your Documents folder.

Xcode will automatically make a new folder for the project using the Product Name that you entered in the previous step (in your case BullsEye), so you don't need to make a new folder yourself.

At the bottom there is a checkbox that says, "Create Git repository on My Mac". You can ignore this for now. You'll learn about the Git version control system later on.

➤ Press **Create** to finish.

Xcode will now create a new project named BullsEye, based on the Single View Application template, in the folder you specified.

When it is done, the screen should look something like this:

The main Xcode window at the start of your project

There may be small differences with what you're seeing on your own computer if you're using a version of Xcode newer than my version. Rest assured, any differences will only be superficial.

Note: If you don't see a file named ViewController.swift in the list on the left but instead have ViewController.h and ViewController.m, then you picked the wrong language (Objective-C) when you created the project. Start over and be sure to choose Swift as the programming language.

Run your project

➤ Press the **Run** button in the top-left corner.

Press Run to launch the app

> **Note:** If this is the first time you're using Xcode, it may ask you to enable developer mode. Click **Enable** and enter your password to allow Xcode to make these changes.
>
> Also, make sure that you do not have your iPhone or iPad plugged in at this point to your computer, for example, for charging. If you do, it might switch to the actual device instead of the Simulator for running the app and since you are not yet set up for running on device, this could result in errors that might leave you scratching your head :]

Xcode will labor for a bit and then launch your brand new app in the iOS Simulator. The app may not look like much yet – and there is not anything you can do with it either – but this is an important first milestone in your journey!

What an app based on the Single View Application template looks like

If Xcode says "Build Failed" or "Xcode cannot run using the selected device" when you press the Run button, then make sure the picker at the top of the window says **BullsEye > iPhone SE** (or any other model number) and not **Generic iOS Device**:

Making Xcode run the app on the Simulator

If your iPhone is currently connected to your Mac via USB cable, Xcode may have attempted to run the app on your iPhone and that may not work without some additional setting up. I'll show you how to get the app to run on your iPhone so you can show it off to your friends soon, but for now just stick with the Simulator.

➤ Next to the Run button is the **Stop** button (the square thingy). Press that to exit the app.

On your phone (or even the simulator) you'd use the home button to exit an app (on the Simulator you could also use the **Hardware → Home** item from the menu bar or use the handy ⇧+⌘+H shortcut), but that won't actually terminate the app. It will disappear from the Simulator's screen but the app stays suspended in the Simulator's memory, just as it would on a real iPhone.

Until you press Stop, Xcode's activity viewer at the top says "Running BullsEye on iPhone SE":

The Xcode activity viewer

It's not really necessary to stop the app, as you can go back to Xcode and make changes to the source code while the app is still running. However, these changes will not become active until you press Run again. That will terminate any running version of the app, build a new version, and launch it in the Simulator.

What happens when you press Run?

Xcode will first *compile* your source code – that is: translate it – from Swift into machine code that the iPhone (or the Simulator) can understand. Even though the programming language for writing iOS apps is Swift or Objective-C, the iPhone itself doesn't speak those languages. A translation step is necessary.

The compiler is the part of Xcode that converts your Swift source code into executable binary code. It also gathers all the different components that make up the app – source files, images, storyboard files, and so on – and puts them into the "application bundle".

This entire process is also known as *building* the app. If there are any errors (such as spelling mistakes for method names), the build will fail. If everything goes according to plan, Xcode copies the application bundle to the Simulator or the iPhone and launches the app. All that from a single press of the Run button.

Add a button

I'm sure you're as unimpressed as I am with an app that just displays a dull white screen :] So, let's make it a bit more interesting by adding a button to it.

The left pane of the Xcode window is named the **Navigator area**. The row of icons along the top lets you select a specific navigator. The default navigator is the **Project navigator**, which shows the files in your project.

The organization of these files roughly corresponds to the project folder on your hard disk, but that isn't necessarily always so. You can move files around and put them into new groups and organize away to your heart's content. We'll talk more about the different files in your project later.

➤ In the **Project navigator**, find the item named **Main.storyboard** and click it once to select it:

The Project navigator lists the files in the project

Like a superhero changing his/her clothes in a phone booth, the main editing pane now transforms into the **Interface Builder**. This tool lets you drag-and-drop user interface components such as buttons to create the UI of your app. (OK, bad analogy, but Interface Builder is a super tool in my opinion.)

➤ If it's not already blue, click the **Hide or show utilities** button in Xcode's toolbar.

Click this button to show the Utilities pane

These toolbar buttons change the appearance of Xcode. This one in particular opens a new pane on the right side of the Xcode window.

Your Xcode should now look something like this:

Editing Main.storyboard in Interface Builder

This is the *storyboard* for your app. The storyboard contains the designs for all of your app's screens, and shows the navigation flow in your app from one screen to another.

Currently, the storyboard contains just a single screen or *scene*, represented by a rectangle in the middle of the Interface Builder canvas.

> **Note:** If you don't see the rectangle labeled "View Controller" but only an empty white canvas, then use your mouse or trackpad to scroll the storyboard around a bit. Trust me, it's in there somewhere! Also make sure your Xcode window is large enough. Interface Builder takes up a lot of space…

The scene currently has the size of an iPhone 8. To keep things simple, you will first design the app for the iPhone SE, which has a slightly smaller screen. Later you'll also make the app fit on the larger iPhone models.

➤ At the bottom of the Interface Builder window, click **View as: iPhone 8** to open up the following panel:

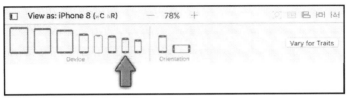

Choosing the device type

Select the **iPhone SE**, the second smallest iPhone, thus resizing the preview UI you see in Interface Builder to be set to that of an iPhone SE. You'll notice that the scene's rectangle now becomes a bit smaller, corresponding to the screen size of the iPhone 5, iPhone 5s, and iPhone SE models.

➤ In the Xcode toolbar, make sure it says **BullsEye > iPhone SE** (next to the Stop button). If it doesn't then click it and pick iPhone SE from the list:

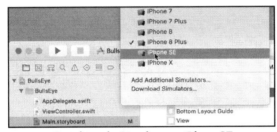

Switching the Simulator to iPhone SE

Now when you run the app, it will run on the iPhone SE Simulator (try it out!).

Back to the storyboard:

➤ At the bottom of the Utilities pane you will find the **Object Library** (make sure the third button, the one that looks like a circle, is selected):

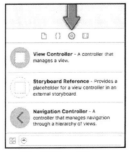

The Object Library

Scroll through the items in the Object Library's list until you see **Button**. (Alternatively, you can type the word "button" in to the search/filter box at the bottom of the Object Library.)

➤ Click on **Button** and drag it into the working area, on top of the scene's rectangle.

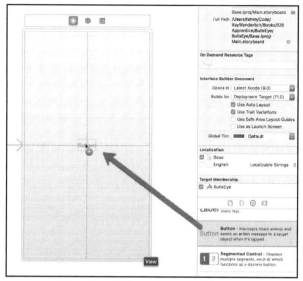

Dragging the button on top of the scene

That's how easy it is to add new buttons, just drag & drop. That goes for all other user interface elements too. You'll be doing a lot of this, so take some time to get familiar with the process.

➤ Drag-and-drop a few other controls, such as labels, sliders, and switches, just to get the hang of it.

This should give you some idea of the UI controls that are available in iOS. Notice that the Interface Builder helps you to layout your controls by snapping them to the edges of the view and to other objects. It's a very handy tool!

➤ Double-click the button to edit its title. Call it Hit Me!

The button with the new title

It's possible that your button has a border around it:

The button with a bounds rectangle

This border is not part of the button, it's just there to show you how large the button is. You can turn these rectangles on or off using the **Editor → Canvas → Show Bounds Rectangles** menu option.

When you're done playing with Interface Builder, press the Run button from Xcode's toolbar. The app should now appear in the Simulator, complete with your "Hit Me!" button. However, when you tap the button it doesn't do anything yet. For that you'll have to write some Swift code!

The source code editor

A button that doesn't do anything when tapped is of no use to anyone. So, let's make it show an alert popup. In the finished game the alert will display the player's score, but for now we shall limit ourselves to a simple text message (the traditional "Hello, World!").

➤ In the **Project navigator**, click on **ViewController.swift**.

The Interface Builder will disappear and the editor area now contains a bunch of brightly colored text. This is the Swift source code for your app:

The source code editor

Note: If your Xcode editor window does not show the line numbers as in the screenshot above, and you'd actually like to see the line numbers, from the menu bar choose **Xcode** → **Preferences...** → **Text Editing** and go to the **Editing** tab. There, you should see a **Line numbers** checkbox under **Show** - check it.

➤ Add the following lines directly above the very last } bracket in the file:

```
@IBAction func showAlert() {
}
```

The source code for **ViewController.swift** should now look like this:

```
//
//  ViewController.swift
//  BullsEye
//
//  Created by <you> on <date>.
//  Copyright © <year> <your organization>. All rights reserved.
//

import UIKit

class ViewController: UIViewController {

  override func viewDidLoad() {
    super.viewDidLoad()
    // Do any additional setup after loading the view, typically
from a nib.
  }

  override func didReceiveMemoryWarning() {
    super.didReceiveMemoryWarning()
    // Dispose of any resources that can be recreated.
  }

  @IBAction func showAlert() {
  }
}
```

Before I can tell you what this all means, I have to introduce the concept of a view controller.

Xcode will autosave

You don't have to save your files after you make changes to them because Xcode will automatically save any modified files when you press the Run button.

Nevertheless, Xcode isn't the most stable piece of software out there and occasionally it may crash on you before it has had a chance to save your changes.

Therefore, I still like to press ⌘+S on a regular basis to save my files.

View controllers

You've edited the **Main.storyboard** file to build the user interface of the app. It's only a button on a white background, but a user interface nonetheless. You also added source code to **ViewController.swift**.

These two files – the storyboard and the Swift file – together form the design and implementation of a *view controller*. A lot of the work in building iOS apps is making view controllers. The job of a view controller is to manage a single screen in your app.

Take a simple cookbook app, for example. When you launch the cookbook app, its main screen lists the available recipes. Tapping a recipe opens a new screen that shows the recipe in detail with an appetizing photo and cooking instructions. Each of these screens is managed by a view controller.

The view controllers in a simple cookbook app

What these two screens do is very different. One is a list of several items; the other presents a detail view of a single item.

That's why you need two view controllers: one that knows how to deal with lists, and another that can handle images and cooking instructions. One of the design principles of iOS is that each screen in your app gets its own view controller.

Currently *Bull's Eye* has only one screen (the white one with the button) and thus only needs one view controller. That view controller is simply named "ViewController" and the storyboard and Swift file work together to implement it. (If you are curious, you can check the connection between the screen and the code for it by switching to the Identity inspector on the right sidebar of Xcode in the storyboard view. The class value shows the current class associated with the storyboard scene.)

Simply put, the Main.storyboard file contains the design of the view controller's user interface, while ViewController.swift contains its functionality – the logic that makes the user interface work, written in the Swift language.

Because you used the Single View Application template, Xcode automatically created the view controller for you. Later you will add a second screen to the game and you will create your own view controller for that.

Make connections

The line of source code you have just added to ViewController.swift lets Interface Builder know that the controller has a "showAlert" action, which presumably will show an alert popup. You will now connect the button on the storyboard to that action in your source code.

➤ Click **Main.storyboard** to go back into Interface Builder.

In Interface Builder, there should be a second pane on the left, next to the navigator area, the **Document Outline**, that lists all the items in your storyboard. If you do not see that pane, click the small toggle button in the bottom-left corner of the Interface Builder canvas to reveal it.

The button that shows the Document Outline pane

➤ Click the **Hit Me button** once to select it.

With the Hit Me button selected, hold down the **Control** key, click on the button and drag up to the **View Controller** item in the Document Outline. You should see a blue line going from the button up to View Controller.

(Instead of holding down Control, you can also right-click and drag, but don't let go of the mouse button before you start dragging.)

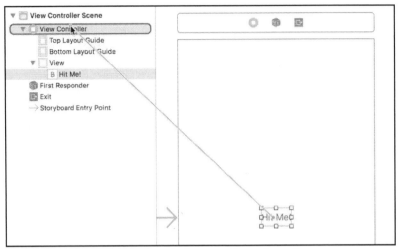

Ctrl-drag from the button to View Controller

Once you're on View Controller, let go of the mouse button and a small menu will appear. It contains two sections, "Action Segue" and "Sent Events", with one or more options below each. You're interested in the **showAlert** option under Sent Events. The Sent Events section shows all possible actions in your source code that can be hooked up to your storyboad and **showAlert** is the name of the action that you added earlier in the source code of **ViewController.swift**.

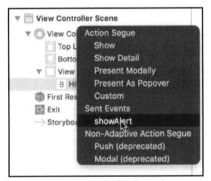

The popup menu with the showAlert action

➤ Click on **showAlert** to select it. This instructs Interface Builder to make a connection between the button and the line @IBAction func showAlert().

From now on, whenever the button is tapped the showAlert action will be performed. That is how you make buttons and other controls do things: you define an action in the view controller's Swift file and then you make the connection in Interface Builder.

You can see that the connection was made by going to the **Connections inspector** in the Utilities pane on the right side of the Xcode window.

➤ Click the small arrow-shaped button at the top of the pane to switch to the Connections inspector:

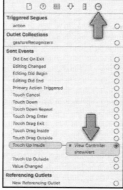

The inspector shows the connections from the button to any other objects

In the Sent Events section, the "Touch Up Inside" event is now connected to the showAlert action. You can also see the connection in the Swift file.

➤ Select **ViewController.swift** to edit it.

Notice how to the left of the line with `@IBAction func showAlert()`, there is a solid circle? Click on that circle to reveal what this action is connected to.

```
override func didReceiveMemoryWarning() {
    super.didReceiveMemoryWarning()
    // Dispose of any resources that can be
}

@IBAction func showAlert() {
}
}
```

A solid circle means the action is connected to something

Act on the button

You now have a screen with a button. The button is hooked up to an action named showAlert that will be performed when the user taps the button.

Currently, however, the action is empty and nothing will happen (try it out by running the app again, if you like). You need to give the app more instructions.

➤ In **ViewController.swift**, modify showAlert to look like the following:

```
@IBAction func showAlert() {
  let alert = UIAlertController(title: "Hello, World",
                               message: "This is my first app!",
                      preferredStyle: .alert)
```

```
    let action = UIAlertAction(title: "Awesome", style: .default,
                               handler: nil)

  alert.addAction(action)

  present(alert, animated: true, completion: nil)
}
```

The new lines of code implement the actual alert display functionality.

The commands between the { } brackets tell the iPhone what to do, and they are performed from top to bottom.

The code in showAlert creates an alert with a title "Hello, World", a message "This is my first app!" and a single button labeled "Awesome".

If you're not sure about the distinction between the title and the message: both show text, but the title is slightly bigger and in a bold typeface.

➤ Click the **Run** button from Xcode's toolbar. If you didn't make any typos, your app should launch in the Simulator and you should see the alert box when you tap the button.

The alert popup in action

Congratulations, you've just written your first iOS app! What you just did may have been mostly gibberish to you, but that shouldn't matter. We take it one small step at a time.

You can strike off the first two items from the to-do list already: putting a button on the screen and showing an alert when the user taps the button.

Take a little break, let it all sink in, and come back when you're ready for more! You're only just getting started...

> **Note:** Just in case you get stuck, I have provided the complete Xcode projects which are snapshots of the project as at the beginning and end of each chapter. That way you can compare your version of the app to mine, or – if you really make a mess of things – continue from a version that is known to work.

You can find the project files for each chapter in the corresponding folder.

Problems?

If Xcode gives you a "Build Failed" error message after you press Run, then make sure you typed in everything correctly. Even the smallest mistake could potentially confuse Xcode. It can be quite overwhelming at first to make sense of the error messages that Xcode spits out. A small typo at the top of a source file can produce several errors elsewhere in that file.

Typical mistakes are differences in capitalization. The Swift programming language is case-sensitive, which means it sees `Alert` and `alert` as two different names. Xcode complains about this with a "<something> undeclared" or "Use of unresolved identifier" error.

When Xcode says things like "Parse Issue" or "Expected <something>" then you probably forgot a curly bracket } or parenthesis) somewhere. Not matching up opening and closing brackets is a common error.

Tip: In Xcode, there are multiple ways to find matching brackets to see if they line up. If you move the text cursor over a closing bracket, Xcode will highlight the corresponding opening bracket, or vice versa. You could also hold down the ⌘ key and move your mouse cursor over a line with a curly bracket and Xcode will highlight the full block from the opening curly bracket to the closing curly bracket (or vice versa) - nifty!

Xcode shows you the complete block for curly brackets

Tiny details are very important when you're programming. Even one single misplaced character can prevent the Swift compiler from building your app.

Fortunately, such mistakes are easy to find.

Xcode makes sure you can't miss errors

When Xcode detects an error it switches the pane on the left from the Project navigator, to the **Issue navigator**, which shows all the errors and warnings that Xcode has found. (You can go back to the project files list using the small buttons at the top.)

In the above screenshot, apparently, I forgot a comma somewhere.

Click on the error message in the Issue navigator and Xcode takes you to the line in the source code with the error. Sometimes, it even suggests a fix to resolve it:

```
20      let action = UIAlertAction(title: "Awesome", style: .default
21                                 handler: nil)                        ⊗ Expected ';' separator ⊗
22
23      alert.addAction(action)                                          Insert ';'          Fix
24
25      present(alert, animated: true, completion: nil)
26    }
27  }
```

Fix-it suggests a solution to the problem

Sometimes it's a bit of a puzzle to figure out what exactly you did wrong when your build fails - fortunately, Xcode lends a helping hand.

Errors and warnings

Xcode makes a distinction between errors (red) and warnings (yellow). Errors are fatal. If you get one, you cannot run the app till the error is fixed. Warnings are informative. Xcode just says, "You probably didn't mean to do this, but go ahead anyway."

In my opinion, it is best to treat all warnings as if they were errors. Fix the warning before you continue and only run your app when there are zero errors and zero warnings. That doesn't guarantee the app won't have any bugs, but at least they won't be silly ones :]

The anatomy of an app

It might be good at this point to get some sense of what goes on behind the scenes of an app.

An app is essentially made up of **objects** that can send messages to each other. Many of the objects in your app are provided by iOS, for example the button – a `UIButton` object – and the alert popup – a `UIAlertController` object. Some objects you will have to program yourself, such as the view controller.

These objects communicate by passing messages to each other. When the user taps the Hit Me button in the app, for example, that `UIButton` object sends a message to your view controller. In turn the view controller may message more objects.

On iOS, apps are *event-driven*, which means that the objects listen for certain events to occur and then process them.

As strange as it may sound, an app spends most of its time doing… absolutely nothing. It just sits there waiting for something to happen. When the user taps the screen, the app springs to action for a few milliseconds and then it goes back to sleep again until the next event arrives.

Your part in this scheme is that you write the source code for the actions that will be performed when your objects receive the messages for such events.

In the app, the button's Touch Up Inside event is connected to the view controller's showAlert action. So when the button recognizes it has been tapped, it sends the showAlert message to your view controller.

Inside showAlert, the view controller sends another message, addAction, to the UIAlertController object. And to show the alert, the view controller sends the present message.

Your whole app will be made up of objects that communicate in this fashion.

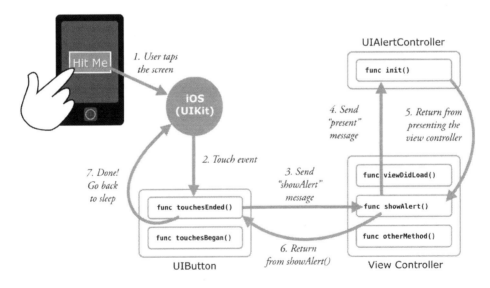

The general flow of events in an app

Maybe you have used PHP or Ruby scripts on your web site. This event-based model is different from how a PHP script works. The PHP script will run from top-to-bottom, executing the statements one-by-one until it reaches the end and then it exits.

Apps, on the other hand, don't exit until the user terminates them (or they crash!). They spend most of their time waiting for input events, then handle those events and go back to sleep.

Input from the user, mostly in the form of touches and taps, is the most important source of events for your app, but there are other types of events as well. For example, the operating system will notify your app when the user receives an incoming phone call, when it has to redraw the screen, when a timer has counted down, and many more.

Everything your app does is triggered by some event.

You can find the project files for the app up to this point under **02 - The One-Button App** in the Source Code folder.

Chapter 3: Slider and Labels

Now that you have accomplished the first task of putting a button on the screen and making it show an alert, you'll simply go down the task list and tick off the other items.

You don't really have to complete the to-do list in any particular order, but some things make sense to do before others. For example, you cannot read the position of the slider if you don't have a slider yet.

So let's add the rest of the controls – the slider and the text labels – and turn this app into a real game!

When you're done, the app will look like this:

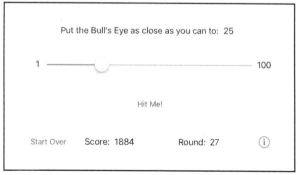

The game screen with standard UIKit controls

Hey, wait a minute... that doesn't look nearly as pretty as the game I promised you! The difference is that these are the standard UIKit controls. This is what they look like straight out of the box.

You've probably seen this look before because it is perfectly suitable for regular apps. But because the default look is a little boring for a game, you'll put some special sauce on top later to spiff things up.

In this chapter, you'll cover the following:

- **Portrait vs. landscape:** Switch your app to landscape mode.

- **Objects, data and methods:** A quick primer on the basics of object oriented programming.

- **Add the other controls:** Add the rest of the controls necessary to complete the user interface of your app.

Portrait vs. landscape

Notice that in the previous screenshot, the dimensions of the app have changed: the iPhone is tilted on its side and the screen is wider but less tall. This is called *landscape* orientation.

You've no doubt seen landscape apps before on the iPhone. It's a common display orientation for games but many other types of apps work in landscape mode too, usually in addition to the regular "upright" *portrait* orientation.

For instance, many people prefer to write emails with their device flipped over because the wider screen allows for a bigger keyboard and easier typing.

In portrait orientation, the iPhone SE screen consists of 320 points horizontally and 568 points vertically. For landscape these dimensions are switched.

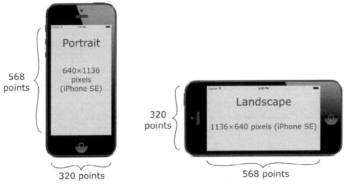

Screen dimensions for portrait and landscape orientation

So what is a *point*?

On older devices – up to the iPhone 3GS and corresponding iPod touch models, as well as the first iPads – one point corresponds to one pixel. As a result, these low-resolution devices don't look very sharp because of their big, chunky pixels.

I'm sure you know what a pixel is? In case you don't, it's the smallest element that a screen is made up of. (That's how the word originated, a shortened form of pictures, PICS or PIX + ELement = PIXEL.) The display of your iPhone is a big matrix of pixels that each can have their own color, just like a TV screen. Changing the color values of these pixels produces a visible image on the display. The more pixels, the better the image looks.

On the high-resolution Retina display of the iPhone 4 and later models, one point actually corresponds to two pixels horizontally and vertically, so four pixels in total. It packs a lot of pixels in a very small space, making for a much sharper display, which accounts for the popularity of Retina devices.

On the Plus devices it's even crazier: they have a 3x resolution with *nine* pixels for every point. Insane! You need to be eagle-eyed to make out the individual pixels on these fancy Retina HD displays. It becomes almost impossible to make out where one pixel ends and the next one begins, that's how miniscule they are!

It's not only the number of pixels that differs between the various iPhone and iPad models. Over the years they have received different form factors, from the small 3.5-inch screen in the beginning all the way up to 12.9-inches on the iPad Pro model.

The form factor of the device determines the width and height of the screen in points:

Device	Form factor	Screen dimension in points
iPhone 4s and older	3.5"	320 x 480
iPhone 5, 5c, 5s, SE	4"	320 x 568
iPhone 6, 6s, 7, 8	4.7"	375 x 667
iPhone 6, 6s, 7, 8 Plus	5.5"	414 x 736
iPhone X	5.8"	375 x 812
iPad, iPad mini	9.7" and 7.9"	768 x 1024
iPad Pro	10.5"	834 x 1112
iPad Pro	12.9"	1024 x 1366

In the early days of iOS, there was only one screen size. But those days of "one size fits all" are long gone. Now we have a variety of screen sizes to deal with.

UIKit and other frameworks

iOS offers a lot of building blocks in the form of frameworks or "kits". The UIKit framework provides the user interface controls such as buttons, labels and navigation bars. It manages the view controllers and generally takes care of anything else that deals with your app's user interface. (That is what UI stands for: User Interface.)

If you had to write all that stuff from scratch, you'd be busy for a long while. Instead, you can build your app on top of the system-provided frameworks and take advantage of all the work the Apple engineers have already put in.

Any object you see whose name starts with UI, such as `UIButton`, comes from UIKit. When you're writing iOS apps, UIKit is the framework you'll spend most of your time with, but there are others as well.

Examples of other frameworks are Foundation, which provides many of the basic building blocks for building apps; Core Graphics for drawing basic shapes such as lines, gradients and images on the screen; AVFoundation for playing sound and video; and many others.

The complete set of frameworks for iOS is known collectively as Cocoa Touch.

Remember that UIKit works with points instead of pixels, so you only have to worry about the differences between the screen sizes measured in points. The actual number of pixels is only important for graphic designers because images are still measured in pixels.

Developers work in points, designers work in pixels.

The difference between points and pixels can be a little confusing, but if that is the only thing you're confused about right now then I'm doing a pretty good job. ;-)

For the time being, you'll work with just the iPhone SE screen size of 320×568 points – just to keep things simple. Later on you'll also make the game fit on the other iPhone screens.

Convert the app to landscape

To switch the app from portrait to landscape, you have to do two things:

1. Make the view in **Main.storyboard** landscape instead of portrait.

2. Change the **Supported Device Orientations** setting of the app.

➤ Open **Main.storyboard**. In Interface Builder, in the **View as: iPhone SE** panel, change **Orientation** to landscape:

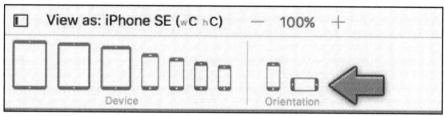

Changing the orientation in Interface Builder

This changes the dimensions of the view controller. It also puts the button off-center.

➤ Move the button back to the center of the view because an untidy user interface just won't do in this day and age.

The view in landscape orientation

That takes care of the view layout.

➤ Run the app on the iPhone SE Simulator. Note that the screen does not show up as landscape yet, and the button is no longer in the center.

➤ Choose **Hardware → Rotate Left** or **Rotate Right** from the Simulator's menu bar at the top of the screen, or hold ⌘ and press the left or right arrow keys on your keyboard. This will flip the Simulator around.

Now, everything will look as it should.

Notice that in landscape orientation the app no longer shows the iPhone's status bar. This gives apps more room for their user interfaces.

To finalize the orientation switch, you should do one more thing. There is a configuration option that tells iOS what orientations your app supports. New apps that you make from a template always support both portrait and landscape orientations.

➤ Click the blue **BullsEye** project icon at the top of the **Project navigator**. The editor pane of the Xcode window now reveals a bunch of settings for the project.

➤ Make sure that the **General** tab is selected:

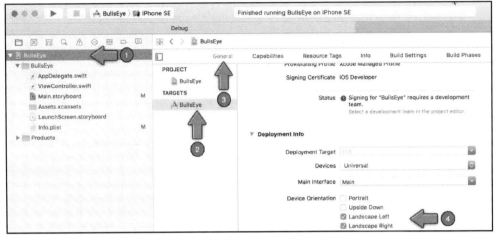

The settings for the project

In the **Deployment Info** section, there is an option for **Device Orientation**.

➤ Check only the **Landscape Left** and **Landscape Right** options and leave the Portrait and Upside Down options unchecked.

Run the app again and it properly launches in the landscape orientation right from the start.

Objects, data and methods

Time for some programming theory. Yes, you cannot escape it. :]

Swift is a so-called "object-oriented" programming language, which means that most of the stuff you do involves objects of some kind. I already mentioned a few times that an app consists of objects that send messages to each other.

When you write an iOS app, you'll be using objects that are provided for you by the system, such as the UIButton object from UIKit, and you'll be making objects of your own, such as view controllers.

Objects

So what exactly *is* an object? Think of an object as a building block of your program.

Programmers like to group related functionality into objects. *This* object takes care of parsing a file, *that* object knows how to draw an image on the screen, and *that* object over there can perform a difficult calculation.

Each object takes care of a specific part of the program. In a full-blown app you will have many different types of objects (tens or even hundreds).

Even your small starter app already contains several different objects. The one you have spent the most time with so far is ViewController. The Hit Me button is also an object, as is the alert popup. And the text values that you put on the alert – "Hello, World" and "This is my first app!" – are also objects.

The project also has an object named AppDelegate - you're going to ignore that for the moment, but feel free to look at its source if you're curious. These object thingies are everywhere!

Data and methods

An object can have both *data* and *functionality*:

- An example of data is the Hit Me button that you added to the view controller earlier. When you dragged the button into the storyboard, it actually became part of the view controller's data. Data *contains* something. In this case, the view controller contains the button.

- An example of functionality is the showAlert action that you added to respond to taps on the button. Functionality *does* something.

The button itself also has data and functionality. Examples of button data are the text and color of its label, its position on the screen, its width and height, and so on. The button also has functionality: it can recognize that the user tapped on it and will trigger an action in response.

The thing that provides functionality to an object is commonly called a *method*. Other programming languages may call this a "procedure" or "subroutine" or "function". You will also see the term function used in Swift; a method is simply a function that belongs to an object.

Your showAlert action is an example of a method. You can tell it's a method because the line says func (short for "function") and the name is followed by parentheses:

All method definitions start with the word func and have parentheses

If you look through the rest of **ViewController.swift** you'll see several other methods, such as `viewDidLoad()` and `didReceiveMemoryWarning()`.

These currently don't do much; the Xcode template placed them there for your convenience. These specific methods are often used by view controllers, so it's likely that you will need to fill them in at some point.

The concept of methods may still feel a little weird, so here's an example:

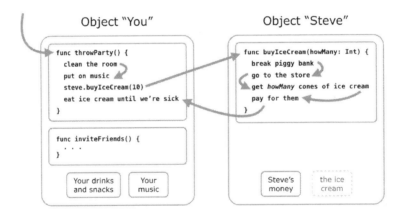

Every party needs ice cream!

You (or at least an object named "You") want to throw a party, but you forgot to buy ice cream. Fortunately, you have invited the object named Steve who happens to live next door to a convenience store. It won't be much of a party without ice cream, so at some point during your party preparations you send object Steve a message asking him to bring some ice cream.

The computer now switches to object Steve and executes the commands from his `buyIceCream()` method, one by one, from top to bottom.

When the `buyIceCream()` method is done, the computer returns to your `throwParty()` method and continues with that, so you and your friends can eat the ice cream that Steve brought back with him.

The Steve object also has data. Before he goes to the store he has money. At the store he exchanges this money data for other, much more important, data: ice cream! After making that transaction, he brings the ice cream data over to the party (if he eats it all along the way, your program has a bug).

Messages

"Sending a message" sounds more involved than it really is. It's a good way to think conceptually of how objects communicate, but there really aren't any pigeons or mailmen involved. The computer simply jumps from the throwParty() method to the buyIceCream() method and back again.

Often the terms "calling a method" or "invoking a method" are used instead. That means the exact same thing as sending a message: the computer jumps to the method you're calling and returns to where it left off when that method is done.

The important thing to remember is that objects have methods (the steps involved in buying ice cream) and data (the actual ice cream and the money to buy it with).

Objects can look at each other's data (to some extent anyway, just like Steve may not approve if you peek inside his wallet) and can ask other objects to perform their methods. That's how you get your app to do things. (But not all data from an object can be inspected by other objects and/or code - this is an area known as access control and you'll learn about this later.)

Add the other controls

Your app already has a button but you still need to add the rest of the UI controls, also known as "views". Here is the screen again, this time annotated with the different types of views:

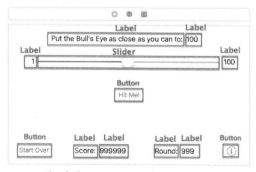

The different views in the game screen

As you can see, I put placeholder values into some of the labels (for example, "999999"). That makes it easier to see how the labels will fit on the screen when they're actually used. The score label could potentially hold a large value, so you'd better make sure the label has room for it.

➤ Try to re-create the above screen on your own by dragging the various controls from the Object Library on to your scene. You'll need a few new Buttons, Labels, and a Slider. You can see in the screenshot above how big the items should (roughly) be. It's OK if you're a few points off.

To tweak the settings of these views, you use the **Attributes inspector**. You can find this inspector in the right-hand pane of the Xcode window:

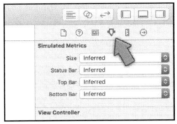

The Attributes inspector

The inspector area shows various aspects of the item that is currently selected. The Attributes inspector, for example, lets you change the background color of a label or the size of the text on a button. You've already seen the Connections inspector that showed the button's actions. As you become more proficient with Interface Builder, you'll be using all of these inspector panes to configure your views.

➤ Hint: the ⓘ button is actually a regular Button, but its **Type** is set to **Info Light** in the Attributes inspector:

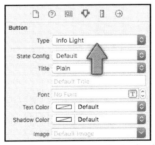

The button type lets you change the look of the button

➤ Also use the Attributes inspector to configure the **slider**. Its minimum value should be 1, its maximum 100, and its current value 50.

The slider attributes

When you're done, you should have 12 user interface elements in your scene: one slider, three buttons and a whole bunch of labels. Excellent!

➤ Run the app and play with it for a minute. The controls don't really do much yet (except for the button that should still pop up the alert), but you can at least drag the slider around.

You can now tick a few more items off the to-do list, all without any programming! That is going to change really soon, because you will have to write Swift code to actually make the controls do anything.

The slider

The next item on your to-do list is: "Read the value of the slider after the user presses the Hit Me button."

If, in your messing around in Interface Builder, you did not accidentally disconnect the button from the showAlert action, you can modify the app to show the slider's value in the alert popup. (If you did disconnect the button, then you should hook it up again first. You know how, right?)

Remember how you added an action to the view controller in order to recognize when the user tapped the button? You can do the same thing for the slider. This new action will be performed whenever the user drags the slider.

The steps for adding this action are largely the same as before.

➤ First, go to **ViewController.swift** and add the following at the bottom, just before the final closing curly bracket:

```
@IBAction func sliderMoved(_ slider: UISlider) {
  print("The value of the slider is now: \(slider.value)")
}
```

➤ Second, go to the storyboard and Control-drag from the slider to View Controller in the Document Outline. Let go of the mouse button and select **sliderMoved:** from the popup. Done!

Just to refresh your memory, the Document Outline sits on the left-hand side of the Interface Builder canvas. It shows the view hierarchy of the storyboard. Here you can see that the View Controller contains a view (succinctly named View) which in turn contains the sub-views you've added: the buttons and labels.

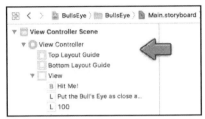

The Document Outline shows the view hierarchy of the storyboard

Remember, if the Document Outline is not visible, click the little icon at the bottom of the Xcode window to reveal it:

This button shows or hides the Document Outline

When you connect the slider, make sure to Control-drag to View Controller (the yellow circle icon), not View Controller Scene at the very top. If you don't see the yellow circle icon, then click the arrow in front of View Controller Scene (called the "disclosure triangle") to expand it.

If all went well, the `sliderMoved:` action is now hooked up to the slider's Value Changed event. This means the `sliderMoved()` method will be called every time the user drags the slider to the left or right.

You can verify that the connection was made by selecting the slider and looking at the **Connections inspector**:

The slider is now hooked up to the view controller

Note: Did you notice that the `sliderMoved:` action has a colon in its name but `showAlert` does not? That's because the `sliderMoved()` method takes a single parameter, `slider`, while `showAlert()` does not have any parameters. If an action method has a parameter, Interface Builder adds a `:` to the name. You'll learn more about parameters and how to use them soon.

➤ Run the app and drag the slider.

As soon as you start dragging, the Xcode window opens a new pane at the bottom, the **Debug area**, showing a list of messages:

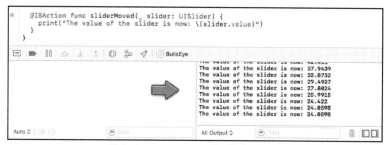

Printing messages in the Debug area

Note: If for some reason the Debug area does not show up, you can always show (or hide) the Debug area by using the appropriate toolbar button on the top right corner of the Xcode window. You will notice from the above screenshot that the Debug area is split into two panes. You can control which of the panes is shown/ hidden by using the two blue square icons shown above in the bottom right corner.

Show Debug area

If you swipe the slider all the way to the left, you should see the value go down to 1. All the way to the right, the value should stop at 100.

The `print()` function is a great help to show you what is going on in the app. Its entire purpose is to write a text message to the **Console** - the right-hand pane in the Debug area. Here, you used `print()` to verify that you properly hooked up the action to the slider and that you can read the slider value as the slider is moved.

I often use `print()` to make sure my apps are doing the right thing before I add more functionality. Printing a message to the Console is quick and easy.

> **Note:** You may see a bunch of other messages in the Console too. This is debug output from UIKit and the iOS Simulator. You can safely ignore these messages.

Strings

To put text in your app, you use something called a "string". The strings you have used so far are:

```
"Hello, World"
"This is my first app!"
"Awesome"
"The value of the slider is now: \(slider.value)"
```

The first three were used to make the `UIAlertController`; the last one you used with `print()`.

Such a chunk of text is called a string because you can visualize the text as a sequence of characters, as if they were pearls in a necklace:

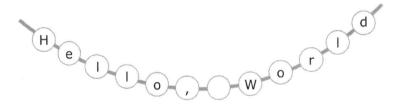

A string of characters

Working with strings is something you need to do all the time when you're writing apps, so over the course of this book you'll get quite experienced in using strings.

In Swift, to create a string, simply put the text in between double quotes. In other languages you can often use single quotes as well, but in Swift they must be double quotes. And they must be plain double quotes, not typographic "smart quotes".

To summarize:

```
// This is the proper way to make a Swift string:
"I am a good string"

// These are wrong:
'I should have double quotes'
```

```
''Two single quotes do not make a double quote''
"My quotes are too fancy"
@"I am an Objective-C string"
```

Anything between the characters \(and) inside a string is special. The `print()` statement used the string, `"The value of the slider is now: \ (slider.value)"`. Think of the `\( ... )` as a placeholder: `"The value of the slider is now: X"`, where X will be replaced by the value of the slider.

Filling in the blanks this way is a very common way to build strings in Swift.

Variables

Printing information with `print()` to the Console is very useful during development of the app, but it's absolutely useless to the user because they can't see the Console when the app is running on a device.

Let's improve this to show the value of the slider in the alert popup. So how do you get the slider's value into `showAlert()`?

When you read the slider's value in `sliderMoved()`, that piece of data disappears when the action method ends. It would be handy if you could remember this value until the user taps the Hit Me button.

Fortunately, Swift has a building block for exactly this purpose: the *variable*.

➤ Open **ViewController.swift** and add the following at the top, directly below the line that says `class ViewController`:

```
var currentValue: Int = 0
```

You have now added a variable named `currentValue` to the view controller object.

The code should look like this (I left out the method code, also known as the method implementations):

```
import UIKit

class ViewController: UIViewController {
  var currentValue: Int = 0

  override func viewDidLoad() {
    . . .
  }

  override func didReceiveMemoryWarning() {
    . . .
  }
```

```
    @IBAction func showAlert() {
      . . .
    }

    @IBAction func sliderMoved(_ slider: UISlider) {
      . . .
    }
  }
```

It is customary to add the variables above the methods, and to indent everything with a tab, or two to four spaces. Which one you use is largely a matter of personal preference. I like to use two spaces. (You can configure this in Xcode's preferences panel. From the menu bar choose **Xcode** → **Preferences…** → **Text Editing** and go to the **Indentation** tab.)

Remember when I said that a view controller, or any object really, could have both data and functionality? The showAlert() and sliderMoved() actions are examples of functionality, while the currentValue variable is part of the view controller's data.

A variable allows the app to remember things. Think of a variable as a temporary storage container for a single piece of data. Similar to how there are containers of all sorts and sizes, data comes in all kinds of shapes and sizes.

You don't just put stuff in the container and then forget about it. You will often replace its contents with a new value. When the thing that your app needs to remember changes, you take the old value out of the box and put in the new value. That's the whole point behind variables: they can *vary*. For example, you will update currentValue with the new position of the slider every time the slider is moved. The size of the storage container and the sort of values the variable can remember are determined by its *data type*, or just *type*.

You specified the type Int for the currentValue variable, which means this container can hold whole numbers (also known as "integers") between at least minus two billion and plus two billion. Int is one of the most common data types. There are many others though, and you can even make your own.

Variables are like children's toy blocks:

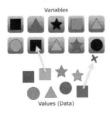

Variables are containers that hold values

The idea is to put the right shape in the right container. The container is the variable and its type determines what "shape" fits. The shapes are the possible values that you can put into the variables.

You can change the contents of each box later as long as the shape fits. For example, you can take out a blue square from a square box and put in a red square - the only thing you have to make sure is that both are squares.

But you can't put a square in a round hole: the data type of the value and the data type of the variable have to match.

I said a variable is a *temporary* storage container. How long will it keep its contents? Unlike meat or vegetables, variables won't spoil if you keep them for too long – a variable will hold onto its value indefinitely, until you put a new value into that variable or until you destroy the container altogether.

Each variable has a certain lifetime (also known as its *scope*) that depends on exactly where in your program you defined that variable. In this case, currentValue sticks around for just as long as its owner, ViewController, does. Their fates are intertwined.

The view controller, and thus currentValue, is there for the duration of the app. They don't get destroyed until the app quits. Soon you'll also see variables that are short-lived (also known as "local" variables).

Enough theory, let's make this variable work for us.

➤ Change the contents of the sliderMoved() method in **ViewController.swift** to the following:

```
@IBAction func sliderMoved(_ slider: UISlider) {
    currentValue = lroundf(slider.value)
}
```

You removed the print() statement and replaced it with this line:

```
currentValue = lroundf(slider.value)
```

What is going on here?

You've seen slider.value before, which is the slider's position at a given moment. This is a value between 1 and 100, possibly with digits behind the decimal point. And currentValue is the name of the variable you have just created.

To put a new value into a variable, you simply do this:

```
variable = the new value
```

This is known as "assignment". You *assign* the new value to the variable. It puts the shape into the box. Here, you put the value that represents the slider's position into the currentValue variable.

Functions

But what is the lroundf thing? Recall that the slider's value can be a non-whole number. You've seen this with the print() output in the Console as you moved the slider.

However, this game would be really hard if you made the player guess the position of the slider with an accuracy that goes beyond whole numbers. That will be nearly impossible to get right!

To give the player a fighting chance, you use whole numbers only. That is why currentValue has a data type of Int, because it stores *integers*, a fancy term for whole numbers.

You use the function lroundf() to round the decimal number to the nearest whole number and you then store that rounded-off number in currentValue.

Functions and methods

You've already seen that methods provide functionality, but *functions* are another way to put functionality into your apps (the name sort of gives it away, right?). Functions and methods are how Swift programs combine multiple lines of code into single, cohesive units.

The difference between the two is that a function doesn't belong to an object while a method does. In other words, a method is exactly like a function – that's why you use the func keyword to define them – except that you need to have an object to use the method. But regular functions, or *free functions* as they are sometimes called, can be used anywhere.

Swift provides your programs with a large library of useful functions. The function lroundf() is one of them and you'll be using quite a few others as you progress. print() is also a function, by the way. You can tell because the function name is always followed by parentheses that possibly contain one or more parameters.

➤ Now change the showAlert() method to the following:

```swift
@IBAction func showAlert() {
  let message = "The value of the slider is: \(currentValue)"

  let alert = UIAlertController(title: "Hello, World",
```

```
                            message: message,      // changed
                   preferredStyle: .alert)

    let action = UIAlertAction(title: "OK",         // changed
                               style: .default,
                               handler: nil)

    alert.addAction(action)

    present(alert, animated: true, completion: nil)
}
```

The line with `let message =` is new. Also note the other two small changes marked by comments.

> **Note:** Anything appearing after two slashes `//` (and up to the end of that particular line) in Swift source code is treated as a comment - a note by the developer to themselves, or to other developers. The Swift compiler generally ignores comments - they are there for the convenience of humans.

As before, you create and show a `UIAlertController`, except this time its message says: "The value of the slider is: X", where X is replaced by the contents of the `currentValue` variable (a whole number between 1 and 100).

Suppose `currentValue` is 34, which means the slider is about one-third to the left. The new code above will convert the string `"The value of the slider is: \(currentValue)"` into `"The value of the slider is: 34"` and put that into a new object named `message`.

The old `print()` did something similar, except that it printed the result to the Console. Here, however, you do not wish to print the result but show it in the alert popup. That is why you tell the `UIAlertController` that it should now use this new string as the message to display.

➤ Run the app, drag the slider, and press the button. Now the alert should show the actual value of the slider.

The alert shows the value of the slider

Cool. You have used a variable, `currentValue`, to remember a particular piece of data, the rounded-off position of the slider, so that it can be used elsewhere in the app, in this case in the alert's message text.

If you tap the button again without moving the slider, the alert will still show the same value. The variable keeps its value until you put a new one into it.

Your first bug

There is a small problem with the app, though. Maybe you've noticed it already. Here is how to reproduce the problem:

➤ Press the Stop button in Xcode to completely terminate the app, then press Run again. Without moving the slider, immediately press the Hit Me button.

The alert now says: "The value of the slider is: 0". But the slider's knob is obviously at the center, so you would expect the value to be 50. You've discovered a bug!

> **Exercise:** Think of a reason why the value would be 0 in this particular situation (start the app, don't move the slider, press the button).

Answer: The clue here is that this only happens when you don't move the slider. Of course, without moving the slider the `sliderMoved()` message is never sent and you never put the slider's value into the `currentValue` variable.

The default value for the `currentValue` variable is 0, and that is what you are seeing here.

➤ To fix this bug, change the declaration of `currentValue` to:

```
var currentValue: Int = 50
```

Now the starting value of `currentValue` is 50, which should be the same value as the slider's initial position.

➤ Run the app again and verify that the bug is fixed.

You can find the project files for the app up to this point under **03 - Slider and Labels** in the Source Code folder.

Chapter 4: Outlets

You've built the user interface for *Bull's Eye* and you know how to find the current position of the slider. That already knocks quite a few items off the to-do list. This chapter takes care of a few other items from the to-do list and covers the following items:

- **Improve the slider:** Set the initial slider value (in code) to be whatever value set in the storyboard instead of assuming an initial value.

- **Generate the random number:** Generate the random number to be used as the target by the game.

- **Add rounds to the game:** Add the ability to start a new round of the game.

- **Display the target value:** Display the generated target number on screen.

Improve the slider

You completed storing the value of the slider into a variable and showing it via an alert. That's great, but you can still improve on it a little.

What if you decide to set the initial value of the slider in the storyboard to something other than 50, say 1 or 100? Then currentValue would be wrong again because the app always assumes it will be 50 at the start. You'd have to remember to also fix the code to give currentValue a new initial value.

Take it from me, that kind of thing is hard to remember, especially when the project becomes bigger and you have dozens of view controllers to worry about, or when you haven't looked at the code for weeks.

Get the initial slider value

To fix this issue once and for all, you're going to do some work inside the `viewDidLoad()` method in **ViewController.swift**. That method currently looks like this:

```swift
override func viewDidLoad() {
  super.viewDidLoad()
  // Do any additional setup after loading the view,
  // typically from a nib.
}
```

When you created this project based on Xcode's template, Xcode inserted the `viewDidLoad()` method into the source code. You will now add some code to it.

The `viewDidLoad()` message is sent by UIKit immediately after the view controller loads its user interface from the storyboard file. At this point, the view controller isn't visible yet, so this is a good place to set instance variables to their proper initial values.

➤ Change `viewDidLoad()` to the following:

```swift
override func viewDidLoad() {
  super.viewDidLoad()
  currentValue = lroundf(slider.value)
}
```

The idea is that you take whatever value is set on the slider in the storyboard (whether it is 50, 1, 100, or anything else) and use that as the initial value of `currentValue`.

Recall that you need to round off the number, because `currentValue` is an `Int` and integers cannot take decimal (or fractional) numbers.

Unfortunately, Xcode immediately complains about these changes even before you try to run the app.

```
33  class ViewController: UIViewController {
34    var currentValue: Int = 50
35
36    override func viewDidLoad() {
37      super.viewDidLoad()
38      currentValue = lroundf(slider.value)          ⊗ Use of unresolved identifier 'slider'
39    }
```

Xcode error message about missing identifier

Note: Xcode tries to be helpful and it analyzes the program for mistakes as you're typing. Sometimes you may see temporary warnings and error messages that will go away when you complete the changes that you're making.

Don't be too intimidated by these messages; they are only short-lived while the code is in a state of flux.

The above happens because `viewDidLoad()` does not know of anything named `slider`.

Then why did this work earlier, in `sliderMoved()`? Let's take a look at that method again:

```
@IBAction func sliderMoved(_ slider: UISlider) {
    currentValue = lroundf(slider.value)
}
```

Here you do the exact same thing: you round off `slider.value` and put it into `currentValue`. So why does it work here but not in `viewDidLoad()`?

The difference is that in the code above, `slider` is a *parameter* of the `sliderMoved()` method. Parameters are the things inside the parentheses following a method's name. In this case, there's a single parameter named `slider`, which refers to the `UISlider` object that sent this action message.

Action methods can have a parameter that refers to the UI control that triggered the method. This is convenient when you wish to refer to that object in the method, just as you did here (the object in question being the `UISlider`).

When the user moves the slider, the `UISlider` object basically says, "Hey view controller, I'm a slider object and I just got moved. By the way, here's my phone number so you can get in touch with me."

The `slider` parameter contains this "phone number" but it is only valid for the duration of this particular method.

In other words, `slider` is *local*; you cannot use it anywhere else.

Locals

When I first introduced variables, I mentioned that each variable has a certain lifetime, known as its *scope*. The scope of a variable depends on where in your program you defined that variable.

There are three possible scope levels in Swift:

1. **Global scope.** These objects exist for the duration of the app and are accessible from anywhere.

2. **Instance scope.** This is for variables such as `currentValue`. These objects are alive for as long as the object that owns them stays alive.

3. **Local scope.** Objects with a local scope, such as the `slider` parameter of `sliderMoved()`, only exist for the duration of that method. As soon as the execution of the program leaves this method, the local objects are no longer accessible.

Let's look at the top part of showAlert():

```
@IBAction func showAlert() {
    let message = "The value of the slider is: \(currentValue)"

    let alert = UIAlertController(title: "Hello, World",
                                message: message,
                          preferredStyle: .alert)

    let action = UIAlertAction(title: "OK", style: .default,
                              handler: nil)
    . . .
```

Because the message, alert, and action objects are created inside the method, they have local scope. They only come into existence when the showAlert() action is performed and cease to exist when the action is done.

As soon as the showAlert() method completes, i.e. when there are no more statements for it to execute, the computer destroys the message, alert, and action objects and their storage space is cleared out.

The currentValue variable, however, lives on forever... or at least for as long as the ViewController does (which is until the user terminates the app). This type of variable is named an *instance variable*, because its scope is the same as the scope of the object instance it belongs to.

In other words, you use instance variables if you want to keep a certain value around, from one action event to the next.

Set up outlets

So, with this newly-gained knowledge of variables and their scope, how do you fix the error that you encountered?

The solution is to store a reference to the slider as a new instance variable, just like you did for currentValue. Except that this time, the data type of the variable is not Int, but UISlider. And you're not using a regular instance variable but a special one called an *outlet*.

➤ Add the following line to **ViewController.swift**:

```
@IBOutlet weak var slider: UISlider!
```

It doesn't really matter where this line goes, just as long as it is somewhere inside the brackets for class ViewController. I usually put outlets with the other instance variables - at the top of the class implementation.

This line tells Interface Builder that you now have a variable named `slider` that can be connected to a `UISlider` object. Just as Interface Builder likes to call methods "actions", it calls these variables outlets. Interface Builder doesn't see any of your other variables, only the ones marked with `@IBOutlet`.

Don't worry about `weak` or the exclamation point for now. Why these are necessary will be explained later on. For now, just remember that a variable for an outlet needs to be declared as `@IBOutlet weak var` and has an exclamation point at the end. (Sometimes you'll see a question mark instead; all this hocus pocus will be explained in due time.)

Once you add the `slider` variable, you'll notice that the Xcode error goes away. Does that mean that you can run your app now? Try it and see what happens.

The app crashes on start with an error similar to the following:

```
class ViewController: UIViewController {
  @IBOutlet weak var slider: UISlider!
  var currentValue: Int = 50

  override func viewDidLoad() {
    super.viewDidLoad()
    currentValue = lroundf(slider.value)    Thread 1: EXC_BAD_INSTRUCTION (code=EXC_I386_INV...
  }

  override func didReceiveMemoryWarning() {
    super.didReceiveMemoryWarning()
    // Dispose of any resources that can be recreated.
  }

  @IBAction func showAlert() {
    let message = "The value of the slider is: \(currentValue)"

    let alert = UIAlertController(title: "Hello, World",
                                  message: message,
                                  preferredStyle: .alert)

    let action = UIAlertAction(title: "OK", style: .default,
                               handler: nil)

    alert.addAction(action)

    present(alert, animated: true, completion: nil)
```

```
self = (BullsEye.ViewController) 0x00007f9c71b06870   fatal error: unexpectedly found nil while unwrapping an
                                                      Optional value
                                                      2017-06-12 06:36:46.482782+0530 BullsEye[63987:10389599] fatal
                                                      error: unexpectedly found nil while unwrapping an Optional
                                                      value
                                                      (lldb)
```

App crash when outlet is not connected

So, what happened?

Remember that an outlet has to be *connected* to something in the storyboard. You defined the variable, but you didn't actually set up the connection yet. So, when the app ran and `viewDidLoad()` was called, it tried to find the matching connection in the storyboard and could not - and crashed.

Let's set up the connection in storyboard now.

➤ Open the storyboard. Hold **Control** and click on the **slider**. Don't drag anywhere though, a menu should pop up that shows all the connections for this slider. (Instead of Control-clicking you can also right-click once.)

This popup menu works exactly the same as the Connections inspector. I just wanted to show you this alternative approach.

➤ Click on the open circle next to **New Referencing Outlet** and drag to **View Controller**:

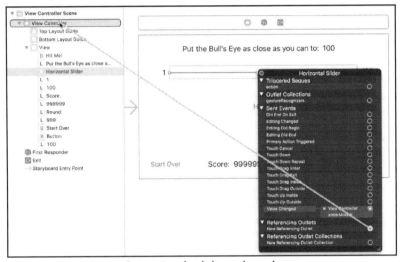

Connecting the slider to the outlet

➤ In the popup that appears, select **slider**.

This is the outlet that you just added. You have successfully connected the slider object from the storyboard to the view controller's slider outlet.

Now that you have done all this set up work, you can refer to the slider object from anywhere inside the view controller using the slider variable.

With these changes in place, it no longer matters what you choose for the initial value of the slider in Interface Builder. When the app starts, currentValue will always correspond to that setting.

➤ Run the app and immediately press the Hit Me! button. It correctly says: "The value of the slider is: 50". Stop the app, go into Interface Builder and change the initial value of the slider to something else, say, 25. Run the app again and press the button. The alert should read 25 now.

> **Note:** When you change the slider value, (or the value in any Interface Builder field), remember to tab out of field when you make a change. If you make the change bur your cursor remains in the field, the change might not take effect. This is something which can trip you up often :]

Put the slider's starting position back to 50 when you're done playing.

> **Exercise:** Give `currentValue` an initial value of 0 again. Its initial value is no longer important – it will be overwritten in `viewDidLoad()` anyway – but Swift demands that all variables always have some value and 0 is as good as any.

Comments

You've seen green text that begin with `//` a few times now. As I explained earlier briefly, these are comments. You can write any text you want after the `//` symbol as the compiler will ignore such lines from the `//` to the end of the line completely.

```
// I am a comment! You can type anything here.
```

Anything between the `/*` and `*/` markers is considered a comment as well. The difference between `//` and `/* */` is that the former only works on a single line, while the latter can span multiple lines.

```
/*
   I am a comment as well!
   I can span multiple lines.
*/
```

The `/* */` comments are often used to temporarily disable whole sections of source code, usually when you're trying to hunt down a pesky bug, a practice known as "commenting out". (You can use the **Cmd-/** keyboard shortcut to comment/uncomment the currently selected lines, or if you have nothing selected, the current line.)

The best use for comment lines is to explain how your code works. Well-written source code is self-explanatory but sometimes additional clarification is useful. Explain to whom? To yourself, mostly.

Unless you have the memory of an elephant, you'll probably have forgotten exactly how your code works when you look at it six months later. Use comments to jog your memory.

Generate the random number

You still have quite a ways to go before the game is playable. So, let's get on with the next item on the list: generating a random number and displaying it on the screen.

Random numbers come up a lot when you're making games because games often need to have some element of unpredictability. You can't really get a computer to generate numbers that are truly random and unpredictable, but you can employ a *pseudo-random generator* to spit out numbers that at least appear to be random. You'll use my favorite, `arc4random_uniform()`.

Before you generate the random value though, you need a place to store it.

➤ Add a new variable at the top of **ViewController.swift**, with the other variables:

```
var targetValue: Int = 0
```

If you don't tell the compiler what kind of variable `targetValue` is, then it doesn't know how much storage space to allocate for it, nor can it check if you're using the variable properly everywhere.

Variables in Swift must always have a value, so here you give it the initial value 0. That 0 is never used in the game; it will always be overwritten by the random value you'll generate at the start of the game.

I hope the reason is clear why you made `targetValue` an instance variable.

You want to calculate the random number in one place – like in `viewDidLoad()` – and then remember it until the user taps the button, in `showAlert()` when you have to check this value against what the user selected.

Next, you need to generate the random number. A good place to do this is when the game starts.

➤ Add the following line to `viewDidLoad()` in **ViewController.swift**:

```
targetValue = 1 + Int(arc4random_uniform(100))
```

The complete `viewDidLoad()` should now look like this:

```
override func viewDidLoad() {
    super.viewDidLoad()
    currentValue = lroundf(slider.value)
    targetValue = 1 + Int(arc4random_uniform(100))
}
```

3

What did you do here? You call the `arc4random_uniform()` function to get an arbitrary integer (whole number) between 0 and 99.

Why is the highest value 99 when the code says 100, you ask? That is because `arc4random_uniform()` treats the upper limit as exclusive. It only goes up-to 100, not up-to-and-including. To get a number that is truly in the range 1 - 100, you add 1 to the result of `arc4random_uniform()`.

Display the random number

➤ Change `showAlert()` to the following:

```
@IBAction func showAlert() {
  let message = "The value of the slider is: \(currentValue)" +
                "\nThe target value is: \(targetValue)"

  let alert = . . .
}
```

Tip: Whenever you see **. . .** in a source code listing I mean that as shorthand for: this part didn't change. Don't go replacing the existing code with an actual ellipsis! :]

You've simply added the random number, which is now stored in `targetValue`, to the message string. This should look familiar to you by now: the `\(targetValue)` placeholder is replaced by the actual random number.

The `\n` character sequence is new. It means that you want to insert a special "new line" character at that point, which will break up the text into two lines so the message is a little easier to read.

➤ Run the app and try it out!

The alert shows the target value on a new line

Note: Earlier you've used the + operator to add two numbers together (just like how it works in math) but here you're also using + to glue different bits of text into one big string.

> Swift allows the use of the same operator for different tasks, depending on the data types involved. If you have two integers, + adds them up. But with two strings, + concatenates, or combines, them into a longer string.
>
> Programming languages often use the same symbols for different purposes, depending on the context. After all, there are only so many symbols to go around :]

Add rounds to the game

If you press the Hit Me button a few times, you'll notice that the random number never changes. I'm afraid the game won't be much fun that way.

This happens because you generate the random number in `viewDidLoad()` and never again afterwards. The `viewDidLoad()` method is only called once when the view controller is created during app startup.

The item on the to-do list actually said: "Generate a random number *at the start of each round*". Let's talk about what a round means in terms of this game.

When the game starts, the player has a score of 0 and the round number is 1. You set the slider halfway (to value 50) and calculate a random number. Then you wait for the player to press the Hit Me button. As soon as they do, the round ends.

You calculate the points for this round and add them to the total score. Then you increment the round number and start the next round. You reset the slider to the halfway position again and calculate a new random number. Rinse, repeat.

Start a new round

Whenever you find yourself thinking something along the lines of, "At this point in the app we have to do such and such," then it makes sense to create a new method for it. This method will nicely capture that functionality in a self-contained unit of its own.

➤ With that in mind, add the following new method to **ViewController.swift**.

```
func startNewRound() {
   targetValue = 1 + Int(arc4random_uniform(100))
   currentValue = 50
   slider.value = Float(currentValue)
}
```

It doesn't really matter where you put it, as long as it is inside the `ViewController` implementation (within the class curly brackets), so that the compiler knows it belongs to the `ViewController` object.

It's not very different from what you did before, except that you moved the logic for setting up a new round into its own method, `startNewRound()`. The advantage of doing this is that you can execute this logic from more than one place in your code.

Use the new method

First, you'll call this new method from `viewDidLoad()` to set up everything for the very first round. Recall that `viewDidLoad()` happens just once when the app starts up, so this is a great place to begin the first round.

➤ Change `viewDidLoad()` to:

```
override func viewDidLoad() {
   super.viewDidLoad()
   startNewRound()
}
```

Note that you've removed some of the existing statements from `viewDidLoad()` and replaced them with just the call to `startNewRound()`.

You will also call `startNewRound()` after the player pressed the Hit Me! button, from within `showAlert()`.

➤ Make the following change to `showAlert()`:

```
@IBAction func showAlert() {
   . . .

   startNewRound()
}
```

The call to `startNewRound()` goes at the very end, right after `present(alert, …)`.

Until now, the methods from the view controller have been invoked for you by UIKit when something happened: `viewDidLoad()` is performed when the app loads, `showAlert()` is performed when the player taps the button, `sliderMoved()` when the player drags the slider, and so on. This is the event-driven model we talked about earlier.

It is also possible to call methods directly, which is what you're doing here. You are sending a message from one method in the object to another method in that same object.

In this case, the view controller sends the `startNewRound()` message to itself in order to set up the new round. The iPhone will then go to that method and execute its statements one-by-one. When there are no more statements in the method, it returns to the calling method and continues with that – either `viewDidLoad()`, if this is the first time, or `showAlert()` for every round after.

Different ways to call methods

Sometimes you may see method calls written like this:

```
self.startNewRound()
```

That does the exact same thing as just `startNewRound()` without `self.` in front. Recall how I just said that the view controller sends the message to itself? Well, that's exactly what `self` means.

To call a method on an object you'd normally write:

```
receiver.methodName(parameters)
```

The `receiver` is the object you're sending the message to. If you're sending the message to yourself, then the receiver is `self`. But because sending messages to `self` is very common, you can also leave this special keyword out for most cases.

To be fair, this isn't exactly the first time you've called methods. `addAction()` is a method on `UIAlertController` and `present()` is a method that all view controllers have, including yours.

When you write Swift programs, a lot of what you do is calling methods on objects, because that is how the objects in your app communicate.

The advantages of using methods

I hope you can see the advantage of putting the "new round" logic into its own method. If you didn't, the code for `viewDidLoad()` and `showAlert()` would look like this:

```
override func viewDidLoad() {
  super.viewDidLoad()

  targetValue = 1 + Int(arc4random_uniform(100))
  currentValue = 50
  slider.value = Float(currentValue)
}

@IBAction func showAlert() {
  . . .

  targetValue = 1 + Int(arc4random_uniform(100))
  currentValue = 50
```

```
    slider.value = Float(currentValue)
}
```

Can you see what is going on here? The same functionality is duplicated in two places. Sure, it is only three lines of code, but often, the code you would have to duplicate will be much larger.

And what if you decide to make a change to this logic (as you will shortly)? Then you will have to make this change in two places as well.

You might be able to remember to do so if you recently wrote this code and it is still fresh in memory, but if you have to make that change a few weeks down the road, chances are that you'll only update it in one place and forget about the other.

Code duplication is a big source of bugs. So, if you need to do the same thing in two different places, consider making a new method for it.

Naming methods

The name of the method also helps to make it clear as to what it is supposed to be doing. Can you tell at a glance what the following does?

```
targetValue = 1 + Int(arc4random_uniform(100))
currentValue = 50
slider.value = Float(currentValue)
```

You probably have to reason your way through it: "It is calculating a new random number and then resets the position of the slider, so I guess it must be the start of a new round."

Some programmers will use a comment to document what is going on (and you can do that too), but in my opinion the following is much clearer than the above block of code with an explanatory comment:

```
startNewRound()
```

This line practically spells out for you what it will do. And if you want to know the specifics of what goes on in a new round, you can always look up the startNewRound() method and look inside.

Well-written source code speaks for itself. I hope I have convinced you of the value of making new methods!

➤ Run the app and verify that it calculates a new random number between 1 and 100 after each tap on the button.

You should also have noticed that after each round the slider resets to the halfway position. That happens because `startNewRound()` sets `currentValue` to 50 and then tells the slider to go to that position. That is the opposite of what you did before (you used to read the slider's position and put it into `currentValue`), but I thought it would work better in the game if you start from the same position in each round.

> **Exercise:** Just for fun, modify the code so that the slider does not reset to the halfway position at the start of a new round.

Type conversion

By the way, you may have been wondering what `Float(...)` and `Int(...)` do in these lines:

```
targetValue = 1 + Int(arc4random_uniform(100))
slider.value = Float(currentValue)
```

Swift is a *strongly typed* language, meaning that it is really picky about the shapes that you can put into the boxes. For example, if a variable is an `Int` you cannot put a `Float`, or a non-whole number, into it, and vice versa.

The value of a `UISlider` happens to be a `Float` – you've seen this when you printed out the value of the slider – but `currentValue` is an `Int`. So the following won't work:

```
slider.value = currentValue
```

The compiler considers this an error. Some programming languages are happy to convert the `Int` into a `Float` for you, but Swift wants you to be explicit about such conversions.

When you say `Float(currentValue)`, the compiler takes the integer number that's stored in `currentValue` and puts it into a new `Float` value that it can pass on to the `UISlider`.

Something similar happens with `arc4random_uniform()`, where the random number gets converted to an `Int` first before it can be stored in `targetValue`.

Because Swift is stricter about this sort of thing than most other programming languages, it is often a source of confusion for newcomers to the language. Unfortunately, Swift's error messages aren't always very clear about what part of the code is wrong or why.

Just remember, if you get an error message saying, "cannot assign value of type 'something' to type 'something else'" then you're probably trying to mix incompatible data types. The solution is to explicitly convert one type to the other, as you've done here.

Display the target value

Great, you figured out how to calculate the random number and how to store it in an instance variable, targetValue, so that you can access it later.

Now you are going to show that target number on the screen. Without it, the player won't know what to aim for and that would make the game impossible to win…

Set up the storyboard

When you made the storyboard, you already added a label for the target value (top-right corner). The trick is to put the value from the targetValue variable into this label. To do that, you need to accomplish two things:

1. Create an outlet for the label so you can send it messages

2. Give the label new text to display

This will be very similar to what you did with the slider. Recall that you added an @IBOutlet variable so you could reference the slider anywhere from within the view controller. Using this outlet variable you could ask the slider for its value, through slider.value. You'll do the same thing for the label.

➤ In **ViewController.swift**, add the following line below the other outlet:

```
@IBOutlet weak var targetLabel: UILabel!
```

➤ In **Main.storyboard**, click to select the correct label - the one at the very top that says "100".

➤ Go to the **Connections inspector** and drag from **New Referencing Outlet** to the yellow circle at the top of your view controller in the central scene. (You could also drag to the **View Controller** in the Document Outline - there are many ways to do the same thing.)

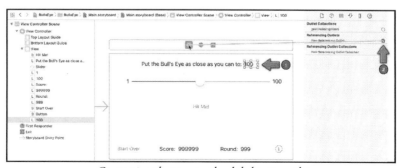

Connecting the target value label to its outlet

➤ Select **targetLabel** from the popup, and the connection is made.

Display the target value via code

➤ Now on to the good stuff. Add the following method below `startNewRound()` in **ViewController.swift**:

```swift
func updateLabels() {
  targetLabel.text = String(targetValue)
}
```

You're putting this logic into its own method because it's something you might use from different places.

The name of the method makes it clear what it does: it updates the contents of the labels. Currently it's just setting the text of a single label, but later on you will add code to update the other labels as well (total score, round number).

The code inside `updateLabels()` should have no surprises for you, although you may wonder why you cannot simply do:

```swift
targetLabel.text = targetValue
```

The answer again is that you cannot put a value of one data type into a variable of another type - the square peg just won't go in the round hole.

The `targetLabel` outlet references a `UILabel` object. The `UILabel` object has a `text` property, which is a `String` object. So, you can only put `String` values into `text`, but `targetValue` is an `Int`. A direct assignment won't fly because an `Int` and a `String` are two very different kinds of things.

So, you have to convert the `Int` into a `String`, and that is what `String(targetValue)` does. It's similar to what you've done before with `Float(...)` and `Int(...)`.

Just in case you were wondering, you could also convert `targetValue` to a `String` by using it as a string with a placeholder like you've done before:

```swift
targetLabel.text = "\(targetValue)"
```

Which approach you use is a matter of taste. Either approach will work fine.

Notice that `updateLabels()` is a regular method – it is not attached to any UI controls as an action – so it won't do anything until you actually call it. (You can tell because it doesn't say `@IBAction` anywhere.)

Action methods vs. normal methods

So what is the difference between an action method and a regular method?

Answer: Nothing.

An action method is really just the same as any other method. The only special thing is the @IBAction specifier. This allows Interface Builder to see the method so you can connect it to your buttons, sliders, and so on.

Other methods, such as viewDidLoad(), don't have the @IBAction specifier. This is good because all kinds of mayhem would occur if you hooked these up to your buttons.

This is the simple form of an action method:

```
@IBAction func showAlert()
```

You can also ask for a reference to the object that triggered this action, via a parameter:

```
@IBAction func sliderMoved(_ slider: UISlider)
@IBAction func buttonTapped(_ button: UIButton)
```

But the following method cannot be used as an action from Interface Builder:

```
func updateLabels()
```

That's because it is not marked as @IBAction and as a result Interface Builder can't see it. To use updateLabels(), you will have to call it yourself.

Call the method

The logical place to call updateLabels() would be after each call to startNewRound(), because that is where you calculate the new target value. So, you could always add a call to updateLabels() in viewDidLoad() and showAlert(), but there's another way too!

What is this other way, you ask? Well, if updateLabels() is always (or at least in your current code) called after startNewRound(), why not call updateLabels() directly from startNewRound() itself? That way, instead of having two calls in two separate places, you can have a single call.

➤ Change startNewRound() to:

```
func startNewRound() {
    targetValue = 1 + Int(arc4random_uniform(100))
    currentValue = 50
    slider.value = Float(currentValue)
```

```
        updateLabels()  // Add this line
}
```

You should be able to type just the first few letters of the method name, like **upd**, and Xcode will show you a list of suggestions matching what you typed. Press **Enter** (or **Tab**) to accept the suggestion (if you are on the right item - or scroll the list to find the right item and then press Enter):

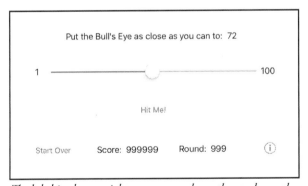

```
72    func startNewRound() {
73        targetValue = 1 + Int(arc4random_uniform(100))
74        currentValue = 50
75        slider.value = Float(currentValue)
76        upd
```
```
 M    Void updateLabels()
 M    Void updateFocusIfNeeded()
 M    Void updateViewConstraints()
 M    Void updateUserActivityState(activity: NSUserActivity)
 V    Int32 VQ_UPDATE
 V    Int32 MNT_UPDATE
 V    Int32 KERN_UPDATEINTERVAL
 M    Bool shouldUpdateFocus(in: UIFocusUpdateContext)
```

Xcode autocomplete offers suggestions

Also worth noting is that you don't have to start typing the method (or property) name you're looking from the beginning - Xcode uses fuzzy search and typing "date" or "label" should help you find "updateLabels" just as easily.

➤ Run the app and you'll actually see the random value on the screen. That should make it a little easier to aim for.

Put the Bull's Eye as close as you can to: 72

1 ————————————⚪———————— 100

Hit Me!

Start Over   Score: 999999   Round: 999   ⓘ

The label in the top-right corner now shows the random value

You can find the project files for the app up to this point under **04 - Outlets** in the Source Code folder.

Chapter 5: Rounds and Score

OK, so you have made quite a bit of progress on the game and the to-do list is getting ever shorter :] So what's next on the list now that you can generate a random number and display it on screen?

A quick look at the task list shows that you now have to "compare the value of the slider to that random number and calculate a score based on how far off the player is". Let's get to it!

This chapter covers the following:

- **Get the difference:** Calculate the difference between the target value and the value that the user selected.

- **Other ways to calculate the difference:** Other approaches to calculating the difference.

- **What's the score?:** Calculate the user's score based on the difference value.

- **The total score:** Calculate the player's total score over multiple rounds.

- **Display the score:** Display the player score on screen.

- **One more round…:** Implement updating the round count and displaying the current round on screen.

Get the difference

Now that you have both the target value (the random number) and a way to read the slider's position, you can calculate how many points the player scored.

The closer the slider is to the target, the more points for the player.

To calculate the score for each round, you look at how far off the slider's value is from the target:

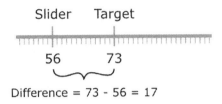

Difference = 73 - 56 = 17

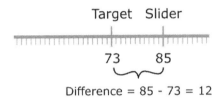

Difference = 85 - 73 = 12

Calculating the difference between the slider position and the target value

A simple approach to finding the distance between the target and the slider is to subtract currentValue from targetValue.

Unfortunately, that gives a negative value if the slider is to the right of the target because now currentValue is greater than targetValue.

You need some way to turn that negative value into a positive value – or you end up subtracting points from the player's score (unfair!).

Doing the subtraction the other way around – currentValue minus targetValue – won't always solve things either because then, the difference will be negative if the slider is to the left of the target instead of the right.

Hmm, it looks like we're in trouble here…

> **Exercise:** How would you frame the solution to this problem if I asked you to solve it in natural language? Don't worry about how to express it in computer language for now, just think it through in plain English.

I came up with something like this:

- *If the slider's value is greater than the target value, then the difference is: slider value minus the target value.*

- *However, if the target value is greater than the slider value, then the difference is: target value minus the slider value.*

- *Otherwise, both values must be equal, and the difference is zero.*

This will always lead to a difference that is a positive number, because you always subtract the smaller number from the larger one.

Do the math:

If the slider is at position 60 and the target value is 40, then onscreen the slider is to the right of the target value, and the difference is 60 - 40 = 20.

However, if the slider is at position 10 and the target is 30, then the slider is to the left of the target and has a smaller value. The difference here is 30 - 10 = also 20.

Algorithms

What you've just done is come up with an *algorithm*, which is a fancy term for a series of steps for solving a computational problem. This is only a very simple algorithm, but it is one nonetheless.

There are many famous algorithms, such as *quicksort* for sorting a list of items and *binary search* for quickly searching through such a sorted list. Other people have already invented many algorithms that you can use in your own programs - that'll save you a lot of thinking!

However, in the programs that you write, you'll probably have to come up with a few algorithms of your own at some time or other. Some are simple such as the one above; others can be pretty hard and might cause you to throw up your hands in despair. But that's part of the fun of programming :]

The academic field of Computer Science concerns itself largely with studying algorithms and finding better ones.

You can describe any algorithm in plain English. It's just a series of steps that you perform to calculate something. Often, you can perform that calculation in your head or on paper, the way you did above. But for more complicated algorithms doing that might take you forever, so at some point you'll have to convert the algorithm to computer code.

The point I'm trying to make is this: if you ever get stuck and you don't know how to make your program calculate something, take a piece of paper and try to write out the steps in English. Set aside the computer for a moment and think the steps through. How you would perform this calculation by hand?

Once you know how to do that, converting the algorithm to code should be a piece of cake.

The difference algorithm

Getting back to your cxode, it is possible you came up with a different way to solve this little problem, and I'll show you two alternatives in a minute, but let's convert this one to computer code first:

```
var difference: Int
if currentValue > targetValue {
  difference = currentValue - targetValue
} else if targetValue > currentValue {
  difference = targetValue - currentValue
} else {
  difference = 0
}
```

The `if` construct is new. It allows your code to make decisions and it works much like you would expect from English. Generally, it works like this:

```
if something is true {
  then do this
} else if something else is true {
  then do that instead
} else {
  do something when neither of the above are true
}
```

Basically, you put a *logical condition* after the `if` keyword. If that condition turns out to be true, for example `currentValue` is greater than `targetValue`, then the code in the block between the { } brackets is executed.

However, if the condition is not true, then the computer looks at the `else if` condition and evaluates that. There may be more than one `else if`, and it tries them one by one from top to bottom until one proves to be true.

If none of the conditions are found to be valid, then the code in the `else` block is executed.

In the implementation of this little algorithm, you first create a local variable named `difference` to hold the result. This will either be a positive whole number or zero, so an Int will do:

```
var difference: Int
```

Then you compare the `currentValue` against the `targetValue`. First, you determine if `currentValue` is greater than `targetValue`:

```
if currentValue > targetValue {
```

The > is the *greater-than* operator. The condition `currentValue > targetValue` is considered true if the value stored in the `currentValue` variable is at least one higher than the value stored in the `targetValue` variable. In that case, the following line of code is executed:

```
difference = currentValue - targetValue
```

Here you subtract `targetValue` (the smaller one) from `currentValue` (the larger one) and store the difference in the `difference` variable.

Notice how I chose variable names that clearly describe what kind of data the variables contain. Often you will see code such as this:

```
a = b - c
```

It is not immediately clear what this is supposed to mean, other than that some arithmetic is taking place. The variable names "a", "b" and "c" don't give any clues as to their intended purpose or what kind of data they might contain.

Back to the `if` statement. If `currentValue` is equal to or less than `targetValue`, the condition is untrue (or *false* in computer-speak) and the program will skip the code block and move on to the next condition:

```
} else if targetValue > currentValue {
```

The same thing happens here as before, except that now the roles of `targetValue` and `currentValue` are reversed. The computer will only execute the following line when `targetValue` is the greater of the two values:

```
difference = targetValue - currentValue
```

This time you subtract `currentValue` from `targetValue` and store the result in the `difference` variable.

There is only one situation you haven't handled yet, and that is when `currentValue` and `targetValue` are equal. If this happens, the player has put the slider exactly at the position of the target random number, a perfect score.

In that case the difference is 0:

```
} else {
  difference = 0
}
```

Since at this point you've already determined that one value is not greater than the other, nor is it smaller, you can only draw one conclusion: the numbers must be equal.

Display the difference

➤ Let's put this algorithm into action. Add it to the top of showAlert():

```
@IBAction func showAlert() {
  var difference: Int
  if currentValue > targetValue {
    difference = currentValue - targetValue
  } else if targetValue > currentValue {
    difference = targetValue - currentValue
  } else {
    difference = 0
  }

  let message = "The value of the slider is: \(currentValue)" +
                "\nThe target value is: \(targetValue)" +
                "\nThe difference is: \(difference)"
  . . .
}
```

Just so you can see that it works, you add the difference value to the alert message as well.

➤ Run it and see for yourself.

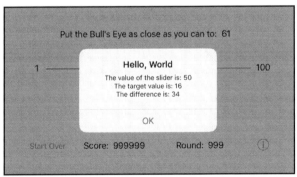

The alert shows the difference between the target and the slider

Simplifying the algorithm

I mentioned earlier that there are other ways to calculate the difference between currentValue and targetValue as a positive number. The above algorithm works well but it is eight lines of code. I think we can come up with a simpler approach that takes up fewer lines.

The new algorithm goes like this:

1. *Subtract the target value from the slider's value.*

2. *If the result is a negative number, then multiply it by -1 to make it a positive number.*

Here you no longer avoid the negative number since computers can work just fine with negative numbers. You simply turn it into a positive number.

> **Exercise:** Convert the above algorithm into source code. Hint: the English description of the algorithm contains the words "if" and "then", which is a pretty good indication you'll have to use an if statement.

You should have arrived at something like this:

```
var difference = currentValue - targetValue
if difference < 0 {
  difference = difference * -1
}
```

This is a pretty straightforward translation of the new algorithm.

You first subtract the two variables and put the result into the difference variable.

Notice that you can create the new variable and assign the result of a calculation to it, all in one line. You don't need to put it onto two different lines, like so:

```
var difference: Int
difference = currentValue - targetValue
```

Also, in the one-liner version you didn't have to tell the compiler that difference takes Int values. Because both currentValue and targetValue are Ints, Swift is smart enough to figure out that difference should also be an Int.

This feature is called *type inference* and it's one of the big selling points of Swift.

Once you have the subtraction result, you use an if statement to determine whether difference is negative, i.e. less than zero. If it is, you multiply by -1 and put the new result – now a positive number – back into the difference variable.

When you write,

```
difference = difference * -1
```

the computer first multiplies difference's value by -1. Then it puts the result of that calculation back into difference. In effect, this overwrites difference's old contents (the negative number) with the positive number.

Because this is a common thing to do, there is a handy shortcut:

```
difference *= -1
```

The *= operator combines * and = into a single operation. The end result is the same: the variable's old value is gone and it now contains the result of the multiplication.

You could also have written this algorithm as follows:

```
var difference = currentValue - targetValue
if difference < 0 {
  difference = -difference
}
```

Instead of multiplying by -1, you now use the negation operator to ensure difference's value is always positive. This works because negating a negative number makes it positive again. (Ask a math professor if you don't believe me.)

Use the new algorithm

➤ Give these new algorithms a try. You should replace the old stuff at the top of showAlert() as follows:

```
@IBAction func showAlert() {
  var difference = currentValue - targetValue
  if difference < 0 {
    difference = difference * -1
  }

  let message = . . .
}
```

When you run this new version of the app (try it!), it should work exactly the same as before. The result of the computation does not change, only the technique you used changed.

Another variation

The final alternative algorithm I want to show you uses a function.

You've already seen functions a few times before: you used arc4random_uniform() when you made random numbers and lroundf() for rounding off the slider's decimals.

To make sure a number is always positive, you can use the abs() function.

If you took math in school you might remember the term "absolute value", which is the value of a number without regard to its sign.

That's exactly what you need here, and the standard library contains a convenient function for it, which allows you to reduce this entire algorithm down to a single line of code:

```
let difference = abs(targetValue - currentValue)
```

It really doesn't matter whether you subtract `currentValue` from `targetValue` or the other way around. If the number is negative, `abs()` turns it positive. It's a handy function to remember.

➤ Make the change to `showAlert()` and try it out:

```
@IBAction func showAlert() {
   let difference = abs(targetValue - currentValue)

   let message = . . .
}
```

It doesn't get much simpler than that!

Exercise: Something else has changed… can you spot it?

Answer: You wrote **let** `difference` instead of **var** `difference`.

Variables and constants

Swift makes a distinction between variables and *constants*. Unlike a variable, the value of a constant, as the name implies, cannot change.

You can only put something into the box of a constant once and cannot replace it with something else afterwards.

The keyword `var` creates a variable while `let` creates a constant. That means `difference` is now a constant, not a variable.

In the previous algorithms, the value of `difference` could possibly change. If it was negative, you turned it positive. That required `difference` to be a variable, because only variables can have their value change.

Now that you can calculate the whole thing in a single line, `difference` will never have to change once you've given it a value. In that case, it's better to make it a constant with `let`. (Why is that better? It makes your intent clear, which in turn helps the Swift compiler understand your program better.)

By the same token, `message`, `alert`, and `action` are also constants (and have been all along!). Now you know why you declared these objects with `let` instead of `var`. Once they've been given a value, they never need to change.

Constants are very common in Swift. Often, you only need to hold onto a value for a very short time. If in that time the value never has to change, it's best to make it a constant (`let`) and not a variable (`var`).

What's the score?

Now that you know how far off the slider is from the target, calculating the player's score for each round is easy.

➤ Change `showAlert()` to:

```
@IBAction func showAlert() {
    let difference = abs(targetValue - currentValue)
    let points = 100 - difference

    let message = "You scored \(points) points"
    . . .
}
```

The maximum score you can get is 100 points if you put the slider right on the target and the difference is zero. The further away from the target you are, the fewer points you earn.

➤ Run the app and score some points!

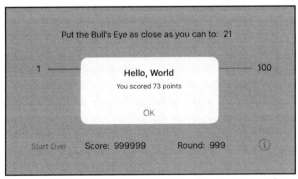

The alert with the player's score for the current round

Exercise: Because the maximum slider position is 100 and the minimum is 1, the biggest difference is 100 - 1 = 99. That means the absolute worst score you can have in a round is 1 point. Explain why this is so. (Eek! It requires math!)

The total score

In this game, you want to show the player's total score on the screen. After every round, the app should add the newly scored points to the total and then update the score label.

Store the total score

Because the game needs to keep the total score around for a long time, you will need an instance variable.

➤ Add a new `score` instance variable to **ViewController.swift**:

```
class ViewController: UIViewController {

    var currentValue: Int = 0
    var targetValue: Int = 0
    var score = 0                    // add this line
```

Did you notice that? Unlike the other two instance variables, you did not state that `score` is an `Int`!

If you don't specify a data type, Swift uses *type inference* to figure out what type you meant. Because 0 is a whole number, Swift assumes that `score` should be an integer, and therefore automatically gives it the type `Int`. Handy!

Note: If you are not sure about the inferred type of a variable, there is an easy way to find out. Simply hold down the **Alt** key and hover your cursor over the variable in question. The variable will be highlighted in blue and your cursor will turn into a question mark. Now, click on the variable and you will get a handy pop up which tells you the type of the variable as well as the source file in which the variable was declared.

Discover the inferred type for a variable

In fact, now that you know about type inference, you don't need to specify Int for the other instance variables either:

```
var currentValue = 0
var targetValue = 0
```

➤ Make the above changes.

Thanks to type inference, you only have to list the name of the data type when you're not giving the variable an initial value. But most of the time, you can safely make Swift guess at the type.

I think type inference is pretty sweet! It will definitely save you some, uh, typing (in more ways than one!).

Update the total score

Now showAlert() can be amended to update this score variable.

➤ Make the following changes:

```
@IBAction func showAlert() {
    let difference = abs(targetValue - currentValue)
    let points = 100 - difference

    score += points          // add this line

    let message = "You scored \(points) points"
    . . .
}
```

Nothing too shocking here. You just added the following line:

```
score += points
```

This adds the points that the user scored in this round to the total score. You could also have written it like this:

```
score = score + points
```

Personally, I prefer the shorthand += version, but either one is okay. Both accomplish exactly the same thing.

Display the score

In order to show your current score, you're going to do exactly the same thing that you did for the target label: hook up the score label to an outlet and put the score value into the label's text property.

> **Exercise:** See if you can do the above without my help. You've already done these things before for the target value label, so you should be able to repeat these steps by yourself for the score label.

Done? You should have done the following. You add this line to **ViewController.swift**:

```
@IBOutlet weak var scoreLabel: UILabel!
```

Then you connect the relevant label on the storyboard (the one that says 999999) to the new scoreLabel outlet.

Unsure how to connect the outlet? There are several ways to make connections from user interface objects to the view controller's outlets:

- Control-click on the object to get a context-sensitive popup menu. Then drag from New Referencing Outlet to View Controller (you did this with the slider).

- Go to the Connections Inspector for the label. Drag from New Referencing Outlet to View Controller (you did this with the target label).

- Control-drag **from** View Controller to the label (give this one a try now) - doing it the other way, Control-dragging from the label to the view controller, won't work.

There is more than one way to skin a cat, or, connect outlets :]

Great, that gives you a scoreLabel outlet that you can use to display the score. Now where in the code can you do that? In updateLabels(), of course.

➤ Back in **ViewController.swift**, change updateLabels() to the following:

```
func updateLabels() {
  targetLabel.text = String(targetValue)
  scoreLabel.text = String(score)      // add this line
}
```

Nothing new here. You convert the score – which is an Int – into a String and then pass that string to the label's text property. In response to that, the label will redraw itself with the new score.

➤ Run the app and verify that the points for this round are added to the total score label whenever you tap the button.

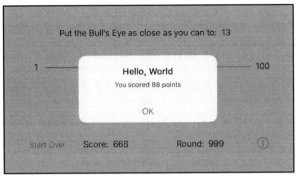

The score label keeps track of the player's total score

One more round...

Speaking of rounds, you also have to increment the round number each time the player starts a new round.

> **Exercise:** Keep track of the current round number (starting at 1) and increment it when a new round starts. Display the current round number in the corresponding label. I may be throwing you into the deep end here, but if you've been able to follow the instructions so far, then you've already seen all the pieces you will need to pull this off. Good luck!

If you guessed that you had to add another instance variable, then you were right. You should have added the following line (or something similar) to **ViewController.swift**:

```
var round = 0
```

It's also OK if you included the name of the data type, even though that is not strictly necessary:

```
var round: Int = 0
```

Also add an outlet for the label:

```
@IBOutlet weak var roundLabel: UILabel!
```

As before, you should connect the label to this outlet in Interface Builder.

Don't forget to make those connections

Forgetting to make the connections in Interface Builder is an often-made mistake, especially by yours truly.

It happens to me all the time that I make the outlet for a button and write the code to deal with taps on that button, but when I run the app it doesn't work. Usually it takes me a few minutes and some head scratching to realize that I forgot to connect the button to the outlet or the action method.

You can tap on the button all you want, but unless that connection exists your code will not respond.

Finally, `updateLabels()` should be modified like this:

```
func updateLabels() {
  targetLabel.text = String(targetValue)
  scoreLabel.text = String(score)
  roundLabel.text = String(round)    // add this line
}
```

Did you also figure out where to increment the `round` variable?

I'd say the `startNewRound()` method is a pretty good place. After all, you call this method whenever you start a new round. It makes sense to increment the round counter there.

➤ Change `startNewRound()` to:

```
func startNewRound() {
  round += 1              // add this line
  targetValue = ...
}
```

Note that when you declared the `round` instance variable, you gave it a default value of 0. Therefore, when the app starts up, `round` is initially 0. When you call `startNewRound()` for the very first time, it adds 1 to this initial value and as a result, the first round is properly counted as round 1.

➤ Run the app and try it out. The round counter should update whenever you press the Hit Me! button.

The round label counts how many rounds have been played

You're making great progress, well done!

You can find the project files for the app up to this point under **05 - Rounds and Score** in the Source Code folder. If you get stuck, compare your version of the app with these source files to see if you missed anything.

Chapter 6: Polish

At this point, your game is fully playable. The gameplay rules are all implemented and the logic doesn't seem to have any big flaws. As far as I can tell, there are no bugs either. But there's still some room for improvement.

This chapter will cover the following:

- **Tweaks:** Small UI tweaks to make the game look and function better.
- **The alert:** Updating the alert view functionality so that the screen updates *after* the alert goes away.
- **Start over:** Resetting the game to start afresh.

Tweaks

Obviously, the game is not very pretty yet and you will get to work on that soon. In the mean time, there are a few smaller tweaks you can make.

The alert title

Unless you already changed it, the title of the alert still says "Hello, World!" You could give it the name of the game, *Bull's Eye*, but I have a better idea. What if you change the title depending on how well the player did?

If the player put the slider right on the target, the alert could say: "Perfect!" If the slider is close to the target but not quite there, it could say, "You almost had it!" If the player is way off, the alert could say: "Not even close..." And so on. This gives the player a little more feedback on how well they did.

> **Exercise:** Think of a way to accomplish this. Where would you put this logic and how would you program it? Hint: there are an awful lot of "if's" in the preceding sentences.

The right place for this logic is `showAlert()`, because that is where you create the `UIAlertController`. You already do some calculations to create the message text and now you will do something similar for the title text.

➤ Here is the changed method in its entirety - replace the existing method with it:

```
@IBAction func showAlert() {
  let difference = abs(targetValue - currentValue)
  let points = 100 - difference
  score += points

  // add these lines
  let title: String
  if difference == 0 {
    title = "Perfect!"
  } else if difference < 5 {
    title = "You almost had it!"
  } else if difference < 10 {
    title = "Pretty good!"
  } else {
    title = "Not even close..."
  }

  let message = "You scored \(points) points"

  let alert = UIAlertController(title: title,  // change this
                               message: message,
                               preferredStyle: .alert)

  let action = UIAlertAction(title: "OK", style: .default,
                             handler: nil)
  alert.addAction(action)
  present(alert, animated: true, completion: nil)

  startNewRound()
}
```

You create a new local string named `title`, which will contain the text that is set for the alert title. Initially, this `title` doesn't have any value. (We'll discuss the `title` variable and how it is set up a bit more in detail just a little further on.)

To decide which title text to use, you look at the difference between the slider position and the target:

- If it equals 0, then the player was spot-on and you set `title` to "Perfect!" .

- If the difference is less than 5, you use the text "You almost had it!"

- A difference less than 10 is "Pretty good!"

- However, if the difference is 10 or greater, then you consider the player's attempt "Not even close..."

Can you follow the logic here? It's just a bunch of `if` statements that consider the different possibilities and choose a string in response.

When you create the `UIAlertController` object, you now give it this `title` string instead of a fixed text.

Constant initialization

In the above code, did you notice that `title` was declared explicitly as being a `String` value? And did you ask yourself why type inference wasn't used there instead? Also, you might have noticed that `title` is actually a constant and yet the code appears to set its value in multiple places. How does that work?

The answer to all of these questions lies in how constants (or `let` values, if you prefer) are initialized in Swift.

You could certainly have used type inference to declare the type for `title` by setting the initial declaration to:

```
let title = ""
```

But do you see the issue there? Now you've actually set the value for `title` and since it's a constant, you can't change the value again. So, the following lines where the `if` condition logic sets a value for `title` would now throw a compiler error since you are trying to set a value to a constant which already has a value. (Go on, try it in your own project! You know you want to ... :])

One way to fix this would be to declare `title` as a variable rather than a constant. Like this:

```
var title = ""
```

The above would work fine, and the compiler error would go away and everything would work fine. But you've got to ask yourself, do you really need a variable there? Or, would a constant do? I personally prefer to use constants where possible since they have less risk of unexpected side-effects because the value was accidentally changed in some fashion - for example, because one of your team members changed the code to use a variable that you had originally depended on being unchanged. That is why the code was written the way it was. But you can decide to carve out your own path since either approach would work.

But if you do declare `title` as a constant, how is it that your code above assigns multiple values to it? The secret is in the fact that while there are indeed multiple values being assigned to `title` , only one value would be assigned per each call to `showAlert` since the branches of an `if` condition are mutually exclusive. So, since `title` starts out without a value (the `let title: String` line only assigns a type, not a value), as long as the code ensures that `title` would always be initialized to a value before the value stored in `title` is accessed, the compiler will not complain.

Again, you can test for this by removing the `else` condition in the block of code where a value is assigned to `title`. Since an `if` condition is only one branch of a test, you need an `else` branch in order for the tests (and the assignment to `title`) to be exhaustive. So, if you remove the `else` branch, Xcode will immediately complain with an error like: "Constant 'title' used before being initialized".

```
59      let title: String
60      if difference == 0 {
61        title = "Perfect!"
62      } else if difference < 5 {
63        title = "You almost had it!"
64      } else if difference < 10 {
65        title = "Pretty good!"
66 //     } else {
67 //       title = "Not even close..."
68      }
69
70      let message = "You scored \(points) points"
71
72      let alert = UIAlertController(title: title,      ⓘ Constant 'title' used before being initialized
73                                   message: message,
74                                   preferredStyle: .alert)
```

A constant needs to be initialized exhaustively

Run the app and play the game for a bit. You'll see that the title text changes depending on how well you're doing. That `if` statement sure is handy!

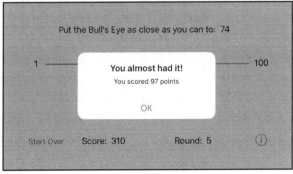

The alert with the new title

Bonus points

> **Exercise:** Give players an additional 100 bonus points when they get a perfect score. This will encourage players to really try to place the bull's eye right on the target. Otherwise, there isn't much difference between 100 points for a perfect score and 98 or 95 points if you're close but not quite there.
>
> Now there is an incentive for trying harder – a perfect score is no longer worth just 100 but 200 points! Maybe you can also give the player 50 bonus points for being just one off.

➤ Here is how I would have made these changes:

```
@IBAction func showAlert() {
  let difference = abs(targetValue - currentValue)
  var points = 100 - difference      // change let to var

  let title: String
  if difference == 0 {
    title = "Perfect!"
    points += 100                    // add this line
  } else if difference < 5 {
    title = "You almost had it!"
    if difference == 1 {             // add these lines
      points += 50
    }
  } else if difference < 10 {
    title = "Pretty good!"
  } else {
    title = "Not even close..."
  }
  score += points                    // move this line here
  . . .
}
```

You should notice a few things:

- In the first `if` you'll see a new statement between the curly brackets. When the difference is equal to zero, you now not only set `title` to "Perfect!" but also award an extra 100 points.

- The second `if` has changed too. There is now an `if` inside another `if`. Nothing wrong with that! You want to handle the case where `difference` is 1 in order to give the player bonus points. That happens inside the new `if` statement.

After all, if the difference is more than 0 but less than 5, it could be 1 (but not necessarily all the time). Therefore, you perform an additional check to see if the difference truly was 1, and if so, add 50 extra points.

- Because these new `if` statements add extra points, `points` can no longer be a constant; it now needs to be a variable. That's why you changed it from `let` to `var`.

- Finally, the line `score += points` has moved below the `if`s. This is necessary because the app updates the `points` variable inside those `if` statements (if the conditions are right) and you want those additional points to count towards the final score.

If your code is slightly different, then that's fine too, as long as it works! There is often more than one way to program something, and if the results are the same, then any approach is equally valid.

➤ Run the app to see if you can score some bonus points!

Raking in the points...

Local variables recap

I would like to point out once more the difference between local variables and instance variables. As you should know by now, a local variable only exists for the duration of the method that it is defined in, while an instance variable exists as long as the view controller (or any object that owns it) exists. The same thing is true for constants.

In `showAlert()`, there are six locals and you use three instance variables:

```
let difference = abs(targetValue - currentValue)
var points = 100 - difference
let title = . . .
score += points
let message = . . .
let alert = . . .
let action = . . .
```

Exercise: Point out which are the locals and which are the instance variables in the showAlert() method. Of the locals, which are variables and which are constants?

Locals are easy to recognize, because the first time they are used inside a method their name is preceded with let or var:

```
let difference = . . .
var points = . . .
let title = . . .
let message = . . .
let alert = . . .
let action = . . .
```

This syntax creates a new variable (var) or constant (let). Because these variables and constants are created inside the method, they are locals.

Those six items – difference, points, title, message, alert, and action – are restricted to the showAlert() method and do not exist outside of it. As soon as the method is done, the locals cease to exist.

You may be wondering how difference, for example, can have a different value every time the player taps the Hit Me button, even though it is a constant – after all, aren't constants given a value just once, never to change afterwards?

Here's why: each time a method is invoked, its local variables and constants are created anew. The old values have long been discarded and you get brand new ones.

When showAlert() is called, it creates a completely new instance of difference that is unrelated to the previous one. That particular constant value is only used until the end of showAlert() and then it is discarded.

The next time showAlert() is called after that, it creates yet another new instance of difference (as well as new instances of the other locals points, title, message, alert, and action). And so on… There's some serious recycling going on here!

But inside a single invocation of showAlert(), difference can never change once it has a value assigned. The only local in showAlert() that can change is points, because it's a var.

The instance variables, on the other hand, are defined outside of any method. It is common to put them at the top of the file:

```
class ViewController: UIViewController {
   var currentValue = 0
   var targetValue = 0
   var score = 0
```

```
    var round = 0
```

As a result, you can use these variables inside any method, without the need to declare them again, and they will keep their values till the object holding them (the view controller in this case) ceases to exist.

If you were to do this:

```
@IBAction func showAlert() {
   let difference = abs(targetValue - currentValue)
   var points = 100 - difference

   var score = score + points        // doesn't work!
   . . .
}
```

Then things wouldn't work as you'd expect them to. Because you now put var in front of score, you have made it a new local variable that is only valid inside this method.

In other words, this won't add points to the *instance variable* score but to a new *local variable* that also happens to be named score. The instance variable score never gets changed, even though it has the same name.

Obviously that is not what you want to happen here. Fortunately, the above won't even compile. Swift knows there's something fishy about that line.

> **Note:** To make a distinction between the two types of variables, so that it's always clear at a glance how long they will live, some programmers prefix the names of instance variables with an underscore.
>
> They would name the variable _score instead of just score. Now there is less confusion because names beginning with an underscore won't be mistaken for being locals. This is only a convention. Swift doesn't care one way or the other how you spell your instance variables.
>
> Other programmers use different prefixes, such as "m" (for member) or "f" (for field) for the same purpose. Some even put the underscore *behind* the variable name. Madness!

The alert

There is something that bothers me about the game. You may have noticed it too...

As soon as you tap the Hit Me! button and the alert pops up, the slider immediately jumps back to its center position, the round number increments, and the target label already gets the new random number.

What happens is that the new round already gets started while you're still watching the results of the last round. That's a little confusing (and annoying).

It would be better to wait on starting the new round until *after* the player has dismissed the alert popup. Only then is the current round truly over.

Asynchronous code execution

Maybe you're wondering why this isn't already happening? After all, in `showAlert()` you only call `startNewRound()` after you've shown the alert popup:

```
@IBAction func showAlert() {
  . . .
  let alert = UIAlertController(. . .)
  let action = UIAlertAction(. . .)
  alert.addAction(action)

  // Here you make the alert visible:
  present(alert, animated: true, completion: nil)

  // Here you start the new round:
  startNewRound()
}
```

Contrary to what you might expect, `present(alert:animated:completion:)` doesn't hold up execution of the rest of the method until the alert popup is dismissed. That's how alerts on other platforms tend to work, but not on iOS.

Instead, `present(alert:animated:completion:)` puts the alert on the screen and immediately returns control to the next line of code in the method. The rest of the `showAlert()` method is executed right away, and the new round already starts before the alert popup has even finished animating.

In programmer-speak, alerts work *asynchronously*. We'll talk much more about that in a later chapter, but what it means for you right now is that you don't know in advance when the alert will be done. But you can bet it will be well after `showAlert()` has finished.

Alert event handling

So, if your code execution can't wait in showAlert() until the popup is dismissed, then how do you wait for it to close?

The answer is simple: events! As you've seen, a lot of the programming for iOS involves waiting for specific events to occur – buttons being tapped, sliders being moved, and so on. This is no different. You have to wait for the "alert dismissed" event somehow. In the mean time, you simply do nothing.

Here's how it works:

For each button on the alert, you have to supply a UIAlertAction object. This object tells the alert what the text on the button is – "OK" – and what the button looks like (you're using the default style here):

```
let action = UIAlertAction(title: "OK", style: .default,
  handler: nil)
```

The third parameter, handler, tells the alert what should happen when the button is pressed. This is the "alert dismissed" event you've been looking for.

Currently handler is nil, which means nothing happens. To change this, you'll need to give the UIAlertAction some code to execute when the button is tapped. When the user finally taps OK, the alert will remove itself from the screen and jump to your code. That's your cue to take it from there.

This is also known as the *callback* pattern. There are several ways this pattern manifests on iOS. Often you'll be asked to create a new method to handle the event. But here you'll use something new: a *closure*.

➤ Change the bottom bit of showAlert() to:

```
@IBAction func showAlert() {
  . . .
  let alert = UIAlertController(. . .)

  let action = UIAlertAction(title: "OK", style: .default,
                    handler: { action in
                               self.startNewRound()
                    })

  alert.addAction(action)
  present(alert, animated: true, completion: nil)
}
```

Two things have happened here:

1. You removed the call to `startNewRound()` from the bottom of the method. (Don't forget this part!)

2. You placed it inside a block of code that you gave to `UIAlertAction`'s `handler` parameter.

Such a block of code is called a closure. You can think of it as a method without a name. This code is not performed right away. Rather, it's performed only when the OK button is tapped. This particular closure tells the app to start a new round (and update the labels) when the alert is dismissed.

➤ Run it and see for yourself. I think the game feels a lot better this way.

> **Self**
>
> You may be wondering why in the handler block you did `self.startNewRound()` instead of just writing `startNewRound()` like before.
>
> The `self` keyword allows the view controller to refer to itself. That shouldn't be too strange a concept. When you say, "I want ice cream," you use the word "I" to refer to yourself. Similarly, objects can talk about (or to) themselves as well.
>
> Normally you don't need to use `self` to send messages to the view controller, even though it is allowed. The exception: inside closures you *do* have to use `self` to refer to the view controller.
>
> This is a rule in Swift. If you forget `self` in a closure, Xcode doesn't want to build your app (try it out). This rule exists because closures can "capture" variables, which comes with surprising side effects. You'll learn more about that in later chapters.

Start over

No, you're not going to throw away the source code and start this project all over! I'm talking about the game's "Start Over" button. This button is supposed to reset the score and start over from the first round.

One use of the Start Over button is for playing against another person. The first player does ten rounds, then the score is reset and the second player does ten rounds. The player with the highest score wins.

> **Exercise:** Try to implement the Start Over button on your own. You've already seen how you can make the view controller react to button presses, and you should be able to figure out how to change the score and round variables.

How did you do? If you got stuck, then follow the instructions below.

The new method

First, add a method to **ViewController.swift** that starts a new game. I suggest you put it near startNewRound() because the two are conceptually related.

➤ Add the new method:

```
func startNewGame() {
   score = 0
   round = 0
   startNewRound()
}
```

This method resets score and round to zero, and starts a new round as well.

Notice that you set round to 0 here, not to 1. You use 0 because incrementing the value of round is the first thing that startNewRound() does.

If you were to set round to 1, then startNewRound() would add another 1 to it and the first round would actually be labeled round 2.

So, you begin at 0, let startNewRound() add one and everything works great.

(It's probably easier to figure this out from the code than from my explanation. This should illustrate why we don't program computers in English.)

You also need an action method to handle taps on the Start Over button. You could write a new method like the following:

```
@IBAction func startOver() {
   startNewGame()
}
```

But you'll notice that this method simply calls the previous method you added :] So, why not cut out the middleman? You can simply change the method you added previously to be an action instead, like this:

```
@IBAction func startNewGame() {
   score = 0
   round = 0
```

```
    startNewRound()
  }
```

You could follow either of the above approaches since both are valid. Personally, I like to have less code since that means there's less stuff to maintain (and less of a chance of screwing something up :]). Sometimes, there could also be legitimate reasons for having a seperate action method which calls your own method, but in this particular case, it's better to keep things simple.

Just to keep things consistent, in `viewDidLoad()` you should replace the call to `startNewRound()` with `startNewGame()`. Because `score` and `round` are already 0 when the app starts, it won't really make any difference to how the app works, but it does make the intention of the source code clearer. (If you wonder if you can call an `IBAction` method directly instead of hooking it up to an action in the storyboard, yes, you certainly can do so.)

➤ Make this change:

```
override func viewDidLoad() {
  super.viewDidLoad()
  startNewGame()          // this line changed
}
```

Connect the outlet

Finally, you need to connect the Start Over button to the action method.

➤ Open the storyboard and Control-drag from the **Start Over** button to **View Controller**. Let go of the mouse button and pick **startNewGame** from the popup if you opted to have `startNewGame()` as the action method. Otherwise, pick the name of your action method .

That connects the button's Touch Up Inside event to the action you have just defined.

➤ Run the app and play a few rounds. Press Start Over and the game puts you back at square one.

Tip: If you're losing track of what button or label is connected to what method, you can click on **View Controller** in the storyboard to see all the connections that you have made so far.

You can either right-click on View Controller to get a popup, or simply view the connections in the **Connections inspector**. This shows all the connections for the view controller.

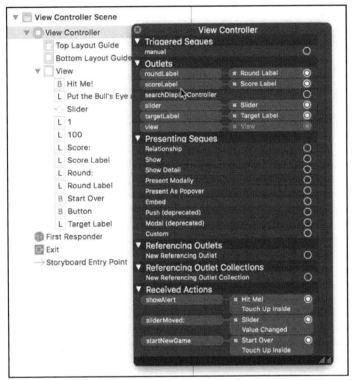

All the connections from View Controller to the other objects

Now your game is pretty polished and your task list is getting ever shorter :]

You can find the project files for the current version of the app under **06 - Polish** in the Source Code folder.

Chapter 7: The New Look

Bull's Eye is looking good, the gameplay elements are done, and there's one item left in your to-do list - "Make it look pretty".

You have to admit the game still doesn't look great. If you were to put this on the App Store in its current form, I'm not sure many people would be excited to download it. Fortunately, iOS makes it easy for you to create good-looking apps, so let's give *Bull's Eye* a makeover and add some visual flair.

This chapter covers the following:

- **Landscape orientation revisited:** Project changes to make landscape orientation support work better.

- **Spice up the graphics:** Replace the app UI with custom graphics to give it a more polished look.

- **The about Screen:** Add an about screen to the app and make it look spiffy.

Landscape orientation revisited

First, let's quickly revisit another item in the to-do list - "Put the app in landscape orientation." You already did this, right? But there's a little bit of clean up to be done with regards to that item.

Apps in landscape mode do not display the iPhone status bar, unless you tell them to. That's great for your app - games require a more immersive experience and the status bar detracts from that.

Even though the system automatically handles not showing the status bar for your game, there is still one thing you can do to improve the way *Bull's Eye* handles the status bar.

➤ Go to the **Project Settings** screen and scroll down to **Deployment Info**. Under **Status Bar Style**, check the option **Hide status bar**.

This will ensure that the status bar is hidden during application launch.

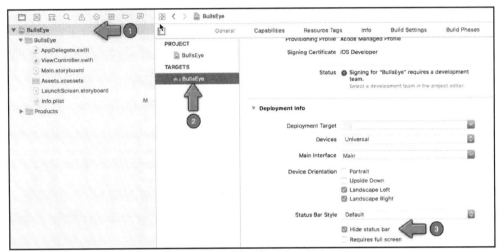

Hiding the status bar when the app launches

It's a good idea to hide the status bar while the app is launching. It takes a few seconds for the operating system to load the app into memory and start it up, and during that time the status bar remains visible, unless you hide it using this option.

It's only a small detail, but the difference between a mediocre app and a great app is that great apps get all the small details right.

➤ That's it. Run the app and you'll see that the status bar is history.

Info.plist

Most of the options from the Project Settings screen, such as the supported device orientations and whether the status bar is visible during launch, get stored in your app's Info.plist file.

Info.plist is a configuration file inside the application bundle that tells iOS how the app will behave. It also describes certain characteristics of the app, such as the version number, that don't really fit anywhere else.

With some earlier versions of Xcode, you often had to edit Info.plist by hand, but with the latest Xcode versions this is hardly necessary anymore. You can make most of the changes directly from the Project Settings screen.

However, it's good to know that Info.plist exists and what it looks like.

➤ Go to the **Project navigator** and select the file named **Info.plist** to take a peek at its contents.

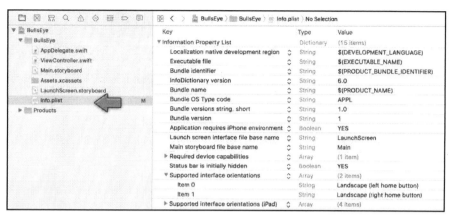

The Info.plist file is just a list of configuration options and their values. Most of these may not make sense to you, but that's OK – they don't always make sense to me either.

Notice the option **Status bar is initially hidden**. It has the value YES. This is the option that you just changed.

Spice up the graphics

Getting rid of the status bar is only the first step. We want to go from this:

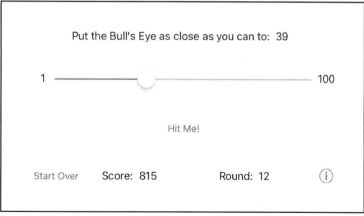

Yawn…

To something that's more like this:

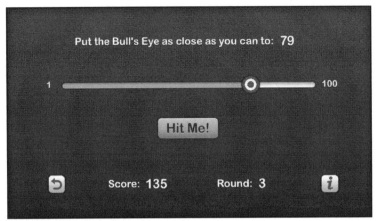

Cool :-)

The actual controls don't change. You'll simply use images to smarten up their look, and you will also adjust the colors and typefaces.

You can put an image in the background, on the buttons, and even on the slider, to customize the appearance of each. The images you use should generally be in PNG format, though JPG files would work too.

Add the image assets

If you are artistically challenged, then don't worry, I have provided a set of images for you. But if you do have mad Photoshop skillz, then by all means feel free to design (and use) your own images.

The Resources folder that comes with this book contains a subfolder named Images. You will first import these images into the Xcode project.

➤ In the **Project navigator**, find **Assets.xcassets** and click on it.

This is known as the asset catalog for the app and it contains all the app's images. Right now, it is empty and contains just a placeholder for the app icon, which you'll add soon.

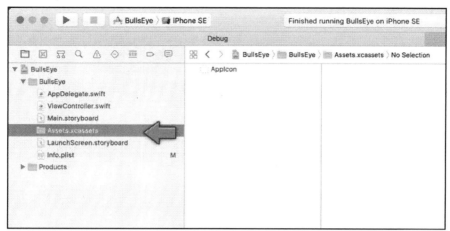

The asset catalog is initially empty

➤ At the bottom of the secondary pane, the one with AppIcon, there is a + button. Click it and then select the **Import...** option:

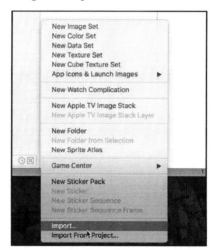

Choose Import to put existing images into the asset catalog

Xcode shows a file picker. Select the **Images** folder from the resources and press ⌘+A to select all the files inside this folder.

Choosing the images to import

Click **Open** and Xcode copies all the image files from that folder into the asset catalog:

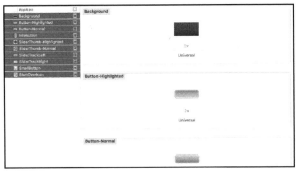

The images are now inside the asset catalog

If Xcode added a folder named "Images" instead of the individual image files, then try again and this time make sure that you select the files inside the Images folder rather than the folder itself before you click Open.

> **Note:** Instead of using the **Import…** menu option as above, you could also simply drag the necessary files from Finder on to the Xcode asset catalog view. As ever, there's more than one way to do the same thing in Xcode.

1x, 2x, and 3x displays

Currently, each image set in the asset catalog has a slot for a "2x" image, but you can also specify 1x and 3x images. Having multiple versions of the same image in varying sizes allows your apps to support the wide variety of iPhone and iPad displays in existence.

1x is for low-resolution screens, the ones with the big, chunky pixels. There are no low-resolution devices in existence that can actually run iOS 11 – they are too old to bother with – so you're not likely to come across many 1x images anymore. 1x is only a concern if you're working on an app that still needs to support iOS 9 or older.

2x is for high-resolution Retina screens. This covers most modern iPhones, iPod touches, and iPads. Retina images are twice as big as the low-res images, hence the 2x. The images you imported just now are 2x images.

3x is for the super high-resolution Retina HD screen of the iPhone Plus devices. If you want your app to have extra sharp images on these top-of-the-line iPhone models, then you can drop them into the "3x" slot in the asset catalog.

There is a special naming convention for image files. If the filename ends in **@2x** or **@3x** then that's considered the Retina or Retina HD version. Low-resolution 1x images have no special name (you don't have to write @1x).

★ ★ ★

Put up the wallpaper

Let's begin by changing the drab white background in *Bull's Eye* to something more fancy.

➤ Open **Main.storyboard**. Go into the **Object Library** and locate an **Image View**. (Tip: if you type "image" into the search box at the bottom of the Object Library, it will quickly filter out all the other views.)

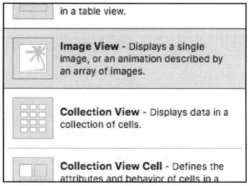

The Image View control in the Object Library

➤ Drag the image view on top of the existing user interface. It doesn't really matter where you put it, as long as it's inside the Bull's Eye View Controller.

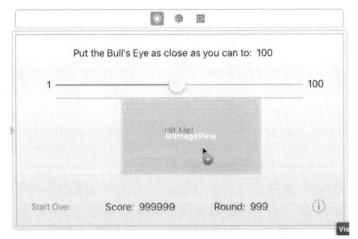

Dragging the Image View into the view controller

➤ With the image view still selected, go to the **Size inspector** (that's the one next to the Attributes inspector) and set X and Y to 0, Width to 568 and Height to 320.

This will make the image view cover the entire screen.

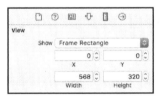

The Size inspector settings for the Image View

➤ Go to the **Attributes inspector** for the image view. At the top there is an option named **Image**. Click the downward arrow and choose **Background** from the list.

This will put the image named "Background" from the asset catalog into the image view.

Setting the background image on the Image View

There is only one problem: the image now covers all the other controls. There is an easy fix for that; you have to move the image view behind the other views.

➤ In the **Editor** menu in Xcode's menu bar at the top of the screen, choose **Arrange** →
Send to Back.

Sometimes Xcode gives you a hard time with this (it still has a few bugs) and you might
not see the Send to Back item enabled. If so, try de-selecting the Image View and then
selecting it again. Now the menu item should be available.

Alternatively, pick up the image view in the Document Outline and drag it to the top of
the list of views, just below View, to accomplish the same thing. (The items in the
Document Outline view are listed so that the backmost item is at the top of the list and
the frontmost one is at the bottom.)

Your interface should now look something like this:

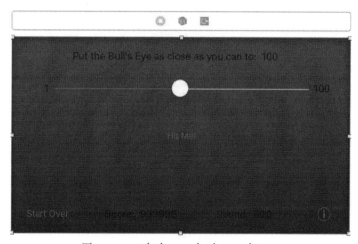

The game with the new background image

That takes care of the background. Run the app and marvel at the new graphics.

Change the labels

Because the background image is quite dark, the black text labels have become hard to
read. Fortunately, Interface Builder lets you change their color. While you're at it, you
might change the font as well.

➤ Still in the storyboard, select the label at the top, open the **Attributes inspector** and
click on the **Color** item - there are two parts to the item, so you need to click on the
actual color and not the text part.

Setting the text color on the label

This opens the Color Picker, which has several ways to select colors. I prefer the sliders (second tab). If all you see is a gray scale slider, then select RGB Sliders from the select box at the top.

➤ Pick a pure white color, Red: 255, Green: 255, Blue: 255, Opacity: 100%.

➤ Click on the **Shadow** item from the Attributes inspector. This lets you add a subtle shadow to the label. By default this color is transparent (also known as "Clear Color") so you won't see the shadow. Using the Color Picker, choose a pure black color that is half transparent, Red: 0, Green: 0, Blue: 0, Opacity: 50%.

Note: Sometimes when you change the Color or Shadow attributes, the background color of the view also changes. This is a bug in Xcode. Put it back to Clear Color if that happens.

➤ Change the **Shadow Offset** to Width: 0, Height: 1. This puts the shadow below the label.

The shadow you've chosen is very subtle. If you're not sure that it's actually visible, then toggle the height offset between 1 and 0 a few times. Look closely and you should be able to see the difference. As I said, it's very subtle.

➤ Click on the [T] icon of the **Font** attribute. This opens the Font Picker.

By default the System font is selected. That uses whatever is the standard system font for the user's device. The system font is nice enough but we want something more exciting for this game.

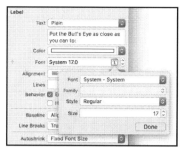

Font picker with the System font

➤ Choose **Font: Custom**. That enables the Family field. Choose **Family: Arial Rounded MT Bold**. Set the Size to 16.

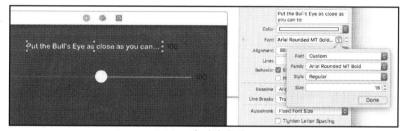

Setting the label's font

➤ The label also has an attribute **Autoshrink**. Make sure this is set to **Fixed Font Size**.

If enabled, Autoshrink will dynamically change the size of the font if the text is larger than will fit into the label. That is useful in certain apps, but not in this one. Instead, you'll change the size of the label to fit the text rather than the other way around.

➤ With the label selected, press ⌘= on your keyboard, or choose **Size to Fit Content** from the **Editor** menu.

(If the Size to Fit Content menu item is disabled, then de-select the label and select it again. Sometimes Xcode gets confused about what is selected. Poor thing.)

The label will now become slightly larger or smaller so that it fits snugly around the text. If the text got cut off when you changed the font, now all the text will show again.

You don't have to set these properties for the other labels one by one; that would be a big chore. You can speed up the process by selecting multiple labels and then applying these changes to that entire selection.

➤ Click on the **Score:** label to select it. Hold ⌘ and click on the **Round:** label. Now both labels will be selected. Repeat what you did above for these labels:

• Set Color to pure white, 100% opaque.

- Set Shadow to pure black, 50% opaque.

- Set Shadow Offset to width 0, height 1.

- Set Font to Arial Rounded MT Bold, size 16.

- Make sure Autoshrink is set to Fixed Font Size.

As you can see, in my storyboard the text no longer fits into the Score and Round labels:

The font is too large to fit all the text in the Score and Round labels

You can either make the labels larger by dragging their handles to resize them manually, or you can use the **Size to Fit Content** option (⌘=). I prefer the latter because it's less work.

Tip: Xcode is smart enough to remember the colors you have used recently. Instead of going into the Color Picker all the time, you can simply choose a color from the Recently Used Colors menu.

Click the tiny arrows at the end of the color field (or, if there is a text name for the color, click on the text part) and the menu will pop up:

Quick access to recently used colors and several handy presets

Exercise: You still have a few labels to go. Repeat what you just did for the other labels. They should all become white, have the same shadow and have the same font. However, the two labels on either side of the slider (1 and 100) will have font size 14, while the other labels (the ones that will hold the target value, the score and the round number) will have font size 20 so they stand out more.

Because you've changed the sizes of some of the labels, your carefully constructed layout may have been messed up a bit. You may want to clean it up a little.

At this point, the game screen should look something like this:

What the storyboard looks like after styling the labels

All right, it's starting to look like something now. By the way, feel free to experiment with the fonts and colors. If you want to make it look completely different, then go right ahead. It's your app!

The buttons

Changing the look of the buttons works very much the same way.

➤ Select the **Hit Me!** button. In the **Size inspector** set its Width to 100 and its Height to 37.

➤ Center the position of the button on the inner circle of the background image.

➤ Go to the **Attributes inspector**. Change **Type** from System to **Custom**.

A "system" button just has a label and no border. By making it a custom button, you can style it any way you wish.

➤ Still in the **Attributes inspector**, press the arrow on the **Background** field and choose **Button-Normal** from the list.

➤ Set the **Font** to **Arial Rounded MT Bold**, size 20.

➤ Set the **Text Color** to red: 96, green: 30, blue: 0, opacity: 100%. This is a dark brown color.

➤ Set the **Shadow Color** to pure white, 50% opacity. The shadow offset should be Width 0, Height 1.

Blending in

Setting the opacity to anything less than 100% will make the color slightly transparent (with opacity of 0% being fully transparent). Partial transparency makes the color blend in with the background and makes it appear softer.

Try setting the shadow color to 100% opaque pure white and notice the difference.

This finishes the setup for the Hit Me! button in its "default" state:

The attributes for the Hit Me button in the default state

Buttons can have more than one state. When you tap a button and hold it down, it should appear "pressed down" to let you know that the button will be activated when you lift your finger. This is known as the *highlighted* state and is an important visual cue to the user.

➤ With the button still selected, click the **State Config** setting and pick **Highlighted** from the menu. Now the attributes in this section reflect the highlighted state of the button.

➤ In the **Background** field, select **Button-Highlighted**.

➤ Make sure the highlighted **Text Color** is the same color as before (red 96, green 30, blue 0, or simply pick it from the Recently Used Colors menu). Change the **Shadow Color** to half-transparent white again.

➤ Check the **Reverses On Highlight** option. This will give the appearance of the label being pressed down when the user taps the button.

You could change the other properties too, but don't get too carried away. The highlight effect should not be too jarring.

The attributes for the highlighted Hit Me button

To test the highlighted look of the button in Interface Builder you can toggle the **Highlighted** box in the **Control** section, but make sure to turn it off again or the button will initially appear highlighted when the screen is shown.

That's it for the Hit Me! button. Styling the Start Over button is very similar, except you will replace its title text with an icon.

➤ Select the **Start Over** button and change the following attributes:

• Set Type to Custom.

• Remove the text "Start Over" from the button.

• For Image choose **StartOverIcon**

• For Background choose **SmallButton**

• Set Width and Height to 32.

You won't set a highlighted state on this button - let UIKit take care of this. If you don't specify a different image for the highlighted state, UIKit will automatically darken the button to indicate that it is pressed.

➤ Make the same changes to the ⓘ button, but this time choose **InfoButton** for the image.

The user interface is almost done. Only the slider is left…

Almost done!

The slider

Unfortunately, you can only customize the slider a little bit in Interface Builder. For the more advanced customization that this game needs – putting your own images on the thumb and the track – you have to resort to writing source code.

Everything you have done so far in Interface Builder you could also have done in code. Setting the color on a button, for example, can be done by sending the setTitleColor() message to the button. (You would normally do this in viewDidLoad.)

However, I find that doing visual design work is much easier and quicker in a visual editor such as Interface Builder than writing the equivalent source code. But for the slider you have no choice.

➤ Go to **ViewController.swift**, and add the following to viewDidLoad():

```swift
let thumbImageNormal = UIImage(named: "SliderThumb-Normal")!
slider.setThumbImage(thumbImageNormal, for: .normal)

let thumbImageHighlighted = UIImage(named: "SliderThumb-
Highlighted")!
slider.setThumbImage(thumbImageHighlighted, for: .highlighted)

let insets = UIEdgeInsets(top: 0, left: 14, bottom: 0, right:
14)

let trackLeftImage = UIImage(named: "SliderTrackLeft")!
let trackLeftResizable =
                trackLeftImage.resizableImage(withCapInsets:
insets)
slider.setMinimumTrackImage(trackLeftResizable, for: .normal)

let trackRightImage = UIImage(named: "SliderTrackRight")!
let trackRightResizable =
                trackRightImage.resizableImage(withCapInsets:
insets)
slider.setMaximumTrackImage(trackRightResizable, for: .normal)
```

This sets four images on the slider: two for the thumb and two for the track. (And if you're wondering what the "thumb" is, that's the little circle in the center of the slider, the one that you drag around to set the slider value.)

The thumb works like a button so it gets an image for the normal (un-pressed) state and one for the highlighted state.

The slider uses different images for the track on the left of the thumb (green) and the track to the right of the thumb (gray).

➤ Run the app. You have to admit it looks fantastic now!

The game with the customized slider graphics

To .png or not to .png

If you recall, the images that you imported into the asset catalog had filenames like **SliderThumb-Normal@2x.png** and so on.

When you create a `UIImage` object, you don't use the original filename but the name that is listed in the asset catalog, **SliderThumb-Normal**.

That means you can leave off the **@2x** bit and the **.png** file extension.

Tip: Xcode now has a handy new feature that makes it really easy to add images in your code. Instead of writing:

```
let thumbImageNormal = UIImage(named: "SliderThumb-Normal")
```

You can now type:

```
let thumbImageNormal = Sli
```

And Xcode's autocomplete will kick in and show a list of suggestions to complete the text `Sli`, including any images whose names start with those letters.

Xcode autocomplete also shows images

Pick **SliderThumb-Normal** from the list and it will add a tiny icon of the image into the code! This tiny icon is known as an *image literal*. If you do the same for the other images, your code will look like this:

```
// Customize slider
let thumbImageNormal = ◉
slider.setThumbImage(thumbImageNormal, for: .normal)

let thumbImageHighlighted = ◉
slider.setThumbImage(thumbImageHighlighted, for: .highlighted)

let insets = UIEdgeInsets(top: 0, left: 14, bottom: 0, right: 14)

let trackLeftImage = ◉
let trackLeftResizable =
  trackLeftImage.resizableImage(withCapInsets: insets)
slider.setMinimumTrackImage(trackLeftResizable, for: .normal)

let trackRightImage = ◉
let trackRightResizable =
  trackRightImage.resizableImage(withCapInsets: insets)
slider.setMaximumTrackImage(trackRightResizable, for: .normal)
```

The images are now part of your source code

Give it a try! I really like how it shows a tiny thumbnail of the image right in the code.

Run your app once again to verify that adding the image literals did not change the functionality of the game in any way. It shouldn't, but it's always good to be sure, right?

The About Screen

Your game looks awesome and your to-do list is done. So, does this mean that you are done with *Bull's Eye*?

Not so fast :] Remember the ⓘ button on the game screen? Try tapping it. Does it do anything? No?

Ooops! Looks as if we forgot to add any functionality to that button :] It's time to rectify that - let's add an "about" screen to the game which shows some information about the game and have it display when the user taps on the ⓘ button.

Initially, the screen will look something like this (but we'll prettify it soon enough):

*** Bull's Eye ***

Welcome to the awesome game of Bull's Eye where you can win points and fame by dragging a slider.

Your goal is to place the slider as close as possible to the target value. The closer you are, the more points you score. Enjoy!

Close

The new About screen

This new screen contains a *text view* with the gameplay rules and a button to close the screen.

Most apps have more than one screen, even very simple games. So, this is as good a time as any to learn how to add additional screens to your apps.

I have pointed it out a few times already: each screen in your app will have its own view controller. If you think "screen", think "view controller".

Xcode automatically created the main `ViewController` object for you, but you'll have to create the view controller for the About screen yourself.

Add a new view controller

➤ Go to Xcode's **File** menu and choose **New → File...** In the window that pops up, choose the **Cocoa Touch Class** template (if you don't see it then make sure **iOS** is selected at the top).

Choosing the file template for Cocoa Touch Class

Click **Next**. Xcode gives you some options to fill out:

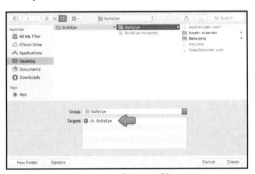

The options for the new file

Choose the following:

- Class: **AboutViewController**

- Subclass of: **UIViewController**

- Also create XIB file: Leave this box unchecked.

- Language: **Swift**

Click **Next**. Xcode will ask you where to save this new view controller.

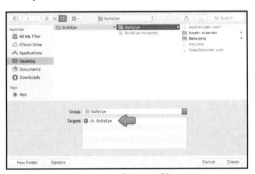

Saving the new file

➤ Choose the **BullsEye** folder (this folder should already be selected).

Also make sure **Group** says **BullsEye** and that there is a checkmark in front of BullsEye in the list of **Targets**. (If you don't see this panel, click the Options button at the bottom of the dialog.)

➤ Click **Create**.

Xcode will create a new file and add it to your project. As you might have guessed, the new file is **AboutViewController.swift**.

Design the view controller in Interface Builder

To design this new view controller, you need to pay a visit to Interface Builder.

➤ Open **Main.storyboard**. There is no scene representing the About view controller in the storyboard yet. So, you'll have to add this first.

➤ From the **Object Library**, choose **View Controller** and drag it on to the canvas, to the right of the main View Controller.

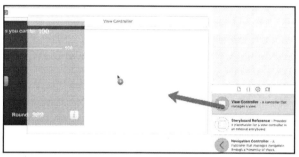

Dragging a new View Controller from the Object Library

This new view controller is totally blank. You may need to rearrange the storyboard so that the two view controllers don't overlap. Interface Builder isn't very tidy about where it puts things.

➤ Drag a new **Button** on to the screen and give it the title **Close**. Put it somewhere in the bottom center of the view (use the blue guidelines to help with positioning).

➤ Drag a **Text View** on to the view and make it cover most of the space above the button.

You can find these components in the Object Library. If you don't feel like scrolling, you can filter the components by typing in the field at the bottom:

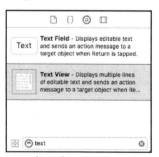

Searching for text components

Note that there is also a Text Field, which is a single-line text component - that's not what you want. You're looking for Text View, which can contain multiple lines of text.

After dragging both the text view and the button on to the canvas, it should look something like this:

The About screen in the storyboard

➤ Double-click the text view to make its content is editable. By default, the Text View contains a bunch of Latin placeholder text (also known as "Lorem Ipsum").

Copy-paste this new text into the Text View:

```
*** Bull's Eye ***

Welcome to the awesome game of Bull's Eye where you can win
points and fame by dragging a slider.

Your goal is to place the slider as close as possible to the
target value. The closer you are, the more points you score.
Enjoy!
```

You can also paste that text into the Attributes inspector's **Text** property for the text view if you find that easier.

➤ Make sure to uncheck the **Editable** checkbox in the Attribute Inspector. Otherwise, the user can actually type into the text view and you don't want that.

The Attributes inspector for the text view

That's the design of the screen done for now.

Show the new view controller

So how do you open this new About screen when the user presses the ⓘ button? Storyboards have a neat trick for this: *segues* (pronounced "seg-way" like the silly scooters). A segue is a transition from one screen to another. They are really easy to add.

➤ Click the ⓘ button in the **View Controller** to select it. Then hold down **Control** and drag over to the **About** screen.

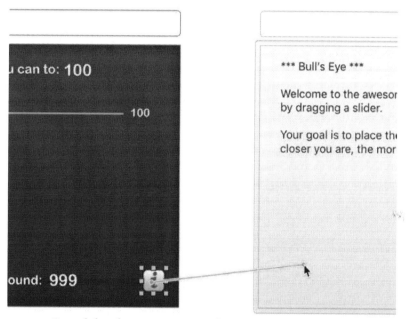

Control-drag from one view controller to another to make a segue

➤ Let go of the mouse button and a popup appears with several options. Choose **Present Modally**.

Choosing the type of segue to create

Now an arrow will appear between the two screens. This arrow represents the segue from the main scene to the About scene.

➤ Click the arrow to select it. Segues also have attributes. In the **Attributes inspector**, choose **Transition, Flip Horizontal**. That is the animation that UIKit will use to move between these screens.

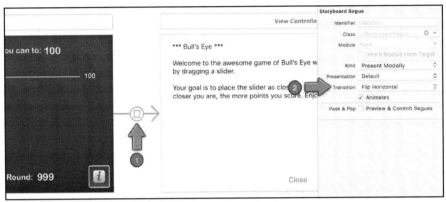

Changing the attributes for the segue

➤ Now you can run the app. Press the ⓘ button to see the new screen.

The About screen appears with a flip animation

The About screen should appear with a neat animation. Good, that seems to work.

Dismiss the About view controller

However, there is an obvious shortcoming here: tapping the Close button seems to have no effect. Once the user enters the About screen they can never leave… that doesn't sound like good user interface design to me, does it?

The problem with segues is that they only go one way. To close this screen, you have to hook up some code to the Close button. As a budding iOS developer you already know how to do that: use an action method!

This time you will add the action method to `AboutViewController` instead of `ViewController`, because the Close button is part of the About screen, not the main game screen.

➤ Open **AboutViewController.swift** and replace its contents with the following:

```swift
import UIKit

class AboutViewController: UIViewController {

  @IBAction func close() {
    dismiss(animated: true, completion: nil)
  }
}
```

This code in the `close()` action method tells UIKit to close the About screen with an animation.

If you had said `dismiss(animated: false, …)`, then there would be no page flip and the main screen would instantly reappear. From a user experience perspective, it's often better to show transitions from one screen to another via an animation.

That leaves you with one final step, hooking up the Close button's Touch Up Inside event to this new `close` action.

➤ Open the storyboard and Control-drag from the **Close** button to the About scene's View Controller. Hmm, strange, the **close** action should be listed in this popup, but it isn't. Instead, this is the same popup you saw when you made the segue:

The "close" action is not listed in the popup

Exercise: Bonus points if you can spot the error. It's a very common – and frustrating! – mistake.

The problem is that this scene in the storyboard doesn't know yet that it is supposed to represent the `AboutViewController`.

Set the class for a view controller

You first added the AboutViewController.swift source file, and then dragged a new view controller on to the storyboard. But, you haven't told the storyboard that the design for this new view controller, in fact, belongs to `AboutViewController`. (That's why in the Document Outline it just says View Controller and not About View Controller.)

➤ Fortunately, this is easily remedied. In Interface Builder, select the About scene's **View Controller** and go to the **Identity inspector** (that's the button to the left of the Attributes inspector).

➤ Under **Custom Class**, type **AboutViewController**.

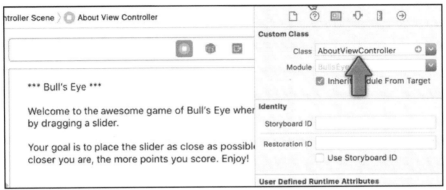

The Identity inspector for the About screen

Xcode should auto-complete this for you once you type the first few characters. If it doesn't, then double-check that you really have selected the View Controller and not one of the views inside it. (The view controller should also have a blue border on the storyboard to indicate it is selected.)

Now you should be able to connect the Close button to the action method.

➤ Control-drag from the **Close** button to **About View Controller** in the Document Outline (or to the yellow circle at the top of the scene in storyboard). This should be old hat by now. The popup menu now does have an option for the **close** action (under Sent Events). Connect the button to that action.

➤ Run the app again. You should now be able to return from the About screen.

OK, that does get us a working about screen, but it does look a little plain doesn't it? What if you added some of the design changes you made to the main screen?

> **Exercise:** Add a background image to the About screen. Also, change the Close button on the About screen to look like the Hit Me! button and play around with the Text View properties in the Attribute Inspector. You should be able to do this by yourself now. Piece of cake! Refer back to the instructions for the main screen if you get stuck.

When you are done, you should have an About screen which looks something like this:

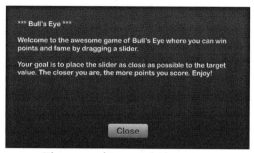

The new and improved About screen

That looks good, but it could be better :] So how do you improve upon it?

Use a web view for HTML content

➤ Now select the **text view** and press the **Delete** key on your keyboard. (Yep, you're throwing it away, and after all those changes, too! But don't grieve for the Text View too much, you'll replace it with something better next.)

➤ Put a **Web View** in its place (as always, you can find this view in the Object Library).

A web view, as its name implies, can show web pages. All you have to do is give it a URL to a web site or the name of a file to load. The web view object is named `UIWebView`.

For this app, you will make it display a static HTML page from the application bundle, so it won't actually have to go online and download anything.

➤ Go to the **Project navigator** and right-click on the **BullsEye** group (the yellow folder). From the menu, choose **Add Files to "BullsEye"**…

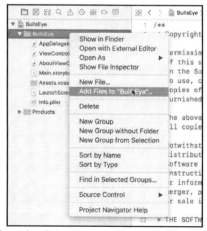

Using the right-click menu to add existing files to the project

➤ In the file picker, select the **BullsEye.html** file from the Resources folder. This is an HTML5 document that contains the gameplay instructions.

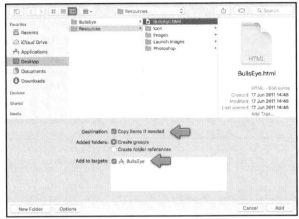

Choosing the file to add

Make sure that **Copy items if needed** is selected and that under **Add to targets**, there is a checkmark in front of **BullsEye**. (If you don't see these options, click the Options button at the bottom of the dialog.)

➤ Press **Add** to add the HTML file to the project.

➤ In **AboutViewController.swift**, add an outlet for the web view:

```
class AboutViewController: UIViewController {
  @IBOutlet weak var webView: UIWebView!
  . . .
}
```

➤ In the storyboard file, connect the UIWebView to this new outlet. The easiest way to do this is to Control-drag from **About View Controller** (in the Document Outline) to the **Web View**.

(If you do it the other way around, from the Web View to About View Controller, then you'll connect the wrong thing and the web view will stay empty when you run the app.)

➤ In **AboutViewController.swift**, add a viewDidLoad() implementation:

```
override func viewDidLoad() {
  super.viewDidLoad()

  if let url = Bundle.main.url(forResource: "BullsEye",
                              withExtension: "html") {
    if let htmlData = try? Data(contentsOf: url) {
      let baseURL = URL(fileURLWithPath: Bundle.main.bundlePath)
```

```
webView.load(htmlData, mimeType: "text/html",
             textEncodingName: "UTF-8",
                          baseURL: baseURL)
      }
    }
  }
```

This displays the HTML file using the web view.

The code may look scary but what goes on is not really that complicated: first it finds the **BullsEye.html** file in the application bundle, then loads it into a `Data` object, and finally it asks the web view to show the contents of this data object.

➤ Run the app and press the info button. The About screen should appear with a description of the gameplay rules, this time in the form of an HTML document:

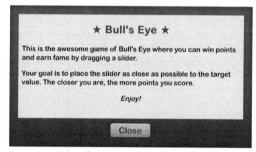

The About screen in all its glory

Congrats! This completes the game. All the functionality is there and – as far as I can tell – there are no bugs to spoil the fun.

You can find the project files for the finished app under **07 - The New Look** in the Source Code folder.

Chapter 8: The Final App

You might be thinking, "OK, *Bull's Eye* is now done, and I can move on to the next app!" If you were, I'm afraid you are in for disappointment - there's just a teensy bit more to do in the game.

"What? What's left to do? We finished the task list!" you say? You are right. The game is indeed complete. However, all this time, you've been developing and testing for a 4" iPhone screen found on devices such as the iPhone 5, 5c, and SE. But what about other iPhones such as the 4.7-inch iPhone, the 5.5-inch iPhone Plus, or the 5.8-inch iPhone X which have bigger screens? Or the iPad with its multiple screen sizes? Will the game work correctly on all these different screen sizes?

And if not, shouldn't we fix it?

This chapter covers the following:

- **Support different screen sizes:** Ensure that the app will run correctly on all the different iPhone and iPad screen sizes.

- **Crossfade:** Add some animation to make the transition to the start of a new game a bit more dynamic.

- **The icon:** Add the app icon.

- **Display name:** Set the display name for the app.

- **Run on device:** How to configure everything to run your app on an actual device.

Support different screen sizes

First, let's check if there is indeed an issue running Bull's Eye on a device with a larger screen. It's always good to verify that there's inded an issue before we do extra work, right? Why fix it, if it isn't broken? :]

➤ To see how the app looks on a larger screen, run the app on an iPhone simulator like the **iPhone 8**. You can switch between Simulators using the selector at the top of the Xcode window:

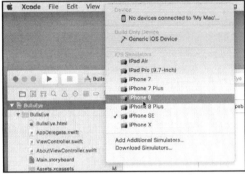

Using the scheme selector to switch to the iPhone 8 Simulator

The result might not be what you expected:

On the iPhone 8 Simulator, the app doesn't fill up the entire screen

Obviously, this won't do. Not everybody is going to be using a 4" iOS device. And you don't want the game to display on only part of the screen for the rest of the people!

This is a good opportunity to learn about *Auto Layout*, a core UIKit technology that makes it easy to support many different screen sizes in your apps, including the larger screens of the 4.7-inch, 5.5-inch, and 5.8-inch iPhones, and the iPad.

Tip: You can use the **Window** → **Scale** menu to resize a simulator if it doesn't fit on your screen. Some of those simulators, like the iPad one, can be monsters! Also, with Xcode 9 onwards, you can resize a simulator window by simply dragging on one corner of the window - just like you do to resize any other window on macOS.

Interface Builder has a few handy tools to help you make the game fit on any screen.

The background image

➤ Go to **Main.storyboard**. Open the **View as:** panel at the bottom and choose the **iPhone 8** device. (You may need to change the orientation back to landscape.)

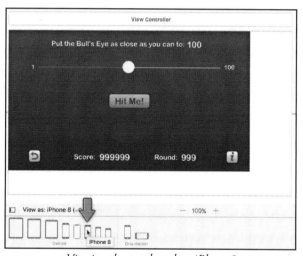

Viewing the storyboard on iPhone 8

The storyboard should look like your screen from when you ran on the iPhone 8 Simulator. This shows you how changes on the storyboard affect the bigger iPhone screens.

First, let's fix the background image. At its normal size, the image is too small to fit on the larger screens.

This is where Auto Layout comes to the rescue.

➤ In the storyboard, select the **Background image view** on the main **View Controller** and click the small **Add New Constraints** button at the bottom of the Xcode window:

The Add New Constraints button

This button lets you define relationships, called *constraints*, between the currently selected view and other views in the scene. When you run the app, UIKit evaluates these constraints and calculates the final layout of the views. This probably sounds a bit abstract, but you'll see soon enough how it works in practice.

In order for the background image to stretch from edge-to-edge on the screen, the left, top, right, and bottom edges of the image should be flush against the screen edges. The way to do this with Auto Layout is to create two alignment constraints, one horizontal and one vertical.

➤ In the **Add New Constraints** menu, set the **left**, **top**, **right**, and **bottom** spacing to zero and make sure that the red I-beam markers next to (or below) each item is enabled. (The red I-beams are used to specify which constraints are enabled when adding new constraints.):

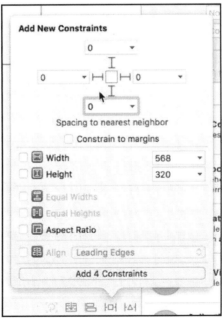

Using the Add New Constraints menu to position the background image

➤ Press **Add 4 Constraints** to finish. The background image will now cover the view fully. (Press Undo and Redo a few times to see the difference.)

The background image now covers the whole view

You might have also noticed that the Document Outline now has a new item called **Constraints**:

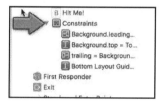

The new Auto Layout constraints appear in the Document Outline

There should be four constraints listed there, one for each edge of the image.

▶ Run the app again on the iPhone 8 Simulator and also on the iPhone SE Simulator. In both cases, the background should display correctly now. (Of course, the other controls are still off-center, but we'll fix that soon.)

If you use the **View as:** panel to switch the storyboard back to the iPhone SE, the background should display correctly there too.

Compiler warnings

When you run the app after adding your first autolayout constraints, sometimes you might see some compiler warnings similar to this:

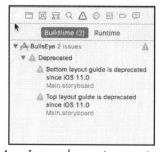

Auto Layout deprecation warnings

If this happens to you, that is because in iOS 11 there were some changes to how autolayout works and how constraints are set up. In previous versions of iOS, you had markers called *top layout guide* and *bottom layout guide* which defined the usable area of a screen. These guides were useful in setting your own views to stretch to the top edge (or the bottom of edge) of the screen without covering any on-screen elements provided by the OS such as navigation bars or tab bars.

However, in iOS 11, they introduced a new layout mechanism which was more flexible than the previously used top and bottom layout guides. These new layout guides are known as the *safe area layout guides*.

So how do you use these new safe area layout guides, you ask? Simple enough, you just have to enable them for your storyboard :]

Switch to your **storyboard**, select your view controller, and then on the right-hand pane, go to the **File Inspector**.

Enable Safe Area Layout Guides

Under the **Interface Builder Document** section, there should be a checkbox for **Use Safe Area Layout Guides** - check it. That's it, you are now using safe area layout guides in your storyboard and the compiler warnings should go away!

If you do not see the **Use Safe Area Layout Guides** checkbox, make sure that you have the view controller selected - that particular option appears only when you have a view controller selected.

The About screen

Let's repeat the background image fix for the About screen, too.

➤ Use the **Add New Constraints** button to pin the About screen's background image view to the parent view.

The background image is now fine. Of course, the Close button and web view are still completely off.

➤ In the storyboard, drag the **Close** button so that it snaps to the center of the view as well as the bottom guide.

Interface Builder shows a handy guide, the dotted blue line, near the edges of the screen, which is useful for aligning objects by hand.

The dotted blue lines are guides that help position your UI elements

You want to create a centering constraint that keeps the Close button in the middle of the screen, regardless of how wide the screen is.

➤ Click the **Close** button to select it. From the **Align** menu (which is to the left of the Add New Constraints button), choose **Horizontally in Container** and click **Add 1 Constraint**.

The Align menu

Interface Builder now draws a red bar to represent the constraint, and a red box around the button as well.

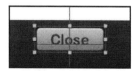

The Close button has red constraints

That's a problem: the bars are all supposed to be blue, not red. Red indicates that something is wrong with the constraints, usually that there aren't enough of them.

The thing to remember is this: for each view, there must always be enough constraints to define both its position and its size. The Close button already knows its size – you typed this into the Size inspector earlier – but for its position there is only a constraint for the X-coordinate (the alignment in the horizontal direction). You also need to add a constraint for the Y-coordinate.

As you've noticed, there are different types of constraints - there are alignment constraints and spacing constraints, like the ones you added via the Add New Constraints button.

➤ With the **Close** button still selected, click on the **Add New Constraints** button.

You want the Close button to always sit at a distance of 20 points from the bottom of the screen.

➤ In the **Add New Constraints** menu, in the **Spacing to nearest neighbor** section, set the bottom spacing to **20** and make sure that the I-beam above the text box is enabled.

The red I-beams decide the sides that are pinned down

➤ Click **Add 1 Constraint** to finish.

The red constraints will now turn blue, meaning that everything is OK:

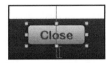

The constraints on the Close button are valid

If at this point you don't see blue bars but orange ones, then something's still wrong with your Auto Layout constraints:

The views are not positioned according to the constraints

This happens when the constraints are valid (otherwise the bars would be red) but the view is not in the right place in the scene. The dashed orange box off to the side is where Auto Layout has calculated the view should be, based on the constraints you have given it.

To fix this issue, select the **Close** button again and click the **Update Frames** button at the bottom of the Interface Builder canvas.

The Update Frames button

You can also use the **Editor → Resolve Auto Layout Issues → Update Frames** item from the menu bar.

The Close button should now always be perfectly centered, regardless of the device screen size.

> **Note:** What happens if you don't add any constraints to your views? In that case, Xcode will automatically add constraints when it builds the app. That is why you didn't need to bother with any of this before.
>
> However, these default constraints may not always do what you want. For example, they will not automatically resize your views to accommodate larger (or smaller) screens. If you want that to happen, then it's up to you to add your own constraints. (Afterall, Auto Layout can't read your mind!)
>
> As soon as you add just one constraint to a view, Xcode will no longer add any other automatic constraints to that view. From then on you're responsible for adding enough constraints so that UIKit always knows what the position and size of the view will be.

There is one thing left to fix in the About screen and that is the web view.

➤ Select the **Web View** and open the **Add New Constraints** menu. First, make sure **Constrain to margins** is unchecked. Then click all four I-beam icons so they become solid red and set their spacing to 20 points, except the bottom one which should be 8 points:

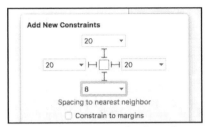

Creating the constraints for the web view

➤ Finish by clicking **Add 4 Constraints**.

There are now four constraints on the web view - indicated by the blue bars on each side:

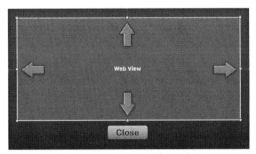

The four constraints on the web view

Three of these pin the web view to the main view, so that it always resizes along with it, and one connects it to the Close button. This is enough to determine the size and position of the web view in any scenario.

Fix the rest of the main scene

Back to the main game scene, which still needs some work.

The game looks a bit lopsided now on bigger screens. You will fix that by placing all the labels, buttons, and the slider into a new "container" view. Using Auto Layout, you'll center that container view in the screen, regardless of how big the screen is.

➤ Select all the labels, buttons, and the slider. You can hold down ⌘ and click them individually, but an easier method is to go to the **Document Outline**, click on the first view (for me that is the "Put the Bull's Eye as close as you can to:" label), then hold down Shift and click on the last view (in my case the Hit Me! button):

Selecting the views from the Document Outline

You should have selected everything but the background image view.

➤ From Xcode's menu bar, choose **Editor** → **Embed In** → **View**. This places the selected views inside a new container view:

The views are embedded in a new container view

This new view is completely white, which is not what you want eventually, but it does make it easier to add the constraints.

➤ Select the newly added **container view** and open the **Add New Constraints** menu. Check the boxes for **Width** and **Height** in order to make constraints for them and leave the width and height at the values specified by Interface Builder. Click **Add 2 Constraints** to finish.

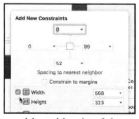

Pinning the width and height of the container view

Interface Builder now draws several bars around the view that represent the Width and Height constraints that you just made, but they are red. Don't panic! It only means there are not enough constraints yet. No problem, you'll add the missing constraints next.

➤ With the container view still selected, open the **Align menu**. Check the **Horizontally in Container** and **Vertically in Container** options. Click **Add 2 Constraints**.

All the Auto Layout bars should be blue now and the view is perfectly centered.

➤ Finally, change the **Background** color of the container view to **Clear Color** (in other words, 100% transparent).

You now have a layout that works correctly on any iPhone display! Try it out:

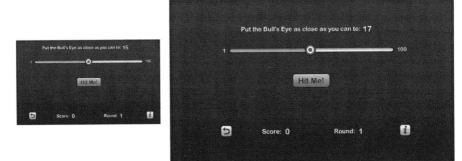

The game running on 4-inch and 5.5-inch iPhones

Auto Layout may take a while to get used to. Adding constraints in order to position UI elements is a little less obvious than just dragging them into place.

But this also buys you a lot of power and flexibility, which you need when you're dealing with devices that have different screen sizes.

You'll learn more about Auto Layout in the other parts of *The iOS Apprentice.*

Exercise: As you try the game on different devices, you might notice something - the controls for the game are always centered on screen, but they do not take up the whole area of the screen on bigger devices! This is because you set the container view for the controls to be a specific size. If you want the controls to change position and size depending on how much screen space is available, then you have to remove the container view (or set it to resize depending on screen size) and then set up the necessary autolayout constraints for each control separately.

Are you up to the challenge of doing this on your own?

Crossfade

There's one final bit of knowledge I want to impart before calling the game complete - Core Animation. This technology makes it very easy to create really sweet animations, with just a few lines of code, in your apps. Adding subtle animations (with emphasis on subtle!) can make your app a delight to use.

You will add a simple crossfade after the Start Over button is pressed, so the transition back to round one won't seem so abrupt.

➤ In **ViewController.swift**, add the following line at the top, right below the other import:

```
import QuartzCore
```

Core Animation lives in its own framework, QuartzCore. With the `import` statement you tell the compiler that you want to use the objects from this framework.

➤ Change `startNewGame()` to:

```
@IBAction func startNewGame() {
  ...
  startNewRound()
  // Add the following lines
  let transition = CATransition()
  transition.type = kCATransitionFade
  transition.duration = 1
  transition.timingFunction = CAMediaTimingFunction(name:

kCAMediaTimingFunctionEaseOut)
  view.layer.add(transition, forKey: nil)
}
```

Everything after the comment telling you to add the following lines, all the `CATransition` stuff, is new.

I'm not going to go into too much detail here. Suffice it to say you're setting up an animation that crossfades from what is currently on the screen to the changes you're making in `startNewRound()` – reset the slider to center position and reset the values of the labels.

➤ Run the app and move the slider so that it is no longer in the center. Press the Start Over button and you should see a subtle crossfade animation.

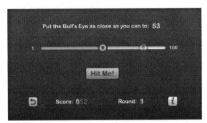

The screen crossfades between the old and new states

The icon

You're almost done with the app, but there are still a few loose ends to tie up. You may have noticed that the app has a really boring white icon. That won't do!

➤ Open the asset catalog (**Assets.xcassets**) and select **AppIcon**:

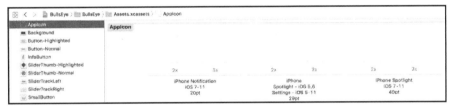

The AppIcon group in the asset catalog

This has ten groups for the different types of icons the app needs.

➤ In Finder, open the **Icon** folder from the resources. Drag the **Icon-40.png** file into the first slot, **iPhone Notification 20pt**:

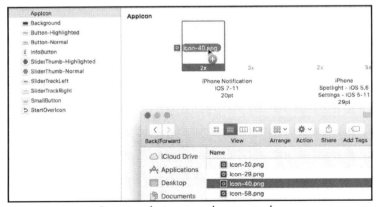

Dragging the icon into the asset catalog

You may be wondering why you're dragging the Icon-40.png file and not the Icon-20.png into the slot for 20pt. Notice that this slot says **2x**, which means it's for Retina devices and on Retina screens one point counts as two pixels. So, 20pt = 40px. And the 40 in the icon name is for the size of the icon in pixels. Makes sense?

➤ Drag the **Icon-60.png** file into the **3x** slot next to it. This is for the iPhone Plus devices with their 3x resolution.

➤ For **iPhone Spotlight & Settings 29pt**, drag the **Icon-58.png** file into the 2x slot and **Icon-87.png** into the 3x slot. (What, you don't know your times table for 29?)

➤ For **iPhone Spotlight 40pt**, drag the **Icon-80.png** file into the 2x slot and **Icon-120.png** into the 3x slot.

➤ For **iPhone App 60pt**, drag the **Icon-120.png** file into the 2x slot and **Icon-180.png** into the 3x slot.

That's four icons in two different sizes. Phew!

The other AppIcon groups are mostly for the iPad.

➤ Drag the specific icons (based on size) into the proper slots for iPad. Notice that the iPad icons need to be supplied in 1x as well as 2x sizes (but not 3x). You may need to do some mental arithmetic here to figure out which icon goes into which slot!

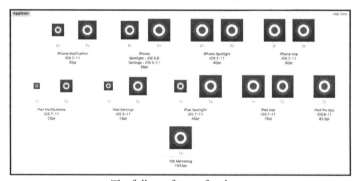

The full set of icons for the app

➤ Run the app and close it. You'll see that the icon has changed on the Simulator's springboard. If not, remove the app from the Simulator and try again (sometimes the Simulator keeps using the old icon and re-installing the app will fix this).

The icon on the Simulator's springboard

Display name

One last thing. You named the project **BullsEye** and that is the name that shows up under the icon. However, I'd prefer to spell it "**Bull's Eye**".

There is only limited space under the icon and for apps with longer names you have to get creative to make the name fit. For this game, however, there is enough room to add the space and the apostrophe.

➤ Go to the **Project Settings** screen. The very first option is **Display Name**. Change this to **Bull's Eye**.

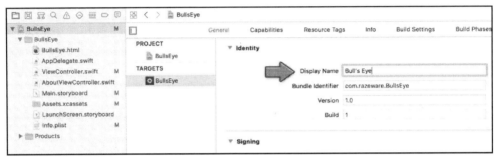

Changing the display name of the app

Like many of the project's settings you can also find the display name in the app's Info.plist file. Let's have a look.

➤ From the **Project navigator**, select **Info.plist**.

The display name of the app in Info.plist

The row **Bundle display name** contains the new name you've just entered.

> **Note:** If **Bundle display name** is not present, the app will use the value from the field **Bundle name**. That has the special value "$(PRODUCT_NAME)", meaning

Xcode will automatically put the project name, BullsEye, in this field when it adds the Info.plist to the application bundle. By providing a **Bundle display name** you can override this default name and give the app any name you want.

➤ Run the app and quit it to see the new name under the icon.

The bundle display name setting changes the name under the icon

Awesome, that completes your very first app!

You can find the project files for the finished app under **08 - The Final App** in the Source Code folder.

Run on device

So far, you've run the app on the Simulator. That's nice and all but probably not why you're learning iOS development. You want to make apps that run on real iPhones and iPads! There's hardly a thing more exciting than running an app that you made on your own phone. And, of course, to show off the fruits of your labor to other people!

Don't get me wrong: developing your apps on the Simulator works very well. When developing, I spend most of my time with the Simulator and only test the app on my iPhone every so often.

However, you do need to run your creations on a real device in order to test them properly. There are some things the Simulator simply cannot do. If your app needs the iPhone's accelerometer, for example, you have no choice but to test that functionality on an actual device. Don't sit there and shake your Mac!

Until a few years back, you needed a paid Developer Program account to run apps on your iPhone. Since Xcode 7, however, you can do it for free. All you need is an Apple ID. And the latest Xcode makes it easier than ever before.

Configure your device for development

➤ Connect your iPhone, iPod touch, or iPad to your Mac using a USB cable.

➤ From the Xcode menu bar select **Window** → **Devices and Simulators** to open the Devices and Simulators window.

Mine looks like this (I'm using an iPhone 6s):

The Devices and Simulators window

On the left is a list of devices that are currently connected to my Mac and which can be used for development.

➤ Click your device name to select it.

If this is the first time you're using the device with Xcode, the Devices window will say something like, "iPhone is not paired with your computer." To pair the device with Xcode, you need to unlock the device first (hold the home button). After unlocking, an alert will pop up on the device asking you to trust the computer you're trying to pair with. Tap on **Trust** to continue.

Xcode will now refresh the page and let you use the device for development. Give it a few minutes (see the progress bar in the main Xcode window). If it takes too long, you may need to unplug the device and plug it back in.

At this point it's possible you may get the error message, "An error was encountered while enabling development on this device." You'll need to unplug the device and reboot it. Make sure to restart Xcode before you reconnect the device.

Also, note the checkbox which says **Connect via network**? That checkbox (gasp!) allows you to run and debug code on your iPhone over WiFi! Yes, that's new in Xcode 9. (I still prefer to do my debugging with my phone connected via USB cable since the last time I checked, the over network debugging was very slow. But your mileage may vary - so give it a try...)

Cool, that is the device sorted.

Add your developer account to Xcode

The next step is setting up your Apple ID with Xcode. It's OK to use the same Apple ID that you're already using with iTunes and your iPhone, but if you run a business, you might want to create a new Apple ID to keep things separate. Of course, if you've already registered for a paid Developer Program account, you should use that Apple ID.

➤ Open the **Accounts** pane in the Xcode Preferences window:

The Accounts preferences

➤ Click the + button at the bottom and select **Add Apple ID** from the list of options.

Xcode Account Type selection

Xcode will ask for your Apple ID:

Adding your Apple ID to Xcode

➤ Type your Apple ID username and password and click **Sign In**.

Xcode verifies your account details and adds it to the stored list of accounts.

> **Note:** It's possible that Xcode is unable to use the Apple ID your provided - for example, if it has been used with a Developer Program account in the past that is

now expired. The simplest solution is to make a new Apple ID. It's free and only takes a few minutes. appleid.apple.com

You still need to tell Xcode to use this account when building your app.

Code signing

➤ Go to the **Project Settings** screen for your app target. In the **General** tab go to the **Signing** section.

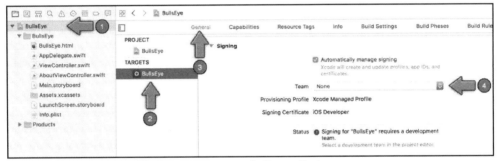

The Signing options in the Project Settings screen

In order to allow Xcode to put an app on your iPhone, the app must be *digitally signed* with your **Development Certificate**. A *certificate* is an electronic document that identifies you as an iOS application developer and is valid only for a specific amount of time.

Apps that you want to submit to the App Store must be signed with another certificate, the **Distribution Certificate**. To use the distribution certificate you must be a member of the paid Developer Program, but using the development certificate is free.

In addition to a valid certificate, you also need a **Provisioning Profile** for each app you make. Xcode uses this profile to sign the app for use on your particular device (or devices). The specifics don't really matter, just know that you need a provisioning profile or the app won't go on your device.

Making the certificates and provisioning profiles used to be a really frustrating and error-prone process. Fortunately, those days are over: Xcode now makes it really easy. When the **Automatically manage signing** option is enabled, Xcode will take care of all this business with certificates and provisioning profiles and you don't have to worry about a thing.

➤ Click on **Team** to select your Apple ID.

Xcode will now automatically register your device with your account, create a new Development Certificate, and download and install the Provisioning Profile on your device. These are all steps you had to do by hand in the past, but now Xcode takes care of all that.

You could get some signing errors like these:

Signing/team set up errors

The app's Bundle Identifier – or App ID as it's called here – must be unique. If another app is already using that identifier, then you cannot use it anymore. That's why you're supposed to start the Bundle ID with your own domain name. The fix is easy: change the Bundle Identifier field to something else and try again.

It's also possible you get this error (or something similar):

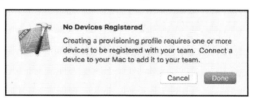

No devices registered

Xcode must know about the device that you're going to run the app on. That's why I asked you to connect your device first. Double-check that your iPhone or iPad is still connected to your Mac and that it is listed in the Devices window.

Run on device

If everything goes smoothly, go back to Xcode's main window and click on the box in the toolbar to change where you will run the app. The name of your device should be in that list somewhere.

On my system it looks like this:

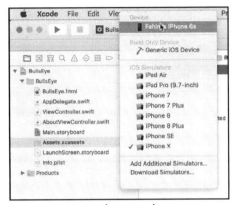

Setting the active device

You're all set and ready to go!

➤ Press **Run** to launch the app.

At this point you may get a popup with the question "codesign wants to sign using key … in your keychain". If so, answer with **Always Allow**. This is Xcode trying to use the new Development Certificate you just created - you just need to give it permission first.

Does the app work? Awesome! If not, read on…

When things go wrong…

There are a few things that can go wrong when you try to put the app on your device, especially if you've never done this before, so don't panic if you run into problems.

The device is not connected

Make sure your iPhone, iPod touch, or iPad is connected to your Mac. The device must be listed in Xcode's Devices window and there should not be a yellow warning icon.

The device does not trust you

You might get this warning:

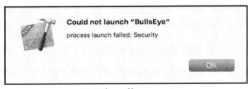

Quick, call security!

On the device itself there will be a popup with the text, "Untrusted Developer. Your device management settings do not allow using apps from developer …".

If this happens, open the Settings app on the device and go to **General** → **Profile**. Your Apple ID should be listed in that screen. Tap it, followed by the Trust button. Then try running the app again.

The device is locked

If your phone locks itself with a passcode after a few minutes, you might get this warning:

The app won't run if the device is locked

Simply unlock your device (hold the home button or type in the 4-digit passcode) and press Run again.

Signing certificates

If you're curious about these certificates, then open the **Preferences** window and go to the **Accounts** tab. Select your account and click the **Manage Certificates…** button in the bottom-right corner.

This brings up another panel, listing your signing certificates:

The Manage Certificates panel

When you're done, close the panel and go to the **Devices and Simulators** window.

You can see the provisioning profiles that are installed on your device by right-clicking the device name and choosing **Show Provisioning Profiles**.

The provisioning profiles on your device

The "iOS Team Provisioning Profile: *" is the thing that allows you to run the app on your device. (By the way, they call it the "team" profile because often there is more than one developer working on an app and they can all share the same profile.)

You can have more than one certificate and provisioning profile installed. This is useful if you're on multiple development teams or if you prefer to manage the provisioning profiles for different apps by hand.

To see how Xcode chooses which profile and certificate to sign your app with, go to the **Project Settings** screen and switch to the **Build Settings** tab. There are a lot of settings in this list, so filter them by typing **signing** in the search box. (Also make sure **All** is selected, not Basic.)

The screen will look something like this:

The Code Signing settings

Under **Code Signing Identity** it says **iOS Developer**. This is the certificate that Xcode uses to sign the app. If you click on that line, you can choose another certificate. Under **Provisioning Profile** you can change the active profile. Most of the time you won't need to change these settings, but at least you know where to find them now.

And that concludes everything you need to know about running your app on an actual device.

The end... or the beginning?

It has been a bit of a journey to get to this point – if you're new to programming, you've had to get a lot of new concepts into your head. I hope your brain didn't explode!

At least you should have gotten some insight into what it takes to develop an app.

I don't expect you to understand exactly everything that you did, especially not the parts that involved writing Swift code. It is perfectly fine if you didn't, as long as you're enjoying yourself and you sort of get the basic concepts of objects, methods and variables.

If you were able to follow along and do the exercises, you're in good shape!

I encourage you to play around with the code a bit more. The best way to learn programming is to do it, and that includes making mistakes and messing things up. I hereby grant you full permission to do so! Maybe you can add some cool new features to the game (and if you do, please let me know).

In the Source Code folder for this book you can find the complete source code for the *Bull's Eye* app. If you're still unclear about some of what you did, it might be a good idea to look at this cleaned up source code.

If you're interested in how I made the graphics, then take a peek at the Photoshop files in the Resources folder. The wood background texture was made by Atle Mo from subtlepatterns.com.

If you're feeling exhausted after all that coding, pour yourself a drink and put your feet up for a bit. You've earned it! On the other hand, if you just can't wait to get to grips with more code, let's move on to our next app!

Section 2: Checklists

This section builds upon what you learnt in the previous chapter by introducing you to your second app. *Checklists* takes you from a single-screen app to a multi-screen app where you learn the concepts of navigation flow, displaying data lists, and the idea of modeling and persisting your data.

If you want to build any sort of list-based iOS app, this section is a good starting point for learning the basics. Of course, even if you aren't building a list-based app, this section has some basic concepts such as handling the navigation flow from one screen to another (and back again) that would be very useful to an apprentice iOS developer.

Chapter 9: Table Views

Chapter 10: The Data Model

Chapter 11: Navigation Controllers

Chapter 12: Add Item Screen

Chapter 13: Delegates and Protocols

Chapter 14: Edit Items

Chapter 15: Saving and Loading

Chapter 16: Lists

Chapter 17: Improved Data Model

Chapter 18: User Defaults

Chapter 19: UI Improvements

Chapter 20: Local Notifications

Ready to get started on your next app? Let's go!

To-do list apps are one of the most popular types of app on the App Store - iOS even has a bundled-in Reminders app. Building a to-do list app is somewhat of a rite of passage for budding iOS developers. So, it makes sense that you create one as well.

Your own to-do list app, *Checklists*, will look like this when you're finished:

The finished Checklists app

The app lets you organize to-do items into lists and then check off these items once you've completed them. You can also set a reminder on a to-do item that will make the iPhone pop up an alert on the due date, even when the app isn't running.

As far as to-do list apps go, *Checklists* is very basic, but don't let that fool you. Even a simple app such as this already has five different screens and a lot of complexity behind the scenes.

This chapter covers the following:

- **Table views and navigation controllers:** A basic introduction to navigation controllers and table views.

- **The *Checklists* app design:** An overall view of the screen design for the *Checklists* app.

- **Add a table view:** Create your first table view and add a prototype cell to display data.

- **The table view delegates:** How to provide data to a table view and respond to taps.

Table views and navigation controllers

Checklists will introduce you to two of the most commonly used UI (user interface) elements in iOS apps: the table view and the navigation controller.

A **table view** shows a list of things. The three screens above all use a table view. In fact, all of this app's screens use table views. This component is extremely versatile and the most important one to master in iOS development.

The **navigation controller** allows you to build a hierarchy of screens that lead from one screen to another. It adds a navigation bar at the top with a title and a back button.

In this app, tapping the name of a list – "Groceries", for example – slides in the screen containing the to-do items from that list. The button in the upper-left corner takes you back to the previous screen with a smooth animation. Moving between those screens is the job of the navigation controller.

Navigation controllers and table views are often used together.

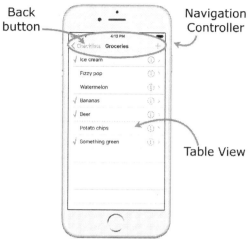

Back button

Navigation Controller

Table View

The grey bar at the top is the navigation bar. The list of items is the table view.

Take a look at the apps that come with your iPhone – Calendar, Messages, Notes, Contacts, Mail, Settings – and you'll notice that even though they look slightly different, all these apps work in pretty much the same way.

That's because they all use table views and navigation controllers:

These are all table views inside navigation controllers

(The Music app also has a *tab bar* at the bottom, something you'll learn about later on.)

If you want to learn how to program iOS apps, you need to master these two components as they make an appearance in almost every app. That's exactly what you'll focus on in this section of the book. You'll also learn how to pass data from one screen to another, a very important topic that often puzzles beginners.

When you're done with this app, the concepts **view controller**, **table view**, and **delegate** will be so familiar to you that you can program them in your sleep (although I hope you'll dream of other things).

This is a very long read with a lot of source code, so take your time to let it all sink in. I encourage you to experiment with the code that you'll be writing. Change stuff and see what it does, even if it breaks the app.

Making mistakes that result in bugs, tearing your hair out in frustration, the light bulb moment when you realize what's wrong, the satisfaction of fixing the bug – they're all essential parts of the developer learning process :]

There's no doubt: playing with code is the quickest way to learn!

By the way, if something is unclear to you – for example, you may wonder why method names in Swift look so funny – then don't panic! Have some faith and keep going... everything will be explained in due course.

The Checklists app design

Just so you know what you're in for, here is an overview of how the *Checklists* app will work:

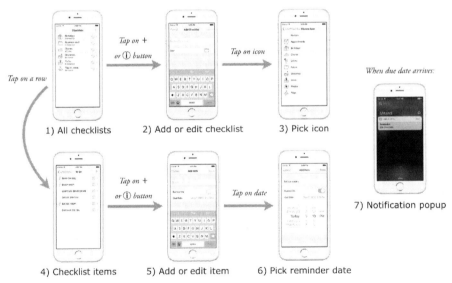

All the screens of the Checklists app

The main screen of the app shows all your "checklists" (1). You can create multiple lists to organize your to-do items.

A checklist has a name, an icon, and zero or more to-do items. You can edit the name and icon of a checklist in the Add/Edit Checklist screen (2) and (3).

You tap on the checklist's name to view its to-do items (4).

A to-do item has a description, a checkmark to indicate that the item is done, and an optional due date. You can edit the item in the Add/Edit Item screen (5).

iOS will automatically notify the user of checklist items that have their "remind me" option set (6), even if the app isn't running (7). That's a pretty advanced feature, but I think you'll be up for the task.

You can find the full source code of this app in the Source Code folder, so have a play with it to get a feel for how it works.

Done playing? Then let's get started!

> **Important:** The *iOS Apprentice* projects are for **Xcode 9.0** and better only. If you're still using an older version of Xcode, please update to the latest version of Xcode from the Mac App Store.
>
> But don't get carried away either – often Apple makes beta versions available of upcoming Xcode releases. Please do *not* use an Xcode beta to follow along. Often, the beta versions break things in unexpected ways and you'll only end up confused. Stick to the official versions for now!

Add a table view

Seeing as table views are so important, you will start out by examining how they work. Making lists has never been this much fun!

Because smart developers split up the workload into small, simple steps, this is what you're going to do in this chapter:

1. Put a table view on the app's screen.

2. Put data into that table view.

3. Allow the user to tap a row in the table to toggle a checkmark on and off.

Once you have these basics up and running, you'll keep adding new functionality over the next few chapters until you end up with a full-blown app.

Create the project

➤ Launch Xcode and start a new project. Choose the **Single View Application** template.

Choosing the Xcode template

Xcode will ask you to fill out a few options:

Choosing the template options

➤ Fill out these options as follows:

• Product Name: **Checklists**

• Team: Since you already set up your developer account for the previous app (you did, didn't you?) you can select your team here - or, you can just leave this at the default setting.

• Organization Name: Your name or the name of your company

• Organization Identifier: Use your own identifier here, using reverse domain name notation

• Language: **Swift**

• Use Core Data, Include Unit Tests, Include UI Tests: these should be off.

➤ Press **Next** and choose a location for the project.

You can run the app if you want, but as you might remember from the *Bull's Eye* app, at this point it is just a white screen.

Set the app orientation

Checklists will run in portrait orientation only. However, the default project that Xcode just generated also includes landscape support.

➤ Click on the Checklists project item at the top of the project navigator and go to the **General** tab. Under **Deployment Info**, **Device Orientation**, make sure that only **Portrait** is selected.

The Device Orientation setting

With the landscape options disabled, rotating the device will no longer have any effect. The app always stays in portrait orientation.

Upside down

There is also an Upside Down orientation but you typically won't use it.

If your app supports Upside Down, users are able to rotate their iPhone so that the home button is at the top of the screen instead of at the bottom.

That may be confusing, especially when the user receives a phone call: the microphone is at the wrong end with the phone upside down.

---

iPad apps, on the other hand, are supposed to support all four orientations including upside-down.

Edit the storyboard

Xcode created a basic app that consists of a single view controller. Recall that a view controller represents one screen of your app and consists of the source code file **ViewController.swift** and a user interface design in **Main.storyboard**.

The storyboard contains the designs of all your app's view controllers inside a single document, with arrows showing the flow between them. In storyboard terminology, each view controller is named a *scene*.

You already used a storyboard in *Bull's Eye* but in this app you will unlock the full power of storyboarding.

➤ Click on **Main.storyboard** to open Interface Builder.

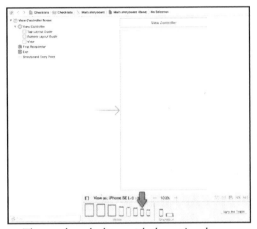

The storyboard editor with the app's only scene

By default, the scene will have the dimensions of a 5.5" iPhone. I used the **View as:** panel at the bottom to switch to the slightly smaller **iPhone SE** because that takes up less room in the book. However, it does not matter which device size you choose to edit the storyboard: the app will automatically resize to fit all iPhone models.

➤ Select **View Controller** in the Document Outline on the left.

Tip: Recall that the Document Outline shows the view hierarchy of all the scenes in the storyboard. If you cannot see the Document Outline, then click the small square button at the bottom of the Interface Builder window to toggle its visibility.

This button shows and hides the Document Outline

➤ Press **delete** on your keyboard to remove the **View Controller Scene** from the storyboard. The canvas should be empty and the Document Outline say "No Scenes".

You do this because you don't want a regular view controller but a **table view controller**. This is a special type of view controller that makes working with table views a little easier.

The view controller code

But remember, the scene on the storyboard is just half the equation - there's also the Swift code file. And the type specified in code has to match the scene's type. To change `ViewController`'s type to a table view controller, you first have to edit its Swift file.

➤ Click on **ViewController.swift** to open it in the source code editor. Change the following line from this:

```
class ViewController: UIViewController {
```

To this:

```
class ChecklistViewController: UITableViewController {
```

With this change you tell the Swift compiler that your own view controller is now a `UITableViewController` object instead of a regular `UIViewController`.

Remember that everything starting with "UI" is part of UIKit. These pre-fabricated components serve as the building blocks for your own app.

When Xcode made the project, it assumed you wanted the `ViewController` object to be built on top of a basic `UIViewController`, but here you're changing it to use the `UITableViewController` building block instead.

You also renamed `ViewController` to `ChecklistViewController` to give it a more descriptive name. This is your own object – you can tell because its name *doesn't* start with UI.

Over the course of this app, you will add data and functionality to the `ChecklistViewController` object to make the app actually do things. You'll also add several new view controllers to the app.

➤ In the Project navigator on the left, click once to select **ViewController.swift**, and then click again to edit its name. (Don't double-click too fast or you'll open the Swift file inside a new source code editor window.)

Change the filename to **ChecklistViewController.swift**:

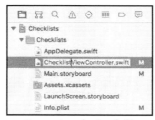

Renaming the Swift file

You might get a warning: "The document could not be saved. The file has been changed by another application." Click **Save Anyway** to make it go away.

Set the view controller class in the storyboard

➤ Go back to the storyboard and drag a **Table View Controller** from the Object Library (bottom-right corner) on to the canvas:

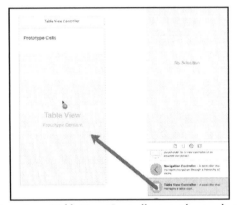

Dragging a Table View Controller into the storyboard

This adds a new Table View Controller scene to the storyboard.

➤ Go to the **Identity inspector** (the third tab in the inspectors pane on the right of the Xcode window) and under **Custom Class** type **ChecklistViewController** (or choose it using the dropdown list).

Tip: When you do this, make sure the actual Table View Controller is selected, not the Table View inside it. There should be a thin blue border around the scene.

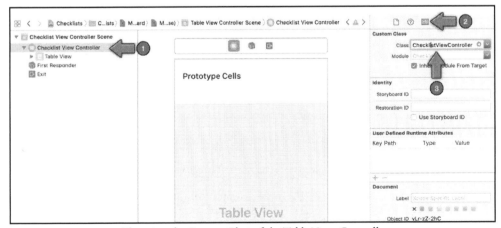

Changing the Custom Class of the Table View Controller

The name of the scene in the Document Outline on the left should change to "Checklist View Controller Scene". You have successfully changed `ChecklistViewController` from a regular view controller object into a table view controller.

As its name implies, and as you can see in the storyboard, the view controller contains a Table View object. We'll go into the difference between controllers and views soon, but for now, remember that the controller is the whole screen while the table view is the object that actually draws the list.

Set the initial view controller

If there is no big arrow pointing towards your new table view controller, then go to the **Attributes inspector** and check **Is Initial View Controller**.

The arrow points at the initial view controller

The initial view controller is the first screen that your users will see. Without one of these, iOS won't know which view controller to load from your storyboard when the app starts up and you'll end up staring at a black screen.

➤ Run the app on the Simulator.

You should see an empty list. This is the table view. You can drag the list up and down but it doesn't contain any data yet.

The app now uses a table view controller

By the way, it doesn't really matter which Simulator you use. Table views resize themselves to the dimensions of the device, and the app will work equally well on the small iPhone SE or the huge iPhone X.

Personally, I use the iPhone SE Simulator because it's compact, but remember that you can open any of the simulators and then simply resize the simulator window by dragging on the corners, just like you resize any macOS window.

> **Note:** When you build the app, Xcode gives the warning "Prototype table cells must have reuse identifiers". Don't worry about this for now, we'll fix it soon.

The anatomy of a table view

First, let's talk a bit more about table views. A `UITableView` object displays a list of items.

> **Note:** I'm not sure why it's named a *table*, because a table is commonly thought of as a spreadsheet-type object that has multiple rows and multiple columns, whereas the `UITableView` only has rows. It's more of a list than a table, but I guess we're stuck with the name now. UIKit also provides a `UICollectionView` object that works similar to a `UITableView` but allows for multiple columns.

There are two styles of tables: "plain" and "grouped". They work mostly the same, but there are a few small differences. The most visible difference is that rows in the grouped style table are placed into boxes (the groups) on a light gray background.

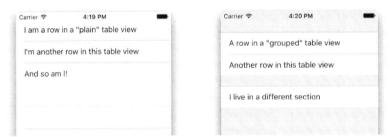

A plain-style table (left) and a grouped table (right)

The plain style is used for rows that all represent something similar, such as contacts in an address book where each row contains the name of one person.

The grouped style is used when the items in the list can be organized by a particular attribute, like book categories for a list of books. The grouped style table could also be used to show related information which doesn't necessarily have to stand together - like the address information, contact information, and e-mail information for a contact.

You will use both table styles in the *Checklists* app.

The data for a table comes in the form of **rows**. In the first version of *Checklists*, each row will correspond to a to-do item that you can check off when you're done with it.

You can potentially have many rows (even tens of thousands) but that kind of design isn't recommended. Most users will find it incredibly annoying to scroll through ten thousand rows to find the one they want. And who can blame them?

Tables display their data in **cells**. A cell is related to a row but it's not exactly the same. A cell is a view that shows a row of data that happens to be visible at that moment. If your table can show 10 rows at a time on the screen, then it only has 10 cells, even though there may be hundreds of rows of actual data.

Whenever a row scrolls off the screen and becomes invisible, its cell will be re-used for a new row that becomes visible.

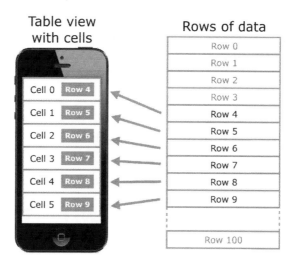

Cells display the contents of rows

Add a prototype cell

In the past, you had to put in quite a bit of effort to create cells for your tables. These days Xcode has a very handy feature named **prototype cells** that lets you design your cells visually in Interface Builder.

➤ Open the storyboard and click the empty cell (the white row below the Prototype Cells label) to select it.

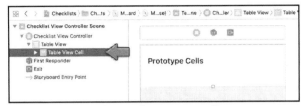

Selecting the prototype cell

Sometimes it can be hard to see exactly what is selected, so keep an eye on the Document Outline to make sure you've picked the right thing.

➤ Drag a **Label** from the Object Library on to the white area in the table view representing the cell. Make sure the label spans the entire width of the cell (but leave a small margin on the sides).

Adding the label to the prototype cell

> **Note:** If you simply drag the label on to the table view, it might not work. You need to drag the label on to the cell itself. You can check where the label ended up on the Document Outline. It has to be inside the Content View for the table view cell.

Besides the label you will also add a checkmark to the cell's design. The checkmark is provided by something called the **accessory**, a built-in view that appears on the right side of the cell. You can choose from a few standard accessory controls or provide your own.

➤ Select the **Table View Cell** again. In the **Attributes inspector**, set the **Accessory** field to **Checkmark**:

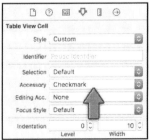

Changing the accessory to get a checkmark

(If you don't see this option, then make sure you selected the Table View Cell, not the Content View or Label below it.)

Your design should now look something like this:

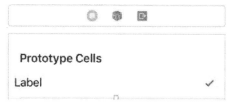

The design of the prototype cell: a label and a checkmark

Note: You may want to resize the label a bit so that it doesn't overlap the checkmark.

You also need to set a **reuse identifier** on the cell. This is an internal name that the table view uses to find free cells to reuse when rows scroll off the screen and new rows must become visible.

The table needs to assign cells for those new rows, and recycling existing cells is more efficient than creating new cells. This technique is what makes table views scroll smoothly.

Reuse identifiers are also important for when you want to display different types of cells in the same table. For example, one type of cell could have an image and a label and another could have a label and a button. You would give each cell type its own identifier, so the table view can assign the right cell for a given row type.

Checklists has only one type of cell but you still need to give it an identifier.

➤ Type **ChecklistItem** into the Table View Cell's **Identifier** field (you can find this in the **Attributes inspector**).

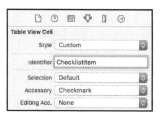

Giving the table view cell a reuse identifier

➤ Run the app and you'll see… zip, zilch, nada - exactly the same as before :] The table is still empty.

This is because you only added a cell design to the table, not actual data. Remember that the cell is just the visual representation of the row, not the actual data. To add data to the table, you have to write some code.

The table view delegates

➤ Switch to **ChecklistViewController.swift** and add the following methods just before the closing bracket at the bottom of the file:

```
override func tableView(_ tableView: UITableView,
       numberOfRowsInSection section: Int) -> Int {
  return 1
}

override func tableView(_ tableView: UITableView,
            cellForRowAt indexPath: IndexPath) ->
            UITableViewCell {

  let cell = tableView.dequeueReusableCell(
                    withIdentifier: "ChecklistItem",
                              for: indexPath)
  return cell
}
```

These methods look a bit more complicated than the ones you've seen in *Bull's Eye*, but that's because each takes two parameters and returns a value to the caller. Other than that, they work the same way as the methods you've dealt with before.

Protocols

The above two methods are part of `UITableView`'s **data source** protocol.

What's a protocol, you ask? Well, its a standard set of methods that a class must adhere to - a protocol to be followed, so to speak. It allows code to be written in such a way that you know that a given class would implement certain methods (with specific parameters of a given type) but where you don't need to know all the implementation details of the class - such as all it's methods. A protocol usually allows you to add functionality for a certain type of operation to a class - for example, handling data for a table view.

The data source is the link between your data and the table view. Usually, the view controller plays the role of data source and implements the necessary methods. So, essentially, the view controller is acting as a delegate on behalf of the table view. (This is the delegate pattern that we've talked about before - where an object does some work on behalf of another object.)

The table view needs to know how many rows of data it has and how it should display each of those rows. But you can't simply dump that data into the table view's lap and be done with it. You don't say: "Dear table view, here are my 100 rows, now go show them on the screen."

Instead, you say to the table view: "This view controller is now your data source. You can ask it questions about the data anytime you feel like it."

Once it is hooked up to a data source – i.e. your view controller – the table view sends a `numberOfRowsInSection` message to find out how many data rows there are.

And when the table view needs to draw a particular row on the screen it sends a `cellForRowAt` message to ask the data source for a cell.

You see this pattern all the time in iOS: one object does something on behalf of another object. In this case, the `ChecklistViewController` works to provide the data to the table view, but only when the table view asks for it.

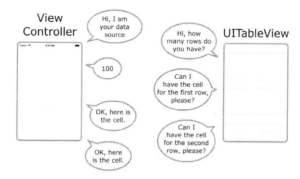

The dating ritual of a data source and a table view

Your implementation of `tableView(_:numberOfRowsInSection:)` – the first method that you added – returns the value 1. This tells the table view that you have just one row of data.

The `return` statement is very important in Swift. It allows a method to send data back to its caller. In the case of `tableView(_:numberOfRowsInSection:)`, the caller is the `UITableView` object and it wants to know how many rows are in the table.

The statements inside a method usually perform some kind of computation using instance variables and any data received through the method's parameters. When the method is done, `return` says, "Hey, I'm done. Here is the answer I came up with." The return value is often called the *result* of the method.

For `tableView(_:numberOfRowsInSection:)` the answer is really simple: there is only one row, so `return 1`.

Now that the table view knows it has one row to display, it calls the second method you added – `tableView(_:cellForRowA:t)` – to obtain a cell for that row. This method grabs a copy of the prototype cell and gives that back to the table view, again with a `return` statement.

Inside `tableView(_:cellForRowAt:)` is also where you would normally put the row data into the cell, but the app doesn't have any row data yet.

➤ Run the app and you'll see there is a single cell in the table:

The table now has one row

Method signatures

In the above text, you might have noticed some special notation for the method names, like `tableView(_:numberOfRowsInSection:)` or `tableView(_:cellForRowAt:)`. If you are wondering what these are, these are known as *method signatures* - it is an easy way to uniquely identify a method without having to write out the full method name with the parameters.

The method signature identifies where each parameter would be (and the parameter name, where necessary) by separating out the parameters with a colon. In the method for `tableView(_:numberOfRowsInSection:)` for example, you might notice an underscore for the first parameter - that means that that method does not need to have the parameter name specified when calling the method - it is simply a convenience in Swift where the parameter can generally be inferred from the method name. (You might have more questions about this - but we'll come back to that later.)

If you are not sure about the signature for a method, take a look at the Xcode **Jump bar** (the tiny toolbar right above the source editor) and click on the last item of the file path elements to get a list of methods (and properties) in the current source file.

```
⊞  <  >   📄 Checklists ⟩ ▦ Checklists ⟩ ◢ ChecklistViewController.sw    ☰ ChecklistViewController
42      // Dispose of any resources that can be       Ⓜ viewDidLoad()
43  }                                                 Ⓜ didReceiveMemoryWarning()
44                                                    Ⓜ tableView(_:numberOfRowsInSection:)
45  override func tableView(_ tableView: UITa         Ⓜ tableView(_:cellForRowAt:)
46                  numberOfRowsInSec                 Ⓜ tableView(_:didSelectRowAt:)
47      return 100
48  }
49
50  override func tableView(_ tableView: UITableView,
51                  cellForRowAt indexPath: IndexPath) -> UITableViewCell {
```

The Jump Bar shows the method signatures

Also, do note that in the above examples, `tableView` is not the method name - or rather, `tableView` by itself is not the method name. The method name is the `tableView` plus the parameter list - everything up to the closing bracket for the parameter list. That's how you get multiple unique methods such as `tableView(_:numberOfRowsInSection:)` and `tableView(_:cellForRowAt:)` eventhough they all look as if they are methods called `tableName` - the complete signature uniquely identifies the method, if that makes sense?

> **Exercise:** Modify the app so that it shows five rows.

That shouldn't have been too hard:

```
override func tableView(_ tableView: UITableView,
    numberOfRowsInSection section: Int) -> Int {
  return 5
}
```

If you were tempted to go into the storyboard and duplicate the prototype cell five times, then you were confusing cells with rows :]

When you make `tableView(_:numberOfRowsInSection:)` return the number 5, you tell the table view that there will be five rows.

The table view then sends the `cellForRowAt` message five times, once for each row. Because `tableView(_:cellForRowAt:)` currently just returns a copy of the prototype cell, your table view will show five identical rows:

The table now has five identical rows

There are several ways to create cells in `tableView(_:cellForRowAt:)`, but by far the easiest approach is what you've done here:

1. Add a prototype cell to the table view in the storyboard.

2. Set a reuse identifier on the prototype cell.

3. Call `tableView.dequeueReusableCell(withIdentifier:for:)`. This makes a new copy of the prototype cell if necessary, or, recycles an existing cell that is no longer in use.

Once you have a cell, you should fill it up with the data from the corresponding row and give it back to the table view. That's what you'll do in the next section.

Putting row data into the cells

Currently, the rows (or rather the cells) all contain the placeholder text "Label". Let's add some unique text for each row.

➤ Open the storyboard and select the **Label** inside the table view cell. Go to the **Attributes inspector** and set the **Tag** field to 1000.

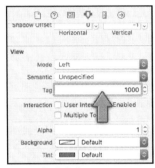

Set the label's tag to 1000

A *tag* is a numeric identifier that you can give to a user interface control in order to uniquely identify it later. Why the number 1000? No particular reason. It should be something other than 0, as that is the default value for all tags. 1000 is as good a number as any.

Double-check to make sure you set the tag on the *Label*, not on the Table View Cell or its Content View. It's a common mistake to set the tag on the wrong view and then the results won't be what you expected!

➤ In **ChecklistViewController.swift**, change tableView(_:cellForRowAt:) to the following:

```
override func tableView(_ tableView: UITableView,
        cellForRowAt indexPath: IndexPath)
        -> UITableViewCell {

  let cell = tableView.dequeueReusableCell(
                     withIdentifier: "ChecklistItem",
                                     for: indexPath)

  // Add the following code
  let label = cell.viewWithTag(1000) as! UILabel

  if indexPath.row == 0 {
```

```
        label.text = "Walk the dog"
    } else if indexPath.row == 1 {
        label.text = "Brush my teeth"
    } else if indexPath.row == 2 {
        label.text = "Learn iOS development"
    } else if indexPath.row == 3 {
        label.text = "Soccer practice"
    } else if indexPath.row == 4 {
        label.text = "Eat ice cream"
    }
    // End of new code block

    return cell
}
```

You've already seen the first line. This gets a copy of the prototype cell – either a new one or a recycled one – and puts it into a local constant named `cell`:

```
let cell = tableView.dequeueReusableCell(
                    withIdentifier: "ChecklistItem",
                              for: indexPath)
```

(Recall that this is a constant because it's declared with `let`, not `var`. It is local because it's defined inside a method.)

But what is this `indexPath` thing?

`IndexPath` is simply an object that points to a specific row in the table. When the table view asks the data source for a cell, you can look at the row number inside the `indexPath.row` property to find out the row for which the cell is intended.

> **Note:** As I mentioned before, it is also possible for tables to group rows into sections. In an address book app you might sort contacts by last name. All contacts whose last name starts with "A" are grouped into their own section, all contacts whose last name starts with "B" are in another section, and so on.
>
> To find out which section a row belongs to, you'd look at the `indexPath.section` property. The *Checklists* app has no need for this kind of grouping, so you'll ignore the `section` property of `IndexPath` for now.

The first new line that you've just added is:

```
let label = cell.viewWithTag(1000) as! UILabel
```

Here you ask the table view cell for the view with tag 1000. That is the tag you just set on the label in the storyboard. So, this returns a reference to the corresponding `UILabel`.

Using tags is a handy trick to get a reference to a UI element without having to make an @IBOutlet variable for it.

> **Exercise:** Why can't you simply add an @IBOutlet variable to the view controller and connect the cell's label to that outlet in the storyboard? After all, that's how you created references to the labels in *Bull's Eye*... so why won't that work here?

Answer: There will be more than one cell in the table and each cell will have its own label. If you connected the label from the prototype cell to an outlet on the view controller, that outlet could only refer to the label from *one* of these cells, not all of them. Since the label belongs to the cell and not to the view controller as a whole, you can't make an outlet for it on the view controller. Confused? We'll circle around to this topic soon, so don't worry about it for now.

Back to the code. The next bit shouldn't give you too much trouble:

```
if indexPath.row == 0 {
  label.text = "Walk the dog"
} else if indexPath.row == 1 {
  label.text = "Brush my teeth"
} else if indexPath.row == 2 {
  label.text = "Learn iOS development"
} else if indexPath.row == 3 {
  label.text = "Soccer practice"
} else if indexPath.row == 4 {
  label.text = "Eat ice cream"
}
```

You have seen this if – else if – else structure before. It simply looks at the value of indexPath.row, which contains the row number, and changes the label's text accordingly. The cell for the first row gets the text "Walk the dog", the cell for the second row gets the text "Brush my teeth", and so on.

> **Note:** Computers generally start counting at 0 for lists of items. If you have a list of 4 items, they are counted as 0, 1, 2 and 3. It may seem a little silly at first, but that's just the way programmers do things.
>
> For the first row in the first section, indexPath.row is 0. The second row has row number 1, the third row is row 2, and so on.
>
> Counting from 0 may take some getting used to, but after a while it becomes second nature and you'll start counting at 0 even when you're out for groceries :]

➤ Run the app - it now has five rows, each with its own text:

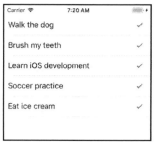

The rows in the table now have their own text

That is how you write the `tableView(_:cellForRowAt:)` method to provide data to the table. You first get a `UITableViewCell` object and then change the contents of that cell based on the row number of the `indexPath`.

Just for the heck of it, let's put 100 rows into the table.

➤ Make `tableView(_:numberOfRowsInSection:)` return 100.

➤ Also, change the code you added earlier to the following:

```
if indexPath.row % 5 == 0 {
  label.text = "Walk the dog"
} else if indexPath.row % 5 == 1 {
  label.text = "Brush my teeth"
} else if indexPath.row % 5 == 2 {
  label.text = "Learn iOS development"
} else if indexPath.row % 5 == 3 {
  label.text = "Soccer practice"
} else if indexPath.row % 5 == 4 {
  label.text = "Eat ice cream"
}
```

This uses the **remainder operator** (also known as the **modulo operator**), represented by the % sign, to determine what row you're on.

The % operator returns the remainder of a division. You may remember this from doing math in school. For example 13 % 4 = 1, because four goes into thirteen 3 times with a remainder of 1. However, 12 % 4 is 0 because there is no remainder.

The first row, as well as the sixth, eleventh, sixteenth and so on, will show the text "Walk the dog". The second, seventh and twelfth row will show "Brush my teeth". The third, eight and thirteenth row will show "Learn iOS development". And so on…

I think you get the picture: every five rows these lines repeat. Rather than typing in all the possibilities all the way up to a hundred, you let the computer calculate this for you (afterall, that is what they are good at):

```
First row:     0 % 5 = 0
Second row:    1 % 5 = 1
Third row:     2 % 5 = 2
Fourth row:    3 % 5 = 3
Fifth row:     4 % 5 = 4

Sixth row:     5 % 5 = 0  (same as first row)    *** The sequence
Seventh row:   6 % 5 = 1  (same as second row)       repeats here
Eighth row:    7 % 5 = 2  (same as third row)
Ninth row:     8 % 5 = 3  (same as fourth row)
Tenth row:     9 % 5 = 4  (same as fifth row)

Eleventh row: 10 % 5 = 0  (same as first row)    *** The sequence
Twelfth row:  11 % 5 = 1  (same as second row)       repeats again
and so on...
```

If this makes no sense to you at all, then feel free to ignore it. You're just using this trick to quickly fill up a large table with data.

➤ Run the app and you should see this:

The table now has 100 rows

Note: To scroll through this table view on the Simulator, you have to pretend you're using an actual iPhone. Click the mouse to "grab" the table view and then drag up or down. Simply swiping without clicking first — the way you'd normally scroll things on the Mac — doesn't work.

Exercise: How many cells do you think this table view uses?

Answer: There are a 100 rows, but only about 14 (or more, depending on the device screen height) fit on the screen at a time. If you count the number of visible rows in the screenshot above you'll get up to 13, but it's possible to scroll the table in such a way that the top cell is still visible while a new cell is pulled in from below. So that makes at least 14 cells.

If you scroll really fast, then I guess it is possible that the table view needs to make a few more temporary cells, but I'm not sure about that. Is this important to know? Not really. You should let the table view take care of juggling the cells behind the scenes. All you have to do is give the table view a cell when it asks for it and fill it up with the data for the corresponding row.

You'll usually have fewer cells than rows. If the app always made a cell for each row, iOS would run out of memory really fast, especially on large tables. Because not all rows can be visible at once, that would be very wasteful and slow. iOS is a good citizen and recycles cells whenever it can.

Now you know why `UITableView` makes the distinction between rows – the data, of which you'll usually have lots – and cells – the visible representation of that data on the screen, of which there are only about a dozen.

As the song goes, "Rows and cells, rows and cells, tables all the way. Oh what fun it is to learn about new things every day!"

Strange crashes?

A common question on the *iOS Apprentice* forums is, "I'm just following along with the book and suddenly my app crashes… What went wrong?"

If that happens to you, then make sure you haven't set a *breakpoint* on your code by accident. A breakpoint is a debugging tool that stops your program at a specific line and jumps into the Xcode debugger. It may appear like a crash, but your program simply paused.

A breakpoint looks like a blue arrow in the left-hand margin (also known as the **gutter**) of the source editor:

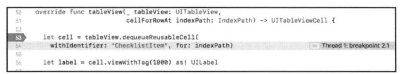

The blue arrow sets a breakpoint

If your app suddenly pauses and the source editor shows a blue arrow on a particular line, then you simply hit a breakpoint. Sometimes people click in the margin by mistake and set a breakpoint without even realizing it (I've certainly done that!).

To remove the breakpoint, drag it out of the Xcode window. Or, you can deactivate a breakpoint by simply clicking on it - it will still be there, ready to be activated again by a click, but will not pause code execution. A deactivated breakpoint is indicated by a faded blue arrow.

A deactivated breakpoint

By the way, the forums for this book are at forums.raywenderlich.com, so drop by if you have any questions.

Tap on the rows

When you tap on a row , the cell color changes to indicate it is selected. The cell remains selected till you tap another row. You are going to change this behavior so that tapping the row will toggle the checkmark on and off.

A tapped row stays gray

Taps on rows are handled by the table view's **delegate**. Remember I said before that in iOS you often find objects doing something on behalf of other objects? The data source is one example of this, but the table view also depends on another little helper, the table view delegate.

The concept of delegation is very common in iOS. An object will often rely on another object to help it out with certain tasks. This *separation of concerns* keeps the system simple, as each object does only what it is good at and lets other objects take care of the rest. The table view offers a great example of this.

Because every app has its own requirements for what its data looks like, the table view must be able to deal with lots of different types of data. Instead of making the table view very complex, or requiring that you modify it to suit your own apps, the UIKit designers have chosen to delegate the duty of providing the cells to display to another object, the data source.

The table view doesn't really care who its data source is or what kind of data your app deals with, just that it can send the cellForRowAt message and receive a cell in return.

This keeps the table view component simple and moves the responsibility for handling the data to where it belongs: in your code.

Likewise, the table view knows how to recognize when the user taps a row, but what it should do in response depends on the app. In this app, you'll make it toggle the checkmark; another app will likely do something totally different.

Using the delegation system, the table view can simply send a message that a tap occurred and let the delegate sort it out.

Usually, components will have just one delegate. But the table view splits up its delegate duties into two separate helpers: the UITableViewDataSource for putting rows into the table, and the UITableViewDelegate for handling taps on the rows and several other tasks.

➤ To see this, open the storyboard and **Control-click** on the table view to bring up its connections.

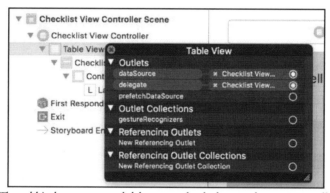

The table's data source and delegate are hooked up to the view controller

You can see that the table view's data source and delegate are both connected to the view controller. That is standard practice for a UITableViewController. (You can also use table views in a basic UIViewController but then you'll have to connect the data source and delegate manually.)

➤ Add the following method to **ChecklistViewController.swift**:

```
override func tableView(_ tableView: UITableView,
        didSelectRowAt indexPath: IndexPath) {

  tableView.deselectRow(at: indexPath, animated: true)
}
```

The tableView(_:didSelectRowAt:) method is one of the table view delegate methods and gets called whenever the user taps on a cell. Run the app and tap a row – the cell briefly turns gray and then becomes de-selected again.

➤ Let's make `tableView(_:didSelectRowAt:)` toggle the checkmark. Change the method to the following:

```swift
override func tableView(_ tableView: UITableView,
                       didSelectRowAt indexPath: IndexPath) {

  if let cell = tableView.cellForRow(at: indexPath) {
    if cell.accessoryType == .none {
      cell.accessoryType = .checkmark
    } else {
      cell.accessoryType = .none
    }
  }

  tableView.deselectRow(at: indexPath, animated: true)
}
```

The checkmark is part of the cell (the accessory, remember?). So, you first need to find the `UITableViewCell` object for the tapped row. You simply ask the table view: what is the cell at this `indexPath` you've given me?

It is theoretically possible that there is no cell at the specified index-path, for example if that row isn't visible. So, you need to use the special `if let` statement.

The `if let` tells Swift that you only want to perform the the code inside the `if` condition only if there really is a `UITableViewCell` object. In this app there always will be one – after all, that's what the user just tapped – but Swift doesn't know that.

Once you have the `UITableViewCell` object, you look at the cell's accessory type, which you can access via the `accessoryType` property. If it is "none", then you change the accessory to a checkmark; if it is already a checkmark, you change it back to none.

> **Note:** In the above code, to find the cell you call `tableView.cellForRow(at:)`.
>
> It's important to realize this is not the same method as the data source method `tableView(_:cellForRowAt:)` that you added earlier.
>
> Despite the similar names they are different methods in different objects, performing different tasks. Tricky, eh?
>
> The purpose of your data source method is to deliver a new (or recycled) cell object to the table view when a row becomes visible. You never call this method yourself; only the `UITableView` may call its data source methods.
>
> The purpose of `tableView.cellForRow(at:)` is also to return a cell object, but this is an existing cell for a row that is currently being displayed. It won't create any new cells. If there is no cell for that row yet, it will return the special value `nil`, meaning that no cell could be found. (You use the `if let` statement to "catch" such `nil` values.)

Remember how I said methods should have clear, descriptive names? UIKit is generally pretty good with its names, but this is a case where a very similar name used in two different places can lead to confusion and despair. Beware this pitfall!

➤ Run the app and try it out. You should be able to toggle the checkmarks on the rows. Sweet!

You can now tap on a row to toggle the checkmark

Note: If the checkmark does not appear or disappear right away but only after you select *another* row, then make sure the method name is not `tableview(_:didDeselectRowAt:)`! You want `didSelect`, not `didDeselect`. Xcode's autocompletion may have fooled you into picking the wrong method name.

Unfortunately, the app has a bug. Here's how to reproduce it:

➤ Tap a row to remove the checkmark. Scroll that row off the screen and scroll back again (try scrolling really fast). The checkmark has reappeared!

In addition, the checkmark seems to spontaneously disappear from other rows. What is going on here?

Again, it's a matter of cells vs. rows: you have toggled the checkmark on the cell but the cell may be reused for another row when you're scrolling. Whether a checkmark is set or not should be a property of a given row (or rather, the data underlying that row), not the cell.

Instead of using the cell's accessory to remember to show a checkmark or not, you need some way to keep track of the checked status for each row. That means it's time to expand the data source and make it use a proper *data model*, which is the topic of the next section.

Methods with multiple parameters

Most of the methods you used in the *Bull's Eye* app took only one parameter or did not have any parameters at all, but these new table view data source and delegate methods take two:

```
override func tableView(
        _ tableView: UITableView,              // parameter 1
        numberOfRowsInSection section: Int)    // parameter 2
        -> Int {                               // return value
    . . .
}
override func tableView(
        _ tableView: UITableView,              // parameter 1
        cellForRowAt indexPath: IndexPath)     // parameter 2
        -> UITableViewCell {                   // return value
    . . .
}
override func tableView(
        _ tableView: UITableView,              // parameter 1
        didSelectRowAt indexPath: IndexPath) { // parameter 2
    . . .
}
```

The first parameter is the `UITableView` object on whose behalf these methods are invoked. This is done for convenience, so you won't have to make an `@IBOutlet` in order to send messages back to the table view.

For `numberOfRowsInSection` the second parameter is the section number. For `cellForRowAt` and `didSelectRowAt` it is the index-path.

Methods are not limited to just one or two parameters, they can have many. But for practical reasons two or three is usually more than enough, and you won't see many methods with more than five parameters.

In other programming languages a method typically looks like this:

```
Int numberOfRowsInSection(UITableView tableView, Int section) {
    . . .
}
```

In Swift we do it a little bit differently, mostly to be compatible with the iOS frameworks, which are all written in the Objective-C programming language. Let's take a look again at `numberOfRowsInSection`:

```
override func tableView(_ tableView: UITableView,
        numberOfRowsInSection section: Int) -> Int {
    . . .
}
```

The method signature for the above method, as discussed before, is tableView(_:numberOfRowsInSection:). If you say that out loud (without the underscores and colons, of course), it actually makes sense. It asks for the number of rows in a particular section of a particular table view.

The first parameter looks like this:

```
_ tableView: UITableView
```

The name of this parameter is tableView. The name is followed by a colon and the parameter's type, UITableView.

The second parameter looks like this:

```
numberOfRowsInSection section: Int
```

This one has two names, numberOfRowsInSection and section.

You use the first name, numberOfRowsInSection, when calling the method. This is the *external* parameter name. Inside the method itself you use the second name, section, known as the *local* parameter name. The data type of this parameter is Int.

The _ underscore is used when you don't want a parameter to have an external name. You'll often see the _ on the first parameter of methods that come from Objective-C frameworks. With such methods the first parameter only has one name but the other parameters have two. Strange? Yes.

It makes sense if you've ever programmed in Objective-C but no doubt it looks weird if you're coming from another language. Once you get used to it, you'll find that this notation is actually quite readable.

Sometimes people with experience in other languages get confused because they think that ChecklistViewController.swift contains three functions that are all named tableView(). But that's not how it works in Swift: the names of the parameters are part of the full method name. That's why these three methods are actually named:

```
tableView(_:numberOfRowsInSection:)
tableView(_:cellForRowAt:)
tableView(_:didSelectRowAt:)
```

By the way, the return type of the method is at the end, after the -> arrow. If there is no arrow, as in tableView(_:didSelectRowAt:), then the method is not supposed to return a value.

Phew! That was a lot of new stuff to take in, so I hope you're still with me. If not, then take a break and start at the beginning again. You're being introduced to a whole bunch of new concepts all at once and that can be overwhelming.

But don't worry, it's OK if everything doesn't make perfect sense yet. As long as you get the gist of what's going on, you're good to go.

If you want to check your work up to this point, you can find the project files for the app under **09 - Table Views** in the Source Code folder.

Chapter 10: The Data Model

In the previous chapter, you created a table view for *Checklists*, got it to display rows of items, and added the ability to mark items as completed (or not completed). However, this was all done using hardcoded, fake data. This would not do for a real to-do app since your users want to store their own custom to-do items.

In order to store, manage, and display to-do information efficiently, you need a data model that allows you to store (and access) to-do information easily. And that's what you're going to do in this chapter.

This chapter covers the following:

- **Model-View-Controller:** A quick explanation of the MVC fundamentals which are central to iOS programming.

- **The data model:** Creating a data model to hold the data for *Checklists*.

- **Clean up the code:** Simplify your code so that it is easier to understand and maintain.

Model-View-Controller

First, a tiny detour into programming-concept-land so that you understand some of the principles behind using a data model. No book on programming for iOS can escape an explanation of **Model-View-Controller**, or MVC for short.

MVC is one of the three fundamental design patterns of iOS. You've already seen the other two: *delegation*, making one object do something on behalf of another; and *target-action*, connecting events such as button taps to action methods.

The Model-View-Controller pattern states that the objects in your app can be split into three groups:

- **Model objects.** These objects contain your data and any operations on the data. For example, if you were writing a cookbook app, the model would consist of the recipes. In a game, it would be the design of the levels, the player score, and the positions of the monsters.

  The operations that the data model objects perform are sometimes called the *business rules* or the *domain logic*. For *Checklists*, the checklists and their to-do items form the data model.

- **View objects.** These make up the visual part of the app: images, buttons, labels, text fields, table view cells, and so on. In a game, the views form the visual representation of the game world, such as the monster animations and a frag counter.

  A view can draw itself and responds to user input, but it typically does not handle any application logic. Many views, such as UITableView, can be re-used in many different apps because they are not tied to a specific data model.

- **Controller objects.** The controller is the object that connects your data model objects to the views. It listens to taps on the views, makes the data model objects do some calculations in response, and updates the views to reflect the new state of your model. The controller is in charge. On iOS, the controller is called the "view controller".

Conceptually, this is how these three building blocks fit together:

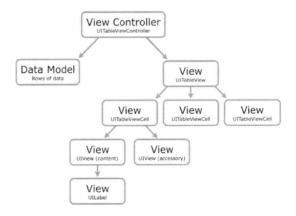

How Model-View-Controller works

The view controller has one main view, accessible through its view property, that contains a bunch of subviews. It is not uncommon for a screen to have dozens of views all at once. The top-level view usually fills the whole screen. You design the layout of the view controller's screen in the storyboard.

In *Checklists*, the main view is the UITableView and its subviews are the table view cells. Each cell also has several subviews of its own, namely the text label and the accessory.

Generally, a view controller handles one screen of the app. If your app has more than one screen, each of these is handled by its own view controller and has its own views. Your app flows from one view controller to another.

You will often need to create your own view controllers, but iOS also comes with ready-to-use view controllers, such as the image picker controller for photos, the mail compose controller that lets you write email, and the tweet sheet for sending Twitter messages.

Views vs. view controllers

Remember that a view and a view controller are two different things.

A view is an object that draws something on the screen, such as a button or a label. The view is what you see.

The view controller is what does the work behind the scenes. It is the bridge that sits between your data model and the views.

A lot of beginners give their view controllers names such as FirstView or MainView. That is very confusing! If something is a view controller, its name should end with "ViewController", not "View".

I sometimes wish Apple had left the word "view" out of "view controller" and just called it "controller" as that is a lot less misleading.

The data model

So far, you've put a bunch of fake data into the table view. The data consists of a text string and a checkmark that can be on or off.

As you saw in the previous chapter, you cannot use the cells to remember the data as cells get re-used all the time and their old contents get overwritten.

Table view cells are part of the view. Their purpose is to display the app's data, but that data actually comes from somewhere else: the data model.

Remember this well: the rows are the data, the cells are the views. The table view controller is the thing that ties them together through the act of implementing the table view's data source and delegate methods.

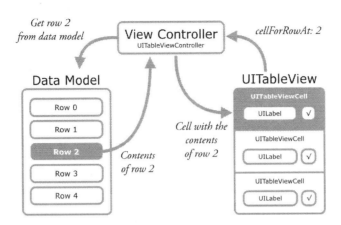

The table view controller (data source) gets the data from the model and puts it into the cells

The data model for this app will be a list of to-do items. Each of these items will get its own row in the table.

For each to-do item you need to store two pieces of information: the text ("Walk the dog", "Brush my teeth", "Eat ice cream") and whether the checkmark is set or not.

That is two pieces of information per row, so you need two variables for each row.

The first iteration

First, I'll show you the cumbersome way to program this. It will work but it isn't very smart. Even though this is not the best approach, I'd still like you to follow along and copy-paste the code into Xcode and run the app so that you understand how this approach works.

Understanding why this approach is problematic will help you appreciate the proper solution better.

➤ In **ChecklistViewController.swift**, add the following constants right after the `class ChecklistViewController` line.

```
class ChecklistViewController: UITableViewController {
   let row0text = "Walk the dog"
   let row1text = "Brush teeth"
   let row2text = "Learn iOS development"
   let row3text = "Soccer practice"
   let row4text = "Eat ice cream"
   . . .
```

These constants are defined outside of any method (they are not "local"), so they can be used by all of the methods in `ChecklistViewController`.

➤ Change the data source methods to:

```swift
override func tableView(_ tableView: UITableView,
      numberOfRowsInSection section: Int) -> Int {
  return 5
}

override func tableView(_ tableView: UITableView,
            cellForRowAt indexPath: IndexPath)
            -> UITableViewCell {
  let cell = tableView.dequeueReusableCell(
                    withIdentifier: "ChecklistItem",
                                for: indexPath)
  let label = cell.viewWithTag(1000) as! UILabel

  if indexPath.row == 0 {
    label.text = row0text
  } else if indexPath.row == 1 {
    label.text = row1text
  } else if indexPath.row == 2 {
    label.text = row2text
  } else if indexPath.row == 3 {
    label.text = row3text
  } else if indexPath.row == 4 {
    label.text = row4text
  }
  return cell
}
```

➤ Run the app. It still shows the same five rows as originally.

What have you done here? For every row, you have added a constant with the text for that row. Together, those five constants are your data model. (You could have used variables instead of constants, but since the values won't change for this particular example, it's better to use constants.)

In `tableView(_:cellForRowAt:)` you look at `indexPath.row` to figure out which row to draw, and put the text from the corresponding constant into the cell.

Handle checkmarks

Now, let's fix the checkmark toggling logic. You no longer want to toggle the checkmark on the cell but at the row (or data) level. To do this, you add five new instance variables to keep track of the "checked" state of each of the rows. (This time the values have to be variables instead of constants since you will be changing the checked/unchecked state for each row.) These new variables are also part of your data model.

➤ Add the following instance variables:

```
var row0checked = false
var row1checked = false
var row2checked = false
var row3checked = false
var row4checked = false
```

These variables have the data type `Bool`. You've seen the data types `Int` (whole numbers), `Float` (decimal/fractional numbers), and `String` (text) before. A `Bool` variable can hold only two possible values: `true` or `false`.

`Bool` is short for "boolean", after Englishman George Boole who long ago invented a kind of logic that forms the basis of all modern computing. The fact that computers talk in ones and zeros is largely due to him.

You use `Bool` variables to remember whether something is true (1) or not (0). As a convention, the names of boolean variables often start with the verb "is" or "has", as in `isHungry` or `hasIceCream`.

The instance variable `row0checked` is `true` if the first row has its checkmark set and `false` if it doesn't. Likewise, `row1checked` reflects whether the second row has a checkmark or not. The same thing goes for the instance variables for the other rows.

> **Note:** How does the compiler know that the type of these variables is `Bool`? You never specified that anywhere.
>
> Remember *type inference* from your code in *Bulls's Eye*? Because you said `var row0checked = false`, Swift assumes that you intended to make this a `Bool`, as `false` is valid only for `Bool` values.

The delegate method that handles taps on table cells will now use these new instance variables to determine whether the checkmark for a row needs to be toggled on or off.

The code in `tableView(_:didSelectRowAt:)` should be something like the following. *Don't make these changes just yet!* Just try to understand what happens first.

```
override func tableView(_ tableView: UITableView,
        didSelectRowAt indexPath: IndexPath) {

  if let cell = tableView.cellForRow(at: indexPath) {
    if indexPath.row == 0 {
      row0checked = !row0checked
      if row0checked {
        cell.accessoryType = .checkmark
      } else {
```

```
          cell.accessoryType = .none
        }
  } else if indexPath.row == 1 {
    row1checked = !row1checked
    if row1checked {
      cell.accessoryType = .checkmark
    } else {
      cell.accessoryType = .none
    }
  } else if indexPath.row == 2 {
    row2checked = !row2checked
    if row2checked {
      cell.accessoryType = .checkmark
    } else {
      cell.accessoryType = .none
    }
  } else if indexPath.row == 3 {
    row3checked = !row3checked
    if row2checked {
      cell.accessoryType = .checkmark
    } else {
      cell.accessoryType = .none
    }
  } else if indexPath.row == 4 {
    row4checked = !row4checked
    if row4checked {
      cell.accessoryType = .checkmark
    } else {
      cell.accessoryType = .none
    }
  }
}
  tableView.deselectRow(at: indexPath, animated: true)
}
```

It should be clear that the code looks at `indexPath.row` to find the row that was tapped, and then performs some logic with the corresponding "row checked" instance variable. But there's also some new stuff you may not have seen before.

Let's look at the first `if indexPath.row` statement in detail:

```
if indexPath.row == 0 {
  row0checked = !row0checked
  if row0checked {
    cell.accessoryType = .checkmark
  } else {
    cell.accessoryType = .none
  }
} . . .
```

If `indexPath.row` is 0, the user tapped on the very first row and the corresponding instance variable is `row0checked`.

You do the following to flip that boolean value around:

```
row0checked = !row0checked
```

The ! symbol is the **logical not** operator. There are a few other logical operators that work on `Bool` values, such as **and** and **or**, which you'll encounter soon enough.

What ! does is simple: it reverses the meaning of the value. If `row0checked` is `true`, then ! makes it `false`. Conversely, `!false` is `true`.

Think of ! as "not": not yes is no and not no is yes. Yes?

Once you have the new value of `row0checked`, you can use it to show or hide the checkmark:

```
if row0checked {
  cell.accessoryType = .checkmark
} else {
  cell.accessoryType = .none
}
```

The same logic is used for the other four rows.

In fact, the other rows use the *exact* same logic. The only thing that is different between each of these code blocks is the name of the "row checked" instance variable.

Because the code looks so familiar from one `if` statement to the next, we can improve upon it.

➤ Replace the current `tableView(_:didSelectRowAt:)` implementation with the following:

```
override func tableView(_ tableView: UITableView,
          didSelectRowAt indexPath: IndexPath) {

  if let cell = tableView.cellForRow(at: indexPath) {
    var isChecked = false

    if indexPath.row == 0 {
      row0checked = !row0checked
      isChecked = row0checked
    } else if indexPath.row == 1 {
      row1checked = !row1checked
      isChecked = row1checked
    } else if indexPath.row == 2 {
      row2checked = !row2checked
      isChecked = row2checked
```

```
        } else if indexPath.row == 3 {
          row3checked = !row3checked
          isChecked = row3checked
        } else if indexPath.row == 4 {
          row4checked = !row4checked
          isChecked = row4checked
        }

        if isChecked {
          cell.accessoryType = .checkmark
        } else {
          cell.accessoryType = .none
        }
      }
    tableView.deselectRow(at: indexPath, animated: true)
}
```

Now isn't that a lot shorter than the previous iteration (that you weren't supposed to type in)?

Notice how the logic that sets the checkmark on the cell has moved to the bottom of the method. There is now only one place where this happens.

To make this possible, you store the value of the "row checked" instance variable into the isChecked local variable. This temporary variable is just used to remember whether the selected row needs a checkmark or not.

By using a local variable you were able to remove a lot of duplicated code, which is a good thing. You've taken the logic that all rows had in common and moved it out of the if statements into a single place.

Note: Code duplication makes programs a lot harder to read. Worse, it invites subtle mistakes that cause hard-to-find bugs. Always be on the lookout for opportunities to remove duplicate code!

Exercise: There was actually a bug in the previous, longer version of this method – did you spot it? That's what happens when you use copy-paste to create duplicate code, like I did when I wrote that method.

➤ Run the app and observe… that it still doesn't work very well. Initially, you have to tap a couple of times on a row to actually make the checkmark go away.

What's wrong here? Simple: when you declared the rowXchecked variables you set their values to false.

So `row0checked` and the others indicate that there is no checkmark on their row, but the table draws one anyway. That's because you enabled the checkmark accessory on the prototype cell.

In other words: the data model (the "row checked" variables) and the views (the checkmarks inside the cells) are out-of-sync.

There are a few ways you could try to fix this: you could set the `Bool` variables to `true` to begin with, or you could remove the checkmark from the prototype cell in the storyboard.

Neither is a foolproof solution. What goes wrong here isn't so much that you initialized the "row checked" values wrong or designed the prototype cell wrong, but that you didn't set the cell's `accessoryType` property to the right value in `tableView(_:cellForRowAt:)`.

When you are asked for a new cell, you always should configure all of its properties. The call to `tableView.dequeueReusableCell(withIdentifier:)` could return a cell that was previously used for a row with a checkmark. If the new row shouldn't have a checkmark, then you have to remove it from the cell at this point (and vice versa).

Let's fix that.

➤ Add the following method to **ChecklistViewController.swift**:

```swift
func configureCheckmark(for cell: UITableViewCell,
                        at indexPath: IndexPath) {
  var isChecked = false

  if indexPath.row == 0 {
    isChecked = row0checked
  } else if indexPath.row == 1 {
    isChecked = row1checked
  } else if indexPath.row == 2 {
    isChecked = row2checked
  } else if indexPath.row == 3 {
    isChecked = row3checked
  } else if indexPath.row == 4 {
    isChecked = row4checked
  }

  if isChecked {
    cell.accessoryType = .checkmark
  } else {
    cell.accessoryType = .none
  }
}
```

This new method looks at the cell for a certain row, specified as usual by `indexPath`, and makes the checkmark visible if the corresponding "row checked" variable is `true`, or hides the checkmark if the variable is `false`.

This logic should look very familiar! The only difference with before is that here you don't toggle the state of the "row checked" variable. You only read it and then set the cell's accessory.

You'll call this method from `tableView(_:cellForRowAt:)`, just before you return the cell.

➤ Change `tableView(_:cellForRowAt:)` to the following (recall that **. . .** means that the existing code at that spot doesn't change):

```
override func tableView(_ tableView: UITableView,
        cellForRowAt indexPath: IndexPath)
        -> UITableViewCell {
    . . .

    configureCheckmark(for: cell, at: indexPath)
    return cell
}
```

➤ Run the app again.

Now the app works just fine. Initially all the rows are unchecked. Tapping a row checks it, tapping it again unchecks it. The rows and cells are now always in sync. This code guarantees that each cell always has the value that corresponds to its underlying data row.

External and internal parameter names

The new `configureCheckmark` method has two parameters, `for` and `at`. Its full name is therefore `configureCheckmark(for:at:)`.

`for` and `at` are the *external* names of these parameters.

Adding short prepositions such as "at", "with", or "for" is very common in Swift. It makes the name of the method sound like a proper English phrase: "configure checkmark for this cell at that index-path". Doesn't it just roll off your tongue?

When you call the method, you always have to include those external parameter names:

```
configureCheckmark(for: someCell, at: someIndexPath)
```

Here, `someCell` is a variable that refers to a `UITableViewCell` object. Likewise, `someIndexPath` is a variable of type `IndexPath`.

You can't write the following:

```
configureCheckmark(someCell, someIndexPath)
```

This won't compile. The app doesn't have a configureCheckmark method that doesn't take parameter names, only configureCheckmark(for:at:). The for and at are an integral part of the method name!

Inside the method you use the *internal* labels cell and indexPath to refer to the parameters.

```
func configureCheckmark(for cell: UITableViewCell,
                        at indexPath: IndexPath) {
  if indexPath.row == 0 {
    . . .
  }

  cell.accessoryType = .checkmark
  . . .
}
```

You can't write if at.row == 0 or for.accessoryType = .checkmark. That also sounds a little odd, doesn't it?

This split between external and internal labels is unique to Swift and Objective-C and takes some getting used to if you're familiar with other languages.

This naming convention primarily exists so that Swift can talk to older Objective-C code, and this is a good thing since most of the iOS frameworks are still written in Objective-C.

Simplify the code

Why was configureCheckmark(for:at:) set up as a method of its own anyway? Well, because you can use it to simplify tableView(_:didSelectRowAt:).

Notice how similar these two methods currently are. That's another case of code duplication that you can get rid of!

You can simplify didSelectRowAt by letting configureCheckmark(for:at:) do some of the work.

➤ Replace tableView(_:didSelectRowAt:) with the following:

```
override func tableView(_ tableView: UITableView,
            didSelectRowAt indexPath: IndexPath) {

  if let cell = tableView.cellForRow(at: indexPath) {
```

```
    if indexPath.row == 0 {
        row0checked = !row0checked
    } else if indexPath.row == 1 {
        row1checked = !row1checked
    } else if indexPath.row == 2 {
        row2checked = !row2checked
    } else if indexPath.row == 3 {
        row3checked = !row3checked
    } else if indexPath.row == 4 {
        row4checked = !row4checked
    }

    configureCheckmark(for: cell, at: indexPath)
    }
    tableView.deselectRow(at: indexPath, animated: true)
}
```

This method no longer sets or clears the checkmark from the cell, but only toggles the "checked" state in the data model and then calls `configureCheckmark(for:at:)` to update the view.

➤ Run the app again and it should still work.

➤ Change the declarations of the instance variables to the following and run the app again:

```
var row0checked = false
var row1checked = true
var row2checked = true
var row3checked = false
var row4checked = true
```

Now rows 1, 2 and 4 (the second, third and fifth rows) initially have a checkmark while the others don't.

The data model and the table view cells are now always in-sync

The approach that we've taken here to remember which rows are checked or not works just fine... when there's five rows of data.

But what if you have 100 rows and they all need to be unique? Should you add another 95 "row text" and "row checked" variables to the view controller, as well as that many additional if statements? I hope not!

There is a better way: arrays.

Arrays

An **array** is an ordered list of objects. If you think of a variable as a container of one value (or one object) then an array is a container for multiple objects.

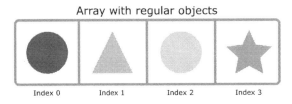

Arrays are ordered lists containing multiple objects

Of course, the array itself is also an object (named Array) that you can put into a variable. And because arrays are objects, arrays can contain other arrays.

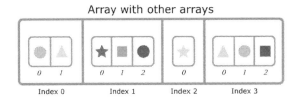

Arrays can also include other arrays

The objects inside an array are indexed by numbers, starting at 0 as usual. To ask the array for the first object, you write array[0]. The second object is at array[1], and so on.

The array is *ordered*, meaning that the order of the objects it contains matters. The object at index 0 always comes before the object at index 1.

> **Note:** An array is a *collection* object. There are several other collection objects and they all organize their objects in a different fashion. Dictionary, for example, contains *key-value pairs*, just like a real dictionary contains a list of words and a description for each of those words. You'll use some of these other collection types in later chapters.

The organization of an array is very similar to the rows for a table – they are both lists of objects in a particular order – so it makes sense to put your data model's rows into an array.

Arrays store one object per index, but your rows currently consist of two separate pieces of data: the text and the checked state. It would be easier if you made a single object for each row, because then the row number from the table simply becomes the index in the array.

The second iteration

Let's combine the text and checkmark state into a new object of your own!

➤ Select the **Checklists** group in the project navigator and right click. Choose **New File…** from the popup menu:

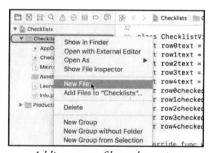

Adding a new file to the project

Under the **Source** section choose **Swift File**:

Choosing the Swift File class template

Click **Next** to continue. Save the new file as **ChecklistItem** (you don't really need to add the **.swift** file extension since it will be automatically added for you).

Saving the new Swift file

Press **Create** to add the new file to the project.

➤ Add the following to the new **ChecklistItem.swift** file, below the import line:

```
class ChecklistItem {
    var text = ""
    var checked = false
}
```

What you see here is the absolute minimum amount of code you need in order to make a new object. The class keyword names the object and the two lines with var add data items (instance variables) to it.

The text property will store the description of the checklist item (the text that will appear in the table view cell's label) and the checked property determines whether the cell gets a checkmark or not.

> **Note:** You may be wondering what the difference is between the terms *property* and *instance variable* – we've used both to refer to an object's data items. You'll be glad to hear that these two terms are interchangeable.
>
> In Swift terminology, a property is a variable or constant that is used in the context of an object. That's exactly what an instance variable is.
>
> (In Objective-C, properties and instance variables are closely related but not quite the same thing. In Swift they are the same.)

That's all for **ChecklistItem.swift** for now. The ChecklistItem object currently only serves to combine the text and the checked variables into one object. Later you'll do more with it.

Before you try using an array, replace the String and Bool instance variables in the view controller with these new ChecklistItem objects to see how that approach would work.

➤ In **ChecklistViewController.swift**, remove the old properties (both the `let` and `var` values) and replace them with `ChecklistItem` objects:

```swift
class ChecklistViewController: UITableViewController {
  var row0item: ChecklistItem
  var row1item: ChecklistItem
  var row2item: ChecklistItem
  var row3item: ChecklistItem
  var row4item: ChecklistItem
```

These replace the `row0text`, `row0checked`, etc. instance variables.

Because some methods in the view controller still refer to these old variables, Xcode will throw up multiple errors at this point. Before you can run the app again, you need to fix these errors. So, let's do that now.

> **Note:** I generally encourage you to type in the code from this book by hand (instead of copy-pasting), because that gives you a better feel for what you're doing, but in the following instances it's easier to just copy-paste from the PDF.
>
> Unfortunately, copying from the PDF sometimes adds strange or invisible characters that confuse Xcode. It's best to first paste the copied text into a plain text editor such as TextMate and then copy that into Xcode.
>
> Of course, if you're reading the print edition of this book, copying & pasting from the book isn't going to work, but you can still use copy-paste to save yourself some effort. Make the changes on one line and then copy that line to create the other lines. Copy-paste is a programmer's best friend, but don't forget to update the lines you pasted to use the correct variable names!

➤ In `tableView(_:cellForRowAt:)`, replace the `if` statements with the following:

```swift
if indexPath.row == 0 {
  label.text = row0item.text
} else if indexPath.row == 1 {
  label.text = row1item.text
} else if indexPath.row == 2 {
  label.text = row2item.text
} else if indexPath.row == 3 {
  label.text = row3item.text
} else if indexPath.row == 4 {
  label.text = row4item.text
}
```

➤ In `tableView(_:didSelectRowAt:)`, again change the `if` statement block to:

```
if indexPath.row == 0 {
    row0item.checked = !row0item.checked
} else if indexPath.row == 1 {
    row1item.checked = !row1item.checked
} else if indexPath.row == 2 {
    row2item.checked = !row2item.checked
} else if indexPath.row == 3 {
    row3item.checked = !row3item.checked
} else if indexPath.row == 4 {
    row4item.checked = !row4item.checked
}
```

➤ And finally, in `configureCheckmark(for:at:)`, change the `if` block to:

```
if indexPath.row == 0 {
    isChecked = row0item.checked
} else if indexPath.row == 1 {
    isChecked = row1item.checked
} else if indexPath.row == 2 {
    isChecked = row2item.checked
} else if indexPath.row == 3 {
    isChecked = row3item.checked
} else if indexPath.row == 4 {
    isChecked = row4item.checked
}
```

Basically, all of the above changes do one thing - instead of using the separate `row0text` and `row0checked` variables, you now use `row0item.text` and `row0item.checked`.

That takes care of all of the errors except for one. Xcode complains that "Class ChecklistViewController has no initializers." This was not a problem before, so what has gone wrong?

Initialize objects

Previously, you gave the "row text" and "row checked" variables a value when you declared them, like so:

```
let row0text = "Walk the dog"
var row0checked = false
```

With the new `ChecklistItem` object you can't do that because a `ChecklistItem` consists of more than one value.

Instead you used what's known as a *type annotation* to tell Swift that `row0Item` is an object of type `ChecklistItem`.

```
var row0item: ChecklistItem
```

But at this point `row0item` doesn't have a value yet, it's just an empty container for a `ChecklistItem` object.

And that's a problem: in Swift programs, all variables should always have an explicit value – the containers can never be undefined.

If you can't give the variable a value right away when you declare it, then you have to give it a value inside an *initializer* method - as the name implies, an initializer method, initializes (or sets up) the object when it first comes into existence.

➤ Add the following to **ChecklistViewController.swift**. The initializer is a special type of method (which is why it doesn't start with the word `func`). It is customary to place it near the top of the file, just below the instance variables.

```
required init?(coder aDecoder: NSCoder) {
  row0item = ChecklistItem()
  row0item.text = "Walk the dog"
  row0item.checked = false

  row1item = ChecklistItem()
  row1item.text = "Brush my teeth"
  row1item.checked = true

  row2item = ChecklistItem()
  row2item.text = "Learn iOS development"
  row2item.checked = true

  row3item = ChecklistItem()
  row3item.text = "Soccer practice"
  row3item.checked = false

  row4item = ChecklistItem()
  row4item.text = "Eat ice cream"
  row4item.checked = true

  super.init(coder: aDecoder)
}
```

Every object in Swift has an `init` method, or initializer. Some objects even have more than one initializer.

The `init` method is called by Swift when the object comes into existence.

For the view controller, that happens when it is loaded from the storyboard during app startup. At that point, its `init?(coder)` method is called.

That makes `init?(coder)` a great place for putting values into any variables that still need them (soon you'll learn more about what the "coder" parameter is for).

Inside `init?(coder)`, you first create a new `ChecklistItem` object:

```
row0item = ChecklistItem()
```

And then set its properties:

```
row0item.text = "Walk the dog"
row0item.checked = false
```

You repeat this for the other four rows. Each row gets its own `ChecklistItem` object that you store in its own instance variable.

This is essentially doing the same thing as before, except that this time the `text` and `checked` variables are not separate instance variables of the view controller but properties of a `ChecklistItem` object.

➤ Run the app just to make sure that everything still works.

Putting the `text` and `checked` properties into their own `ChecklistItem` object already improved the code, but it is still a bit unwieldy.

With the current approach, you need to keep around a `ChecklistItem` instance variable for each row. That's not ideal, especially if you want more than just a handful of rows.

Time to bring that array into play!

➤ In **ChecklistViewController.swift**, remove all the instance variables and replace them with a single array variable named `items`:

```
class ChecklistViewController: UITableViewController {

    var items: [ChecklistItem]
```

Instead of five different instance variables, one for each row, you now have just one variable for the array.

This looks similar to how you declared the previous variables but this time there are square brackets around `ChecklistItem`. Those square brackets indicate that the variable is going to be an array containing `ChecklistItem` objects.

➤ Make the following changes to `init?(coder:)`:

```
required init?(coder aDecoder: NSCoder) {
    items = [ChecklistItem]()              // add this line

    let row0item = ChecklistItem()         // let
    row0item.text = "Walk the dog"
    row0item.checked = false
    items.append(row0item)                 // add this line
```

```
    let row1item = ChecklistItem()                  // let
    row1item.text = "Brush my teeth"
    row1item.checked = true
    items.append(row1item)                          // add this line

    let row2item = ChecklistItem()                  // let
    row2item.text = "Learn iOS development"
    row2item.checked = true
    items.append(row2item)                          // add this line

    let row3item = ChecklistItem()                  // let
    row3item.text = "Soccer practice"
    row3item.checked = false
    items.append(row3item)                          // add this line

    let row4item = ChecklistItem()                  // let
    row4item.text = "Eat ice cream"
    row4item.checked = true
    items.append(row4item)                          // add this line

    super.init(coder: aDecoder)
}
```

This is not so different from before, except that you first create – or *instantiate* – the array object:

```
items = [ChecklistItem]()
```

You've seen that the notation [ChecklistItem] means an array of ChecklistItem objects. But that is just the data type of the items variable; it is not the actual array object yet.

To get the array object you have to construct it first. That is what the parentheses () are for: they tell Swift to make the new array object.

The data type is like the brand name of a car. Just saying the words "Porsche 911" out loud doesn't magically get you a new car – you actually have to go to the dealer to buy one.

The parentheses () behind the type name are like going to the object dealership to buy an object of that type. The parentheses tell Swift's object factory, "Build me an object of the type array-with-ChecklistItems."

It is important to remember that just declaring that you have a variable does not automatically make the corresponding object for you. The variable is just the container for the object. You still have to instantiate the object and put it into the container. The variable is the box and the object is the thing inside the box.

So until you order an actual array-of-`ChecklistItem`s object from the factory and put that into `items`, the variable is empty. And empty variables are a big no-no in Swift.

Just to drive this point home:

```
// This declares that items will hold an array of ChecklistItem
// objects but it does not actually create that array.
// At this point, items does not have a value yet.
var items: [ChecklistItem]

// This instantiates the array. Now items contains a valid array
// object, but the array has no objects inside it yet.
items = [ChecklistItem]()
```

Note: You can simplify the above two lines by combininig them. When you declare the `items` variable, you can also instantiate it by having the declaration be: `var items: [ChecklistItem]()`. That is perfectly acceptable. I have separated the two steps out above for the sake of clarity. Feel free to instantiate variables when they are declared if you like - I generally do.

Each time you make a `ChecklistItem` object, you also add it to the array:

```
// This instantiates a new ChecklistItem object. Notice the ().
let row0item = ChecklistItem()

// Set values for the data items inside the new object.
row0item.text = "Walk the dog"
row0item.checked = false

// This adds the ChecklistItem object to the items array.
items.append(row0item)
```

Notice that you're also using the parentheses here to create each of the individual `ChecklistItem` objects.

It's also important that `row0item` and the others are now local to the `init` method. They are no longer valid instance variable names (because you removed those earlier). That's why you need to use the `let` keyword; without it, the app won't compile.

At the end of `init?(coder)`, the `items` array contains five `ChecklistItem` objects. This is your new data model.

Simplify the code - again

Now that you have all your rows in the `items` array, you can simplify the table view data source and delegate methods once again.

➤ Change these methods:

```
override func tableView(_ tableView: UITableView,
            cellForRowAt indexPath: IndexPath)
            -> UITableViewCell {
  let cell = tableView.dequeueReusableCell(
                      withIdentifier: "ChecklistItem",
                                 for: indexPath)

  let item = items[indexPath.row]        // Add this

  let label = cell.viewWithTag(1000) as! UILabel
  // Replace everything after the above line with the following
  label.text = item.text
  configureCheckmark(for: cell, at: indexPath)
  return cell
}
```

```
override func tableView(_ tableView: UITableView,
            didSelectRowAt indexPath: IndexPath) {

  if let cell = tableView.cellForRow(at: indexPath) {
    // Replace everything inside this `if` condition
    // with the following
    let item = items[indexPath.row]
    item.checked = !item.checked

    configureCheckmark(for: cell, at: indexPath)
  }
  tableView.deselectRow(at: indexPath, animated: true)
}
```

```
func configureCheckmark(for cell: UITableViewCell,
                  at indexPath: IndexPath) {
  // Replace full method implementation
  let item = items[indexPath.row]

  if item.checked {
    cell.accessoryType = .checkmark
  } else {
    cell.accessoryType = .none
  }
}
```

That's a lot simpler than what you had before! Each method is now only a handful of lines long.

In each method, you do:

```
let item = items[indexPath.row]
```

This asks the array for the `ChecklistItem` object at the index that corresponds to the row number. Once you have that object, you can simply look at its `text` and `checked` properties and do whatever you need to do.

If the user were to add 100 to-do items to this list, none of this code would need to change. It works equally well with five items as with a hundred (or a thousand).

Speaking of the number of items, you can now change `numberOfRowsInSection` to return the actual number of items in the array, instead of a hard-coded number.

➤ Change the `tableView(_:numberOfRowsInSection:)` method to:

```
override func tableView(_ tableView: UITableView,
        numberOfRowsInSection section: Int) -> Int {
    return items.count
}
```

Not only is the code a lot shorter and easier to read, it can now also handle an arbitrary number of rows. That is the power of arrays!

➤ Run the app and see for yourself. It should still do exactly the same as before but internal structure of the code is way better.

> **Exercise:** Add a few more rows to the table. You should only have to change `init?(coder)` for this to work.

Clean up the code

There are a few more things you can do to improve the source code.

➤ Replace `configureCheckmark(for:at:)` with this one:

```
func configureCheckmark(for cell: UITableViewCell,
                        with item: ChecklistItem) {
    if item.checked {
        cell.accessoryType = .checkmark
    } else {
        cell.accessoryType = .none
    }
}
```

Instead of an index-path, you now directly pass the `ChecklistItem` object to the method.

Note that now the full name of the method becomes
configureCheckmark(for:with:) and that's how you will call it from other places in
the app.

Why did you change this method? Previously it received an index-path and then did the
following to find the corresponding ChecklistItem:

```
let item = items[indexPath.row]
```

But in both cellForRowAt and didSelectRowAt you already do that. So, it's simpler
to pass that ChecklistItem object directly to configureCheckmark instead of making
it do the same work twice. Anything that simplifies the code is good.

➤ Also add this new method:

```
func configureText(for cell: UITableViewCell,
                   with item: ChecklistItem) {
  let label = cell.viewWithTag(1000) as! UILabel
  label.text = item.text
}
```

This sets the checklist item's text on the cell's label. Previously you did that in
cellForRowAt but it's clearer to put that in its own method.

➤ Update tableView(_:cellForRowAt:) so that it calls these new methods:

```
override func tableView(_ tableView: UITableView,
            cellForRowAt indexPath: IndexPath)
            -> UITableViewCell {
  let cell = tableView.dequeueReusableCell(
                      withIdentifier: "ChecklistItem",
                                 for: indexPath)

  let item = items[indexPath.row]

  configureText(for: cell, with: item)
  configureCheckmark(for: cell, with: item)
  return cell
}
```

➤ Also update tableView(_:didSelectRowAt:):

```
override func tableView(_ tableView: UITableView,
                        didSelectRowAt indexPath: IndexPath) {

  if let cell = tableView.cellForRow(at: indexPath) {
    let item = items[indexPath.row]
    item.toggleChecked()
    configureCheckmark(for: cell, with: item)
```

```
    }
    tableView.deselectRow(at: indexPath, animated: true)
  }
```

The above calls a new method named `toggleChecked()` on the item object longer instead of modifying the `ChecklistItem`'s `checked` property directly.

You will need to add this new method to the `ChecklistItem` object since Xcode should already be complaining about the method not being there.

➤ Open **ChecklistItem.swift** and add the following method (just below the property declarations and before the closing curly bracket):

```
func toggleChecked() {
  checked = !checked
}
```

Naturally, your own objects can also have methods. As you can see, this method does exactly what `didSelectRowAt` used to do, except that you've added this bit of functionality to `ChecklistItem` instead.

A good object-oriented design principle is that you should let objects change their own state as much as possible. Previously, the view controller implemented this toggling behavior but now `ChecklistItem` knows how to toggle itself on or off.

➤ Run the app. It should still work exactly the same as before, but the code is a lot better. You can now have lists with thousands of to-do items, for those especially industrious users.

Clean up that mess!

So what's the point of making all of these changes if the app still works exactly the same? For one, the code is much cleaner and that helps with avoiding bugs. By using an array you've also made the code more flexible. The table view can now handle any number of rows.

You'll find that when you are programming you are constantly restructuring your code to make it better. It's impossible to do the whole thing 100% perfect from the get go.

So you write code until it becomes messy and then you clean it up. After a little while it becomes a big mess again and you clean it up again. The process for cleaning up code is called *refactoring* and it's a cycle that never ends.

There are a lot of programmers who never refactor their code. The result is what we call "spaghetti code" and it's a horrible mess to maintain.

If you haven't looked at your code for several months but need to add a new feature or fix a bug, you may need some time to read it through to understand again how everything fits together. This task becomes that much harder when you have spaghetti code.

So, it's in your own best interest to write code that is as clean as possible.

If you want to check your work, you can find the project files for the current version of the app in the folder **10-The Data Model** in the Source Code folder.

Chapter 11: Navigation Controllers

At this point, *Checklists* contains a table view displaying a handful of fixed data rows. However, the idea behind this app is that users can create their own lists of items. Therefore, you need to give the user the ability to add to-do items.

In this chapter you'll expand the app to have a **navigation bar** at the top. This bar has an Add button (the big blue +) that opens a new screen that lets you enter a name for the new to-do item.

When you tap Done, the new item will be added to the list.

The + button in the navigation bar opens the Add Item screen

Presenting a new screen to add items is a common pattern in a lot of apps. Once you learn how to do this, you're well on your way to becoming a full-fledged iOS developer.

This chapter covers the following:

- **Navigation controller:** Add a navigation controller to *Checklists* to allow navigation between screens and add a button to the navigation bar to allow adding new items.

- **Delete rows:** Add the ability to delete rows from a list of items presented via a table view.

- **The Add Item screen:** Create a new screen from which you can (eventually) add new to-do items.

Navigation controller

First, let's add the navigation bar. You may have seen in the Object Library that there is an object named Navigation Bar. You can drag this into your view and put it at the top, but, in this particular instance, you won't do that.

Instead, you will embed your view controller inside a **navigation controller**.

Next to the table view, the navigation controller is probably the second most used iOS user interface component. It is the thing that lets you go from one page to another:

A navigation controller in action

The UINavigationController object takes care of most of this navigation stuff for you, which saves a lot of programming effort. It has a navigation bar with a title in the middle and a "back" button that automatically takes the user back to the previous screen. You can put a button of your own on the right.

Add a navigation controller

Adding a navigation controller is really easy.

➤ Open **Main.storyboard** and select the **Checklist View Controller**.

➤ From the menu bar at the top of the screen, choose **Editor** → **Embed In** → **Navigation Controller**.

Putting the view controller inside a navigation controller

That's it. Interface Builder has now added a new Navigation Controller scene and made a relationship between it and your view controller.

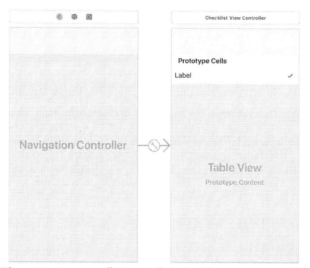

The navigation controller is now linked with your view controller

When the app starts up, the Checklist View Controller is automatically put inside a navigation controller.

➤ Run the app and try it out.

The app now has a navigation bar at the top

The only thing different (visually) is that the app now has a navigation bar at the top.

Set the navigation bar title

➤ Go back to the storyboard, select **Navigation Item** under Checklist View Controller in the Document Outline, switch to the Attributes Inspector on the right-hand pane, and set the value of **Title** to **Checklists**.

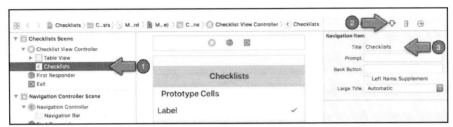

Changing the title in the navigation bar

What you're doing here is changing a **Navigation Item** object that was automatically added to the view controller when you chose the Embed In command.

The Navigation Item object contains the title and buttons that appear in the navigation bar when this view controller becomes active. Each embedded view controller has its own Navigation Item that it uses to configure what shows up in the navigation bar.

When the navigation controller slides a new view controller in, it replaces the contents of the navigation bar with the new view controller's Navigation Item.

Run your app and your screen should look something like this:

Navigation bar with title

Display large titles

Before iOS 11, that was all you could do in terms of setting up the navigation bar title. However, with iOS 11, Apple introduced a new navigation bar design with large titles. Large titles are not enabled by default, but you can enable them quite easily with just a checkbox in storyboard, or a single line of code. So, let's do that!

➤ Switch to **ChecklistViewController.swift** and add the following line to viewDidLoad, right after the existing super.viewDidLoad() line:

```
navigationController?.navigationBar.prefersLargeTitles = true
```

There are a few interesting things in that bit of code but we don't want to get into all of it now. For now, the important things to remember are these:

1. Generally, there is a single navigation controller for a given navigation flow.

2. A single navigation controller could present multiple view controllers as part of its navigation flow.

3. Each view controller in a navigation hierarchy has a reference to the navigation controller which presented it.

Given the above information, the previous code snippet simply uses the view controller's reference to the navigation controller to access the navigation bar for the app. Then, it sets the prefersLargeTitles property on the navigation bar to true. And it is this property, as the name implies, which enables large titles on iOS 11.

> **Note:** If you wanted to make the same change via storyboard instead of code, you'd select the Navigation Bar under your Navigation Controller in your storyboard and set the **Prefers Large Titles** checkbox in the **Attributes inspector**.

Run your app again. Do you see a difference?

Navigation bar with large title

> **Note:** Apple does not recommend using large titles for all of your screens. Rather, their recommendation is to use large titles on your main screen and any other subsequent screens where it might make sense to have a prominent title. You will learn how to turn off large titles for secondary views later on.

Interesting, huh? Of course, you might wonder why there is so much space above the title - that seems like a waste of space, right? That space will be utilized by the navigation items - the back button on the left (if you are in a secondary screen), and any other button you assign to the right.

Add a navigation button to add items

Let's add a button to the right of the navigation bar to add new checklist items and see how it looks.

➤ Open your main storyboard.

➤ Go to the Object Library and look for **Bar Button Item**. Drag it into the right-side slot of the navigation bar. (Be sure to use the navigation bar on the Checklist View Controller, not the one from the navigation controller!)

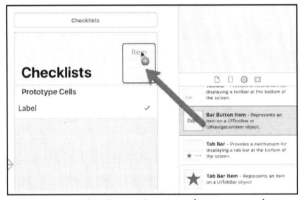

Dragging a Bar Button Item into the navigation bar

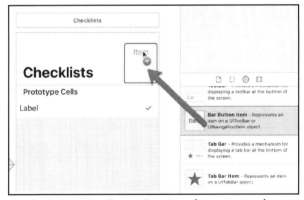

Dragging a Bar Button Item into the navigation bar

Note: You will see large titles on the navigation bar as in the above screenshot only if you enabled large titles via the storyboard. If you enable large titles via code, you will only see the small text title on the navigation bar.

By default, this new button is named "Item" but for this app you want it to have a big + sign.

➤ In the **Attributes inspector** for the bar button item, choose **System Item: Add**.

Bar Button Item attributes

If you look through the list for the System Item dropdown, you'll see a lot of predefined bar button types: Add, Compose, Reply, Camera, and so on. You can use these in your own apps, but be sure to use them only for their intended purpose - you shouldn't use the camera icon on a button that sends an email, for example. Improper use of these icons may lead Apple to reject your app from the App Store. And that sucks.

OK, that gives us a button. If you run the app, it should look like this:

The app with the Add button

Now it looks a little less bare, right? If you are still not happy with the amount of space taken up by large titles, you can always turn off large titles, but do note that when you have a screenful of items and you need to scroll to see more information, the large title will retract into the top navigation bar and give you the "classic"-look navigation bar. So you might want to try this out a bit before deciding to disable it.

Make the navigation button do something

Now, if you tap on your new add button, it doesn't actually do anything. That's because you haven't hooked it up to an action. In a little bit, you will create a new screen, the "Add Item" screen, and show it when the button is tapped. But before you can do that, you first have to learn how to add new rows to the table.

Let's hook up the Add button to an action. You got plenty of exercise with this for *Bull's Eye*, so it should be child's play for you by now.

➤ Add a new action method to **ChecklistViewController.swift**:

```swift
@IBAction func addItem() {
}
```

You're leaving the method empty for the moment, but it needs to be there so you have something to connect the button to.

➤ Open the storyboard and connect the Add button to this action. To do this, **Control-drag** from the + button to the yellow circle in the bar above the view (this circle represents the Checklist View Controller):

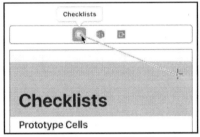

Control-drag from Add button to Checklist View Controller

Actually, you can Control-drag from the Add button to almost anywhere in the same scene to make the connection.

➤ After dragging, pick **addItem** from the popup (under **Sent Actions**):

Connecting to the addItem action

➤ Let's give addItem() something to do. Back in **ChecklistViewController.swift**, add some code to the method as follows:

```
@IBAction func addItem() {
   let newRowIndex = items.count

   let item = ChecklistItem()
   item.text = "I am a new row"
   item.checked = false
   items.append(item)

   let indexPath = IndexPath(row: newRowIndex, section: 0)
   let indexPaths = [indexPath]
   tableView.insertRows(at: indexPaths, with: .automatic)
}
```

The new code creates a new ChecklistItem object and adds it to the data model (the items array). You also have to tell the table view, "I've inserted a row at this index, please update yourself."

Let's review the code section-by-section:

```
let newRowIndex = items.count
```

You need to know what the index of the new row in your array would be. This is necessary in order to properly update the table view later.

When you start the app there are 5 items in the array and 5 rows on the screen. Computers start counting at 0, so the existing rows have indexes 0, 1, 2, 3 and 4. To add the new row to the end of the array, the index for that new row must be 5.

In other words, when you add a row to the end of an array, the index for the new row is always equal to the number of items currently in the array. Let that sink in for a second.

You store the index for the new row in the local constant newRowIndex. This can be a constant instead of a variable because it never has to change.

The following few lines should look familiar:

```
let item = ChecklistItem()
item.text = "I am a new row"
item.checked = false
items.append(item)
```

You have seen this code before in init?(coder). It creates a new ChecklistItem object and adds it to the end of the array.

The data model now consists of 6 ChecklistItem objects inside the items array. Note that at this point newRowIndex is still 5 even though items.count is now 6. That's why you read the item count and stored this value in newRowIndex *before* you added the new item to the array.

Just adding the new `ChecklistItem` object to the data model's array isn't enough. You have to tell the table view about this new row so it can add a new cell for that row.

```
let indexPath = IndexPath(row: newRowIndex, section: 0)
```

As you know by now, table views use index-paths to identify rows. So, you first make an `IndexPath` object that points to the new row, using the row number from the `newRowIndex` variable. This index-path object now points to row 5 (in section 0).

The next line creates a new, temporary array holding just the one index-path item:

```
let indexPaths = [indexPath]
```

You use the table view method `insertRows(at:with:)` to tell the table view about the new row. While you only have one inserted row here, as its name implies, this method actually lets you insert multiple rows at the same time, if you wanted to.

So, instead of a single `IndexPath` object, you need to pass an array of index-paths to the method. Fortunately, it is easy to create an array that contains a single index-path object by writing `[indexPath]`. The notation `[]` creates a new `Array` object that contains the objects between the brackets.

Finally, you tell the table view to insert this new row. The `with: .automatic` parameter makes the table view use a nice animation when it inserts the row:

```
tableView.insertRows(at: indexPaths, with: .automatic)
```

To recap, you:

1. Created a new `ChecklistItem` object.

2. Added it to the data model.

3. Inserted a new row for it in the table view.

When you call `tableView.insertRows(at:with:)` to insert a new row, the table view makes a cell for this new row by calling your `tableView(_:cellForRowAt:)` data source method. (But it only does this if the new row is actually in the visible portion of the table view.)

➤ Try it out. You can now add many new rows to the table. You can also tap these new rows to turn their checkmarks on and off again. When you scroll the table up and down, the checkmarks stay with the proper rows.

After adding new rows with the + button

> **Note:** If you were concerned by the change to large titles, also notice how the large title becomes a smaller title (and vice versa) when you scroll up and down.

Remember, the rows always have to be added to both your data model and the table view. When you send the `insertRows(at:with:)` message to the table view, you say: "Hey table, my data model has a bunch of new items added to it."

This is important! If you forget to tell the table view about your new items or if you tell the table view there are new items, but you don't actually add them to your data model, then your app will crash. The data model and the table view always have to be in sync.

> **Exercise:** Give the new items checkmarks by default.

Delete rows

While you're at it, you might as well give users the ability to delete rows.

A common way to do this in iOS apps is "swipe-to-delete". You swipe your finger over a row and a Delete button slides into view. A tap on the Delete button confirms the removal, tapping anywhere else will cancel.

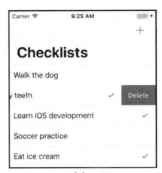

Swipe-to-delete in action

Swipe-to-delete

Swipe-to-delete is very easy to implement.

➤ Add the following method to **ChecklistViewController.swift**. Just to keep things organized, I suggest you put this near the other table view delegate methods.

```
override func tableView(
                _ tableView: UITableView,
        commit editingStyle: UITableViewCellEditingStyle,
          forRowAt indexPath: IndexPath) {
  // 1
  items.remove(at: indexPath.row)

  // 2
  let indexPaths = [indexPath]
  tableView.deleteRows(at: indexPaths, with: .automatic)
}
```

When the `commitEditingStyle` method is present in your view controller (it is a method defined by the table view data source protocol), the table view will automatically enable swipe-to-delete. All you have to do is:

1. Remove the item from the data model.

2. Delete the corresponding row from the table view.

This mirrors what you did in `addItem()`. Again, you make a temporary array with the index-path object and then tell the table view to remove the rows with an animation.

➤ Run the app to try it out!

Destroying objects

When you call `items.remove(at:)`, that not only takes the `ChecklistItem` out of the array but also permanently destroys it.

We'll talk more about this later on, but if there are no more references to an object, it is automatically destroyed. As long as a `ChecklistItem` object sits inside an array, that array has a reference to it.

But when you pull that `ChecklistItem` out of the array, the reference goes away and the object is destroyed. Or in computer-speak, it is *deallocated*.

What does it mean for an object to be destroyed? Each object occupies a small section of the computer's memory. When you create an object instance, a chunk of memory is reserved to hold the object's data.

If the object is deallocated, that memory becomes available again and will eventually be occupied by new objects. After it has been deleted, the object does not exist in memory any more and you can no longer use it.

On older versions of iOS, you had to take care of this memory bookkeeping by hand. Fortunately times have changed for the better. Swift uses a mechanism called **Automatic Reference Counting**, or **ARC**, to manage the lifetime of the objects in your app, freeing you from having to worry about that bookkeeping. I like not having to worry about things!

The Add Item screen

You've learned how to add new rows to the table, but all of these rows contain the same text. You will now change the `addItem()` action to open a new screen that lets the user enter their own text for new `ChecklistItems`.

The Add Item screen

Add a new view controller to the storyboard

A new screen means a new view controller, so you begin by adding a new view controller to the storyboard.

➤ Go to the Object Library and drag a new **Table View Controller** (not a regular view controller) on to the storyboard canvas.

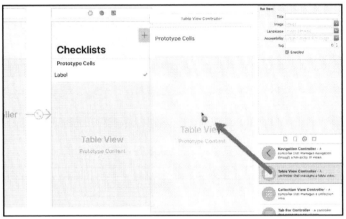

Dragging a new Table View Controller into the canvas

You may need to zoom out to fit everything properly. Right-click on the canvas to get a popup with zoom options, or use the - **100%** + controls at the bottom of the Interface Builder canvas. (You can also double-click on an empty spot in the canvas to zoom in or out. Or, if you have a Trackpad, simply pinch with two fingers to zoom in or out.)

➤ With the new view controller in place, select the **Add button** from the Checklist View Controller. **Control-drag** to the new view controller.

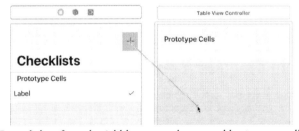

Control-drag from the Add button to the new table view controller

Let go of the mouse and a list of options pops up.

The Action Segue popup

The options in this menu are the different types of connections you can make between the Add button and the new screen.

➤ Choose **Show** from the menu.

As I mentioned when adding the About screen for *Bull's Eye*, this type of connection is named a segue.

The segue is represented by the arrow between the two view controllers:

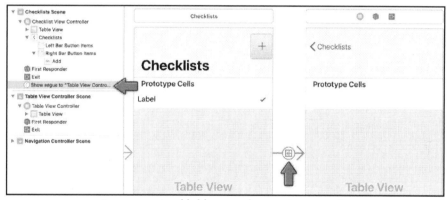

A new segue is added between the two view controllers

➤ Run the app to see what it does.

When you press the Add button, a new empty table view slides in from the right. You can press the back button – the one that says "Checklists" – at the top to go back to the previous screen.

The screen that shows up after you press the Add button

You didn't even have to write much code and you now have yourself a working navigation controller where you can go from one screen to another!

> **Note:** Xcode may be giving you the warning, "Prototype table cells must have reuse identifiers". You might remember this issue from before - you will fix this issue soon.

Note that the Add button no longer adds a new row to the table. That connection has been broken and is replaced by the segue. Just in case, you should remove the button's connection with the `addItem` action.

➤ Select the Add button, go to the **Connections inspector** and press X next to `addItem`.

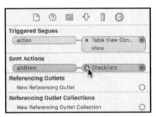

Removing the addItem action from the Add button

Notice that this inspector also shows the connection with the segue that you've just made (under **Triggered Segues**).

Segue Types

When showing the new view controller above, you opted for a Show segue. But what does it mean? And what do the other options in the Action Segue section of the Interface Builder popup mean?

Here is a brief explanation of each type of segue:

• **Show:** Pushes the new view controller onto the navigation stack so that the new view controller is at the top of the navigation stack. It also provides a back button to return to the previous view controller. If the view controllers are not embedded in a navigation controller, then the new view controller will be presented modally (see Present Modally in the list below as to what this means).

  Example: Navigating folders in the *Mail* app

• **Show Detail:** For use in a split view controller (you'll learn more about those when developing the last app in this book). The new view controller replaces the detail view controller of the split view when in an expanded two-column interface. Otherwise, if in single-column mode, it will push in a navigation controller.

Example: In *Messages*, tapping a conversation will show the conversation details - replacing the view controller on the right when in a two-column layout, or push the conversation when in a single column layout

- **Present Modally:** Presents the new view controller to cover the previous view controller - most commonly used to present a view controller that covers the entire screen on iPhone, or on iPad it's common to present it as a centered box that darkens the presenting view controller. Usually, if you had a navigation bar at the top or a tab bar at the bottom, those are covered by the modal view controller too.

  Example: Selecting Touch ID & Passcode in *Settings*

- **Present as Popover:** When run on an iPad, the new view controller appears in a popover, and tapping anywhere outside of this popover will dismiss it. On an iPhone, will present the new view controller modally over the full screen.

  Example: Tapping the + button in *Calendar*

- **Custom:** Allows you to implement your own custom segue and have control over its behavior. (You will learn more about this in a later chapter.)

Customize the navigation bar

So now you have a new table view controller that slides into the screen when you press the Add button. However, this is not quite what you want.

Data input screens usually have a navigation bar with a Cancel button on the left and a Done button on the right. (In some apps the button on the right is called Save or Send.) Pressing either of these buttons will close the screen, but only Done will save your changes.

➤ First, drag a Navigation Item on to the new scene.

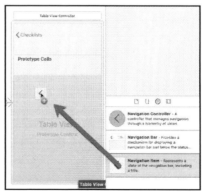

Add a navigation item to the view controller

If you check the Document Outline before you drag the Navigation Item on, you will notice that the new table view controller scene does not have a Navigation Item. So, we are not able to customize the storyboard elements for this table view controller - such as the navigation buttons, or the title, without the Navigation Item. Which is the reason for adding one.

➤ Next, drag two **Bar Button Items** on to the navigation bar, one to the left slot (removing the existing back button) and one to the right slot.

The navigation bar items for the new screen

➤ In the **Attributes inspector** for the left button choose **System Item: Cancel**.

➤ For the right button choose **Done** for both **System Item** and **Style** attributes.

Don't type anything into the button's Title field. The Cancel and Done buttons are built-in button types that automatically use the proper text. If your app runs on an iPhone where the language is set to something other than English, these predefined buttons are automatically translated into the user's language.

➤ Double-click the navigation bar for the new table view controller to edit its title and change it to **Add Item**. (You can also change this via the Attributes inspector as you did before.)

➤ Run the app, tap the Add button on the main screen, and you'll see that your new screen has Cancel and Done buttons.

The Cancel and Done buttons in the app

The new buttons look good, but (as you would have noticed from the storyboard if you had enabled large titles from the storyboard) the title is huge! If Apple recommends using large titles only on main screens, we probably should change this screen to have smaller titles. But how do we do that?

While some view controller (or table view controller) customizations can be done via storyboard (and this one can too), some require writing some code. Our new view controller does not have a matching source file. So, in the next section we'll create the source file and add the custom code instead of doing the changes via storyboard just so you know how to do it via code.

> **Note:** If you'd prefer to make the change via storyboard, then simply select the Navigation Item for the new view controller, go to the **Attributes inspector** and select **Never** from the **Large Title** dropdown.

Make your own view controller class

You created a custom view controller in *Bull's Eye* for the About screen. Do you remember how to do it on your own? If not, here are the steps:

➤ Right-click on the Checklists group (the yellow folder) in the project navigator and choose **New File...** Choose the **Cocoa Touch Class** template.

➤ In the next dialog, set the Class to **AddItemViewController** and Subclass to **UITableViewController** (when you change the subclass, the class name will automatically change - so either set the subclass first or change the class name back after the change). Leave the language at **Swift** (or change it back if it is not set to Swift).

➤ Save the file to your project folder, which should be the default location.

➤ The file should have a lot of source and commented code - this is known as *boilerplate code*, or code that is generally always needed. In this particular case, you don't need most of it. So remove everything except for viewDidLoad (and remove the comments from inside viewDidLoad as well) so that your code looks like this:

```swift
import UIKit

class AddItemViewController: UITableViewController {
  override func viewDidLoad() {
    super.viewDidLoad()
  }
}
```

This tells Swift that you have a new object for a table view controller that goes by the name of AddItemViewController. You'll add the rest of the code soon. First, you have to let the storyboard know about this new view controller too.

➤ In the storyboard, select the Add Item table view controller and go to the **Identity inspector**. Under **Custom Class**, type **AddItemViewController**.

This tells the storyboard that the view controller from this scene is actually your new `AddItemViewController` object.

Changing the class name of the AddItemViewController

Don't forget this step! Without it, the Add Item screen will simply not work.

Make sure that it is really the view controller that is selected before you change the fields in the Identity inspector (the scene needs to have a blue border). A common mistake is to select the table view and change that.

Turn off large titles

Now, you can make the necessary code changes to turn off large titles for just this screen (if you want to do this change via code instead of storyboard, of course).

➤ Add the following line to the end of `viewDidLoad` in **AddItemViewController.swift**:

```
navigationItem.largeTitleDisplayMode = .never
```

The above code customizes the Navigation Item for the Add Item screen, to never show large titles. Try running the app now.

Large titles begone!

Make the navigation buttons work

Much better, right? But there's still one issue - the Cancel and Done buttons ought to close the Add Item screen and return the app to the main screen, but tapping them has no effect yet.

Exercise: Do you know why the Cancel and Done buttons do not return you to the main screen?

Answer: Because those buttons have not yet been hooked up to any actions!

You will now implement the necessary action methods in **AddItemViewController.swift**.

➤ Add these new cancel() and done() action methods:

```
@IBAction func cancel() {
  navigationController?.popViewController(animated: true)
}

@IBAction func done() {
  navigationController?.popViewController(animated: true)
}
```

This tells the navigation controller to close the Add Item screen with an animation and to go back to the previous screen, which in this case is the main screen.

You still need to hook up the Cancel bar button to the cancel() action and the Done bar button to the done() action.

➤ Open the storyboard and find the Add Item View Controller. **Control-drag** from the bar buttons to the yellow circle icon and pick the proper action from the popup menu.

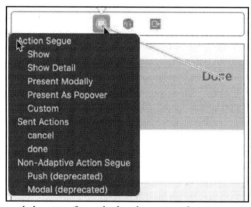

Control-dragging from the bar button to the view controller

➤ Run the app to try it out. The Cancel and Done buttons now return the app to the main screen.

What do you think happens to the AddItemViewController object when you dismiss it? After the view controller disappears from the screen, its object is destroyed and the memory it was using is reclaimed by the system.

Every time the user opens the Add Item screen, the app makes a new instance of it. This means a view controller object is only alive for the duration that the user is interacting with it; there is no point in keeping it around afterwards.

Container view controllers

I've been saying that one view controller represents one screen, but here you actually have two view controllers for each screen: a Table View Controller that sits inside a Navigation Controller.

The Navigation Controller is a special type of view controller that acts as a container for other view controllers. It comes with a navigation bar and has the ability to easily go from one screen to another, by sliding them in and out of sight. The container essentially "wraps around" these screens.

The Navigation Controller is just the frame that contains the view controllers that do the real work, which are known as the "content" controllers. Here, the ChecklistViewController provides the content for the first screen; the content for the second screen comes from the AddItemViewController.

Another often-used container is the Tab Bar Controller, which you'll see in the next app.

On the iPad, container view controllers are even more commonplace. View controllers on the iPhone are full-screen but on the iPad they often occupy only a portion of the screen, such as the content of a popover or one of the panes in a split-view.

This completes the implementation of the navigation functionality for your app's two screens. If at any point you got stuck, you can refer to the project files for the app from the **11 - Navigation Controllers** folder in the Source Code folder.

Chapter 12: Add Item Screen

Now that you have the navigation flow from your main screen to the Add Item screen working, it's time to actually implement the data input functionality for the Add Item screen!

Let's change the look of the Add Item screen. Currently it is an empty table with a navigation bar on top, but I want it to look like this:

What the Add Item screen will look like when you're done

This chapter covers the following:

- **Static table cells:** Add a static table view cell to the table to display the text field for data entry.

- **Read from the text field:** Access the contents of the text field.

- **Polish it up:** Improve the look and functionality of the Add Item screen.

Static table cells

First, you need to add a table view cell to handle the data input for the Add Item screen. As is generally the case with UI changes, you start with the storyboard.

Storyboard changes

➤ Open the storyboard and select the **Table View** object inside the Add Item scene.

➤ In the **Attributes inspector**, change the **Content** setting from Dynamic Prototypes to **Static Cells**.

Changing the table view to static cells

You use static cells when you know beforehand how many sections and rows the table view will have. This is handy for screens that require the user to enter data, such as the one you're building here.

With static cells, you can design the rows directly in the storyboard. For a table with static cells you don't need to provide a data source, and you can hook up the labels and other controls from the cells directly to outlets on the view controller.

As you can see in the Document Outline, the table view now has a Table View Section object under it, and three Table View Cells in that section. (You may need to expand the Table View item first by clicking the disclosure triangle.)

The table view has a section with three static cells

➤ Click on the bottom two cells and delete them (press the **delete** key on your keyboard). You only need one cell for now.

➤ Select the Table View again and in the **Attributes inspector** set its **Style** to **Grouped**. That gives us the look we want.

The table view with grouped style

Next up, you'll add a text field component inside the table view cell that lets the user type text.

➤ Drag a **Text Field** object into the cell and size it up nicely.

➤ In the **Attributes inspector** for the text field, set the **Border Style** to **no border** (select the dotted box):

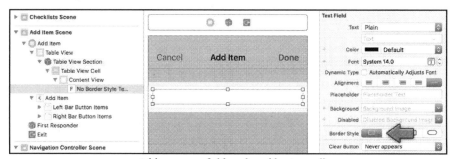

Adding a text field to the table view cell

➤ Run the app and press the + button to open the Add Item screen. Tap on the cell and you'll see the keyboard slide in from the bottom of the screen.

Any time you make a text field active, the keyboard automatically appears. You can type into the text field by tapping on the letters. (On the Simulator, you can simply type using your Mac's keyboard.)

You can now type text into the table view cell

> **Note:** If the keyboard does not appear in the Simulator, press ⌘K or use the
> **Hardware → Keyboard → Toggle Software Keyboard** menu option. You can also
> use your normal Mac keyboard to type into the text field, even if the on-screen
> keyboard is not visible. If that doesn't work, also select **Hardware → Keyboard →
> Connect Hardware Keyboard** from the menu.

Disable cell selection

Look what happens when you tap just outside the text field's area, but still in the cell (try
tapping in the margins that surround the text field):

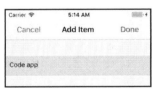

Whoops, that looks a little weird

The row turns gray because you selected it. Oops, that's not what you want - you should
disable selections for this row. You can do this easily via code by adding the following
table view delegate method to **AddItemViewController.swift**:

```
override func tableView(_ tableView: UITableView,
          willSelectRowAt indexPath: IndexPath)
          -> IndexPath? {
  return nil
}
```

When the user taps on a cell, the table view sends the delegate a `willSelectRowAt` message that says: "Hi delegate, I am about to select this particular row."

By returning the special value `nil`, the delegate answers: "Sorry, but you're not allowed to!"

Return to sender

You've seen the `return` statement a few times now. You use `return` to send a value from a method back to the method that called it.

Let's take a more detailed look at what happens.

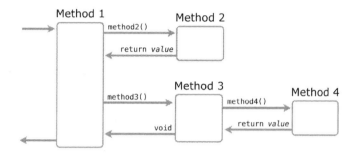

Methods call other methods and receive values in return.

You cannot just return any value. The value you return must be of the data type that is specified after the –> arrow that follows the method name.

For example, `tableView(_:numberOfRowsInSection:)` must return an `Int` value:

```
override func tableView(_ tableView: UITableView,
       numberOfRowsInSection section: Int) -> Int {
    return 1
}
```

If instead your code was like this:

```
override func tableView(_ tableView: UITableView,
       numberOfRowsInSection section: Int) -> Int {
    return "1"
}
```

Then, the compiler would give an error message, as `"1"` is a string, not an `Int`. To a human reader they look similar and you can easily understand the intent, but Swift isn't that tolerant. Data types have to match or they just aren't allowed.

Your most recent version of this method looks like this:

```
override func tableView(_ tableView: UITableView,
       numberOfRowsInSection section: Int) -> Int {
   return items.count
}
```

That is also a valid return statement because items is an Array and the count property from Array is also of the type Int.

The tableView(_:cellForRowAt:) method is supposed to return a UITableViewCell object:

```
override func tableView(_tableView: UITableView,
          cellForRowAt indexPath: IndexPath)
          -> UITableViewCell {

   let cell = tableView.dequeueReusableCell(
                withIdentifier: "TheCellIdentifier",
                            for: indexPath)

   . . .
   return cell
}
```

The local constant cell contains a UITableViewCell object, so it's OK to return the value of cell from the method.

The tableView(_:willSelectRowAt:) method is supposed to return an IndexPath object. However, you can also make it return "nil", which means no object.

```
override func tableView(_ tableView: UITableView,
          willSelectRowAt indexPath: IndexPath) -> IndexPath? {
   return nil
}
```

That's what the ? behind IndexPath is for: The question mark tells Swift that you can also return nil from this method. Note that returning nil from a method is only allowed if there is a question mark (or exclamation point) behind the return type. A type declaration with a question mark behind it is known as an *optional*. (You'll learn more about optionals in the next chapter.)

The special value nil represents "no value" but it's used to mean different things throughout the iOS SDK. Sometimes it means "nothing found" or "don't do anything". Here it means that the row should not be selected when the user taps it.

How do you know what nil means for a certain method? You can find that in the documentation of the method in question.

In the case of `willSelectRowAt`, the iOS documentation says:

> Return Value: An index-path object that confirms or alters the selected row. Return an IndexPath object other than indexPath if you want another cell to be selected. Return nil if you don't want the row selected.

This means you can either:

1. Return the same index-path you were given. This confirms that this row can be selected.

2. Return another index-path in order to select a different row.

3. Return `nil` to prevent the row from being selected, which is what you did.

So remember, you need to use the `return` statement to exit a method that expects to return something. If you forget, then Xcode will give the following error: "Missing return in a function expect to return".

You've also seen methods that do not return anything:

```
@IBAction func addItem()
```

and:

```
func configureCheckmark(for cell: UITableViewCell,
                        with item: ChecklistItem)
```

These methods do not have an arrow (–>) indicating a return value. Such a method does not pass a value back to the caller and therefore does not need a `return` statement. (You can still use `return` to exit from such methods, but the `return` statement should not be followed by a value.)

Strictly speaking, even methods without a return type *do* return a value, an *empty tuple*. Think of this as a special object that embodies the concept of "nothing". (Don't confuse this with *nil*, which is an actual value.)

You sometimes see this written as:

```
func methodThatDoesNotReturnValue() -> ()

func anotherMethodThatDoesNotReturnValue() -> Void
```

The notation for an empty tuple is (), so in this context the parentheses mean there is no return value. The term `Void` is a synonym for ().

But really, if a method does not return anything it's just as easy to leave out the -> arrow. Also note that @IBAction methods never return a value - this is a rule.

While it's already impossible to select the row, as you've just told the table view you won't allow it, there is one more thing you need to do to prevent the row from going gray. In fact, most of the time, this second change is enough to not show cell selection, even without the code change above.

Table view cells have a selection color property. Even if you make it impossible for a row to be selected, sometimes UIKit still briefly draws the cell gray when you tap it. Therefore, it is best to also disable this selection color.

➤ In the storyboard, select the table view cell and go to the **Attributes inspector**. Set the **Selection** attribute to **None**.

Now if you run the app, it is impossible to select the row and make it turn gray. Try and prove me wrong! :]

Read from the text field

You have a text field in a table view cell that the user can type into, but how do you read the text that the user has typed?

Add an outlet for the text field

When the user taps Done, you need to get that text and somehow put it into a new ChecklistItem and add it to the list of to-do items. This means the done() action needs to be able to refer to the text field.

You already know how to refer to controls from within your view controller: use an outlet. When you added outlets for the previous app, I told you to type in the @IBOutlet declaration in the source file and make the connection in the storyboard.

I'm going to show you a trick now that will save you some typing. You can let Interface Builder do all of this automatically by Control-dragging from the control in question directly into your source code file!

➤ First, go to the storyboard and select the **Add Item View Controller**. Then open the **Assistant editor** using the toolbar button on the top right. This button looks like two circles.

Click the toolbar button to open the Assistant editor

This may make the screen a little crowded – there might now be up to five horizontal panels open. If you're running out of space, you might want to close the Project navigator, the Utilities pane, and/or the Document Outline using the relevant toolbar buttons.

The Assistant editor opens a new pane on the right of the screen by default (it might give you horizontal split views instead, if you have changed your default view settings). In the Jump Bar (the bar below the toolbar) it should say **Automatic** and the Assistant editor should be displaying the **AddItemViewController.swift** file:

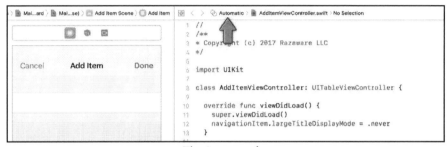

The Assistant editor

"Automatic" means the Assistant editor tries to figure out what other file is related to the one you're currently editing. When you're editing a storyboard, the related file is generally the selected view controller's Swift file.

(Sometimes Xcode can be a little dodgy here. If it shows you something other than **AddItemViewController.swift**, then click in the Jump Bar and manually select the correct file.)

➤ With the storyboard and the Swift file side by side, select the text field. Then **Control-drag** from the text field into the Swift file.

Control-dragging from the text field into the Swift file

When you let go, a popup appears:

The popup that lets you add a new outlet

➤ Choose the following options:

• Connection: Outlet

• Name: **textField**

• Type: UITextField

• Storage: Weak

> **Note:** If "Type" does not say UITextField, but instead says UITableViewCell or UIView, then you selected the wrong thing.
>
> Make sure you're Control-dragging from the text field inside the cell, not the cell itself. Granted, it's kinda hard to see, being white on white. If you're having trouble selecting the text field, click that area several times in succession.
>
> You can also Control-drag from "No Border Style Text Field" in the Document Outline.

➤ Press **Connect** and voila, Xcode automatically inserts an @IBOutlet for you and connects it to the text field object.

In code it looks like this:

```
@IBOutlet weak var textField: UITextField!
```

Just by dragging you have successfully hooked up the text field object with a new property named textField. How easy was that?

Read the contents of the text field

Now you'll modify the done() action to write the contents of this text field to the Xcode Console, the pane at the bottom of the screen where print() messages show up. This is a quick way to verify that you can actually read what the user typed.

➤ In **AddItemViewController.swift**, change done() to:

```
@IBAction func done() {
    // Add the following line
    print("Contents of the text field: \(textField.text!)")

    navigationController?.popViewController(animated:true)
}
```

You can make these changes directly inside the Assistant editor. It's very handy that you can edit the source code and the storyboard side-by-side.

➤ Run the app, press the + button and type something in the text field. When you press Done, the Add Item screen should close and Xcode should reveal the Debug pane with a message like this:

```
Contents of the text field: Hello, world!
```

Great, so that works. print() should be an old friend by now. It's one of my faithful debugging companions :]

Recall that you can print the value of a variable by placing it inside \(and) in a string. Here you used \(textField.text!) to print out the contents of the text field's text property. (I'll explain what the exclamation point is for later.)

> **Note:** Because the iOS Simulator already outputs a lot of debug messages of its own, it may be a bit hard to find your print() messages in the Console. Luckily there is a Filter box at the bottom that lets you search for your own messages.

Polish it up

Before you write the code to take the text and insert it as a new item into the items list, let's improve the design and workings of the Add Item screen a little.

Give the text field focus on screen opening

For instance, it would be nice if you didn't have to tap on the text field in order to bring up the keyboard. It would be more convenient if the keyboard automatically showed up on the screen opening.

➤ To accomplish this, add a new method to **AddItemViewController.swift**.

```
override func viewWillAppear(_ animated: Bool) {
  super.viewWillAppear(animated)
  textField.becomeFirstResponder()
}
```

The view controller receives the `viewWillAppear()` message just before it becomes visible. That is a perfect time to make the text field active. You do this by sending it the `becomeFirstResponder()` message.

If you've done programming on other platforms, this is often called "giving the control focus". In iOS terminology, the control becomes the *first responder.*

➤ Run the app and go to the Add Item screen; you can start typing right away.

(Again, note that the keyboard may not appear on the Simulator. Press ⌘+K to bring it up. The keyboard will always appear when you run the app on an actual device, though.)

It's often little features like this that make an app a joy to use. Having to tap on the text field before you can start typing gets old really fast. In this fast-paced age, using their mobiles on the go, users don't have the patience for that. Such minor annoyances may be reason enough for users to switch to a competitor's app. I always put a lot of effort into making my apps as frictionless as possible.

Style the text field

With that in mind, let's style the input field a bit.

➤ Open the storyboard and select the text field. Go to the **Attributes inspector** and set the following attributes:

- Placeholder: **Name of the Item**
- Font: System 17
- Adjust to Fit: Uncheck this
- Capitalization: Sentences
- Return Key: Done

The text field attributes

There are several options here that let you configure the keyboard that appears when the text field becomes active.

If this were a field that only allowed numbers, for example, you would set the Keyboard Type to Number Pad. If it were an email address field, you'd set it to E-mail Address. For our purposes, the Default keyboard is appropriate.

You can also change the text that is displayed on the keyboard's Return Key. By default it says "return" but you set it to "Done". This is just the text on the button; it doesn't automatically close the screen. You still have to make the keyboard's Done button trigger the same action as the Done button from the navigation bar.

Handle the keyboard Done button

➤ Make sure the text field is selected and open the **Connections inspector**. Drag from the **Did End on Exit** event to the view controller and pick the **done** action.

If you still have the Assistant editor open, you can also drag directly to the source code for the done() method.

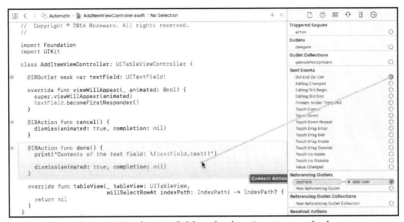

Connecting the text field to the done() action method

To see the connections for the **done** action, click on the circle in the gutter next to the method name. The popup shows that **done( )** is now connected to both the bar button and the text field:

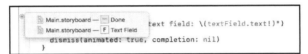

Viewing the connections for the done() method

➤ Run the app. Pressing Done on the keyboard will now close the screen and print the text to the debug area.

The keyboard now has a big blue Done button

Disallow empty input

Now that you have user input working, It's always good to validate what the user entered to make sure that the input is acceptable. For instance, what should happen if the user immediately taps the Done button on the Add Item screen without entering any text?

Adding a to-do item to the list that has no description text is not very useful. So, in order to prevent this, you should disable the Done button when no text has been typed yet.

Of course, you have two Done buttons to take care of, one on the keyboard, and one in the navigation bar. Let's start with the Done button from the keyboard as this is the simplest one to fix.

➤ On the **Attributes inspector** for the text field, check **Auto-enable Return Key**.

That's it. Now when you run the app, the Done button on the keyboard is disabled when there is no text in the text field. Try it out!

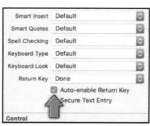

The Auto-enable Return Key option disables the return key when there is no text

For the Done button in the navigation bar, you have to do a little more work. You have to check the contents of the text field after every keystroke to see if it is now empty or not. If it is, then you disable the button.

The user can always press Cancel, but Done only works when there is text.

In order to listen to changes to the text field – which may come from taps on the keyboard but also from cut/paste – you need to make the view controller a delegate for the text field.

The text field will send events to its delegate to let it know what is going on. The delegate, which will be the `AddItemViewController`, can then respond to these events and take appropriate actions.

A view controller is allowed to be the delegate for more than one object. The `AddItemViewController` is already a delegate (and data source) for the `UITableView` (because it is a `UITableViewController`). Now it will also become the delegate for the text field object, `UITextField`.

These are two different delegates and you make the view controller play both roles. Later on you'll add even more delegates for this app.

How to become a delegate

Delegates are used everywhere in the iOS SDK, so it's good to remember that it always takes three steps to become a delegate.

1. You declare yourself capable of being a delegate. To become the delegate for `UITextField` you need to include `UITextFieldDelegate` in the `class` line for the

view controller. This tells the compiler that this particular view controller can actually handle the notification messages that the text field sends to it.

2. You let the object in question, in this case the UITextField, know that the view controller wishes to become its delegate. If you forget to tell the text field that it has a delegate, it will never send you any notifications.

3. Implement the delegate methods. It makes no sense to become a delegate if you're not responding to the messages you're being sent!

Often, delegate methods are optional, so you don't need to implement all of them. For example, UITextFieldDelegate actually declares seven different methods but you only care about textField(_:shouldChangeCharactersIn:replacementString:) for this app.

➤ In **AddItemViewController.swift**, add UITextFieldDelegate to the class declaration:

```
class AddItemViewController: UITableViewController,
  UITextFieldDelegate
```

The view controller now says, "I can be a delegate for text field objects."

You also have to let the text field know that you have a delegate for it.

➤ Go to the storyboard and select the text field.

There are several different ways in which you can hook up the text field's delegate outlet to the view controller. I prefer to go to its **Connections inspector** and drag from **delegate** to the view controller's little yellow icon:

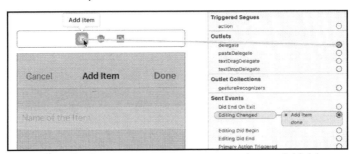

Drag from the Connections inspector to connect the text field delegate

You also have to add an outlet for the Done bar button item, so you can send it messages from within the view controller in order to enable or disable it.

➤ Open the **Assistant editor** and make sure **AddItemViewController.swift** is visible in the assistant pane.

➤ **Control-drag** from the Done bar button into the Swift file and let go. Name the new outlet doneBarButton.

This adds the following outlet:

```
@IBOutlet weak var doneBarButton: UIBarButtonItem!
```

➤ Add the following to **AddItemViewController.swift**, at the bottom (before the final curly brace):

```
func textField(_ textField: UITextField,
               shouldChangeCharactersIn range: NSRange,
               replacementString string: String) -> Bool {

  let oldText = textField.text!
  let stringRange = Range(range, in:oldText)!
  let newText = oldText.replacingCharacters(in: stringRange,
                                            with: string)
  if newText.isEmpty {
    doneBarButton.isEnabled = false
  } else {
    doneBarButton.isEnabled = true
  }
  return true
}
```

This is one of the UITextField delegate methods. It is invoked every time the user changes the text, whether by tapping on the keyboard or via cut/paste.

First, you figure out what the new text will be:

```
let oldText = textField.text!
let stringRange = Range(range, in:oldText)!
let newText = oldText.replacingCharacters(in: stringRange, with:
string)
```

The textField(_:shouldChangeCharactersIn:replacementString:) delegate method doesn't give you the new text, only which part of the text should be replaced (the range) and the text it should be replaced with (the replacement string).

You need to calculate what the new text will be by taking the text field's text and doing the replacement yourself. This gives you a new string object that you store in the newText constant.

NSRange vs. Range and NSString vs. String

In the above code, you get a parameter as NSRange and you convert it to a Range value. If you are wondering what a range is, the clue is in the name :] A range object gives you a range of values, or in this case, a range of characters - with a lower bound and an upper bound.

So, why did we convert the original NSRange value to a Range value, you ask? NSRange is an Objective-C structure whereas Range is its Swift equivalent - they are similar, but not exactly the same. So, while an NSRange parameter is used by the UITextField (which internally, and historically, is Objective-C based) in its delegate method, in our Swift code, if we wanted to do any String operations, such as replacingCharacters, then we need a Range value instead. Swift methods generally use Range values and do not understand NSRange values, which is why we converted the NSRange value to a Swift-understandable Range value.

There was a different way to approach this problem as well - though it might not be as "Swift-y" :] We could have converted the Swift String value into its Objective-C equivalent - NSString. Since Swift is still young, it's String handling methods aren't as good … but they are getting better. NSString is considered by some to be more powerful and often easier to use than Swift's own String.

String and NSString are "bridged", meaning that you can use NSString in place of String. And NSString too has a replacingCharacters(in:with:) method, and that method takes an NSRange as a parameter!

So, you could have simply converted the String value to an NSString value and then used the NSString replacingCharacters(in:with:) method with the passed in range value instead of the above code.

But personally, I prefer to use Swift types and classes in my code as much as possible. So, I opted to go with the solution above :]

By the way, String isn't the only thing that is bridged to an Objective-C type. Another example is Array and its Objective-C counterpart NSArray. Because the iOS frameworks are written in a different language than Swift, sometimes these little Objective-C holdovers pop up when you least expect them.

Once you have the new text, you check if it's empty, and enable or disable the Done button accordingly:

```
if newText.isEmpty {
  doneBarButton.isEnabled = false
} else {
  doneBarButton.isEnabled = true
}
```

However, you could simplify the above code even further. Since `newText.isEmpty` returns a `true` or `false` value, you can discard the `if` condition and use the value returned by `newText.isEmpty` to decide whether the Done button should be enabled or not.

```
doneBarButton.isEnabled = !newText.isEmpty
```

Basically, if the text is not empty, enable the button. Otherwise, don't enable it. That's much more compact, and concise, right?

Remember this trick – whenever you see code like this,

```
if some condition {
  something = true
} else {
  something = false
}
```

you can write it simply as:

```
something = (some condition)
```

In practice it doesn't really matter which version you use. I prefer the shorter one; that's what the pros do. Just remember that comparison operators such as == and > always return `true` or `false`, so the extra `if` really isn't necessary.

➤ Run the app and type some text into the text field. Now remove that text and you'll see that the Done button in the navigation bar properly gets disabled when the text field becomes empty.

One problem: The Done button is initially enabled when the Add Item screen opens, but there is no text in the text field at that point. So, it really should be disabled. This is simple enough to fix.

➤ In the storyboard, select the **Done** bar button and go to the **Attributes inspector**. Uncheck the **Enabled** box.

The Done button is now properly disabled when you first enter the Add Item screen:

The Done button is not enabled if there is no text

Using FileMerge to compare files

You can compare your own work with my version of the app using the FileMerge tool.

Open this tool from the Xcode menu bar, under **Xcode → Open Developer Tool → FileMerge**:

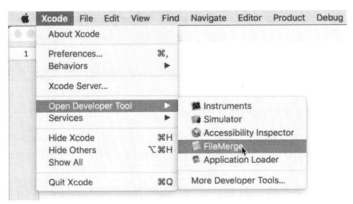

You give FileMerge two files or folders to compare:

After working hard for a few seconds or so, FileMerge tells you what is different:

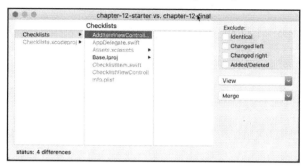

Double-click on a filename from the list to view the differences between the two files:

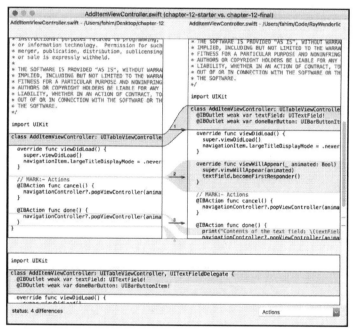

FileMerge is a wonderful tool for spotting the differences between two files or even entire folders. I use it all the time!

If something from the book doesn't work as it should, then do a "diff" – that's what you're supposed to call it – between your own files and the ones from the Source Code folder to see if you can find any anomalies.

You can find the project files for the app up to this point under **12 - Add Item Screen** in the Source Code folder.

Chapter 13: Delegates and Protocols

You now have an Add Item screen with a keyboard that lets the user enter text. The app also properly validates the input so that you'll never end up with text that is empty.

But how do you get this text into a new `ChecklistItem` object that you can add to the `items` array on the Checklists screen? That is the topic that this chapter will explore.

Add new ChecklistItems

In order for a new item addition to work, you'll have to get the Add Item screen to notify the Checklist View Controller of the new item addition. This is one of the fundamental tasks that every iOS app needs to do: sending messages from one view controller to another.

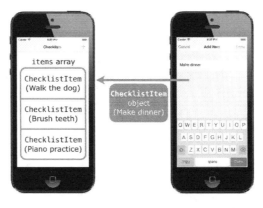

Sending a ChecklistItem object to the screen with the items array

The messy way

> **Exercise:** How would you tackle this problem? The done() method needs to create a new ChecklistItem object with the text from the text field (easy), then add it to the items array and the table view in ChecklistViewController (not so easy).

Maybe you came up with something like this:

```
class AddItemViewController: UITableViewController, . . . {

  // This variable refers to the other view controller
  var checklistViewController: ChecklistViewController

  @IBAction func done() {
    // Create the new checklist item object
    let item = ChecklistItem()
    item.text = textField.text!

    // Directly call a method from ChecklistViewController
    checklistViewController.add(item)
  }
}
```

In this scenario, AddItemViewController has a variable that refers to the ChecklistViewController, and done() calls its add() method with the new ChecklistItem object.

This will work, but it's not the iOS way. The big downside to this approach is that it shackles these two view controller objects together.

As a general principle, if screen A launches screen B then you don't want screen B to know too much about the screen that invoked it (A). The less B knows of A, the better.

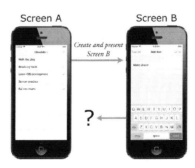

Screen A knows all about screen B, but B knows nothing of A

Giving `AddItemViewController` a direct reference to `ChecklistViewController` prevents you from opening the Add Item screen from somewhere else in the app. It can only ever talk back to `ChecklistViewController`. That's a big disadvantage.

You won't actually need to do this in *Checklists*, but in many apps it's common for one screen to be accessible from multiple places. For example, a login screen that appears after the user has been logged out due to inactivity. Or, a details screen that shows more information about a tapped item, no matter where that item is located in the app (you'll see an example of this in the next app).

Therefore, it's best if `AddItemViewController` doesn't know anything about `ChecklistViewController`.

But if that's the case, then how can you make the two communicate?

The solution is to make your own *delegate*.

The delegate way

You've already seen delegates in a few different places: the table view has a delegate that responds to taps on the rows; the text field has a delegate that you used to validate the length of the text; and the app also has something named the `AppDelegate` (see the project navigator).

You can't turn a corner in this place without bumping into a delegate…

The delegate pattern is commonly used to handle the situation you find yourself in: Screen A opens screen B. At some point screen B needs to communicate back to screen A, usually when it closes.

The solution is to make screen A the delegate of screen B, so that B can send its messages to A whenever it needs to.

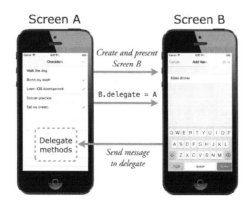

Screen A launches screen B and becomes its delegate

The cool thing about the delegate pattern is that screen B doesn't really know anything about screen A. It just knows that *some* object is its delegate, but doesn't really care who that is. Just like how UITableView doesn't really care about your view controller, only that it delivers table view cells when the table view asks for them.

This principle, where screen B is independent of screen A and yet can still talk to it, is called *loose coupling* and is considered good software design practice.

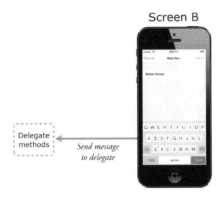

This is what Screen B sees: only the delegate part, not the rest of screen A

You will use the delegate pattern to let the AddItemViewController send notifications back to the ChecklistViewController, without it having to know anything about the latter.

Delegates go hand-in-hand with *protocols*, a prominent feature of the Swift language.

The delegate protocol

➤ At the top of **AddItemViewController.swift**, add this in after the import line (but before the class line - it is not part of the AddItemViewController object):

```
protocol AddItemViewControllerDelegate: class {
  func addItemViewControllerDidCancel(
                        _ controller: AddItemViewController)
  func addItemViewController(
                  _ controller: AddItemViewController,
          didFinishAdding item: ChecklistItem)
}
```

This defines the AddItemViewControllerDelegate protocol. You should recognize the lines inside the protocol { ... } block as method declarations, but unlike the previous methods you've seen, these don't have any source code in them. The protocol just lists the names of the methods.

Think of the delegate protocol as a contract between screen B, in this case the Add Item View Controller, and any screens that wish to use it.

Protocols

In Swift, a *protocol* doesn't have anything to do with computer networks or meeting royalty. It is simply a name for a group of methods.

A protocol normally doesn't implement any of the methods it declares. It just says: any object that conforms to this protocol must implement methods X, Y and Z. (There are special cases where you might want to provide a default implementation for a protocol, but that's an advanced topic that we don't need to get into right now :])

The two methods listed in the `AddItemViewControllerDelegate` protocol are:

• `addItemViewControllerDidCancel(_:)`

• `addItemViewController(_:didFinishAdding:)`

Delegates often have very long method names!

The first method is for when the user presses Cancel, the second is for when they press Done. In the latter case, the `didFinishAdding` parameter passes along the new `ChecklistItem` object.

To make the `ChecklistViewController` conform to this protocol, it must provide implementations for these two methods. From then on, you can refer to `ChecklistViewController` using the protocol name, instead of the class name.

(If you've programmed in other languages before, you may recognize protocols as being very similar to "interfaces".)

In `AddItemViewController`, you can use the following to refer back to `ChecklistViewController`:

```
var delegate: AddItemViewControllerDelegate
```

The variable `delegate` is nothing more than a reference to *some* object that implements the methods of the `AddItemViewControllerDelegate` protocol. You can send messages to the object referenced by the `delegate` variable without knowing what kind of object it really is.

Of course, *you* know the object referenced by `delegate` is the `ChecklistViewController`, but `AddItemViewController` doesn't need to be aware of that. All it sees is some object that implements its delegate protocol.

If you wanted to, you could make some other object implement the protocol and `AddItemViewController` would be perfectly OK with that. That's the power of delegation: you have removed – or *abstracted* away – the dependency between the AddItemViewController and the rest of the app.

It may seem a little overkill for a simple app such as this, but delegates are one of the cornerstones of iOS development. The sooner you master them, the better!

Notify the delegate

You're not done yet in **AddItemViewController.swift**. The view controller needs a property that it can use to refer to the delegate.

➤ Add this inside the AddItemViewController class, below the outlets:

```
weak var delegate: AddItemViewControllerDelegate?
```

It looks like a regular instance variable declaration, with two differences: weak and the question mark.

Delegates are usually declared as being *weak* – not a statement of their moral character but a way to describe the relationship between the view controller and its delegate. Delegates are also *optional* (the question mark - which you learnt a bit about in the previous chapter).

You'll learn more about those things in a moment.

➤ Replace the cancel() and done() actions with the following:

```
@IBAction func cancel() {
    delegate?.addItemViewControllerDidCancel(self)
}

@IBAction func done() {
    let item = ChecklistItem()
    item.text = textField.text!
    item.checked = false

    delegate?.addItemViewController(self, didFinishAdding: item)
}
```

Let's look at the changes you made. When the user taps the Cancel button, you send the addItemViewControllerDidCancel(_:) message back to the delegate.

You do something similar for the Done button, except that the message is addItemViewController(_:didFinishAdding:) and you pass along a new ChecklistItem object that has the text string from the text field.

> **Note:** It is customary for the delegate methods to have a reference to their owner as the first (or only) parameter.
>
> Doing this is not required, but still a good idea. For example, in the case of table views, it may happen that an object is the delegate or data source for more than one table view. In that case, you need to be able to distinguish between those table views. To allow for this, the table view delegate methods have a parameter for the UITableView object that sent the notification. Having this reference also saves you from having to make an @IBOutlet for the table view.
>
> That explains why you pass self to your delegate methods. Recall that self refers to the object itself, in this case AddItemViewController. It's also why all the delegate method names start with addItemViewController.

➤ Run the app and try the Cancel and Done buttons. They no longer work!

I hope you're not too surprised… The Add Item screen now depends on a delegate to make it close, but you haven't told the Add Item screen who its delegate is yet.

That means the delegate property has no value and the messages aren't being sent to anyone – there is no one listening for them.

Optionals

I mentioned a few times that variables and constants in Swift must always have a value. In other programming languages the special symbol nil or NULL is often used to indicate that a variable has no value. This is not allowed in Swift for normal variables.

The problem with nil and NULL is that they are a frequent cause of crashing apps. If an app attempts to use a variable that is nil when you don't expect it to be nil, the app will crash. This is the dreaded "null pointer dereference".

Swift stops this by preventing you from using nil with regular variables.

However, sometimes a variable does need to have "no value". In that case you can make it an *optional*. You mark something as optional in Swift using either a question mark ? or an exclamation point !.

Only variables that are made optional can have the value nil.

You've already seen the question mark used with IndexPath?, the return type of tableView(_:willSelectRowAt:). Returning nil from this method is a valid response; it means that the table should not select a particular row.

The question mark tells Swift that it's OK for the method to return nil instead of an actual IndexPath object.

Variables that refer to a delegate are usually marked as optional too. You can tell because there is a question mark behind the type:

```
weak var delegate: AddItemViewControllerDelegate?
```

Thanks to the ? it's perfectly acceptable for a delegate to be nil.

You may be wondering why the delegate would ever be nil. Doesn't that negate the idea of having a delegate in the first place? There are two reasons.

Often, delegates are truly optional; a UITableView works fine even if you don't implement any of its delegate methods (but you do need to provide at least some of its data source methods).

More importantly, when AddItemViewController is loaded from the storyboard and instantiated, it won't know right away who its delegate is. Between the time the view controller is loaded and the delegate is assigned, the delegate variable will be nil. And variables that can be nil, even if it is only temporary, must be optionals.

When delegate is nil, you don't want cancel() or done() to send any of the messages. Doing that would crash the app because there is no one to receive the messages.

Swift has a handy shorthand for skipping the work when delegate is not set:

```
delegate?.addItemViewControllerDidCancel(self)
```

Here the ? tells Swift not to send the message if delegate is nil. You can read this as, "Is there a delegate? Then send the message." This practice is called *optional chaining* and it's used a lot in Swift.

In this app it should never happen that delegate is nil – that would get users stuck on the Add Item screen. But Swift doesn't know that. So you'll have to pretend that it can happen anyway and use optional chaining to send messages to the delegate.

Optionals aren't common in other programming languages, so they may take some getting used to. I find that optionals do make programs clearer – most variables never have to be nil, so it's good to prevent them from becoming nil and avoid these potential sources of bugs.

Remember, if you see ? or ! in a Swift program, you're dealing with optionals. In the course of this app I'll come back to this topic a few more times and explain the finer points of using optionals in more detail.

Conform to the delegate protocol

Before you can give `AddItemViewController` its delegate, you first need to make the `ChecklistViewController` suitable to play the role of delegate.

➤ In **ChecklistViewController.swift**, change the class line to the following (this goes all on one line):

```
class ChecklistViewController: UITableViewController,
                              AddItemViewControllerDelegate {
```

This tells the compiler that `ChecklistViewController` now promises to do the things from the `AddItemViewControllerDelegate` protocol. Or, in programming terminology, that it *conforms* to the `AddItemViewControllerDelegate` protocol.

At this point, Xcode should throw up an error: "Type ChecklistViewController does not conform to protocol AddItemViewControllerDelegate."

Xcode warns about not conforming to protocol

That is correct: you still need to add the methods that are listed in `AddItemViewControllerDelegate`. With the latest Xcode, there is an easy way to get started with fixing this issue - see that "Fix" button? Simply click it :]

Xcode will add in the stubs (the bare minimum code) for the missing methods. You will have to add in the actual implementation for each method, of course.

➤ Add the implementations for the protocol methods to `ChecklistViewController`:

```
func addItemViewControllerDidCancel(
                    _ controller: AddItemViewController) {
  navigationController?.popViewController(animated:true)
}

func addItemViewController(
            _ controller: AddItemViewController,
        didFinishAdding item: ChecklistItem) {
  navigationController?.popViewController(animated:true)
}
```

Currently, both methods simply close the Add Item screen. This is what the `AddItemViewController` used to do in its `cancel()` and `done()` actions. You've simply moved that responsibility to the delegate.

The code that puts the new `ChecklistItem` object into the table view is yet to be added. You'll do that in a moment, but there's something else you need to do first.

Delegates in five easy steps

These are the steps for setting up the delegate pattern between two objects, where object A is the delegate for object B, and object B will send messages back to A. The steps are:

1 - Define a delegate `protocol` for object B.

2 - Give object B a `delegate` optional variable. This variable should be **weak**.

3 - Update object B to send messages to its delegate when something interesting happens, such as the user pressing the Cancel or Done buttons, or when it needs a piece of information. You write `delegate?.methodName(self, . . .)`

4 - Make object A conform to the delegate protocol. It should put the name of the protocol in its `class` line and implement the methods from the protocol.

5 - Tell object B that object A is now its delegate.

You've done steps 1 - 4, so there is just one more thing you need to do - step 5: tell `AddItemViewController` that `ChecklistViewController` is its delegate.

The proper place to do that is in the `prepare(for:sender:)` method, also known as *prepare-for-segue*.

The `prepare(for:sender:)` method is invoked by UIKit when a segue from one screen to another is about to be performed. Recall that the segue is the arrow between two view controllers in the storyboard.

Using prepare-for-segue allows you to pass data to the new view controller before it is displayed. Usually you'll do this by setting its properties.

➤ Add this method to **ChecklistViewController.swift**:

```
override func prepare(for segue: UIStoryboardSegue,
                      sender: Any?) {
  // 1
  if segue.identifier == "AddItem" {
    // 2
    let controller = segue.destination
                  as! AddItemViewController
    // 3
```

```
    controller.delegate = self
  }
}
```

This is what the above code does, step-by-step:

1. Because there may be more than one segue per view controller, it's a good idea to give each one a unique identifier and to check for that identifier first to make sure you're handling the correct segue. Swift's == comparison operator works on not just numbers but also on strings and most other types of objects.

2. The new view controller to be displayed can be found in `segue.destination`, but `destination` is of type `UIViewContoller` since the new view controller could be any view controller sub-class.

   So, you *cast* `destination` to `AddItemViewController` to get a reference to an object with the right type. (The `as!` keyword is known as a *type cast* or a *downcast* since you are casting an object of one type to a different type.

   Do note that if you downcast objects of completely different types, you might get a `nil` value. The casting works here because `AddItemViewController` is a sub-class of `UIViewContoller`.)

3. Once you have a reference to the `AddItemViewController` object, you set its `delegate` property to `self` and the connection is complete. This tells `AddItemViewController` that from now on, the object identified as `self` is its delegate. But what is "self" here? Well, since you're editing **ChecklistViewController.swift**, `self` refers to `ChecklistViewController`.

Excellent! `ChecklistViewController` is now the delegate of `AddItemViewController`. It took some work, but you're almost set now - except for one teensy thing :]

Set the segue identifier

See the segue identifier that is checked in the code above? Where was it set? The answer is, that it wasn't. We need to set the identifier in order for the above code to work.

➤ Open the storyboard and select the segue between the Checklist View Controller and the Add Item View Controller.

➤ In the **Attributes inspector**, type **AddItem** into the **Identifier** field:

Naming the segue between the Checklists scene and the Add Item scene

➤ Run the app to see if it works. (Make sure the storyboard is saved before you press Run, or the app may crash.)

Pressing the + button will perform the segue to the Add Item screen with the Checklists screen set as its delegate.

When you press Cancel or Done, AddItemViewController sends a message to its delegate, ChecklistViewController. Currently the delegate simply closes the Add Item screen. But now that you know it works, you can make it do more.

Let's add the new ChecklistItem to the data model and the table view. Finally!

Add new to-do items

➤ Change the implementation of the didFinishAdding delegate method in **ChecklistViewController.swift** to the following:

```
func addItemViewController(
          _ controller: AddItemViewController,
      didFinishAdding item: ChecklistItem) {
   let newRowIndex = items.count
   items.append(item)

   let indexPath = IndexPath(row: newRowIndex, section: 0)
   let indexPaths = [indexPath]
   tableView.insertRows(at: indexPaths, with: .automatic)
   navigationController?.popViewController(animated:true)
}
```

This is basically the same as what you did in addItem() before. In fact, I simply copied the contents of addItem() and pasted that into this method with some slight modifications. Compare the two methods and see for yourself.

The only difference is that you no longer create the `ChecklistItem` object here; that happens in the `AddItemViewController`. You merely insert this new object into the `items` array.

As before, you tell the table view you have a new row for it and then close the Add Items screen.

➤ Remove `addItem()` from **ChecklistViewController.swift** as you no longer need this method.

Just to make sure, open the storyboard and double-check that the + button is no longer connected to the `addItem` action. You should have already removed the connection to the action when you set up the segue to the Add Items scene, but it doesn't hurt to check since bad things happen if buttons are connected to methods that no longer exist…

(You can check this in the Connections inspector for the + button, under **Sent Actions**. Nothing should be connected there. Only the segue under Triggered Segues should be present.)

➤ Run the app and you should be able to add your own items to the list!

You can finally add new items to the to-do list

Weak

I still owe you an explanation about the **weak** keyword. Relationships between objects can be weak or strong. You use weak relationships to avoid what is known as an *ownership cycle*.

When object A has a strong reference to object B, and at the same time object B also has a strong reference back to A, then these two objects are involved in a dangerous kind of romance: an ownership cycle.

Normally, an object is destroyed – or *deallocated* – when there are no more strong references to it. But because A and B have strong references to each other, they keep each other alive.

The result is a potential *memory leak* where an object that ought to be destroyed, isn't, and the memory for its data is never reclaimed. With enough such leaks, iOS will run out of available memory and your app will crash. I told you it was dangerous!

Due to the strong references between them, A owns B and at the same time, B also owns A:

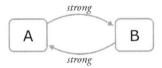

To avoid ownership cycles you can make one of these references weak.

In the case of a view controller and its delegate, screen A usually has a strong reference to screen B, but B only has a weak reference back to its delegate, A.

Because of the weak reference, B no longer owns A:

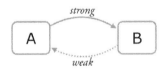

Now there is no ownership cycle.

Such cycles can occur in other situations too, but they are most common with delegates. Therefore, delegates are always made weak.

(There is another relationship type, unowned, that is similar to weak and can be used for delegates too. The difference is that weak variables are allowed to become nil again. You may forget this right now.)

@IBOutlets are usually also declared with the weak keyword. This isn't done to avoid an ownership cycle, but to make it clear that the view controller isn't really the owner of the views from the outlets.

In the course of this book, you'll learn more about weak, strong, optionals, and the relationships between objects. These are important concepts in Swift, but they may take a while to make sense. If you don't understand them immediately, don't lose any sleep over it!

You can find the project files for the app up to this point under **13 - Delegates and Protocols** in the Source Code folder.

Chapter 14: Edit Items

Adding new items to the list is a great step forward for the app, but there are usually three things an app needs to do with data:

1. Add new items (which you've tackled).

2. Deleting items (you allow that with swipe-to-delete).

3. Editing existing items (uhh…).

The last is useful when you want to rename an item from your list - we all make typos.

This chapter covers the following:

- **Edit items:** Edit existing to-do items via the app interface.

- **Refactor the code:** Using Xcode's built-in refactoring capability to rename code to be easily identifiable.

- **One more thing:** Fix missed code changes after the code refactoring using the Find navigator.

Edit items

You could make a completely new Edit Item screen but it would work mostly the same as the Add Item screen. The only difference is that it doesn't start out empty - instead, it works with an existing to-do item.

So, let's re-use the Add Item screen and make it capable of editing an existing `ChecklistItem` object.

Editing a to-do item

For the edit option, when the user presses Done, you won't have to make a new `ChecklistItem` object, instead, you will simply update the text in the existing `ChecklistItem`.

You'll also tell the delegate about these changes so that it can update the text label of the corresponding table view cell.

> **Exercise:** What changes would you need to make to the Add Item screen to enable it to edit existing items?

Answer:

1. The screen title must be changed to **Edit Item**.

2. You must be able to pass it an existing `ChecklistItem` object.

3. You have to place the `ChecklistItem`'s text into the text field.

4. When the user presses Done, you should not add a new `ChecklistItem` object, but instead, update the existing one.

There is a bit of a user interface problem, though… How will the user actually open the Edit Item screen? In many apps that is done by tapping on the item's row, but in *Checklists* that already toggles the checkmark on or off.

To solve this problem, you'll have to revise the UI a little first.

Revise the UI to allow editing

When a row is given two functions, the standard approach is to use a **detail disclosure button** for the secondary task:

The detail disclosure button

Tapping the row itself will still perform the row's main function, in this case, toggling the checkmark. But tapping the disclosure button will open the Edit Item screen.

> **Note:** An alternative approach is in Apple's *Reminders* app, where the checkmark is on the left and tapping only this part of the row will toggle the checkmark. Tapping anywhere else in the row will bring up the Edit screen for that item.
>
> There are also apps that can toggle the whole screen into "Edit mode" and then let you change the text of an item inline. Which solution you choose depends on what works best for your data.

➤ Go to the table view cell in the storyboard for the Checklists scene and in the **Attributes inspector** set its **Accessory** to **Detail Disclosure**.

Instead of the checkmark, you'll now see a chevron (>) and a blue info button on the cell. This means you'll have to place the checkmark somewhere else.

The new checkmark

➤ Drag a new **Label** on to the cell and place it to the left of the text label. Give it the following attributes:

- Text: √ (you can type this with **Alt/Option+V**)
- Font: Helvetica Neue, Bold, size 22
- Tag: 1001

You've given this new label its own tag, so you can easily find it later.

If typing Option-V does not work for you, or you'd prefer a different image, choose **Edit → Emoji & Symbols** from the Xcode menu bar. Use the search bar to search for "check" – or whatever takes your fancy. (Note that not all of these special symbols may actually work on your iPhone.)

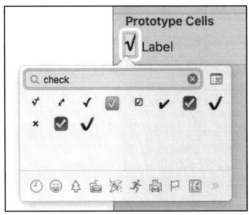

The Emoji & Symbols palette

➤ Resize the text label so that it doesn't overlap the checkmark or the disclosure button. It should be about 215 points wide.

The design of the prototype cell now should look similar to this:

The new design of the prototype cell

➤ In **ChecklistViewController.swift**, change `configureCheckmark(for:with:)` to:

```swift
func configureCheckmark(for cell: UITableViewCell,
                        with item: ChecklistItem) {
  let label = cell.viewWithTag(1001) as! UILabel

  if item.checked {
    label.text = "√"
  } else {
    label.text = ""
  }
}
```

Instead of setting the cell's `accessoryType` property, this now changes the text in the new label.

➤ Run the app and you'll see that the checkmark has moved to the left. There is also a blue detail disclosure button on the right. Tapping the row still toggles the checkmark, but tapping the blue button doesn't do anything.

The checkmarks are now on the other side of the cell

The edit screen segue

Next, you're going to make the detail disclosure button open the Add/Edit Item screen. This is pretty simple because Interface Builder also allows you to make a segue for a disclosure button.

➤ Open the storyboard. Select the table view cell for the Checklists scene and **Control-drag** to the Add Item scene to make a segue. From the popup, choose **Show** from the **Accessory Action** section (not from Selection Segue):

Making a segue from the detail disclosure button

There should now be two segues going from the Checklists screen to the navigation controller. One is triggered by the + button, the other by the detail disclosure button from the prototype cell.

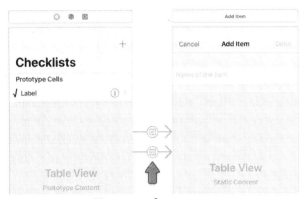

Two arrows for two segues

For the app to make a distinction between these two segues, they must have unique identifiers.

➤ Give this new segue the identifier **EditItem** (in the **Attributes inspector**).

If you run the app now, tapping the blue ⓘ button will also open the Add Item screen. But the Cancel and Done buttons won't work.

Exercise: Can you explain why not?

Answer: You haven't set the delegate yet. Remember that you set the delegate in `prepare(for:sender:)`, but only for when the + button is tapped to perform the "AddItem" segue. You haven't done the same for this new "EditItem" segue.

Before you do that, you should first make the Add Item screen capable of editing existing `ChecklistItem` objects.

Update the Add Item screen to handle editing

➤ Add a new property for a `ChecklistItem` object below the other instance variables in **AddItemViewController.swift**:

```
var itemToEdit: ChecklistItem?
```

This variable contains the existing `ChecklistItem` object that the user will edit. But when adding a new to-do item, `itemToEdit` will be `nil`. That is how the view controller will make the distinction between adding and editing.

Because `itemToEdit` can be `nil`, it needs to be an optional. That explains the question mark.

➤ Update `viewDidLoad()` in **AddItemViewController.swift** as follows:

```
override func viewDidLoad() {
  . . .
  if let item = itemToEdit {
    title = "Edit Item"
    textField.text = item.text
  }
}
```

Recall that `viewDidLoad()` is called by UIKit when the view controller is loaded from the storyboard, but before it is shown on the screen. That gives you time to put the user interface in order.

In editing mode, when `itemToEdit` is not `nil`, you change the title in the navigation bar to "Edit Item". You do this by changing the `title` property.

Each view controller has a number of built-in properties and this is one of them. The navigation controller looks for the `title` property and automatically changes the text in the navigation bar.

You also set the text in the text field to the value from the item's `text` property.

if let

You cannot use optionals like you would regular variables. For example, if `viewDidLoad()` had the following code:

```
    textField.text = itemToEdit.text
```

Xcode would complain with the error message, "Value of optional type ChecklistItem? not unwrapped".

That's because `itemToEdit` is the optional version of `ChecklistItem`.

In order to use it, you first need to *unwrap* the optional. You do that with the following special syntax:

```
  if let temporaryConstant = optionalVariable {
    // temporaryConstant now contains the unwrapped value
    // of the optional variable
  }
```

If the optional is not `nil`, then the code inside the `if` statement is performed.

There are a few other ways to read the value of an optional, but using `if let` is the safest: if the optional has no value – i.e. it is `nil` – then the code inside the `if let` block is skipped over.

The new code you added to `viewDidLoad` can also be written like this:

```
if let itemToEdit = itemToEdit {
  title = "Edit Item"
  textField.text = itemToEdit.text
}
```

Looks a bit weird, does it? Why are we assigning the value from `itemToEdit` back again to `itemToEdit`? And how come the compiler doesn't complain about optional unwrapping now if we write the code like that?

The above practice is called *variable shadowing* - you create a "shadow" instance of the `itemToEdit` variable just for the duration of the `if` condition and that shadow instance is an unwrapped instance of the originally optional `itemToEdit` variable.

So, when you refer to `itemToEdit` when assigning text to the text field, you are actually referring to the unwrapped instance of the variable instead of the original optional instance.

This might be a bit confusing if you are new to Swift and optionals. So, whether you use variable shadowing to unwrap optionals, or not, is entirely up to you. Personally, I prefer shadowing because then the code is clear about the variable being referred to in the code at all times since the same variable name is used for both the optional and unwrapped versions.

The `AddItemViewController` is now capable of recognizing when it needs to edit an item. If the `itemToEdit` property is given a `ChecklistItem` object, then the screen magically changes into the Edit Item screen.

But where do you set that `itemToEdit` property? In prepare-for-segue, of course! That's the ideal place for placing values into the properties of the new screen before it becomes visible.

Set the item to be edited

➤ Change `prepare(for:sender:)` in **ChecklistViewController.swift** to the following:

```
override func prepare(for segue: UIStoryboardSegue,
                      sender: Any?) {
  if segue.identifier == "AddItem" {
    . . .

  } else if segue.identifier == "EditItem" {
    let controller = segue.destination
                    as! AddItemViewController
    controller.delegate = self
```

```
    if let indexPath = tableView.indexPath(
                        for: sender as! UITableViewCell) {
      controller.itemToEdit = items[indexPath.row]
    }
  }
}
```

As before, you get the `AddItemViewController` via the segue's `destination`.

You also set the view controller's `delegate` property so you're notified when the user taps Cancel or Done. Nothing new there. This is the same as for the `AddItem` segue.

This is the interesting new bit:

```
if let indexPath = tableView.indexPath(
                    for: sender as! UITableViewCell){
  controller.itemToEdit = items[indexPath.row]
}
```

You're in the `prepare(for:sender:)` method, which has a parameter named `sender`. This parameter contains a reference to the control that triggered the segue, in this case, the table view cell whose disclosure button was tapped.

You use that `UITableViewCell` object to find the table view row number by looking up the corresponding index path using `tableView.indexPath(for:)`.

The return type of `indexPath(for:)` is `IndexPath?`, an optional, meaning it can possibly return `nil`. That's why you need to unwrap this optional value with `if let` before you can use it.

Once you have the index path, you obtain the `ChecklistItem` object to edit, and you assign this to `AddItemViewController`'s `itemToEdit` property.

Sending data between view controllers

We've talked about screen B (the Add/Edit Item screen) passing data back to screen A (the Checklists screen) via delegates. But here, you're passing a piece of data the other way around – from screen A to screen B – namely, the `ChecklistItem` to edit.

Data transfer between view controllers works two ways:

1. From A to B. When screen A opens screen B, A can give B the data it needs. You simply make a new instance variable in B's view controller. Screen A then puts an object into this property right before it makes screen B visible, usually in `prepare(for:sender:)`.

2. From B to A. To pass data back from B to A you use a delegate.

This illustration shows how screen A sends data to screen B by putting it into B's properties, and how screen B sends data back to the delegate:

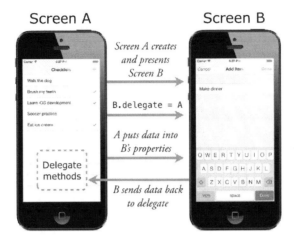

I hope the flow between view controllers is starting to make sense to you now. You're going to do this sort of thing a few more times in this app, just to make sure you get comfortable with it.

Making iOS apps is all about creating view controllers and sending messages between them, so you want this to become second nature.

► With these steps done, you can now run the app. A tap on the + button opens the Add Item screen as before. But tap the accessory button on an existing row and the screen that opens is named Edit Item. It already contains the to-do item's text:

Editing an item

Enable the Done button for edits

One small problem: the Done button in the navigation bar is initially disabled. This is because you originally set it to be disabled in the storyboard.

➤ Change `viewDidLoad()` in **AddItemViewController.swift** to fix this:

```
override func viewDidLoad() {
  super.viewDidLoad()

  if let item = itemToEdit {
    title = "Edit Item"
    textField.text = item.text
    doneBarButton.isEnabled = true     // add this line
  }
}
```

When in edit mode, you simply enable the Done button since you are guaranteed to be passed some text for the item.

The problems don't end here, though. Run the app, tap a row to edit it, and press Done. Instead of changing the text on the existing item, a brand new to-do item with the new text is added to the list.

How come? You didn't write the code yet to update the data model! So, the delegate always thinks it needs to add a new row.

To solve this, you will add a new method to the delegate protocol.

Handle edits in the delegate protocol

➤ Add the following line to the `protocol` section in **AddItemViewController.swift**:

```
func addItemViewController(_ controller: AddItemViewController,
                didFinishEditing item: ChecklistItem)
```

The full protocol now looks like this:

```
protocol AddItemViewControllerDelegate: class {
  func addItemViewControllerDidCancel(
                _ controller: AddItemViewController)
  func addItemViewController(
                _ controller: AddItemViewController,
              didFinishAdding item: ChecklistItem)
  func addItemViewController(
                _ controller: AddItemViewController,
              didFinishEditing item: ChecklistItem)
}
```

There is a method that is invoked when the user presses Cancel and two methods for when the user presses Done.

After adding a new item you call didFinishAdding, but when editing an existing item, the new didFinishEditing method should now be called instead.

By using different methods the delegate (the ChecklistViewController) can make a distinction between those two situations.

➤ In **AddItemViewController.swift**, change the done() method to:

```
@IBAction func done() {
  if let itemToEdit = itemToEdit {
    itemToEdit.text = textField.text!
    delegate?.addItemViewController(self,
              didFinishEditing: itemToEdit)

  } else {
    let item = ChecklistItem()
    item.text = textField.text!
    item.checked = false
    delegate?.addItemViewController(self, didFinishAdding: item)
  }
}
```

First the code checks whether the itemToEdit property contains an object - you should recognize the if let syntax for unwrapping an optional.

If the optional is not nil, you put the text from the text field into the existing ChecklistItem object and then call the new delegate method.

In the case that itemToEdit *is* nil, the user is adding a new item and you do the stuff you did before (inside the else block).

Implement the new delegate method

➤ Try to build the app. It won't work.

Xcode says "Build Failed" but there don't seem to be any error messages in **AddItemViewController.swift**. So what went wrong?

You can see all errors and warnings from Xcode in the **Issue navigator**.

Xcode warns about incomplete implementation

The error is apparently in `ChecklistViewController` because it does not implement a method from the protocol. That is not so strange because you just added the new `addItemViewController(_:didFinishEditing:)` method to the delegate protocol. But you did not yet tell the view controller, which plays the role of the delegate, what to do with it.

> **Note:** The exact error message in my version of Xcode is "Method … has different argument names from those required by protocol …". That's a bit of a strange error message, wouldn't you say? It doesn't really describe what's wrong, just what Swift is confused about.
>
> As you write your own apps, you'll probably run into other strange or even undecipherable Swift error messages. This should get better in time. The Swift compiler is quite new at the job and still needs to work on its bedside manner.

➤ Add the following to **ChecklistViewController.swift** and the compiler error will be history:

```swift
func addItemViewController(
          _ controller: AddItemViewController,
      didFinishEditing item: ChecklistItem) {
  if let index = items.index(of: item) {
    let indexPath = IndexPath(row: index, section: 0)
    if let cell = tableView.cellForRow(at: indexPath) {
      configureText(for: cell, with: item)
    }
  }
  navigationController?.popViewController(animated:true)
}
```

The `ChecklistItem` object already has the new text – it was put there by `done()` – and the cell for it already exists in the table view. But you do need to update the label for its table view cell.

So, in this new method you look for the cell that corresponds to the `ChecklistItem` object and, using the `configureText(for:with:)` method you wrote earlier, tell it to refresh its label.

The first statement is the most interesting:

```
if let index = items.index(of: item) {
```

In order to create the `IndexPath` that you need to retrieve the cell, you first need to find the row number for this `ChecklistItem`. The row number is the same as the index of the `ChecklistItem` in the `items` array - you can use the `index(of:)` method to return that index.

Now, it won't happen here, but in theory it's possible that you use `index(of:)` on an object that is not actually in the array. To account for the possibility, `index(of:)` does not return a normal value, it returns an optional. If the object is not part of the array, the returned value is `nil`.

That's why you need to use `if let` here to unwrap the return value from `index(of:)`.

➤ Try to build the app. Oops, I guess I spoke too soon! Xcode has found another reason to complain: "Cannot invoke index with an argument list of type blah blah blah". What does *that* mean?

New Xcode error

This error is displayed because you can't use `index(of:)` on just any array (or collection of objects). An object has to be "equatable" if you are to use `index(of:)` on an array of that object type. This is because `index(of:)` must be able to somehow compare the object that you're looking for against the objects in the array, to see if they are equal.

Your `ChecklistItem` object does not have any functionality for that yet. There are a few ways you can fix this, but we'll go for the easy one.

➤ In **ChecklistItem.swift**, change the class line to:

```
class ChecklistItem: NSObject {
```

If you've programmed in Objective-C before, you'll be familiar with `NSObject`.

Almost all objects in Objective-C programs are based on `NSObject`. It's the most basic building block provided by iOS, and it offers a bunch of useful functionality that standard Swift objects don't have.

You can write many Swift programs without having to resort to `NSObject`, but in times like these it comes in handy.

Building `ChecklistItem` on top of `NSObject` is enough to satisfy the "equatable" requirement. In a later chapter, when you learn about saving the checklist items, you would have had to make `ChecklistItem` an `NSObject` anyway. So, this is a good solution for this app.

➤ Run the app again and verify that editing items works now. Excellent!

Refactor the code

At this point, you have an app that can add new items and edit existing items using the combined Add/Edit Item screen. Pretty sweet!

Given the recent changes, I don't think the name `AddItemViewController` is appropriate anymore as this screen is now used to both add and edit items.

I suggest you rename it to `ItemDetailViewController`.

Rename the view controller

Most IDEs (or Integrated Development Environments) such as Xcode have a feature named *refactoring*, which allows you to change the name of a class, method, or variable through the entire project safely. Unfortunately, the refactoring functionality in Xcode did not work correctly for several years with Swift source files :[

The good news is that as of Xcode 9, the refactoring functionaliy in Xcode has not only been restored for Swift files, but it has been re-written from the ground up to work for most of the source code types you would generally work on in Xcode!

Yes, I hear you saying, "Enough of the sales pitch, show me how to refactor!" There are a couple of ways to access the refactor functionality, but the easiest is to simply **right-click** (or, **Control-click**) on any class name, method, or variable.

You'll get a menu similar to this:

The Xcode context menu

You should notice two things about the above screenshot:

1. Notice how the class name (or method name, or variable name) that was under your cursor when you right-clicked was highlighted? That indicates that the highlighted name is the one that would be renamed.

2. Notice the **Rename...** option on the menu? It's this menu option which provides the refactor functionality.

➤ If you right-clicked over the AddItemViewController class name, select the **Rename...** option now. (If you right-clicked elsewhere, first move your cursor over the class name, right-click, and then select Rename...). You should get a screen similar to the following:

Xcode rename view

The new screen shows you all the files and instances (including the storyboard and file names) in the project where the particular name you selected is used. Also notice how the name at the instance where you right-clicked is now editable.

Start typing in the new name you want and you'll notice that all the matching names for all the other instances in the view update in real-time. Cool!

Xcode real-time renaming

When you've entered the correct name and verified that everything will be updated correctly, just click the **Rename** button on the top right corner and you're done :] It's as simple as that!

> **Note:** While the refactoring worked flawlessly most of the time, I've sometimes had Xcode do all the refactoring correctly except for renaming the file itself. If this does happen to you, you might have to rename the file manually.

Test the code after a refactor

Let's see if everything works correctly now.

➤ Press ⌘+B to compile the app.

> **Note:** Getting a "Build Failed" error? Sometimes this does happen after a massive change across the whole project like this. The first thing to try is to use the Xcode menu's **Product → Clean** option and try building again. It should work in most cases at that point.

Because you made quite a few changes all over the place, it's a good idea to clean up the debris and detritus from old compiler runs so that Xcode picks up all the new changes. You don't have to be paranoid about this, but it's good practice to clean house once in a while.

➤ From Xcode's menu bar choose **Product → Clean**. When the clean is done, choose **Product → Build** (or simply press the Run button).

If there are no build issues, run the app again and test the various features just to make sure everything still works! (If the build succeeds but Xcode still shows red error icons in your source file, then close the project and open it again, or restart Xcode. Restarting Xcode is the solution that Almost Always Works™. And if it doesn't, restarting your computer is the last resort. That does get rid of even the most stubborn issues.)

One more thing

The rename process appears to have gone through flawlessly, your app works fine when you test it, and there are no crashes. So, everything should be fine and you can move on to the next feature in the app, right?

Well … not quite :] Switch to **ItemDetailViewController.swift** and check the protocol definition at the top. What do you see?

```
33
34   protocol AddItemViewControllerDelegate: class {
35     func addItemViewControllerDidCancel(_ controller: ItemDetailViewController)
36     func addItemViewController(_ controller: ItemDetailViewController, didFinishAdding item:
             ChecklistItem)
37     func addItemViewController(_ controller: ItemDetailViewController, didFinishEditing item:
             ChecklistItem)
38   }
```

The protocol name has not changed after renaming

Looks as if the protocol name, `AddItemViewControllerDelegate`, did not change when you renamed `AddItemViewController`.

If you think about it, it makes sense. `AddItemViewControllerDelegate` is a different entity than `AddItemViewController`. So all the renaming did was to change the all the references to `AddItemViewController` class, not the `AddItemViewControllerDelegate` protocol.

You can easily change the name of the protocol to `ItemDetailViewControllerDelegate` by using Xcode's rename functionality yet again. But you'll notice that that only changes the protocol name itself - not the protocol method names. Hmm … this is getting to be a lot of work!

You can try renaming each protocol method separately and Xcode's rename functionality will do a good job with the renaming, but you'd have to do this three times for the three methods. This could get really time consuming, especially if you were dealing with a protocol with lots of methods. There's an easier way.

What is this easier way? To use Xcode's search and replace functionality, of course! As you'll notice, all that remains to change in the `ItemDetailViewControllerDelegate` is the method names, all of which begin with `addItemViewController`. So, if you can search for the term `addItemViewController` across the entire project and replace it with `itemDetailViewController`, you should be done!

Here's how you do it:

➤ Switch to the **Find navigator** (fourth tab in the navigator pane).

➤ Click on **Find** to change it to **Replace**.

➤ Change Ignoring Case to **Matching Case**.

➤ Type as the search text: **addItemViewController**. Important: Make sure you spell it exactly like this since your search term is going to be case-sensitive!

➤ Type in the replacement field: **itemDetailViewController**, again making sure that you type it exactly.

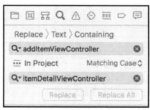

The search & replace options

➤ Press **return** on your keyboard to start the search. This doesn't replace anything yet.

The Find navigator shows the files containing matches for the search term. You should see two Swift source files in this list.

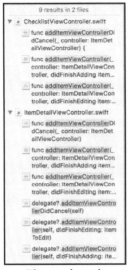

The search results

➤ Click on any item in the file list above to be taken to that particular match in the relevant file with the match highlighted in the source code:

The results list allows you to verify each match

Have a look through the search results just to make sure Xcode isn't doing anything you'll regret later. It should only rename everything that says `addItemViewController` to `itemDetailViewController`.

➤ If you are satisfied that the matches are correct, click **Replace All**. (You could also select only some results in the list and then click **Replace** to have only those results be changed.)

I always repeat the search afterwards, ignoring case, to make sure I didn't skip anything by accident.

Now Run the app and test its functionality once again to make sure that everything works. If it does, you are done with this particular task, finally :]

Iterative development

If you think this approach to development we've taken so far is a little messy, then you're absolutely right. You started out with one design, but as you continued development you found out that things didn't work out so well in practice, and that you had to refactor your approach a few times to find a way that works. This is actually how software development goes in practice.

You first build a small part of your app and everything looks and works fine. Then you add the next small part on top of that and suddenly everything breaks down. The proper thing to do is to go back and restructure your entire approach so that everything is hunky-dory again… Until the next change you need to make.

Software development is a constant process of refinement. In this book I didn't want to just give you a perfect piece of code and explain how each part works. That's not how software development happens in the real world.

Instead, you're working your way from zero to a full app, exactly the way a pro developer would, including the mistakes and dead ends.

Isn't it possible to create a design up-front – sometimes called a "software architecture design" – that deals with all of these situations, something like a blueprint for software?

I don't believe in such designs. Sure, it's always good to plan ahead. Before writing this book, I made a few quick sketches of how I imagined each app would turn out. That was useful to envision the amount of work, but as usual, some of my assumptions and guesses turned out to be wrong and the design stopped being useful about halfway in. And this is only a simple app!

That doesn't mean you shouldn't spend any time on planning and design — just not too much. Simply start somewhere and keep going until you get stuck, then backtrack and improve on your approach. This is called *iterative development* and it's usually faster and provides better results than meticulous up-front planning.

You can find the project files for the app up to this point under **14 - Edit Items** in the Source Code folder.

Chapter 15: Saving and Loading

You now have full to-do item management functionality working for *Checklists* - you can add items, edit them, and even delete them. However, any new to-do items that you add to the list cease to exist when you terminate the app (by pressing the Stop button in Xcode, for example). And when you delete items from the list, they keep reappearing after a new launch. That's not how a real app should behave!

So, it's time to consdider *data persistence* - or, to put it simply, saving and loading items ...

In this chapter you wil cover the following:

- **The need for data persistence:** A quick look at why you need data persistence.

- **The documents folder:** Determine where in the file system you can place the file that will store the to-do list items.

- **Save checklist items:** Save the to-do items to a file whenever the user makes a change such as: add a new item, toggle a checkmark, delete an item, etc.

- **Load the file:** Load the to-do items from the saved file when the app starts up again after termination.

The need for data persistence

Thanks to the multitasking nature of iOS, an app stays in memory when you close it and go back to the home screen or switch to another app. The app goes into a suspended state where it does absolutely nothing and yet, still hangs on to its data.

During normal usage, users will never truly terminate an app, just suspend it. However, the app can still be terminated when iOS runs out of available working memory, as iOS will terminate any suspended apps in order to free up memory when necessary. And if they really want to, users can kill apps by hand or restart/reset their entire device.

Just keeping the list of items in memory is not good enough because there is no guarantee that the app will remain in memory forever, whether active or suspended.

Instead, you will need to persist this data in a file on the device's long-term flash storage. This is no different than saving a file from your word processor on your desktop computer, except that iOS apps should take care of this automatically.

The user shouldn't have to press a Save button just to make sure unsaved data is safely placed in long-term storage.

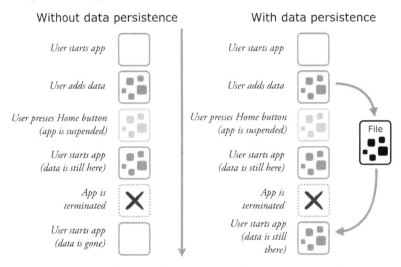

Apps need to persist data just in case the app is terminated

So let's get crackin' on that data persistence functionality!

The documents folder

iOS apps live in a sheltered environment known as the **sandbox**. Each app has its own folder for storing files but cannot access the directories or files of any other app.

This is a security measure, designed to prevent malicious software such as viruses from doing any damage. If an app can only change its own files, it cannot modify (or affect) any other part of the system.

Your apps can store files in the "Documents" folder in the app's sandbox.

The contents of the Documents folder are backed up when the user syncs their device with iTunes or iCloud.

When you release a new version of your app and users install the update, the Documents folder is left untouched. Any data the app has saved into this folder stays there when the app is updated.

In other words, the Documents folder is the perfect place for storing your user's data files.

Get the save file path

Let's look at how this works.

➤ Add the following methods to **ChecklistViewController.swift**:

```
func documentsDirectory() -> URL {
   let paths = FileManager.default.urls(for: .documentDirectory,
                                         in: .userDomainMask)
   return paths[0]
}

func dataFilePath() -> URL {
   return documentsDirectory().appendingPathComponent(
                               "Checklists.plist")
}
```

The documentsDirectory() method is something I've added for convenience. There is no standard method you can call to get the full path to the Documents folder, so I rolled my own.

The dataFilePath() method uses documentsDirectory() to construct the full path to the file that will store the checklist items. This file is named **Checklists.plist** and it lives inside the Documents folder.

Notice that both methods return a URL object. iOS uses URLs to refer to files in its filesystem. Where websites use http:// or https:// URLs, to refer to a file you use a file:// URL.

Note: Double check to make sure your code says .documentDirectory and not .documentationDirectory. Xcode's autocomplete can easily trip you up here!

➤ Still in **ChecklistViewController.swift**, add the following two print statements to the bottom of init?(coder:), below the call to super.init():

```
required init?(coder aDecoder: NSCoder) {
  . . .
  super.init(coder: aDecoder)

  print("Documents folder is \(documentsDirectory())")
  print("Data file path is \(dataFilePath())")
}
```

➤ Run the app. Xcode's Console will now show you where your app's Documents folder is actually located.

If I run the app from the Simulator, on my system it shows something like this:

```
Documents folder is file:///Users/fahim/Library/Developer/
CoreSimulator/Devices/CA23DAEA-DF30-43C3-8611-E713F96D4780/
data/Containers/Data/Application/CA115C3A-E1FB-4EF9-A776-
F434DAB8029E/Documents/
Data file path is file:///Users/fahim/Library/Developer/
CoreSimulator/Devices/CA23DAEA-DF30-43C3-8611-E713F96D4780/
data/Containers/Data/Application/CA115C3A-E1FB-4EF9-A776-
F434DAB8029E/Documents/Checklists.plist
```

Console output showing Documents folder and data file locations

If you run it on your iPhone, the path will look somewhat different. Here's what mine says:

```
Documents folder is file:///var/mobile/Applications/
FDD50B54-9383-4DCC-9C19-C3DEBC1A96FE/Documents

Data file path is file:///var/mobile/Applications/
FDD50B54-9383-4DCC-9C19-C3DEBC1A96FE/Documents/Checklists.plist
```

As you'll notice, the folder name is a random 32-character ID. Xcode picks this ID when it installs the app on the Simulator or the device. Anything inside that folder is part of the app's sandbox.

Browse the documents folder

For the rest of this app, run the app on the Simulator instead of a device. That makes it easier to look at the files you'll be writing into the Documents folder. Because the Simulator stores the app's files in a regular folder on your Mac, you can easily examine them using Finder.

➤ Open a new Finder window by clicking on the Desktop and typing **⌘+N** (or, by clicking the Finder icon in your dock, if you have one.). Then press **⌘+Shift+G** (or, select **Go → Go to Folder…** from the menu), copy the Documents folder path from Xcode Console, and paste the full path to the Documents folder in the dialog. (Don't include the **file://** bit. The path starts with **/Users/yourname/…**)

The Finder window will go to that folder. Keep this window open so you can verify that the Checklists.plist file is actually created when you get to that part.

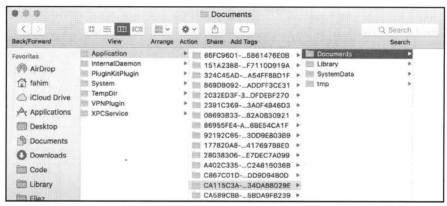

The app's directory structure in the Simulator

Tip: If you want to navigate to the Simulator's app directory by traversing your folder structure, then you should know that the Library folder, which is in your home folder, is normally hidden. Hold down the Alt/Option key and click on Finder's Go menu (or hold down the Alt key while the Go menu is open). This will reveal a shortcut to the Library folder on the Go menu.

You can see several folders inside the app's sandbox folder:

• The Documents folder where the app will put its data files. Currently the Documents folder is empty.

• The Library folder has cache files and preferences files. The contents of this folder are managed by the operating system.

• The SystemData folder, as the name implies is for use by the operating system to store any system level information relevant to the app.

• The tmp folder is for temporary files. Sometimes apps need to create files for temporary usage. You don't want these to clutter up your Documents folder, so tmp is a good place to put them. iOS will clear out this folder from time to time.

It is also possible to get an overview of the Documents folder of apps on your device.

➤ On your device, go to **Settings** → **General** → **iPhone Storage**, scroll down to the list of installed apps (you might have to wait for the list to load) and tap the name of an app.

You'll now see the size of the contents of its Documents folder (but not the actual content):

Viewing the Documents folder info on the device

Save checklist items

In this section you are going to write code that saves the list of to-do items to a file named Checklists.plist when the user adds a new item or edits an existing item. Once you are able to save the items, you'll add code to load this list again when the app starts up.

Plist files

So what is a **.plist** file?

You've already seen a file named Info.plist in the *Bull's Eye* lesson. All apps have one, including the *Checklists* app (see the project navigator). Info.plist contains several configuration options that give iOS additional information about the app, such as what name to display under the app's icon on the home screen.

"plist" stands for Property List and it is an XML file format that stores structured data, usually in the form of a list of settings and their values. Property List files are very common in iOS. They are suitable for many types of data storage, and best of all, they are simple to use. What's not to like?

To save the checklist items, you'll use Swift's `Codable` protocol, which lets objects which support the `Codable` protocol to store themselves in a structured file format.

You actually don't have to care much about that format. In this case it happens to be a .plist file but you're not directly going to mess with that file. All you care about is that the data gets stored in some kind of file in the app's Documents folder, but you'll leave the technical details to `Codable`.

While `Codable` is a new protocol introduced in Swift 4, you have already used its Objective-C cousin, `NSCoder`, behind the scenes because that's exactly how storyboards work. When you add a view controller to a storyboard, Xcode uses the `NSCoder` system to write this object to a file (encoding). Then when your application starts up, it uses `NSCoder` again to read the objects from the storyboard file (decoding). The `Codable` protocol works similarly.

The process of converting objects to files and back again is also known as **serialization**. It's a big topic in software engineering.

I like to think of this whole process as freezing objects. You take a living object and freeze it so that it is suspended in time. You store that frozen object into a file on the device's flash drive where it will spend some time in cryostasis. Later, you can read that file into memory and defrost the object to bring it back to life again.

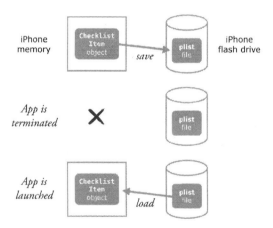

The process of freezing (saving) and unfreezing (loading) objects

Save data to a file

➤ Add the following method to **ChecklistViewController.swift**:

```
func saveChecklistItems() {
   // 1
   let encoder = PropertyListEncoder()
   // 2
   do {
```

```
    // 3
    let data = try encoder.encode(items)
    // 4
    try data.write(to: dataFilePath(),
            options: Data.WritingOptions.atomic)
    // 5
  } catch {
    // 6
    print("Error encoding item array!")
  }
}
```

This method takes the contents of the items array, converts it to a block of binary data, and then writes this data to a file. Let's take the commented lines step-by-step to understand the code:

1. First create an instance of PropertyListEncoder which will encode the items array and all the ChecklistItems in it into some sort of binary data format that can be written to a file.

2. The do keyword, which you have not encountered before, sets up a block of code to catch Swift errors. Swift handles errors under certain conditions by *throwing* an error. In such cases, you need a block of code to catch the error and to handle it. The do keyword indicates the start of such a block. You will see the error catching code after comment #5, where the catch keyword can be seen.

3. The encoder you created in earlier is used to try to encode the items array. The encode method throws a Swift error if it is unable to encode the data for some reason - for example, the data is not in the expected format, or it is corrupted etc. The try keyword indicates that the call to encode can fail and if that happens, that it will throw an error. (If you do not have the try keyword before a call to a method which throws an error, you will get an Xcode error. Try it and see.)If the call to encode fails, execution will immediately jump to the catch block instead of proceeding on to the next line.

4. If the data constant was successfully created by the call to encode in the previous line, then you write the data to a file using the file path returned by a call to dataFilePath(). Note that the write method also can throw an error. So again, you have to precede the method call with another try statement.

5. The catch statement indicates the block of code to be executed if an error was thrown by any line of code in the enclosing do block.

6. Handle the caught error. Here, you simply print out an error mesage to the Xcode Console.

It's not really important that you understand how PropertyListEncoder works internally. The format that it stores the data in is not relevant. All you care about is that it allows you to put your objects into a file and read them back later.

You have to call this new saveChecklistItems() method whenever the list of items is modified.

Exercise: Where in the source code would you call this method?

Answer: Look at where the items array is modified. This happens inside the ItemDetailViewControllerDelegate methods. That's where the party's at!

➤ Add a call to saveChecklistItems() to the end of these methods in **ChecklistViewController.swift**:

```swift
func itemDetailViewController(
              _ controller: ItemDetailViewController,
      didFinishAdding item: ChecklistItem) {
  . . .
  saveChecklistItems()
}
```

```swift
func itemDetailViewController(
              _ controller: ItemDetailViewController,
      didFinishEditing item: ChecklistItem) {
  . . .
  saveChecklistItems()
}
```

➤ Let's not forget the swipe-to-delete function:

```swift
override func tableView(
              _ tableView: UITableView,
      commit editingStyle: UITableViewCellEditingStyle,
        forRowAt indexPath: IndexPath) {
  . . .
  saveChecklistItems()
}
```

➤ And toggling the checkmark on a row on or off:

```swift
override func tableView(_ tableView: UITableView,
          didSelectRowAt indexPath: IndexPath) {
  . . .
  saveChecklistItems()
}
```

The Codable protocol

Just encoding the items array using PropertyListEncoder is not enough. If you were to run the app now and do something that results in a save, such as tapping a row to flip the checkmark, the app will crash (try it out):

Xcode error about Codable support

The Xcode window has switched to the *debugger* and points out which line caused the crash, more or less, but the error message in the source editor is not very helpful. However, if you look at the Console, you'll see a much more descriptive error indicating the issue:

```
fatal error: Array<ChecklistItem> does not conform to Encodable
because ChecklistItem does not conform to Encodable.: file /
Library/Caches/com.apple.xbs/Sources/swiftlang/
swiftlang-900.0.43/src/swift/stdlib/public/core/Codable.swift,
line 3280
```

According to the above error, the PropertyListEncoder was unable to encode the items array because ChecklistItem does not conform to the Encodable protocol. Now you might be wondering where Encodable came from since I only talked about a Codable protocol before.

The thing is, Codable is a protocol which combines two other protocols - Encodable and Decodable. Basically, the Codable protocol encompasses both sides of the seriallization process. But since at this point what you wanted to do was encode something, you get an error about the missing `Encodable` protocol support. If you later tried to decode a `ChecklistItem` you'd get an error about the missing `Decodable` protocol support as well.

Just to clarify, most standard Swift objects and structures support the `Codable` protocol by default. So, you don't get an error here for the `items` array itself. But `ChecklistItem` is a custom object that we created. The issue is with `ChecklistItem` and it is very easy to fix :]

➤ Switch to **ChecklistItem.swift** and modify the `class` line as follows:

```
class ChecklistItem: NSObject, Codable {
```

In the above, you tell the compiler that `ChecklistItem` will conform to the `Codable` protocol. That's all you need to do!

"Now, hold on," I hear you say. "We had to implement methods to support a protocol before. How come we don't have to do that here?"

Remember how I mentioned in a previous chapter that protocols can have default implementations? No? OK, it was in the **Delegates and Protocols** chapter in the section about protocols :] Sometimes, it is useful to have a default implementation for a protocol to provide functionality that would make things easier - or would cover a lot of standard scenarios.

In our case, all of the properties of `ChecklistItem` are standard Swift types and Swift already knows how to encode/decode those types. So, we can simply piggyback on things without having to write any code of our own to implement encoding/decoding in `ChecklistItem`. Handy, eh?

Verify the saved file

➤ Run the app again and tap a row to toggle a checkmark. The app didn't crash? Good!

➤ Go to the Finder window that has the app's Documents directory open:

The Documents directory now contains a Checklists.plist file

There is now a **Checklists.plist** file in the Documents folder, which contains the items from the list.

You can look inside this file if you want, but the contents won't make much sense. Even though it is XML, this file wasn't intended to be read by humans, only by something like PropertyListDecoder, the counterpart to the PropertyListEncoder that we already used.

If you're having trouble viewing the XML, it may be because the plist file isn't stored as text but as a binary format. Some text editors support this file format and can read it as if it were text (TextWrangler is a good one and is a free download on the Mac App Store).

You can also use Finder's Quick Look feature to view the file. Simply select the file in Finder and press the space bar.

Naturally, you can also open the plist file with Xcode.

➤ Right-click the Checklists.plist file and choose **Open With** → **Xcode**.

Checklist.plist in Xcode

It still won't make much sense but it's fun to look at anyway.

Expand some of the rows and you'll see that the names of the ChecklistItems are in there as well as their checked/unchecked state. But exactly how all these data items fit together, might not make much sense to you just yet.

"NS" objects

Objects whose name start with the "NS" prefix, like NSObject, NSString, or NSCoder, are provided by the Foundation framework. NS stands for NextStep, the operating system from the 1990's that later became Mac OS X and which also forms the basis of iOS.

If you are curious about exactly how objects such as NSObbject and NSString work, you can Alt/Option-click any item in your source code to bring up a popup with a brief description. And this works for non-NS prefixed objects too :] In fact, you can look up details about any class, object, variable, or method this way in Xcode.

I use this all the time to remind myself of how to use framework objects and their methods. You can click on any of the blue color items since they are links to more detailed documentation on the topic. That will take you to the Developer Documenation app which lets you read up further on the selected subject.

It's good to have a general idea of what objects are available in the frameworks, but no one can remember all the specifics. So get into the habit of looking up the documentation for any new objects and methods that you encounter. It'll help you learn the iOS frameworks that much quicker!

Load the file

Saving is all well and good, but pretty useless by itself. So, let's also implement the loading of the Checklists.plist file. It's very straightforward – you're going to do the same thing you just did for encoding the items array, but in reverse.

Read data from a file

➤ Switch to **ChecklistViewController.swift** andd add the following new method:

```swift
func loadChecklistItems() {
  // 1
  let path = dataFilePath()
  // 2
  if let data = try? Data(contentsOf: path) {
    // 3
    let decoder = PropertyListDecoder()
    do {
      // 4
      items = try decoder.decode([ChecklistItem].self,
                                 from: data)
    } catch {
      print("Error decoding item array!")
    }
  }
}
```

Let's go through this step-by-step:

1. First you put the results of `dataFilePath()` in a temporary constant named `path`.

2. Try to load the contents of Checklists.plist into a new `Data` object. The `try?` command attempts to create the `Data` object, but returns `nil` if it fails. That's why you put it in an `if let` statement.

   Why would it fail? If there is no Checklists.plist then there are obviously no `ChecklistItem` objects to load. This is what happens when the app is started up for the very first time. In that case, you'll skip the rest of this method.

   Also, do notice that this is another way to use the `try` statement - instead of enclosing the `try` statement within a `do` block, like you did previously, you can have a `try?` statement which indicates that the `try` could fail and if it does, that it will return `nil`. Whether you use the `do` block approach or this one, is completely up to you.

3. When the app does find a Checklists.plist file, you'll load the entire array and its contents from the file using a `PropertyListDecoder`. So, create the decoder instance.

4. Load the saved data back into `items` using the decoder's `decode` method. The only item of interest here would be the first parameter passed to `decode`. The decoder needs to know what type of data will be the result of the decode operation and you let it know by indicating that it will be an array of `ChecklistItem` objects.

This populates the array with exact copies of the `ChecklistItem` objects that were frozen into the Checklists.plist file.

You now have your `loadChecklistItems()` method, but it needs to be called from somewhere in order for this to work. There are several places from which you can do this.

Take a look at the current coder in **ChecklistViewController.swift** - you have `init?(coder:)` which currently populates the static data displayed by the app, but you also have `viewDidLoad()` which is called when the view controller is first loaded. So which should you use?

The difference between the two is this - `init?(coder:)` is called only when the view controller is created from a storyboard. However, view controllers could also be instantiated from code, as you'll find out later. So, in the second case, depending on how you write your code, `init?(coder:)` might not be called, but `viewDidLoad()` will always be called for a view controller no matter how the view controller was created.

So, my vote is to delete the `init?(coder:)` implementation (to get rid of the static data that is loaded on app start up), and to call `loadChecklistItems()` from `viewDidLoad()`. (If you decide to go the other way, do remember to clean up `init?`

(`coder:`) so as to remove the static item loading.)

Load the saved data on app start

Here's what you need to do:

➤ Change the following line in **ChecklistViewController.swift** (at the very top):

```
var items: [ChecklistItem]
```

To:

```
var items = [ChecklistItem]()
```

The only difference between the two is that in the former, you declare `items` as being an array of `ChecklistItem` objects, but you don't initialize it, in the latter, you initialize `items` to be an empty `CheklistItem` array.

Now, when `ChecklistViewController` is created, it would have `items` initialized to an empty array instead of you having to do this explicitly in an `init` method or in `viewDidLoad`. Personally, I find it easier and simpler to have variable (or constant) declarations and initializations at the same place where possibble. Again, you can follow whichever practice which best suits you - there is no right or wrong way :]

➤ Remove the `init?(coder:)` method from **ChecklistViewController.swift**.

Now that you initialize the `items` array at the top of the class, you don't have any code in `init?(coder:)` that is useful. So, you can delete all the static item creation code (and the method itself) to clean up your code a bit.

➤ Add a call to `loadChecklistItems()` in `viewDidLoad()` so that the method looks like this:

```
override func viewDidLoad() {
    super.viewDidLoad()
    // Enable large titles
    navigationController?.navigationBar.prefersLargeTitles = true
    // Load items
    loadChecklistItems()
}
```

You don't need to add the comments in there but its always good to have some comments in your source so that you can understand your own code a month or two (or a few years) down the line :]

All that's changed in the above is the addition of a call to `loadChecklistItems()` to ensure that the saved item data is loaded back when the view controller is first loaded.

➤ Run the app and make some changes to the to-do items. Press Stop to terminate the app. Start it again and notice that your changes are still there.

➤ Stop the app again. Go to the Finder window with the Documents folder and remove the Checklists.plist file. Run the app once more. You should now have an empty list of items.

➤ Add an item and notice that the Checklists.plist file re-appears.

Awesome! You've written an app that not only lets you add and edit data, but which also persists the data between sessions. These techniques form the basis of many, many apps.

Being able to use a navigation controller, show secondary screens, and pass data around through delegates are essential iOS development skills.

Initializers

Methods named `init` are special in Swift. They are only used when you're creating new objects, to make those new objects ready for use.

Think of it as having bought new clothes. The clothes are in your possession (the memory for the object is allocated) but they're still in the bag. You need to go change and put the new clothes on (initialization) before you're ready to go out and party.

When you write the following to create a new object,

```
let item = ChecklistItem()
```

Swift first allocates a chunk of memory big enough to hold the new object and then calls `ChecklistItem`'s `init()` method with no parameters.

It is pretty common for objects to have more than one init method. Which one is used depends on the circumstances.

For example, amongst the `init` methods for `UITableViewController` you'll find - `init(nibName:bundle:)`, `init(style:)` and the one you've already seen, `init?(coder:)`. As you've already learnt, `init?(coder:)` is used when the view controller is instantiated from a storyboard. But you can also create a `UITableViewController` instance directly by calling either `init(nibName:bundle:)` or `init(style:)`. So, how you initialize an object depends on the circumstances.

The implementations of these `init` methods, whether they're just called `init()` or `init?(coder:)` or something else, always follow the same series of steps. When you write your own `init` methods, you need to stick to those steps as well.

This is the standard way to write an `init` method:

```
init() {
    // Put values into your instance variables and constants.

    super.init()

    // Other initialization code, such as calling methods, goes
    here.
}
```

Note that unlike other methods, `init` does not have the `func` keyword.

Sometimes you'll see it written as `override init` or `required init?`. That is necessary when you're adding the `init` method to an object that is a subclass of some other object. Much more about that later.

The question mark is for when `init?` can potentially fail and return a `nil` value instead of a real object. You can imagine that decoding an object can fail if not enough information is present in the plist file.

Inside the `init` method, you first need to make sure that all your instance variables and constants have a value. Recall that in Swift all variables must always have a value, except for optionals.

When you declare an instance variable you can give it an initial value (or initialize it), like so:

```
var checked = false
```

It's also possible to write just the variable name and its type (or declare the variable), but not give the variable a value yet:

```
var checked: Bool
```

In the latter case, you have to give this variable a value in your `init` method:

```
init() {
    checked = false
    super.init()
}
```

You must use either one of these approaches; if you don't give the variable a value at all, Swift considers this an error. The only exception is optionals, they do not need to have a value (in which case they are `nil`).

Once you've given all your instance variables and constants values, you call `super.init()` to initialize the object's superclass. If you haven't done any object-oriented programming at all, you may not know what a *superclass* is. That's fine; we'll completely ignore this topic till later.

Just remember that sometimes objects need to send messages to something called `super` and if you forget to do this, bad things are likely to happen.

After calling `super.init()`, you can do additional initialization, such as calling the object's own methods. You're not allowed to do that before the call to `super.init()` because Swift has no guarantee that your object's variables all have proper values until then.

You don't always need to provide an `init` method. If your `init` method doesn't need to do anything – if there are no instance variables to fill in – then you can leave it out completely and the compiler will provide one for you. As an example, take a look at `ChecklistItem` - it doesn't have an `init()` method since all its variables are initialized when they are declared.

Swift's rules for initializers can be a bit complicated, but fortunately the compiler will remind you when you forget to provide an `init` method.

What next?

Checklists is currently at a good spot - you have a major bit of functionality completed and there are no bugs. This is a good time to take a break, put your feet up, and daydream about all the cool apps you'll soon be writing :]

It's also smart to go back and repeat those parts you're still a bit fuzzy about. Don't rush through these chapters – there are no prizes for finishing first. Rather than going fast, take your time to truly understand what you've been doing.

As always, feel free to change the app and experiment. Breaking things is allowed – even encouraged – here at iOS Apprentice Academy!

You can find the project files for the app up to this point under **15 - Saving and Loading** in the Source Code folder.

Chapter 16: Lists

Just to make sure you truly get everything you've done so far, next up, you'll expand the app with new features that more or less repeat what you just did.

But I'll also throw in a few twists to keep it interesting...

The app is named *Checklists* for a reason: it allows you to keep more than one list of to-do items. So far though, the app has only supported a single list. Now you'll add the capability to handle multiple checklists.

In order to complete the functionality for this chapter, you will need two new screens, and that means two new view controllers:

1. `AllListsViewController` shows all the user's lists.

2. `ListDetailViewController` allows adding a new list and editing the name and icon of an existing list.

This chapter covers the following:

- **The All Lists view controllers:** Add a new view controller to show all the lists of to-do items.

- **The All Lists UI:** Complete the user interface for the All Lists screen.

- **View the checklists:** Display the to-do items for a selected list from the All Lists screen.

- **Manage checkists:** Add a view controller to add/edit checklists.

The All Lists view controller

You will first add `AllListsViewController`. This becomes the new main screen of the app.

When you're done, this is what it will look like:

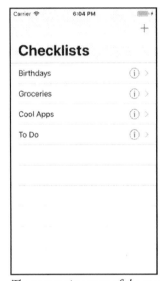

The new main screen of the app

This screen is very similar to what you created before. It's a table view controller that shows a list of `Checklist` objects (not `ChecklistItem` objects).

From now on, I will refer to this screen as the "All Lists" screen, and to the screen that shows the to-do items from a single checklist as the "Checklist" screen.

Add the new view controller

➤ Right-click the Checklists group in the project navigator and choose **New File**. Choose the **Cocoa Touch Class** template (under iOS, Source).

In the next step, choose the following options:

- Class: **AllListsViewController**
- Subclass of: **UITableViewController**
- Also create XIB file: Make sure this is **not** checked
- Language: **Swift**

Choosing the options for the new view controller

> **Note:** Make sure the "Subclass of" field is set to **UITableViewController**, not "UIViewController". Also be careful that Xcode didn't rename what you typed into Class to "AllListsTableViewController" with the extra word "Table" when you change the "Subclass of" value. It can be sneaky like that...

➤ Press **Next** and then **Create** to finish.

As you might remember from a previous chapter, the Xcode template for a table view controller puts a lot of stuff in this new file that you don't need. The template assumes you'll fill in this placeholder code (known as *boilerplate* code) before you run the app. Let's clean that up first.

You'll also put some fake data in the table view just to get it up and running. As you know by now, I always like to take as small a step as possible and then run the app to see if it's working. Once everything works, you can move forward and put in the real data.

Clean up the boilerplate code

➤ In **AllListsViewController.swift**, remove the `numberOfSections(in:)` method. Without it, there will always be a single section in the table view.

➤ Change the `tableView(_:numberOfRowsInSection:)` method to:

```
override func tableView(_ tableView: UITableView,
      numberOfRowsInSection section: Int) -> Int {
   return 3
}
```

➤ Implement the `tableView(_:cellForRowAt:)` method to put some text into the cells, just so there is something to see.

Note that the boilerplate code already contains a commented-out version of this method. You can uncomment it by removing the /* and */ surrounding the method, and make your changes there.

```
override func tableView(_ tableView: UITableView,
```

```
                          cellForRowAt indexPath: IndexPath) ->
UITableViewCell {

    let cell = makeCell(for: tableView)
    cell.textLabel!.text = "List \(indexPath.row)"
    return cell
}
```

In `ChecklistViewController` the table view used prototype cells that you designed in Interface Builder. Just for the fun of it, in `AllListsViewController` you are taking a different approach where you'll create the cells in code instead.

➤ That requires you to add the following helper method:

```
func makeCell(for tableView: UITableView) -> UITableViewCell {
    let cellIdentifier = "Cell"
    if let cell =
            tableView.dequeueReusableCell(withIdentifier:
cellIdentifier) {
        return cell
    } else {
        return UITableViewCell(style: .default,
                               reuseIdentifier: cellIdentifier)
    }
}
```

Later on I'll explain in more detail how this works, but for now recognize that you're using `dequeueReusableCell(withIdentifier:)` here too. If it returns `nil`, there is no cell that can be recycled and you construct a new one with `UITableViewCell(style:reuseIdentifier:)`.

The reason you put this logic into a separate method is so that it keeps the code in `tableView(_:cellForRowAt:)` simple and clean. I find it more readable that way.

➤ Remove all the commented-out cruft from **AllListsViewController.swift**. Xcode puts it there to be helpful, but it also makes a mess of things.

Special comments

You might have noticed lines like the following in the boilerplate code in **AllListsViewController.swift**:

```
// MARK: - Table view data source
```

If you were wondering what they were, here's the scoop. Of course, you already know that they are comments, because the lines being with //, but they are not *just* comments. As the keyword at the beginning of the comment line, MARK, indicates, they are markers. But markers for what?

They are markers to organize the code and for you to find a section of code (for example, a set of related methods, like for table view delegates) via the Xcode Jump Bar. Take a look at the method list for **AllListsViewController.swift** in the Xcode Jump Bar:

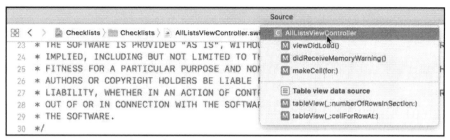

The Xcode Jump Bar with code organization

Notice the separator line in the middle of the list of methods? Do you notice the bolded text title right after? Does that seem familiar?

The text you provide after the MARK: keyword defines how the section title is displayed in the menu. If you put in a hyphen (-), you get a separator line followed by any text after the hyphen as the section title. If you don't provide a hyphen but provide some text, then you simply get a section title but no separator. If you provide neither, then you just get a section icon with no text and no separator. (Try these out.)

There are a couple of other comment tags besides MARK: that you can use in your Swift files. These are TODO: and FIXME:. The first is generally used to indicate portions of your code that need to be completed, while the latter is used to mark portions of code that need re-writing or fixing.

Consider using these tags to organize your code better. When you are in a hurry and need to find that particular bit of code in a long source file, they come in very handy. I certainly use them all the time in my own code :]

Storyboard changes

The final step is to add the new view controller to the storyboard.

➤ Open the storyboard and drag a new **Table View Controller** onto the canvas. Put it somewhere near the initial navigation controller.

➤ **Control-drag** from the navigation controller to this new table view controller:

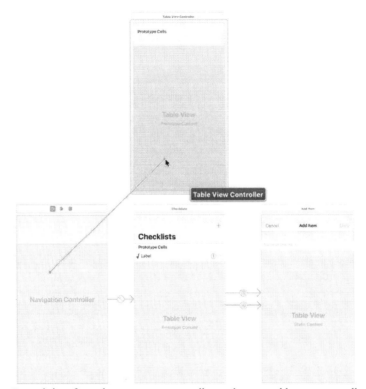

Control-drag from the navigation controller to the new table view controller

From the popup menu choose **Relationship Segue - root view controller**:

Relationships are also segues

This will break the existing connection between the navigation controller and the ChecklistViewController so that "Checklists" is no longer the app's main screen.

➤ Select the new table view controller and set its **Class** in the **Identity inspector** to **AllListsViewController**.

➤ Select the new view controller's Navigation Item in the Document Outline and then change its title to **Checklists** via the Attributes Inspector.

This may make Xcode rename the view controller in the Document Outline from All Lists View Controller to just Checklists. (Sometimes it won't happen till you restart Xcode.) This is a bit confusing because there's a Checklists view controller already.

It's simple enough to fix the scene names. Normally, the scene name is based on either the underlying view controller name or the navigation item title. But you can set whatever you want as the scene name by simply changing the displayed title on the Document Outline :]

➤ Tap the new view controller in the Document Outline (the yellow circle, not the rectangle representing the scene) and then tap it again to put the title into edit mode. Then, just rename it to **All Lists**.

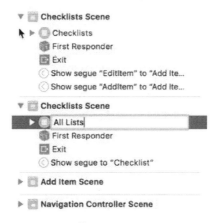

Rename scene

➤ Repeat the above step to rename the remaining Checklists scene to **Checklist** (note the missing "s" at the end).

You may want to reorganize your storyboard at this point to make everything look neat again. The All Lists scene goes in between the other scenes.

As I mentioned, you're not going to use prototype cells for this table view. It would be perfectly fine if you did, and as an exercise you could rewrite the code to use prototype cells later, but I want to show you another way of making table view cells.

➤ Delete the empty prototype cell from the All Lists scene. (Simply select the Table View Cell and press **delete** on your keyboard.)

➤ **Control-drag** from the yellow circle icon at the top of All Lists scene on to the Checklist scene and create a **Show** segue.

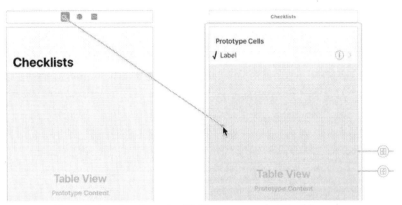

Control-dragging from the All Lists scene to the Checklist scene

This adds a "push" transition from the All Lists screen to the Checklist screen. It also puts the navigation bar back on the Checklist scene (the one on the right).

➤ Double-click the navigation bar on the Checklist scene to change its title to (**Name of the Checklist**). This is just placeholder text.

Note that the new segue isn't attached to any button or table view cell.

There is nothing on the All Lists screen that you can tap or otherwise interact with in order to trigger this segue. That means you have to perform the segue programmatically.

Perform a segue via code

➤ Click on the new segue to select it, go to the **Attributes inspector** and give it the identifier **ShowChecklist**.

The segue **Kind** should be **Show (e.g. Push)** because you're pushing the Checklist View Controller onto the navigation stack when performing this segue.

➤ In **AllListsViewController.swift**, add the `tableView(_:didSelectRowAt:)` method:

```swift
override func tableView(_ tableView: UITableView,
          didSelectRowAt indexPath: IndexPath) {
  performSegue(withIdentifier: "ShowChecklist", sender: nil)
}
```

Recall that this table view delegate method is invoked when you tap a row.

Previously, a tap on a row would automatically perform the segue because you had hooked up the segue to the prototype cell. However, the table view for this screen isn't using prototype cells. Therefore, you have to perform the segue manually.

That's simple enough: just call performSegue(withIdentifier:sender:) with the name of the segue and things will start moving.

➤ Run the app. It now looks like this:

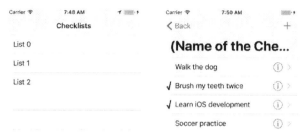

The first version of the All Lists screen (left). Tapping a row opens the Checklist screen (right).

Tap a row and the familiar ChecklistViewController slides into the screen.

You can tap the "Back" button in the top-left to go back to the main list. Now you're truly using the power of the navigation controller!

Fix the titles

Notice something about the titles on the two screens? (This only happens if you configured large titles via code. If you have been setting large titles via storyboard, then you simply have to change the Navigation Item setting on the Checklist scene and ignore the rest of the "Fix the titles" section.)

The second screen, Checklist, has the large title while the first one doesn't! This is because we originally set up large titles for ChecklistViewController.swift.

Exercise: Can you fix the titles on your own so that the large titles are enabled by AllListsViewController.swift and the Checklist screen does not show a large title?

The change is simple enough to implement.

➤ Move the following lines of code from viewDidLoad in **ChecklistViewController.swift** to viewDidLoad in **AllListsViewController.swift**:

```
// Enable large titles
navigationController?.navigationBar.prefersLargeTitles = true
```

➤ Add this code to viewDidLoad in **ChecklistViewController.swift**:

```
// Disable large titles for this view controller
navigationItem.largeTitleDisplayMode = .never
```

In each case, the comments explain what the code does :]

Run the app again and you should see that the titles now display correctly.

Carrier 🔋	8:01 AM	▓▓▓▸	Carrier 🔋	8:03 AM	▓▓▸
			‹ Back	(Name of the Checklist) ＋	
Checklists			Walk the dog		ⓘ ›
			✓ Brush my teeth twice		ⓘ ›
List 0			✓ Learn iOS development		ⓘ ›
List 1			Soccer practice		ⓘ ›
List 2					

The All Lists screen now shows large titles.

The All Lists UI

You're going to duplicate most of the functionality from the Checklist View Controller for this new All Lists screen.

There will be a + button at the top that lets users add new checklists, they can do swipe-to-delete, and they can tap the disclosure button to edit the name of the checklist.

Of course, you'll also save the array of Checklist objects to the Checklists.plist file.

As you've already seen how this works, we'll go through the steps a bit quicker this time.

The data model

You begin by creating a data model object that represents a checklist.

➤ Add a new file to the project based on the **Cocoa Touch Class** template. Name it **Checklist** and make it a subclass of **NSObject**. (Also make sure that the language is set to **Swift**.)

This adds the file Checklist.swift to the project.

Just like ChecklistItem, you're building Checklist on top of NSObject. As you found out previously, this is a requirement when you need to compare objects (in order to find a list item in an array of lists).

➤ Give **Checklist.swift** a name property:

```swift
import UIKit

class Checklist: NSObject {
  var name = ""
}
```

Next, you'll give `AllListsViewController` an array that will store these new `Checklist` objects.

➤ Add a new instance variable to **AllListsViewController.swift**:

```
var lists = [Checklist]()
```

This is an array that will hold the `Checklist` objects.

> **Note:** You can also write the above as follows:
>
> ```
> var lists = Array<Checklist>()
> ```
>
> The version with the square brackets is what's known as *syntactic sugar* for the complete notation, which is `Array<`*type of the objects to put in the array*`>`.
>
> You will see both forms used in Swift programs and they do exactly the same thing. Because arrays are used a lot, the designers of Swift included the handy shorthand with the square brackets.

As a first step, you will fill this new array with test data, which you'll do from `viewDidLoad()` as before. Remember that UIKit automatically invokes this method when the view controller is first loaded.

Dummy data

In **AllListsViewController.swift** you could add the following to `viewDidLoad()` (don't actually add it just yet, just read along with the description):

```
// 1
var list = Checklist()
list.name = "Birthdays"
lists.append(list)

// 2
list = Checklist()
list.name = "Groceries"
lists.append(list)

list = Checklist()
list.name = "Cool Apps"
lists.append(list)

list = Checklist()
list.name = "To Do"
lists.append(list)
```

You've seen something very much like it a while ago when you added the fake test data to ChecklistViewController. Here is what it does step-by-step:

1. Create a new Checklist object, give it a name, and add it to the array.

2. You create three more Checklist objects. Because you declared the local variable list as var instead of let, you can re-use it.

Notice how this is performing the same two steps for every new Checklist object you're creating?

```
list = Checklist()
list.name = "Name of the checklist"
```

It seems likely that every Checklist you'll ever make will also have a name. You can make this a requirement by writing your own init method that takes the name as a parameter. Then you can simply write:

```
list = Checklist(name: "Name of the checklist")
```

➤ Go to **Checklist.swift** and add the new init method:

```
init(name: String) {
    self.name = name
    super.init()
}
```

This initializer takes one parameter, name, and places it into the property called name.

Notice that while the parameter and property are both named name - they are two distinct entities. So, you use self.name to refer to the property (or instance variable, if you prefer that term).

If you used this code instead:

```
init(name: String) {
    name = name
    super.init()
}
```

Then Swift wouldn't understand that the first name referred to the property.

To disambiguate, you use self. Recall that self refers to the object that you're in, so self.name means the name variable of the current Checklist object.

➤ Go back to **AllListsViewController.swift** and add the following code to the end of `viewDidLoad()`, for real this time:

```
override func viewDidLoad() {
  . . .
  // Add placeholder data
  var list = Checklist(name: "Birthdays")
  lists.append(list)

  list = Checklist(name: "Groceries")
  lists.append(list)

  list = Checklist(name: "Cool Apps")
  lists.append(list)

  list = Checklist(name: "To Do")
  lists.append(list)
}
```

That's a bit shorter than what I showed you before, and it guarantees that new Checklist objects will now always have their name property filled in.

Note that you don't write:

```
var list = Checklist.init(name: "Birthdays")
```

Even though the method is named `init`, it's not a regular method. Initializers are only used to construct new objects and you write that as:

```
var object = ObjectName(parameter1: value1, parameter2:
value2, . . .)
```

Depending on the parameters that you specified, Swift will locate the corresponding `init` method and call that.

Clear? Great! Let's continue building the All Lists screen.

Display data in table view

➤ Change the `tableView(_:numberOfRowsInSection:)` method to return the number of objects in the new array:

```
override func tableView(_ tableView: UITableView,
      numberOfRowsInSection section: Int) -> Int {
  return lists.count
}
```

➤ Finally, change `tableView(_:cellForRowAt:)` to fill in the cells for the rows:

```
override func tableView(_ tableView: UITableView,
            cellForRowAt indexPath: IndexPath)
            -> UITableViewCell {
  let cell = makeCell(for: tableView)
  // Update cell informaiton
  let checklist = lists[indexPath.row]
  cell.textLabel!.text = checklist.name
  cell.accessoryType = .detailDisclosureButton

  return cell
}
```

➤ Run the app. It should look like this:

The table view shows Checklist objects

It has a table view with cells representing `Checklist` objects. The rest of the screen doesn't do much yet, but it's a start.

The many ways to make table view cells

Creating a new table view cell in `AllListsViewController` is a little more involved than how it was done in `ChecklistViewController`. There you just did the following to obtain a new table view cell:

```
let cell = tableView.dequeueReusableCell(
            withIdentifier: "ChecklistItem", for: indexPath)
```

But here you have a whole chunk of code to accomplish the same:

```
let cellIdentifier = "Cell"
if let cell =
      tableView.dequeueReusableCell(
                        withIdentifier: cellIdentifier) {
  return cell
} else {
  return UITableViewCell(style: .default,
```

```
                        reuseIdentifier: cellIdentifier)
    }
```

The call to dequeueReusableCell(withIdentifier:) is still there, except that previously the storyboard had a prototype cell with that identifier and now it doesn't.

If the table view cannot find a cell to re-use (and it won't until it has enough cells to fill the entire visible area), this method will return nil and you have to create your own cell by hand. That's what happens in the else branch.

There are actually two versions of dequeueReusableCell, one with an extra for parameter that takes an IndexPath, and one without. Here you're using the one without. The difference is that dequeueReusableCell(withIdentifier:for:) only works with prototype cells. If you tried to use it here, it would crash the app.

There are four ways that you can make table view cells:

1. Using prototype cells. This is the simplest and quickest way. You did this in ChecklistViewController.

2. Using static cells. You did this for the Add/Edit Item screen. Static cells are limited to screens where you know in advance which cells you'll have. The big advantage with static cells is that you don't need to provide any of the data source methods (cellForRowAt etc.).

3. Using a *nib* file. A nib (also known as a XIB) is like a mini storyboard that only contains a single customized UITableViewCell object. This is very similar to using prototype cells, except that you can do it outside of a storyboard.

4. By hand, what you did above. This is how you were supposed to do it in the early days of iOS. Chances are, you'll run across code examples that do it this way, especially from older articles and books. It's a bit more work, but also offers you the most flexibility.

When you create a cell by hand, you specify a certain **cell style**, which gives you a cell with a preconfigured layout that already has labels and an image view.

For the All Lists scene you're using the "Default" style. Later on you'll switch it to "Subtitle", which gives the cell a second, smaller label below the main label.

Using standard cell styles means you don't have to design your own cell layout. For many apps these standard layouts are sufficient, so that saves you some work.

Prototype cells and static cells can also use these standard cell styles. The default style for a prototype or static cell is "Custom", which requires you to use your own labels, but you can change that to one of the built-in styles via Interface Builder.

And finally, a gentle warning: Sometimes I see code that creates a new cell for every row rather than trying to reuse cells. Don't do that! Always ask the table view first whether it has a cell available that can be recycled, using one of the dequeueReusableCell methods.

Creating a new cell for each row will cause your app to slow down, as object creation is slower than simply re-using an existing object. Creating all these new objects also takes up more memory, a precious commodity on mobile devices. For the best performance, reuse those cells!

View the checklists

Right now, the data model consists of the lists array from AllListsViewController that contains a handful of Checklist objects. There is also a separate items array in ChecklistViewController with ChecklistItem objects.

You may have noticed that when you tap the name of a list, the Checklist screen slides into view but it currently always shows the same to-do items, regardless of which list you tapped on.

Each checklist should really have its own to-do items. You'll work on that later on, as this requires a significant change to the data model.

As a start, let's set the title of the Checklist screen to reflect the chosen checklist.

Set the title of the screen

➤ Add a new instance variable to **ChecklistViewController.swift**:

```
var checklist: Checklist!
```

I'll explain why the exclamation mark is necessary in a moment.

➤ Change viewDidLoad in **ChecklistViewController.swift** to:

```
override func viewDidLoad() {
   . . .
   title = checklist.name
}
```

This changes the title of the screen, which is shown in the navigation bar, to the name of the Checklist object.

You'll pass the necessary Checklist object to ChecklistViewController when the segue is performed.

➤ In **AllListsViewController.swift**, update `tableView(_:didSelectRowAt:)` to the following:

```
override func tableView(_ tableView: UITableView,
          didSelectRowAt indexPath: IndexPath) {
  let checklist = lists[indexPath.row]
  performSegue(withIdentifier: "ShowChecklist",
                    sender: checklist)
}
```

As before, you use `performSegue()` to start the segue. This method has a `sender` parameter that you previously set to `nil`. Now you'll use it to send along the `Checklist` object from the row that the user tapped on.

You can put anything you want into `sender`. If the segue is performed by the storyboard (rather than manually like you do here) then `sender` will refer to the control that triggered it, for example, the `UIBarButtonItem` object for the Add button, or the `UITableViewCell` for a row in the table.

But because you start this particular segue by hand, you can put whatever is most convenient into `sender`.

Putting the `Checklist` object into the `sender` parameter doesn't pass it to `ChecklistViewController` yet. That happens in "prepare-for-segue", which you still need to add for this view controller.

➤ Add the `prepare(for:sender:)` method to **AllListsViewController.swift**:

```
override func prepare(for segue: UIStoryboardSegue,
                      sender: Any?) {
  if segue.identifier == "ShowChecklist" {
    let controller = segue.destination
                     as! ChecklistViewController
    controller.checklist = sender as! Checklist
  }
}
```

You've seen this method before. `prepare(for:sender:)` is called right before the segue happens. Here you get a chance to set the properties of the new view controller before it becomes visible.

Inside `prepare(for:sender:)`, you need to pass the `ChecklistViewController` the `Checklist` object from the row that the user tapped. That's why you put that object in the `sender` parameter earlier.

(You could have temporarily stored the `Checklist` object in an instance variable instead, but passing it along in the `sender` parameter is much easier and cleaner.)

All of this happens a short time after `ChecklistViewController` is instantiated but just before `ChecklistViewController`'s view is loaded. That means its `viewDidLoad()` method is called after `prepare(for:sender:)`.

At this point, the view controller's `checklist` property is set to the `Checklist` object from `sender`, and `viewDidLoad()` can set the title of the screen accordingly.

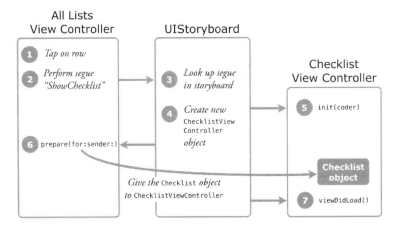

The steps involved in performing a segue

This sequence of events is why the `checklist` property is declared as `Checklist!` with an exclamation point. That allows its value to be temporarily `nil` until `viewDidLoad()` happens.

`nil` is normally not an allowed value for non-optional variables in Swift but by using the `!` you override that.

Does this sound an awful lot like optionals? The exclamation point turns `checklist` into a special kind of optional. It's very similar to optionals with a question mark, but you don't have to write `if let` to unwrap it.

Such *implicitly unwrapped* optionals should be used sparingly and with care, as they do not have any of the anti-crash protection that normal optionals do.

➤ Run the app and notice that when you tap the row for a checklist, the next screen properly displays the checklist title.

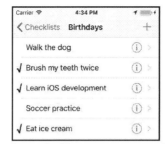

The name of the chosen checklist now appears in the navigation bar

Note that passing the `Checklist` object to the `ChecklistViewController` does not make a copy of it.

You only pass the view controller a *reference* to that object – any changes the user makes to that `Checklist` object are also seen by `AllListsViewController`.

Both view controllers have access to the exact same `Checklist` object. You'll use that to your advantage later in order to add new `ChecklistItems` to the selected `Checklist`.

Type Casts

In `prepare(for:sender:)` you do this:

```
override func prepare(for segue: UIStoryboardSegue,
                      sender: Any?) {
  . . .
  controller.checklist = sender as! Checklist
  . . .
}
```

What is that `as! Checklist` bit?

If you've been paying attention – of course you have! – then you've seen this "as something" used quite a few times now. This is known as a *type cast*.

A type cast tells Swift to interpret a value as having a different data type.

(It's the opposite of what happens to certain actors in the movies. For them, typecasting results in always playing the same character; in Swift, a type cast actually changes the character of an object.)

Here, `sender` has type `Any?`, meaning that it can be any sort of object: a `UIBarButtonItem`, a `UITableViewCell`, or in this case, a `Checklist`. Thanks to the question mark it can even be `nil`.

But the `controller.checklist` property always expects a `Checklist` object – it wouldn't know what to do with a `UITableViewCell`... Hence, Swift demands that you only put `Checklist` objects into the `checklist` property.

By writing `sender as! Checklist`, you tell Swift that it can safely treat `sender` as a `Checklist` object and to force unwrap it (since the `sender` is an optional).

Another example of a typecast is:

```
let controller = segue.destination as! ChecklistViewController
```

The segue's `destination` property refers to the view controller on the receiving end of the segue. But obviously the engineers at Apple could not predict beforehand that we would call it `ChecklistViewController`.

So you have to cast it from its generic type (`UIViewController`) to the specific type used in this app (`ChecklistViewController`) before you can access any of its properties.

Similar to the `as!` type cast, there is also `as?` with a question mark. This is for casting optionals, or when the type cast is allowed to fail. You'll see some examples of that later.

Don't worry if any of this goes over your head right now. You'll see plenty more examples of type casting in action.

The main reason you need all these type casts is for interoperability with the iOS frameworks that are written in Objective-C. Swift is less forgiving about types than Objective-C and requires you to be much more explicit about types.

Manage checklists

Let's quickly add the Add Checklist / Edit Checklist screen. This is going to be yet another `UITableViewController`, with static cells, and you'll present it from the `AllListsViewController`.

If the previous sentence made perfect sense to you, then you're getting the hang of this!

Add the view controller

➤ Add a new file to the project, **ListDetailViewController.swift**. You can use the **Swift File** template for this since you'll be adding the complete view controller implementation by hand.

➤ Add the following to **ListDetailViewController.swift**:

```
import UIKit

protocol ListDetailViewControllerDelegate: class {
  func listDetailViewControllerDidCancel(
```

```
            _ controller: ListDetailViewController)
   func listDetailViewController(
          _ controller: ListDetailViewController,
          didFinishAdding checklist: Checklist)

   func listDetailViewController(
          _ controller: ListDetailViewController,
          didFinishEditing checklist: Checklist)
}

class ListDetailViewController: UITableViewController,
                               UITextFieldDelegate {
  @IBOutlet weak var textField: UITextField!
  @IBOutlet weak var doneBarButton: UIBarButtonItem!

  weak var delegate: ListDetailViewControllerDelegate?

  var checklistToEdit: Checklist?
}
```

I simply took the contents of **ItemDetailViewController.swift** and changed the names. Also, instead of a property for a `ChecklistItem` you're now dealing with a `Checklist`.

➤ Add the `viewDidLoad()` method:

```
override func viewDidLoad() {
  super.viewDidLoad()
  // Disable large titles for this view controller
  navigationItem.largeTitleDisplayMode = .never

  if let checklist = checklistToEdit {
    title = "Edit Checklist"
    textField.text = checklist.name
    doneBarButton.isEnabled = true
  }
}
```

This changes the title of the screen if the user is editing an existing checklist, and it puts the checklist's name into the text field already.

➤ Also add the `viewWillAppear()` method to pop up the keyboard:

```
override func viewWillAppear(_ animated: Bool) {
  super.viewWillAppear(animated)
  textField.becomeFirstResponder()
}
```

The Cancel and Done buttons

➤ Add the action methods for the Cancel and Done buttons:

```
// MARK:- Actions
@IBAction func cancel() {
    delegate?.listDetailViewControllerDidCancel(self)
}

@IBAction func done() {
    if let checklist = checklistToEdit {
        checklist.name = textField.text!
        delegate?.listDetailViewController(self,
                        didFinishEditing: checklist)
    } else {
        let checklist = Checklist(name: textField.text!)
        delegate?.listDetailViewController(self,
                        didFinishAdding: checklist)
    }
}
```

This should look familiar as well. It's essentially the same as what the Add/Edit Item screen does.

To create the new Checklist object in done(), you use its init(name:) method and pass the contents of textField.text as the name parameter.

You cannot write this the way you did for ChecklistItems – this won't work:

```
let checklist = Checklist()
checklist.name = textField.text!
```

Because Checklist does not have an init() method that takes no parameters, writing Checklist() results in a compiler error. It only has an init(name:) method, and you must always use that initializer to create new Checklist objects.

Other functionality

➤ Also make sure the user cannot select the table cell with the text field:

```
// MARK:- TableView Delegates
override func tableView(_ tableView: UITableView,
            willSelectRowAt indexPath: IndexPath) -> IndexPath? {
    return nil
}
```

➤ And finally, add the text field delegate method that enables or disables the Done button depending on whether the text field is empty or not.

```
// MARK:- UITextField Delegates
func textField(_ textField: UITextField,
               shouldChangeCharactersIn range: NSRange,
               replacementString string: String) -> Bool {

  let oldText = textField.text!
  let stringRange = Range(range, in:oldText)!
  let newText = oldText.replacingCharacters(in: stringRange,
                                            with: string)
  doneBarButton.isEnabled = !newText.isEmpty
  return true
}
```

Again, this is the same as what you did in `ItemDetailViewController`.

Let's create the user interface for this new view controller in Interface Builder.

The storyboard

➤ Open the storyboard. Drag a new **Table View Controller** from the Object Library on to the canvas and move it below the other view controllers.

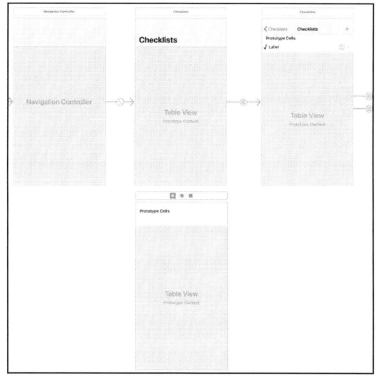

Adding a new table view controller to the canvas

➤ Select the new Table View Controller and go to the **Identity inspector**. Change its class to **ListDetailViewController**.

➤ **Control-drag** from the yellow cirlce at the top of the All Lists scene to the new scene. Select **Show** from the Manual Segue section of the popup menu.

➤ Add a Navigation Item to the new scene.

➤ Change the navigation bar title from "Title" to **Add Checklist**. (The new scene should now appear as Add Checklist scene in the Document Outline.)

➤ Select the Navigation Item and set **Large Title** in the Attributes inspector to **Never**.

➤ Add **Cancel** and **Done** bar button items and hook them up to the action methods in the Add Checklist scene. Also connect the Done button to the **doneBarButton** outlet and uncheck its **Enabled** option.

Remember, you can Control-drag from a button to the view controller to connect it to an action method. To connect an outlet, do it the other way around: Control-drag from the view controller to the button.

Tip: My Xcode acted a bit buggy and wouldn't let me drop the bar buttons on the navigation bar. If this happens to you too, drop them on the navigation item – now called Add Checklist – in the Document Outline. You can also Control-drag in the Document Outline to make the connections to the actions and the outlet.

➤ Change the table view to **Static Cells**, style **Grouped**. You only need one cell, so remove the bottom two.

➤ Drop a new **Text Field** on to the cell. Here are the configuration options:

• Border Style: none

• Font size: 17

• Placeholder text: **Name of the List**

• Adjust to Fit: disabled

• Capitalization: Sentences

• Return Key: Done

• Auto-enable Return key: check

➤ Control-drag from the view controller to the Text Field and connect it to the **textField** outlet.

➤ Then Control-drag the other way around, from the Text Field back to the view controller, and choose **delegate** under **Outlets**. Now the view controller is the delegate for the text field.

➤ Connect the text field's **Did End on Exit** event to the **done** action on the view controller.

This completes setting up the new view controller to be the Add / Edit Checklist screen:

The finished design of the ListDetailViewController

Connect the view controllers

➤ Go to the **All Lists** scene (the one titled "Checklists") and drag a **Bar Button Item** on to its navigation bar. Change it to an **Add** button.

➤ **Control-drag** from this new bar button to the Add Checklist scene below to add a new **Show** segue.

➤ Click on the new segue and name it **AddChecklist**.

➤ Click on the other segue (the one not connected the the Add buton) and name it **EditChecklist**.

Your storyboard should now look something like this:

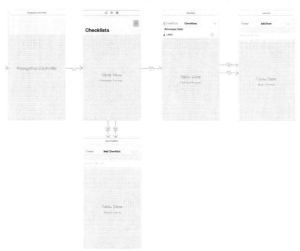

The full storyboard: 1 navigation controller, 4 table view controllers

Set up the delegates

Almost there. You still have to make the `AllListsViewController` the delegate for the
`ListDetailViewController` and then you're done. Again, it's very similar to what you
did before.

➤ Declare the All Lists view controller to conform to the delegate protocol by adding
`ListDetailViewControllerDelegate` to its class line.

You do this in **AllListsViewController.swift**:

```swift
class AllListsViewController: UITableViewController,
                              ListDetailViewControllerDelegate {
```

➤ Still in **AllListsViewController.swift**, extend `prepare(for:sender:)` to:

```swift
override func prepare(for segue: UIStoryboardSegue,
                        sender: Any?) {
  if segue.identifier == "ShowChecklist" {
    . . .
  } else if segue.identifier == "AddChecklist" {
    let controller = segue.destination
                        as! ListDetailViewController
    controller.delegate = self
  }
}
```

The first `if` doesn't change. You've added a second `if` for the new "AddChecklist" segue
that you just defined in the storyboard. As before, you look for the view controller and
set its `delegate` property to `self`.

➤ Next, implement the following delegate methods in **AllListsViewController.swift**:

```swift
// MARK:- List Detail View Controller Delegates
func listDetailViewControllerDidCancel(
                _ controller: ListDetailViewController) {
  navigationController?.popViewController(animated: true)
}

func listDetailViewController(
                _ controller: ListDetailViewController,
    didFinishAdding checklist: Checklist) {
  let newRowIndex = lists.count
  lists.append(checklist)

  let indexPath = IndexPath(row: newRowIndex, section: 0)
  let indexPaths = [indexPath]
  tableView.insertRows(at: indexPaths, with: .automatic)

  navigationController?.popViewController(animated: true)
```

```
}

func listDetailViewController(
                _ controller: ListDetailViewController,
    didFinishEditing checklist: Checklist) {
  if let index = lists.index(of: checklist) {
    let indexPath = IndexPath(row: index, section: 0)
    if let cell = tableView.cellForRow(at: indexPath) {
      cell.textLabel!.text = checklist.name
    }
  }
  navigationController?.popViewController(animated: true)
}
```

These methods are called when the user presses Cancel or Done inside the new Add/Edit Checklist screen.

None of this code should surprise you. It's exactly what you did before but now for the ListDetailViewController and Checklist objects.

➤ Also add the table view data source method that allows the user to delete checklists:

```
override func tableView(
               _ tableView: UITableView,
    commit editingStyle: UITableViewCellEditingStyle,
    forRowAt indexPath: IndexPath) {
  lists.remove(at: indexPath.row)

  let indexPaths = [indexPath]
  tableView.deleteRows(at: indexPaths, with: .automatic)
}
```

➤ Run the app. Now you can add new checklists and delete them again:

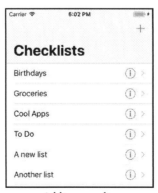

Adding new lists

> **Note:** If the app crashes, then go back and make sure you made all the connections properly in Interface Builder. It's really easy to miss just one tiny thing, but even the tiniest of mistakes can bring the app crashing down in flames…

You can't edit the names of existing lists yet. That requires one last addition to the code.

To bring up the Edit Checklist screen, the user taps the blue accessory button in the `ChecklistViewController` that triggered a segue. You could use a segue here too. If you want to go that route, you've already set up a segue named "EditChecklist" on the storyboard that you can use for this purpose. But I want to show you another way.

This time you're not going to use a segue at all, but load the new view controller by hand from the storyboard. Just because you can.

Load a view controller via code

➤ Add the following `tableView(_:accessoryButtonTappedForRowWith:)` method to **AllListsViewController.swift**. This method comes from the table view delegate protocol and the name is hopefully obvious enough for you to guess what it does.

```
override func tableView(_ tableView: UITableView,
    accessoryButtonTappedForRowWith indexPath: IndexPath) {

  let controller = storyboard!.instantiateViewController(
                   withIdentifier: "ListDetailViewController")
                   as! ListDetailViewController
  controller.delegate = self

  let checklist = lists[indexPath.row]
  controller.checklistToEdit = checklist

  navigationController?.pushViewController(controller,
                                    animated: true)
}
```

In this method, you create the view controller object for the Add/Edit Checklist screen and push it on to the navigation stack. This is roughly equivalent to what a segue would do behind the scenes. The view controller is embedded in a storyboard and you have to ask the storyboard object to load it.

Where did you get that storyboard object? As it happens, each view controller has a `storyboard` property that refers to the storyboard the view controller was loaded from. You can use that property to do all kinds of things with the storyboard, such as instantiating other view controllers.

The `storyboard` property is optional because view controllers are not always loaded from a storyboard. But this one is, which is why you can use ! to *force unwrap* the optional. It's like using `if let`, but because you can safely assume `storyboard` will not be `nil` in this app, you don't have to unwrap it inside an `if` statement.

The call to `instantiateViewController(withIdentifier:)` takes an identifier string, `ListDetailViewController`. That is how you ask the storyboard to create the new view controller. In your case, this will be the `ListDetailViewController`.

You still have to set this identifier on the navigation controller; otherwise the storyboard won't be able to find it. (And if you try to run the app without setting the identifier, it will crash.)

➤ Open the storyboard and select the List Detail View Controller. Go to the **Identity inspector** and set **Storyboard ID** to **ListDetailViewController**:

Setting the storyboard identifier

➤ That should do the trick. Run the app and tap some detail disclosure buttons.

(If the app crashes, make sure the storyboard is saved before you press Run.)

Are you still with me?

If at this point your eyes are glazing over and you feel like giving up: don't.

Learning new things is hard and programming doubly so. Set the book aside, sleep on it, and come back in a few days.

Chances are that in the mean time you'll have an a-ha! moment where the thing that didn't make any sense suddenly becomes clear as day.

If you have specific questions, join us on the forums. I usually check in a few times a day to help people out and so do many members of our community. Don't be embarrassed to ask for help! forums.raywenderlich.com

You can find the project files for the app up to this point under **16 - Lists** in the Source Code folder.

Chapter 17: Improved Data Model

Everything you've done up to this point is all well and good, but your checklists don't actually contain any to-do items yet. Or rather, if you select a checklist, you see the same old items for every list! There is no connection between the selected list and the items displayed for that list.

It's time for you to fix that.

This chapter covers the following steps:

- **The new data model:** Update the data model so that the to-do items for a list are saved along with the list.

- **Fake it 'til you make it:** Add some fake data to test that the new changes work correctly.

- **Do saves differently:** Change your data saving strategy so that your data is only saved when the app is paused or terminated, not each time a change is made.

- **Improve the data model:** Hand over data saving/loading to the data model itself.

The new data model

So far, the list of to-do items and the actual checklists have been separate from each other.

Let's change the data model to look like this:

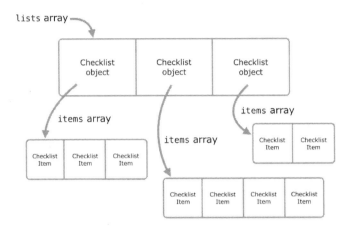

Each Checklist object has an array of ChecklistItem objects

There will still be the `lists` array that contains all the `Checklist` objects, but each of these `Checklist` instances will have its own array of `ChecklistItem` objects.

The to-do item array

➤ Add a new property to **Checklist.swift**:

```
class Checklist: NSObject {
    var name = ""
    var items = [ChecklistItem]()    // add this line
    . . .
```

This creates a new empty array that can hold `ChecklistItem` objects and assigns it to the `items` property.

If you're a stickler for completeness, you can also write it as follows:

```
var items: [ChecklistItem] = [ChecklistItem]()
```

I personally don't like this way of declaring variables because it violates the "DRY" principle – Don't Repeat Yourself. Fortunately, thanks to Swift's type inference, you can save yourself some keystrokes.

Another way you'll see it written sometimes is:

```
var items: [ChecklistItem] = []
```

The notation [] means: make an empty array of the specified type. There is no type inference at play there since you have to specify the type explicitly. If you don't specify a type and write the above line as:

```
var items = []
```

You will get an error since the compiler cannot determine the type of the array. That makes sense, right? Regardless of the way you choose to write it, the Checklist object now contains an array of ChecklistItem objects. Initially, that array is empty.

Pass the array

Earlier you fixed prepare(for:sender:) in AllListsViewController.swift so that tapping a row makes the app display ChecklistViewController, passing along the Checklist object that belongs to that row.

Currently ChecklistViewController still gets the ChecklistItem objects that it displays from its own private items array. You will change that so it reads from the items array inside the Checklist object instead.

➤ Remove the items instance variable from **ChecklistViewController.swift.**

➤ Then, anywhere it says items, change it to say checklist.items instead.

```
override func tableView(_ tableView: UITableView,
      numberOfRowsInSection section: Int) -> Int {
  return checklist.items.count
}
```

```
override func tableView(_ tableView: UITableView,
          cellForRowAt indexPath: IndexPath)
          -> UITableViewCell {
  . . .
  let item = checklist.items[indexPath.row]
  . . .
}
```

```
override func tableView(_ tableView: UITableView,
          didSelectRowAt indexPath: IndexPath) {
  . . .
  let item = checklist.items[indexPath.row]
  . . .
}
```

```
override func tableView(
            _ tableView: UITableView,
    commit editingStyle: UITableViewCellEditingStyle,
      forRowAt indexPath: IndexPath) {

  checklist.items.remove(at: indexPath.row)
  . . .
}
```

```
func itemDetailViewController(
              _ controller: ItemDetailViewController,
        didFinishAdding item: ChecklistItem) {
  let newRowIndex = checklist.items.count
  checklist.items.append(item)
  . . .
}
```

```
func itemDetailViewController(
                _ controller: ItemDetailViewController,
        didFinishEditing item: ChecklistItem) {

  if let index = checklist.items.index(of:item) {
  . . .
}
```

```
override func prepare(for segue: UIStoryboardSegue,
                      sender: Any?) {
    . . .
    controller.itemToEdit = checklist.items[indexPath.row]
    . . .
}
```

➤ Delete the following methods from **ChecklistViewController.swift**. (Tip: You may want to set aside the code from these methods in a temporary file somewhere; shortly you'll be using them again in a slightly modified form.)

- `func documentsDirectory()`
- `func dataFilePath()`
- `func saveChecklistItems()`
- `func loadChecklistItems()`

You added these methods to load and save the checklist items from a file. That is no longer the responsibility of this view controller. It is better from a design perspective for the Checklist object to do that.

Loading and saving data model objects really belongs in the data model itself, rather than in a controller.

But before you get to that, let's first test whether these changes were successful. Xcode is throwing up a few errors because you still call saveChecklistItems() and loadChecklistItems() from several places in the code. You should remove those lines, as you will soon be saving the items from a different place.

➤ Remove the lines that call saveChecklistItems() and loadChecklistItems().

➤ Press ⌘+B to make sure the app builds without errors.

Fake it 'til you make it

Let's add some fake data to the various Checklist objects so that you can test whether this new design actually works.

Add fake to-do data

In AllListsViewController's viewDidLoad() you already put fake Checklist objects into the lists array. It's time to add something new to this method.

➤ Add the following to the bottom of **AllListsViewController.swift**'s viewDidLoad():

```
// Add placeholder item data
for list in lists {
  let item = ChecklistItem()
  item.text = "Item for \(list.name)"
  list.items.append(item)
}
```

This introduces something you haven't seen before: the for in statement. Like if, this is a special language construct.

Programming language constructs

For the sake of review, let's go over the programming language stuff you've already seen. Most modern programming languages offer at least the following basic building blocks:

• The ability to remember values by storing things into variables. Some variables are simple, such as Int and Bool. Others can store objects (ChecklistItem, UIButton) or even collections of objects (Array).

• The ability to read values from variables and use them for basic arithmetic (multiply, add) and comparisons (greater than, not equals, etc).

• The ability to make decisions. You've already seen the if statement, but there is also a switch statement that is shorthand for if with many else ifs.

- The ability to group functionality into units such as methods and functions. You can call those methods and receive back a result value that you can then use in further computations.

- The ability to bundle functionality (methods) and data (variables) together into objects.

- The ability to execute a one or more lines of code inside a do block and to catch any errors thrown via a try statement. (Or, to simply bypass the do block by using a try? statement instead.)

- The ability to repeat a set of statements more than once. This is what the for in statement does. There are other ways to perform repetitions as well: while and repeat. Endlessly repeating things is what computers are good at.

Everything else is built on top of these building blocks. You've seen most of these already, but repetitions (or **loops** in programmer talk) are new.

If you grok the concepts from this list, you're well on your way to becoming a software developer. And if not, well, just hang in there!

Let's go through that for loop line-by-line:

```
for list in lists {
  . . .
}
```

This means the following: for every Checklist object in the lists array, perform the statements between the curly braces.

The first time through the loop, the temporary list variable will hold a reference to the Birthdays checklist, as that is the first Checklist object that you created and added to the lists array.

Inside the loop you do:

```
let item = ChecklistItem()
item.text = "Item for \(list.name)"
list.items.append(item)
```

This should be familiar. You first create a new ChecklistItem object. Then you set its text property to "Item for Birthdays" because the \(...) placeholder gets replaced with the name of the Checklist object, list.name, which is "Birthdays".

Finally, you add this new ChecklistItem to the Birthdays Checklist object, or rather, to its items array.

That concludes the first pass through this loop. Now the `for in` statement will look at the `lists` array again and sees that there are three more `Checklist` objects in that array. So it puts the next one, Groceries, into the `list` variable and the process repeats.

This time the text is "Item for Groceries", which is put into its own `ChecklistItem` object that goes into the `items` array of the Groceries `Checklist` object.

After that, the loop adds a new `ChecklistItem` with the text "Item for Cool Apps" to the Cool Apps checklist, and "Item for To Do" to the To Do checklist.

Then there are no more objects left to look at in the `lists` array and the loop ends.

Using loops will often save you a lot of time. You could have written this code as follows:

```
var item = ChecklistItem()
item.text = "Item for Birthdays"
lists[0].items.append(item)

item = ChecklistItem()
item.text = "Item for Groceries"
lists[1].items.append(item)

item = ChecklistItem()
item.text = "Item for Cool Apps"
lists[2].items.append(item)

item = ChecklistItem()
item.text = "Item for To Do"
lists[3].items.append(item)
```

That's very repetitive, which is a good sign it's better to use a loop. Imagine if you had 100 `Checklist` objects… would you be willing to copy-paste that code a hundred times? I'd rather use a loop.

Most of the time you won't even know in advance how many objects you'll have, so it's impossible to write it all out by hand. By using a loop you don't need to worry about that. The loop will work just as well for three items as for three hundred.

As you can imagine, loops and arrays work quite well together.

➤ Run the app. You'll see that each checklist now has its own set of items.

Play with it for a minute, remove items, add items, and verify that each list indeed is completely separate from the others.

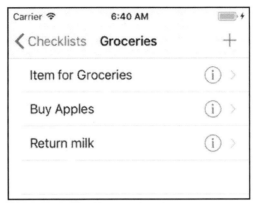

Each Checklist now has its own items

The new load/save code

Let's put the load/save code back in. This time you'll make `AllListsViewController` do the loading and saving.

➤ Add the following to **AllListsViewController.swift** (you may want to copy this from that temporary file, but be sure to make the changes mentioned in the comments):

```swift
func documentsDirectory() -> URL {
  let paths = FileManager.default.urls(for: .documentDirectory,
                                       in: .userDomainMask)
  return paths[0]
}

func dataFilePath() -> URL {
  return documentsDirectory().appendingPathComponent(
                                "Checklists.plist")
}

// this method is now called saveChecklists()
func saveChecklists() {
  let encoder = PropertyListEncoder()
  do {
    // You encode lists instead of "items"
    let data = try encoder.encode(lists)
    try data.write(to: dataFilePath(),
             options: Data.WritingOptions.atomic)
  } catch {
    print("Error encoding item array!")
  }
}

// this method is now called loadChecklists()
func loadChecklists() {
  let path = dataFilePath()
```

```
if let data = try? Data(contentsOf: path) {
  let decoder = PropertyListDecoder()
  do {
    // You decode to an object of [Checklist] type to lists
    lists = try decoder.decode([Checklist].self, from: data)
  } catch {
    print("Error decoding item array!")
  }
 }
}
```

This is mostly identical to what you had before in `ChecklistViewController`, except that you load and save the `lists` array instead of the `items` array. Note that the decode type is now `[Checklist].self` instead of `[ChecklistItem].self`. Also, the names of the methods changed slightly.

➤ Change `viewDidLoad()` to:

```
override func viewDidLoad() {
  super.viewDidLoad()
  // Enable large titles
  navigationController?.navigationBar.prefersLargeTitles = true
  // Load data
  loadChecklists()
}
```

This gets rid of the test data you put there earlier and makes the `loadChecklists()` method do all the work.

You also have to make the `Checklist` object support the `Codable` protocol - but that's just a simple change.

➤ Add the `Codable` protocol in **Checklist.swift**:

```
class Checklist: NSObject, Codable {
```

➤ **Important:** Before you run the app, remove the old **Checklists.plist** file from the Simulator's Documents folder.

If you don't, the app will most probably throw up an error message in the Console about the an error decoding because the internal format of the file no longer corresponds to the new data you're loading and saving. This is because the new Swift `Codable` protocol handles data encoding/decoding in a safe fashion.

With older version of this book, where the `Codable` protocol was not available, you had to encode/decode data in a different fashion. That approach used to crash the app if the Checklists.plist file was not removed and the data was in a different format.

Weird crashes

When I first wrote this book, I didn't think to remove the Checklists.plist file before running the app. That was a mistake, but the app appeared to work fine… until I added a new checklist. At that point the app aborted with a strange error message from UITableView that made no sense at all.

I started to wonder whether I tested the code properly. But then I thought of the old file, removed it and ran the app again. It worked perfectly. Just to make sure it was the fault of that file, I put a copy of the old file back and ran the app again. Sure enough, when I tried to add a new checklist it crashed.

The explanation for this kind of error is that somehow the code managed to load the old file, even though its format no longer corresponded to the new data model. This put the table view into a bad state. Any subsequent operations on the table view caused the app to crash.

You'll run into this type of bug every so often, where the crash isn't directly caused by what you're doing but by something that went wrong earlier on. These kinds of bugs can be tricky to solve, because you can't fix them until you find the true cause.

There is a section devoted to debugging techniques towards the end of the book because it's inevitable that you'll introduce bugs in your code. Knowing how to find and eradicate them is an essential skill that any programmer should master – if only to save you a lot of time and aggravation!

➤ Run the app and add a checklist and a few to-do items.

➤ Exit the app (with the Stop button) and run it again. You'll see that the list is empty again. All your to-do items are gone!

You can add all the checklists and items you want, but nothing gets saved anymore. What's going on here?

Do saves differently

Previously, you saved the data whenever the user changed something: adding a new item, deleting an item, and toggling a checkmark all caused Checklists.plist to be re-saved. That used to happen in ChecklistViewController.

However, you just moved the saving logic to `AllListsViewController`. How do you make sure changes to the to-do items get saved now? The `AllListsViewController` doesn't know when a checkmark is toggled on or off.

You could give `ChecklistViewController` a reference to the `AllListsViewController` and have it call its `saveChecklists()` method whenever the user changes something, but that introduces a *child-parent dependency* and you've been trying hard to avoid those (ownership cycles, remember?).

Parents and their children

The terms *parent* and *child* are common in software development.

A parent is an object higher up in some hierarchy; a child is an object lower in the hierarchy.

In this case, the "hierarchy" represents the navigation flow between the different screens of the app.

The All Lists screen is the parent of the Checklist screen, because All Lists was "born" first. It creates a new `ChecklistViewController` "baby" every time the user views the item list for a checklist.

Likewise, All Lists is also the parent of the List Detail screen. The Item Detail screen, however, is the child of the Checklist view controller.

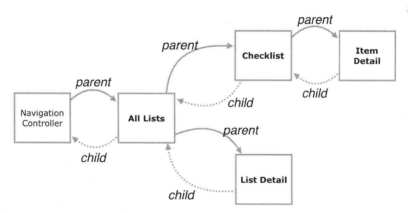

Generally speaking, it's OK if the parent knows everything about its children, but not the other way around (just like in real life, every parent has horrible secrets they don't want their kids to know about... or so I've been told).

As a result, you don't want parent objects to be dependent on their child objects, but the other way around is fine. So `ChecklistViewController` asking `AllListsViewController` to do things is a big no-no.

The new saving strategy

You may think: ah, I could use a delegate for this. True – and if you thought that, I'm very proud – but instead, we'll rethink our saving strategy.

Is it really necessary to save changes all the time? While the app is running, the data model sits in working memory and is always up-to-date.

The only time you have to load anything from the file (the long-term storage memory) is when the app first starts up, but never afterwards. From then on you always make the changes to the objects in the working memory.

But when changes are made, the file becomes out-of-date. That is why you save those changes – to keep the file in sync with what is in memory.

The reason you save to a file is so that you can restore the data model in working memory after the app gets terminated. But until that happens, the data in the short-term working memory will do just fine.

You just need to make sure that you save the data to the file just before the app gets terminated. In other words, the only time you save is when you actually need to keep the data safe.

Not only is this more efficient, especially if you have a lot of data, it also is simpler to program. You no longer need to worry about saving every time the user makes a change to the data, only right before the app terminates.

There are three situations in which an app can terminate:

1. While the user is running the app. This doesn't happen very often anymore, but earlier versions of iOS did not support multitasking apps. Receiving an incoming phone call, for example, would kill the currently running app. As of iOS 4, the app will simply be suspended and sent to the background when that happens.

   There are still situations where iOS may forcefully terminate a running app, for example, if the app becomes unresponsive or runs out of memory.

2. When the app is suspended. Most of the time iOS keeps running apps around for a long time. Their data is frozen in memory and no computations are taking place. (When you resume a suspended app, it literally continues from where it left off.)

   Sometimes the OS needs to make room for an app that requires a lot of working memory – often a game – and then it simply kills the suspended apps and wipes them from memory. The suspended apps are not notified of this.

3. The app crashes. There are ways to detect crashes but handling them can be very tricky. Trying to deal with the crash may actually make things worse. The best way to avoid crashes is to make no programming mistakes! :]

Fortunately for us, iOS will inform the app about significant changes such as, "you are about to be terminated", and, "you are about to be suspended". You can listen for these events and save your data at that point. That will ensure the on-file representation of the data model is always up-to-date when the app does terminate.

Save changes on app termination

The ideal place for handling app termination notifications is inside the **application delegate**. You haven't spent much time with this object before, but every app has one. As its name implies, it is the delegate object for notifications that concern the app as a whole.

This is where you receive the "app will terminate" and "app will be suspended" notifications.

In fact, if you look inside **AppDelegate.swift**, you'll see the methods:

```
func applicationDidEnterBackground(_ application: UIApplication)
```

And:

```
func applicationWillTerminate(_ application: UIApplication)
```

There are a few others, but these are the ones you need. (The Xcode template put helpful comments inside these methods, so you know what to do with them.)

Now the trick is, how do you call `AllListsViewController`'s `saveChecklists()` method from these delegate methods? The app delegate does not know anything about `AllListsViewController` yet.

You have to use some trickery to find the All Lists View Controller from within the app delegate.

➤ Add this new method to **AppDelegate.swift**:

```
func saveData() {
    let navigationController = window!.rootViewController
                              as! UINavigationController
    let controller = navigationController.viewControllers[0]
                 as! AllListsViewController
    controller.saveChecklists()
}
```

The `saveData()` method looks at the `window` property to find the `UIWindow` object that contains the storyboard.

UIWindow is the top-level container for all your app's views. There is only one UIWindow object in your app (unlike desktop apps, which usually have multiple windows).

> **Exercise:** Can you explain why you wrote window! with an exclamation point?

Unwrapping optionals

At the top of AppDelegate.swift you can see that window is declared as an optional:

```
var window: UIWindow?
```

To *unwrap* an optional you normally use the if let syntax:

```
if let w = window {
  // if window is not nil, w is the real UIWindow object
  let navigationController = w.rootViewController
}
```

As a shorthand you can use *optional chaining*:

```
let navigationController = window?.rootViewController
```

If window is nil, then the app won't even bother to look at the rest of the statement and navigationController will also be nil.

For apps that use a storyboard (and most of them do), you're guaranteed that window is never nil, even though it is an optional. UIKit promises that it will put a valid reference to the app's UIWindow object inside the window variable when the app starts up.

So why is it an optional? There is a brief moment between when the app is launched and the storyboard is loaded where the window property does not have a valid value yet. And if a variable can be nil – no matter how briefly – then Swift requires it to be an optional.

If you're *sure* an optional will not be nil when you're going to use it, you can *force unwrap* it by adding an exclamation point:

```
let navigationController = window!.rootViewController
```

That's exactly what you're doing in the saveData() method. Force unwrapping is the simplest way to deal with optionals, but it comes with a danger: if you're wrong and the optional *is* nil, the app will crash. Use with caution!

(You've actually used force unwrapping already when you read the text from the UITextField objects in the Item Detail and List Detail view controllers. The

UITextField text property is an optional String but it will never be nil, which is why you can read it with textField.text! – the exclamation point converts the optional String value to a regular String.)

Normally you don't need to do anything with your UIWindow, but in cases such as this you have to ask it for its rootViewController. The "root" or "initial" view controller is the very first scene from the storyboard, the navigation controller all the way over on the left.

You can see this in Interface Builder because this navigation controller has the big arrow pointing at it. This is the one:

The navigation controller is the window's root view controller

(The Attributes inspector for this navigation controller also has the **Is Initial View Controller** box checked, that's the same thing. In the Document Outline it is called the Storyboard Entry Point.)

Once you have the navigation controller, you can find the AllListsViewController. After all, that's the view controller that is embedded in the navigation controller.

Unfortunately, the UINavigationController does not have a "rootViewController" property of its own, so you have to look into its viewControllers array to find it:

```
let controller = navigationController.viewControllers[0]
                 as! AllListsViewController
```

As usual, a type cast is necessary because the viewControllers array does not know anything about the exact types of your own view controllers. Once you have a reference to AllListsViewController you can call its saveChecklists() method.

It's a bit of work to dig through the window and navigation controller to find the view controller you need, but that's life as an iOS developer.

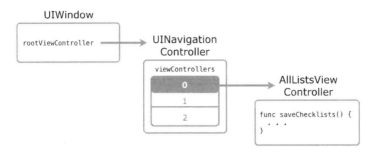

From the root view controller to the AllListsViewController

> **Note:** By the way, the `UINavigationController` does have a `topViewController` property, but you cannot use it here: the "top" view controller is the screen that is currently displaying, which may be the `ChecklistViewController` if the user is looking at to-do items. You don't want to send the `saveChecklists()` message to that screen – it has no method to handle that message and the app will crash!

➤ Change the `applicationDidEnterBackground()` and `applicationWillTerminate()` methods to call `saveData()`:

```
func applicationDidEnterBackground(_ application: UIApplication)
{
  saveData()
}

func applicationWillTerminate(_ application: UIApplication) {
  saveData()
}
```

➤ Run the app, add some checklists, add items to those lists, and set some checkmarks.

➤ Press the Simulator's home button (or press **Shift+⌘+H**, or pick **Hardware → Home** from the Simulator's menu bar) to make the app go to the background. This simulates what happens when a user taps the home button on their iPhone.

Look inside the app's Documents folder using Finder. There should be a new Checklists.plist file there.

➤ Press Stop in Xcode to terminate the app. Run the app again and your data should still be there. Awesome!

Xcode's Stop button

Important note: When you press Xcode's Stop button, the application delegate will *not* receive the `applicationWillTerminate(_:)` notification. Xcode kills the app immediately, without mercy.

Therefore, to test the saving behavior, always simulate a tap on the home button to make the app go into the background before you press Stop. If you don't to that, you'll lose your data. *Caveat developer.*

Improve the data model

The above code works, but you can still do a little better. You have made data model objects for `Checklist` and `ChecklistItem` but the code for loading and saving the Checklists.plist file currently lives in `AllListsViewController`. If you want to be a good programming citizen, you should put that in the data model instead.

The DataModel class

I prefer to create a top-level `DataModel` object for many of my apps. For this app, `DataModel` will contain the array of `Checklist` objects. You can move the code for loading and saving data to this new `DataModel` object.

➤ Add a new file to the project using the **Swift File** template. Save it as **DataModel.swift** (you don't need to make this a subclass of anything).

➤ Change **DataModel.swift** to the following:

```swift
import Foundation

class DataModel {
  var lists = [Checklist]()
}
```

This defines the new `DataModel` object and gives it a `lists` property.

Unlike `Checklist` and `ChecklistItem`, `DataModel` does not need to be built on top of `NSObject`. It also does not need to conform to the `Codable` protocol.

`DataModel` will take over the responsibilities for loading and saving the to-do lists from `AllListsViewController`.

➤ Cut the following methods out of **AllListsViewController.swift** and paste them into **DataModel.swift**:

- func documentsDirectory()

- func dataFilePath()

- func saveChecklists()

- func loadChecklists()

➤ Add an init() method to **DataModel.swift**:

```
init() {
  loadChecklists()
}
```

This makes sure that as soon as the DataModel object is created, it will attempt to load Checklists.plist.

You don't have to call super.init() because DataModel does not have a superclass (it is not built on NSObject).

Switch to **AllListsViewController.swift** and make the following changes:

➤ Remove the lists instance variable.

➤ Remove the call to loadChecklists() in viewDidLoad.

➤ Add a new instance variable:

```
var dataModel: DataModel!
```

The ! is necessary because dataModel will temporarily be nil when the app starts up. It doesn't have to be a true optional – with ? – because once dataModel is given a value, it will never become nil again.

Xcode still finds a number of errors in **AllListsViewController.swift**. You can no longer reference the lists variable directly, because it no longer exists. Instead, you'll have to ask the DataModel for its lists property.

➤ Wherever the code for AllListsViewController says lists, replace it with dataModel.lists. You need to do this in the following methods:

- tableView(_:numberOfRowsInSection:)

- tableView(_:cellForRowAt:)

- tableView(_:didSelectRowAt:)

- tableView(_:commit:forRowAt:)

- `tableView(_:accessoryButtonTappedForRowWith:)`

- `listDetailViewController(_:didFinishAdding:)`

- `listDetailViewController(_:didFinishEditing:)`

Phew, that's a big list! Fortunately, the change is very simple.

To recap, you created a new `DataModel` object that owns the array of `Checklist` objects and knows how to load and save the checklists and their items.

Instead of its own array, the `AllListsViewController` now uses this `DataModel` object, which it accesses through the `dataModel` property.

Create the DataModel object

But where does this `DataModel` object get created? There is no place in the code that currently does `dataModel = DataModel()`.

The best place for this is in the app delegate. You can consider the app delegate to be the top-level object in your app. Therefore it makes sense to make it the "owner" of the data model.

The app delegate then passes this `DataModel` object to any view controllers that need to use it.

➤ In **AppDelegate.swift**, add a new property:

```
let dataModel = DataModel()
```

This creates the `DataModel` object and puts it in a constant named `dataModel`.

Even though `AllListsViewController` also has an instance variable named `dataModel`, these two things are totally separate from each other. Here you're only putting the `DataModel` object into `AppDelegate`'s `dataModel` property.

➤ Simplify the `saveData()` method to just this:

```
func saveData() {
   dataModel.saveChecklists()
}
```

If you run the app now, it will crash at once because `AllListsViewController`'s own reference to `DataModel` is still `nil`. I told you those `nil`s were no-gooders!

The best place to share the `DataModel` instance with `AllListsViewController` is in the `application(_:didFinishLaunchingWithOptions:)` method, which gets called as soon as the app starts up.

➤ Change that method to:

```
func application(_ application: UIApplication,
      didFinishLaunchingWithOptions launchOptions:
      [UIApplicationLaunchOptionsKey: Any]?) -> Bool {

  let navigationController = window!.rootViewController
                            as! UINavigationController
  let controller = navigationController.viewControllers[0]
                   as! AllListsViewController
  controller.dataModel = dataModel

  return true
}
```

This finds the AllListsViewController by looking in the storyboard (as before) and then sets its dataModel property. Now the All Lists screen can access the array of Checklist objects again.

➤ Do a clean build (**Product → Clean**) and run the app. Verify that everything still works. It does? Great!

Still confused about var and let?

If var makes a variable and let makes a constant, then why were you able to do this in AppDelegate.swift:

```
let dataModel = DataModel()
```

You'd think that when something is constant it cannot change, right? Then how come the app lets you add new Checklist objects to DataModel? Obviously the DataModel object *can* be changed…

Here's the trick: Swift makes a distinction between **value types** and **reference types**, and let works a bit differently for both.

An example of a value type is Int. Once you create a constant of type Int you can never change it afterwards:

```
let i = 100
i = 200        // not allowed
i += 1         // not allowed

var j = 100
j = 200        // allowed
j += 1         // allowed
```

The same goes for other value types such as `Float`, `String`, and even `Array`. They are called value types because the variable or constant directly stores their value.

When you assign the contents of one variable to another, the value is copied into the new variable:

```
var s = "hello"
var u = s          // u has its own copy of "hello"
s += " there"      // s and u are now different
```

But objects that you define with the keyword `class` (such as `DataModel`) are reference types. The variable or constant does not contain the actual object, only a reference to the object.

```
var d = DataModel()
var e = d               // e refers to the same object as d
d.lists.remove(at: 0)   // this also changes e
```

You can also write this using `let` and it would do the exact same thing:

```
let d = DataModel()
let e = d               // e refers to the same object as d
d.lists.remove(at: 0)   // this also changes e
```

So what is the difference between `var` and `let` for reference types?

When you use `let` it is not the object that is constant but the *reference* to the object. That means you cannot do this:

```
let d = DataModel()
d = someOtherDataModel   // error: cannot change the reference
```

The constant d can never point to another object, but the object itself can still change.

It's OK if you have trouble wrapping your head around this. The distinction between value types and reference types is an important idea in software development, but it also is something which takes a while to understand.

My suggestion is that you use `let` whenever you can and change to `var` when the compiler complains. Note that optionals always need to be `var`, because being an optional implies that it can change its value at some point.

You can find the project files for the app up to this point under **17 - Improved Data Model** in the Source Code folder.

Chapter 18: User Defaults

You now have an app that lets you create lists and add to-do items to those lists. All of this data is saved to long-term storage so that even if the app gets terminated, nothing is lost.

There are some improvements (both to the user interface and to the code) that you can make, though.

This chapter covers the following:

- **Remember the last open list:** Improve the user-experience by remembering the last open list on app re-launch.

- **Defensive programming:** Adding in checks to guard against possible crashes - coding defensively instead of reacting to crashes later.

- **The first-run experience:** Improving the first-run experience for the user so that the app looks more polished and user-friendly.

Remember the last open list

Imagine the user is on the Birthdays checklist and switches to another app. The *Checklists* app is now suspended. It is possible that at some point the app gets terminated and is removed from memory. When the user reopens the app some time later, it no longer is on Birthdays but on the main screen. Because it was terminated, the app didn't simply resume where it left off, but got launched anew.

You might be able to get away with this, as apps don't get terminated often (unless your users play a lot of games that eat up memory), but little things like this matter in iOS apps.

Fortunately, it's fairly easy to remember whether the user has opened a checklist and to switch to it when the app starts up.

Use UserDefaults

You could store this information in the Checklists.plist file, but for simple settings such as this, there is the UserDefaults object.

UserDefaults works like a *dictionary*, which is a collection object for storing key-value pairs. You've already seen the array collection, which stores an ordered list of objects. The dictionary is another very common collection that looks like this:

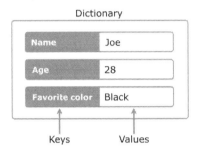

A dictionary is a collection of key-value pairs

Dictionaries in Swift are handled by the Dictionary object (who would've guessed?).

You can put objects into the dictionary under a reference key and then retrieve it later using that key. This is, in fact, how Info.plist works.

The Info.plist file is read into a dictionary and then iOS uses the various keys (on the left hand) to obtain the values (on the right hand). Keys are usually strings but values can be any type of object.

To be accurate, UserDefaults isn't a true dictionary, but it certainly acts like one.

When you insert new values into UserDefaults, they are saved somewhere in your app's sandbox. So, these values persist even after the app terminates.

You don't want to store huge amounts of data inside UserDefaults, but it's ideal for small things like settings – and for remembering what screen the app was on when it closed.

This is what you are going to do:

1. On the segue from the main screen, AllListsViewController, to the checklist screen, ChecklistViewController, you write the row index of the selected list into UserDefaults. This is how you'll remember which checklist was active.

You could have saved the name of the checklist instead of the row index, but what would happen if two checklists have the same name? Unlikely, but not impossible. Using the row index guarantees that you'll always select the proper one.

2. When the user presses the back button to return to the main screen, you have to remove this value from `UserDefaults` again. It is common to set a value such as this to -1 to mean "no value".

    Why -1? You start counting rows at 0, so you can't use 0. Positive numbers are also out of the question, unless you use a huge number such as 1000000 as it's very unlikely the user will make that many checklists. -1 is not a valid row index – and because it's a negative value it looks weird, making it easy to spot during debugging.

    (If you're wondering why you're not using an optional for this – good question! – the answer is that `UserDefaults` cannot handle optionals. Sad face.)

3. If the app starts up and the value from `UserDefaults` isn't -1, the user was previously viewing the contents of a checklist and you have to manually perform a segue to the `ChecklistViewController` for the corresponding row.

Phew, it's more work to explain this in English than writing the actual code. ;-)

Let's start with the segue from the main screen. Recall that this segue is triggered from code rather than from the storyboard.

➤ In **AllListsViewController.swift**, change `tableView(_:didSelectRowAt:)` to the following:

```
override func tableView(_ tableView: UITableView,
        didSelectRowAt indexPath: IndexPath) {
  // add this line:
  UserDefaults.standard.set(indexPath.row, forKey:
"ChecklistIndex")

  let checklist = dataModel.lists[indexPath.row]
  performSegue(withIdentifier: "ShowChecklist", sender:
checklist)
}
```

In addition to what this method did before, you now store the index of the selected row into `UserDefaults` under the key "ChecklistIndex".

Navigation controller delegate

To be notified when the user presses the back button on the navigation bar, you have to become a delegate of the navigation controller. Being the delegate means that the navigation controller tells you when it pushes or pops view controllers on the navigation stack.

The logical place for this delegate is the `AllListsViewController`.

➤ Add the delegate protocol to the `class` line in **AllListsViewController.swift**:

```
class AllListsViewController: UITableViewController,
                             ListDetailViewControllerDelegate,
                             UINavigationControllerDelegate {
```

As you can see, a view controller can be a delegate for many objects at once.

`AllListsViewController` is now the delegate for both the `ListDetailViewController` and the `UINavigationController`, but also implicitly for the `UITableView` (because it is a table view controller).

➤ Add the following delegate method to **AllListsViewController.swift**:

```
func navigationController(
                _ navigationController: UINavigationController,
            willShow viewController: UIViewController,
                        animated: Bool) {

  // Was the back button tapped?
  if viewController === self {
    UserDefaults.standard.set(-1, forKey: "ChecklistIndex")
  }
}
```

This method is called whenever the navigation controller shows a new screen.

If the back button was pressed, the new view controller is `AllListsViewController` itself and you set the "ChecklistIndex" value in `UserDefaults` to -1, meaning that no checklist is currently selected.

Equal or identical

To determine whether the `AllListsViewController` is the newly activated view controller, you wrote:

```
if viewController === self {
```

Yep, it's not a typo, that's three equals signs in a row.

Previously to compare objects you used only two equals signs:

```
if segue.identifier == "AddItem" {
```

You may be wondering what the difference is between these two operators. It's a subtle but important question about identity. (Who said programmers couldn't be philosophical?)

If you use ==, you're checking whether two variables have the same value.

With === you're checking whether two variables refer to the exact same object.

Imagine two people who are both called Joe. They're different people who just happen to have the same name.

If we'd compare them using joe1 === joe2 then the result would be false, as they're not the same person.

But joe1.name == joe2.name would be true.

On the other hand, if I'm telling you an amusing (or embarrassing!) story about Joe and this story seems awfully familiar to you, then maybe we happen to know this same Joe.

In that case, joe1 === joe2 would be true as well.

By the way, the above code would have worked just fine if you had written,

```
if viewController == self
```

with just two equals signs. For objects such as view controllers, equality is tested by comparing the references, just like === would do. But technically speaking, === is more correct here than ==.

Show the last open list

The only thing that remains is to check at startup which checklist you need to show and then perform the segue manually. You'll do that in viewDidAppear().

➤ Add the viewDidAppear() method to **AllListsViewController.swift**:

```
override func viewDidAppear(_ animated: Bool) {
  super.viewDidAppear(animated)

  navigationController?.delegate = self

  let index = UserDefaults.standard.integer(
                                forKey: "ChecklistIndex")
  if index != -1 {
    let checklist = dataModel.lists[index]
    performSegue(withIdentifier: "ShowChecklist",
                        sender: checklist)
  }
}
```

UIKit automatically calls this method after the view controller has become visible.

First, the view controller makes itself the delegate for the navigation controller.

Every view controller has a built-in `navigationController` property. To access it you use the notation `navigationController?.delegate` because the navigation controller is optional.

(You could also have written `navigationController!` instead of ?. The difference between the two is that ! will crash the app if this view controller was ever to be shown outside of a `UINavigationController`, while ? won't crash but simply ignore the rest of that line. For our app, this does not matter.)

Then it checks `UserDefaults` to see whether it has to perform the segue.

If the value of the "ChecklistIndex" setting is -1, then the user was on the app's main screen before the app was terminated, and we don't have to do anything.

However, if the value of the "ChecklistIndex" setting is *not* -1, then the user was previously viewing a checklist and the app should segue to that screen. As before, you place the relevant `Checklist` object into the `sender` parameter of `performSegue(withIdentifier:sender:)`.

The `!=` operator means: not equal. It is the opposite of the `==` operator. If you're mathematically-inclined, with some imagination `!=` looks like ≠. (Some languages use `<>` for not equal but that won't work in Swift.)

> **Note:** It may not be immediately obvious what's going on here.
>
> `viewDidAppear()` isn't just called when the app starts up but also every time the navigation controller slides the main screen back into view.
>
> Checking whether to restore the checklist screen needs to happen only once when the app starts, so why did you put this logic in `viewDidAppear()` if it gets called more than once?
>
> Here's the reason:
>
> The very first time `AllListsViewController`'s screen becomes visible, you don't want the `navigationController(_:willShow:animated:)` delegate method to be called yet, as that would always overwrite the old value of "ChecklistIndex" with -1, before you've had a chance to restore the old screen.
>
> By waiting to register `AllListsViewController` as the navigation controller delegate until it is visible, you avoid this problem. `viewDidAppear()` is the ideal place for that, so it makes sense to do it from that method.

However, as mentioned, `viewDidAppear()` also gets called after the user presses the back button to return to the All Lists screen. That shouldn't have any unwanted side effects, such as triggering the segue again.

Naturally, the navigation controller calls `navigationController(_:willShow:animated:)` when the back button is pressed, but this happens before `viewDidAppear()`. The delegate method always sets the value of "ChecklistIndex" back to -1, and as a result, `viewDidAppear()` does not trigger a segue again.

And so it all works out... The logic that you added to `viewDidAppear()` only does its job once during app startup. There are other ways to solve this particular issue but this approach is simple, so I like it.

Is all of this going way over your head? Don't fret about it. To get a better idea of what's going on, sprinkle `print()` statements around the various methods to see in which order they get called. Change things around to see what the effect is. Jumping into the code and playing with it is the quickest way to learn!

Double-check that all the lines with `UserDefaults` use the same key name, "ChecklistIndex". If one of them is misspelled, `UserDefaults` is reading from and writing to different items.

➤ Run the app and go to a checklist screen. Exit to the home screen via the Home button, followed by Stop to quit the app.

Tip: You need to exit to the home screen first because `UserDefaults` may not immediately save its settings to disk, and therefore, you may lose your changes if you kill the app from within Xcode.

Note: Does the app crash for you at this point? That happens if you didn't add any lists or to-do items yet. That's the exact problem we'll solve in the next section. You can either comment out the code in `viewDidAppear()`, add some to-do items, and enable the code again to try it. Or, simply move on to the next section.

➤ Run the app again and you'll notice that Xcode immediately switches to the screen where you were last at. Cool, huh?

Defensive programming

➤ Now do the following: stop the app and delete it from the Simulator by holding down on the app icon until it starts to wiggle and then deleting it.

Then, run the app again from within Xcode and watch it crash:

```
fatal error: Index out of range
```

The app crashes in `viewDidAppear()` on the line:

```
let checklist = dataModel.lists[index]
```

What's going on here? Apparently, the value of `index` is not -1, because the code entered the `if` statement.

As it turns out `index` is 0, even though there should be nothing in `UserDefaults` yet because this is a fresh install of the app. The app didn't write anything in the "ChecklistIndex" key yet.

Here's the thing: `UserDefaults`'s `integer(forKey:)` method returns 0 if it cannot find the value for the key you specified. But in this app, 0 is a valid row index.

At this point, the app doesn't have any checklists yet. So, index 0 does not exist in the `lists` array. That is why the app crashes.

What should happen instead, is that `UserDefaults` returns -1 if nothing is set yet for "ChecklistIndex", because to your app -1 means: show the main screen instead of a specific checklist.

Set a default value for a UserDefaults key

Fortunately, `UserDefaults` will let you set default values for the default values. Yep, you read that correctly. Let's do that in the `DataModel` object.

➤ Add the following method to **DataModel.swift**:

```swift
func registerDefaults() {
  let dictionary = [ "ChecklistIndex": -1 ]

  UserDefaults.standard.register(defaults: dictionary)
}
```

This creates a new `Dictionary` instance and adds the value -1 for the key "ChecklistIndex".

The square bracket notation is not only used to make arrays, but also dictionaries. The difference is that for a dictionary it always looks like,

```
[ key1: value1, key2: value2, . . . ]
```

while an array is just:

```
[ value1, value2, value3, . . . ]
```

UserDefaults will use the values from this dictionary if you ask it for a key but it cannot find anything under that key.

➤ Change **DataModel.swift**'s init() to call this new method:

```
init() {
   loadChecklists()
   registerDefaults()
}
```

➤ Run the app again. Now, it should no longer crash.

Why did you do this in DataModel? Well, I don't really like to sprinkle all of these calls to UserDefaults throughout the code.

Clean up the code

In fact, let's move all of the UserDefaults stuff into DataModel.

➤ Add the following to **DataModel.swift**:

```
var indexOfSelectedChecklist: Int {
   get {
      return UserDefaults.standard.integer(
                          forKey: "ChecklistIndex")
   }
   set {
      UserDefaults.standard.set(newValue,
                          forKey: "ChecklistIndex")
   }
}
```

This does something you haven't seen before. It appears to declare a new instance variable indexOfSelectedChecklist of type Int, but what are these get { } and set { } blocks?

This is an example of a *computed property*.

There isn't any storage allocated for this property (so it's not really a variable). Instead, when the app tries to read the value of indexOfSelectedChecklist, the code in the get block is performed. And when the app tries to put a new value into indexOfSelectedChecklist, the set block is performed.

From now on, you can simply use indexOfSelectedChecklist and it will automatically update UserDefaults. How cool is that?

You're doing this so the rest of the code won't have to worry about UserDefaults anymore. The other objects just have to use the indexOfSelectedChecklist property on DataModel.

Hiding implementation details is an important object-oriented programming principle, and this is one way to do it.

If you decide later that you want to store these settings somewhere else, for example, in a database, or in iCloud, then you only have to change this in one place, in DataModel. The rest of the code will be oblivious to these changes. That's a good thing.

➤ Update the code in **AllListsViewController.swift** to use this new computed property:

```
override func viewDidAppear(_animated: Bool) {
  super.viewDidAppear(animated)

  navigationController?.delegate = self

  let index = dataModel.indexOfSelectedChecklist // change this
  if index != -1 {
    let checklist = dataModel.lists[index]
    performSegue(withIdentifier: "ShowChecklist",
                     sender: checklist)
  }
}
```

```
override func tableView(_ tableView: UITableView,
          didSelectRowAt indexPath: IndexPath) {
  // change this line
  dataModel.indexOfSelectedChecklist = indexPath.row

  let checklist = dataModel.lists[indexPath.row]
  performSegue(withIdentifier: "ShowChecklist",
                   sender: checklist)
}
```

```
func navigationController(
          _ navigationController: UINavigationController,
          willShow viewController: UIViewController,
                      animated: Bool) {
  if viewController === self {
```

```
      dataModel.indexOfSelectedChecklist = -1    // change this
    }
  }
```

The intent of the code is now much clearer. `AllListsViewController` no longer has to worry about the "how" – storing values in `UserDefaults` – and can simply focus on the "what" – changing the index of the selected checklist.

➤ Run the app again and make sure everything still works.

A subtle bug

It's pretty nice that the app now remembers what screen you were on, but this new feature has also introduced a subtle bug in the app. Here's how to reproduce it:

➤ Start the app and add a new checklist. Also, add a new to-do item to this list. Now kill the app from within Xcode.

Because you did not exit to the home screen first, the new checklist and its item were not saved to Checklists.plist.

However, there is a (small) chance that `UserDefaults` did save its changes to disk and now thinks this new list is selected. That's a problem because that list doesn't exist anymore (it never made it into Checklists.plist).

`UserDefaults` will save its changes at indeterminate times. So, it could have saved before you terminated the app.

➤ Run the app again and – if you're lucky? – it will crash with:

```
fatal error: Index out of range
```

If you can't get this error to appear, add the following line to the `set` block of `indexOfSelectedChecklist` and try again. This forces `UserDefaults` to save its changes every time `indexOfSelectedChecklist` changes:

```
set {
  UserDefaults.standard.set(newValue,
                forKey: "ChecklistIndex")
  UserDefaults.standard.synchronize()
}
```

The reason for the crash is that `UserDefaults` and the contents of Checklists.plist are out-of-sync. `UserDefaults` thinks the app needs to select a checklist that doesn't actually exist. Every time you run the app it will now crash. Yikes!

This situation shouldn't really happen during regular usage. It happened because you used the Xcode Stop button to kill the app before it had a chance to save the plist file.

Under normal circumstances, the user would press the home button. As the app goes into the background, it properly saves both Checklists.plist and UserDefaults and everything is in sync again.

However, the OS can always decide to terminate the app and then this same situation could occur.

Even though there's only a small chance that this can go wrong in practice, you should really protect the app against this. These are the kinds of bug reports you don't want to receive because often, you have no idea what the user did to make it happen.

This is where the practice of *defensive programming* becomes important. Your code should always check for such boundary cases and be able to gracefully handle them even if they are unlikely to occur.

In our case, you can easily fix AllListsViewController's viewDidAppear() method to deal with this situation.

➤ Change the if statement in viewDidAppear() to:

```
if index >= 0 && index < dataModel.lists.count {
```

Instead of just checking for index != −1, you now do a more precise check to determine whether index is valid. It should be between 0 and the number of checklists in the data model. If not, then you simply don't segue.

This prevents dataModel.lists[index] from asking for an object at an index that doesn't exist.

You haven't seen the && operator before. This symbol means "logical and". It is used as follows:

```
if something && somethingElse {
  // do stuff
}
```

This reads: if something is true **and** something else is also true, then do stuff.

In viewDidAppear() you only perform the segue when index is 0 or greater and also less than the number of checklists, which means it's only valid if it lies in between those two values.

With this defensive check in place, you're guaranteed that the app will not try to segue to a checklist that doesn't exist, even if the data is out-of-sync.

Note: Even though the app remembers what checklist the user was on, it won't bother to remember whether the user had the Add/Edit Checklist or Add/Edit Item screen open.

These kinds of data input screens are supposed to be temporary. You open them to make a few changes and then close them again. If the app goes to the background and is terminated, then it's no big deal if the data input screen disappears.

At least, that is true for this app. If you have an app that allows the user to make many complicated edits in an input screen, you may want to persist those changes when the app closes so the user won't lose all their work in case the app is killed.

In this chapter you used UserDefaults to remember which screen was open, but iOS actually has a dedicated API for this kind of thing, State Preservation and Restoration. You can read more about this on raywenderlich.com/117471/state-restoration-tutorial.

The first-run experience

Let's use UserDefaults for something else. It would be nice if the first time you ran the app it created a default checklist for you, simply named "List", and switched over to that list. This enables you to start adding to-do items right away.

That's how the standard Notes app works too: you can start typing a note right after launching the app for the very first time, but you can also go one level back in the navigation hierarchy to see a list of all notes.

Check for first run

To implement the above feature, you need to keep track in UserDefaults whether this is the first time the user runs the app. If it is, you create a new Checklist object.

You can perform all of this logic inside DataModel.

It's a good idea to add a new default setting to the registerDefaults() method. The key for this value is "FirstTime".

➤ Change the registerDefaults() method in **DataModel.swift** (don't miss the comma after the first line of the dictionary):

```
func registerDefaults() {
  let dictionary: [String:Any] = [ "ChecklistIndex": -1,
                                   "FirstTime": true ]
```

```
    UserDefaults.standard.register(defaults: dictionary)
}
```

The "FirstTime" setting can be a boolean value because it's either true (this is the first time) or false (this is any other than the first time).

The value of "FirstTime" needs to be true if this is the first launch of the app after a fresh install.

Also, note that there's now a type declaration for `dictionary`. Why was that added? Try removing the type declaration, the : `[String:Any]` bit, and see what happens. Xcode will throw up an error.

This is because originally, there was one value in the dictionary and it was an `Int`. But when you introduced the `FirstTime` key, its corresponding value is a `Bool`. Now your dictionary has a mixed set of values - an `Int` and a `Bool`. So, at this point, the compiler is unsure whether you meant to have a mixed bag of values, or if it was a mistake on your part. So it wants you to explicitly indicate what the dictionary type is, and that's why you declare it as `[String:Any]`, to indicate that the value could indeed be of any type.

➤ Still in **DataModel.swift**, add a new `handleFirstTime()` method:

```
func handleFirstTime() {
   let userDefaults = UserDefaults.standard
   let firstTime = userDefaults.bool(forKey: "FirstTime")

   if firstTime {
      let checklist = Checklist(name: "List")
      lists.append(checklist)

      indexOfSelectedChecklist = 0
      userDefaults.set(false, forKey: "FirstTime")
      userDefaults.synchronize()
   }
}
```

Here you check `UserDefaults` for the value of the "FirstTime" key. If the value for "FirstTime" is true, then this is the first time the app is being run. In that case, you create a new `Checklist` object and add it to the array.

You also set `indexOfSelectedChecklist` to 0, which is the index of this newly added `Checklist` object, to make sure the app will automatically segue to the new list in `AllListsViewController`'s `viewDidAppear()` method.

Finally, you set the value of "FirstTime" to false, so this code won't be executed again the next time the app starts up.

➤ Call this new method from `DataModel`'s `init()`:

```
init() {
  loadChecklists()
  registerDefaults()
  handleFirstTime()
}
```

➤ Remove the app from the Simulator and run it again from Xcode.

Because it's the first time you run the app (at least from the app's perspective) after a fresh install, it will automatically create a new checklist named List and switch to it.

Organizing Source Files

At this point, your Project navigator probably lists your files something like this:

Project navigator file listing

It's a bit messy since it's hard to find where a given file is. Sure, you know exactly where each file is now, but what happens when you have 20 or 30 files in there? Or a hundred?

Xcode does provide a few different ways to organize your files.

The first thing you can do is a simple alphabetical sorting of files so that you can find a given file quickly - since it will be in alphabetical order. That is simple enough to accomplish.

➤ Right-click (or Control-click) on the yellow **Checklists** folder. A context menu should pop up.

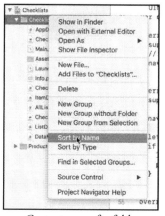

Context menu for folder

➤ Select **Sort by Name**.

Voila! All the files inside the Checklists folder are now in alphabetical order.

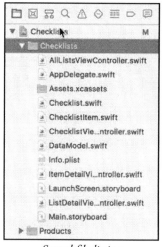

Sorted file listing

That certainly makes finding files a lot easier, but what if you had 20 or 30 files? Or even a hundred? You would still have to do a lot of scrolling around to find the exact file you wanted.

Xcode does provide a filter field at the bottom of the Navigator pane that you can use to filter files in the current list by name. You can type in, for example, "Controller" and it will display only the files with "Controller" in the file name. (You can click the little circle icon with an "x" in the filter field to clear the filter.)

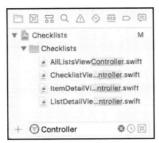

Filter file list by name

But you can do better :] You can also organize your files into virtual folders, called *groups*, so that you can organize the files by functionality. For example, you can put all your view controllers together into a folder called View Controllers, the data models into a Data Models folder and so on ...

You probably noticed the New Group menu option on the folder context menu when you right-clicked on the Checklists folder earlier. That's what you need to use in order to create a new group. Simply create a new group (or three), drag files into the group and you should be set.

You could quite easily organize the file listing from above to look something like this:

Organized file listing

You can find the project for the app up to this point under **18 - UserDefaults** in the Source Code folder.

Chapter 19: UI Improvements

Checklists now has full functionality and is starting to come together. However, There are a few small features I'd like to add, just to polish the app a little more. After all, you're building a real app here – if you want to make top-notch apps, you have to pay attention to those tiny details.

This chapter covers the following:

- **Show counts:** Show the number of to-do items remaining for each list.

- **Sort the lists:** Sort the list of checklist items alphabetically.

- **Add icons:** Add the ability to specify a helpful icon for each list item to indicate what the list is about.

- **Make the app look good:** Improve how the app looks by making a few basic colour changes to give it its own unique style.

- **Support all iOS devices:** Add support for the different screen sizes present on the various iOS devices.

Show counts

On the main screen, for each checklist, the app will show the number of to-do items that do not have checkmarks yet:

Each checklist shows how many items are still left to-do

Count the unchecked items

First, you need a way to count these items.

➤ Add the following method to **Checklist.swift**:

```
func countUncheckedItems() -> Int {
  var count = 0
  for item in items where !item.checked {
    count += 1
  }
  return count
}
```

With this method you can ask any `Checklist` object how many of its `ChecklistItem` objects do not yet have their checkmark set. The method returns this count as an `Int` value.

You use a `for in` to loop through the `ChecklistItem` objects from the `items` array. If an `item` object has its `checked` property set to false, you increment the local variable `count` by 1.

Remember that the `!` operator negates the result. So if `item.checked` is true, then `!item.checked` will make it false. You should read it as "where not item.checked".

> **Note:** If the `!` symbol is written in front of something then it is the logical **not** operator, as you see here. When the `!` is written behind something, it's related to optionals. This is another example of a symbol that has more than one meaning in Swift. The correct interpretation depends on the context where it is being used.

When the loop is over and you've looked at all the objects, you return the total value of the count to the caller.

> **Exercise:** What would happen if you used `let` instead of `var` to make the `count` variable?

Answer: When `count` is a constant, Swift won't let you change its value, so the line that does `+= 1` will show an error message.

By the way, you could also have written the loop as follows:

```
for item in items {
  if !item.checked {
    count += 1
  }
}
```

This uses the more familiar `if` statement instead. Personally, I like the brevity of the `for in where` loop, but using an `if` is just as valid.

Display the unchecked item count

➤ Go to **AllListsViewController.swift** and in `makeCell(for:)` change `style: .default` to `style: .subtitle`.

The rest of the code stays the same, except you now use `.subtitle` for the cell style instead of `.default`. The "subtitle" cell style adds a second, smaller label below the main label. You can use the cell's `detailTextLabel` property to access this subtitle label.

➤ That happens in `tableView(_:cellForRowA:t)`. Add the following line just before `return cell`:

```
cell.detailTextLabel!.text =
            "\(checklist.countUncheckedItems()) Remaining"
```

You call the `countUncheckedItems()` method on the `Checklist` object and put the count into a new string that you display using the `detailTextLabel`.

As usual, you use `\(...)` to do the string interpolation. Notice that you can even call methods inside interpolated strings. Sweet!

Force unwrapping

To put text into the cell's labels, you wrote:

```
cell.textLabel!.text = someString
cell.detailTextLabel!.text = anotherString
```

The ! is necessary because `textLabel` and `detailTextLabel` are optionals.

The `textLabel` property is only present on table view cells that use one of the built-in cell styles; it is `nil` on custom cell designs. Likewise, not all of the cell styles have a detail label and `detailTextLabel` will be `nil` in those cases.

Here you're using the "Subtitle" cell style, which is guaranteed to have both labels. Because these optionals will never be `nil` for a "Subtitle" cell, you can use ! to *force unwrap* them. This turns the optional into an actual object that you can use.

Be careful with this, though… using ! on an optional that *is* `nil` will crash your app immediately.

You could also have written the above code as:

```
if let label = cell.textLabel {
   label.text = someString
}
if let label = cell.detailTextLabel {
   label.text = anotherString
}
```

That is safer – no chance of crashing here – but also a bit more cumbersome. Writing ! is just more convenient in this case.

➤ Run the app. For each checklist it will now show how many items still remain unchecked.

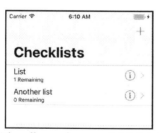

The cells now have a subtitle label

Update the unchecked item count on changes

One problem: The to-do count never changes. If you toggle a checkmark on or off, or add new items, the "to do" count remains the same. That's because you create these table view cells once and never update their labels. (Try it out!)

> **Exercise:** Think of all the situations that will cause this "still to do" count to change.

Answer:

- The user toggles a checkmark on an item. When the checkmark is set, the count goes down. When the checkmark gets removed, the count goes up again.

- The user adds a new item. New items don't have their checkmark set, so adding a new item should increment the count.

- The user deletes an item. The count should go down but only if that item had no checkmark.

These changes all happen in the `ChecklistViewController` but the "still to do" label is shown in the `AllListsViewController`.

So, how do you let the All Lists View Controller know about this?

If you thought, "That's easy, let's use a delegate!", then you're starting to get the hang of this. You could make a new `ChecklistViewControllerDelegate` protocol that sends messages when the following things happen:

- The user toggles a checkmark on an item

- The user adds a new item

- The user deletes an item

But what would the delegate – which would be `AllListsViewController` – do in response? It would simply set some new text on the cell's `detailTextLabel` in all cases.

The delegate approach sounds good, but you're going to cheat and not use a delegate at all :] There is a simpler solution, and a smart programmer always picks the simplest way to solve a problem.

➤ Go to **AllListsViewController.swift** and add the `viewWillAppear()` method to do the following:

```
override func viewWillAppear(_ animated: Bool) {
  super.viewWillAppear(animated)
  tableView.reloadData()
}
```

Don't confuse this method with `viewDidAppear()`. The difference is in the verb: *will* versus *did*. `viewWillAppear()` is called before `viewDidAppear()`, when the view is about to become visible but the animation hasn't started yet. `viewDidAppear()` is called after the view is visible on the screen and the animation has completed. There may be half a second or so difference between them as the animation takes place.

The iOS API often does this: there is a "will" method that is invoked before something happens and a "did" method that is invoked after that something happenes. Sometimes you need to do things before, sometimes after, and having two methods gives you the ability to choose whichever situation works best for you.

> **API (ay-pee-eye)** stands for Application Programming Interface. When people say "the iOS API" they mean all the frameworks, objects, protocols and functions that are provided by iOS that you as a programmer can use to write apps.
>
> The iOS API consists of everything from UIKit, Foundation, Core Graphics, and so on. Likewise, when people talk about "the Facebook API" or "the Google API", they mean the services that these companies provide that allow you to write apps for those platforms.

Here, viewWillAppear() tells the table view to reload its entire contents. That will cause tableView(_:cellForRowAt:) to be called again for every visible row.

When you tap the back button on the ChecklistViewController's navigation bar, the AllListsViewController screen will slide back into view. Just before that happens, viewWillAppear() is called. Thanks to the call to tableView.reloadData() the app will update all of the table cells, including the detailTextLabels.

Reloading all of the cells may seem like overkill, but in this situation you can easily get away with it. It's unlikely the All Lists screen will contain many rows (say, less than 100) and only about 14 visible cells, so reloading them is quite fast. And it saves you some work of having to make yet another delegate.

Sometimes a delegate is the best solution; sometimes you just reload the entire table.

➤ Run the app and test that it works!

Display a completion message when all items are done

> **Exercise.** Change the label to read "All Done!" when there are no more to-do items left to check.

Answer: Change the relevant code in tableView(_:cellForRowAt:) to:

```
let count = checklist.countUncheckedItems()
if count == 0 {
  cell.detailTextLabel!.text = "All Done!"
} else {
  cell.detailTextLabel!.text = "\(count) Remaining"
}
```

You put the count into a local constant because you refer to it twice. Calculating the count once and storing it into a temporary constant is more optimal than doing the same calculation twice.

Display an indicator when there are no items in a list

Exercise: Now update the label to say "No Items" when the list is empty.

Answer:

```
let count = checklist.countUncheckedItems()
if checklist.items.count == 0 {
  cell.detailTextLabel!.text = "(No Items)"
} else if count == 0 {
  cell.detailTextLabel!.text = "All Done!"
} else {
  cell.detailTextLabel!.text = "\(count) Remaining"
}
```

Just looking at the result of countUncheckedItems() is not enough. If this returns 0, you don't know whether that means all items are checked off or if the list has no items at all. You also need to look at the total number of items in the checklist, with checklist.items.count.

The text in the detail label changes depending on how many items are checked off

Little details like these matter – they make your app more fun to use. Ask yourself, what would make you feel better about having done your chores, the rather bland message "0 Remaining" or the joyous exclamation "All Done!"?

A short diversion into Functional Programming

Swift is primarily an object-oriented language. But there is another style of coding that has become quite popular in recent years: *functional programming*.

The term "functional" means that programs can be expressed purely in terms of mathematical functions that transform data.

Unlike the methods and functions in Swift, these mathematical functions are not allowed to have "side effects". For any given inputs, a function should always produce the same output. Methods are much less strict.

Even though Swift is not a purely functional language, it does let you use certain functional programming techniques in your apps. They can really make your code a lot shorter.

For example, let's look at `countUncheckedItems()` again:

```swift
func countUncheckedItems() -> Int {
  var count = 0
  for item in items where !item.checked {
    count += 1
  }
  return count
}
```

That's quite a bit of code for something that's fairly simple. You can actually write this in a single line of code:

```swift
func countUncheckedItems() -> Int {
  return items.reduce(0) { cnt,
                    item in cnt + (item.checked ? 0 : 1) }
}
```

`reduce()` is a method that looks at each item and performs the code in the { } block. Initially, the `cnt` variable contains the value 0, but after each item it is incremented by either 0 or 1, depending on whether the item was checked.

Incidentally, the `item.checked ? 0 : 1` bit is a simpler way to do an `if` … `else` block - the `? .. :..` construct is known as a *ternary conditional operator* - if the first part (the bit before the ?) evaluates to true, then the result of the expression would be the item after the ?. Otherwise, the result is the item after the :. It can be very handy in a lot of places to write simpler, more succinct code.

When `reduce()` is done, its return value is the total count of unchecked items.

You don't have to remember any of this for now, but it's pretty cool to see that Swift allows you to express this kind of algorithm very succinctly.

Sort the lists

Another thing you often need to do with lists is sort them in some particular order.

Let's sort the list of checklists by name. Currently when you add a new checklist it is always appended to the end of the table, regardless of alphabetical order.

When do you do the sorting?

Before we figure out how to sort an array, let's think about when you need to perform this sort:

• When a new checklist is added

• When a checklist is renamed

There is no need to re-sort when a checklist is deleted because that doesn't have any impact on the order of the other objects.

Currently you handle these two situations in AllListsViewController's implementation of "didFinishAdding" and "didFinishEditing".

➤ Change these methods to the following:

```
func listDetailViewController(
                _ controller: ListDetailViewController,
     didFinishAdding checklist: Checklist) {
   dataModel.lists.append(checklist)
   dataModel.sortChecklists()
   tableView.reloadData()
   navigationController?.popViewController(animated: true)
}

func listDetailViewController(
                _ controller: ListDetailViewController,
     didFinishEditing checklist: Checklist) {
   dataModel.sortChecklists()
   tableView.reloadData()
   navigationController?.popViewController(animated: true)
}
```

You were able to remove a whole bunch of stuff from both methods because you now always do reloadData() on the table view.

It is no longer necessary to insert the new row manually, or to update the cell's textLabel. Instead you simply call tableView.reloadData() to refresh the entire table's contents.

Again, you can get away with this because the table will only hold a handful of rows. If this table had hundreds of rows, a more advanced approach might be necessary. (You could figure out where the new or renamed `Checklist` object should be inserted and just update that row.)

The sorting algorithm

The `sortChecklists()` method on `DataModel` is new and you still need to add it. But before that, we need to have a short discussion about how sorting works.

When you sort a list of items, the app will compare the items one-by-one to figure out what the proper order is. But what does it mean to compare two `Checklist` objects?

In *Checklists* we obviously want to sort them by name, but we need some way to tell the app that's what we mean.

➤ Add the following method to **DataModel.swift**:

```
func sortChecklists() {
  lists.sort(by: { checklist1, checklist2 in
    return checklist1.name.localizedStandardCompare(
        checklist2.name) == .orderedAscending })
}
```

Here you tell the `lists` array that the `Checklists` it contains should be sorted using some specific logic.

That logic is provided in the shape of a *closure*. You can tell it's a closure by the { } brackets around the sorting code:

```
lists.sort(by: { /* the sorting code goes here */ })
```

You've briefly seen closures with the alert box in the *Bull's Eye* app. They wrap a piece of source code into an anonymous, inline method.

The purpose of the closure is to determine whether one `Checklist` object comes before another, based on our rules for sorting.

The sort algorithm will repeatedly ask one `Checklist` object from the list how it compares to the other `Checklist` objects using the logic from the closure, and then shuffle them around until the array is sorted.

This allows `sort()` to sort the contents of the array in any order you desire. If you wanted to sort on other criteria, all you'd have to do is change the logic inside the closure.

The actual sorting code is this:

```
checklist1.name.localizedStandardCompare(
    checklist2.name) == .orderedAscending
```

To compare these two `Checklist` objects, you're only looking at their names.

The `localizedStandardCompare(_:)` method compares the two name strings while ignoring lowercase vs. uppercase (so "a" and "A" are considered equal) and taking into consideration the rules of the current *locale*.

A locale is an object that knows about country and language-specific rules. Sorting in German may be different than sorting in English, for example.

That's all you have to do to sort the array: call `sort()` and give it a closure with the logic that compares two `Checklist` objects.

➤ Just to make sure the existing lists are also sorted in the right order, you should also call `sortChecklists()` when the plist file is loaded:

```
func loadChecklists() {
    . . .
    lists = try decoder.decode([Checklist].self, from: data)
    sortChecklists()           // Add this
  } catch {
    . . .
  }
}
```

➤ Run the app and add some new checklists. Change their names and notice that the list is always sorted alphabetically.

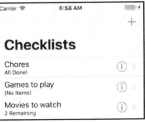

New checklists are always sorted alphabetically

Add icons

Because true iOS developers can't get enough of view controllers and delegates, let's add a new property to the `Checklist` object that lets you choose an icon. We're really going to cement these principles in your mind!

When you're done, the Add/Edit Checklist screen will look like this:

You can assign an icon to a checklist

You are going to add a row to the Add/Edit Checklist screen that opens a new screen for picking an icon. This icon picker is a new view controller and you will show it by pushing it on to the navigation stack, just like your previous view controllers.

Add the icons to the project

The Resources folder for the book contains a folder named **Checklist Icons** with a selection of PNG images that depict different categories.

The various checklist icon images

➤ Add the images from this folder to the asset catalog. Select **Assets.xcassets** in the project navigator, click the + button at the bottom and choose **Import…**

Importing new images into the asset catalog

Navigate to the **Checklist Icons** folder and select all the files inside:

Selecting the image files to import

Note: Make sure to select the actual image files, not just the folder.

Click **Open** to import the images. The asset catalog should now look like this:

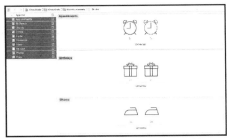

The asset catalog after importing the checklist icons

Each image comes with a 2x version for Retina devices and a 3x version for the iPhone Plus with the Retina HD screen.

As I pointed out in the previously, you don't need low-resolution 1x graphics anymore. All iPhone, iPad, and iPod touch devices that can run iOS 11 have Retina 2x or 3x screens.

Update the data model

➤ Add the following property to **Checklist.swift**:

```
var iconName = ""
```

The `iconName` variable holds the filename of the icon image.

The above code initializes `iconName` to have no icon set by default. But what if you actually wanted to create new `Checklist` objects with a default icon set?

It's very easy to implement a default icon. Say, you want all new checklists to have the "Appointments" icon - then change the above line to this:

```
var iconName = "Appointments"
```

And that's all you need to do :]

Display the icon

At this point, you just want to see that you can make an icon – any icon – show up in the table view. When that works, you can worry about letting the user pick their own icons. (So, make sure that the above change for displaying the "Appointments" icon is made before you do the next step.)

➤ Change `tableView(_:cellForRowAt:)` in **AllListsViewController.swift** to put the icon into the table view cell:

```
override func tableView(_ tableView: UITableView,
          cellForRowAt indexPath: IndexPath)
          -> UITableViewCell {
  . . .

  cell.imageView!.image = UIImage(named: checklist.iconName)
  return cell
}
```

Cells using the standard `.subtitle` cell style come with a built-in `UIImageView` on the left. You can simply pass it an image and it will be displayed automatically. Easy peasy.

> **Note:** When you run the app, you will not see any of your previoulsy saved checklist items. Can you guess why? The addition of `iconName` changed the `Checklist` object and the previously saved information for the object is no longer valid. So, the decoder will run into issues when trying to decode the previously saved file and so, you will end up with no saved items. Sorry.

➤ Run the app, create a few checklists and now each of them should have an alarm clock icon.

The checklists have an icon

The default icon

Now that you know it works, you can now change `Checklist` to give each `Checklist` object an icon named "No Icon" by default.

➤ In **Checklist.swift**, change the `iconName` declaration to:

```
var iconName = "No Icon"
```

The "No Icon" image is a fully transparent PNG image with the same dimensions as the other icons. Using a transparent image is necessary to make all the checklists line up properly, even if they have no icon.

If you were to set `iconName` to an empty string instead, the image view in the table view cell would remain empty and the text would align with the left margin of the screen. That looks bad when other cells do have icons:

Using an empty image to properly align the text labels (right)

The icon picker class

Now, let's create the icon picker screen.

➤ Add a new Swift file to the project. Name it **IconPickerViewController**.

➤ Replace the contents of **IconPickerViewController.swift** with:

```swift
import UIKit

protocol IconPickerViewControllerDelegate: class {
  func iconPicker(_ picker: IconPickerViewController,
              didPick iconName: String)
}

class IconPickerViewController: UITableViewController {
  weak var delegate: IconPickerViewControllerDelegate?
}
```

This defines the `IconPickerViewController` object, which is a table view controller, and a delegate protocol that it uses to communicate with other objects in the app.

➤ Add a constant (inside the class brackets) to hold the array of icons:

```
let icons = [ "No Icon", "Appointments", "Birthdays", "Chores",
   "Drinks", "Folder", "Groceries", "Inbox", "Photos", "Trips" ]
```

This is an array that contains a list of icon names. These strings are both the text you will show on the screen and the name of the PNG file inside the asset catalog.

The icons array is the data model for this table view. Note that it is a non-mutable array (it is defined with let and arrays are "value" types), because the user cannot add or delete icons.

This new view controller is a UITableViewController, so you have to implement the data source methods for the table view.

➤ Add the following methods to the source file:

```
// MARK:- Table View Delegates
override func tableView(_ tableView: UITableView,
       numberOfRowsInSection section: Int) -> Int {
  return icons.count
}
```

This simply returns the number of icons in the array.

```
override func tableView(_ tableView: UITableView,
           cellForRowAt indexPath: IndexPath)
           -> UITableViewCell {

  let cell = tableView.dequeueReusableCell(
                           withIdentifier: "IconCell",
                                      for: indexPath)

  let iconName = icons[indexPath.row]
  cell.textLabel!.text = iconName
  cell.imageView!.image = UIImage(named: iconName)

  return cell
}
```

Here you obtain a table view cell and give it a title and an image. You will design this cell in the storyboard momentarily. It will be a prototype cell with the "Default" cell style (or "Basic" as it is called in Interface Builder). Cells with this style already contain a text label and an image view, which is very convenient.

The icon picker storyboard changes

➤ Open the storyboard. Drag a new **Table View Controller** from the Object Library and place it next to the Add Checklist scene.

➤ In the **Identity inspector**, change the class of this new table view controller to **IconPickerViewController**.

➤ Select the prototype cell and set its **Style** to **Basic** and its (re-use) **Identifier** to **IconCell**.

That takes care of the design for the icon picker. Now you need to have some place to call it from. To do this, you will add a new row to the Add Checklist screen.

➤ Go to the **Add Checklist View Controller** and add a new section to the table view. You can do this by changing the **Sections** value in the **Attributes inspector** for the table view from 1 to 2. This will duplicate the existing section.

➤ Delete the Text Field from the new cell; you don't need it.

➤ Add a **Label** to this cell and change its text to **Icon**.

➤ Set the cell's **Accessory** to **Disclosure Indicator**. That adds a gray chevron.

➤ Add an **Image View** to the right of the cell. Make it 36 × 36 points big. (Tip: use the Size inspector for this.)

➤ Use the **Assistant Editor** to add an outlet property for this image view to **ListDetailViewController.swift** and name it **iconImageView**.

Now that you've finished the designs for both screens, you can connect them via a segue.

➤ **Control-drag** from the "Icon" table view cell to the Icon Picker View Controller and add a segue of type **Selection Segue – Show**. (Make sure you're dragging from the Table View Cell, not its Content View or any of the other subviews. If you are unable to do this accurately from the scene, remember that you can also Control-drag from the Document Outline.)

➤ Give the segue the identifier **PickIcon**.

➤ Thanks to the segue, the new view controller has been given a navigation bar. (However, it might not have a Navigation Item - if it doesn't, drag one from the Object Library on to the Icon Picker scene.) Double-click the navigation bar and change its title to **Choose Icon**.

This part of the storyboard should now look like this:

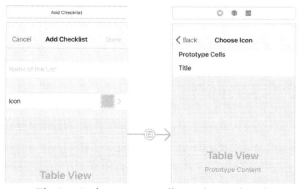

The Icon Picker view controller in the storyboard

Display the icon picker

➤ In **ListDetailViewController.swift**, change the `willSelectRowAt` table view delegate method to:

```
override func tableView(_ tableView: UITableView,
          willSelectRowAt indexPath: IndexPath)
          -> IndexPath? {
  if indexPath.section == 1 {
    return indexPath
  } else {
    return nil
  }
}
```

Without this change you cannot tap the "Icon" cell to trigger the segue.

Previously this method always returned `nil`, which meant tapping on rows was not possible. Now, however, you want to allow the user to tap the Icon cell, so this method should return the index-path for that cell.

Because the Icon cell is the only row in the second section, you only have to check `indexPath.section`. There is no need to check the row number too. Users still can't select the cell with the text field (from section 0).

➤ Run the app and verify that there is now an Icon row in the Add/Edit Checklist screen. Tapping it will open the Choose Icon screen and show a list of icons.

The icon picker screen

Handle icon selection

You can press the back button to go back but selecting an icon doesn't do anything yet. It just colors the row gray but doesn't put the icon into the checklist.

To make this work, you have to hook up the icon picker to the Add/Edit Checklist screen through its own delegate protocol.

➤ First, add an instance variable in **ListDetailViewController.swift**:

```
var iconName = "Folder"
```

You use this variable to keep track of the chosen icon name.

Even though the Checklist object now has an iconName property, you cannot keep track of the chosen icon in the Checklist object for the simple reason that you may not always have a Checklist object, i.e. when the user is adding a new checklist.

So, you'll store the icon name in a temporary variable and copy that into the Checklist's iconName property at the right time.

You should initialize the iconName variable with something reasonable. Let's go with the folder icon. This is only necessary for new Checklists, which get the Folder icon by default.

➤ Update viewDidLoad() to the following:

```
override func viewDidLoad() {
  . . .
  if let checklist = checklistToEdit {
    . . .
    iconName = checklist.iconName            // add this
  }
```

```
    iconImageView.image = UIImage(named: iconName) // add this
  }
```

This has two new lines: If the `checklistToEdit` optional is not `nil`, then you copy the `Checklist` object's icon name into the `iconName` instance variable. You also load the icon's image file into a new `UIImage` object and set it on the `iconImageView` so it shows up in the Icon row.

Earlier you created a push segue named "PickIcon". You still need to implement `prepare(for:sender:)` in order to tell the `IconPickerViewController` that this screen is now its delegate.

➤ First, add the name of that protocol to the `class` line in **ListDetailViewController.swift**:

```
class ListDetailViewController: UITableViewController,
      UITextFieldDelegate, IconPickerViewControllerDelegate {
```

➤ Next, add the implementation of the method from that delegate protocol:

```
// MARK:- Icon Picker View Controller Delegate
func iconPicker(_ picker: IconPickerViewController,
        didPick iconName: String) {
  self.iconName = iconName
  iconImageView.image = UIImage(named: iconName)
  navigationController?.popViewController(animated: true)
}
```

This puts the name of the chosen icon into the `iconName` variable to remember it, and also updates the image view with the new image.

After you do all that, you use `popViewController(animated:)` to "pop" the Icon Picker View Controller off the navigation stack.

Recall that `navigationController` is an optional property of the view controller, so you need to use ? (or !) to access the actual `UINavigationController` object.

➤ Now, add the following method to **ListDetailViewController.swift**:

```
// MARK:- Navigation
override func prepare(for segue: UIStoryboardSegue,
                      sender: Any?) {
  if segue.identifier == "PickIcon" {
    let controller = segue.destination
                     as! IconPickerViewController
    controller.delegate = self
  }
}
```

This code should have no big surprises for you.

➤ Change the done() action so that it puts the chosen icon name into the Checklist object when the user closes the screen:

```
@IBAction func done() {
  if let checklist = checklistToEdit {
    checklist.name = textField.text!
    checklist.iconName = iconName                 // add this
    delegate?.listDetailViewController(self,
                      didFinishEditing: checklist)
  } else {
    let checklist = Checklist(name: textField.text!)
    checklist.iconName = iconName                 // add this
    delegate?.listDetailViewController(self,
                      didFinishAdding: checklist)
  }
}
```

Finally, you must change IconPickerViewController to actually call the delegate method when a row is tapped.

➤ Add the following method to the bottom of **IconPickerViewController.swift**:

```
override func tableView(_ tableView: UITableView,
          didSelectRowAt indexPath: IndexPath) {
  if let delegate = delegate {
    let iconName = icons[indexPath.row]
    delegate.iconPicker(self, didPick: iconName)
  }
}
```

And that's it. You can now set icons on the Checklist objects.

To recap, you:

• Added a new view controller object.

• Designed its user interface in the storyboard editor.

• Hooked it up to the Add/Edit Checklist screen using a segue and a delegate.

Those are the basic steps you need to take with any new screen that you add.

➤ Run the app to try it out.

You can now give each list its own icon

Achievement unlocked: users can pick icons!

Code refactoring

There's still a small improvement you can make to the code. In done(), you currently do this:

```
let checklist = Checklist(name: textField.text!)
checklist.iconName = iconName
```

Setting the icon name can be considered part of the initialization of Checklist, so it would be nice if you could pass the icon name to the Checklist initializer. And you can :]

➤ Switch to **Checklist.swift** and modify the init method as follows:

```
init(name: String, iconName: String = "No Icon") {
    self.name = name
    self.iconName = iconName
    super.init()
}
```

The modified init method looks almost the same as the previous one except for taking a new iconName parameter and assigning it to the object's iconName property.

But what is the = "No Icon" bit after the second parameter? That's called a *default parameter value*. When you specify a default parameter value for a method, when the method is called, you can omit the parameters with default values and the method call would still work, but the default values would be used for the parameters that were omitted. Nifty, huh?

➤ In **ListDetailViewController.swift**'s done() method, replace the code that creates the new Checklist object with this (and remove the line after that which sets the iconName property):

```
let checklist = Checklist(name: textField.text!,
                          iconName: iconName)
```

➤ Build the app to verify it still works.

> **Exercise:** Give `ChecklistItem` an `init(text:)` method that is used instead of the parameter-less `init()`. Or how about an `init(text:checked:)` method?

Make the app look good

For *Checklists*, you're going to keep things simple as far as fancying up the graphics goes. The standard look of navigation controllers and table views is perfectly adequate, although a little bland. In the next apps you'll see how you can customize the look of these UI elements.

Change the tint color

Even though this app uses the stock visuals, there is a simple trick to give the app its own personality: changing the **tint color**.

The tint color is what UIKit uses to indicate that things, such as buttons, can be interacted with. The default tint color is a medium blue.

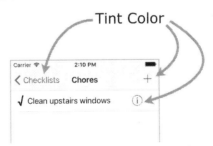

The buttons all use the same tint color

Changing the tint color is pretty easy.

➤ Open the storyboard and go to the **File inspector** (the first tab).

➤ Click **Global Tint** to open the color picker and choose Red: 4, Green: 169, Blue: 235. That makes the tint color a lighter shade of blue.

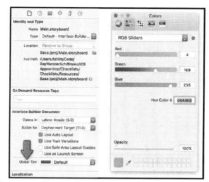

Changing the Global Tint color for the storyboard

Tip: If the color picker only shows a black & white bar, then click the dropdown at the top that says Gray Scale Slider and change it to **RGB Sliders**.

Set the color of the checkmark

It would also look nice if the checkmark wasn't black but used the tint color too.

➤ To make that happen, add the following line to configureCheckmark(for:with:) in **ChecklistViewController.swift**:

```
label.textColor = view.tintColor
```

➤ Run the app. It already looks a lot more interesting:

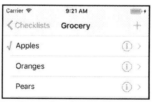

The tint color makes the app less plain looking

Add app icons

No app is complete without an icon. The Resources folder for this app contains a folder named **Icon** with the app icon image in various sizes. Notice that it uses the same blue as the tint color.

➤ Add these icons to the asset catalog (**Assets.xcassets**). Recall that icons go into the **AppIcon** section. Simply drag them from the Finder into the slots.

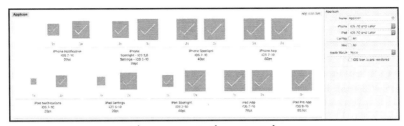

The app icons in the asset catalog

Set the launch image

Apps should also have a launch image or launch file. Showing a static picture of the app's UI will give the illusion of the app is loading faster than it really is. It's all smoke and mirrors.

The Xcode template includes the file **LaunchScreen.storyboard** that is used as the launch file. With some effort you could make this look like the initial screen of the app, but there's an easier solution.

➤ Open the **Project Settings** screen. In the **General** tab, scroll down to the **App Icons and Launch Images** section.

➤ In the **Launch Screen File** box, press the arrow and select **Main.storyboard**.

Changing the launch screen file

This tells the app you'll be using the design from the storyboard as the launch file.

Upon startup, the app finds the initial view controller and converts it into a static launch image. For this app that is the All Lists View Controller inside its navigation controller.

➤ Delete **LaunchScreen.storyboard** from the project.

➤ From the **Product** menu choose **Clean**. It's also a good idea to delete the app from the Simulator just so it no longer has any copies of the old launch file lying around (hold down on the icon until it starts to wiggle, just like on a real iPhone).

➤ Run the app. Just before the real UI appears you should briefly see the following launch screen:

The empty launch screen

The launch screen simply has a navigation bar and an empty table view. This gives the illusion the app's UI has already been loaded, though in reality, that the data hasn't been filled in yet.

Using a proper launch screen makes the app look more professional – and faster!

For many apps, you can simply use the main storyboard as the launch file, making it a no-brainer to add.

Support all iOS devices

The app should run without major problems on all current iOS devices, from the smallest (iPhone SE) to the largest (iPad Pro). Table view controllers are very flexible and will automatically resize to fit the screen, no matter how large or small. Give it a try in the different Simulators!

Well, I said no *major* problems. But there are still a few tweaks you can make here and there.

Update the Add Checklist rows for larger screens

So far, I've been showing you screenshots of the iPhone SE simulator, and I also designed my screens in Interface Builder using the dimensions of the iPhone SE. But what happens when you run the app on a larger simulator such as the iPhone 8 Plus or the iPhone X?

The icon is in the wrong place

The icon is no longer nicely aligned on the right. Also try typing some text: it gets cut off because the text field is too small. Why does this happen?

When you design the user interface for your app in Interface Builder, it doesn't automatically fit all possible screen sizes, only the one you're designing for. You need to help Interface Builder out and tell it how to adjust your UI for different screen sizes. As you saw before with *Bull's Eye*, that's where Auto Layout comes in.

What you want to happen is that the image view stays glued to the right edge of the screen, always at the same distance from the disclosure indicator. When the view controller grows or shrinks to fit the iPhone screen, the image view should move along with it.

The solution is to add Auto Layout constraints to the image view that tell the app what the relationship is between the image view and the edges of its parent view.

➤ Select the **Icon Image View**. Bring up the **Add New Constraints menu** using the icon at the bottom of the canvas.

➤ First, uncheck **Constrain to margins**.

➤ Activate the bars at the top and the right so they turn red.

➤ Put checkmarks in front of **Width** and **Height**.

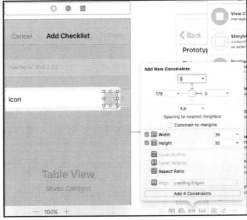

Adding constraints to the Image View

➤ Finally, click **Add 4 Constraints** to finish.

The image view should now look like this:

The Image View with the constraints

Make sure the bars representing the constraints are blue. If they are orange or red you may have forgotten something in the Add New Constraints menu. (Either try again or use the **Editor** → **Resolve Auto Layout Issues** → **Update Frames** menu item.)

The most important constraint is the one on the right. This tells UIKit that the right-hand side of the image view should always stick to the right-hand edge of the table view cell's content view.

In other words, no matter how wide or narrow the screen is, the image view will always have the same location relative to the disclosure indicator.

The other three constraints – top, width, and height – were necessary only because all views must always have enough constraints to determine their position and size.

If you don't specify any constraints of your own, Interface Builder will come up with reasonable default constraints. But as soon as you add just one custom constraint, you'll have to add the others too.

➤ To verify that your changes do the right thing you don't necessarily need to run the app in the simulator. Use the **View as:** panel at the bottom to switch between the different iPhone models right inside Interface Builder. If your constraints are correct, then the icon should always be in the right place.

While you're at it, you might as well fix the text field so that it stretches the entire width of the screen.

➤ Select the **Text Field** and in the **Add New Constraints menu** activate the four bars so they all become red:

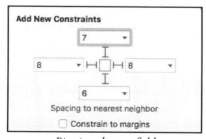

Pinning the text field

These options will make the text field stick to the sides of the table view cell. (The numbers here don't really matter, so it's fine if your numbers are slightly different. The important thing is that there are four red bars indicating the four active constraints.)

➤ Also do this for the text field on the Add/Edit Item screen.

Now you can type all the way to the edge and then the text will start scrolling:

Type to your heart's content

Let's say you enter a long text value. What happens to that text when it gets shown in the other table view?

There is no problem on the All Lists screen:

Built-in cell styles automatically resize

This table view uses the built-in "Subtitle" cell style, which automatically resizes to fit the width of the screen. It also truncates the text with … when it becomes too large.

Update to-do items list for larger screens

For the to-do items table, however, the picture doesn't look so rosy. The text gets cut off before the end of the screen on larger devices:

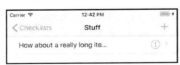

The text gets cut off

Because this is a custom prototype cell design, you'll have to add some constraints to stop this from happening.

➤ In the storyboard, go to the Checklist screen and select the label inside the prototype cell.

➤ First use **Editor → Size to Fit Content** to give the label its ideal size. That makes it a lot smaller, but that's OK. Without doing this first you may run into issues on the next steps. (Don't worry if doing this also moves the label.)

You want to pin the label to the right edge of the content view so it sticks to the disclosure button. Let's make that constraint first.

➤ Open the **Add New Constraints menu** and uncheck **Constrain to margins**.

➤ Activate the red I-beam on the **left**. Keep the value at what is suggested if you are happy with the spacing between the label and the checkmark before it.

➤ Activate the red I-beam on the **right**. Give it the value 0 so there is no spacing between the label and the disclosure button.

➤ Click **Add 1 Constraint** to add the new constraint.

Pinning the label

Hmm … that moves everything right and the label has a red outline around it:

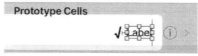

The label doesn't have enough constraints yet

Remember that you always need to specify enough constraints to determine the position and size of a view. Here you only have enough for the label to position itself horizontally, but what about vertically?

➤ With the label still selected, open the **Align menu** (next to Add New Constraints). Check **Vertically in Container** and click **Add 1 Constraint**.

Centering the label vertically

Now everything turns blue again. The label has a valid position, both X and Y.

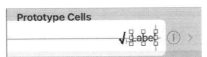

All blue bars but still in the wrong place

Note: Even though you didn't specify any constraints for the label's size, the bars are all blue. How come they are not red or orange?

Without size constraints, the label uses its contents – the text and the font – to calculate how big needs to be. This is called the *intrinsic content size*.

UI components with an intrinsic size, such as UILabel, don't need to have Width or Height constraints, but this is only valid if you've used Size to Fit Content to reset the label to its intrinsic size first.

Unfortunately, the label is now right aligned. That's not what you wanted... the label should be on the left and just as wide as the cell's content view.

The easiest way to make this happen is to constraints to the checkmark icon to glue it to the left edge of the screen as well. However, do note that the checkmark label changes size depending on whether the checkmark is set or not. So you can't depend on the label's intrinsic content size here. (Otherwise, when the checkmark is not showing, the text for thos rows would be slightly shifted to the left.)

➤ Instead, you'll set the **left** spacing for the checkmark label as well as a specific **width**.

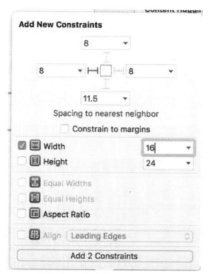

Checkmark label constraints

The label now stretches to be as wide as the table view cell.

There's one more thing to be done - you need to vertically center the checkmark. Easy enough since you are now a master of auto layout, right?

➤ With the checkmark label still selected, open the **Align menu** (next to Add New Constraints). Check **Vertically in Container** and click **Add 1 Constraint**.

➤ Run the app and the label should properly truncate:

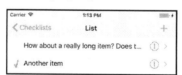

The label uses as much room as it can

You can find the project for the app up to this point under **19 - UI Improvements** in the Source Code folder.

Chapter 20: Local Notifications

I hope you're still with me! We have discussed in great detail view controllers, navigation controllers, storyboards, segues, table views and cells, and the data model. These are all essential topics to master if you want to build iOS apps because almost every app uses these building blocks.

In this chapter you're going to expand the app to add a new feature: **local notifications**, using the iOS User Notifications framework. A local notification allows the app to schedule a reminder to the user that will be displayed even when the app is not running.

You will add a "due date" field to the `ChecklistItem` object and then remind the user about this deadline with a local notification.

If this sounds like fun, then keep reading. :-)

The steps for this chapter are as follows:

- **Try it out:** Try out a local notification just to see how it works.

- **Set a due date:** Allow the user to pick a due date for to-do items.

- **Due date UI:** Create a date picker control.

- **Schedule local notifications:** Schedule local notifications for the to-do items, and update them when the user changes the due date.

Try it out

Before you wonder about how to integrate local notifications with *Checklists*, let's just schedule a local notification and see what happens.

By the way, local notifications are different from *push* notifications (also known as *remote* notifications). Push notifications allow your app to receive messages about external events, such as your favorite team winning the World Series.

Local notifications are more similar to an alarm clock: you set a specific time and then it "beeps".

Get permission to display local notifications

An app is only allowed to show local notifications after it has asked the user for permission. If the user denies permission, then any local notifications for your app simply won't appear. You only need to ask for permission once, so let's do that first.

➤ Open **AppDelegate.swift** and add an new import to the top of the file:

```
import UserNotifications
```

This tells Xcode that we're going to use the User Notifications framework.

➤ Add the following to the method
`application(_:didFinishLaunchingWithOptions:)`, just before the `return true` line:

```
// Notification authorization
let center = UNUserNotificationCenter.current()
center.requestAuthorization(options: [.alert, .sound]) {
  granted, error in
  if granted {
    print("We have permission")
  } else {
    print("Permission denied")
  }
}
```

Recall that `application(_:didFinishLaunchingWithOptions:)` is called when the app starts up. It is the *entry point* for the app, the first place in the code where you can do something after the app launches.

Because you're just playing with these local notifications now, this is a good place to ask for permission.

You tell iOS that the app wishes to send notifications of type "alert" with a sound effect. Later you'll put this code into a more appropriate place.

Things that start with a dot

Throughout the app you've seen things like `.none`, `.checkmark`, and `.subtitle` – and now `.alert` and `.sound`. These are *enumeration* symbols.

An enumeration, or enum for short, is a data type that consists of a list of possible symbols and their values.

For example, the `UNAuthorizationOptions` enum contains the symbols:

```
.badge
.sound
.alert
.carPlay
```

You can combine these names in an array to define what sort of notifications the app will show to the user. Here you've chosen the combination of an alert and a sound effect by writing `[.alert, .sound]`.

It's easy to spot when an enum is being used because of the dot in front of the symbol name. This is actually shorthand notation; you could also have written it like this:

```
center.requestAuthorization(options:
   [UNAuthorizationOptions.alert, UNAuthorizationOptions.sound])
{
   . . .
```

Fortunately, Swift is smart enough to realize that `.alert` and `.sound` are from the enum `UNAuthorizationOptions`, so you can save yourself some keystrokes.

➤ Run the app. You should immediately get a popup asking for permission:

The permission dialog

Tap **Allow**. The next time you run the app you won't be asked again; iOS remembers your choice.

(If you tapped Don't Allow – naughty! – then you can always reset the Simulator to get the permissions dialog again. You can also change the notification options via the *Settings* app.)

Show a test local notification

➤ Stop the app and add the following code to the end of `didFinishLaunchingWithOptions` (but before the `return`):

```
let content = UNMutableNotificationContent()
content.title = "Hello!"
content.body = "I am a local notification"
content.sound = UNNotificationSound.default()

let trigger = UNTimeIntervalNotificationTrigger(
                                    timeInterval: 10,
                                        repeats: false)
let request = UNNotificationRequest(
                        identifier: "MyNotification",
                           content: content,
                           trigger: trigger)
center.add(request)
```

This creates a new local notification. Because you wrote `timeInterval: 10`, it will fire exactly 10 seconds after the app has started.

The `UNMutableNotificationContent` describes what the local notification will say. Here, you set an alert message to be shown when the notification fires. You also set a sound.

Finally, you add the notification to the `UNUserNotificationCenter`. This object is responsible for keeping track of all the local notifications and displaying them when they are up.

➤ Run the app. Immediately after it has started, exit to the home screen.

Wait 10 seconds… I know, it seems like an eternity! After an agonizing 10 seconds a message should pop up:

The local notification message

➤ Tap the notification to go back to the app.

And that's a local notification. Pretty cool, huh?

Why did I want you to exit to the home screen? iOS will only show a notification alert if the app is not currently active.

➤ Stop the app and run it again. This time don't press Home and just wait.

Well, don't wait too long – nothing will happen. The local notification does get fired, but it is not shown to the user. To handle this situation, we must listen somehow to interesting events that concern these notifications. How? Through a delegate, of course!

Handle local notification events

➤ Add the following to **AppDelegate**'s `class` declaration:

```
class AppDelegate: UIResponder, UIApplicationDelegate,
                UNUserNotificationCenterDelegate {
```

This makes **AppDelegate** the delegate for the `UNUserNotificationCenter`.

➤ Also add the following method to **AppDelegate.swift**:

```
// MARK:- User Notification Delegates
func userNotificationCenter(
                _ center: UNUserNotificationCenter,
    willPresent notification: UNNotification,
    withCompletionHandler completionHandler:
    @escaping (UNNotificationPresentationOptions) -> Void) {
  print("Received local notification \(notification)")
}
```

This method will be invoked when the local notification is posted and the app is still running. You won't do anything here except log a message to the debug pane.

When your app is active and in the foreground, it is supposed to handle any fired notifications in its own manner. Depending on the type of app, it may make sense to react to the notification, for example to show a message to the user or to refresh the screen.

➤ Finally, tell the `UNUserNotificationCenter` that **AppDelegate** is now its delegate. You do this in `application(_:didFinishLaunchingWithOptions:)` (add this after you ask for permission - perhaps when permission is granted?):

```
center.delegate = self
```

➤ Run the app again and just wait (don't press Home).

After 10 seconds you should see a message in the Xcode Console. It displays something like this:

```
Received local notification <UNNotification: 0x7ff54af135e0;
date:
2016-07-11 14:21:27 +0000, request:
<UNNotificationRequest: . . .
identifier: MyNotification, content: <UNNotificationContent: . .
.
title: Hello!, subtitle: (null), body: I am a local
notification,
. . .
```

All right, now you know that it works, you should remove the test code from **AppDelegate.swift** because you don't really want to schedule a new notification every time the user starts the app.

➤ Remove the the local notification code from didFinishLaunchingWithOptions, but keep these lines:

```
let center = UNUserNotificationCenter.current()
center.delegate = self
```

You can also keep the userNotificationCenter(_:willPresent:withCompletionHandler:) method, as it will come in handy when debugging the local notifications.

Set a due date

Let's think about how the app will handle these notifications. Each ChecklistItem will get a due date field (a Date object, which specifies a date and time) and a Bool that says whether the user wants to be reminded of this item or not.

Users might not want to be reminded of everything, so you shouldn't schedule local notifications unless the user asks for it. Such a Bool variable is often called a *flag*. Let's name it shouldRemind.

When do you schedule a notification?

First, let's figure out how and when to schedule the notifications. I can think of the following situations:

• When the user adds a new ChecklistItem object that has the shouldRemind flag set, you must schedule a new notification.

- When the user changes the due date on an existing `ChecklistItem`, the old notification (if there is one) should be cancelled and a new one scheduled in its place (if `shouldRemind` is still set).

- When the user toggles the `shouldRemind` flag from on to off, the existing notification should be cancelled. The other way around, from off to on, should schedule a new notification.

- When the user deletes a `ChecklistItem`, its notification, if it had one, should be cancelled.

- When the user deletes an entire `Checklist`, all the notifications for those items, if there are any, should be cancelled.

This makes it obvious that you don't need just a way to schedule new notifications, but also a way to cancel them.

You should probably also check that you don't create notifications for to-do items whose due dates are in the past. I'm sure iOS is smart enough to ignore those notifications, but let's be good citizens anyway.

Associate to-do items with notifications

We need some way to associate `ChecklistItem` objects with their local notifications. This requires some changes to our data model.

When you schedule a local notification, you create a `UNNotificationRequest` object. It is tempting to put the `UNNotificationRequest` object as an instance variable in `ChecklistItem`, so you always know what it is. However, this is not the correct approach.

Instead, you'll use an *identifier*. When you create a local notification, you need to give it an identifier, which is just a `String`. It doesn't really matter what is in this string, as long as it is unique for each notification.

To cancel a notification at a later point, you don't use the `UNNotificationRequest` object but the identifier you gave it. The right approach is to store this identifier in the `ChecklistItem` object.

Even though the identifier for the local notification is a `String`, you'll give give each `ChecklistItem` an identifier that is simply a number. You'll also save this item ID in the Checklists.plist file. When it's time to schedule or cancel a local notification, you'll turn that number into a string. Then, you can easily find the notification when you have the `ChecklistItem` object, or the `ChecklistItem` object when you have the notification object.

Assigning numeric IDs to objects is a common approach when creating data models – it is very similar to giving records in a relational database a numeric primary key, if you're familiar with that sort of thing.

➤ Add these properties to **ChecklistItem.swift**:

```
var dueDate = Date()
var shouldRemind = false
var itemID: Int
```

Note that you called the last variable `itemID` and not simply "id". The reason is that `id` is a special keyword in Objective-C, and this could cause trouble if you ever wanted to mix your Swift code with Objective-C code.

The `dueDate` and `shouldRemind` variables have initial values, but `itemID` does not. That's why you had to specify the type for `itemID` – it's an `Int` – but not for the other two variables since Swift will infer the type for those based on the initial value.

Xcode will complain at this point since `Checklist` has no initilizer which sets up `itemID` and it has no initial value. In order to correct this, you need to add a new method to `DataModel` to generate a unique item ID.

➤ Hop on over to **DataModel.swift** and add a new method:

```
class func nextChecklistItemID() -> Int {
   let userDefaults = UserDefaults.standard
   let itemID = userDefaults.integer(forKey: "ChecklistItemID")
   userDefaults.set(itemID + 1, forKey: "ChecklistItemID")
   userDefaults.synchronize()
   return itemID
}
```

You're using your old friend `UserDefaults` again.

This method gets the current "ChecklistItemID" value from `UserDefaults`, adds 1 to it, and writes it back to `UserDefaults`. It returns the previous value to the caller.

The method also does `userDefaults.synchronize()` to force `UserDefaults` to write these changes to disk immediately, so they won't get lost if you kill the app from Xcode before it had a chance to save.

This is important because you never want two or more `ChecklistItems` to get the same ID.

You could add a default value for "ChecklistItemID" to the `registerDefaults()` method so as to customize the start value for the item ID, but you really don't have to in this case :] Remember that if there is no existing value for "ChecklistItemID", you'd get 0 back from a call to `UserDefaults` (if you didn't provide a defualt value via registerDefaults()). That is good enough for your use since your IDs would then start at 0 and count up.

The first time nextChecklistItemID() is called, it will return the ID 0. The second time it is called it will return the ID 1, the third time it will return the ID 2, and so on. The number is incremented by one each time. You can call this method a few billion times before you run out of unique IDs.

Class methods vs. instance methods

If you are wondering why you wrote,

```
class func nextChecklistItemID()
```

and not just:

```
func nextChecklistItemID()
```

then I'm glad you're paying attention. :-)

Adding the class keyword means that you can call this method without having a reference to an instance of the DataModel object.

With a class method, you do:

```
itemID = DataModel.nextChecklistItemID()
```

Instead of:

```
itemID = dataModel.nextChecklistItemID()
```

This is because ChecklistItem objects do not have a dataModel property with a reference to a DataModel object. You could certainly pass them such a reference, but I decided that using a *class method* was easier.

The declaration of a class method begins with class func. This kind of method applies to the class as a whole.

So far you've been using *instance methods*. They just have the word func (without class) and work only on a specific instance of that class.

We haven't discussed the difference between classes and instances before, and you'll get into that in more detail later in the book. For now, just remember that a method starting with class func allows you to call methods on an object even when you don't have a reference to that object.

I had to make a trade-off: is it worth giving each `ChecklistItem` object a reference to the `DataModel` object, or can I get away with a simple class method? To keep things simple, I chose the latter. It's certainly possible that, if you were to develop this app further, it would make more sense to give `ChecklistItem` a `dataModel` property instead.

➤ Now, switch back to **ChecklistItem.swift** and add an `init()` method to fix the initial Xcode error:

```
override init() {
  itemID = DataModel.nextChecklistItemID()
  super.init()
}
```

This asks the `DataModel` object for a new item ID whenever the app creates a new `ChecklistItem` object.

Display the new IDs

For a quick test to see if assigning these IDs works, you can add them to the text that is shown in the `ChecklistItem` cell label. This is just a temporary thing for testing purposes, as users couldn't care less about the internal identifier of these objects.

➤ In **ChecklistViewController.swift**, change the `configureText(for:with:)` method to:

```
func configureText(for cell: UITableViewCell,
                with item: ChecklistItem) {
  let label = cell.viewWithTag(1000) as! UILabel
  //label.text = item.text
  label.text = "\(item.itemID): \(item.text)"
}
```

I have commented out the original line because you want to reuse it later. The new one uses \(...) to add the to-do item's `itemID` property to the text.

Before you run the app, do note that you have changed the format of the `ChecklistItem` (and thus, by extension the Checklists.plist file) and so your existing data will not display when you run the app.

➤ Run the app and add some checklist items. Each new item should get a unique identifier. Exit to the home screen (to make sure everything is saved properly) and stop the app.

Run the app again and add some new items; the IDs for these new items should start counting at where they left off.

The items with their IDs. Note that the item with ID 3 was deleted in this example.

OK, that takes care of the IDs. Now lets add the "due date" and "should remind" fields to the Add/Edit Item screen.

(Keep `configureText(for:with:)` the way it is for the time being; that will come in handy with testing the notifications.)

Due date UI

You will add settings for the two new fields to the Add/Edit Item screen and make it look like this:

The Add/Edit Item screen now has Remind Me and Due Date fields

The due date field will require some sort of date picker control. iOS comes with a cool date picker view that you'll add into the table view.

The UI changes

➤ Add the following outlets to **ItemDetailViewController.swift**:

```
@IBOutlet weak var shouldRemindSwitch: UISwitch!
@IBOutlet weak var dueDateLabel: UILabel!
```

➤ Open the storyboard and select the Table View in the Add Item scene.

➤ Add a new section to the table. The easiest way to do this is to increment the **Sections** field in the **Attributes inspector**. This duplicates the existing section and cell.

➤ Remove the Text Field from the new cell. Select the new section in the Document Outline and then increment its **Rows** value to 2 in the **Attributes inspector**.

You will now design the new cells to look as follows:

The new design of the Add/Edit Item screen

➤ Add a **Label** to the first cell and set its text to **Remind Me**. Set the font to **System**, size **17**.

➤ Also drag a **Switch** control into the cell. Hook it up to the `shouldRemindSwitch` outlet on the view controller. In the Attributes inspector, set its Value to **Off** so it is no longer green.

➤ Pin the Switch to the **top** and **right** edges of the table view cell. This makes sure the control will be visible regardless of the width of the device's screen.

➤ The third cell has two labels: Due Date on the left and the label that will hold the actual chosen date on the right. You don't have to add these labels yourself: simply set the **Style** of the cell to **Right Detail** and rename Title to **Due Date**.

➤ The label on the right should be hooked up to the `dueDateLabel` outlet.

You may need to move the Remind Me label and the switch around a bit to align them nicely with the labels from the "due date" cell. Tip: select the "Due Date" and "Detail" labels and look in the Size inspector what their margins are (should be 16 points from the edges).

Display the due date

Let's write the code for dispalying the due date.

➤ Add a new dueDate instance variable to **ItemDetailViewController.swift**:

```
var dueDate = Date()
```

For a new ChecklistItem item, the due date is right now, i.e. Date(). That sounds reasonable but by the time the user has filled in the rest of the fields and pressed Done, that due date will be in the past.

But you do have to suggest something here. An alternative default value could be this time tomorrow, or ten minutes from now, but in most cases the user will have to pick their own due date anyway.

➤ Add a new updateDueDateLabel() method to the file:

```
func updateDueDateLabel() {
   let formatter = DateFormatter()
   formatter.dateStyle = .medium
   formatter.timeStyle = .short
   dueDateLabel.text = formatter.string(from: dueDate)
}
```

To convert the Date value to text, you use a DateFormatter object.

The way it works is very straightforward: you give it a style for the date component and a separate style for the time component, and then ask it to format the Date object.

You can play with different styles here, but space in the label is limited. So, you can't fit in the full month name, for example.

The cool thing about DateFormatter is that it takes the current locale into consideration so the time will look good to the user no matter where they are on the globe.

➤ Change viewDidLoad() as follows:

```
override func viewDidLoad() {
   . . .
   if let item = itemToEdit {             // Change name
   . . .
```

```
        shouldRemindSwitch.isOn = item.shouldRemind  // add this
        dueDate = item.dueDate                        // add this
    }

    updateDueDateLabel()                              // add this
}
```

If there already is an existing `ChecklistItem` object, you set the switch control to on or off, depending on the value of the object's `shouldRemind` property. If the user is adding a new item, the switch is initially off (you did that in the storyboard).

You also get the due date from the `ChecklistItem`.

Update edited values

➤ The last thing to change in this file is the `done()` action. Replace the current code with:

```
@IBAction func done() {
  if let item = itemToEdit {
    item.text = textField.text!

    item.shouldRemind = shouldRemindSwitch.isOn  // add this
    item.dueDate = dueDate                        // add this

    delegate?.itemDetailViewController(self,
                       didFinishEditing: item)
  } else {
    let item = ChecklistItem()
    item.text = textField.text!
    item.checked = false

    item.shouldRemind = shouldRemindSwitch.isOn  // add this
    item.dueDate = dueDate                        // add this

    delegate?.itemDetailViewController(self,
                       didFinishAdding: item)
  }
}
```

Here you put the value of the switch control and the `dueDate` instance variable back into the `ChecklistItem` object when the user presses the Done button.

➤ Run the app and change the position of the switch control. The app will remember this setting when you terminate it (but be sure to exit to the home screen first).

The due date row doesn't really do anything yet, however. In order to make that work, you first have to create a date picker.

> **Note:** Maybe you're wondering why you're using an instance variable for the `dueDate` but not for `shouldRemind`.
>
> You don't need one for `shouldRemind` because it's easy to get the state of the switch control: you just look at its `isOn` property, which is either `true` or `false`.

> However, it is hard to read the chosen date back out of the `dueDateLabel` because the label stores text (a `String`), not a `Date`. So it's easier to keep track of the chosen date separately in a `Date` instance variable.

The date picker

You will not create a new view controller for the date picker. Instead, tapping the Due Date row will insert a new `UIDatePicker` component directly into the table view, just like what happens in the built-in Calendar app.

The date picker in the Add Item screen

➤ Add a new instance variable to **ItemDetailViewController.swift**, to keep track of whether the date picker is currently visible:

```
var datePickerVisible = false
```

➤ Add the `showDatePicker()` method:

```
func showDatePicker() {
  datePickerVisible = true

  let indexPathDatePicker = IndexPath(row: 2, section: 1)
  tableView.insertRows(at: [indexPathDatePicker], with: .fade)
}
```

This sets the new instance variable to `true`, and tells the table view to insert a new row below the Due Date cell. This new row will contain the `UIDatePicker`.

The question is: where does the cell for this new date picker row come from? You can't put it into the table view as a static cell already because then it would always be visible. You only want to show it after the user taps the Due Date row.

Xcode has a feature where you can add additional views to a scene that are not immediately visible. That's a great solution to this problem!

➤ Open the storyboard and go to the **Add Item** scene. From the Object Library, pick up a new **Table View Cell**. Don't drag it on to the view controller itself but on to the scene dock at the top:

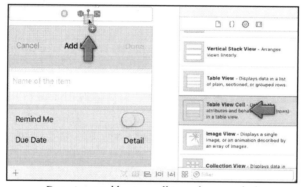

Dragging a table view cell into the scene dock

Now, the storyboard should look like this:

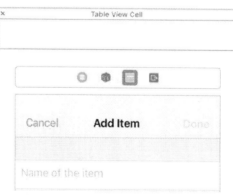

The new table view cell sits in its own area

The new Table View Cell object belongs to the scene but it is not (yet) part of the scene's table view.

The cell is a bit too small to fit a date picker, so first you'll make it bigger.

➤ Select the Table View Cell and in the **Size inspector** set the **Height** to 217. The date picker is 216 points tall, plus one point for the separator line at the bottom of the cell.

➤ In the **Attributes inspector**, set **Selection** to **None** so this cell won't turn gray when you tap on it.

➤ From the Object Library, drag a **Date Picker** into the cell. It should fit exactly.

➤ Use the **Add New Constraints menu** to glue the Date Picker to the four sides of the cell. Turn off **Constrain to margins** and then select the four I-beams to make them red (they all should be 0).

When you're done, the new cell looks like this:

The finished date picker cell

So how do you get this cell into the table view? First, make two new outlets and connect them to the cell and the date picker, respectively. That way you can refer to these views from code.

➤ Add these lines to **ItemDetailViewController.swift**:

```
@IBOutlet weak var datePickerCell: UITableViewCell!
@IBOutlet weak var datePicker: UIDatePicker!
```

➤ Switch back to the storyboard and simply Control-drag from the yellow circle icon for the view controller to the gray icon for the Table View Cell, and select the **datePickerCell** outlet.

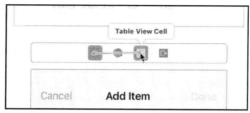

Control-drag between the icons in the scene dock

➤ To connect the date picker, Control-drag from the yellow icon to the big Date Picker above it and select the **datePicker** outlet.

Display the date picker

Great! Now that you have outlets for the cell and the date picker inside it, you can write the code to add them to the table view.

Normally, you would implement the `tableView(_:cellForRowAt:)` method, but remember that this screen uses a table view with static cells. Such a table view does not have a data source and therefore does not use `cellForRowAt`.

If you look in **ItemDetailViewController.swift** you won't find that method anywhere. However, with a bit of trickery you can override the data source for a static table view and provide your own methods.

➤ Add the `tableView(_:cellForRowAt:)` method to **ItemDetailViewController.swift**:

```swift
override func tableView(_ tableView: UITableView,
             cellForRowAt indexPath: IndexPath)
             -> UITableViewCell {
  if indexPath.section == 1 && indexPath.row == 2 {
    return datePickerCell
  } else {
    return super.tableView(tableView, cellForRowAt: indexPath)
  }
}
```

Danger: You shouldn't really mess around too much with this method when it's being used by a static table view, because it may interfere with the inner workings of those static cells. But if you're careful you can get away with it.

The `if` statement checks whether `cellForRowAt` is being called with the index-path for the date picker row. If so, it returns the new `datePickerCell` that you just designed. This is safe to do because the table view from the storyboard doesn't know anything about row 2 in section 1, so you're not interfering with an existing static cell.

For any index-paths that are not the date picker cell, this method will call through to super (which is UITableViewController). This is the trick that makes sure the other static cells still work.

➤ You also need to override tableView(_:numberOfRowsInSection:):

```
override func tableView(_ tableView: UITableView,
        numberOfRowsInSection section: Int) -> Int {
  if section == 1 && datePickerVisible {
    return 3
  } else {
    return super.tableView(tableView,
      numberOfRowsInSection: section)
  }
}
```

If the date picker is visible, then section 1 has three rows. If the date picker isn't visible, you can simply pass through to the original data source.

➤ Likewise, you also need to provide the tableView(_:heightForRowAt:) method:

```
override func tableView(_ tableView: UITableView,
            heightForRowAt indexPath: IndexPath) -> CGFloat {
  if indexPath.section == 1 && indexPath.row == 2 {
    return 217
  } else {
    return super.tableView(tableView, heightForRowAt: indexPath)
  }
}
```

So far the cells in your table views all had the same height (44 points), but this is not a hard requirement. By providing the heightForRowAt method you can give each cell its own height. The UIDatePicker component is 216 points tall, plus 1 point for the separator line, making for a total row height of 217 points.

The date picker is only made visible after the user taps the Due Date cell, which happens in tableView(_:didSelectRowAt:).

➤ Add that method:

```
override func tableView(_ tableView: UITableView,
            didSelectRowAt indexPath: IndexPath) {
  tableView.deselectRow(at: indexPath, animated: true)
  textField.resignFirstResponder()

  if indexPath.section == 1 && indexPath.row == 1 {
    showDatePicker()
  }
}
```

This calls `showDatePicker()` when the index-path indicates that the Due Date row was tapped. It also hides the on-screen keyboard if that was visible.

Make the Due Date row tappable

At this point you have most of the pieces in place, but the Due Date row isn't actually tap-able yet. That's because **ItemDetailViewController.swift** already has a `willSelectRowAt` method that always returns `nil`, causing taps on all rows to be ignored.

➤ Change `tableView(_:willSelectRowAt:)` to:

```
override func tableView(_ tableView: UITableView,
            willSelectRowAt indexPath: IndexPath) -> IndexPath? {
  if indexPath.section == 1 && indexPath.row == 1 {
    return indexPath
  } else {
    return nil
  }
}
```

Now the Due Date row responds to taps, but the other rows don't.

➤ Run the app to try it out. Add a new checklist item and tap the Due Date row.

Oop!. The app crashes. After some investigating, I found that when you override the data source for a static table view cell, you also need to provide the delegate method `tableView(_:indentationLevelForRowAt:)`.

That's not a method you'd typically use, but because you're messing with the data source for a static table view, you do need to override it. I told you this was a little tricky.

➤ Add the new delegate method:

```
override func tableView(_ tableView: UITableView,
    indentationLevelForRowAt indexPath: IndexPath) -> Int {
  var newIndexPath = indexPath
  if indexPath.section == 1 && indexPath.row == 2 {
    newIndexPath = IndexPath(row: 0, section: indexPath.section)
  }
  return super.tableView(tableView,
          indentationLevelForRowAt: newIndexPath)
}
```

The reason the app crashed on this method was that the standard data source doesn't know anything about the cell at row 2 in section 1 (the one with the date picker), because that cell isn't part of the table view's design in the storyboard.

So after inserting the new date picker cell, the data source gets confused and it crashes the app. To fix this, you have to trick the data source into believing there really are three rows in that section when the date picker is visible.

➤ Run the app again. This time the date picker cell shows up where it should:

The date picker appears in a new cell

Listen for date picker events

Interacting with the date picker *should* change the date in the Due Date row, but currently this has no effect whatsover on the Due Date row (try it out: spin the wheels).

You have to listen to the date picker's "Value Changed" event. That event gets sent whenever the picker wheels settle on a new value. For that, you need to add a new action method.

➤ Add the action method to **ItemDetailViewController.swift**:

```
@IBAction func dateChanged(_ datePicker: UIDatePicker) {
   dueDate = datePicker.date
   updateDueDateLabel()
}
```

This is pretty simple. It updates the `dueDate` instance variable with the new date and then updates the text on the Due Date label.

➤ In the storyboard, Control-drag from the Date Picker to the view controller and select the **dateChanged:** action method. Now everything is properly hooked up. (You can verify that the action method is indeed connected to the date picker's Value Changed event by looking at the Connections inspector.)

➤ Run the app to try it out. When you turn the wheels on the date picker, the text in the Due Date row updates too. Cool.

However, when you edit an existing to-do item, the date picker does not show the date from that item. It always starts on the current date and time.

➤ Add the following line to the bottom of showDatePicker():

```
datePicker.setDate(dueDate, animated: false)
```

This passes the proper date to the UIDatePicker component.

➤ Verify that it works: click on the ⓘ button from an existing to-do item, preferably one you made a while ago, and confirm that the date picker shows the same date and time as the Due Date label. Excellent!

Change the date label color when the date picker is active

Speaking of the label, it would be nice if this becomes highlighted when the date picker is active. You can use the tint color for this (that's also what the Calendar app does).

➤ Replace the contents of showDatePicker() with this:

```
func showDatePicker() {
  datePickerVisible = true

  let indexPathDateRow = IndexPath(row: 1, section: 1)
  let indexPathDatePicker = IndexPath(row: 2, section: 1)

  if let dateCell = tableView.cellForRow(at: indexPathDateRow) {
    dateCell.detailTextLabel!.textColor =
          dateCell.detailTextLabel!.tintColor
  }

  tableView.beginUpdates()
  tableView.insertRows(at: [indexPathDatePicker], with: .fade)
  tableView.reloadRows(at: [indexPathDateRow], with: .none)
  tableView.endUpdates()

  datePicker.setDate(dueDate, animated: false)
}
```

This sets the textColor of the detailTextLabel to the tint color. It also tells the table view to reload the Due Date row. Without that, the separator lines between the cells don't update properly.

Because you're doing two operations on the table view at the same time – inserting a new row and reloading another – you need to put that code in between calls to beginUpdates() and endUpdates(), so that the table view can animate everything at the same time.

➤ Run the app. The date now appears in blue:

The date label appears in the tint color while the date picker is visible

Hide the date picker

When the user taps the Due Date row again, the date picker should disappear. If you try that right now the app will crash – what did you expect? This won't win it many favorable reviews.

➤ Add a new `hideDatePicker()` method:

```
func hideDatePicker() {
  if datePickerVisible {
    datePickerVisible = false

    let indexPathDateRow = IndexPath(row: 1, section: 1)
    let indexPathDatePicker = IndexPath(row: 2, section: 1)

    if let cell = tableView.cellForRow(at: indexPathDateRow) {
      cell.detailTextLabel!.textColor = UIColor.black
    }
    tableView.beginUpdates()
    tableView.reloadRows(at: [indexPathDateRow], with: .none)
    tableView.deleteRows(at: [indexPathDatePicker], with: .fade)
    tableView.endUpdates()
  }
}
```

This does the opposite of `showDatePicker()`. It deletes the date picker cell from the table view and restores the color of the date label to the original color.

➤ Change `tableView(_:didSelectRowAt:)` to toggle between the visible and hidden states.

```
override func tableView(_ tableView: UITableView,
          didSelectRowAt indexPath: IndexPath) {
  . . .
  if indexPath.section == 1 && indexPath.row == 1 {
    if !datePickerVisible {
      showDatePicker()
    } else {
      hideDatePicker()
    }
  }
}
```

There is another situation where it's a good idea to hide the date picker: when the user taps inside the text field.

It won't look very nice if the keyboard partially overlaps the date picker, so you might as well hide it. The view controller is already the delegate for the text field, making this easy.

➤ Add the textFieldDidBeginEditing(_:) method:

```
func textFieldDidBeginEditing(_ textField: UITextField) {
  hideDatePicker()
}
```

And with that you have a cool inline date picker!

➤ Run the app and verify that hiding the date picker works for both scenarios.

Schedule local notifications

One of the principles of object-oriented programming is that objects should do as much as possible themselves. Therefore, it makes sense that the ChecklistItem object should schedule its own notifications.

Schedule notifications

➤ Add the following method to **ChecklistItem.swift**:

```
func scheduleNotification() {
  if shouldRemind && dueDate > Date() {
    print("We should schedule a notification!")
  }
}
```

This compares the due date on the item with the current date. You can always get the current time by making a new Date object.

The statement `dueDate > Date()` compares the two dates and returns `true` if `dueDate` is in the future and `false` if it is in the past.

If the due date is in the past, the `print()` will not be performed.

Note the use of the && "and" operator. You only print the text when the Remind Me switch is set to "on" *and* the due date is in the future.

You will call this method when the user presses the Done button after adding or editing a to-do item.

➤ In the `done()` action in **ItemDetailViewController.swift**, add the following line just before the call to `didFinishEditing` and also before `didFinishaAdding`:

```
item.scheduleNotification()
```

➤ Run the app and try it out. Add a new item, set the switch to ON but don't change the due date. Press Done.

There should be no message in the Console because the due date has already passed (it is several seconds in the past by the time you press Done).

➤ Add another item, set the switch to ON, and choose a due date in the future.

When you press Done now, the text "We should schedule a notification!" should appear in the Console.

Now that you've verified the method is called in the proper place, let's actually schedule a new local notification object for the following three scenarios: adding a to-do item, editing a to-to item, deleting a to-do item.

Add a to-do item

➤ In **ChecklistItem.swift**, change `scheduleNotification()` to:

```swift
func scheduleNotification() {
  if shouldRemind && dueDate > Date() {
    // 1
    let content = UNMutableNotificationContent()
    content.title = "Reminder:"
    content.body = text
    content.sound = UNNotificationSound.default()

    // 2
    let calendar = Calendar(identifier: .gregorian)
    let components = calendar.dateComponents(
                      [.month, .day, .hour, .minute],
                      from: dueDate)
    // 3
```

```
        let trigger = UNCalendarNotificationTrigger(
                                    dateMatching: components,
                                        repeats: false)
        // 4
        let request = UNNotificationRequest(
              identifier: "\(itemID)", content: content,
                  trigger: trigger)
        // 5
        let center = UNUserNotificationCenter.current()
        center.add(request)

        print("Scheduled: \(request) for itemID: \(itemID)")
    }
}
```

You've seen this code before when you tried out local notifications for the first time, but there are a few differences.

1. Put the item's text into the notification message.

2. Extract the month, day, hour, and minute from the dueDate. We don't care about the year or the number of seconds – the notification doesn't need to be scheduled with millisecond precision, on the minute is precise enough.

3. To test local notifications you used a UNTimeIntervalNotificationTrigger, which scheduled the notification to appear after a number of seconds. Here, you're using a UNCalendarNotificationTrigger, which shows the notification at the specified date.

4. Create the UNNotificationRequest object. Important here is that we convert the item's numeric ID into a String and use it to identify the notification. That is how you'll be able to find this notification later in case you need to cancel it.

5. Add the new notification to the UNUserNotificationCenter.

Xcode is not so impressed with this new code and gives a bunch of error messages.

What is wrong here? UNUserNotificationCenter and the other objects are provided by the User Notifications framework – you can tell by the "UN" prefix in their names.

However, ChecklistItem hasn't used any code from that framework until now. The only framework objects it has used, NSObject and Codable, came from another framework, Foundation.

➤ To tell ChecklistItem about the User Notifications framework, you need to add the following line to the top of the file, below the other import:

```
import UserNotifications
```

Now the errors disappear like snow in the sun.

There's another small problem, though. If you've reset the Simulator recently, then the app no longer has permission to send local notifications.

➤ Try it out. Run the app, add a new checklist item, set the due date a minute into the future, and press Done. You might not see a notification.

Even if you do see a notification, since the authorization request code is no longer there, *Checklists* certainly won't have permission on your user devices.

When you were just messing around at the beginning of this chapter, you placed the permission request code in the AppDelegate and ran it immediately upon launch. That's not recommended.

Don't you just hate those apps that prompt you for ten different things before you've even had a chance to properly look at them? Let's be a bit more user friendly with our own app!

➤ Add the following method to **ItemDetailViewController.swift**:

```
@IBAction func shouldRemindToggled(_ switchControl: UISwitch) {
  textField.resignFirstResponder()

  if switchControl.isOn {
    let center = UNUserNotificationCenter.current()
    center.requestAuthorization(options: [.alert, .sound]) {
      granted, error in
      // do nothing
    }
  }
}
```

When the switch is toggled to ON, this prompts the user for permission to send local notifications. Once the user has given permission, the app won't put up a prompt again.

➤ Also add an import UserNotifications or the above method won't compile.

➤ Open the storyboard and connect the **shouldRemindToggled:** action to the switch control.

➤ Test it out. Run the app, add a new checklist item, set the due date a minute into the future, press Done and exit to the home screen.

Wait one minute (patience...) and the notification should appear. Pretty cool!

The local notification when the app is in the background

That takes care of the adding a new item scenario. There are two others left.

Edit an existing item

When the user edits an item, the following situations can occur with the Remind Me switch:

- Remind Me was switched off and is now switched on. You have to schedule a new notification.

- Remind Me was switched on and is now switched off. You have to cancel the existing notification.

- Remind Me stays switched on but the due date changes. You have to cancel the existing notification and schedule a new one.

- Remind Me stays switched on but the due date doesn't change. You don't have to do anything.

- Remind Me stays switched off. Here you also don't have to do anything.

Of course, in all those situations you'll only schedule the notification if the due date is in the future.

Phew, that's quite a list. It's always a good idea to take stock of all possible scenarios before you start programming because this gives you a clear picture of everything you need to tackle.

It may seem like you need to write a lot of logic here to deal with all these situations, but actually it turns out to be quite simple.

First you'll look if there is an existing notification for this to-do item. If there is, you simply cancel it. Then you determine whether the item should have a notification and if so, you schedule a new one.

That should take care of all the above situations, even if sometimes you simply could have left the existing notification alone. The algorithm is crude, but effective.

➤ Add the following method to **ChecklistItem.swift**:

```
func removeNotification() {
  let center = UNUserNotificationCenter.current()
```

```
    center.removePendingNotificationRequests(
                        withIdentifiers: ["\(itemID)"])
  }
```

This removes the local notification for this `ChecklistItem`, if it exists. Note that `removePendingNotificationRequests()` requires an array of identifiers, so we first put our `itemID` into a string with `\(...)` and then into an array using `[]`.

➤ Call this new method from to the top of `scheduleNotification()`:

```
func scheduleNotification() {
  removeNotification()
  . . .
}
```

Let's try it out.

➤ Run the app and add a to-do item with a due date two minutes into the future. A new notification will be scheduled. Go to the home screen and wait until it shows up.

➤ Edit the item and change the due date to three minutes into the future. The old notification will be removed and a new one scheduled for the new time.

➤ Add a new to-do item with a due date two minutes into the future. Edit the to-do item but now set the switch to OFF. The old notification will be removed and no new notification will be scheduled.

➤ Edit again and put the time a few minutes into the future but don't change anything else; no new notification will be scheduled because the switch is still off.

These tests should also work if you terminate the app in between.

Delete a to-do item

There is one last case to handle: deletion of a `ChecklistItem`. This can happen in two ways:

1. The user can delete an individual item using swipe-to-delete.

2. The user can delete an entire checklist, in which case all its `ChecklistItem` objects are also deleted.

An object is notified when it is about to be deleted using the `deinit` message. You can simply implement this method, look if there is a scheduled notification for this item, and then cancel it.

➤ Add the following to **ChecklistItem.swift**:

```
deinit {
  removeNotification()
}
```

That's all you have to do. The special `deinit` method will be invoked when you delete an individual `ChecklistItem` but also when you delete a whole `Checklist` – because all its `ChecklistItems` will be destroyed as well, as the array they are in is deallocated.

➤ Run the app and try it out. First, schedule some notifications a minute or so into the future and then remove that to-do item or its entire checklist. Wait until the due date comes and you shouldn't get a notification.

Once you're convinced everything works, you can remove the `print()` statements. They are only temporary for debugging purposes. You probably don't want to leave them in the final app. The `print()` statements won't hurt, but the end user can't see those messages anyway.

➤ Also remove the item ID from the label in the `ChecklistViewController` – that was only used for debugging.

That's a wrap!

Things should be starting to make sense by now. I've thrown you into the deep end by writing an entire app from scratch. We've touched on a number of advanced topics already, but hopefully you were able to follow along quite well with what we've been doing. Kudos for sticking with it until the end!

It's OK if you're still a bit fuzzy on the details. Sleep on it for a bit and keep tinkering with the code. Programming requires its own way of thinking and you won't learn that overnight. Don't be afraid to do this app again from the start – it will make more sense the second time around!

This section focused mainly on UIKit and its most important controls and patterns. In the next section we'll take a few steps back to talk more about the Swift language itself. And of course, you'll build another cool app.

Here is the final storyboard for *Checklists*:

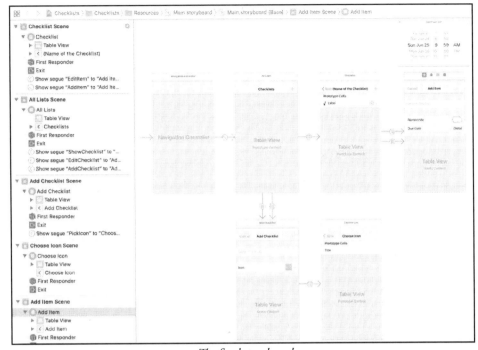

The final storyboard

Completing all of that is pretty impressive! Give yourself a well-deserved pat on the back :]

Take a break, and when you're ready, continue on to the next section, where you'll make an app that knows its place! :-)

Haven't had enough yet? Here are some challenges to sink your teeth into:

> **Exercise:** Display the due date in the table view cells, under the text of the to-do item.

> **Exercise:** Sort the to-do items list based on the due date. This is similar to what you did with the list of `Checklists` except that now you're sorting `ChecklistItem` objects and you'll be comparing `Date` objects instead of strings.

You can find the final project files for the Checklists app under **20 - Local Notifications** in the Source Code folder.

Section 3: My Locations

With this third section and the *MyLocations* app, you get into Swift programming in earnest.

Sure you've already done coding in the previous two sections, but this section starts off with a good review of all the Swift coding principles you've learned so far and adds to it by introducing some new concepts too.

In addition to that, you learn about using GPS coordinates, displaying data on maps, and using the iOS image picker to take photos using your camera or to pick existing images from your photo album. There's a lot of valuable general information on Swift development as well as specific information about building location-aware apps.

Chapter 21: Swift Review

Chapter 22: Get Location Data

Chapter 23: Use Location Data

Chapter 24: Objects vs. Classes

Chapter 25: The Tag Location Screen

Chapter 26: Adding Polish

Chapter 27: Saving Locations

Chapter 28: The Locations Tab

Chapter 29: Maps

Chapter 30: Image Picker

Chapter 31: Polishing the App

Chapter 21: Swift Review

You have made great progress! You've learnt the basics of Swift programming and created two applications from scratch. You are on the threshold of creating your next app.

But, a good building needs a good foundation. And in order to strengthen the foundations of your Swift knowledge, you first need some additional theory. There is still a lot more to learn about Swift and object-oriented programming!

In the previous chapters I've shown you a fair bit of the Swift programming language already, but not quite everything. Previously, it was good enough if you could more-or-less follow along with what we were doing, but now is the time to fill in the gaps in theory. So, let's do a little refresher on what we've talked about so far.

In this chapter, you will learn the following:

- **Variables, constants, and types:** the difference between variables and constants, and what a type is.

- **Methods and functions:** what are methods and functions, are they the same thing?

- **Making decisions:** an explanation of the various programming constructs that can be used in the decision making process for your programs.

- **Loops:** how do you loop through a list of items?

- **Objects:** all you ever wanted to know about Objects - what they are, their component parts, how to use them, and how not to abuse them.

- **Protocols:** the nitty, gritty details about protocols.

Variables, constants, and types

Variables and types

A **variable** is a temporary container for a specific type of value:

```
var count: Int
var shouldRemind: Bool
var text: String
var list: [ChecklistItem]
```

The **data type**, or just **type**, of a variable determines what kind of values it can contain. Some variables hold simple values such as Int or Bool, others hold more complex objects such as String or Array.

The basic types you've used so far are: Int for whole numbers, Float for numbers with decimals (also known as *floating-point* numbers), and Bool for boolean values (true or false).

There are a few other fundamental types as well:

- Double. Similar to a Float but with more precision. You will use Doubles later on for storing latitude and longitude data.

- Character. Holds a single character. A String is a collection of Characters.

- UInt. A variation on Int that you may encounter occasionally. The U stands for "unsigned", meaning the data type can hold positive values only. It's called unsigned because it cannot have a negative sign (-) in front of the number. UInt can store numbers between 0 and 18 quintillion, but no negative numbers.

- Int8, UInt8, Int16, UInt16, Int32, UInt32, Int64, UInt64. These are all variations on Int. The difference is in how many bytes they have available to store their values. The more bytes, the bigger the values they can store. In practice, you almost always use Int, which uses 8 bytes for storage on a 64-bit platform (a fact that you may immediately forget) and can fit positive and negative numbers up to about 19 digits. Those are big numbers!

- CGFloat. This isn't really a Swift type but a type defined by the iOS SDK. It's a decimal point number like Float and Double. For historical reasons, this is used throughout UIKit for floating-point values. (The "CG" prefix stands for the Core Graphics framework.)

Swift is very strict about types, more so than many other languages. If the type of a variable is Int, you cannot put a Float value into it. The other way around also won't work: an Int won't go into a Float.

Even though both types represent numbers of some sort, Swift won't automatically convert between different number types. You always need to convert the values explicitly.

For example:

```
var i = 10
var f: Float
f = i          // error
f = Float(i)   // OK
```

You don't always need to specify the type when you create a new variable. If you give the variable an initial value, Swift uses **type inference** to determine the type:

```
var i = 10              // Int
var d = 3.14            // Double
var b = true            // Bool
var s = "Hello, world"  // String
```

The integer value `10`, the floating-point value `3.14`, the boolean `true` and the string `"Hello, world"` are named **literal constants** or just **literals**.

Note that using the value 3.14 in the example above leads Swift to conclude that you want to use a `Double` here. If you intended to use a `Float` instead, you'd have to write:

```
var f: Float = 3.14
```

The `: Float` bit is called a **type annotation**. You use it to override the guess made by Swift's type inference mechanism, since it doesn't always get things right.

Likewise, if you wanted the variable `i` to be a `Double` instead of an `Int`, you'd write:

```
var i: Double = 10
```

Or a little shorter, by giving the value 10 a decimal point:

```
var i = 10.0
```

These simple literals such as `10`, `3.14`, or `"Hello world"`, are useful only for creating variables of the basic types – `Int`, `Double`, `String`, and so on. To use more complex types, you'll need to **instantiate** an object first.

When you write the following,

```
var item: ChecklistItem
```

it only tells Swift you want to store a `ChecklistItem` object into the `item` variable, but it does not create that `ChecklistItem` object yet.

For that you need to write:

```
item = ChecklistItem()
```

This first reserves memory to hold the object's data, followed by a call to `init()` to properly set up the object for use. Reserving memory is also called **allocation**; filling up the object with its initial value(s) is **initialization**.

The whole process is known as **instantiating** the object – you're making an object **instance**. The instance is the block of memory that holds the values of the object's variables (that's why they are called "instance variables", get it?).

Of course, you can combine the above into a single line:

```
var item = ChecklistItem()
```

Here you left out the `: ChecklistItem` type annotation because Swift is smart enough to realize that the type of `item` should be `ChecklistItem`.

However, you can't leave out the `()` parentheses – this is how Swift knows that you want to make a new `ChecklistItem` instance.

Some objects allow you to pass **parameters** to their `init` method. For example:

```
var item = ChecklistItem(text: "Charge my iPhone", checked:
false)
```

This calls the corresponding `init(text:checked:)` method to prepare the newly allocated `ChecklistItem` object for usage.

You've seen two types of variables: **local variables**, whose existence is limited to the method they are declared in, and **instance variables** (also known as "ivars", or properties) that belong to the object and therefore can be used from within any method.

The lifetime of a variable is called its **scope**. The scope of a local variable is smaller than that of an instance variable. Once the method ends, any local variables are destroyed.

```
class MyObject {
   var count = 0        // an instance variable

   func myMethod() {
     var temp: Int     // a local variable
      temp = count     // OK to use the instance variable here
   }

   // the local variable "temp" doesn't exist outside the method
 }
```

If you have a local variable with the same name as an instance variable, then it is said to **shadow** (or **hide**) the instance variable. You should avoid these situations as they can lead to subtle bugs where you may not be using the variable that you think you are:

```swift
class MyObject {
    var count = 7       // an instance variable

    func myMethod() {
        var count = 42   // local variable "hides" instance variable
        print(count)     // prints 42
    }
}
```

Some developers place an underscore in front of their instance variable names to avoid this problem: _count instead of count. An alternative is to use the keyword self whenever you want to access an instance variable:

```swift
func myMethod() {
    var count = 42
    print(self.count)    // prints 7
}
```

Constants

Variables are not the only code elements that can hold values. A variable is a container for a value that is allowed to *change* over the course of the app being run.

For example, in a note-taking app, the user can change the text of the note. So, you'd place that text into a String variable. Every time the user edits the text, the variable is updated.

Sometimes, you'll just want to store the result of a calculation or a method call into a temporary container, after which this value will never change. In that case, it is better to make this container a **constant** rather than a variable.

The following values cannot change once they've been set:

```swift
let pi = 3.141592
let difference = abs(targetValue - currentValue)
let message = "You scored \(points) points"
let image = UIImage(named: "SayCheese")
```

If a constant is local to a method, it's allowed to give the constant a new value the next time the method is called. The value from the previous method invocation is destroyed when that method ends, and the next time the app enters that method you're creating a new constant with a new value (but with the same name). Of course, for the duration of that method call, the constant's value must remain the same.

Tip: My suggestion is to use `let` for everything. That is the right solution 90% of the time. When you get it wrong, the Swift compiler will warn that you're trying to change a constant. Only then should you change it to a `var`. This ensures you're not making things variable that don't need to be.

Value types vs. reference types

When working with basic values such as integers and strings – so called **value types** – a constant created with `let` cannot be changed once it has been given a value:

```
let pi = 3.141592
pi = 3                 // not allowed
```

However, with objects that are **reference types**, it is only the reference that is constant. The object itself can still be changed:

```
let item = ChecklistItem()
item.text = "Do the laundry"
item.checked = false
item.dueDate = yesterday
```

But this is not allowed:

```
let anotherItem = ChecklistItem()
item = anotherItem   // cannot change the reference
```

So how do you know what is a reference type and what is a value type?

Objects defined as `class` are reference types, while objects defined as `struct` or `enum` are value types. In practice, this means most of the objects from the iOS SDK are reference types but things that are built into the Swift language, such as `Int`, `String`, and `Array`, are value types. (More about this important difference later.)

Collections

A variable stores only a single value. To keep track of multiple objects, you can use a **collection** object. Naturally, I'm talking about arrays (`Array`) and dictionaries (`Dictionary`), both of which you've seen previously.

An **array** stores a list of objects. The objects it contains are ordered sequentially and you retrieve them by index.

```
// an array of ChecklistItem objects:
var items: Array<ChecklistItem>

// Or, using shorthand notation:
```

```
var items: [ChecklistItem]

// making an instance of the array:
items = [ChecklistItem]()

// accessing an object from the array:
let item = items[3]
```

You can write an array as Array<Type> or [Type]. The first one is the official version, the second is "syntactic sugar" that is a bit easier to read. (Unlike other languages, in Swift you don't write Type[]. The type name goes inside the brackets.)

A **dictionary** stores key-value pairs. An object, usually a string, is the key that retrieves another object.

```
// a dictionary that stores (String, Int) pairs, for example a
// list of people's names and their ages:
var ages: Dictionary<String, Int>

// Or, using shorthand notation:
var ages: [String: Int]

// making an instance of the dictionary:
ages = [String: Int]()

// accessing an object from the dictionary:
var age = dict["Jony Ive"]
```

The notation for retrieving an object from a dictionary looks very similar to reading from an array – both use the [ ] brackets. For indexing an array, you always use a positive integer, but for a dictionary you typically use a string.

There are other sorts of collections as well, but array and dictionary are the most common ones.

Generics

Array and Dictionary are known as **generics**, meaning that they are independent of the type of thing you want to store inside these collections.

You can have an Array of Int objects, but also an Array of String objects – or an Array of any kind of object, really (even an array of other arrays).

That's why you have to specify the type of object to store inside the array, before you can use it. In other words, you cannot write this:

```
var items: Array   // error: should be Array<TypeName>
var items: []      // error: should be [TypeName]
```

There should always be the name of a type inside the [ ] brackets or following the word Array in < > brackets. (If you're coming from Objective-C, be aware that the < > mean something completely different there.)

For `Dictionary`, you need to supply two type names: one for the type of the keys and one for the type of the values.

Swift requires that all variables and constants have a value. You can either specify a value when you declare the variable or constant, or by assigning a value inside an `init` method.

Optionals

Sometimes it's useful to have a variable that can have no value, in which case you need to declare it as an **optional**:

```
var checklistToEdit: Checklist?
```

You cannot use this variable immediately; you must always first test whether it has a value or not. This is called **unwrapping** the optional:

```
if let checklist = checklistToEdit {
   // "checklist" now contains the real object
} else {
   // the optional was nil
}
```

The `age` variable from the dictionary example in the previous section is actually an optional, because there is no guarantee that the dictionary contains the key "Jony Ive". Therefore, the type of `age` is `Int?` instead of just `Int`.

Before you can use a value from a dictionary, you need to unwrap it first using `if let`:

```
if let age = dict["Jony Ive"] {
   // use the value of age
}
```

If you are 100% sure that the dictionary contains a given key, you can also use **force unwrapping** to read the corresponding value:

```
var age = dict["Jony Ive"]!
```

With the ! you tell Swift, "This value will not be `nil`. I'll stake my reputation on it!" Of course, if you're wrong and the value *is* `nil`, the app will crash and your reputation is down the drain. Be careful with force unwrapping!

A slightly safer alternative to force unwrapping is **optional chaining**. For example, the following will crash the app if the `navigationController` property is `nil`:

```
navigationController!.delegate = self
```

But this won't:

```
navigationController?.delegate = self
```

Anything after the ? will simply be ignored if `navigationController` does not have a value. It's equivalent to writing:

```
if navigationController != nil {
  navigationController!.delegate = self
}
```

It is also possible to declare an optional using an exclamation point instead of a question mark. This makes it an **implicitly unwrapped** optional:

```
var dataModel: DataModel!
```

Such a value is potentially unsafe because you can use it as a regular variable without having to unwrap it first. If this variable has the value `nil` when you don't expect it – and don't they always – your app will crash.

Optionals exist to guard against such crashes, and using ! undermines the safety of using optionals.

However, sometimes using implicitly unwrapped optionals is more convenient than using pure optionals. Use them when you cannot give the variable an initial value at the time of declaration, nor in `init()`.

But once you've given the variable a value, you really ought not to make it `nil` again. If the value can become `nil` again, it's better to use a true optional with a question mark.

Methods and functions

You've learned that objects, the basic building blocks of all apps, have both data and functionality. Instance variables and constants provide the data, **methods** provide the functionality.

When you call a method, the app jumps to that section of the code and executes all the statements in the method one-by-one. When the end of the method is reached, the app jumps back to where it left off:

```
let result = performUselessCalculation(314)
print(result)

. . .

func performUselessCalculation(_ a: Int) -> Int {
  var b = Int(arc4random_uniform(100))
  var c = a / 2
  return (a + b) * c
}
```

Methods often return a value to the caller, usually the result of a computation or looking up something in a collection. The data type of the result value is written after the -> arrow. In the example above, it is Int. If there is no -> arrow, the method does not return a value (also known as returning Void).

Methods are **functions** that belong to an object, but there are also standalone functions such as print() and arc4random_uniform().

Functions serve the same purpose as methods – they bundle functionality into small re-usable units – but live outside of any objects. Such functions are also called *free* functions or *global* functions.

These are examples of methods:

```
// Method with no parameters, no return a value.
override func viewDidLoad()

// Method with one parameter, slider. No return a value.
// The keyword @IBAction means that this method can be connected
// to a control in Interface Builder.
@IBAction func sliderMoved(_ slider: UISlider)

// Method with no parameters, returns an Int value.
func countUncheckedItems() -> Int

// Method with two parameters, cell and item, no return value.
// Note that the first parameter has an extra label, for,
// and the second parameter has an extra label, with.
func configureCheckmarkFor(for cell: UITableViewCell,
                        with item: ChecklistItem)

// Method with two parameters, tableView and section.
// Returns an Int. The _ means the first parameter does not
// have an external label.
override func tableView(_ tableView: UITableView,
      numberOfRowsInSection section: Int) -> Int

// Method with two parameters, tableView and indexPath.
// The question mark means it returns an optional IndexPath
// object (may also return nil).
```

```
override func tableView(_ tableView: UITableView,
          willSelectRowAt indexPath: IndexPath) -> IndexPath?
```

To call a method on an object, you write `object.method(parameters)`. For example:

```
// Calling a method on the lists object:
lists.append(checklist)

// Calling a method with more than one parameter:
tableView.insertRows(at: indexPaths, with: .fade)
```

You can think of calling a method as *sending a message* from one object to another: "Hey `lists`, I'm sending you the `append` message for this `checklist` object."

The object whose method you're calling is known as the *receiver* of the message.

It is very common to call a method from the same object. Here, `loadChecklists()` calls the `sortChecklists()` method. Both are members of the `DataModel` object.

```
class DataModel {
  func loadChecklists() {
    . . .
    sortChecklists()  // this method also lives in DataModel
  }

  func sortChecklists() {
    . . .
  }
}
```

Sometimes this is written as:

```
func loadChecklists() {
  . . .
  self.sortChecklists()
}
```

The `self` keyword makes it clear that the `DataModel` object itself is the receiver of this message.

> **Note:** In this book I leave out the `self` keyword for method calls, because it's not necessary to have it. Objective-C developers are very attached to `self`, so you'll probably see it used a lot in Swift too. It is a topic of heated debate in developer circles, but except for a few specific scenarios, the compiler doesn't really care whether you use `self` or not.

Inside a method you can also use `self` to get a reference to the object itself:

```
@IBAction func cancel() {
  delegate?.itemDetailViewControllerDidCancel(self)
}
```

Here `cancel()` sends a reference to the object (i.e. `self`) along to the delegate, so the delegate knows who sent this `itemDetailViewControllerDidCancel()` message.

Also note the use of **optional chaining** here. The `delegate` property is an optional, so it can be `nil`. Using the question mark before the method call will ensure nothing bad happens if `delegate` is not set.

Parameters

Often methods have one or more **parameters**, so they can work with multiple data items. A method that is limited to a fixed set of data is not very useful or reusable. Consider `sumValuesFromArray()`, a method that has no parameters:

```
class MyObject {
  var numbers = [Int]()

  func sumValuesFromArray() -> Int {
    var total = 0
    for number in numbers {
      total += number
    }
    return total
  }
}
```

Here, `numbers` is an instance variable. The `sumValuesFromArray()` method is tied closely to that instance variable, and is useless without it.

Suppose you add a second array to the app that you also want to apply this calculation to. One approach is to copy-paste the above method and change the name of the variable to that of the new array. That certainly works, but it's not smart programming!

It's better to give the method a parameter that lets you pass in the array object you wish to examine. Then the method becomes independent from any instance variables:

```
func sumValues(from array: [Int]) -> Int {
  var total = 0
  for number in array {
    total += number
  }
  return total
}
```

Now you can call this method with any [Int] (or Array<Int>) object as its parameter.

This doesn't mean methods should never use instance variables, but if you can make a method more general by giving it a parameter, then that is usually a good idea.

Often methods use two names for their parameters, the **external label** and the **internal label**. For example:

```
func downloadImage(for searchResult: SearchResult,
                   withTimeout timeout: TimeInterval,
                   andPlaceOn button: UIButton) {
    . . .
}
```

This method has three parameters: searchResult, timeout, and button. Those are the internal parameter names you'd use in the code inside the method.

The external labels become part of the method name. The full name for the method is downloadImage(for:withTimeout:andPlaceOn:). Method names in Swift are often quite long!

To call this method, you'd use the external labels:

```
downloadImage(for: result, withTimeout: 10,
              andPlaceOn: imageButton)
```

Sometimes you'll see a method whose first parameter does not have an external label, but has an _ underscore instead:

```
override func tableView(_ tableView: UITableView,
       numberOfRowsInSection section: Int) -> Int
```

This is often the case with delegate methods. It's a holdover from the Objective-C days, where the label for the first parameter was embedded in the first part of the method name. For example, in Objective-C the downloadImage() method example above would be named downloadImageForSearchResult(). These kinds of names should become less and less common in the near future.

Swift is pretty flexible with how it lets you name your methods, but it's smart to stick to the established conventions.

Inside a method you can do the following things:

• Create local variables and constants.

• Do basic arithmetic with mathematical operators such as +, −, *, /, and %.

• Put new values into variables (both local and instance variables).

- Call other methods.
- Make decisions with `if` or `switch` statements.
- Perform repetitions with the `for` or `while` statements.
- Return a value to the caller.

Let's look at the `if` and `for` statements in more detail.

Making decisions

The `if` statement looks like this:

```
if count == 0 {
   text = "No Items"
} else if count == 1 {
   text = "1 Item"
} else {
   text = "\(count) Items"
}
```

The expression after `if` is called the **condition**. If a condition is true then the statements in the following { } block are executed. The `else` section gets performed if none of the conditions are true.

Comparison Operators

You use **comparison operators** to perform comparisons between two values:

`==`   equal to

`!=`   not equal

`>`   greater than

`>=`   greater than or equal

`<`   less than

`<=`   less than or equal

```
let a = "Hello, world"
let b = "Hello," + " world"
print(a == b)                    // prints true
```

When you use the == operator, the contents of the objects are compared. The above code only returns true if a and b have the same value:

This is different from Objective-C, where == is only true if the two objects are the exact same instance in memory. However, in Swift == compares the values of the objects, not whether they actually occupy the same spot in memory. (If you need to do that use ===, the identity operator.)

Logical Operators

You can use **logical** operators to combine two expressions:

a && b is true if both a *and* b are true

a || b is true when either a *or* b is true (or both)

There is also the logical **not** operator, !, that turns true into false, and false into true. (Don't confuse this with the ! that is used with optionals.)

You can group expressions with ( ) parentheses:

```
if ((this && that) || (such && so)) && !other {
    // statements
}
```

This reads as:

```
if ((this and that) or (such and so)) and not other {
    // statements
}
```

Or if you want to see clearly in which order these operations are performed:

```
if (
        (this and that)
            or
        (such and so)
    )
    and
        (not other)
```

Of course, the more complicated you make it, the harder it is to remember exactly what you're doing!

switch statement

Swift has another very powerful construct in the language for making decisions, the switch statement:

```
switch condition {
    case value1:
```

```
     // statements

  case value2:
     // statements

  case value3:
     // statements

  default:
     // statements
}
```

It works the same way as an if statement with a bunch of else ifs. The following is equivalent:

```
if condition == value1 {
  // statements
} else if condition == value2 {
  // statements
} else if condition == value3 {
  // statements
} else {
  // statements
}
```

In such a situation, the switch statement would be more convenient to use. Swift's version of switch is much more powerful than the one in Objective-C. For example, you can match on ranges and other patterns:

```
switch difference {
  case 0:
    title = "Perfect!"
  case 1..<5:
    title = "You almost had it!"
  case 5..<10:
    title = "Pretty good!"
  default:
    title = "Not even close..."
}
```

The ..< is the **half-open range** operator. It creates a range between the two numbers, but the top number is exclusive. So the half-open range 1..<5 is the same as the **closed range 1...4**.

You'll see the switch statement in action a little later on.

return statement

Note that `if` and `return` can be used to return early from a method:

```swift
func divide(_ a: Int, by b: Int) -> Int {
  if b == 0 {
    print("You really shouldn't divide by zero")
    return 0
  }
  return a / b
}
```

This can even be done for methods that don't return a value:

```swift
func performDifficultCalculation(list: [Double]) {
  if list.count < 2 {
    print("Too few items in list")
    return
  }

  // perform the very difficult calculation here
}
```

In this case, `return` simply means: "We're done with the method". Any statements following the `return` are skipped and execution immediately returns to the caller.

You could also have written it like this:

```swift
func performDifficultCalculation(list: [Double]) {
  if list.count < 2 {
    print("Too few items in list")
  } else {
    // perform the very difficult calculation here
  }
}
```

Which approach you use is up to personal preference. I prefer an early `return` when it avoids multiple nested blocks of code with multiple levels of indentation since that makes the code look cleaner :]

For example, sometimes you see code like this:

```swift
func someMethod() {
  if condition1 {
    if condition2 {
      if condition3 {
        // statements
      } else {
        // statements
      }
```

```
    } else {
       // statements
    }
  } else {
    // statements
  }
}
```

This can become very hard to read, so I like to restructure that kind of code as follows:

```
func someMethod() {
  if !condition1 {
    // statements
    return
  }

  if !condition2 {
    // statements
    return
  }

  if !condition3 {
    // statements
    return
  }

  // statements
}
```

Both do exactly the same thing, but I find the second one much easier to understand. (Note that the conditions now use the ! operator to invert their meaning.)

Swift even has a dedicated feature, guard, to help write this kind of code. It looks like this:

```
func someMethod() {
  guard condition1 else {
    // statements
    return
  }
  guard condition2 else {
    // statements
    return
  }
  . . .
```

As you become more experienced, you'll start to develop your own taste for what looks good and what is readable code.

Loops

You've seen the `for in` statement for looping through an array:

```
for item in items {
  if !item.checked {
    count += 1
  }
}
```

Which can also be written as:

```
for item in items where !item.checked {
  count += 1
}
```

This performs the statements inside the `for in` block once for each object from the `items` array matching the condition provided by the `where` clause.

Note that the scope of the variable `item` is limited to just this `for` statement. You can't use it outside this statement, so its lifetime is even shorter than a local variable.

Looping through number ranges

Some languages, including Swift 2, have a `for` statement that looks like this:

```
for var i = 0; i < 5; ++i {
  print(i)
}
```

When you run this code, it should print:

```
0
1
2
3
4
```

However, as of Swift 3.0 this kind of `for` loop is now removed from the language. Instead, you can loop over a range. This has the same output as above:

```
for i in 0...4 {    // or 0..<5
  print(i)
}
```

By the way, you can also write this loop as:

```
for i in stride(from: 0, to: 5, by: 1) {
  print(i)
}
```

The stride() function creates a special object that represents the range 0 to 5 in increments of 1. If you wanted to show just the even numbers, you could change the by parameter to 2. You can even use stride() to count backwards if you pass by a negative number.

while statement

The for statement is not the only way to perform loops. Another very useful looping construct is the while statement:

```
while something is true {
  // statements
}
```

The while loop keeps repeating the statements until its condition becomes false. You can also write it as follows:

```
repeat {
  // statements
} while something is true
```

In the latter case, the condition is evaluated after the statements have been executed at least once.

You can rewrite the loop that counts the ChecklistItems as follows using a while statement:

```
var count = 0
var i = 0
while i < items.count {
  let item = items[i]
  if !item.checked {
    count += 1
  }
  i += 1
}
```

Most of these looping constructs are really the same, they just look different. Each of them lets you repeat a bunch of statements until some ending condition is met.

Still, using a while is slightly more cumbersome than "for item in items", which is why you'll see for in used most of the time.

There really is no significant difference between using a `for`, `while`, or `repeat while` loop, except that one may be easier to read than the others, depending on what you're trying to do.

> **Note:** `items.count` and `count` in this example are two different things with the same name. The first `count` is a property on the `items` array that returns the number of elements in that array; the second `count` is a local variable that contains the number of unchecked to-do items counted so far.

Just like you can prematurely exit from a method using the `return` statement, you can exit a loop at any time using the `break` statement:

```swift
var found = false
for item in array {
  if item == searchText {
    found = true
    break
  }
}
```

This example loops through the array until it finds an `item` that is equal to the value of `searchText` (presumably both are strings). Then it sets the variable `found` to `true` and jumps out of the loop using `break`. You've found what you were looking for, so it makes no sense to look at the other objects in that array - for all you know there could be hundreds of items.

There is also a `continue` statement that is somewhat the opposite of `break`. It doesn't exit the loop but immediately skips to the next iteration. You use `continue` to say, "I'm done with the current item, let's look at the next one."

Loops can often be replaced by *functional programming* constructs such as `map`, `filter`, or `reduce`. These are functions that operate on a collection, perform some code for each element, and return a new collection (or single value, in the case of `reduce`) with the results.

For example, using `filter` on an array will return items that satisfy a certain condition. To get a list of all the unchecked `ChecklistItem` objects, you'd write:

```swift
var uncheckedItems = items.filter { item in !item.checked }
```

That's a lot simpler than writing a loop. Functional programming is an advanced topic so we won't spend too much time on it here.

Objects

Objects are what it's all about. They combine data with functionality into coherent, reusable units – that is, if you write them properly!

The data is made up of the object's instance variables and constants. We often refer to these as the object's **properties**. The functionality is provided by the object's methods.

In your Swift programs you will use existing objects, such as `String`, `Array`, `Date`, `UITableView`, and you'll also make your own.

To define a new object, you need a bit of code that contains a `class` section:

```swift
class MyObject {
   var text: String
   var count = 0
   let maximum = 100

   init() {
     text = "Hello world"
   }

   func doSomething() {
     // statements
   }
}
```

Inside the brackets for the class, you add properties (the instance variables and constants) and methods.

Properties

There are two types of properties:

- **Stored properties** are the usual instance variables and constants.

- **Computed properties** don't store a value, but perform logic when you read from, or write to, their values.

This is an example of a computed property:

```swift
var indexOfSelectedChecklist: Int {
  get {
    return UserDefaults.standard().
                      integerForKey("ChecklistIndex")
  }
  set {
    UserDefaults.standard().set(newValue,
                      forKey: "ChecklistIndex")
```

```
    }
}
```

The `indexOfSelectedChecklist` property does not store a value like a normal variable would. Instead, every time someone uses this property, it performs the code from the `get` or `set` block.

The alternative would be to write separate `setIndexOfSelectedChecklist()` and `getIndexOfSelectedChecklist()` methods, but that doesn't read as nicely.

If a property name is preceded by the keyword `@IBOutlet`, that means that the property can refer to a user interface element in Interface Builder, such as a label or button. Such properties are usually declared `weak` and optional. Similarly, the keyword `@IBAction` is used for methods that will be performed when the user interacts with the app.

Methods

There are three kinds of methods:

- Instance methods
- Class methods
- Init methods

As mentioned previously, a method is a function that belongs to an object. To call such a method you first need to have an instance of the object:

```
let myInstance = MyObject()      // create the object instance
. . .
myInstance.doSomething()         // call the method
```

You can also have **class methods**, which can be used without an object instance. In fact, they are often used as "factory" methods, to create new object instances:

```
class MyObject {
  . . .

  class func makeObject(text: String) -> MyObject {
    let m = MyObject()
    m.text = text
    return m
  }
}

let myInstance = MyObject.makeObject(text: "Hello world")
```

Init methods, or **initializers**, are used during the creation of new object instances. Instead of the above factory method, you might as well use a custom `init` method:

```
class MyObject {
  . . .

  init(text: String) {
    self.text = text
  }
}

let myInstance = MyObject(text: "Hello world")
```

The main purpose of an `init` method is to set up (or, initialize) the object's properties. Any instance variables or constants that do not have a value yet must be given one in the `init` method.

Swift does not allow variables or constants to have no value (except for optionals), and `init` is your last chance to make this happen.

Objects can have more than one `init` method; which one you use depends on the circumstances.

A `UITableViewController`, for example, can be initialized either with `init?(coder:)` when automatically loaded from a storyboard, with `init(nibName:bundle:)` when manually loaded from a nib file, or with `init(style:)` when constructed without a storyboard or nib. Sometimes you use one, sometimes the other. You can also provide a `deinit` method that gets called just before the object is destroyed.

By the way, `class` isn't the only way to define an object in Swift. It also supports other types of objects such as `structs` and `enums`. You'll learn more about these later, so I won't give away the whole plot here (no spoilers!).

Protocols

Besides objects, you can also define **protocols**. A protocol is simply a list of method names (and possibly, properties):

```
protocol MyProtocol {
  func someMethod(value: Int)
  func anotherMethod() -> String
}
```

A protocol is like a job ad. It lists all the things that a candidate for a certain position in your company should be able to do.

But the ad itself doesn't do the job – it's just words printed in the careers section of the newspaper – so you need to hire an actual employee who can get the job done. That would be an object.

Objects need to indicate that they conform to a protocol:

```
class MyObject: MyProtocol {
    . . .
}
```

This object now has to provide an implementation for the methods listed in the protocol. (If not, it's fired!)

From then on, you can refer to this object as a `MyObject` (because that is its class name) but also as a `MyProtocol` object:

```
var m1: MyObject = MyObject()
var m2: MyProtocol = MyObject()
```

To any part of the code using the m2 variable, it doesn't matter that the object is really a `MyObject` under the hood. The type of m2 is `MyProtocol`, not `MyObject`.

All your code sees is that m2 is *some* object conforming to `MyProtocol`, but it's not important what sort of object that is.

In other words, you don't really care that your employee may also have another job on the side, as long as it doesn't interfere with the duties you've hired him, or her, for.

Protocols are often used to define **delegates**, but they come in handy for other uses as well, as you'll find out later on.

This concludes the quick recap of what you've seen so far of the Swift language. After all that theory, it's time to write some code!

Chapter 22: Get Location Data

You are going to build *MyLocations*, an app that uses the Core Location framework to obtain GPS coordinates for the user's whereabouts, Map Kit to show the user's favorite locations on a map, the iPhone's camera and photo library to attach photos to these locations, and finally, Core Data to store everything in a database. Phew, that's a lot of stuff!

The finished app looks like this:

The MyLocations app

MyLocations lets you keep a list of spots that you find interesting. Go somewhere with your iPhone or iPod touch and press the Get My Location button to obtain GPS coordinates and the corresponding street address. Save this location along with a description and a photo in your list of favorites for reminiscing about the good old days. Think of this app as a "location album" instead of a photo album.

To make the workload easier to handle, you'll split up the project into smaller chunks:

1. You will first figure out how to obtain GPS coordinates from the Core Location framework and how to convert these coordinates into an address, a process known as **reverse geocoding**. Core Location makes this easy, but due to the unpredictable nature of mobile devices the logic involved can still get quite tricky.

2. Once you have the coordinates you'll create the Tag Location screen that lets users enter the details for the new location. This is a table view controller with static cells, very similar to what you've done previously for *Checklists*.

3. You'll store the location data into a Core Data store. For the last app you saved app data into a .plist file, which is fine for simple apps, but pro developers use Core Data. It's not as scary as it sounds!

4. Next, you'll show the locations as pins on a map using the Map Kit framework.

5. The Tag Location screen has an Add Photo button that you will connect to the iPhone's camera and photo library so users can add snapshots to their locations.

6. Finally, you'll make the app look good using custom graphics. You will also add sound effects and some animations to the mix.

Of course, you are not going to do all of that at once :] In this chatper, you will do the following:

- **Get GPS Coordinates:** Create a tab bar-based app and set up the UI for the first tab.

- **CoreLocation:** Use the CoreLocation framework to get the user's current location.

- **Display coordinates:** Display location information on screen.

When you're done with this chapter, the app will look like this:

The first screen of the app

Get GPS coordinates

First, you'll create the *MyLocations* project in Xcode and then use the Core Location framework to find the latitude and longitude of the user's location.

Create project

➤ Fire up Xcode and make a new project. Choose the **Tabbed Application** template.

Choosing the Tabbed Application template

➤ Fill in the options as follows:

• Product Name: **MyLocations**

• Organization Name: Your name or the name of your company

• Organization Identifier: Your own identifier in reverse domain notation

• Language: **Swift**

• Include Unit Tests and Include UI Tests: unchecked

➤ Save the project.

If you run the app, it looks like this:

The app from the Tabbed Application template

The app has a tab bar along the bottom with two tabs: First and Second.

Even though it doesn't do much yet, the app already employs three view controllers:

1. The *root controller* is a `UITabBarController` that contains the tab bar and performs the switching between the different screens.

2. A view controller for the First tab.

3. A view controller for the Second tab.

The two tabs each have their own view controller. By default, the Xcode template names them `FirstViewController` and `SecondViewController`.

At this point, the storyboard looks like this:

The storyboard from the Tabbed Application template

I already had to zoom it out to fit the whole thing on my screen. Storyboards are great, but they sure take up a lot of space!

As before, you'll be editing the storyboard using the iPhone SE dimensions, and later you'll make the app work on other screen sizes as well.

➤ In the **View as:** pane at the bottom, choose **iPhone SE**.

➤ Also, check the **Use Safe Area Layout Guides** checkbbox (if it is not already checked) for the storyboard in the **File inspector**. (This isn't very important yet, but will come into play later when you start using auto layout. And if you don't see the **Use Safe Area Layout Guides** checkbox, try clicking on a view controller first.)

The first tab

In this chapter, you'll be working with the first tab only. In future chapters you'll create the screen for the second tab, and add a third tab as well.

Let's give FirstViewController a better name.

Remember the refactoring tricke you learnt previously? That's what you'll use here since that renames both the file and any references to it anywhere in the project.

➤ Open **FirstViewController.swift**, hover your mouse cursor over the word FirstViewController in the class line, right-click (or Control-click) and select **Rename…** from the context menu.

➤ Change the name to **CurrentLocationViewController**. This changes the file name, the class name, and the reference to the class in the storyboard - all at once! Nifty, eh?

➤ Go to the **Project Settings** screen and de-select the Landscape Left and Landscape Right settings under **Deployment Info - Device Orientation**. Now the app is portrait-only. (You can enable **Upside Down** at the same time if you like, since this would enable both portrait modes on iPad.)

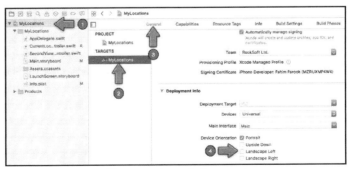

The app only works in portrait

➤ Run the app again just to make sure everything still works.

Whenever I change how things are hooked up in the storyboard, I find it useful to run the app and verify that the change was successful – it's way too easy to forget a step and you want to catch such mistakes right away.

And if you are wondering where you changed things in the storyboard, remember how you renamed the FirstViewController? That change modified the storybaord too :]

As you saw in *Checklists*, a view controller that sits inside a navigation controller has a Navigation Item object that allows it to configure the navigation bar. Tab bars work the same way. Each view controller that represents a tab has a Tab Bar Item object.

➤ Select the **Tab Bar Item** object from the **First Scene** (this is the Current Location View Controller) and go to the **Attributes inspector**. Change the **Title** to **Tag**.

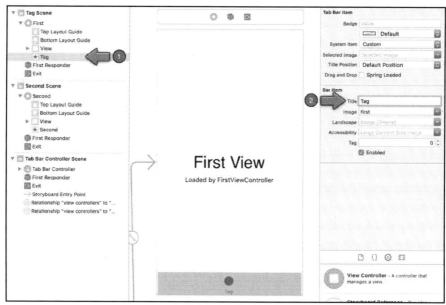

Changing the title of the Tab Bar Item

Later on, you'll also set a new image for the Tab Bar Item too; it currently uses the default image from the template.

First tab UI

You will now design the screen for this first tab. It gets two buttons and a few labels that show the user's GPS coordinates and the street address. To save you some time, you'll add all the outlets in one go.

➤ Add the following to the class in **CurrentLocationViewController.swift**:

```
@IBOutlet weak var messageLabel: UILabel!
@IBOutlet weak var latitudeLabel: UILabel!
@IBOutlet weak var longitudeLabel: UILabel!
@IBOutlet weak var addressLabel: UILabel!
@IBOutlet weak var tagButton: UIButton!
@IBOutlet weak var getButton: UIButton!

@IBAction func getLocation() {
  // do nothing yet
}
```

Design the UI to look something like this:

The design of the Current Location screen

➤ The (**Message label**) at the top should span the whole width of the screen. You'll use this label for status messages while the app is obtaining the GPS coordinates. Set the **Alignment** attribute to centered and connect the label to the messageLabel outlet.

➤ Make the (**Latitude goes here**) and (**Longitude goes here**) labels right-aligned and connect them to the latitudeLabel and longitudeLabel outlets respectively.

➤ The (**Address goes here**) label also spans the whole width of the screen and is **50** points high so it can fit two lines of text. Set its **Lines** attribute to **0** (that means it can display a variable number of lines). Connect this label to the addressLabel outlet.

➤ The **Tag Location** button doesn't do anything yet, but should be connected to the tagButton outlet.

➤ Connect the **Get My Location** button to the getButton outlet, and its Touch Up Inside event to the getLocation action.

➤ Run the app to see the new design in action.

So far, nothing special. With the exception of the tab bar, this is stuff you've seen and done before. Time to add something new: let's play with Core Location!

> **Note:** Because you're initially designing for the iPhone SE screen size, it's best to use the iPhone SE Simulator to run the app. The app won't look good yet on larger screens. You'll fix this later on.

Core Location

Most iOS devices have a way to let you know exactly where you are on the globe, either through communication with GPS satellites, or Wi-Fi and cell tower triangulation. The Core Location framework puts that power in your own hands.

An app can ask Core Location for the user's current latitude and longitude. For devices with a compass, it can also give the heading (you won't be using that for this app). Core Location can also provide continuous location updates while you're on the move.

Get your current location

Getting a location from Core Location is pretty easy, but there are some pitfalls that you need to avoid. Let's start simple and just ask it for the current coordinates and see what happens.

➤ At the top of **CurrentLocationViewController.swift**, add an import statement:

```
import CoreLocation
```

That is all you have to do to add the Core Location framework to your project.

Core Location, like so many other parts of the iOS SDK, works via a delegate, so you should make the view controller conform to the CLLocationManagerDelegate protocol.

➤ Add CLLocationManagerDelegate to the view controller's class line:

```
class CurrentLocationViewController: UIViewController,
                                     CLLocationManagerDelegate {
```

➤ Also add a new property:

```
let locationManager = CLLocationManager()
```

The `CLLocationManager` is the object that will give you the GPS coordinates. You're putting the reference to this object in a constant (using `let`), not a variable (`var`). Once you have created the location manager object, the value of `locationManager` will never have to change.

The new `CLLocationManager` object doesn't give you GPS coordinates right away. To begin receiving coordinates, you have to call its `startUpdatingLocation()` method first.

Unless you're doing turn-by-turn navigation, you don't want your app to continuously receive GPS coordinates. That requires a lot of power and will quickly drain the battery. For this app, you only turn on the location manager when you want a location fix and turn it off again when you've received a usable location.

You'll implement that logic in a minute (it's more complex than you'd think). For now, you're only interested in receiving something from Core Location, just so you know that it works.

➤ Change the `getLocation()` action method to the following:

```
@IBAction func getLocation() {
  locationManager.delegate = self
  locationManager.desiredAccuracy =
              kCLLocationAccuracyNearestTenMeters
  locationManager.startUpdatingLocation()
}
```

This method is hooked up to the Get My Location button. It tells the location manager that the view controller is its delegate and that you want to receive locations with an accuracy of up to ten meters. Then you start the location manager. From that moment on, the `CLLocationManager` object will send location updates to its delegate, i.e. the view controller.

➤ Speaking of the delegate, add the following code too:

```
// MARK: - CLLocationManagerDelegate
func locationManager(_ manager: CLLocationManager,
        didFailWithError error: Error) {
  print("didFailWithError \(error)")
}

func locationManager(_ manager: CLLocationManager,
    didUpdateLocations locations: [CLLocation]) {
  let newLocation = locations.last!
```

```
    print("didUpdateLocations \(newLocation)")
}
```

These are the delegate methods for the location manager. For the time being, you'll simply output a `print()` message to the Console.

➤ Run the app in the Simulator and press the **Get My Location** button.

Oops, nothing seems to happen. That's because you need to ask for permission before accessing location information.

Ask for permission

➤ Add the following lines to the top of `getLocation()`:

```
let authStatus = CLLocationManager.authorizationStatus()

if authStatus == .notDetermined {
  locationManager.requestWhenInUseAuthorization()
  return
}
```

This checks the current authorization status. If it is `.notDetermined`, meaning that this app has not asked for permission yet, then the app will request "When In Use" authorization. That allows the app to get location updates while it is open and the user is interacting with it.

There is also "Always" authorization, which permits the app to check the user's location even when it is not active. That's useful for a navigation app, for example. For most apps, including *MyLocations*, when-in-use is what you want to ask for.

Just adding these lines of code is not enough. You also have to add a special key to the app's Info.plist.

➤ Open **Info.plist** file. Right-click somewhere inside Info.plist and choose **Add Row** from the menu.

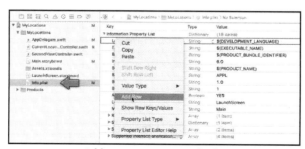

Adding a new row to Info.plist

➤ For the key, type **NSLocationWhenInUseUsageDescription** (or choose **Privacy - Location When In Use Usage Description** from the list).

➤ Type the following text in the Value column:

This app lets you keep track of interesting places. It needs access to the GPS coordinates for your location.

This description tells the user what the app wants to use the location data for.

Key	Type	Value
▼ Information Property List	Dictionary	(16 items)
Localization native development region	String	$(DEVELOPMENT_LANGUAGE)
Privacy - Location When In Use Usage Description ⟳⊕⊖	String	resting places. It needs access to the GPS coordinates for your location.
Executable file	String	$(EXECUTABLE_NAME)
Bundle identifier	String	$(PRODUCT_BUNDLE_IDENTIFIER)

Adding the new item to Info.plist

➤ Run the app again and press the **Get My Location** button.

Core Location will pop up the following alert, asking the user for permission:

Users have to allow your app to use their location

If a user denies the request with the Don't Allow button, then Core Location will never give your app location coordinates.

➤ Press the **Don't Allow** button. Now press Get My Location again.

Xcode's debug area should now show the following message (or something similar):

```
didFailWithError Error Domain=kCLErrorDomain Code=1 "(null)"
```

This comes from the `locationManager(_:didFailWithError:)` delegate method. It's telling you that the location manager wasn't able to obtain a location.

The reason why is described by an `Error` object, which is the standard object that the iOS SDK uses to convey error information. You'll see it in many other places in the SDK (there are plenty of places where things can go wrong!).

This `Error` object has a "domain" and a "code". The domain in this case is `kCLErrorDomain` meaning the error came from Core Location (CL). The code is 1, also identified by the symbolic name `CLError.denied`, which means the user did not allow the app to obtain location information.

> **Note:** The k prefix is often used by the iOS frameworks to signify that a name represents a constant value (I guess whoever came up with this prefix thought it was spelled "konstant"). This is an old convention and you won't see it used much in new frameworks or in Swift code, but it still pops up here and there.

➤ Stop the app from within Xcode and run it again.

When you press the Get My Location button, the app does not ask for permission anymore but immediately gives you the same error message.

Let's make this more user-friendly, as a normal user would never see that print().

Handle permission errors

➤ Add the following method to **CurrentLocationViewController.swift**:

```swift
func showLocationServicesDeniedAlert() {
  let alert = UIAlertController(
    title: "Location Services Disabled",
    message: "Please enable location services for this app in Settings.",
    preferredStyle: .alert)

  let okAction = UIAlertAction(title: "OK", style: .default,
                               handler: nil)
  alert.addAction(okAction)

  present(alert, animated: true, completion: nil)
}
```

This pops up an alert with a helpful hint. This app is pretty useless without access to the user's location, so it should encourage the user to enable location services. (It's not necessarily the user of the app who has denied access to the location data; a systems administrator or parent may have restricted location access.)

➤ To show this alert, add the following lines to getLocation(), just before you set the locationManager's delegate:

```swift
if authStatus == .denied || authStatus == .restricted {
  showLocationServicesDeniedAlert()
  return
}
```

This shows the alert if the authorization status is denied or restricted. Notice the use of || here, the "logical or" operator. showLocationServicesDeniedAlert() will be called if either of those two conditions is true.

➤ Try it out. Run the app and tap **Get My Location**. You should now get the Location Services Disabled alert:

The alert that pops up when location services are not available

Fortunately, users can change their minds and enable location services for your app again. This is done from the iPhone's Settings app.

➤ Open the **Settings** app in the Simulator and go to **Privacy** → **Location Services**.

Location Services in the Settings app

➤ Click **MyLocations** and then **While Using the App** to enable location services again. Switch back to the app (or run it again from Xcode) and press the **Get My Location** button.

When I tried this, the following message appeared in Xcode's debug area:

```
didFailWithError Error Domain=kCLErrorDomain Code=0 "(null)"
```

Again there is an error message but with a different code, 0. This is "location unknown" which means Core Location was unable to obtain a location for some reason.

That is not so strange, as you're running this from the Simulator, which obviously does not have a real GPS. Your Mac may have a way to obtain location information through Wi-Fi but this is not built into the Simulator. Fortunately, there is a way to fake it!

Fake location on the simulator

➤ With the app running, from the Simulator's menu bar at the top of the screen, choose **Debug → Location → Apple**.

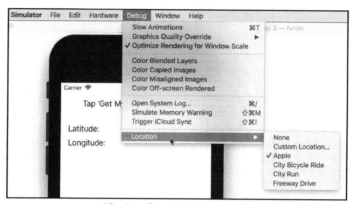

The Simulator's Location menu

You should now see messages like these in the debug area:

```
didUpdateLocations <+37.33259552,-122.03031802> +/- 500.00m
(speed -1.00 mps / course -1.00) @ 6/30/17, 8:19:11 AM India
Standard Time
didUpdateLocations <+37.33241211,-122.03050893> +/- 65.00m
(speed -1.00 mps / course -1.00) @ 6/30/17, 8:19:13 AM India
Standard Time
didUpdateLocations <+37.33240901,-122.03048800> +/- 65.00m
(speed -1.00 mps / course -1.00) @ 6/30/17, 8:19:14 AM India
Standard Time
```

It keeps going on and on, giving the app a new location every second or so. After a short while, the latitude and longitude readings will not change anymore. These particular coordinates point at the Apple headquarters in Cupertino, California.

Look carefully at the coordinates the app is receiving. The first one says "+/- 500.00m", the second one "+/- 65.00m", a little further on "+/- 50.00m" etc. This number keeps getting smaller and smaller until it stops at about "+/- 5.00m".

This is the accuracy of the measurement, expressed in meters. What you see is the Simulator imitating what happens when you ask for a location on a real device.

If you go out with an iPhone and try to obtain location information, the iPhone uses three different ways to find your coordinates. It has onboard cellular, Wi-Fi, and GPS radios that each give it location information at different levels of detail:

• Cell tower triangulation will always work if there is a signal but it's not very precise.

- Wi-Fi positioning works better, but that is only available if there are known Wi-Fi routers nearby. This system uses a big database that contains the locations of wireless networking equipment.

- The very best results come from the GPS (**G**lobal **P**ositioning **S**ystem), but that attempts a satellite communication and is therefore the slowest of the three. It also won't work very well indoors.

So, your device has several ways of obtaining location data, ranging from fast but inaccurate (cell towers, Wi-Fi) to accurate but slow (GPS). And none of these are guaranteed to work. Some devices don't even have a GPS or cellular radio at all and have to rely on just Wi-Fi. Suddenly obtaining a location seems a lot trickier.

Fortunately for us, Core Location does all of the hard work of turning the location readings from its various sources into a useful number. Instead of making you wait for the definitive results from the GPS (which may never come), Core Location sends location data to the app as soon as it gets it, and then follows up with more and more accurate readings.

> **Exercise.** If you have an iPhone, iPod touch or iPad nearby, try the app on your device and see what kind of readings it gives you. If you have more than one device, try the app on all of them and note the differences.

Asynchronous operations

Obtaining a location is an example of an **asynchronous** process.

Sometimes apps need to do things that may take a while. After you start an operation, you have to wait until it gives you the results. If you're unlucky, those results may never come at all!

In the case of Core Location, it can take a second or two before you get the first location reading and then quite a few seconds more to get coordinates that are accurate enough for your app to use.

Asynchronous means that after you start such an operation, your app will continue on its merry way. The user interface is still responsive, new events are being sent and handled, and the user can still tap on things.

The asynchronous process is said to be operating "in the background". As soon as the operation is done, the app is notified through a delegate so that it can process the results.

The opposite is **synchronous** (without the a). If you start an operation that is synchronous, the app won't continue until that operation is done. In effect, the app freezes up.

In the case of CLLocationManager that would cause a big problem: your app would be totally unresponsive for the couple of seconds that it takes to get a location fix. Those kinds of "blocking" operations are often a bad experience for the user.

For example, *MyLocations* has a tab bar at the bottom. If the app blocked while getting the location, switching to another tab during that time would have no effect. The user expects to always be able to change tabs, but now it appears that the app is frozen, or worse, has crashed.

The designers of iOS decided that such behavior is unacceptable and therefore operations that take longer than a fraction of a second should be performed in an asynchronous manner.

For the next app, you'll see more asynchronous processing in action when we talk about network connections and downloading stuff from the Internet.

By the way, iOS has something called the "watchdog timer". If your app is unresponsive for too long, then under certain circumstances, the watchdog timer will kill your app without mercy – so don't do that!

The take-away is this: any operation that takes long enough to be noticeable by the user should be done asynchronously, in the background.

Display coordinates

The locationManager(_:didUpdateLocations:) delegate method gives you an array of CLLocation objects that contain the current latitude and longitude coordinates of the user. (These objects also have some additional information, such as the altitude and speed, but you don't use those in this app.)

You'll take the last CLLocation object from the array – because that is the most recent update – and display its coordinates in the labels that you added to the screen earlier.

➤ Add a new instance variable to **CurrentLocationViewController.swift**:

```
var location: CLLocation?
```

You will store the user's current location in this variable. This needs to be an optional, because it is possible to *not* have a location, for example, when you're stranded out in the Sahara desert somewhere and there is not a cell tower or GPS satellite in sight.

But even when everything works as it should, the value of location will still be nil until Core Location reports back with a valid CLLocation object, which as you've seen, may take a few seconds. So an optional it is.

➤ Change `locationManager(_:didUpdateLocations:)` to:

```
func locationManager(_ manager: CLLocationManager,
    didUpdateLocations locations: [CLLocation]) {
  let newLocation = locations.last!
  print("didUpdateLocations \(newLocation)")

  location = newLocation    // Add this
  updateLabels()            // Add this
}
```

You store the `CLLocation` object that you get from the location manager into the instance variable and call a new `updateLabels()` method.

Keep the `print()` in there because it's handy for debugging.

➤ Add the `updateLabels()` method:

```
func updateLabels() {
  if let location = location {
    latitudeLabel.text = String(format: "%.8f",
                                location.coordinate.latitude)
    longitudeLabel.text = String(format: "%.8f",
                                 location.coordinate.longitude)
    tagButton.isHidden = false
    messageLabel.text = ""
  } else {
    latitudeLabel.text = ""
    longitudeLabel.text = ""
    addressLabel.text = ""
    tagButton.isHidden = true
    messageLabel.text = "Tap 'Get My Location' to Start"
  }
}
```

Because the `location` instance variable is an optional, you use the `if let` syntax to unwrap it.

Note the *shadowing* of the original `location` variable by the unwrapped variable. Inside the `if` statement, `location` now refers to an actual `CLLocation` object that can never be `nil`.

If there is a valid location object, you convert the latitude and longitude, which are values with type `Double`, into strings and put them into the labels.

You've seen *string interpolation* before to put values into strings, so why doesn't this code simply do the following?

```
latitudeLabel.text = "\(location.coordinate.latitude)"
```

That would certainly work, but it doesn't give you any control over how the latitude value appears. For this app, you want both latitude and longitude to be shown with 8 digits behind the decimal point.

For that sort of control, you need to use a *format string*.

Format strings

Like string interpolation, a format string uses placeholders that will be replaced by the actual value during runtime. These placeholders, or *format specifiers*, can be quite intricate.

To create the text for the latitude label you do this:

```
String(format: "%.8f", location.coordinate.latitude)
```

This creates a new String object using the format string "%.8f", and the value to replace in that string, location.coordinate.latitude.

Placeholders always start with a percent (%) sign. Examples of common placeholders are: %d for integer values, %f for floating-point, and %@ for objects.

Format strings are very common in Objective-C code, but less so in Swift because string interpolation is much simpler (but less powerful).

The %.8f format specifier does the same thing as %f: it takes a decimal number and puts it in the string. The .8 means that there should always be 8 digits behind the decimal point.

➤ Run the app, select a location to simulate from the Simulator's **Debug** menu and tap the **Get My Location** button. You'll now see the latitude and longitude appear on the screen.

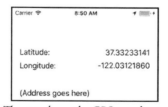

The app shows the GPS coordinates

When the app starts up, it has no location object (location is still nil) and therefore ought to show the "Tap 'Get My Location' to Start" message at the top as a hint to the user. But it doesn't do that yet since the app doesn't call updateLabels() until it receives the first coordinates.

➤ To fix this, also call `updateLabels()` from `viewDidLoad()`:

```
override func viewDidLoad() {
   super.viewDidLoad()
   updateLabels()
}
```

➤ Run the app. Initially, the screen should now say, Tap 'Get My Location' to Start, and the latitude and longitude labels are empty.

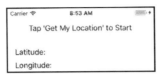

What the app looks like when you start it

You can find the project files for this chapter under **22 – Get Location Data** in the Source Code folder.

Chapter 23: Use Location Data

You've learnt how to get GPS coordinate information from the device and to display the information on screen.

In this chapter, you will learn the following:

- **Handle GPS errors:** Receiving GPS information is an error-prone process. How do you handle the errors?

- **Improve GPS results:** How to improve GPS the accuracy of the GPS results you receive.

- **Reverse geocoding:** Getting the address for a given set of GPS coordinates.

- **Testing on device:** Testing on device to ensure that your app handles real-world scenarios.

- **Support different screen sizes:** Setting up your UI to work on iOS devices with different screen sizes.

Handle GPS errors

Getting GPS coordinates is error-prone. You may be somewhere where there is no clear line-of-sight to the sky (such as inside or in an area with lots of tall buildings), blocking your GPS signal.

There may not be many Wi-Fi routers around you, or they haven't been catalogued yet, so the Wi-Fi radio isn't much help getting a location fix either.

And of course your cellular signal might be so weak that triangulating your position doesn't offer particularly good results either.

All of that is assuming your device actually has a GPS or cellular radio. I just went out with my iPod touch to capture coordinates and get some pictures for this app. In the city center it was unable to obtain a location fix. My iPhone did better, but it still wasn't ideal.

The moral of this story is that your location-aware apps had better know how to deal with errors and bad readings. There are no guarantees that you'll be able to get a location fix, and if you do, then it might still take a few seconds.

This is where software meets the real world. You should add some error handling code to the app to let users know about problems getting those coordinates.

The error handling code

➤ Add these two instance variables to **CurrentLocationViewController.swift**:

```
var updatingLocation = false
var lastLocationError: Error?
```

➤ Change locationManager(_:didFailWithError:) to the following:

```
func locationManager(_ manager: CLLocationManager,
        didFailWithError error: Error) {
  print("didFailWithError \(error)")

  if (error as NSError).code ==
      CLError.locationUnknown.rawValue {
    return
  }

  lastLocationError = error

  stopLocationManager()
  updateLabels()
}
```

The location manager may report errors for a variety of scenarios. You can look at the code property of the Error object to find out what type of error you're dealing with. (You do need to cast to NSError first since that is the subclass of Error that actually contains the code property.)

Some of the possible Core Location errors:

- CLError.locationUnknown - the location is currently unknown, but Core Location will keep trying.

- CLError.denied - the user denied the app permission to use location services.

- CLError.network - there was a network-related error.

There are more (having to do with the compass and geocoding), but you get the point. Lots of reasons for things to go wrong!

> **Note:** These error codes are defined in the `CLError` enumeration. Recall that an enumeration, or enum, is a list of values and names for these values.
>
> The error codes used by Core Location have simple integer values. Rather than using the values 0, 1, 2 and so on in your program, Core Location has given them symbolic names using the `CLError` enum. That makes these codes easier to understand and you're less likely to pick the wrong one.
>
> To convert these names back to an integer value you ask for the `rawValue`.

In your updated `locationManager(_:didFailWithError:)`, you do:

```
if (error as NSError).code == CLError.locationUnknown.rawValue {
    return
}
```

The `CLError.locationUnknown` error means the location manager was unable to obtain a location right now, but that doesn't mean all is lost. It might just need another second or so to get an uplink to the GPS satellite. In the mean time, it's letting you know that, for now, it could not get any location information.

When you get this error, you will simply keep trying until you do find a location or receive a more serious error.

In the case of a more serious error, you store the error object into a new instance variable, `lastLocationError`:

```
lastLocationError = error
```

That way, you can look up later what kind of error you were dealing with. This comes in useful in `updateLabels()`. You'll be extending that method shortly to show the error to the user because you don't want to leave them in the dark about such things.

> **Exercise.** Can you explain why `lastLocationError` is an optional?

Answer: When there is no error, `lastLocationError` will not have a value. In other words, it can be `nil`, and variables that can be `nil` must be optionals in Swift.

Finally, the update to `locationManager(_:didFailWithError:)` adds a new method call:

```
stopLocationManager()
```

Stop location updates

If obtaining a location appears to be impossible for wherever the user currently is on the globe, then you need to tell the location manager to stop. To conserve battery power, the app should power down the iPhone's radios as soon as it doesn't need them anymore.

If this was a turn-by-turn navigation app, you'd keep the location manager running even in the case of a network error, because who knows, a couple of meters ahead you might get a valid location.

For this app, the user will simply have to press the Get My Location button again if they want to try in another spot.

➤ Add the stopLocationManager() method:

```swift
func stopLocationManager() {
  if updatingLocation {
    locationManager.stopUpdatingLocation()
    locationManager.delegate = nil
    updatingLocation = false
  }
}
```

There's an if statement there that checks whether the boolean instance variable updatingLocation is true or false. If it is false, then the location manager isn't currently active and there's no need to stop it.

The reason for having this updatingLocation variable is that you are going to change the appearance of the Get My Location button and the status message label when the app is trying to obtain a location fix, to let the user know the app is working on it.

➤ Put some extra code in updateLabels() to show the error message:

```swift
func updateLabels() {
  if let location = location {
    . . .
  } else {
    . . .
    // Remove the following line
    messageLabel.text = "Tap 'Get My Location' to Start"
    // The new code starts here:
    let statusMessage: String
    if let error = lastLocationError as NSError? {
      if error.domain == kCLErrorDomain &&
          error.code == CLError.denied.rawValue {
        statusMessage = "Location Services Disabled"
```

```
          } else {
            statusMessage = "Error Getting Location"
          }
        } else if !CLLocationManager.locationServicesEnabled() {
          statusMessage = "Location Services Disabled"
        } else if updatingLocation {
          statusMessage = "Searching..."
        } else {
          statusMessage = "Tap 'Get My Location' to Start"
        }
        messageLabel.text = statusMessage
      }
    }
```

The new code determines what to put in the messageLabel at the top of the screen. It uses a bunch of if statements to figure out what the current status of the app is.

If the location manager gave an error, the label will show an error message.

The first error it checks for is CLError.denied (in the error domain kCLErrorDomain, which means Core Location errors). In that case the user has not given this app permission to use the location services. That sort of defeats the purpose of this app but it can happen, and you have to check for it anyway.

If the error code is something else then you simply say "Error Getting Location" as this usually means there was no way of obtaining a location fix.

Even if there was no error, it might still be impossible to get location coordinates if the user disabled Location Services completely on their device (instead of just for this app). You check for that situation with the locationServicesEnabled() method of CLLocationManager.

Suppose there were no errors and everything works fine, then the status label will say "Searching..." before the first location object has been received.

If your device can obtain the location fix quickly, then this text will be visible only for a fraction of a second, but often, it might take a short while to get that first location fix. No one likes waiting, so it's nice to let the user know that the app is actively looking up their location. That is what you're using the updatingLocation boolean for.

> **Note:** You put all this logic into a single method because that makes it easy to change the screen when something has changed. Received a location? Simply call updateLabels() to refresh the contents of the screen. Received an error? Let updateLabels() sort it out...

Start location updates

➤ Also add a new `startLocationManager()` method. (I suggest you put it right above `stopLocationManager()`, to keep related functionality together):

```
func startLocationManager() {
  if CLLocationManager.locationServicesEnabled() {
    locationManager.delegate = self
    locationManager.desiredAccuracy =
                    kCLLocationAccuracyNearestTenMeters
    locationManager.startUpdatingLocation()
    updatingLocation = true
  }
}
```

Starting the location manager used to happen in the `getLocation()` action method. However, because you now have a `stopLocationManager()` method, it makes sense to move the start code into a method of its own, `startLocationManager()`, just to keep things symmetrical.

The only difference from before is that this checks whether the location services are enabled and you set the variable `updatingLocation` to `true` if you did indeed start location updates.

➤ Change `getLocation()` to:

```
@IBAction func getLocation() {
  . . .
  if authStatus == .denied || authStatus == .restricted {
    . . .
  }
  // New code below, replacing existing code after this point
  startLocationManager()
  updateLabels()
}
```

There is one more small change to make. Suppose there was an error and no location could be obtained, but then you walk around for a bit and a valid location comes in. In that case, it's a good idea to remove the old error code.

➤ At the bottom of `locationManager(_:didUpdateLocations:)`, add the following line just before calling `updateLabels()`:

```
lastLocationError = nil
```

This clears out the old error state. After receiving a valid coordinate, any previous error you may have encountered is no longer applicable.

➤ Run the app. While the app is waiting for incoming coordinates, the label at the top should say "Searching..." until it finds a valid coordinate or encounters a fatal error.

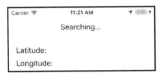

The app is waiting to receive GPS coordinates

Play around with the Simulator's location settings for a while and see what happens when you choose different locations.

Note that changing the Simulator's location to None isn't an error anymore. This still returns the .locationUnknown error code but you ignore that because it's not a fatal error.

Tip: You can also simulate locations from within Xcode. If your app uses Core Location, the bar at the top of the debug area gets an arrow icon. Click on that icon to change the simulated location:

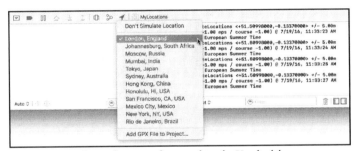

Simulating locations from within the Xcode debugger

Ideally, you should not just test in the Simulator but also on your device, as you're more likely to encounter real errors that way.

Improve GPS results

Cool, you know how to obtain a CLLocation object from Core Location and you're able to handle errors. Now what?

Well, here's the thing: you saw in the Simulator that Core Location keeps giving you new location objects over and over, even though the coordinates may not have changed. That's because the user could be on the move, in which case their GPS coordinates *do* change.

However, you're not building a navigation app. So, for *MyLocations* you just want to get a location that is accurate enough and then you can tell the location manager to stop sending updates.

This is important because getting location updates costs a lot of battery power as the device needs to keep its GPS/Wi-Fi/cellular radios powered up for this. This app doesn't need to ask for GPS coordinates all the time, so it should stop when the location is accurate enough.

The problem is that you can't always get the accuracy you want, so you have to detect this. When the last couple of coordinates you received aren't increasing in accuracy then that is probably as good as it's going to get, and you should let the radio power down.

Get results for a specific accuracy level

➤ Change locationManager(_:didUpdateLocations:) to the following:

```
func locationManager(_ manager: CLLocationManager,
    didUpdateLocations locations: [CLLocation]) {
  let newLocation = locations.last!
  print("didUpdateLocations \(newLocation)")

  // 1
  if newLocation.timestamp.timeIntervalSinceNow < -5 {
    return
  }

  // 2
  if newLocation.horizontalAccuracy < 0 {
    return
  }

  // 3
  if location == nil || location!.horizontalAccuracy >
                        newLocation.horizontalAccuracy {

    // 4
    lastLocationError = nil
    location = newLocation

    // 5
    if newLocation.horizontalAccuracy <=
       locationManager.desiredAccuracy {
      print("*** We're done!")
      stopLocationManager()
    }
    updateLabels()
  }
}
```

Let's take these changes one-by-one:

1. If the time at which the given location object was determined is too long ago (5 seconds in this case), then this is a *cached* result.

    Instead of returning a new location fix, the location manager may initially give you the most recently found location under the assumption that you might not have moved much in the last few seconds (obviously this does not take into consideration people with jet packs).

    You'll simply ignore these cached locations if they are too old.

2. To determine whether new readings are more accurate than previous ones, you'll use the horizontalAccuracy property of the location object. However, sometimes locations may have a horizontalAccuracy that is less than 0. In which case, these measurements are invalid and you should ignore them.

3. This is where you determine if the new reading is more useful than the previous one. Generally speaking, Core Location starts out with a fairly inaccurate reading and then gives you more and more accurate ones as time passes. However, there are no guarantees, so you cannot assume that the next reading truly is always more accurate.

    Note that a larger accuracy value means *less* accurate – after all, accurate up to 100 meters is worse than accurate up to 10 meters. That's why you check whether the previous reading, location!.horizontalAccuracy, is greater than the new reading, newLocation.horizontalAccuracy.

    You also check for location == nil. Recall that location is an optional instance variable that stores the CLLocation object that you obtained in a previous call to "didUpdateLocations". If location is nil, then this is the very first location update you're receiving and in that case you should continue.

    So, if this is the very first location reading (location is nil) or the new location is more accurate than the previous reading, you continue to step 4. Otherwise you ignore this location update.

4. You've seen this part before. It clears out any previous error and stores the new CLLocation object into the location variable.

5. If the new location's accuracy is equal to or better than the desired accuracy, you can call it a day and stop asking the location manager for updates. When you started the location manager in startLocationManager(), you set the desired accuracy to 10 meters (kCLLocationAccuracyNearestTenMeters), which is good enough for this app.

Short circuiting

Because `location` is an optional object, you cannot access its properties directly – you first need to unwrap it. You could do that with `if let`, but if you're sure that the optional is not `nil` you can also *force unwrap* it with `!`.

That's what you are doing in this line:

```
if location == nil || location!.horizontalAccuracy >
                      newLocation.horizontalAccuracy {
```

You wrote `location!.horizontalAccuracy` with an exclamation point instead of just `location.horizontalAccuracy`.

But what if `location == nil`, won't the force unwrapping fail then? Not in this case, because the force unwrap is never performed.

The `||` operator (logical or) tests whether either of the two conditions is true. If the first one is true (`location` is `nil`), it will ignore the second condition. That's called *short circuiting*. There is no need for the app to check the second condition if the first one is already true.

So the app will only look at `location!.horizontalAccuracy` when `location` is guaranteed to be non-`nil`. Blows your mind, eh?

➤ Run the app. First set the Simulator's location to None, then press Get My Location. The screen now says "Searching…"

➤ Switch to location Apple (but don't press Get My Location again). After a brief moment, the screen is updated with GPS coordinates as they come in.

If you check the Xcode Console, you'll get about 10 location updates before it says "*** We're done!" and the location updates stop.

> **Note:** It's possible the above steps won't work for you. If the screen does not say "Searching…" but shows an old set of coordinates instead, then the Simulator is holding on to old location data. This seems to happen when you pick a location from within Xcode (using the arrow in the debug area) instead of the Simulator's Debug menu.
>
> The quickest way to fix this is to quit the Simulator and run the app again (which launches a new Simulator). If you can't get it to work, no worries, it's not that important. Just be aware that the Simulator can be finicky sometimes.

You as the developer can tell from the Console when the location updates stop, but obviously, the user won't see this.

The Tag Location button becomes visible as soon as the first location is received so the user can start saving this location to their library right away, but at this point the location may not be accurate enough yet. So it's nice to show the user when the app has found the most accurate location.

Update the UI

To make this clearer, you are going to toggle the Get My Location button to say "Stop" when the location grabbing is active and switch it back to "Get My Location" when it's done. That gives a nice visual clue to the user. Later on, you'll also show an animated activity spinner that makes this even more obvious.

To change the state of the button, you'll add a configureGetButton() method.

➤ Add the following method to **CurrentLocationViewController.swift**:

```
func configureGetButton() {
  if updatingLocation {
    getButton.setTitle("Stop", for: .normal)
  } else {
    getButton.setTitle("Get My Location", for: .normal)
  }
}
```

It's quite simple: if the app is currently updating the location, then the button's title becomes Stop, otherwise it is Get My Location.

You need to now call configureGetButton() from several different places in your code. If you look closely, you'll notice that wherever you call updateLabels(), you also need to call the new method. So might as well call the new method from within updateLabels(), right?

➤ Add a call to configureGetButton() at the end of updateLabels():

```
func updateLabels() {
  . . .
  configureGetButton()
}
```

➤ Run the app again and perform the same test as before. The button changes to Stop when you press it. When there are no more location updates, it switches back.

The stop button

When a button says "Stop", you naturally expect to be able to press it so you can interrupt the location updates. This is especially so when you're not getting any coordinates at all. Eventually Core Location may give an error, but as a user you may not want to wait for that.

Currently, however, pressing Stop doesn't stop anything. You have to change getLocation() for this, as any taps on the button call this method.

➤ In getLocation(), replace the line with the call to startLocationManager() with the following:

```
if updatingLocation {
  stopLocationManager()
} else {
  location = nil
  lastLocationError = nil
  startLocationManager()
}
```

Again, you're using the updatingLocation flag to determine what state the app is in.

If the button is pressed while the app is already doing the location fetching, you stop the location manager.

Note that you also clear out the old location and error objects before you start looking for a new location.

➤ Run the app. Now pressing the Stop button will put an end to the location updates. You should see no more updates in the Console after you press Stop.

Note: If the Stop button doesn't appear long enough for you to click it, set the location back to None first, tap Get My Location a few times, and then select the Apple location again.

Reverse geocoding

The GPS coordinates you've dealt with so far are just numbers. The coordinates 37.33240904, -122.03051218 don't really mean that much, but the address 1 Infinite Loop in Cupertino, California does.

Using a process known as **reverse geocoding**, you can turn a set of coordinates into a human-readable address. (Regular or "forward" geocoding does the opposite: it turns an address into GPS coordinates. You can do both with the iOS SDK, but for *MyLocations* you only do the reverse one.)

You'll use the CLGeocoder object to turn the location data into a human-readable address and then display that address on screen.

It's quite easy to do this but there are some rules. You're not supposed to send out a ton of these reverse geocoding requests at the same time. The process of reverse geocoding takes place on a server hosted by Apple and it costs them bandwidth and processor time to handle these requests. If you flood their servers with requests, Apple won't be happy.

MyLocations is only supposed to be used occasionally. So theoretically, its users won't be spamming the Apple servers, but you should still limit the geocoding requests to one at a time, and once for every unique location. After all, it makes no sense to reverse geocode the same set of coordinates over and over.

Reverse geocoding needs an active Internet connection and anything you can do to prevent unnecessary use of the iPhone's radios is a good thing for your users.

The implementation

➤ Add the following properties to **CurrentLocationViewController.swift**:

```
let geocoder = CLGeocoder()
var placemark: CLPlacemark?
var performingReverseGeocoding = false
var lastGeocodingError: Error?
```

These mirror what you did for the location manager. CLGeocoder is the object that will perform the geocoding and CLPlacemark is the object that contains the address results.

The placemark variable needs to be an optional because it will have no value when there is no location yet, or when the location doesn't correspond to a street address (I don't think it will respond with "Sahara desert, Africa", but I haven't tried that yet).

You set performingReverseGeocoding to true when a geocoding operation is taking place, and lastGeocodingError will contain an Error object if something went wrong (or nil if there is no error).

➤ You'll put the geocoder to work in `locationManager(didUpdateLocations)`:

```swift
func locationManager(_ manager: CLLocationManager,
    didUpdateLocations locations: [CLLocation]) {
  . . .
  if location == nil || location!.horizontalAccuracy >
                        newLocation.horizontalAccuracy {
    . . .
    if newLocation.horizontalAccuracy <=
      locationManager.desiredAccuracy {
      . . .
    }
    updateLabels()
    // The new code begins here:
    if !performingReverseGeocoding {
      print("*** Going to geocode")

      performingReverseGeocoding = true

      geocoder.reverseGeocodeLocation(newLocation,
                              completionHandler: {
        placemarks, error in
        if let error = error {
          print("*** Reverse Geocoding error: \
(error.localizedDescription)")
          return
        }
        if let places = placemarks {
          print("*** Found places: \(places)")
        }
      })
    }
    // End of the new code
  }
}
```

The app should only perform a single reverse geocoding request at a time. So, first you check whether it is busy by looking at the `performingReverseGeocoding` variable. Then you start the geocoder.

The code looks straightforward enough, right? If you are wondering what the `completionHandler` bit is, harken back to chapter 6 when you used a similar construct to handle a `UIAlertController` action - it's a *closure*.

Closures

Unlike the location manager, `CLGeocoder` does not use a delegate to return results from an operation. Instead, it uses a closure. Closures are an important Swift feature and you can expect to see them all over the place. (For Objective-C programmers, a closure is similar to a "block".)

Closures can have parameters too and here, the parameters for the closure are `placemarks` and `error`, both of which are optionals because either one or the other can be `nil` depending on the situation.

So, while all the code inside the closure does is print out either the list of places or the error, you do have to unwrap each optional before you do that to be sure that you have a value there. Also, do note the `error.localizedDescription` bit which, instead of simply printing out the contents of the `error` variable, outputs a human understandable version of the error (if possible) based on the device's current locale (or language setting).

Unlike the rest of the code in `locationManager(_:didUpdateLocations:)`, the code in the closure is not performed right away. After all, you can only print the geocoding results once the geocoding completes, and that may be several seconds later.

The closure is kept for later by the `CLGeocoder` object and is only performed after `CLGeocoder` finds an address or encounters an error.

So why does `CLGeocoder` use a closure instead of a delegate?

The problem with using a delegate to provide feedback is that you need to write one or more separate methods. For example, for `CLLocationManager` there are the `locationManager(_:didUpdateLocations:)` and `locationManager(_:didFailWithError:)` methods.

By creating separate methods, you move the code that deals with the response away from the code that makes the request. With closures, on the other hand, you can put that handling code in the same place. That makes the code more compact and easier to read. (Some APIs do both, and you have a choice between using a closure or becoming a delegate.)

So when you write,

```
geocoder.reverseGeocodeLocation(newLocation, completionHandler:
{ placemarks, error in
  // put your statements here
}
```

you're telling the `CLGeocoder` object that you want to reverse geocode the location, and that the code in the block following `completionHandler:` should be executed as soon as the geocoding is completed.

The closure itself is:

```
{ placemarks, error in
    // put your statements here
}
```

The items before the in keyword – placemarks and error – are the parameters for this closure and they work just like parameters for a method or a function.

When the geocoder finds a result for the location object that you gave it, it invokes the closure and executes the statements within. The placemarks parameter will contain an array of CLPlacemark objects that describe the address information, and the error variable contains an error message in case something went wrong.

Just to rub it in: the statements in the closure are *not* executed right away when locationManager(_:didUpdateLocations:) is called. Instead, the closure and everything inside it is given to CLGeocoder, which keeps it till later after it has performed the reverse geocoding operation. Only then will it execute the code from the closure.

It's the exact same principle as using delegate methods, except you're not putting the code into a separate method but in a closure.

It's OK if closures have got you scratching your head right now. You'll see them used many more times in the upcoming chapters.

➤ Run the app and pick a location. As soon as the first location is found, you can see in the Console that the reverse geocoder has kicked in (give it a second or two):

```
didUpdateLocations <+37.33233141,-122.03121860> +/- 379.75m
(speed -1.00 mps / course -1.00) @ 7/1/17, 10:31:15 AM India
Standard Time
*** Going to geocode
*** Found places: [Apple Inc., Apple Inc., 1 Infinite Loop,
Cupertino, CA  95014, United States @
<+37.33233141,-122.03121860> +/- 100.00m, region
CLCircularRegion (identifier:'<+37.33233140,-122.03121860>
radius 141.73', center:<+37.33233140,-122.03121860>, radius:
141.73m)]
```

If you choose the Apple location, you'll see that some location readings are duplicates; the geocoder only does the first of those. Only when the accuracy of the reading improves does the app reverse geocode again. Nice!

Note: Several readers reported that if you are in China and are trying to reverse geocode an address that is outside of China, you may get an error and placemarks will be nil. Try a location inside China instead.

Handle reverse geocoding errors

➤ Replace the contents of the geocoding closure with the following:

```
self.lastGeocodingError = error
if error == nil, let p = placemarks, !p.isEmpty {
  self.placemark = p.last!
} else {
  self.placemark = nil
}

self.performingReverseGeocoding = false
self.updateLabels()
```

Just as with the location manager, you store the error object so you can refer to it later, although you use a different instance variable this time, lastGeocodingError.

The next line does something you haven't seen before:

```
if error == nil, let p = placemarks, !p.isEmpty {
```

You know that if let is used to unwrap optionals. Here, placemarks is an optional, so it needs be unwrapped before you can use it or you risk crashing the app when placemarks is nil. The unwrapped placemarks array gets the temporary name p.

The !p.isEmpty bit says that we should only enter this if statement if the array of placemark objects is not empty.

You should read this line as:

```
if there's no error and the unwrapped placemarks array is not
empty {
```

Of course, Swift doesn't speak English, so you have to express this in terms that Swift understands.

You could also have written this as three different, nested if statements:

```
if error == nil {
  if let p = placemarks {
    if !p.isEmpty {
```

But it's just as easy to combine all of these conditions into a single if.

You're doing a bit of **defensive programming** here: you specifically check first whether the array has any objects in it. If there is no error, then it should have at least one object, but you're not going to trust that it always will. Good developers are suspicious!

If all three conditions are met – there is no error, the `placemarks` array is not `nil`, and there is at least one `CLPlacemark` inside this array – then you take the last of those `CLPlacemark` objects:

```
self.placemark = p.last!
```

The `last` property refers to the last item from an array. It's an optional because there is no last item if the array is empty. As an alternative, you can also write `placemarks[placemarks.count - 1]` but that's not as tidy.

Usually there will be only one `CLPlacemark` object in the array, but there is the odd situation where one location coordinate may refer to more than one address. This app can only handle one address at a time. So, you'll just pick the last one, which usually is the only one.

If there was an error during geocoding, you set `self.placemark` to `nil`. Note that you did not do that for the locations. If there was an error there, you kept the previous location object because it may actually be correct (or good enough) and it's better than nothing. But for the address that makes less sense.

You don't want to show an old address, only the address that corresponds to the current location or no address at all.

In mobile development, nothing is guaranteed. You may get coordinates back or you may not, and if you do, they may not be very accurate. The reverse geocoding will probably succeed if there is some type of network connection available, but you also need to be prepared to handle the case where there is none.

And remember, not all GPS coordinates correspond to actual street addresses - there is no corner of 52nd and Broadway in the Sahara desert.

> **Note:** Did you notice that inside the `completionHandler` closure you used `self` to refer to the view controller's properties and methods? This is a Swift requirement.
>
> Closures are said to *capture* all the variables they use and `self` is one of them. You can forget about that immediately, if you like; just know that Swift requires that all captured variables are explicitly mentioned.
>
> As you've seen, outside a closure, you can use `self` to refer to properties and methods, but it's not a requirement. However, you do get a compiler error if you leave out `self` inside a closure. So you don't have much choice there.

Display the address

Let's show the address to the user.

➤ Change `updateLabels()` to:

```
func updateLabels() {
  if let location = location {
    . . .
    // Add this block
    if let placemark = placemark {
      addressLabel.text = string(from: placemark)
    } else if performingReverseGeocoding {
      addressLabel.text = "Searching for Address..."
    } else if lastGeocodingError != nil {
      addressLabel.text = "Error Finding Address"
    } else {
      addressLabel.text = "No Address Found"
    }
    // End new code
  } else {
    . . .
  }
}
```

Because you only do the address lookup once the app has a valid location, you just have to change the code inside the first `if` branch. If you've found an address, you show that to the user, otherwise you show a status message.

The code to format the `CLPlacemark` object into a string is placed in its own method, just to keep the code readable.

➤ Add the `string(from)` method:

```
func string(from placemark: CLPlacemark) -> String {
  // 1
  var line1 = ""

  // 2
  if let s = placemark.subThoroughfare {
    line1 += s + " "
  }

  // 3
  if let s = placemark.thoroughfare {
    line1 += s
  }

  // 4
  var line2 = ""
```

```
    if let s = placemark.locality {
        line2 += s + " "
    }
    if let s = placemark.administrativeArea {
        line2 += s + " "
    }
    if let s = placemark.postalCode {
        line2 += s
    }

    // 5
    return line1 + "\n" + line2
}
```

Let's look at this in detail:

1. Create a new string variable for the first line of text.

2. If the placemark has a subThoroughfare, add it to the string. This is an optional property, so you unwrap it with if let first. Just so you know, subThoroughfare is a fancy name for house number.

3. Adding the thoroughfare (or street name) is done similarly. Note that you put a space between it and subThoroughfare so they don't get glued together.

4. The same logic goes for the second line of text. This adds the locality (the city), administrative area (the state or province), and postal code (or zip code), with spaces between them where appropriate.

5. Finally, the two lines are concatenated (added together) with a newline character in between. The \n adds the line break (or newline) to the string.

➤ In getLocation(), clear out the placemark and lastGeocodingError variables to start with a clean slate. Put this just above the call to startLocationManager():

```
placemark = nil
lastGeocodingError = nil
```

➤ Run the app again. Seconds after a location is found, the address label should be filled in as well.

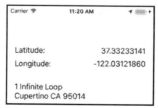

Reverse geocoding finds the address for the GPS coordinates

It's fairly common that street numbers or other details are missing from the address. The CLPlacemark object may contain incomplete information, which is why its properties are all optionals. Geocoding is not an exact science!

Exercise. If you pick the City Bicycle Ride or City Run locations from the Simulator's Debug menu, you should see in the Console that the app jumps through a whole bunch of different coordinates (it simulates someone moving from one place to another). However, the coordinates on the screen and the address label don't change nearly as often. Why is that?

Answer: The logic for *MyLocations* was designed to find the most accurate set of coordinates for a stationary position. You only update the location variable when a new set of coordinates comes in that is more accurate than previous readings. Any new readings with a higher – or the same – horizontalAccuracy value are simply ignored, regardless of what the actual coordinates are.

With the City Bicycle Ride and City Run options, the app doesn't receive the same coordinates with increasing accuracy but a series of completely different coordinates. That means this app doesn't work very well when you're on the move (unless you press Stop and try again), but that's also not what it was intended for.

Note: If you're playing with different locations in the Simulator or from the Xcode debugger menu and you get stuck, then the quickest way to get unstuck is to reset the Simulator. Sometimes it just doesn't want to move to a new location even if you tell it to, and then you have to show it who's the boss!

Testing on device

When I first wrote this code, I had only tested it on the Simulator. It worked fine there. Then, I put it on my iPod touch and guess what? Not so good.

The problem with the iPod touch is that it doesn't have GPS, so it relies only on Wi-Fi to determine the location. But Wi-Fi might not be able to give you accuracy up to ten meters; I got +/- 100 meters at best.

Right now, you only stop the location updates when the accuracy of the reading falls within the desiredAccuracy setting – something that will never actually happen on my iPod touch.

That goes to show that you can't always rely on the Simulator to test your apps. You need to put them on your device and test them in the wild, especially when using device-dependent functionality like location-based APIs. If you have more than one device, then test on all of them!

In order to deal with this situation, you will improve upon the `didUpdateLocations` delegate method.

First fix

➤ Change `locationManager(_:didUpdateLocations:)` to:

```swift
func locationManager(_ manager: CLLocationManager,
  didUpdateLocations locations: [CLLocation]) {
  . . .

  if newLocation.horizontalAccuracy < 0 {
    return
  }

  // New section #1
  var distance = CLLocationDistance(
      Double.greatestFiniteMagnitude)
  if let location = location {
    distance = newLocation.distance(from: location)
  }
  // End of new section #1
  if location == nil || location!.horizontalAccuracy >
                        newLocation.horizontalAccuracy {

    . . .
    if newLocation.horizontalAccuracy <=
      locationManager.desiredAccuracy {
      . . .
      // New section #2
      if distance > 0 {
        performingReverseGeocoding = false
      }
      // End of new section #2
    }

    if !performingReverseGeocoding {
      . . .
    }

  // New section #3
  } else if distance < 1 {
    let timeInterval = newLocation.timestamp.timeIntervalSince(
                                        location!.timestamp)

    if timeInterval > 10 {
      print("*** Force done!")
      stopLocationManager()
```

```
        updateLabels()
    }
    // End of new sectiton #3
  }
}
```

It's a pretty long method now, but only the three highlighted sections were added. This is the first one:

```
var distance = CLLocationDistance(
    Double.greatestFiniteMagnitude)
if let location = location {
  distance = newLocation.distance(from: location)
}
```

This calculates the distance between the new reading and the previous reading, if there was one. We can use this distance to measure if our location updates are still improving.

If there was no previous reading, then the distance is Double.greatestFiniteMagnitude. That is a built-in constant that represents the maximum value that a Double value can have. This little trick gives it a gigantic distance if this is the very first reading. You're doing that so any of the following calculations still work even if you weren't able to calculate a true distance yet.

You also add an if statement later where you stop the location manager:

```
if distance > 0 {
  performingReverseGeocoding = false
}
```

This forces a reverse geocoding for the final location, even if the app is already currently performing another geocoding request.

You absolutely want the address for that final location, as that is the most accurate location you've found. But if some previous location was still being reverse geocoded, this step would normally be skipped.

Simply by setting performingReverseGeocoding to false, you always force the geocoding to be done for this final coordinate.

(Of course, if distance is 0, then this location is the same as the location from a previous reading, and you don't need to reverse geocode it anymore.)

The real improvement is found in the final new section:

```
} else if distance < 1 {
  let timeInterval = newLocation.timestamp.timeIntervalSince(
```

```
                                              location!.timestamp)
    if timeInterval > 10 {
      print("*** Force done!")
      stopLocationManager()
      updateLabels()
    }
  }
```

If the coordinate from this reading is not significantly different from the previous reading and it has been more than 10 seconds since you've received that original reading, then it's a good point to hang up your hat and stop.

It's safe to assume you're not going to get a better coordinate than this and you can stop fetching the location.

This is the improvement that was necessary to make my iPod touch stop scanning after some time. It wouldn't give me a location with better accuracy than +/- 100 meters, but it kept repeating the same one over and over.

I picked a time limit of 10 seconds because that seemed to give good results.

Note that you don't just say:

```
  } else if distance == 0 {
```

The distance between subsequent readings is never exactly 0. It may be something like 0.0017632. Rather than checking for equals to 0, it's better to check for less than a certain distance, in this case one meter.

(By the way, did you notice how you used `location!` to unwrap it before accessing the timestamp property? When the app gt inside this `else-if`, the value of `location` is guaranteed to be non-`nil`, so its safe to force unwrap the optional.)

➤ Run the app and test that everything still works. It may be hard to recreate this situation on the Simulator, but try it on your device inside the house and see what output you see in the Console.

There is another improvement you can make to increase the robustness of this logic, and that is to set a time-out on the whole thing. You can tell iOS to perform a method one minute from now. If by that time the app hasn't found a location yet, you stop the location manager and show an error message.

Second fix

➤ First add a new instance variable:

```
  var timer: Timer?
```

➤ Then change `startLocationManager()` to:

```
func startLocationManager() {
  if CLLocationManager.locationServicesEnabled() {
    . . .
    timer = Timer.scheduledTimer(timeInterval: 60, target: self,
                  selector: #selector(didTimeOut), userInfo: nil,
                  repeats: false)
  }
}
```

The new lines set up a timer object that sends a `didTimeOut` message to `self` after 60 seconds; `didTimeOut` is the name of a method.

A *selector* is the term that Objective-C uses to describe the name of a method, and the `#selector()` syntax is how you create a selector in Swift.

➤ Change `stopLocationManager()` to:

```
func stopLocationManager() {
  if updatingLocation {
    . . .
    if let timer = timer {
      timer.invalidate()
    }
  }
}
```

You have to cancel the timer in case the location manager is stopped before the time-out fires. This happens when an accurate enough location is found within one minute after starting, or when the user taps the Stop button.

➤ Finally, add the `didTimeOut()` method:

```
@objc func didTimeOut() {
  print("*** Time out")
  if location == nil {
    stopLocationManager()
    lastLocationError = NSError(
                    domain: "MyLocationsErrorDomain",
                    code: 1, userInfo: nil)
    updateLabels()
  }
}
```

There's something new about this method - there's a new `@objc` statement before `func` - whatever could it be?

Remember how how `#selector` is an Objective-C concept? (How could you forget, it was just a few paragraphs ago, right?) So, when you use `#selector` to identify a method to call, that method has to be accessible not only from Swift, but from Objective-C as well. The @objc attribute allows you to identify a method (or class, or property, or even enumeration) as being accessible from Objective-C.

So, that's what you've done for didTimeOut - declared it as being accessible from Objective-C.

didTimeOut() is always called after one minute, whether you've obtained a valid location or not – unless stopLocationManager() cancels the timer first.

If after that one minute there still is no valid location, you stop the location manager, create your own error code, and update the screen.

By creating your own NSError object and putting it into the lastLocationError instance variable, you don't have to change any of the logic in updateLabels().

However, you do have to make sure that the error's domain is not kCLErrorDomain because this error object does not come from Core Location but from within your own app.

An error domain is simply a string, so "MyLocationsErrorDomain" will do. For the code I picked 1. The value of code doesn't really matter at this point because you only have one custom error, but you can imagine that when an app becomes bigger, you might need multiple error codes.

Note that you don't always have to use an NSError object; there are other ways to let the rest of your code know that an error occurred. In this case updateLabels() was already using an NSError anyway, so having your own error object just makes sense.

➤ Run the app. Set the Simulator location to None and press **Get My Location**.

After a minute, the debug area should say "*** Time out" and the Stop button reverts to Get My Location. There should also be an error message on the screen:

The error after a time out

Just getting a simple location from Core Location and finding the corresponding street address turned out to be a lot more hassle than it looked. There are many different situations to handle. Nothing is guaranteed, and everything can go wrong. (iOS development sometimes requires nerves of steel!)

To recap, the app either:

• Finds a location with the desired accuracy,

- Finds a location that is not as accurate as you'd like and you don't get any more accurate readings,

- Doesn't find a location at all,

- Or, takes too long finding a location.

The code now handles all these situations, but I'm sure it's not perfect yet. No doubt the logic could be tweaked more, but it will do for the purposes of this book.

I hope it's clear that if you're releasing a location-based app, you need to do a lot of field testing!

Required device capabilities

The **Info.plist** file has a key, **Required device capabilities**, that lists the hardware that your app needs in order to run. This is the key that the App Store uses to determine whether a user can install your app on their device.

The default value is **armv7**, which is the CPU architecture of the iPhone 3GS and later models. If your app requires additional features, such as Core Location to retrieve the user's location, you should list them here.

➤ Add a new item with the value **location-services** to **Info.plist**:

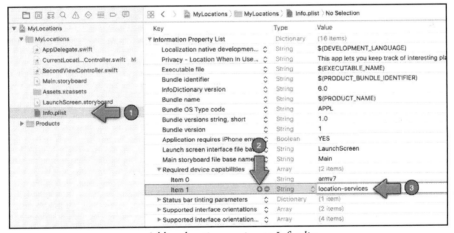

Adding location-services to Info.plist

You could also add the item **gps**, in which case the app requires a GPS receiver. But if you did, users won't be able to install the app on an iPod touch or on certain iPads.

For the full list of possible device capabilities, see the *App Programming Guide for iOS* on the Apple Developer website.

P.S. You can now take the `print()` statements out of the app (or simply comment them out). Personally, I like to keep them in there as they're handy for debugging. In an app that you plan to upload to the App Store, you'll definitely want to remove the `print()` statements when development's complete.

Support different screen sizes

So far, you've been designing and testing the app for the iPhone SE's 4-inch screen.

As discussed previously, older iPhone models with smaller 3.5-inch screens are not supported by iOS 11. However, it used to be that users running the app on an iPad had the OS force the app to use the 3.5-inch dimensions anyway. This too is no longer an issue as of iOS 11 :]

But, if you find work as a professional iOS developer, you may need to support iOS 9 or even iOS 8, and that means it's still necessary for your apps to work on those smaller screens. And there will always be larger screens that you need to support too.

➤ To see what the app looks like on the iPhone 4s, go to **Main.storyboard** and use the **View as** panel at the bottom to switch to the smallest iPhone model.

The 'Get My Location' button is missing on the 3.5-inch screen

It's a good thing you tried this because the Get My Location button is no longer visible. This button was very close to the bottom of the 4-inch screen already, and it simply drops off the screen of smaller devices. You will have to move the button up a bit or end up with 1-star reviews in the App Store.

For the previous apps you used Auto Layout to make the app's user interface resizable. You used the Add New Constraints and Align menus to create constraints that held your views in place. This works well enough, but ask any iOS developer and they'll agree that it can be a bit of a hassle to manage all those constraints, especially as your UI designs grow more complex.

Fortunately, there's a handy shortcut that doesn't require you to make any constraints at all: **autoresizing**.

Autoresizing

Before Auto Layout was available, autoresizing – also known as "springs & struts" – was the main tool for building resizable user interface layouts. It is simple to use, but has its limitations. However, in many cases, autoresizing is more than adequate.

Here's how it works: each view has an autoresizing setting that determines what happens to the size and position of that view when the size of its superview – i.e. the view that contains it – changes. You can make the view stick to any of the four sides of its superview, and resize the view horizontally or vertically to fill up the space in the superview.

As of the writing of this book (iOS 11), you could still easily combine autoresizing with Auto Layout. Instead of making your own layout constraints, you simply set the autoresizing options for your views and UIKit will automatically make constraints for them.

Let's see how this works in practice. You will use autoresizing to keep the Get My Location button at a fixed distance from the bottom of the screen, no matter how large or small that screen is.

➤ First use the **View as** panel to switch back to the **iPhone SE**, so you can see the Get My Location button again.

➤ Select the Get My Location button and go to the **Size inspector**. Change the autoresizing options to the following:

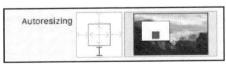

The autoresizing options connect the button to the bottom of its superview

As you can see in the example animation on Xcode, the button (the red box) will now always be positioned relative to the bottom of its superview (the white box).

➤ Use **View as** to switch to the **iPhone 4s** (or open the Preview pane in the Assistant editor). Now the button is visible on 3.5-inch devices as well.

If you find your Tag Location button is now too close to Get My Location, then move the Tag Location button up a bit in the storyboard. Around Y = 250 should be fine.

➤ Now use **View as** to view the app on the iPhone 8 Plus (or run the app in one of the iPhone Plus or iPad Simulators).

The app on the iPhone 8 Plus Simulator

The labels are no longer aligned with the right edge of the screen and the Tag Location button isn't centered. That looks quite messy. Autoresizing to the rescue!

➤ Before you make the following changes, switch back to the **iPhone SE** in the storyboard.

➤ For the (**Message label**) and the **Tag Location** button, change the autoresizing settings to:

The autoresizing settings for the message label and the button

Now the label and the button will always be centered horizontally in the main view.

➤ For the (**Latitude goes here**) and (**Longitude goes here**) labels, change the autoresizing settings to:

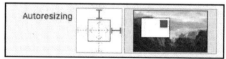

The autoresizing settings for the coordinate labels

This keeps these two labels aligned with the right edge of the screen.

➤ Finally, for the (**Address goes here**) label, change the autoresizing settings to:

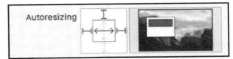

The autoresizing settings for the address label

This stretches the address label to be as wide as the screen allows. Now the app should look decent on any iOS device, no matter the screen size. Try it out!

Attributes and properties

Most of the attributes in Interface Builder's inspectors correspond directly to properties on the selected object. For example, a UILabel has the following attributes:

These are directly related to the following properties:

```
Text          label.text
Color         label.textColor
Font          label.font
Alignment     label.textAlignment
Lines         label.numberOfLines
Enabled       label.isEnabled
Baseline      label.baselineAdjustment
Line Breaks   label.lineBreakMode
```

And so on… As you can see, the names may not always be exactly the same ("Lines" and numberOfLines) but you can easily figure out which property goes with which attribute.

You can find these properties in the documentation for UILabel. From the Xcode **Help** menu, select **Developer Documentation**. Type "uilabel" into the search field to bring up the class reference for UILabel:

The documentation for UILabel does not list properties for all of the attributes from the inspectors. For example, in the Attributes inspector there is a section named "View". The attributes in this section come from UIView, which is the base class of UILabel. So if you can't find a property in the UILabel class, you may need to check the documentation under the "Inherits From" section of the documentation.

You can find the project files for this chapter under **23 – Use Location Data** in the Source Code folder.

Chapter 24: Objects vs. Classes

Time for something new. Up until now I've been calling almost everything an "object". That's not quite correct though. So, it's time for you to brush up on your programming theory a bit more.

In this chapter, you will learn the following:

- **Classes:** The difference between classes and objects.

- **Inheritance:** What class inheritance is and how it works.

- **Overriding methods:** Overriding methods in sub-classes to provide different functionality.

- **Casts:** Casting an object from a subclass to its superclass - how (and why) you do it.

Classes

If you want to use the proper object-oriented programming vernacular, you have to make a distinction between an object and its **class**.

When you do this,

```
class ChecklistItem: NSObject {
    . . .
}
```

You're really defining a class named ChecklistItem, not an object. An object is what you get when you **instantiate** a class:

```
let item = ChecklistItem()
```

The item variable now contains an object of the class ChecklistItem. You can also say: the item variable contains an **instance** of the class ChecklistItem. The terms object and instance mean the same thing.

In other words, "instance of class ChecklistItem" is the **type** of this item variable.

The Swift language and the iOS frameworks already come with a lot of types built-in, but you can also add types of your own by making new classes.

Let's use an example to illustrate the difference between a class and an instance / object.

You and I are both hungry, so we decide to eat some ice cream (my favorite subject next to programming!). Ice cream is the class of food that we're going to eat.

The ice cream class looks like this:

```swift
class IceCream: NSObject {
  var flavor: String
  var scoops: Int

  func eatIt() {
    // code goes in here
  }
}
```

You and I go on over to the ice cream stand and ask for two cones:

```swift
// one for you
let iceCreamForYou = IceCream()
iceCreamForYou.flavor = "Strawberry"
iceCreamForYou.scoops = 2

// and one for me
let iceCreamForMe = IceCream()
iceCreamForMe.flavor = "Pistachio"
iceCreamForMe.scoops = 3
```

Yep, I get more scoops, but that's because I'm hungry from all this explaining. ;-]

Now the app has two instances of IceCream, one for you and one for me. There is just one class that describes what sort of food we're eating – ice cream – but there are two distinct objects. Your object has strawberry flavor, mine pistachio.

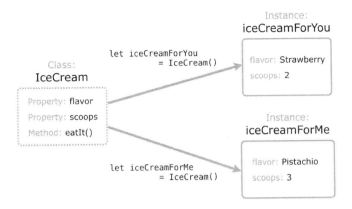

The class is a template for making new instances

The IceCream class is like a template that declares: objects of this type have two properties, flavor and scoops, and a method named eatIt().

Any new instance that is made from this template will have those instance variables and methods, but it lives in its own section of computer memory and therefore has its own values.

If you're more into architecture than food, you can also think of a class as a blueprint for a building. It is the design of the building but not the building itself. One blueprint can make many buildings, and you could paint each one – each instance – a different color if you wanted to.

Inheritance

Sorry, this is not where I tell you that you've inherited a fortune. We're talking about **class inheritance** here, one of the main principles of object-oriented programming.

Inheritance is a powerful feature that allows a class to be built on top of another class. The new class takes over all the data and functionality from that other class and adds its own specializations to it.

Take the IceCream class from the previous example. It is built on NSObject, the fundamental class for iOS frameworks. You can see that in the class line that defines IceCream:

```
class IceCream: NSObject {
```

This means that IceCream is actually the NSObject class with a few additions of its own, namely the flavor and scoops properties and the eatIt() method.

NSObject is the **base class** for almost all other classes in iOS frameworks. Most objects that you'll encounter are made from a class that either directly inherits from NSObject, or from another class that is ultimately based on NSObject. You can't escape it!

You've also seen class declarations that look like this:

```
class ChecklistViewController: UITableViewController
```

The ChecklistViewController class is really a UITableViewController class with your own additions. It does everything a UITableViewController does, plus whatever new data and functionality you've given it.

This inheritance thing is very handy because UITableViewController already does a lot of work for you behind the scenes. It has a table view, it knows how to deal with prototype cells and static cells, and it handles things like scrolling and a ton of other stuff. All you have to do is add your own customizations and you're ready to go.

UITableViewController itself is built on top of UIViewController, which is built on top of something called UIResponder, and ultimately that class is built on NSObject. This is called the *inheritance tree*.

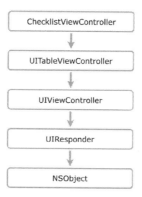

All framework classes stand on the shoulders of NSObject

The big idea here is that each object that is higher up performs a more specialized task than the one below it.

NSObject, the base class, only provides a few basic functions that are needed by all objects. For example, it contains an alloc method that is used to reserve memory space for the object's instance variables, and a basic init method.

UIViewController is the base class for all view controllers. If you want to make your own view controller, you extend UIViewController. To **extend** means that you make a class that inherits from another one. Other commonly used terms are to **derive from** or **to base on** or **to subclass**. These phrases all mean the same thing.

UIViewController does way more than you'd think - you really don't want to write all your own screen and view handling code. If you'd had to program each screen totally from scratch, you'd still be working on lesson 1!

Thank goodness that stuff has been taken care of by very smart people working at Apple and they've bundled it all into UIViewController. You simply make a class that inherits from UIViewController and you get all that functionality for free. You just add your own data and logic to that class and off you go!

If your screen primarily deals with a table view, then you'd subclass UITableViewController instead. This class does everything UIViewController does – because it inherits from it –, but is more specialized for dealing with table views.

You could write all that code by yourself, but why would you, when it's already available in a convenient package? Class inheritance lets you re-use existing code with minimal effort. It can save you a lot of time!

Superclasses and subclasses

When programmers talk about inheritance, they'll often throw around the terms **superclass** and **subclass**.

In the example above, UITableViewController is the immediate superclass of ChecklistViewController, and conversely ChecklistViewController is a subclass of UITableViewController. The superclass is the class you derived from (or extended), while a subclass derives from your class.

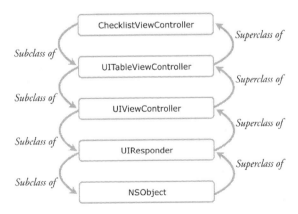

Superclass and subclass

A class in Swift can have many subclasses but only one immediate superclass. Of course, that superclass can have a superclass of its own. There are many different classes that inherit from UIViewController, for example:

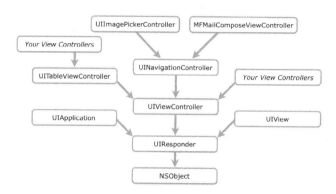

A small portion of the UIKit inheritance tree

Because nearly all classes extend from NSObject, they form a big hierarchy. It is important that you understand this class hierarchy so you can make your own objects inherit from the proper superclasses.

As you'll see later on, there are many other types of hierarchies in programming. For some reason programmers seem to like hierarchies :]

Do note that in Objective-C, all your classes must at least inherit from the NSObject class. This is not the case with Swift. You could also have written the IceCream class as follows:

```
class IceCream {
  . . .
}
```

Now IceCream does not have a base class at all. This is fine in pure Swift code, but you might run into troubled waters if you try to use IceCream instances in combination with iOS frameworks (which are written in Objective-C). So, sometimes you'll have to use the NSObject base class, even if you're writing the app in Swift only.

Inheriting properties (and methods)

Inheriting from a class means your new class gets to use the properties and methods from its superclass.

If you create a new base class Snack:

```
class Snack {
  var flavor: String
  func eatIt() {
    // code goes in here
  }
}
```

And make `IceCream` inherit from that class:

```
class IceCream: Snack {
   var scoops: Int
}
```

Then elsewhere in your code you can do:

```
let iceCreamForMe = IceCream()
iceCreamForMe.flavor = "Chocolate"
iceCreamForMe.scoops = 1
iceCreamForMe.eatIt()
```

This works even though `IceCream` did not explicitly declare an `eatIt()` method or `flavor` instance variable. But `Snack` did! Because `IceCream` inherits from `Snack`, it automatically gets the method and instance variable for free.

Overriding methods

In the previous example, `IceCream` could use the `eatIt()` method implementation from `Snack` for free. But that's not the full story :]

`IceCream` can also provide its own `eatIt()` method if it's important for your app that eating ice cream is different from eating any other kind of snack (for example, you may want to eat it faster, before it melts):

```
class IceCream: Snack {
  var scoops: Int

  override func eatIt() {
    // code goes in here
  }
}
```

Now, when someone calls `iceCreamForMe.eatIt()`, this new version of the method in the `IceCream` class is invoked. Note that Swift requires you to use the `override` keyword in front of any methods that you provide that already exist in the superclass.

A possible implementation of this overridden version of `eatIt()` could look like this:

```
class IceCream: Snack {
   var scoops: Int
   var isMelted: Bool

   override func eatIt() {
     if isMelted {
```

```
      throwAway()
    } else {
      super.eatIt()
    }
  }
}
```

If the ice cream has melted, you want to throw it in the trash. But if it's still edible, you'll call Snack's version of eatIt() using super.

Just like self refers to the current object, the super keyword refers to the object's superclass. That is the reason you've been calling super in various places in your code, to let any superclasses do their thing.

Something that happens often in iOS frameworks is that methods are used for communicating between a class and its subclasses, so that the subclass can perform specific behavior in certain circumstances. That is what methods such as viewDidLoad() and viewWillAppear(_:) are for.

These methods are defined and implemented by UIViewController but your own view controller subclass can override them.

For example, when its screen is about to become visible, the UIViewController class will call viewWillAppear(true). Normally this will invoke the viewWillAppear(_:) method from UIViewController itself, but if you've provided your own version of this method in your subclass, then yours will be invoked instead.

By overriding viewWillAppear(_:), you get a chance to handle this event before the superclass does:

```
class MyViewController: UIViewController {
  override func viewWillAppear(_ animated: Bool) {
    // do your own stuff before super

    // don't forget to call super!
    super.viewWillAppear(animated)

    // do your own stuff after super
  }
}
```

That's how you can tap into the power of your superclass. A well-designed superclass provides such "hooks" that allow you to react to certain events.

Don't forget to call super's version of the method, though. If you neglect this, the superclass will not get its own notification and weird things may happen.

You've also seen override already in the table view data source methods:

```
override func tableView(_ tableView: UITableView,
          didSelectRowAt indexPath: IndexPath) {
  . . .
}
```

UITableViewController, the superclass, already implements these methods. So, if you want to provide your own implementation, you need to override the existing ones.

Note: Inside those table view delegate and data source methods, it's usually not necessary to call super. The iOS API documentation can usually tell you whether you need to call super or not.

Subclass initialization

When making a subclass, the init methods require special care.

If you don't want to change any of the init methods from your superclass or add any new init methods, then it's easy: you don't have to do anything. The subclass will automatically take over the init methods from the superclass.

Most of the time, however, you will want to override an init method or add your own. For example, to put values into the subclass's new instance variables. In that case, you may have to override not just that one init method but all of them.

In the next app you'll create a class named GradientView that extends UIView. That app uses init(frame:) to create and initialize a GradientView object. GradientView overrides this method to set the background color:

```
class GradientView: UIView {
  override init(frame: CGRect) {
    super.init(frame: frame)
    backgroundColor = UIColor.black
  }
  required init?(coder aDecoder: NSCoder) {
    super.init(coder: aDecoder)
  }
  . . .
}
```

But because UIView also has another init method, init?(coder:), GradientView needs to implement that method too even if it doesn't do anything but call super.

Also note that init(frame:) is marked as override, but init?(coder:) is required. The required keyword is used to enforce that every subclass always implements this particular init method.

Swift wants to make sure that subclasses don't forget to add their own stuff to such required `init` methods, even if the app doesn't actually use that particular `init` method, as in the case of `GradientView` – it can be a bit of an over-concerned parent, that Swift.

The rules for inheritance of `init` methods are somewhat complicated – the official Swift Programming Guide devotes many pages to it – but at least if you make a mistake, Xcode will tell you what's wrong and what you should do to fix it.

Private parts

So… does a subclass get to use all the methods from its superclass? Not quite.

`UIViewController` and other UIKit classes have a lot more methods hidden away than you have access to. Often these secret methods do cool things and it is tempting to use them. But they are not part of the official API, making them off-limits for mere mortals such as you and I.

If you ever hear other developers speak of "private APIs" in hushed tones and down dark alleys, then this is what they are talking about.

It is, in theory, possible to call such hidden methods if you know their names, but this is not recommended. It may even get your app rejected from the App Store, as Apple is known to scan apps for usage of these private APIs.

You're not supposed to use private APIs for two reasons:

1. These APIs may have unexpected side effects and not be as robust as their publicly available relatives.

2. There is no guarantee these methods will exist from one version of iOS to the next. Using them is very risky, as your apps may suddenly stop working.

Sometimes, however, using a private API is the only way to access certain functionality on the device. If so, you're out of luck. Fortunately, for most apps the official public APIs are more than enough and you won't need to resort to the private stuff.

So how do you mark your own methods as private, I hear you ask? This could get a bit complicated and is probably best left to a more detailed treatment of the subject. But in simple terms, similar to the `@objc` attribute you used in the previous chapter, there are other attributes that you can use to modify the access control level of Swift classes, methods, or properties.

Two of the most common are `public` and `private`. And hopefully, their names alone give you an understanding as to their intent. In Swift 4, `public` is assumed by default. Which is why you have not had to prefix any of your classes or methods with this attribute.

`private` is what you need if you wanted to hide any of your classes, methods, or properties. But a discussion as to how `private` works in terms of what is hidden if you use the attribute and the advantages of doing so, might be a bit too broad a subject for now :]

Casts

Often your code will refer to an instance not by its own class but by one of its superclasses. That probably sounds very weird, so let's look at an example.

MyLocations has a `UITabBarController` with three tabs, each of which is represented by a view controller. The view controller for the first tab is `CurrentLocationViewController`. Later on you'll add two others, `LocationsViewController` for the second tab, and `MapViewController` for the third.

The designers of iOS obviously didn't know anything about those three particular view controllers when they created `UITabBarController`. The only thing the tab bar controller can reliably depend on is that each tab has a view controller that inherits from `UIViewController`.

So, instead of talking to the `CurrentLocationViewController` class, the tab bar controller only sees its superclass part, `UIViewController`.

As far as the tab bar controller is concerned, it has three `UIViewController` instances and it doesn't know or care about the additions that you've made to each one.

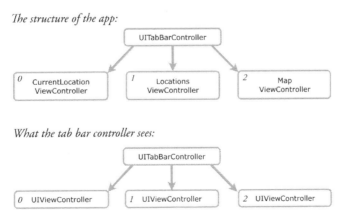

The UITabBarController does not see your subclasses

The same thing goes for `UINavigationController`. To the navigation controller, any new view controllers that get pushed on the navigation stack are all instances of `UIViewController`, nothing more, nothing less.

Sometimes that can be a little annoying. When you ask the navigation controller for one of the view controllers on its stack, it returns a reference to a `UIViewController` instance, even though that is not the full type of that object.

If you want to treat that object as your own view controller subclass instead, you need to **cast** it to the proper type.

Previously you did the following in `prepare(for:sender:)`:

```
let controller = segue.destination as!
                    ItemDetailViewController
controller.delegate = self
```

Here, you wanted to get the segue's destination view controller, which is an instance of `ItemDetailViewController`, and set its `delegate` property.

However, the segue's `destination` property won't give you an object of type `ItemDetailViewController`. The value it returns is of the plain `UIViewController` type, which naturally doesn't have your `delegate` property.

If you were write the above code without the `as! ItemDetailViewController` bit, like so:

```
let controller = segue.destination
```

Then, Xcode would show an error for the line below it. Swift now infers the type of `controller` to be `UIViewController`, but `UIViewController` does not have a `delegate` property. That property is something you added to the subclass, `ItemDetailViewController`.

You know that `destination` refers to an `ItemDetailViewController`, but Swift doesn't. Even though all `ItemDetailViewControllers` are `UIViewControllers`, not all `UIViewControllers` are `ItemDetailViewControllers`!

Just because your friend Chuck has no hair, that doesn't mean all bald guys are named Chuck. Or, that all guys named Chuck have no hair, either :]

To solve this problem, you have to cast the object to the proper type. You as the developer know this particular object is an `ItemDetailViewController`, so you use the `as!` cast operator to tell the compiler, "I want to treat this object as an `ItemDetailViewController`."

With the cast, the code looks like this:

```
let controller = segue.destination as!
                 ItemDetailViewController
```

(You would put this all on a single line in Xcode. Having long descriptive names is great for making the source code more readable, but it also necessitates clumsy line wrapping to make it fit in the book.)

Now, you can treat the value from `controller` as an `ItemDetailViewController` object. But... the compiler can't check whether the thing you're casting really is that kind of object. So, if you're wrong and it's not, your app will most likely crash.

Casts can fail for other reasons, too. For example, the value that you're trying to cast may actually be `nil`. If that's a possibility, it's a good idea to use the `as?` operator to make it an optional cast. You must also store the result of the cast into an optional value or use `if let` to safely unwrap it.

Note that a cast doesn't magically convert one type to another. You can't cast an `Int` to a `String`, for example. You only use a cast to make a type more specific, and the two types have to be compatible for this to work.

Casting is very common in Swift programs because of the Objective-C heritage of the iOS frameworks. You'll be doing a lot of it!

To summarize, there are three kinds of casts you can perform:

1. **as?** for casts that are allowed to fail. This would happen if the object is `nil` or doesn't have a type that is compatible with the one you're trying to cast to. It will try to cast to the new type and if it fails, then no biggie. This cast returns an optional that you can unwrap with `if let`.

2. **as!** for casts between a class and one of its subclasses. This is also known as a *downcast*. As with implicitly unwrapped optionals, this cast is potentially unsafe and you should only use `as!` when you are certain it cannot possibly go wrong. You often need to use this cast when dealing with objects coming from UIKit and other iOS frameworks. Better get used to all those exclamation marks!

3. **as** for casts that can never possibly fail. Swift can sometimes guarantee that a type cast will always work, for example between `NSString` and `String`. In that case you can leave off the ? or the ! and just write `as`.

It can sometimes be confusing to decide which of these three cast operators you need. If so, just type "as" and Xcode will suggest the correct variant. You can rely on Xcode :]

Chapter 25: The Tag Location Screen

There is a big button on the main screen of the app that says **Tag Location**. It only becomes active when GPS coordinates have been captured, and you use it to add a description and a photo to that location.

In this chapter, you'll build the Tag Location screen, but you won't save the location object anywhere yet, that's a topic for another chapter :]

This chapter covers the following:

- **The Screen:** What the finished screen looks like and what it will do.
- **The new view controller:** How to add the new view controller for the screen and to set up the navigation flow.
- **Make the cells:** Create the table view cells for displaying information.
- **Display location info:** Display location info on screen via the new view.
- **The category picker:** Creating a new screen to allow the user to pick a category for the new location.

The screen

The Tag Location screen is a regular table view controller with static cells. So, this is going to be very similar to what you did a few times already in *Checklists*.

The finished Tag Location screen will look like this:

The Tag Location screen

The description cell at the top contains a UITextView for text. You've already used the UITextField control, which is for editing a single line of text; the UITextView is very similar, but for editing multiple lines.

Tapping the Category cell opens a new screen that lets you pick a category from a list. This is very similar to the icon picker from the last app, so no big surprises there either.

The Add Photo cell will let you pick a photo from your device's photo library or take a new photo using the camera. You'll skip this feature for now and build that later on. Let's not get ahead of ourselves and try too much at once!

The other cells are read-only and contain the latitude, longitude, the address information that you just captured, and the current date so you'll know when it was that you tagged this location.

> **Exercise.** Try to implement this screen by yourself using the description I just gave you. You don't have to make the Category and Add Photo buttons work yet.
> Yikes, that seems like a big job! It sure is, but you should be able to pull this off. This screen doesn't do anything you haven't done previously. So if you feel brave, go ahead!

The new view controller

➤ Add a new file to the project using the **Swift File** template. Name the file **LocationDetailsViewController**.

You know what's next: create outlets and connect them to the controls on the storyboard. In the interest of saving time, I'll just give you the code that you're going to end up with.

➤ Replace the contents of **LocationDetailsViewController.swift** with the following:

```swift
import UIKit

class LocationDetailsViewController: UITableViewController {
  @IBOutlet weak var descriptionTextView: UITextView!
  @IBOutlet weak var categoryLabel: UILabel!
  @IBOutlet weak var latitudeLabel: UILabel!
  @IBOutlet weak var longitudeLabel: UILabel!
  @IBOutlet weak var addressLabel: UILabel!
  @IBOutlet weak var dateLabel: UILabel!

  // MARK:- Actions
  @IBAction func done() {
    navigationController?.popViewController(animated: true)
  }

  @IBAction func cancel() {
    navigationController?.popViewController(animated: true)
  }
}
```

Nothing special here, just a bunch of outlet properties and two action methods that both go back to the previous view in the navigation stack.

➤ In the storyboard, select the Current Location View Controller (the Tag Scene), and choose **Editor → Embed In → Navigation Controller** from Xcode's menu bar to put it inside a new navigation controller. (This sets up all the views on that particular tab of the tab view controller to be part of a navigation stack.)

➤ Drag a new **Table View Controller** on to the canvas and put it next to the Tag Scene.

➤ In the **Identity inspector**, change the **Class** attribute of the table view controller to **LocationDetailsViewController** to link it with the source code file you just created.

➤ **Control-drag** from the **Tag Location** button on the Tag Scene to the new view controller and create a **Show** segue. Give the segue the identifier **TagLocation**.

➤ Add a Navigation Item to the Location Details View Controller, and change the title to **Tag Location**.

➤ Switch the table content to **Static Cells** and its style to **Grouped**.

The storyboard should now looks like this:

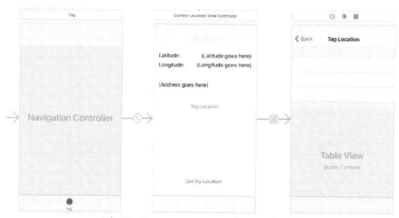

The Tag Location screen in the storyboard

Navigation bar hiding

You'll notice that the Tag Scene (the Current Location View Controller) now has an empty navigation bar area. This is because it is now embedded in a Navigation Controller. You can either set the title (and/or make it a large title), or, you can hide the navigation bar altogether for the first view.

For this particular app design, I think having no titles would look the best. So, you now have to hide the navigation bar at runtime for only the Tag Scene. How do you do it?

Simple enough. It's just a code change :]

➤ Switch to **CurrentLocationViewController.swift** and add a new `viewWillAppear` implementation:

```
override func viewWillAppear(_ animated: Bool) {
  super.viewWillAppear(animated)
  navigationController?.isNavigationBarHidden = true
}
```

All you do is ask the navigation controller to hide the navigation bar when this particular view appears. Simple as that :]

➤ Run the app and make sure the Tag Location button works.

Do you notice an issue when you switch to the Location Details View Controller via the Tag Location button?

The navigation bar on the new screen is hidden as well! Can you guess why this is?

Yep, it's because you hid the navigation controller's navigation bar in the previous screen :] That setting is not a per-screen setting. It affects the navigation bar for the navigation controller from that point onwards for all views dispalyed by the navigation controller.

So how do you fix it? Simple enough, ask the navigation controller to start showing the navigation bar as soon as you exit the view where you hide the navigation bar. And there is a handy `viewWillDisappear` method that you can override in `UIViewController` that's just the place for this kind of code.

➤ Add the following method to **CurrentLocationViewController.swift**:

```
override func viewWillDisappear(_ animated: Bool) {
    super.viewWillAppear(animated)
    navigationController?.isNavigationBarHidden = false
}
```

You simply reverse what you did previously in `viewWillAppear` by asking the navigation controller to show the navigation bar each time the current view disappears from view - usually, either because another view appeared on top of it, or because this view was dismissed in order to go back to a previous view.

➤ Run the app again and make sure that the navigation flow (and the showing/hiding of the navigation bar) works correctly.

Add navigation buttons

Of course, the new screen won't do anything useful yet. Let's add some buttons.

➤ Drag a **Bar Button Item** on to the left slot of the navigation bar. Make it a **Cancel** button and connect it to the **cancel** action. (If you're using the Connections inspector, the thing that you're supposed to connect is the Bar Button Item's "selector", under Sent Actions.)

➤ Also drag a **Bar Button Item** on to the right slot. Set both the **Style** and **System Item** attributes to **Done**, and connect it to the **done** action.

➤ Run the app again and make sure you can close the Tag Location screen from both buttons after you've opened it.

Make the cells

There will be three sections in this table view:

1. The description text view and the category cell. These can be changed by the user.

2. The photo. Initially this cell says Add Photo but once the user has picked a photo, you'll display the actual photo inside the cell. It's good to have that in a section of its own.

3. The latitude, longitude, address, and date rows. These are read-only information.

➤ Open the storyboard. Select the table view and go to the **Attributes inspector**. Change the **Sections** field from 1 to 3.

When you do this, the contents of the first section are automatically copied to the next sections. That isn't quite what you want. So, you'll have to remove some rows here and there. The first section will have 2 rows, the middle section will have just 1 row, and the last section will have 4 rows.

➤ Select one cell in the first section and delete it. (If it won't delete, make sure you selected the whole Table View Cell and not its Content View. The Document Outline can be very useful here.)

➤ Delete two cells from the middle section.

➤ Select the last Table View Section object (that is easiest in the Document Outline) and in the **Attributes inspector** set its **Rows** to 4.

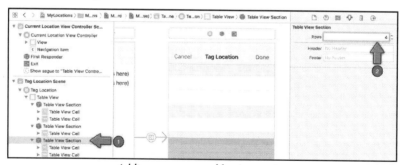

Adding a row to a table view section

(Alternatively, you can drag a new Table View Cell from the Object Library on to the section.)

The right detail cells

The second row from the first section, and the first, second and fourth rows in the last section will all use a standard cell style.

➤ Select these cells (you can select multiple items via the Document Outline by Command-clicking) and set their **Style** attribute to **Right Detail**.

The cells with the Right Detail style

The labels in these standard cell styles are regular UILabels. So, you can select them and change their properties.

➤ Change the titles for the labels on the left, from top to bottom to: **Category**, **Latitude**, **Longitude**, and **Date**.

(If Xcode moves the label when you type into it or cuts off the text, then change the cell style to Left Detail and back again to Right Detail. That seems to fix it.)

➤ Drag a new **Label** into the cell in the middle section (the one that's still empty). You cannot use a standard cell style for this cell. So, you'll design it yourself. Name this label **Add Photo**. (Later on you'll also add an image view to this cell.)

➤ Make sure the font of the label is **System**, size **17**, so it's the same size as the labels from the Right Detail cell style. If necessary, use **Editor → Size to Fit Content** to resize the label to its optimal size.

➤ Put the Add Photo label at X: 16 (in the **Size inspector**) and vertically centered in its cell. You can use the **Editor → Align → Vertically in Container** menu option for this. (If this menu option is grayed out, deselect the label and select it again.)

The table should now look like this:

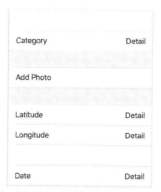

The labels in the Tag Location screen

Note: You're going to make a bunch of changes that are the same for each cell. For some of these, it is easier if you select all the cells at once and then change the setting. That will save you some time.

Unfortunately, some menu items and options are grayed out when you have a multiple selection, so you'll still have to change some of the settings for each cell individually.

Tappable cells

Only the Category and Add Photo cells are tap-able, so you have to set the cell selection color to None on the other cells.

➤ Select all the cells except Category and Add Photo. In the **Attributes inspector**, set **Selection** to **None**.

➤ Select the Category and Add Photo cells and set **Accessory** to **Disclosure Indicator**.

Category and Add Photo now have a disclosure indicator

The address cell

The empty cell in the last section is for the Address label. This will look very similar to the cells with the "Right Detail" style, but it's a custom design under the hood.

➤ Drag a new **Label** into that cell and name it **Address**. Put it on the left. Set the X position to 16, Y position to 11.

➤ Drag another **Label** into the same cell and name it **Detail**. Put it on the right, X position 260, Y position 11.

➤ Make sure the font of both labels is **System**, size **17**.

➤ Change the **Alignment** of the address detail label to right-aligned.

The detail label is special. Most likely the street address will be too long to fit in that small space. So, you'll configure this label to have a variable number of lines. This requires a bit of programming in the view controller to make it work, but you also have to set up this label's attributes properly.

➤ In the **Attributes inspector** for the address detail label, set **Lines** to **0** and **Line Break** to **Word Wrap**. When the number of lines is 0, the label will resize vertically to fit all the text that you put into it, which is exactly what you need.

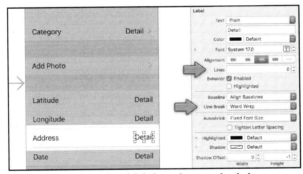

The address detail label can have multiple lines

The description cell

So far, you've left the cell at the top empty. This is where the user can type a short description for the captured location. Currently, there is not much room to type anything. So first, you'll make the cell larger.

➤ Click on the top cell to select it, then go into the **Size inspector** and type **88** into the **Row Height** field.

Changing the height of a row

You can also drag the cell to this new height by the sizing handle at its bottom, but I prefer to simply type in the new value.

The reason I chose 88 is that quite a few iOS screen elements have a size of 44 points. The navigation bar is 44 points high, regular table view cells are 44 points high, and so on. Choosing 44 or a multiple of it keeps the UI looking balanced.

➤ Drag a **Text View** into the cell. Give it the following position and size, X: 16, Y: 10, Width: 288, Height: 68.

➤ By default, Interface Builder puts a whole bunch of Latin placeholder text (Lorem ipsum dolor, etc) into the text view. Replace that text with (**Description goes here**). The user will never see that text, but it's handy to remind yourself what this view is for.

➤ Set the font to **System**, size **17**.

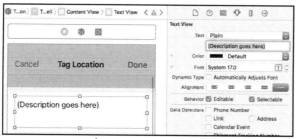

The attributes for the text view

➤ With the text view selected, go to the **Size inspector**. Change the **Autoresizing** settings to the following:

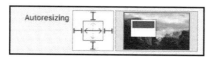

The autoresizing settings for the text view

With the "springs" enabled, the text view will automatically grow larger to fill up the extra space on larger screens.

One more thing to do, and then the layout is complete. Because the top cell doesn't have a label to describe what it does – and the text view will initially be empty as well – the user may not know what it is for.

There really isn't any room to add a label in front of the text view, as you've done for the other rows. So, let's add a header to the section. Table view sections can have a header and footer, and these can either be text or complete views with controls of their own.

➤ Select the top-most Table View Section and in its **Attributes inspector** type **Description** into the **Header** field:

Giving the section a header

That's the layout done. The Tag Location screen should look like this in the storyboard:

The finished design of the Tag Location screen

Now you can actually make the screen do stuff.

Connecting outlets

➤ Connect the Detail labels and the text view to their respective outlets. It should be obvious which one goes where. (Tip: Control-drag from the round yellow icon that represents the view controller to each of the labels. That's the quickest way.)

If you look at the **Connections inspector** for this view controller, you should see the following:

The connections of the Location Details View Controller

➤ Run the app to test whether everything works.

Of course, the screen still says "Detail" in the labels instead of the location's actual coordinates and address because you haven't passed it any data yet. Time to fix that, you reckon?

Display location info

➤ Add two new properties to **LocationDetailsViewController.swift**:

```
var coordinate = CLLocationCoordinate2D(latitude: 0,
                                       longitude: 0)
var placemark: CLPlacemark?
```

You've seen the CLPlacemark class before. It contains the address information – street name, city name, and so on – that you've obtained through reverse geocoding. This is an optional because there is no guarantee that the geocoder finds an address for the given coordinates.

CLLocationCoordinate2D is new. This contains the latitude and longitude from the CLLocation object that you received from the location manager. You only need the latitude and longitude, so there's no point in sending along the entire CLLocation object. The coordinate is not an optional, so you must give it an initial value.

> **Exercise.** Why is coordinate not an optional?

Answer: You cannot tap the Tag Location button unless GPS coordinates have been found. So, you'll never open the LocationDetailsViewController without a valid set of coordinates.

During the segue from the Current Location screen to the Tag Location screen you will fill in these two properties, and then the Tag Location screen can put these values into its labels.

Xcode isn't happy with the two lines you just added. It complains about "Use of unresolved identifier CLLocationCoordinate2D" and "CLPlacemark". That means Xcode does not know anything about these types yet.

That's because they are part of the Core Location framework – and before you can use anything from a framework, you first need to import it.

➤ Add the following import to the file:

```
import CoreLocation
```

Now Xcode's error messages should disappear after a second or two. If they don't, use ⌘+B to build the app again.

Structs

Unlike the objects you've seen before, CLLocationCoordinate2D is not a class, instead, it is a **struct** (short for structure).

Structs are like classes, but a little less powerful. They can have properties and methods, but unlike classes, they cannot inherit from one another.

The definition for CLLocationCoordinate2D is as follows:

```
struct CLLocationCoordinate2D {
    var latitude: CLLocationDegrees
    var longitude: CLLocationDegrees
}
```

This struct has two fields, `latitude` and `longitude`. Both these fields have the data type `CLLocationDegrees`, which is a synonym for `Double`:

```
typealias CLLocationDegrees = Double
```

As you probably remember from before, the `Double` type is one of the primitive types built into Swift. It's like a `Float` but with higher precision.

Don't let these synonyms confuse you; `CLLocationCoordinate2D` is basically this:

```
struct CLLocationCoordinate2D {
   var latitude: Double
   var longitude: Double
}
```

The reason the designers of Core Location used `CLLocationDegrees` instead of `Double` is that "CL Location Degrees" tells you what this type is intended for: it stores the degrees of a location from the Core Location framework.

Underneath the hood it's a `Double`, but as a user of Core Location all you need to care about when you want to store latitude or longitude is that you can use the `CLLocationDegrees` type. The name of the type adds meaning.

UIKit and other iOS frameworks also use structs regularly. Common examples are `CGPoint` and `CGRect`. In fact, `Array` and `Dictionary` are also structs.

Structs are more lightweight than classes. If you just need to pass around a set of values it's often easier to bundle them into a struct and pass that struct around, and that is exactly what Core Location does with coordinates.

Pass data to the details view

Back to the new properties that you just added to `LocationDetailsViewController`. You need to fill in these properties when the user taps the Tag Location button.

➤ Switch to **CurrentLocationViewController.swift** and add the following code:

```
// MARK:- Navigation
override func prepare(for segue: UIStoryboardSegue,
                          sender: Any?) {
   if segue.identifier == "TagLocation" {
      let controller = segue.destination
                       as! LocationDetailsViewController
      controller.coordinate = location!.coordinate
      controller.placemark = placemark
   }
}
```

You've seen how this works before. You use some casting magic to obtain the proper destination view controller and then set its properties. Now when the segue is performed, the coordinate and address are passed on to the Tag Location screen.

Because `location` is an optional, you need to unwrap it before you can access its `coordinate` property. It's perfectly safe to force unwrap at this point because the Tag Location button that triggers the segue won't be visible unless a location is found. At this point, `location` will never be `nil`.

The `placemark` variable is also an optional, but so is the `placemark` property on `LocationDetailsViewController`, so you don't need to do anything special here. You can always assign the value of one optional to another optional without problems.

Now that you have the values, you need to display them in the Tag Location screen.

Display information on the Tag Location screen

`viewDidLoad()` is a good place to display the passed in values on screen.

➤ Add the following code to **LocationDetailsViewController.swift**:

```swift
override func viewDidLoad() {
  super.viewDidLoad()

  descriptionTextView.text = ""
  categoryLabel.text = ""

  latitudeLabel.text = String(format: "%.8f",
                             coordinate.latitude)
  longitudeLabel.text = String(format: "%.8f",
                              coordinate.longitude)

  if let placemark = placemark {
    addressLabel.text = string(from: placemark)
  } else {
    addressLabel.text = "No Address Found"
  }

  dateLabel.text = format(date: Date())
}
```

This simply sets a value for every label. It uses two helper methods that you haven't defined yet: `string(from:)` to format the `CLPlacemark` object into a string, and `format(date:)` to do the same for a `Date` object.

➤ Add the `string(from:)` method:

```swift
// MARK:- Prviate Methods
func string(from placemark: CLPlacemark) -> String {
```

```
    var text = ""

    if let s = placemark.subThoroughfare {
      text += s + " "
    }
    if let s = placemark.thoroughfare {
      text += s + ", "
    }
    if let s = placemark.locality {
      text += s + ", "
    }
    if let s = placemark.administrativeArea {
      text += s + " "
    }
    if let s = placemark.postalCode {
      text += s + ", "
    }
    if let s = placemark.country {
      text += s
    }
    return text
}
```

This is fairly straightforward. It is similar to how you formatted the placemark on the main screen, except that you also include the country here.

Note: You might have noticed the // MARK comments all over the previous sections of code in this chapter. You already know what the // MARK comment does. So, I'm not going to explain that again.

You can feel free to leave the comments out when you type in your own code, but personally, I like to organize my code into identifiables sections as I've done here so that I can navigate my code easily. It's totally up to you whethr you follow what I do, create an organization style of your own, or use no organization at all :]

Date formatting

To format the date, you'll use a DateFormatter object. You've seen this class at work in the previous app. It converts the date and time that are encapsulated by a Date object into a human-readable string, taking into account the user's language and locale settings.

For *Checklists* you created a new instance of DateFormatter every time you wanted to convert a Date to a string. Unfortunately, DateFormatter is a relatively expensive object to create. In other words, it takes a while to initialize this object. If you do that many times over, then it may slow down your app (and drain the phone's battery faster).

It is better to create DateFormatter just once and then re-use that same object over and over. The trick is that you won't create the DateFormatter object until the app actually needs it. This principle is called **lazy loading** and it's a very important pattern for iOS apps - the work that you don't do won't cost any battery power.

In addition, you'll only ever create one instance of DateFormatter. The next time you need to use DateFormatter you won't make a new instance but re-use the existing one.

To pull this off you'll use a *private global* constant. That's a constant that lives outside of the LocationDetailsViewController class (global) but it is only visible inside the **LocationDetailsViewController.swift** file (private).

➤ Add the following to the top of **LocationDetailsViewController.swift**, in between the import and class lines:

```swift
private let dateFormatter: DateFormatter = {
    let formatter = DateFormatter()
    formatter.dateStyle = .medium
    formatter.timeStyle = .short
    return formatter
}()
```

What is going on here? You're creating a new constant named dateFormatter of type DateFormatter, that much should be obvious. This constant is private so it cannot be used outside of this Swift file. (Remember the discussion about private and public attributes in the previous chapter?)

You're also giving dateFormatter an initial value, but what follows the = is not an ordinary value – it looks like a bunch of source code in between { } brackets. That looks like a clousre, doesn't it? That's because it *is* a closure.

Normally, you'd create a new object like this:

```swift
private let dateFormatter = DateFormatter()
```

But to initialize the date formatter it's not enough to just make an instance of DateFormatter, you also want to set the dateStyle and timeStyle properties of this instance.

To create the object and set its properties in one go, you can use a closure:

```swift
private let dateFormatter: DateFormatter = {
    // the code that sets up the DateFormatter object
    return formatter
}()
```

The closure contains the code that creates and initializes the new DateFormatter object, and then returns it. This returned value is what gets put into dateFormatter.

The trick to making this work is the ( ) at the end. Closures are like functions, and to perform the code inside the closure you call it just like you'd call a function.

> **Note:** If you leave out the ( ), Swift thinks you're assigning the closure itself to dateFormatter – in other words, dateFormatter will contain a block of code, not an actual DateFormatter object. That's not what you want.
>
> Instead, you want to assign the *result* of that closure to dateFormatter. To make that happen, you use the ( ) to perform or **evaluate** the closure – this runs the code inside the closure and returns a DateFormatter object.

Using a closure to create and configure an object all at once is a nifty trick; you can expect to see this often in Swift programs.

In Swift, globals are always created in a lazy fashion, which means the code that creates and sets up this DateFormatter object isn't performed until the very first time the dateFormatter global is used in the app.

That happens inside the new format(date:) method.

➤ Add the new method - this code goes inside the class (and I would generally put it in the private methods section created by my previous // MARK comment, for organizational purposes):

```
func format(date: Date) -> String {
  return dateFormatter.string(from: date)
}
```

How simple is that? It just asks the DateFormatter to turn the Date into a String and returns that.

> **Exercise.** How can you verify that the date formatter is really only created once?

Answer: Add a print() just before the return formatter line in the closure. This print() text should appear only once in the Xcode Console.

➤ Run the app. Choose the Apple location from the Simulator's Debug menu. Wait until the street address is visible and then press the Tag Location button.

The coordinates, address and date are all filled in:

Latitude	37.33233141
Longitude	-122.03121860
Address	1
Date	Jul 3, 2017 at 9:24 AM

The Address label is too small to fit the entire address

The address seems to be missing something… only the first part of the address is visible (just the subthoroughfare or street number).

Multi-line address display

You have earlier configured the label to fit multiple lines of text, but the problem is that the table view doesn't know about that. Let's fix that.

There are several different ways to fix this particular issue - for example, table view cells can be set to change their height based on their content size. However, that approach would require adding auto layout constraints to the cell contents so that the content items (like buttons, labels, images etc.) knoiw how to resize themselves.

In this particular instance, since we have a limited number of static rows, it might be simpler to provide specific table view row heights, depending on the row, via a delegate method.

➤ Add the following method to **LocationDetailsViewController.swift**:

```
// MARK: - Table View Delegates
override func tableView(_ tableView: UITableView,
          heightForRowAt indexPath: IndexPath) -> CGFloat {
  if indexPath.section == 0 && indexPath.row == 0 {
    return 88

  } else if indexPath.section == 2 && indexPath.row == 2 {
    addressLabel.frame.size = CGSize(
                     width: view.bounds.size.width - 120,
                     height: 10000)
    addressLabel.sizeToFit()
    addressLabel.frame.origin.x = view.bounds.size.width -
                     addressLabel.frame.size.width - 16
    return addressLabel.frame.size.height + 20

  } else {
    return 44
  }
}
```

This delegate method is called by the table view when it loads its cells. You use it to tell the table view how tall each cell is.

Usually, all the cells have the same height and you can simply set a property on the table view if you wanted to change the height of all the cells at once (using the Row Height attribute in the storyboard or the `tableView.rowHeight` property).

This table view, however, has three different cell heights:

- The Description cell at the top. You already set its height to 88 points in the storyboard.

- The Address cell. The height of this cell is variable. It may be anywhere from one line of text to several, depending on how big the address string is.

- The other cells. They all have the standard cell height of 44 points.

The three branches of the `if` statements in `tableView(_:heightForRowAt:)` correspond to these three situations. Let's take a look at the branch for sizing the Address label:

```
// 1
addressLabel.frame.size = CGSize(
                         width: view.bounds.size.width - 120,
                         height: 10000)
// 2
addressLabel.sizeToFit()
// 3
addressLabel.frame.origin.x = view.bounds.size.width -
                         addressLabel.frame.size.width - 16
// 4
return addressLabel.frame.size.height + 20
```

This uses a bit of trickery to resize the `UILabel` to make all its text fit to the width of the cell (using word-wrapping), and then you use the newly calculated height of that label to determine how tall the cell must be.

The `frame` property is a `CGRect` that describes the position and size of a view.

`CGRect` is a struct that describes a rectangle. This rectangle has an origin made up of a `CGPoint` value with (X, Y) coordinates, and a `CGSize` value for the width and height.

All `UIView` objects – and that includes subclasses such as `UILabel` – have a frame rectangle. Changing the `frame` property is how views are positioned on the screen.

Step-by-step this is what the code does:

1. Change the width of the label to be 120 points less than the width of the screen, which makes it 200 points wide on the iPhone SE.

   Those 120 points that get subtracted account for the "Address" label on the left, the margins at the edges of the cell (16 points each), and some extra space between the two labels.

This code also makes the frame a whopping 10,000 points high. That is done to make the rectangle tall enough to fit a lot of text.

Because you're changing the `frame` property, the multi-line `UILabel` will now word-wrap the text to fit the requested width. This works because you already set the text on the label in `viewDidLoad()`.

2. Now that the label has word-wrapped its contents, you'll have to size the label back to the proper height because you don't want a cell that is 10,000 points tall. Remember the Size to Fit Content menu option from Interface Builder that you can use to resize a label to fit its contents? You can also do that via code with `sizeToFit()`.

3. The call to `sizeToFit()` removed any spare space to the right and bottom of the label. It may also have changed the width so that the text fits inside the label as snugly as possible, and because of that the X-position of the label may no longer be correct.

    A "detail" label like this should be placed against the right edge of the screen with a 16-point margin between them. That's done by changing the `frame`'s `origin.x` position.

4. Now that you know how high the label is, you can add a margin (10 points at the top, 10 points at the bottom) to calculate the full height for the cell.

> **Note:** If you think this is a horrible way to figure out how large the contents are of a multiline label that does word wrapping, then I totally agree. But it works, and that's the important thing!
>
> As I mentioned before, you can use Auto Layout to automatically calculate the height of the address cell using *self-sizing* table view cells. However, using multiline labels in Auto Layout is always a bit finicky. I find it easier to perform the calculations by hand. Besides, doing a little math never hurt anyone... ;-]

➤ Run the app. Now the reverse geocoded address should completely fit in the Address cell (even on larger screens). Try it out with a few different locations.

Latitude	37.33233141
Longitude	-122.03121860
Address	1 Infinite Loop, Cupertino, CA 95014, United States
Date	Jul 3, 2017 at 9:51 AM

The label resizes to fit the address

Frame vs. bounds

In the code above, you do the following:

```
addressLabel.frame.size = CGSize(
                     width: view.bounds.size.width - 120,
                     height: 10000)
```

You use the view's bounds to calculate the address label's frame. Both frame and bounds are of type CGRect, which describes a rectangle. So what is the difference between the bounds and the frame?

The frame describes the position and size of a view in its parent view. If you want to put a 150×50 label at position X: 100, Y: 30, then its frame is (100, 30, 150, 50). To move a view from one position to another, you change its frame property (or its center property - which defines the centered position for the view in its parent -, which in turn will modify the frame).

Where the frame describes the outside of the view, the bounds describe the inside. The X and Y coordinates of the bounds are (0, 0) and the width and height will be the same as the frame. So for the above example, the bounds are (0, 0, 150, 50). It's a matter of perspective.

Sometimes it makes sense to use the bounds; sometimes you need to use the frame. The frame is actually derived from a combination of properties: the center position of the view, the bounds, and any transform that is set on the view. (Transforms are used for rotating or scaling the view.)

When you set Auto Layout constraints on a view, those constraints are used to calculate the view's frame. If a view has constraints, you shouldn't change the frame or bounds properties yourself, or it will conflict with Auto Layout and the results may be unpredictable.

The category picker

When the user taps the Category cell, the app should show a list of category names:

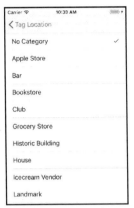

The category picker

The view controller class

This is a new screen, so you need a new view controller. The way this works is very similar to the icon picker from *Checklists*. I'm just going to give you the source code and tell you how to hook it up.

➤ Add a new file to the project named **CategoryPickerViewController.swift**.

➤ Replace the contents of **CategoryPickerViewController.swift** with:

```swift
import UIKit

class CategoryPickerViewController: UITableViewController {
  var selectedCategoryName = ""

  let categories = [
    "No Category",
    "Apple Store",
    "Bar",
    "Bookstore",
    "Club",
    "Grocery Store",
    "Historic Building",
    "House",
    "Icecream Vendor",
    "Landmark",
    "Park"]

  var selectedIndexPath = IndexPath()
```

```swift
  override func viewDidLoad() {
    super.viewDidLoad()

    for i in 0..<categories.count {
      if categories[i] == selectedCategoryName {
        selectedIndexPath = IndexPath(row: i, section: 0)
        break
      }
    }
  }

  // MARK:- Table View Delegates
  override func tableView(_ tableView: UITableView,
        numberOfRowsInSection section: Int) -> Int {
    return categories.count
  }

  override func tableView(_ tableView: UITableView,
             cellForRowAt indexPath: IndexPath) ->
             UITableViewCell {
    let cell = tableView.dequeueReusableCell(
                        withIdentifier: "Cell",
                              for: indexPath)

    let categoryName = categories[indexPath.row]
    cell.textLabel!.text = categoryName

    if categoryName == selectedCategoryName {
      cell.accessoryType = .checkmark
    } else {
      cell.accessoryType = .none
    }
    return cell
  }

  override func tableView(_ tableView: UITableView,
             didSelectRowAt indexPath: IndexPath) {
    if indexPath.row != selectedIndexPath.row {
      if let newCell = tableView.cellForRow(at: indexPath) {
        newCell.accessoryType = .checkmark
      }
      if let oldCell = tableView.cellForRow(
                     at: selectedIndexPath) {
        oldCell.accessoryType = .none
      }
      selectedIndexPath = indexPath
    }
  }
}
```

There's nothing special going on here. This is a table view controller that shows a list of category names. The table gets its rows from the `categories` array.

The only thing worth noting is the `selectedIndexPath` instance variable. When the screen opens it shows a checkmark next to the currently selected category. This comes from the `selectedCategoryName` property, which is filled in when you segue to this screen.

When the user taps a row, you want to remove the checkmark from the previously selected cell and put it in the new cell.

In order to be able to do that, you need to know which row is the currently selected one. You can't use `selectedCategoryName` for this because that is a string, not a row number. Therefore, you first need to find the row number – or index-path – for the selected category name.

That happens in `viewDidLoad()`. You loop through the array of categories and compare the name of each category to `selectedCategoryName`. If they match, you create an index-path object and store it in the `selectedIndexPath` variable. Once a match is found, you can `break` out of the loop because there's no point in looping through the rest of the categories.

Now that you know the row number, you can remove the checkmark for this row in `tableView(_:didSelectRowAt:)` when another row gets tapped.

It's a bit of work for such a small feature, but in a good app it's the details that matter.

There are several different ways of looping through the contents of an array.

You've already seen `for in`, which is used as follows:

```
for category in categories {
```

This puts the name of each category into a temporary constant named `category`.

However, in order to make the index-path object, you don't want the name of the category but the index of that category in the array. So you'll have to loop in a slightly different fashion:

```
for i in 0..<categories.count {
  let category = categories[i]
    . . .
}
```

Thanks to the half-open range operator `..<`, `i` is a number that increments from 0 to `categories.count` − 1. This is a very common pattern for looping through an array if you want to have the index as well.

Another way to do this is to use the `enumerated()` method, for which you'll see an example when you get to the next app. As a quick preview, this is how you'd use it:

```
for (i, category) in categories.enumerated() {
  . . .
}
```

The storyboard scene

➤ Open the storyboard and drag a new **Table View Controller** on to the canvas. Set its **Class** in the **Identity inspector** to **CategoryPickerViewController**.

➤ Change the **Style** of the prototype cell to **Basic**, and give it the re-use identifier **Cell**.

➤ **Control-drag** from the Category cell on the Location Details View Controller to this new view controller and choose **Selection Segue - Show**.

➤ Give the segue the identifier **PickCategory**.

The Category Picker View Controller now has a navigation bar at the top. You could change its title to "Choose Category", but Apple recommends that you do not give view controllers a title if their purpose is obvious. This helps to keep the navigation bar uncluttered.

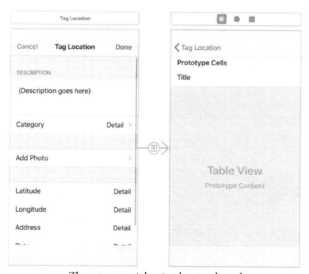

The category picker in the storyboard

That's enough for the storyboard. Now all that remains is to handle the segue.

The Segue

➤ Switch back to **LocationDetailsViewController.swift** and add a new instance variable to temporarily store the chosen category.

```
var categoryName = "No Category"
```

Initially you set the category name to "No Category", which is the category at the top of the list in the category picker.

➤ Change `viewDidLoad()` to put `categoryName` into the label:

```
override func viewDidLoad() {
  . . .
    categoryLabel.text = categoryName        // change this line
  . . .
```

➤ Finally, add the segue handling code:

```
// MARK:- Navigation
override func prepare(for segue: UIStoryboardSegue,
                      sender: Any?) {
  if segue.identifier == "PickCategory" {
    let controller = segue.destination as!
                  CategoryPickerViewController
    controller.selectedCategoryName = categoryName
  }
}
```

This simply sets the `selectedCategoryName` property of the category picker. And with that, the app has categories.

➤ Run the app and play with the category picker.

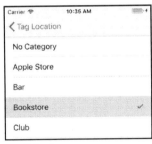

Selecting a new category

Hmm, it doesn't seem to work very well. You can choose a category, but the screen doesn't close when you tap a row. When you press the back button, the category you picked isn't shown on the parent screen.

Exercise. Which piece of the puzzle is missing?

Answer: The `CategoryPickerViewController` currently does not have a way to communicate back to the `LocationDetailsViewController` about the user selection.

I hope that at this point you're thinking, "Of course, dummy! You forgot to give the category picker a delegate protocol. That's why it cannot send any messages to the other view controller." (If so, awesome! You're getting the hang of this.)

A delegate protocol is a fine solution indeed, but I want to show you a handy storyboarding feature that can accomplish the same thing with less work: **unwind segues**.

The unwind segue

In case you were wondering what the orange "Exit" icons in the storyboard are for, you now have your answer: unwind segues.

 Exit

The Exit icon

Where a regular segue is used to open a new screen, an unwind segue closes the active screen. Sounds simple enough. However, making unwind segues is not very intuitive.

The orange Exit icons don't appear to do anything. Try Control-dragging from the prototype cell to the Exit icon, for example. It won't let you make a connection.

First, you have to add a special type of action method to the *destination* of the unwind segue.

➤ In **LocationDetailsViewController.swift**, add the following method:

```
@IBAction func categoryPickerDidPickCategory(
                  _ segue: UIStoryboardSegue) {
  let controller = segue.source as! CategoryPickerViewController
  categoryName = controller.selectedCategoryName
  categoryLabel.text = categoryName
}
```

You can see that this is an action method because it has the `@IBAction` annotation. What's different from a regular action method is the parameter, a `UIStoryboardSegue` object.

Normally, if an action method has a parameter, it points to the control that triggered the action, such as a button or slider. But in order to make an unwind segue, you need to define an action method that takes a `UIStoryboardSegue` parameter.

What happens inside the method is pretty straightforward. You look at the view controller that sent the segue (the `source`), which of course is the

`CategoryPickerViewController`, and then read the value of its
`selectedCategoryName` property. That property contains the category that the user
picked.

Now, to use this new method in the storyboard ...

➤ Open the storyboard. **Control-drag** from the prototype cell to the Exit button. This
time it allows you to make a connection:

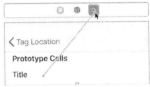

Control-dragging to the Exit icon to make an unwind segue

From the popup choose **Selection Segue - categoryPickerDidPickCategory:**, the name
of the unwind action method you just added.

The popup lists the unwind action methods

(If Interface Builder doesn't let you make a connection, then make sure you're really
Control-dragging from the Cell, not from its Content View or the label.)

Now when you tap a cell in the category picker, the screen closes and this new method is
called.

➤ Run the app to try it out.

That was easy! Well, not quite. Unfortunately, the chosen category is ignored…

That's because `categoryPickerDidPickCategory()` looks at the
`selectedCategoryName` property, but that property isn't set anywhere in your code yet.

You need some kind of mechanism that is invoked when the unwind segue is triggered,
at which point you can fill in the `selectedCategoryName` based on the row that was
tapped.

What might such a mechanism be called? `prepare(for:sender:)`, of course! This
works for segues in both directions.

➤ Add the following method to **CategoryPickerViewController.swift**:

```
// MARK:- Navigation
override func prepare(for segue: UIStoryboardSegue,
                     sender: Any?) {
```

```
if segue.identifier == "PickedCategory" {
    let cell = sender as! UITableViewCell
    if let indexPath = tableView.indexPath(for: cell) {
        selectedCategoryName = categories[indexPath.row]
    }
}
}
```

This looks at the selected index-path and puts the corresponding category name into the `selectedCategoryName` property.

This logic assumes the unwind segue is named "PickedCategory", so you still have to set an identifier on the unwind segue.

Unfortunately, there is no visual representation of that unwind segue in the storyboard. There is no nice, big arrow that you can click on. To select the unwind segue you have to locate it in the Document Outline:

You can find unwind segues in the Document Outline

➤ Select the unwind segue and go to the **Attributes inspector**. Give it the identifier **PickedCategory**.

➤ Run the app. Now the category picker should work properly. As soon as you tap the name of a category, the screen closes and the new category name is displayed.

Unwind segues are pretty cool and are often easier than using a delegate protocol, especially for simple picker screens such as this one.

You can find the project files for this chapter under **25 – Tag Location Screen** in the Source Code folder.

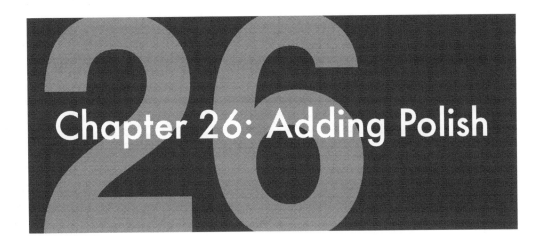

Chapter 26: Adding Polish

Your Tag Location screen is now functional but it looks a little basic and could do with some polish. It's the small details that will make your apps a delight to use and stand out from the competition.

In this chapter, you will learn the following:

- **Improve the user experience:** How to improve the user experience by adding tiny tweaks to your app which gives it some polish.

- **Add a HUD:** How to add a HUD (Heads Up Display) to your app to provide a quick, animated status update.

- **Handle the navigation:** How to continue the navigation flow after displaying the HUD.

Improve the user experience

Take a look at the design of the cell with the Description text view:

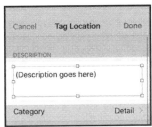

There is a margin between the text view and the cell border

There is a 10-point margin between the text view and the cell border, but because the background of both the cell and the text view are white, the user cannot see where the text view begins (or ends).

It is possible to tap on the cell but be just outside the text view area. That is annoying when you want to start typing: you think that you're tapping in the text view, but the keyboard doesn't appear.

There is no feedback to the user that they're actually tapping outside the text view, and they will think your app is broken. In my opinion, deservedly so.

Keyboard activation for cells

You'll have to make the app a little more forgiving. When the user taps anywhere inside that first cell, the text view should activate, even if the tap wasn't on the text view itself.

➤ Add the following table view delegate methods to **LocationDetailsViewController.swift**:

```swift
override func tableView(_ tableView: UITableView,
          willSelectRowAt indexPath: IndexPath) -> IndexPath? {
  if indexPath.section == 0 || indexPath.section == 1 {
    return indexPath
  } else {
    return nil
  }
}

override func tableView(_ tableView: UITableView,
          didSelectRowAt indexPath: IndexPath) {
  if indexPath.section == 0 && indexPath.row == 0 {
    descriptionTextView.becomeFirstResponder()
  }
}
```

The `tableView(_:willSelectRowAt:)` method limits taps to just the cells from the first two sections. Recall that `||` means "or". So, if the section number equals 0 *or* when it equals 1, you accept the tap on the cell. The third section only has read-only labels - it doesn't need to allow taps.

The `tableView(_:didSelectRowAt:)` method handles the actual taps on the rows. You don't need to respond to taps on the Category or Add Photo rows as these cells are connected to segues.

But if the user taps on the first row of the first section – the row with the description text view –, then you will give the input focus to the text view. Here you use `&&`, meaning "and", to make sure the tap is in the first section *and* also on the first row of that section.

➤ Try it out. Run the app and click or tap somewhere along the edges of the first cell. Any tap inside that first cell should now make the text view active and bring up the keyboard (but remember that on the Simulator you may need to press ⌘+K to make the keyboard visible).

Anything you can do to make screens less frustrating to use, is worth putting in the effort!

Speaking of the text view, once you've activated it, there's no way to get rid of the keyboard! And because the keyboard takes up half of the screen, that can be a bit annoying.

Deactivate the keyboard

It would be nice if the keyboard disappeared after you tapped anywhere else on the screen. As it happens, that is not so hard to implement.

➤ Add the following to the end of `viewDidLoad()` in **LocationDetailsViewController.swift**:

```
// Hide keyboard
let gestureRecognizer = UITapGestureRecognizer(target: self,
                            action: #selector(hideKeyboard))
gestureRecognizer.cancelsTouchesInView = false
tableView.addGestureRecognizer(gestureRecognizer)
```

A **gesture recognizer** is a very handy object that can recognize touch-based actions like taps, swipes, pans and pinches. You simply create the gesture recognizer object, give it a method to call when that particular gesture has been observed to take place, and add the recognizer object to a view.

You're using a `UITapGestureRecognizer`, which as the name implies, recognizes simple taps.

Notice the `#selector()` keyword again:

```
. . . target: self, action: #selector(hideKeyboard)) . .
```

You use this syntax to tell the `UITapGestureRecognizer` that it should call the method named by the `#selector()` whenever the gesture happens.

This pattern is known as **target-action** and you've already used it whenever you've connected `UIButtons`, `UIBarButtonItems`, and other controls to action methods.

The "target" is the object that the message should be sent to, which is often `self`, and "action" is the message to send.

Here you've chosen the message **hideKeyboard** to be sent when a tap is recognized anywhere in the table view, so you also have to implement a method to respond to that message. (Also, remember that selectors have their root in Objective-C and so, any method which is called via a selector has to be accessible from Objective-C.)

➤ Add the hideKeyboard() method to **LocationDetailsViewController.swift**:

```
@objc func hideKeyboard(_ gestureRecognizer:
                        UIGestureRecognizer) {
  let point = gestureRecognizer.location(in: tableView)
  let indexPath = tableView.indexPathForRow(at: point)

  if indexPath != nil && indexPath!.section == 0
                      && indexPath!.row == 0 {
    return
  }
  descriptionTextView.resignFirstResponder()
}
```

Whenever the user taps somewhere in the table view, the gesture recognizer calls this method. Conveniently, it also passes a reference to itself as a parameter, which lets you ask gestureRecognizer where the tap happened.

The gestureRecognizer.location(in:) method returns a CGPoint value indicating the tap position. CGPoint is a common struct that you see all the time in UIKit. It contains two fields, x and y, that describe a position on screen.

Using this CGPoint, you ask the table view which index-path is currently displayed at that position. This is important because you obviously don't want to hide the keyboard if the user tapped in the row with the text view! If the user tapped anywhere else, you hide the keyboard.

Exercise. Does the logic in the if statement make sense to you? Explain how this works.

Answer: It is possible that the user tapped inside the table view, but not on a cell - for example, somewhere in between two sections or on the section header. In that case, indexPath will be nil, making this an optional (of type IndexPath?). And to use an optional, you need to unwrap it somehow, either with if let or with !.

You only want to hide the keyboard if the index-path for the tap is not section 0, row 0, which is the cell with the text view. If the user did tap that particular cell, you bail out of hideKeyboard() with the return statement before the code reaches the call to resignFirstResponder().

> **Note:** You don't want to force unwrap an optional if there's a chance it might be nil or you risk crashing the app. Force unwrapping `indexPath!.section` and `indexPath!.row` may look dangerous here, but it is guaranteed to work thanks to the **short-circuiting** behavior of the && operator.
>
> If `indexPath` equals `nil`, then everything behind the first && is simply ignored. The condition can never become true anymore if one of the terms is false. So when the app gets to look at `indexPath!.section`, you know that the value of `indexPath` is not `nil` at that point.

An alternative way to write this logic is:

```
if indexPath == nil ||
        !(indexPath!.section == 0 && indexPath!.row == 0) {
    descriptionTextView.resignFirstResponder()
}
```

Can you wrap your head around that? Here, the `if` statement checks for the exact opposite. The && and || operators are each other's opposite in Boolean logic and you can often flip the meaning of a condition around by turning && into || by introducing the ! not operator.

You don't need to worry about this so early on in your programming career, but at some point you'll have to learn these rules of Boolean logic. They can be mind-benders!

Of course, you can also use `if let` to safely unwrap `indexPath`. So a third way to write the `if` statement is as follows:

```
if let indexPath = indexPath, indexPath.section != 0 &&
                              indexPath.row != 0 {
    descriptionTextView.resignFirstResponder()
}
```

I just wanted to give you a brief glimpse of the various ways you can write the conditions in `if` statements. There's often more than one way to do something in Swift. So, choose whatever approach you find easiest to understand.

➤ Run the app. Tap in the text view to bring up the keyboard. (If the keyboard doesn't come up, press ⌘+K.) Tap anywhere else in the table view to hide the keyboard again.

The table view can also automatically dismiss the keyboard when the user starts scrolling. You can enable this in the storyboard.

➤ Open the storyboard and select the table view in the Tag Location scene. In the **Attributes inspector** change the **Keyboard** option to **Dismiss on drag**. Now scrolling should also hide the keyboard.

The "Dismiss on drag" option for the keyboard

(If this doesn't work for you, try it on a real device. The keyboard in the Simulator can be a bit wonky.)

➤ Also try the **Dismiss interactively** option. Which one do you like best?

The HUD

There is one more improvement I wish to make to this screen, just to add a little spice. When you tap the Done button to close the screen, the app will show a quick animation to let you know it successfully saved the location:

Before you close the screen it shows an animated checkmark

This type of overlay graphic is often called a HUD, for Heads-Up Display. Apps aren't quite fighter jets, but HUDs are often used to display a progress bar or spinner while files are downloading or another long-lasting task is taking place.

You'll show your own HUD view for a brief second before the screen closes. It adds an extra bit of liveliness to the app.

If you're wondering how you can display anything on top of a table, this HUD is simply a `UIView` subclass. You can add views on top of other views. That's what you've been doing all along, in fact.

The labels are views that are added on top of the cells, which are also views. The cells themselves are added on top of the table view, and the table view in turn is added on top of the navigation controller's content view.

So far, when you've made your own objects, they have always been view controllers or data model objects, but it's also possible to make your own views.

Often, using the standard buttons and labels is sufficient. But when you want to do something that is not available as a standard view, you can always make your own. You either subclass `UIView` or `UIControl` and do your own drawing. That's what you're going to do for the HUD view as well.

Create the HUD view

➤ Add a new file to the project using the **Swift File** template. Name it **HudView**.

Let's build a minimal version of this class just so that you can get something on the screen. When that works, you'll make it look fancy.

➤ Replace the contents of **HudView.swift** with the following:

```swift
import UIKit

class HudView: UIView {
  var text = ""

  class func hud(inView view: UIView,
                  animated: Bool) -> HudView {
    let hudView = HudView(frame: view.bounds)
    hudView.isOpaque = false

    view.addSubview(hudView)
    view.isUserInteractionEnabled = false

    hudView.backgroundColor = UIColor(red: 1, green: 0, blue: 0,
                                       alpha: 0.5)
    return hudView
  }
}
```

The `hud(inView, animated)` method is known as a **convenience constructor**. It creates and returns a new `HudView` instance.

Normally you would create a new `HudView` object by writing:

```
let hudView = HudView()
```

But using the convenience constructor you'd write:

```
let hudView = HudView.hud(inView: parentView, animated: true)
```

A convenience constructor is always a **class method**, i.e. a method that works on the class as a whole and not on any particular instance. You can tell because its declaration begins with `class func` instead of just `func`.

When you call `HudView.hud(inView: parentView, animated: true)` you don't have an instance of `HudView` yet. The whole purpose of this method is to create an instance of the HUD view for you, so you don't have to do that yourself, and to place it on top of another view.

You can see that making an instance is actually the first thing this method does:

```
class func hud(inView view: UIView,
                     animated: Bool) -> HudView {
  let hudView = HudView(frame: view.bounds)
  . . .
  return hudView
}
```

It calls `HudView()`, or actually `HudView(frame:)` which is an `init` method inherited from `UIView`. At the end of the method, the new instance is returned to the caller.

So why use this convenience constructor? As the name implies, for convenience.

Since there are several steps to setting up the view, putting them in the convenience constructor frees you from having to worry about any of that.

One of these additional steps is that this method adds the new `HudView` object as a subview on top of the "parent" view object. This is the navigation controller's view, so the HUD will cover the entire screen.

It also sets the parent view's `isUserInteractionEnabled` property to `false`. While the HUD is showing, you don't want the user to interact with the screen anymore. The user has already pressed the Done button and the screen is in the process of closing.

Most users will leave the screen alone at this point, but there's always some joker who wants to try and break things. By setting `isUserInteractionEnabled` to `false`, the view swallows any touches and all the underlying views become unresponsive.

Just for testing, you set the background color of the HUD to 50% transparent red. That way you can see if it covers the entire screen.

Use the HUD view

Let's add the code to call this funky new HUD, so that you can see it in action.

➤ Change the done() method in **LocationDetailsViewController.swift** to:

```
@IBAction func done() {
   let hudView = HudView.hud(inView: navigationController!.view,
                             animated: true)
   hudView.text = "Tagged"
}
```

This creates a HudView object and adds it to the navigation controller's view with an animation. You also set the text property on the new object.

Previously, done() sent you back to the previous view controller. For testing purposes, you're not going to do that anymore. You want to have enough time to see what the HudView looks like as you build it step-by-step; if you immediately close the screen after showing the HUD, it will be hard to see what's going on (unless you have the ability to slow down time somehow). You'll put back the code that closes the screen later.

➤ Run the app. When you press the Done button, the screen will look like this:

The HUD view covers the whole screen

The app is now totally unresponsive because user interaction is disabled.

When you're working with views, it's a good idea to set the background color to a bright color such as red or blue, so you can see exactly how big a given view is.

Did you, upon looking at the HUD activation code think, "Hey, how come we are using the navigation' controller's view instead of the view from LocationDetailsViewController?" If you did, good on you! It shows that you are starting to understand the composition of view controllers and views and thinking about how they work.

The answer is simple enough to figure out :] Just try it and see what happens. Change the HudView creation line in done() to the following:

```
let hudView = HudView.hud(inView: view, animated: true)
```

Here, instead of the navigation controller's content view, you use the current view controller's view as the parent for the HUD.

➤ Run the app and try the Done button. You should get a screen like this:

The HUD view does not cover the navigation bar

Do you see what happened?

The HUD now only covers the screen area for the LocationDetailsViewController's view - it does not cover the navigation bar. And you know what that means, right? The user can tap on the Cancel or Done buttons and have them respond even if the rest of the screen has user interactions disabled. That can be a problem is certain situations.

Revert your code back to using the navigation controller's view before you forget.

Let's get the HUD view to actually display something on screen instead of the red background.

Draw the HUD view

➤ Remove the backgroundColor line from the hud(inView:animated:) method.

➤ Add the following method to **HudView.swift**:

```
override func draw(_ rect: CGRect) {
  let boxWidth: CGFloat = 96
  let boxHeight: CGFloat = 96

  let boxRect = CGRect(
    x: round((bounds.size.width - boxWidth) / 2),
    y: round((bounds.size.height - boxHeight) / 2),
```

```
        width: boxWidth,
        height: boxHeight)

    let roundedRect = UIBezierPath(roundedRect: boxRect,
                                   cornerRadius: 10)
    UIColor(white: 0.3, alpha: 0.8).setFill()
    roundedRect.fill()
}
```

The draw() method is invoked whenever UIKit wants your view to redraw itself.

Recall that everything in iOS is event-driven. The view doesn't draw anything on screen unless UIKit asks it to draw itself. That means you should never call draw() yourself.

Instead, if you want a view to redraw, you should send it the setNeedsDisplay() message. UIKit will then trigger a draw() when it is ready to perform the drawing. This may seem strange if you're coming from another platform. You may be used to redrawing the screen whenever you feel like it, but on iOS, UIKit is in charge of who gets to draw when.

The above code draws a filled rectangle with rounded corners in the center of the screen. The rectangle is 96 by 96 points (so I suppose it's really a square):

```
let boxWidth: CGFloat = 96
let boxHeight: CGFloat = 96
```

This declares two constants you'll be using in the calculations that follow. You're using constants because it's clearer to refer to the symbolic name boxWidth than the number 96. That number doesn't mean much by itself, but "box width" is a pretty clear description of its purpose.

Additionally, if you were to later decide to change the size of the HUD box, you only have one place in your code where you need to change the width or the height, instead of going through all your code trying to figure out where else you had the width or the height value as a number.

Note that you force the type of these constants to be CGFloat, which is the type used by UIKit to represent decimal numbers. When working with UIKit or Core Graphics (CG, get it?) you use CGFloat instead of the regular Float or Double.

```
let boxRect = CGRect(
    x: round((bounds.size.width - boxWidth) / 2),
    y: round((bounds.size.height - boxHeight) / 2),
    width: boxWidth,
    height: boxHeight)
```

There is CGRect again, the struct that represents a rectangle. You use it to calculate the position for the HUD. The HUD rectangle should be centered horizontally and vertically on the screen. The size of the screen is given by bounds.size (this is the size of HudView itself, which spans the entire screen).

The above calculation uses the round() function to make sure the rectangle doesn't end up on fractional pixel boundaries because that makes the image look fuzzy.

```
let roundedRect = UIBezierPath(roundedRect: boxRect,
  cornerRadius: 10)
UIColor(white: 0.3, alpha: 0.8).setFill()
roundedRect.fill()
```

UIBezierPath is a very handy object for drawing rectangles with rounded corners. You just tell it how large the rectangle is and how round the corners should be. Then you fill the rectangle with an 80% opaque dark gray color.

➤ Run the app. The result should look like this:

The HUD view has a partially transparent background

There are two more things to add to the HUD, a checkmark and a text label. The checkmark is an image.

Display the HUD checkmark

➤ The Resources folder for the book has two files in the **Hud Images** folder, **Checkmark@2x.png** and **Checkmark@3x.png**. Add these files to the asset catalog, **Assets.xcassets**.

You can do this with the + button or simply drag them from Finder on to the Xcode window with the asset catalog open.

➤ Add the following code to the end of draw():

```
// Draw checkmark
if let image = UIImage(named: "Checkmark") {
  let imagePoint = CGPoint(
```

```
    x: center.x - round(image.size.width / 2),
    y: center.y - round(image.size.height / 2) - boxHeight / 8)
  image.draw(at: imagePoint)
}
```

This loads the checkmark image into a UIImage object. Then it calculates the position for that image based on the center coordinate of the HUD view (center) and the dimensions of the image (image.size).

Finally, it draws the image at that position.

➤ Run the app to see the HUD view with the image:

The HUD view with the checkmark image

Note: If you don't see the checkmark when you run the app, and if you did change the done() method to use the view controller's view instead of the navigation controller's content view, make sure that you reverted the code back.

The position calculations are based on the HUD view stretching up to the navigation bar, and if the view size is different, the checkmark will be placed a little above the rounded square. Since the background is mostly white outside the square, and the checkmark is white too, you might not even notice it when it is drawn outside the rounded square :]

Failable initializers

To create the UIImage you used if let to unwrap the resulting object. That's because UIImage(named) is a *failable* initializer.

It is possible that loading the image fails. This could be for one of many different reasons such as there being no image with the specified name, or the file not containing a valid image. You can't fool UIImage into loading something that isn't an image!

That's why UIImage's init(named:) method is really defined as init?(named:). The question mark indicates that this method returns an optional. If there was a problem loading the image, it returns nil instead of a brand spanking new UIImage object.

You'll see these failable initializers throughout the iOS frameworks. One that you have encountered before is init?(coder:). Whenever it is possible that creating a new object will fail, the responsible init method will return an optional that you need to unwrap before you can use it.

Display the HUD text

Usually, to display text in your own view, you'd add a UILabel object as a subview and let UILabel do all the hard work. However, for a view as simple as this, you can also do your own text drawing.

➤ Add the following code to the end of draw() to complete the method:

```
// Draw the text
let attribs = [
    NSAttributedStringKey.font: UIFont.systemFont(ofSize: 16),
    NSAttributedStringKey.foregroundColor: UIColor.white ]

let textSize = text.size(withAttributes: attribs)

let textPoint = CGPoint(
  x: center.x - round(textSize.width / 2),
  y: center.y - round(textSize.height / 2) + boxHeight / 4)

text.draw(at: textPoint, withAttributes: attribs)
```

When drawing text, you first need to know how big the text is so you can figure out where to position it. String has a bunch of handy methods for doing both.

First, you set up a dictionary of attributes for the text that you want to draw, such as the font to be used, the text color etc. Here, you'll use a white "System" font of size 16.

You use these attributes and the string from the text property to calculate how wide and tall the text will be. The result ends up in the textSize constant, which is of type CGSize. (As you'll notice, CGPoint, CGSize, and CGRect are types you use a lot when making your own views.)

Finally, you calculate where to draw the text (textPoint), and then draw it. Quite simple, really.

➤ Run the app to try it out. Lookin' good!

The HUD view with the checkmark and the text

➤ Make sure to test the HUD on the different Simulators. No matter the device dimensions, the HUD should always appear centered in the screen.

OK, you've now got a rounded box with a checkmark, but it's still far from spectacular. Time to liven it up a little with some animation!

Add some animation

You've already seen a bit about animations before – they're really easy to add.

➤ Add the following method to **HudView.swift**:

```
// MARK:- Public methods
func show(animated: Bool) {
  if animated {
    // 1
    alpha = 0
    transform = CGAffineTransform(scaleX: 1.3, y: 1.3)
    // 2
    UIView.animate(withDuration: 0.3, animations: {
      // 3
      self.alpha = 1
      self.transform = CGAffineTransform.identity
    })
  }
}
```

For the *Bull's Eye* app, you made a crossfade animation using the Core Animation framework. UIView, however, has its own animation mechanism. It still uses Core Animation behind the scenes, but it's a little more convenient to use.

The standard steps for doing UIView-based animations are as follows:

1. Set up the initial state of the view before the animation starts. Here you set alpha to 0, making the view fully transparent. You also set the transform to a scale factor of 1.3. We're not going to go into depth on transforms here, but basically, this means the view is initially scaled up to be larger than it normally would be.

2. Call `UIView.animate(withDuration:animations:)` to set up an animation. You pass the method a closure that describes what happens as part the animation. Recall that a closure is a piece of inline code that is not executed right away. UIKit will animate the properties that you change inside the closure from their initial state to the final state.

3. Inside the closure, set up the state of the view as it should be after the animation completes. You set `alpha` to 1, which means the `HudView` is now fully opaque. You also set the `transform` to the "identity" transform, restoring the scale back to normal. Because this code is part of a closure, you need to use `self` to refer to the `HudView` instance and its properties. That's the rule for closures.

The HUD view will quickly fade in as it goes from fully transparent to fully opaque, and it will scale down from 1.3 times its original size to its regular width and height.

This is only a simple animation but it looks quite smart.

➤ Change the `hud(inView:animated:)` method to call `show(animated:)` just before it returns:

```
class func hud(inView view: UIView, animated: Bool) -> HudView {
  . . .
  hudView.show(animated: animated)
  return hudView
}
```

➤ Run the app and marvel at the magic of `UIView` animation.

Improve the animation

You can actually do one better. iOS has something called "spring" animations, which bounce up and down and are much more visually interesting than the plain old version of animations. Using them is very simple.

➤ Replace the `UIView.animate(withDuration:animations:)` code in `show(animated:)` with the following:

```
UIView.animate(withDuration: 0.3, delay: 0,
    usingSpringWithDamping: 0.7, initialSpringVelocity: 0.5,
                  options: [], animations: {
    self.alpha = 1
    self.transform = CGAffineTransform.identity
  }, completion: nil)
```

The code in the closure is still the same – it sets alpha to 1 and restores the identity transform – but this new animation method has a lot more options. Feel free to play with these options to see what they do.

➤ Run the app and watch it bounce. Actually, the effect is very subtle, but subtle is good when it comes to user interfaces. You don't want your users to get seasick from using the app!

Handle the navigation

Back to **LocationDetailsViewController**... You still need to close the screen when the user taps Done.

There's a challenge here: you don't want to dismiss the screen right away. It won't look very good if the screen already closes before the HUD is finished animating. You didn't spend all that time writing `HudView` for nothing – you want to give your users a chance to see it.

You are going to use the **Grand Central Dispatch** framework, or GCD here. GCD is a very handy but somewhat low-level library for handling asynchronous tasks. Telling the app to wait a few seconds before executing some code is a perfect example of an "async" task.

➤ Add these lines to the bottom of the `done()` action method:

```
let delayInSeconds = 0.6
DispatchQueue.main.asyncAfter(deadline: .now() + delayInSeconds,
                             execute: {
  self.navigationController?.popViewController(animated: true)
})
```

Believe it or not, these mysterious incantations tell the app to close the Tag Location screen after 0.6 seconds :]

The magic happens in `DispatchQueue.main.asyncAfter()`. This function takes a closure as its final parameter. Inside that closure, you tell the navigation controller to go back to the previous view controller in the navigation stack. This doesn't happen right away, though. That's the exciting thing about closures: even though this code sits side-by-side with all the other code in the method, everything inside the closure is ignored for now and kept for a later time.

`DispatchQueue.main.asyncAfter()` uses the time given by `.now()` + `delayInSeconds` to schedule the closure for some point in the future. Until then, the app just sits there twiddling its thumbs. (By the way, `.now()` is a shortcut for `DispatchTime.now()`. Swift's type inference already knows that the type of the `when:` parameter is always a `DispatchTime` object, so you don't have to mention `DispatchTime` explicitly.)

After 0.6 seconds, the code from the closure runs and the screen closes.

> **Note:** I spent some time tweaking that number. The HUD view takes 0.3 seconds to fully fade in and then you wait another 0.3 seconds before the screen disappears. That felt right to me. You don't want to close the screen too quickly or the effect from showing the HUD is lost, but it shouldn't take too long either, or it will annoy the user. Animations are cool but they shouldn't make the app more frustrating to use!

➤ Run the app. Press the Done button and watch how the screen disappears. This looks pretty smooth, if I do say so myself.

But wait … the HUD never goes away after the Tag Location screen closes! It still is there after you navigate back to the parent view. This is not good …

> **Exercise:** Can you explain why this happens?

The reason is simple. You added the HUD to the navigation controller's content view, not the Tag Location screen's view. So, even though you've dismissed the Tag Location screen, you still have the HUD displaying because the navigation controller itself is still in existence.

So what do you think you should do to hide the HUD? Remove it from view, of course!

➤ Add the following method to **HudView.swift**:

```
func hide() {
  superview?.isUserInteractionEnabled = true
  removeFromSuperview()
}
```

This method is rather simple. Remember how you disabled user-interactions when showing the HUD? You first re-enable user-interactions and then remove the HudView instance from it's parent view. The only new thing might be superview and that's a reference to a view's parent view - all UIView objects (and sub-classes of UIVew too) have a superview property which identifies the view's parent.

Of course, if you wanted, you could have made the method a bit more complex and interesting by adding some animation to the removal of the HUD. Basically, you'd set up the animation to reverse what you did when you showed the view. But I leave that to you as an exercise :]

Now, you need to call this new method to hide the HUD before you exit the Tag Location screen.

➤ Modify the `DispatchQueue.main.asyncAfter` closure for `done()` in **LocationDetailsViewController.swift**:

```
DispatchQueue.main.asyncAfter(deadline: .now() + delayInSeconds,
                              execute: {
  hudView.hide()    // Add this line
    self.navigationController?.popViewController(animated: true)
})
```

➤ Run the app. Press the Done button and check if the HUD disappears when the Tag Location screen goes away.

Clean up the code

Now I don't know about you, but I find this GCD stuff to be a bit messy. So let's clean up the code and make it easier to understand.

➤ Add a new file to the project using the **Swift File** template. Name the file **Functions.swift**.

➤ Replace the contents of the new file with:

```
import Foundation

func afterDelay(_ seconds: Double, run: @escaping () -> Void) {
    DispatchQueue.main.asyncAfter(deadline: .now() + seconds,
                                  execute: run)
}
```

That looks very much like the code you just added to `done()`, except it now lives in its own function, `afterDelay()`. This is a **free function**, not a method inside an object. So, it can be used from anywhere in your code.

Take a good look at `afterDelay()`'s second parameter, the one named `run`. Its type is `() -> Void`. That's not some weird emoticon; it is Swift notation for a parameter that takes a closure with no arguments and no return value.

The type for a closure generally looks like this:

```
(parameter list) -> return type
```

In this case, both the parameter list and the return value are empty, `()` and `Void`. This can also be written as `Void -> Void`, or even `() -> ()`, but I like the `() -> Void` better because it looks like a function delcaration.

So, whenever you see a -> in the type annotation for a parameter, you know that parameter is a closure.

afterDelay() simply passes this closure along to DispatchQueue.main.asyncAfter().

The annotation @escaping is necessary for closures that are not performed immediately. This is so that Swift knows that it should hold on to this closure for a while.

You may be wondering why you're going through all this trouble. No fear! The reason why will become apparent after you've made the following change...

➤ Go back to **LocationDetailsViewController.swift** and change done() as follows:

```
@IBAction func done() {
  let hudView = HudView.hud(inView: navigationController!.view,
                            animated: true)
  hudView.text = "Tagged"
  afterDelay(0.6, run: {
    hudView.hide()
    self.navigationController?.popViewController(animated: true)
  })
}
```

Now that's the power of Swift! It only takes one look at this code to immediately understand what it does. After a delay, some code is executed.

By moving the nasty GCD stuff into a new function, afterDelay(), you have added a new level of **abstraction** to your code that makes it much easier to follow. Writing good programs is all about finding the right abstractions.

Note: Because the code referring to the navigation controller sits in a closure, it needs to use self. Inside closures you always need to use self explicitly. But, you didn't need to use self for the line referring to the hudView since it is a local variable which would be in existence only within the scope of the done() method.

You can make the code even more concise. Change the code to:

```
afterDelay(0.6) {
  hudView.hide()
  self.navigationController?.popViewController(animated: true)
}
```

Now the closure sits *outside* of the call to afterDelay().

Swift has a handy rule that says you can put a closure outside a function call if it's the last parameter of the function. This is known as **trailing closure syntax**. You will usually see closures being used in this manner because it reads (and looks) better.

➤ Run the app again to make sure the timing still works. Boo-yah!

You can find the project files for this chapter under **26 – Adding Polish** in the Source Code folder.

Chapter 27: Saving Locations

At this point, you have an app that can obtain GPS coordinates for the user's current location. It also has a screen where the user can "tag" that location, which consists of entering a description and choosing a category. Later on, you'll also allow the user to pick a photo.

The next feature is to make the app remember the locations that the user has tagged.

This chapter covers the following:

- **Core Data overview:** A brif overview of what Core Data is and how it works.

- **Add Core Data:** Add the Core Data framework to the app and use it.

- **The data store:** Initializing the data store used by Core Data.

- **Pass the context:** How to pass the context object used to access Core Data between view controllers.

- **Browse the data:** Looking through the saved data.

- **Save the locations:** Saving entered location information using Core Data.

- **Handle Core Data errors:** Handling Core Data errors when there's an issue with saving.

Core Data overview

You have to persist the data for these captured locations somehow - they need to be remembered even when the app terminates.

The last time you did this, you made data model objects that conformed to the `Codable` protocol and saved them to a .plist file. That works fine, but in this lesson I want to introduce you to a framework that can take a lot of work out of your hands: Core Data.

Core Data is an object persistence framework for iOS apps. If you've looked at Core Data before, you may have found the official documentation a little daunting, but the principle is quite simple.

You've learned that objects get destroyed when there are no more references to it. In addition, all objects get destroyed when the app terminates.

With Core Data, you can designate some objects as being persistent so they will always be saved to a **data store**. Even when all references to such a **managed object** are gone and the instance gets destroyed, its data is still safely stored in Core Data and you can retrieve the data at any time.

If you've worked with databases before, then you might be tempted to think of Core Data as a database, but that's a little misleading. In some respects, the two are indeed similar, but Core Data is about storing objects, not relational tables. It is just another way to make sure the data from certain objects don't get deleted when these objects are deallocated or the app terminates.

Add Core Data

Core Data requires the use of a data model. This is a special file that you add to your project to describe the objects that you want to persist. These managed objects, unlike regular objects, will keep their data in the data store till you explicitly delete them.

Create the data model

➤ Add a new file to the project. Choose the **Data Model** template under the **Core Data** section (scroll down in the template chooser):

Adding a Data Model file to the project

➤ Save it as **DataModel**.

This will add a new file to the project, DataModel.xcdatamodeld.

➤ Click **DataModel.xcdatamodeld** in the Project navigator to open the Data Model editor:

The empty data model

For each object that you want Core Data to manage, you have to add an **entity**.

An entity describes which data fields your objects will have. In a sense, it serves the same purpose as a class, but specifically for Core Data's data store. (If you've worked with SQL databases before, you can think of an entity as a table.)

This app will have one entity, Location, which stores all the properties for a location that the user tagged. Each Location will keep track of the following data:

• Latitude and longitude

• Placemark (the street address)

• The date when the location was tagged

• The user's description

- Category

These are the items from the Tag Location screen, except for the photo. Photos can potentially be very big and can take up several megabytes of storage space. Even though the Core Data store can handle big "blobs" of data, it is usually better to store photos as separate files in the app's Documents directory. More about that later.

➤ Click the **Add Entity** button at the bottom of the data model editor. This adds a new entity under the ENTITIES heading. Name it **Location**. (You can rename the entity by clicking its name or from the Data Model inspector pane on the right.)

The new Location entity

The entity detail pane in the center shows three sections: Attributes, Relationships and Fetched Properties. The Attributes are the entity's data fields.

This app only has one entity, but generally, apps will have many entities that are all related to each other somehow. With Relationships and Fetched Properties, you can tell Core Data how your objects depend on each other.

For this app, you will only use the Attributes section.

➤ Click the **Add Attribute** button at the bottom of the editor, or the small + button below the Attributes section. Name the new attribute **latitude** and set its **Type** to **Double**:

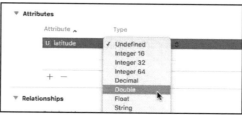

Choosing the attribute type

Attributes are basically the same as properties, and therefore they have a type. You've seen earlier that the latitude and longitude coordinates really have the data type `Double`. So, that's what you're choosing for the attribute as well.

> **Note:** Don't let the change in terminology scare you. Just think:
>
> entity = object (or class)
>
> attribute = property
>
> If you're wondering where you'll define methods in Core Data, then the answer is: you don't. Core Data is only for storing the data portion of objects. That is what an entity describes: the data of an object, and optionally, how that object relates to other objects if you use Relationships and Fetched Properties.
>
> In a short while, you are going to define your own `Location` class by creating a Swift file, just as you've been doing all along. Because it describes a managed object, this class will be associated with the Location entity in the data model. But it's still a regular class, so you can add your own methods to it.

➤ Add the rest of the attributes for the Location entity:

- longitude, type Double

- date, type Date

- locationDescription, type String

- category, type String

- placemark, type Transformable

The data model should look like this when you're done:

All the attributes of the Location entity

Why didn't you just call the description value "description" instead of "locationDescription"? As it turns out, `description` is the name of a method from `NSObject`. If you try to name an attribute "description", then it will cause a naming conflict with the NSObject method since Core Data managed objects are derived from NSObject. Xcode will give you an error message if you try to do this.

The type of the placemark attribute is Transformable. Core Data only supports a limited number of data types right out the box, such as String, Double, and Date. The placemark is a CLPlacemark object and is not in the list of supported data types.

Fortunately, Core Data has a provision for handling arbitrary data types. Any class that conforms to the NSCoding protocol can be stored in a Transformable attribute without additional work. Fortunately for us, CLPlacemark does conform to NSCoding, so you can store it in Core Data with no trouble. (And in case you are wondering, NSCoding is the Objective-C equivalent of the Swift Codable protocol - it allows classes to encode and decode themselves if they support it.)

By default, entity attributes are optional, meaning they can be nil. In our app, the only thing that can be nil is the placemark, in case reverse geocoding failed. It's a good idea to embed this constraint in the data model.

➤ Select the category attribute. In the inspectors panel, switch to the Data Model inspector (third tab). Uncheck the Optional setting:

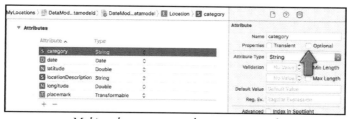

Making the category attribute non-optional

➤ Repeat this for the other attributes, except for placemark. (Tip: you can select multiple attributes at the same time, either by Command+clicking to select individually, or Shift+Clicking to select a range.)

➤ Press ⌘+S to save your changes. Xcode is supposed to do this automatically, but I've found the data model editor to be a little unreliable at times. Better safe than sorry!

You're done with the data model, but there's one more thing to do.

Generate the code

➤ Click on the Location entity to select it and go to the Data Model inspector.

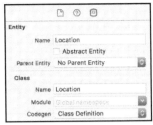

The Data Model inspector

The Class - Name field says "Location". When you retrieve a Location entity from Core Data, it gives you an object of the class `Location` which is derived from `NSManagedObject`. `NSManagedObject` is the base class for all objects that are managed by Core Data. Regular objects inherit from `NSObject`, but Core Data objects extend `NSManagedObject`.

Because using `NSManagedObject` directly is a bit limiting, Xcode helpfully sets you up to use your own `Location` class instead. You're not required to make your own classes for your entities, but it does make Core Data easier to use. So now when you retrieve a Location entity from the data store, Core Data doesn't give you an `NSManagedObject` but an instance of your own `Location` class.

Note also that the Class - Codegen dropdown is set to "Class Definition". Xcode will automatically generate the code for your entity's class with this setting so that you don't have to do any extra work. However, it is useful to understand how to make your own `NSManagedObject` subclass rather than relying on Xcode magic. So, for this app, you'll write the code yourself.

➤ In the inspector, change **Codegen** to **Manual/None**.

Even though you won't be using automatic class generation, Xcode can still lend a helping hand.

➤ From the menu bar, choose **Editor** → **Create NSManagedObject Subclass….**

The assistant will now ask you for which data model and which entity you wish to create the class.

➤ Select **DataModel** and click **Next**. In the next step, make sure **Location** is selected and click **Next** again.

Select the Location entity

➤ Choose a location to save the source files. Press **Create** to finish.

This adds two new files to the project. The first one is named
Location+CoreDataClass.swift and looks something like this:

```
import Foundation
import CoreData

@objc(Location)
public class Location: NSManagedObject {

}
```

As you can see in the `class` line, the `Location` class extends `NSManagedObject` instead
of the regular `NSObject`. You already know what the `public` and `@objc` attributes are
for since you've encountered them before too, but what does the `(Location)` bit do?

That is actually a part of the `@objc` attribute. The Swift compiler uses a mechanism
called *name mangling* to rename method internally so that they can be identified
uniquely. Afterall, if you have two methods named `copyFiles` in the same project, how
does the compiler know which one the code refers to? It has to have a way to identify
each method uniquely so that all method calls are resolved correctly.

Name mangling works fine if your project has only Swift code. But since you can
combine Swift and Objective-C code in the same project, sometimes you run into
trouble in such "hybrid" projects because Objective-C is not able to identify a Swift class
correctly due to name mangling. This happens often when working with archived data
since the archived data saves the class name and you run into issues when Objective-C
can't reconcile the name it receives with a known class.

This is where the `@objc(Location)` (or similar) notation comes into play. The part
inside the brackets, in this case `Location`, tells the compiler that that is the name
Objective-C code will use to refer to this particular class.

You shouldn't have to worry about the above notation at all in this book since you'll be
working with Swift code only. However, it's always a good idea to know things such as
this for when you are a full-blown developer since you most likely will encounter a
"hybrid" project at some point.

The second file that got created is **Location+CoreDataProperties.swift**:

```
import Foundation
import CoreData

extension Location {
 @nonobjc public class func fetchRequest() ->
                    NSFetchRequest<Location> {
    return NSFetchRequest<Location>(entityName: "Location");
  }

  @NSManaged var latitude: Double
  @NSManaged var longitude: Double
  @NSManaged var date: NSDate?
  @NSManaged var locationDescription: String?
  @NSManaged var category: String?
  @NSManaged var placemark: NSObject?
}
```

In this file, Xcode has created properties for the attributes that you specified in the Data Model editor. But what is this extension thing?

With an *extension* you can add additional functionality to an existing object without having to change the original source code for that object. This even works when you don't actually have the source code for those objects. Later on you'll see an example of how you can use an extension to add new methods to objects from iOS frameworks.

Here, the extension is used for another purpose. If you change your Core Data model at some later time and you want to automatically update the code to match those changes, then you can choose **Create NSManagedObject Subclass** again and Xcode will only overwrite what is in **Location+CoreDataProperties.swift** but not anything you added to **Location+CoreDataClass.swift**.

So, it's not a good idea to make changes to **Location+CoreDataProperties.swift** if you plan on overwriting this file later. Unfortunately, Xcode made a few small boo-boos in the types of the properties, so you'll have to make some changes to this file anyway.

The first thing to fix is the placemark variable. Because you made placemark a Transformable attribute, Xcode doesn't really know what kind of object this will be. So, it chose the generic type NSObject. But you know it's going to be a CLPlacemark object. So, you can make things easier for yourself by changing it.

➤ First import Core Location into **Location+CoreDataProperties.swift**:

```
import CoreLocation
```

➤ Then change the `placemark` property to:

```
@NSManaged var placemark: CLPlacemark?
```

You're adding a question mark too, because `placemark` is optional.

➤ Also change the date property from `NSDate` to `Date`:

```
@NSManaged var date: Date
```

The `NSDate` class is what Objective-C uses to represent dates, but in Swift, we work with `Date`, without the "NS". It is also no longer an optional.

➤ Finally, remove the question marks behind the `category` and `locationDescription` properties. Earlier you told Core Data these attributes were not optionals. So, they don't need the question mark.

Because this is a *managed* object, and the data lives inside a data store, Swift will handle `Location`'s variables in a special way. The `@NSManaged` keyword tells the compiler that these properties will be resolved at runtime by Core Data. When you put a new value into one of these properties, Core Data will place that value into the data store for safekeeping, instead of in a regular instance variable.

And if you are wondering, the `@nonobjc` attribute is the reverse of the `@objc` attribute - it makes a class, method, or property not available to Objective-C. Since this came by way of generated boilerplate code, don't worry too much about why you'd want to do that in this particular case :]

This concludes the definition of the data model for *MyLocations*. Now you have to hook it up to a data store.

The data store

On iOS, Core Data stores all of its data into an SQLite database (pronounced "SQL light"). It's OK if you have no idea what SQLite is. You'll take a peek into that database later, but you don't really need to know what goes on inside the data store in order to use Core Data.

However, you need to initialize this data store when the app starts. The code for that is the same for just about any app that uses Core Data and it goes in the app delegate class.

As you learnt previously, the *app delegate* is the object that gets notifications that concern the application as a whole. This is where iOS notifies the app that it has started up, for example.

You're going to make a few changes to the project's `AppDelegate` class.

➤ Open **AppDelegate.swift** and import the Core Data framework at the very top:

```
import CoreData
```

➤ Add the following code inside the `AppDelegate` class (usually at the top where you define properties):

```
lazy var persistentContainer: NSPersistentContainer = {
  let container = NSPersistentContainer(name: "DataModel")
  container.loadPersistentStores(completionHandler: {
    storeDescription, error in
    if let error = error {
      fatalError("Could load data store: \(error)")
    }
  })
  return container
}()
```

This is the code you need to load the data model that you've defined earlier, and to connect it to an SQLite data store.

The goal here is to create a `NSManagedObjectContext` object. That is the object you'll use to talk to Core Data. To get that `NSManagedObjectContext` object, the app needs to do several things:

1. Create an `NSManagedObjectModel` from the Core Data model you created earlier. This object represents the data model during runtime. You can ask it what sort of entities it has, what attributes these entities have, and so on. In most apps, you don't need to use the `NSManagedObjectModel` object directly.

2. Create an `NSPersistentStoreCoordinator` object. This object is in charge of the SQLite database.

3. Finally, create the `NSManagedObjectContext` object and connect it to the persistent store coordinator.

Together, these objects are also known as the "Core Data stack".

Previously, you had to perform the above steps one-by-one in code, which could get a little messy. But as of iOS 10, there is a new object, the `NSPersistentContainer`, that takes care of everything.

That doesn't mean you should immediately forget what you just learned about the `NSManagedObjectModel` and the `NSPersistentStoreCoordinator`, but it does save you from writing a bunch of code.

The code that you just added creates an instance variable persistentContainer of type NSPersistentContainer. To get the NSManagedObjectContext that we're after, you can simply ask the persistentContainer for its viewContext property.

➤ For convenience, add another property to get the NSManagedObjectContext from the persistent container:

```
lazy var managedObjectContext: NSManagedObjectContext =
                self.persistentContainer.viewContext
```

Now we're ready to start using Core Data!

➤ Build the app to make sure it compiles without errors. If you run it you won't notice any difference because you're not actually using Core Data anywhere yet.

Pass the context

When the user presses the Done button in the Tag Location screen, the app currently just closes the screen. Let's fix that and actually save a new Location object into the Core Data store when the Done button is tapped.

I mentioned the NSManagedObjectContext object. This is the object that you use to talk to Core Data. It is often described as a "scratchpad". You first make your changes to the context and then you call its save() method to store those changes permanently in the data store.

This means that every object that needs to do something with Core Data needs to have a reference to the NSManagedObjectContext object.

Get the context

➤ Switch to **LocationDetailsViewController.swift**. First, import Core Data at the top, and then add a new instance variable:

```
var managedObjectContext: NSManagedObjectContext!
```

The problem is: how do you put the NSManagedObjectContext object from the app delegate into this property?

The context object is created by AppDelegate, but AppDelegate has no reference to the LocationDetailsViewController.

That's not so strange since the Location Details view controller doesn't exist until the user taps the Tag Location button. Prior to that, there simply is no LocationDetailsViewController object in existence.

The answer is to pass along the NSManagedObjectContext object during the segue that presents the LocationDetailsViewController. The obvious place for that is prepare(for:sender:) in CurrentLocationViewController.

But then you need to find a way to get the NSManagedObjectContext object into the CurrentLocationViewController in the first place.

I come across a lot of code that does the following:

```
let appDelegate = UIApplication.sharedApplication().delegate
                                            as! AppDelegate
let context = appDelegate.managedObjectContext
// do something with the context
```

From anywhere in your source code, you can get a reference to the context simply by asking the AppDelegate for its managedObjectContext property. Sounds like a good solution, right?

Not quite… Suddenly all your objects are dependent on the app delegate. This introduces a dependency that can make your code very messy really quickly.

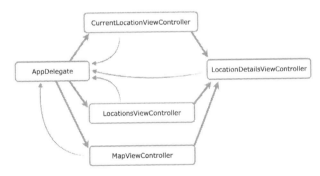

Bad: All classes depend on AppDelegate

As a general design principle, it is best to make your classes depend on each other as little as possible. The fewer interactions there are between the different parts of your program, the simpler it is to understand.

If many of your classes need to reach out to some shared object such as the app delegate, then you may want to rethink your design.

A better solution is to give the NSManagedObjectContext to each object that needs it. Now all the arrows in the diagram go just one way:

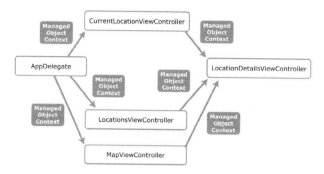

Good: The context object is passed from one object to the next

Using this architecture, `AppDelegate` gives the managed object context to `CurrentLocationViewController`, which in turn will pass it on to the `LocationDetailsViewController` when it performs the segue. This technique is known as *dependency injection*.

This means `CurrentLocationViewController` needs its own property for the `NSManagedObject` context.

➤ Add the following property to **CurrentLocationViewController.swift** (and don't forget to add the Core Data import):

```
var managedObjectContext: NSManagedObjectContext!
```

➤ Add the following to `prepare(for:sender:)`, so that it passes on the context to the Tag Location screen:

```
override func prepare(for segue: UIStoryboardSegue, sender:
Any?) {
  if segue.identifier == "TagLocation" {
    . . .
    // New code
    controller.managedObjectContext = managedObjectContext
  }
}
```

This should also explain why the `managedObjectContext` variable is declared as an implicitly unwrapped optional with the type `NSManagedObjectContext!`.

You should know by now that variables in Swift must always have a value. If they can be `nil` – which means "not a value" – then the variable must be made optional.

If you were to declare `managedObjectContext` without the exclamation point, like this:

```
var managedObjectContext: NSManagedObjectContext
```

Then Swift demands you give it a value in an `init` method. For objects loaded from a storyboard, such as view controllers, that is `init?(coder:)`.

However, `prepare(for:sender:)` happens *after* the new view controller is instantiated, long after the call to `init?(coder:)`. As a result, inside `init?(coder:)` you can't know what the value for `managedObjectContext` will be.

You have no choice but to leave the `managedObjectContext` variable `nil` for a short while until the segue happens, and therefore it must be an optional.

You could also have declared it like this:

```
var managedObjectContext: NSManagedObjectContext?
```

The difference between `?` and `!` is that the former requires you to manually unwrap the value with `if let` every time you want to use it.

That gets annoying fast, especially when you know that `managedObjectContext` will get a proper value during the segue and that it will never become `nil` afterwards again. In that case, the exclamation mark is the best type of optional to use.

These rules for optionals may seem very strict – and possibly confusing – when you're coming from another language such as Objective-C, but they are there for a good reason. By only allowing certain variables to have no value, Swift can make your programs safer and reduce the number of programming mistakes.

The fewer optionals you use, the better, but sometimes you can't avoid them – as in this case with `managedObjectContext`.

Pass the context from AppDelegate

AppDelegate.swift now needs some way to pass the `NSManagedObjectContext` object to `CurrentLocationViewController`.

Unfortunately, Interface Builder does not allow you to make outlets for your view controllers on the App Delegate. Instead, you have to look up these view controllers by digging through the view hierarchy.

➤ Change the `application(_:didFinishLaunchingWithOptions:)` method to:

```
func application(_ application: UIApplication,
      didFinishLaunchingWithOptions launchOptions:
          [UIApplicationLaunchOptionsKey: Any]?) -> Bool {

  let tabController = window!.rootViewController
                          as! UITabBarController

  if let tabViewControllers = tabController.viewControllers {
```

```
    let navController = tabViewControllers[0]
                    as! UINavigationController
    let controller = navController.viewControllers.first
                    as! CurrentLocationViewController
    controller.managedObjectContext = managedObjectContext
  }
  return true
}
```

In order to get a reference to the CurrentLocationViewController, you first have to find the UITabBarController and then look at its viewControllers array.

And since the first controller for the first tab is a navigation controller, then you have to go through the navigation controller's list of controllers to finally get at the CurrentLocationViewController.

Once you have a reference to the CurrentLocationViewController object, you pass it the managedObjectContext. It may not be immediately obvious from looking at the code, but something special happens at this point...

Remember the code for persistentContainer you added to AppDelegate earlier? You probably recognized it as a lazy loading variable since you've encountered something similar before. This is the point at which the closure for the variable is actually executed and a new NSPersistentContainer instance is created.

What actually happens inside the closure is fairly straightforward:

```
  let container = NSPersistentContainer(name: "DataModel")
  container.loadPersistentStores(completionHandler: {
    storeDescription, error in
    if let error = error {
      fatalError("Could load data store: \(error)")
    }
  })
  return container
```

You instantiate a new NSPersistentContainer object with the name of the data model you created earlier, "DataModel". Then you tell it to loadPersistentStores(), which loads the data from the database into memory and sets up the Core Data stack.

There is another closure here, given by the completionHandler parameter. The code in this closure gets invoked when the persistent container is done loading the data. If something went wrong, you print an error message – useful for debugging! – and terminate the app using the function fatalError().

Now that you know what it does, you may be wondering why you didn't just put all of this code into a regular method like this:

```
var persistentContainer: NSPersistentContainer

init() {
  persistentContainer = createPersistentContainer()
}

func createPersistentContainer() -> NSPersistentContainer {
  // all the initialization code here
  return container
}
```

That would certainly be possible, but now the initialization of `persistentContainer` is spread over three different parts of the code: the declaration of the variable, the method that performs all the initialization logic, and the `init` method to tie it all together.

Isn't it nicer to keep all this stuff in one place, rather than in three different places? Swift lets you perform complex initialization right where you declare the variable. I think that's pretty nifty.

There's another thing going on here:

```
lazy var persistentContainer: NSPersistentContainer = { ... }()
```

Notice the `lazy` keyword? That means the entire block of code in the `{ ... }()` closure isn't actually performed right away. The context object won't be created until you ask for it. This is another example of **lazy loading**, Similar to how you handled `DateFormatter` earlier.

The `managedObjectContext` property is also declared `lazy`:

```
lazy var managedObjectContext: NSManagedObjectContext =
                self.persistentContainer.viewContext
```

This is necessary because its initial value comes from `persistentContainer`. It's also necessary to use `self` here to refer to `persistentContainer`. Otherwise, Xcode gives a compiler error.

➤ Run the app. Everything should still be the way it was, but behind the scenes a new database has been created for Core Data.

Browse the data

Core Data stores the data in an SQLite database. That file is named **DataModel.sqlite** and it lives in the app's Library folder. That's similar to the Documents folder that you saw previously.

You can see it in Finder if you go to ~/**Library/Developer/CoreSimulator** and then to the folder that contains the data for *MyLocations* on a particular simulator.

Core Data data store location

➤ The easiest way to find this folder is to add the following to **Functions.swift**:

```
let applicationDocumentsDirectory: URL = {
  let paths = FileManager.default.urls(for: .documentDirectory,
                                       in: .userDomainMask)
  return paths[0]
}()
```

This creates a new global constant, `applicationDocumentsDirectory`, containing the path to the app's Documents directory. It's a global because you're not putting this inside a class. This constant will exist for the duration of the app; it never goes out of scope. You could have made a method for this as you did for *Checklists*, but using a global constant works just as well.

As before, you're using a closure to provide the code that initializes this constant. Like all globals, this is evaluated lazily the very first time it is used.

> **Note:** Globals have a bad reputation. Many programmers avoid them at all costs. The problem with globals is that they create hidden dependencies between the various parts of your program. And dependencies make the program hard to change and hard to debug.
>
> But used well, globals can be very handy. It's feasible that your app will need to know the path to the Documents directory in several different places. Putting it in a global constant is a great way to solve that design problem.

➤ Add the following line to `application(_:didFinishLaunchingWithOptions:)`:

```
print(applicationDocumentsDirectory)
```

On my computer this prints out:

```
file:///Users/fahim/Library/Developer/CoreSimulator/Devices/
CA23DAEA-DF30-43C3-8611-E713F96D4780/data/Containers/Data/
Application/64B60279-41D1-46A4-83A7-492D03C3E5C7/Documents/
```

➤ Open a new Finder window and press **Shift+⌘+G**. Then copy-paste the path without the `file://` bit (note that you leave out only two slashes out of the three...) to go to the Documents folder.

The database is not actually in the Documents folder, so go back one level and enter the **Library** folder, **Application Support**:

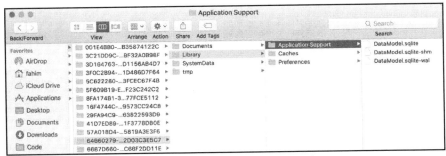

The new database in the app's Documents directory

The **DataModel.sqlite-shm** and **-wal** files are also part of the data store.

This database is still empty because you haven't stored any objects in it yet, but just for the fun of it, you'll take a peek inside.

There are several handy (free!) tools that give you a graphical interface for interacting with your SQLite databases.

Browse the Core Data store using a GUI app

For this app, you will use **Liya** to examine the data store file. Download it from the Mac App Store or cutedgesystems.com/software/liya/.

➤ Start Liya. It asks you for a database connection. Under **Database Type** choose **SQLite**.

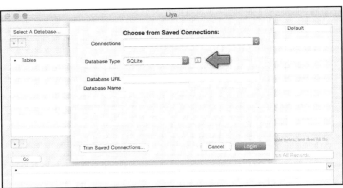

Liya opens with this dialog box

➤ On the right of the Database Type field is a small icon. Click this to open a file picker.

You can navigate to the **CoreSimulator/…/Library/Application Support** folder, but that's a lot of work (it's a very deeply nested folder).

If you have the Finder window still open, it's easier to drag the **DataModel.sqlite** file from Finder directly on to the open file picker. Click **Choose** when you're done.

> **Tip:** You can also right-click the DataModel.sqlite file in Finder and choose **Open With → Liya** from the popup menu.

The **Database URL** field should now contain the app's Document folder and **Database Name** should say DataModel.sqlite:

Connecting to the SQLite database

➤ Click **Login** to proceed.

The screen should look something like this:

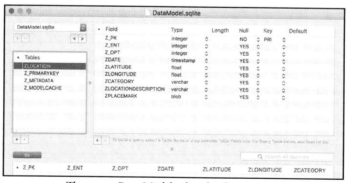

The empty DataModel.sqlite database in Liya

The ZLOCATION table is where your Location objects will be stored. It's currently empty, but on the right you can already see the column names that correspond to your fields: ZDATE, ZLATITUDE, and so on. Core Data also adds its own columns and tables (with the Z_ prefix).

You're not really supposed to change anything in this database by hand, but sometimes using a visual tool like this is handy to see what's going on. You'll come back to Liya once you've inserted new Location objects.

> **Note:** An alternative to Liya is SQLiteStudio, sqlitestudio.pl. You can find more tools, paid and free, on the Mac App Store by searching for "sqlite".

Troubleshoot Core Data issues

There is another handy tool for troubleshooting Core Data. By setting a special flag on the app, you can see the SQL statements that Core Data uses under the hood to talk to the data store.

Even if you have no experience with SQL, this is still valuable information. At least you can use it to tell whether Core Data is doing something or not. To enable this tool, you have to edit the project's **scheme**.

Schemes are how Xcode lets you configure your projects. A scheme is a bunch of settings for building and running your app. Standard projects have just one scheme, but you can add additional schemes, which is handy when your project becomes bigger.

➤ Click on the left part of the **MyLocations > iPhone** bar at the top of the screen and choose **Edit Scheme...** from the menu.

The Edit Scheme... option

The following panel should pop up:

The scheme editor

➤ Choose the **Run** option on the left-hand side.

➤ Select the **Arguments** tab.

➤ In the **Arguments Passed On Launch** section, add the following:

```
-com.apple.CoreData.SQLDebug 1
-com.apple.CoreData.Logging.stderr 1
```

Adding the SQLDebug launch argument

➤ Press **Close** to close this dialog, and run the app.

You should see something like this in the Xcode Console:

```
CoreData: annotation: Connecting to sqlite database file at "/
Users/fahim/Library/Developer/CoreSimulator/Devices/CA23DAEA-
DF30-43C3-8611-E713F96D4780/data/Containers/Data/Application/
B3C8FED1-3218-454F-B86F-1482ED64433A/Library/Application
Support/DataModel.sqlite"
CoreData: sql: SELECT TBL_NAME FROM SQLITE_MASTER WHERE TBL_NAME
= 'Z_METADATA'
CoreData: sql: pragma recursive_triggers=1
CoreData: sql: pragma journal_mode=wal
CoreData: sql: SELECT Z_VERSION, Z_UUID, Z_PLIST FROM Z_METADATA
CoreData: sql: SELECT TBL_NAME FROM SQLITE_MASTER WHERE TBL_NAME
= 'Z_MODELCACHE'
```

This is the debug output from Core Data. If you understand SQL, some of this will look familiar. The specifics don't matter, but it's clear that Core Data is connecting to the data store at this point. Excellent!

Save the locations

You've successfully initialized Core Data and passed the NSManagedObjectContext to the Tag Location screen. Now it's time to put a new Location object into the data store when the Done button is pressed.

➤ Add the following instance variable to **LocationDetailsViewController.swift**:

```
var date = Date()
```

You're adding this variable because you need to store the current date in the new Location object. You only want to make that Date object once.

➤ In viewDidLoad(), change the line that sets the dateLabel's text to:

```
dateLabel.text = format(date: date)
```

This now uses the new property insted of creating the date on the fly.

➤ Change the done() method to the following:

```
@IBAction func done() {
  let hudView = HudView.hud(inView: navigationController!.view,
                            animated: true)
  hudView.text = "Tagged"
  // 1
  let location = Location(context: managedObjectContext)
  // 2
  location.locationDescription = descriptionTextView.text
  location.category = categoryName
  location.latitude = coordinate.latitude
  location.longitude = coordinate.longitude
  location.date = date
  location.placemark = placemark
  // 3
  do {
    try managedObjectContext.save()
    afterDelay(0.6) {
      hudView.hide()
      self.navigationController?.popViewController(
                                      animated: true)
    }
  } catch {
    // 4
    fatalError("Error: \(error)")
  }
}
```

This is where you do all the work:

1. First, you create a new Location instance. Because this is a managed object, you have to use its init(context:) method. You can't just write Location() because then the managedObjectContext won't know about the new object.

2. Once you have created the Location instance, you can use it like any other object. Here you set its properties to whatever the user entered in the screen.

3. You now have a new Location object whose properties are all filled in, but if you were to look in the data store at this point, you'd still see no objects there. That won't happen until you save() the context.

Saving takes any objects that were added to the context, or any managed objects that had their contents changed, and permanently writes these changes to the data store. That's why they call the context a "scratchpad"; its changes aren't persisted until you save them.

The save() method can fail for a variety of reasons and therefore you need to catch any potential errors. That's done using Swift error handling, which you've encountered before.

4. Output the error and then terminate the application via the sytem method fatalError. But where does the error variable that you output come from? This is a local constant that Swift automatically populates with the error that it caught - handy, huh?

➤ Run the app and tag a location. Enter a description and press the Done button.

If everything went well, Core Data will dump a whole bunch of debug information into the debug area:

```
CoreData: sql: BEGIN EXCLUSIVE
. . .
CoreData: sql: INSERT INTO ZLOCATION(Z_PK, Z_ENT, Z_OPT,
ZCATEGORY, ZDATE, ZLATITUDE, ZLOCATIONDESCRIPTION, ZLONGITUDE,
ZPLACEMARK) VALUES(?, ?, ?, ?, ?, ?, ?, ?, ?)
CoreData: sql: COMMIT
. . .
CoreData: annotation: sql execution time: 0.0001s
```

These are the SQL statements that Core Data performs to store the new Location object in the database.

➤ In Liya, refresh the contents of the ZLOCATION table (press the Go button below the Tables list). There should now be one row in that table:

Z_PK	Z_ENT	Z_OPT	ZDATE	ZLATITUDE	ZLONGITUDE	ZCATEGORY	ZLOCATIONDES...
1	1	1	2014-09-26 1...	37,33165083	-122,03029752	Apple Store	Apple HQ

A new row was added to the table

Note: If you don't see any rows in the table, press the Stop button in Xcode first to exit the app. You can also try closing the Liya window and opening a new connection to the database. Sometimes, especially in Xcode 9, the Simulator data folder locations appear to change between app runs - so you might need to set up a new database connection in Liya after each run.

As you can see, the columns in this table contain the property values from the Location object. The only column that is not readable is ZPLACEMARK. Its contents have been encoded as a binary "blob" of data. That is because it's a Transformable attribute and the NSCoding protocol has converted its fields into a binary chunk of data.

If you don't have Liya or are a command line junkie, then there is another way to examine the contents of the database. You can use the Terminal app and the sqlite3 tool, but you'd better know your SQL's from your ABC's if you want to go that route:

Examining the database from the Terminal

Handle Core Data errors

To save the contents of the context to the data store, you did:

```
do {
   try managedObjectContext.save()
   . . .
} catch {
   fatalError("Error: \(error)")
}
```

What if something goes wrong with the save? In that case, code execution jumps to the catch branch and you call the fatalError() function. That will immediately kill the app and return the user to the iPhone's Springboard. That's a nasty surprise for the user, and therefore, not recommended.

The good news is that Core Data only gives an error if you're trying to save something that is not valid. In other words, when there is some bug in your app.

Of course, you'll catch all the bugs during development so users will never experience any, right? The truth is that you'll never catch all the bugs. Some always slip through.

Unfortunately, there isn't much else to do but crash when Core Data does give an error. Something went horribly wrong somewhere and now you're stuck with invalid data. If the app were allowed to continue, things would likely only get worse, as there is no telling what state the app is in. The last thing you want to do is to corrupt the user's data.

However, instead of making the app crash hard with `fatalError()`, it might be nice to tell the user about the issue first so at least they know what is happening. The crash is still inevitable, but now your users will know why the app suddenly stopped working.

In this section, you'll add a popup alert for handling such situations. Again, these errors should happen only during development, but just in case they do occur to an actual user, you'll try to handle it with at least a little bit of grace.

Fake errors for testing purposes

Here's a way to fake such a fatal error, just to illustrate what happens.

➤ Open the data model (**DataModel.xcdatamodeld** in the file list), and select the **placemark** attribute. In the Data Model inspector, uncheck the **Optional** flag.

Making the placemark attribute non-optional

That means `location.placemark` can never be `nil`. This is a constraint that Core Data will enforce. When you try to save a `Location` object to the data store whose `placemark` property is `nil`, Core Data will throw a tantrum. So that's exactly what you're going to do here, just to test your error handling code and to make sure the app fails gracefully.

➤ Run the app. It is possible that the app crashes right away…

What happens is that you have just changed the data model by making changes to the `placemark` attribute. When you launch the app, the `NSPersistentContainer` notices this and tries to perform a "migration" of the SQLite database to the new, updated data model.

The migration may succeed… or not… depending on what is currently in your data store. If you previously tagged a location that did not have a valid address – i.e. whose `placemark` is `nil` – then the migration to the new data model fails. After all, the new data model does not allow for `placemark`s that are `nil`.

If the app crashed for you, then the debug area says why:

```
reason=Cannot migrate store in-place: Validation error missing
attribute
values on mandatory destination attribute, . . .
{entity=Location, attribute=placemark, . . .}
```

The DataModel.sqlite file is out of date with respect to the changed data model, and Core Data can't automatically resolve this issue.

There are two ways to fix this:

1. Simply throw away the DataModel.sqlite file from the Library directory.

2. Remove the entire app from the Simulator.

➤ Remove the DataModel.sqlite file, as well as the –shm and –wal files, and run the app again.

This wasn't actually the crash I wanted to show you, but it's important to know that changing the data model may require you to throw away the database file or Core Data cannot be initialized properly.

> **Note:** Not all is lost if `NSPersistentContainer`'s migration fails. Core Data allows you to perform your own migrations when you release an update to your app with a new data model. Instead of crashing, this mechanism allows you to convert the contents of the user's existing data store to the new model. However, during development, it is just as easy to toss out the old database.

➤ Now here's the trick. Tap the Get My Location button and then tap immediately on Tag Location. If you do that quickly enough, you can beat the reverse geocoder to it and the Tag Location screen will say: "No Address Found". It only says that when `placemark` is `nil`.

If geocoding happens too fast, you can fake this by temporarily commenting out the line `self.placemark = p.last!` in `locationManager(_:didUpdateLocations:)` inside **CurrentLocationViewController.swift**. This will make it seem as if no address was found and the value of `placemark` stays `nil`.

➤ Tap the Done button to save the new `Location` object.

The app will crash:

The app crashes after a Core Data error

In the Console, you can see that it says:

```
The operation couldn't be completed . . .
NSValidationErrorKey=placemark
```

This means the `placemark` attribute did not validate properly. Because you set it to non-optional, Core Data does not accept a placemark value that is `nil`.

Of course, what you've just seen only happens when you run the app from Xcode - when it crashes, the debugger takes over and points at the line with the error. But that's not what the user sees.

➤ Stop the app. Now tap the app's icon in the Simulator to launch the app outside of Xcode. Repeat the same procedure to make the app crash. The app will simply cease functioning and disappear from the screen.

Imagine this happening to a user who just paid 99 cents (or more) for your app. They'll be horribly confused, "What just happened?!" They may even ask for their money back.

It's better to show an alert when this happens. After the user dismisses that alert, you'll still make the app crash, but at least the user knows the reason why. (The alert message should probably ask them to contact you and explain what they did, so you can fix that bug in the next version of your app.)

Alert the user about crashes

➤ Add the following code to **Functions.swift**:

```
let CoreDataSaveFailedNotification =
  Notification.Name(rawValue: "CoreDataSaveFailedNotification")
```

```
func fatalCoreDataError(_ error: Error) {
  print("*** Fatal error: \(error)")
  NotificationCenter.default.post(
      name: CoreDataSaveFailedNotification, object: nil)
}
```

This defines a new global function for handling fatal Core Data errors.

➤ Replace the error handling code in the done() action with:

```
. . .
} catch {
  fatalCoreDataError(error)
}
```

The call to `fatalCoreDataError()` has taken the place of `fatalError()`. So what does that new function do, actually?

It first outputs the error message to the Console using `print()` because it's always useful to log such errors. After dumping the debug info, the function does the following:

```
NotificationCenter.default.post(
      name: CoreDataSaveFailedNotification, object: nil)
```

I've been using the term "notification" to mean any generic event or message being delivered, but the iOS SDK also has an object called the `NotificationCenter` (not to be confused with Notification Center on your iOS device).

The code above uses `NotificationCenter` to post a notification. Any object in your app can subscribe to such notifications and when these occur, `NotificationCenter` will call a certain method in those listener objects.

Using this official notification system is yet another way that your objects can communicate with each other. The handy thing is that the object that sends the notification and the object that receives the notification don't need to know anything about each other. The sender just broadcasts the notification to all and doesn't really care what happens to it. If anyone is listening, great. If not, then that's cool too.

UIKit defines a lot of standard notifications that you can subscribe to. For example, there is a notification that lets you know that the app is about to be suspended after the user taps the Home button.

You can also define your own notifications, and that is what you've done here. The new notification is called `CoreDataSaveFailedNotification`.

The idea is that there is one place in the app that listens for this notification, pops up an alert view, and terminates. The great thing about using `NotificationCenter` is that your Core Data code does not need to care about any of this.

Whenever a saving error occurs, no matter at which point in the app, the
fatalCoreDataError(_:) function sends out this notification, safe in the belief that
some other object is listening for the notification and will handle the error.

So who will actually handle the error? The app delegate is a good place for this. It's the
top-level object in the app and it's always guaranteed to exist.

➤ Add the following method to **AppDelegate.swift**:

```swift
// MARK:- Helper methods
func listenForFatalCoreDataNotifications() {
  // 1
  NotificationCenter.default.addObserver(
    forName: CoreDataSaveFailedNotification,
    object: nil, queue: OperationQueue.main,
    using: { notification in
      // 2
      let message = """
There was a fatal error in the app and it cannot continue.

Press OK to terminate the app. Sorry for the inconvenience.
"""
      // 3
      let alert = UIAlertController(
        title: "Internal Error", message: message,
                      preferredStyle: .alert)

      // 4
      let action = UIAlertAction(title: "OK",
                                 style: .default) { _ in
        let exception = NSException(
          name: NSExceptionName.internalInconsistencyException,
          reason: "Fatal Core Data error", userInfo: nil)
        exception.raise()
      }
      alert.addAction(action)

      // 5
      let tabController = self.window!.rootViewController!
      tabController.present(alert, animated: true,
                            completion: nil)
  })
}
```

Here's how this works step-by-step:

1. Tell NotificationCenter that you want to be notified whenever a
    CoreDataSaveFailedNotification is posted. The actual code that is performed
    when that happens sits in a closure following using:.

2. Set up the error message to display. This could have been done using a normal string by inserting new lines (\n) as you've seen done before, but I thought it might be useful for you to see a new feature in Swift 4 - multiline strings.

    Note that the multiline string starts and ends with a triple quote (""") and that the first line of the string has to start on a new line and the closing triple quotes have to be on a new line as well. You can include new lines and other special characters like quotes within the string. So it can be really handy, even if it looks a little weird :]

3. Create a `UIAlertController` to show the error message and use the multiline string from earlier as the message.

4. Add an action for the alert's OK button. The code for handling the button press is again a closure (these things are everywhere!). Instead of calling `fatalError()`, the closure creates an `NSException` object to terminate the app. That's a bit nicer and it provides more information to the crash log.

5. To show the alert with `present(animated:completion:)` you need a view controller that is currently visible. You simply use the window's `rootViewController` – in this app that is the tab bar controller – since it will be visible at all times as per the current navigation flow of the app.

All that remains is calling this new method so that the notification handler is registered with `NotificationCenter`.

➤ Add the following to `application(_:didFinishLaunchingWithOptions:)`, just before the `return true` statement:

```
listenForFatalCoreDataNotifications()
```

➤ Run the app again and try to tag a location before the street address has been obtained. Even though the app still crashes when you tap the OK button on the alert, at least now it tells the user what's going on:

The app crashes with a message

Again, I should stress that you test your app thoroughly to make sure you're not giving Core Data any objects that do not validate. You want to avoid these save errors at all costs!

Ideally, users should never have to see that alert view, but it's good to have in place because there are no guarantees your app won't have bugs.

> **Note:** You can legitimately use `managedObjectContext.save()` to let Core Data validate user input. There is no requirement that you make your app crash after an unsuccessful save, only if the error was unexpected and definitely shouldn't have happened!
>
> Besides the "optional" flag, there are many more validation settings you can set for your entities. If you let users enter data that needs to go into these attributes, then it's perfectly acceptable to use `save()` to validate input. If it throws an error, then a user input is invalid and you need to handle it.

➤ In the data model, set the **placemark** attribute back to optional (and uncomment the code in **CurrentLocationViewController.swift**, if you did comment out the `placemark` line).

Run the app just to make sure everything works as it should.

You can find the project files for this chapter under **27 – Saving Locations** in the Source Code folder.

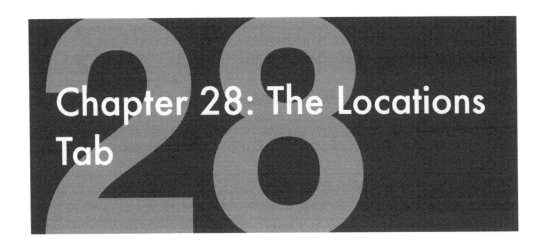

Chapter 28: The Locations Tab

You've set up the data model and given the app the ability to save new locations to the data store. Next, you'll show these saved locations in a table view in the second tab.

The completed Locations screen will look like this:

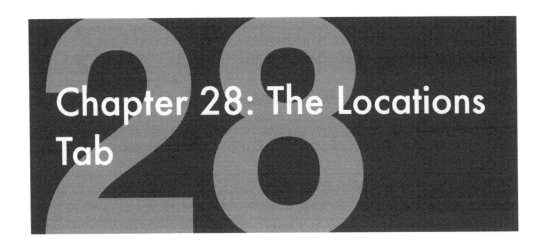

The Locations screen

This chapter covers the following:

- **The locations tab:** Set up the second tab to display a list of saved locations.

- **Create a custom table view cell subclass:** Create a custom table view cell subclass to handle displaying location information.

- **Edit locations:** Add functionality to allow editing of items in the locations list.

- **Use NSFetchedResulsController:** How do you use NSFetchedResultsController to fetch data from your Core Data store?

- **Delete Locations:** Add the ability to the UI to delete locations, thus removing them from the Core Data store as well.

- **Table view sections:** Use built-in Core Data functionality to add the ability to display separate sections based on the location category.

The Locations tab

➤ Open the storyboard editor and delete the **Second Scene**. This is a leftover from the project template and you don't need it.

➤ Drag a new **Navigation Controller** on to the canvas. (This has a table view controller attached to it, which is fine. You'll use that in a second.)

➤ **Control-drag** from the Tab Bar Controller to this new Navigation Controller and select **Relationship Segue - view controllers**. This adds the navigation controller to the tab bar.

➤ The Navigation Controller now has a **Tab Bar Item** that is named "Item". Rename it to **Locations**.

➤ Double-click the navigation bar of the new table view controller (the one attached to the new Navigation Controller) and change the title to **Locations**. (If Xcode gives you trouble, use the Attributes inspector on the Navigation Item instead.)

The storyboard now looks like this:

The storyboard after adding the Locations screen

➤ Run the app and activate the Locations tab. It doesn't show anything useful yet:

The Locations screen in the second tab

Design the table view cell

Before you can show any data in the table, you first have to design the prototype cell.

➤ Set the prototype cell's Reuse Identifier to **LocationCell**.

➤ In the **Size inspector**, change **Row Height** to 57.

➤ Drag two Labels on to the cell. Give the top one the text **Description** and the bottom one the text **Address**. This is just so you know what they are for.

➤ Set the font of the Description label to **System Bold**, size 17. Give this label a tag of 100.

➤ Set the font of the Address label to **System**, size **14**. Set the Text color to black with 50% opacity (so its looks like a medium gray). Give it a tag of 101.

The cell will look something like this:

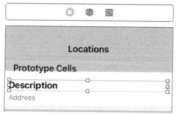

The prototype cell

Make sure that the labels are wide enough to span the entire cell.

Just changing the Row Height of the prototype cell isn't enough; you also have to tell the table view about the height of its rows.

➤ Select the table view and go to the **Size inspector**. Set the **Row Height** field to 57:

Setting the row height on the table view

The basic table view controller

Let's write the code for the view controller. You've seen table view controllers several times now, so this should be easy.

You're going to fake the content first, because it's a good idea to make sure that the prototype cell works before you have to deal with Core Data.

➤ Add a new file to the project and name it **LocationsViewController.swift**.

> **Tip:** If you want to keep your list of source files neatly sorted by name in the project navigator, then right-click the MyLocations group (the yellow folder icon) and choose **Sort by Name** from the menu.

➤ Change the contents of **LocationsViewController.swift** to:

```swift
import UIKit
import CoreData
import CoreLocation

class LocationsViewController: UITableViewController {
  var managedObjectContext: NSManagedObjectContext!

  // MARK: - Table View Delegates
  override func tableView(_ tableView: UITableView,
        numberOfRowsInSection section: Int) -> Int {
    return 1
  }

  override func tableView(_ tableView: UITableView,
              cellForRowAt indexPath: IndexPath) ->
              UITableViewCell {
    let cell = tableView.dequeueReusableCell(
                    withIdentifier: "LocationCell",
                              for: indexPath)

    let descriptionLabel = cell.viewWithTag(100) as! UILabel
    descriptionLabel.text = "If you can see this"

    let addressLabel = cell.viewWithTag(101) as! UILabel
    addressLabel.text = "Then it works!"

    return cell
  }
}
```

You've faked a single row with some placeholder text in the labels. You've also given this class an `NSManagedObjectContext` property even though you won't be using it yet.

➤ Switch to the storyboard, select the Locations scene, and in the **Identity inspector**, change the **Class** of the table view controller to **LocationsViewController**. (Be careful with the auto completion when you're doing this since you also have a LocationsDetailViewController and that might get auto added if you are not careful...)

➤ Run the app to make sure the table view works.

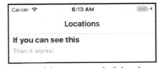

The table view with fake data

Excellent! Now it's time to fill up the table with the Location objects from the data store.

Display Locations from data store

➤ Run the app and tag a handful of locations. If there is no data in the data store, then the app doesn't have much to show…

This new part of the app doesn't know anything yet about the Location objects that you have added to the data store. In order to display them in the table view, you need to obtain references to these objects somehow. You can do that by asking the data store. This is called *fetching*.

➤ First, add a new instance variable to **LocationsViewController.swift**:

```swift
var locations = [Location]()
```

This array will hold the list of Location objects.

➤ Add a viewDidLoad() implementation:

```swift
override func viewDidLoad() {
  super.viewDidLoad()
  // 1
  let fetchRequest = NSFetchRequest<Location>()
  // 2
  let entity = Location.entity()
  fetchRequest.entity = entity
  // 3
  let sortDescriptor = NSSortDescriptor(key: "date",
                                    ascending: true)
  fetchRequest.sortDescriptors = [sortDescriptor]
  do {
    // 4
    locations = try managedObjectContext.fetch(fetchRequest)
  } catch {
    fatalCoreDataError(error)
  }
}
```

This may look daunting but it's actually quite simple. You're going to ask the managed object context for a list of all Location objects in the data store, sorted by date.

1. The NSFetchRequest is the object that describes which objects you're going to fetch from the data store. To retrieve an object that you previously saved to the data store, you create a fetch request that describes the search parameters of the object – or multiple objects – that you're looking for.

2. Here you tell the fetch request you're looking for Location entities.

3. The NSSortDescriptor tells the fetch request to sort on the date attribute, in ascending order. In order words, the Location objects that the user added first will

be at the top of the list. You can sort on any attribute here (later on for this app you'll sort on the Location's category as well).

That completes the fetch request. It took a few lines of code, but basically you said: "Get all Location objects from the data store and sort them by date."

4. Now that you have a fetch request, you can tell the context to execute it. The fetch() method returns an array with the sorted objects, or throws an error in case something went wrong. That's why this happens inside a do-try-catch block.

If everything goes well, you assign the results of the fetch to the locations instance variable.

> **Note:** To create the fetch request you wrote NSFetchRequest<Location>.
>
> The < > mean that NSFetchRequest is a *generic*. Recall that arrays are also generics - to create an array you specify the type of objects that go into the array, either using the shorthand notation [Location], or the longer Array<Location>.
>
> To use an NSFetchRequest, you need to tell it what type of objects you're going to be fetching. Here, you create an NSFetchRequest<Location> so that the result of fetch() is an array of Location objects.

Now that you've loaded the list of Location objects into an instance variable, you can change the table view's data source methods.

➤ Change the data source methods to:

```
override func tableView(_ tableView: UITableView,
       numberOfRowsInSection section: Int) -> Int {
  return locations.count
}
```

```
override func tableView(_ tableView: UITableView,
            cellForRowAt indexPath: IndexPath) ->
            UITableViewCell {
  let cell = tableView.dequeueReusableCell(
                   withIdentifier: "LocationCell",
                               for: indexPath)

  let location = locations[indexPath.row]

  let descriptionLabel = cell.viewWithTag(100) as! UILabel
  descriptionLabel.text = location.locationDescription
```

```
    let addressLabel = cell.viewWithTag(101) as! UILabel
    if let placemark = location.placemark {
      var text = ""
      if let s = placemark.subThoroughfare {
        text += s + " "
      }
      if let s = placemark.thoroughfare {
        text += s + ", "
      }
      if let s = placemark.locality {
        text += s
      }
      addressLabel.text = text
    } else {
      addressLabel.text = ""
    }
    return cell
  }
```

This should have no surprises for you. You get the Location object for the row from the array and then use its properties to fill the labels. Because placemark is an optional, you use if let to unwrap it.

➤ Run the app. Now switch to the Locations tab and… crap! It crashes.

The text in the Console says something like:

```
fatal error: unexpectedly found nil while unwrapping an Optional
value
```

Exercise. What did you forget?

Answer: You added a managedObjectContext property to LocationsViewController, but never gave this property a value. Therefore, there is nothing to fetch Location objects from. (If you already noticed this and were like, "How come we are not passing the value from AppDelegate?", good job! You are really getting the hang of this :])

➤ Switch to **AppDelegate.swift**. In application(_:didFinishLaunchingWithOption:s), change the if let tabBarViewControllers block, as follows:

```
if let tabViewControllers = tabController.viewControllers {
  // First tab
  var navController = tabViewControllers[0]
                     as! UINavigationController
```

```
  let controller1 = navController.viewControllers.first
                    as! CurrentLocationViewController
  controller1.managedObjectContext = managedObjectContext
  // Second tab
  navController = tabViewControllers[1]
                   as! UINavigationController
    let controller2 = navController.viewControllers.first
                    as! LocationsViewController
    controller2.managedObjectContext = managedObjectContext
}
```

There are a couple of minor changes to the existing code - one is to make navController a variable so that it can be re-used for the second tab, and the second is to rename the controller constant to controller1 to separate it from the the second view controller which would be of a different type.

The code for the second tab looks up the LocationsViewController in the storyboard and gives it a reference to the managed object context, similar to what you did for the first tab.

➤ Run the app again and switch to the Locations tab. Core Data properly fetches the objects and shows them on the screen:

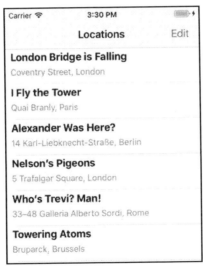

The list of Locations

Note that the list doesn't update yet if you tag a new location. You have to restart the app to see the new Location object appear. You'll solve this later on.

Create a custom table view cell subclass

Using `viewWithTag(_:)` to find the labels from the table view cell works, but it doesn't look very object-oriented to me. It would be much nicer if you could make your own `UITableViewCell` subclass and give it outlets for the labels. Fortunately, you can, and it's pretty easy!

➤ Add a new file to the project using the **Cocoa Touch Class** template. Name it **LocationCell** and make it a subclass of **UITableViewCell**. (Make sure that the class name does not change when you set the subclass - this can be a little annoying.)

➤ Add the following outlets to **LocationCell.swift**, inside the class definition:

```
@IBOutlet weak var descriptionLabel: UILabel!
@IBOutlet weak var addressLabel: UILabel!
```

➤ Open the storyboard and select the prototype cell that you made earlier. In the **Identity inspector**, set **Class** to **LocationCell**.

➤ Now you can connect the two labels to the two outlets. This time the outlets are not on the view controller but on the cell, so use the `LocationCell`'s Connections inspector to connect the `descriptionLabel` and `addressLabel` outlets.

That is all you need to do to make the table view use your own table view cell class. But, you do need to update `LocationsViewController` to make use of it.

➤ In **LocationsViewController.swift**, replace `tableView(cellForRowAt)` with:

```
override func tableView(_ tableView: UITableView,
             cellForRowAt indexPath: IndexPath) ->
             UITableViewCell {
  let cell = tableView.dequeueReusableCell(
                withIdentifier: "LocationCell",
                for: indexPath) as! LocationCell

  let location = locations[indexPath.row]
  cell.configure(for: location)

  return cell
}
```

As before, this asks for a cell using `dequeueReusableCell(withIdentifier:for:)`, but now this will always be a `LocationCell` object instead of a regular `UITableViewCell`. That's why you've added the type cast.

Note that the string `LocationCell` is the re-use identifier from the placeholder cell, but `LocationCell` is the class of the actual cell object that you're getting. They have the same name but one is a `String` and the other is a `UITableViewCell` subclass with extra properties. I hope that's not too confusing.

Once you have the cell reference, you call a new method, `configure(for:)` to put the `Location` object into the table view cell.

➤ Add this new method to **LocationCell.swift**:

```swift
func configure(for location: Location) {
  if location.locationDescription.isEmpty {
    descriptionLabel.text = "(No Description)"
  } else {
    descriptionLabel.text = location.locationDescription
  }

  if let placemark = location.placemark {
    var text = ""
    if let s = placemark.subThoroughfare {
      text += s + " "
    }
    if let s = placemark.thoroughfare {
      text += s + ", "
    }
    if let s = placemark.locality {
      text += s
    }
    addressLabel.text = text
  } else {
    addressLabel.text = String(format:
        "Lat: %.8f, Long: %.8f", location.latitude,
                                 location.longitude)
  }
}
```

Instead of using `viewWithTag(_:)` to find the description and address labels, you now simply use the `descriptionLabel` and `addressLabel` properties of the cell.

➤ Run the app to make sure everything still works. If you have a location without a description the table cell will now say "(No Description)". If there is no placemark, the address label contains the GPS coordinates.

Using a custom subclass for your table view cells, there is no limit to how complex the cell functionality can be.

Edit locations

You will now connect the `LocationsViewController` to the Location Details screen, so that when you tap a row in the table, it lets you edit that location's description and category.

You'll be re-using the `LocationDetailsViewController` but have it edit an existing `Location` object rather than add a new one.

Create edit segue

➤ Go to the storyboard. Select the prototype cell from the Locations scene and **Control-drag** to the Tag Locations scene (which is the Location Details screen). Add a **Show** selection segue and name it **EditLocation**.

At this point the storyboard should look like this:

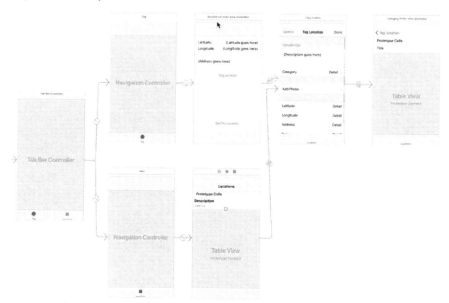

The Location Details screen is now also connected to the Locations screen

There are now two segues from two different screens going to the same view controller.

This is the reason why you should build your view controllers to be as independent of their "calling" controllers as possible. You can then easily re-use them somewhere else in your app.

Soon, you will be calling this same screen from yet another place. In total there will be three segues to it.

➤ Go to **LocationsViewController.swift** and add the following code:

```
// MARK:- Navigation
override func prepare(for segue: UIStoryboardSegue,
                          sender: Any?) {
  if segue.identifier == "EditLocation" {
    let controller = segue.destination
                  as! LocationDetailsViewController
    controller.managedObjectContext = managedObjectContext

    if let indexPath = tableView.indexPath(for: sender
                                    as! UITableViewCell) {
      let location = locations[indexPath.row]
      controller.locationToEdit = location
    }
  }
}
```

This method is invoked when the user taps a row in the Locations screen. It figures out which `Location` object belongs to the row and puts it in the new `locationToEdit` property of `LocationDetailsViewController`. This property doesn't exist yet, but you'll add it in a moment.

The Any type

The type of the `sender` parameter is `Any`. You have seen this type in a few places before. What is it?

Objective-C has a special type, `id`, that means "any object". It's similar to `NSObject` except that it doesn't make any assumptions at all about the underlying type of the object. `id` doesn't have any methods, properties or instance variables, it's a completely naked object reference.

All objects in an Objective-C program can be treated as having type `id`. As a result, a lot of the APIs from iOS frameworks depend on this special `id` type. This is a powerful feature of Objective-C, but unfortunately, a dynamic type like `id` doesn't really fit in a *strongly typed* language such as Swift.

Still, we can't avoid `id` completely because it's so prevalent in iOS frameworks. The Swift equivalent of `id` is the `Any` type.

The `sender` parameter from `prepare(for:sender:)` can be any kind of object, and so has type `Any` (thanks to the question mark it can also be `nil`).

If the segue is triggered from a table view, `sender` is of type `UITableViewCell`. If triggered from a `button`, sender is of type `UIBarButtonItem`, and so on.

Objects that appear as type `Any` are not very useful in that form, and you'll have to tell Swift what sort of object it really is. In the code that you just wrote, `indexPath(for:)` expects a `UITableViewCell` object, not an `Any` object.

You and I both know that `sender` in this case really is a `UITableViewCell` because the only way to trigger this segue is to tap a table view cell. With the `as!` type cast you're giving Swift your word (scout's honor!) that it can safely interpret `sender` as a `UITableViewCell`. Of course, if you were to hook up this segue to something else, such as a button, then this assumption is no longer valid and the app will crash.

Set up the edit view controller

When editing an existing `Location` object, you have to do a few things differently in the `LocationDetailsViewController`. The title of the screen shouldn't be "Tag Location" but "Edit Location". You also must put the values from the existing `Location` object into the various cells.

The value of the new `locationToEdit` property determines whether the screen operates in "add" mode or in "edit" mode.

➤ Add these properties to **LocationDetailsViewController.swift**:

```
var locationToEdit: Location?
var descriptionText = ""
```

`locationToEdit` needs to be an optional because in "add" mode it will be `nil`.

➤ Update `viewDidLoad()` to check whether `locationToEdit` is set:

```
override func viewDidLoad() {
  super.viewDidLoad()
  if let location = locationToEdit {
    title = "Edit Location"
  }
  . . .
}
```

If `locationToEdit` is not `nil`, you're editing an existing `Location` object. In that case, the title of the screen becomes "Edit Location".

> **Note:** Xcode gives a warning on the line `if let location = locationToEdit` because you're not using the value of `location` anywhere. If you click the yellow icon, Xcode suggests that you replace it with `if locationToEdit != nil`. You *will* use `location` in a bit, so ignore Xcode's suggestion.

➤ Also change this line in `viewDidLoad()`:

```
descriptionTextView.text = descriptionText
```

You load the value of the new `descriptionText` variable into the text view.

Now how do you get the values from the `locationToEdit` object into the text view and labels of this view controller? Swift has a really cool **property observer** feature that is perfect for this.

➤ Change the declaration of the `locationToEdit` property to the following:

```
var locationToEdit: Location? {
  didSet {
    if let location = locationToEdit {
      descriptionText = location.locationDescription
      categoryName = location.category
      date = location.date
      coordinate = CLLocationCoordinate2DMake(
        location.latitude, location.longitude)
      placemark = location.placemark
    }
  }
}
```

If a variable has a `didSet` block, then the code in this block is performed whenever you put a new value into that variable. Very handy!

Here, you take the opportunity to fill in the view controller's instance variables with the `Location` object's values.

Because `prepare(for:sender:)` – and therefore `locationToEdit`'s `didSet` – is called before `viewDidLoad()`, this puts the right values on the screen before it becomes visible.

➤ Run the app, go to the Locations tab and tap on a row. The Edit Location screen should now appear with the data from the selected location:

Editing an existing location

➤ Change the description of the location and press Done.

Nothing happened?! Well, that's not quite true. Stop the app and run it again. You will see that a new location has been added with the changed description, but the old one is still there as well.

Fix the edit screen

There are two problems to solve:

1. When editing an existing location you must save changes to the location instead of creating a new entry.

2. The Locations screen doesn't update to reflect any changes to the data.

The first fix is easy.

➤ Still in **LocationDetailsViewController.swift**, change the top part of done():

```
@IBAction func done() {
  let hudView = HudView.hud(inView: . . .)

  let location: Location
  if let temp = locationToEdit {
    hudView.text = "Updated"
    location = temp
  } else {
    hudView.text = "Tagged"
    location = Location(context: managedObjectContext)
  }

  location.locationDescription = descriptionTextView.text
  . . .
```

The change is straightforward: you only ask Core Data for a new Location object if you don't already have one. You also make the text in the HUD say "Updated" when the user is editing an existing Location.

> **Note:** I've been harping on about the fact that Swift requires all non-optional variables and constants to always have a value. But here you declare let location without giving it an initial value. What gives?
>
> Well, the if statement that follows this declaration always puts a value into location, either the unwrapped value of locationToEdit, or a new Location object obtained from Core Data. After the if statement, location is guaranteed to have a value. Swift is cool with that.

➤ Run the app again and edit a location. Now the HUD should say "Updated".

➤ Stop the app and run it again to verify that the object was indeed properly changed. (You can also look at it directly in the SQLite database, of course.)

> **Exercise.** Why do you think the table view isn't being updated after you change a Location object? Tip: Recall that the table view also doesn't update when you tag new locations.

Answer: You fetch the Location objects in viewDidLoad(). But viewDidLoad() is only performed once, when the app starts. After the initial load of the Locations screen, its contents are never refreshed.

In *Checklists*, you solved this by using a delegate and that would be a valid solution here too. The LocationDetailsViewController could tell you through delegate methods that a location has been added or changed. But since you're using Core Data, there is a better way to do this.

Use NSFetchedResultsController

As you are no doubt aware by now, table views are everywhere in iOS apps. A lot of the time when you're working with Core Data, you want to fetch objects from the data store and show them in a table view. And when those objects change, you want to do a live update of the table view in response, to show the changes to the user.

So far, you've filled up the table view by manually fetching the results, but then you also need to manually check for changes and perform the fetch again to update the table. Thanks to NSFetchedResultsController, that suddenly becomes a lot easier.

It works like this: you give NSFetchedResultsController a fetch request, just like the NSFetchRequest you made earlier, and tell it to go fetch the objects. So far nothing new.

But, you don't put the results from that fetch into your own array. Instead, you read them straight from the fetched results controller. In addition, you make the view controller the delegate for the NSFetchedResultsController. Through this delegate, the view controller is informed that objects have been changed, added or deleted so that it can update the table in response.

➤ In **LocationsViewController.swift**, replace the locations instance variable with a new fetchedResultsController variable:

```
lazy var fetchedResultsController:
        NSFetchedResultsController<Location> = {
  let fetchRequest = NSFetchRequest<Location>()

  let entity = Location.entity()
  fetchRequest.entity = entity

  let sortDescriptor = NSSortDescriptor(key: "date",
                              ascending: true)
  fetchRequest.sortDescriptors = [sortDescriptor]

  fetchRequest.fetchBatchSize = 20

  let fetchedResultsController = NSFetchedResultsController(
          fetchRequest: fetchRequest,
    managedObjectContext: self.managedObjectContext,
       sectionNameKeyPath: nil, cacheName: "Locations")

  fetchedResultsController.delegate = self
  return fetchedResultsController
}()
```

This again uses the lazy initialization pattern with a closure to set everything up. It's good to get into the habit of lazily loading objects. You don't allocate them until you first use them. This makes your apps quicker to start and it saves memory.

The code in the closure does the same thing that you used to do in `viewDidLoad()`: it makes an `NSFetchRequest` and gives it an entity and a sort descriptor.

Note: Note that the new variable is not just `NSFetchedResultsController` but `NSFetchedResultsController<Location>`, since it's a generic. You need to tell the fetched results controller what type of objects to fetch.

This is new:

```
fetchRequest.fetchBatchSize = 20
```

If you have a huge table with hundreds of objects, then it requires a lot of memory to keep all of these objects around, even though you can only see a handful of them at a time.

The `NSFetchedResultsController` is pretty smart about this and will only fetch the objects that you can actually see, which cuts down on memory usage. This is all done in the background without you having to worry about it. The fetch batch size setting allows you to tweak how many objects will be fetched at a time.

Once the fetch request is set up, you can create the star of the show:

```
let fetchedResultsController = NSFetchedResultsController(
  fetchRequest: fetchRequest,
  managedObjectContext: self.managedObjectContext,
  sectionNameKeyPath: nil, cacheName: "Locations")
```

The `cacheName` needs to be a unique name that `NSFetchedResultsController` uses to cache the search results. It keeps this cache around even after your app quits, so the next time the fetch request is lightning fast, as the `NSFetchedResultsController` doesn't have to make a round-trip to the database but can simply read from the cache.

We'll talk about the `sectionNameKeyPath` parameter shortly.

The line that sets `fetchedResultsController.delegate` to `self` currently gives an error message because `LocationsViewController` does not conform to the right delegate protocol yet. You'll fix that in minute.

Now that you have a fetched results controller, you clean up `viewDidLoad()`.

➤ Change `viewDidLoad()` like this:

```
override func viewDidLoad() {
  super.viewDidLoad()
  performFetch()
}

// MARK:- Private methods
func performFetch() {
  do {
    try fetchedResultsController.performFetch()
  } catch {
    fatalCoreDataError(error)
  }
}
```

You still perform the initial fetch in `viewDidLoad()`, using the new `performFetch()` helper method. However, if any `Location` objects change after that initial fetch, the `NSFetchedResultsController`'s delegate methods are called to let you know about these changes. I'll show you in a second how that works.

It's always a good idea to explicitly set the delegate to `nil` when you no longer need the `NSFetchedResultsController`, just so you don't get any more notifications that were still pending.

➤ For that reason, add a `deinit` method:

```
deinit {
  fetchedResultsController.delegate = nil
}
```

The deinit method is invoked when this view controller is destroyed. It may not strictly be necessary to nil out the delegate here, but it's a bit of defensive programming that won't hurt.

Note that in this app the LocationsViewController will never actually be deallocated because it's one of the top-level view controllers in the tab bar. Still, it's good to get into the habit of writing deinit methods.

Because you removed the locations array, you should also change the table's data source methods.

➤ Change tableView(_:numberOfRowsInSection:) to:

```
override func tableView(_ tableView: UITableView,
      numberOfRowsInSection section: Int) -> Int {
  let sectionInfo = fetchedResultsController.sections![section]
  return sectionInfo.numberOfObjects
}
```

The fetched results controller's sections property returns an array of NSFetchedResultsSectionInfo objects that describe each section of the table view. The number of rows is found in the section info's numberOfObjects property.

(Currently there is only one section, but in a bit you'll split up the locations by category and then each category gets its own section.)

➤ Change tableView(_:cellForRowAt:) to:

```
override func tableView(_ tableView: UITableView,
            cellForRowAt indexPath: IndexPath) ->
            UITableViewCell {
  let cell = tableView.dequeueReusableCell(
        withIdentifier: "LocationCell",
                  for: indexPath) as! LocationCell

  let location = fetchedResultsController.object(at: indexPath)
  cell.configure(for: location)

  return cell
}
```

Instead of looking into the locations array like you did before, you now ask the fetchedResultsController for the object at the requested index-path. Because it is designed to work closely with table views, NSFetchedResultsController knows how to deal with index-paths, so that's very convenient.

➤ Make the same change in prepare(for:sender:).

There is still one piece of the puzzle missing. You need to implement the delegate methods for `NSFetchedResultsController` in `LocationsViewController`. Let's use an *extension* for that, to keep the code organized.

Organize the code using extensions

An extension lets you add code to an existing class, without having to modify the original class source code. When you make an extension you say, "here are a bunch of extra methods that also need to go into that class", and you can do that even if you didn't write the original class to begin with.

You've seen an extension used in Location+CoreDataProperties.swift. That was done to make it easier for Xcode to regenerate this file without overwriting the contents of Location+CoreDataClass.swift.

You can also use extensions to organize your source code. Here you'll use an extension just for the `NSFetchedResultsControllerDelegate` methods, so they are not all tangled up with `LocationsViewController`'s other code. By putting this code in a separate unit, you keep the responsibilities separate.

This makes it easy to spot which part of `LocationsViewController` plays the role of the delegate. All the fetched results controller delegate stuff happens just in this extension, not in the main body of the class. (You could even place this extension in a separate Swift file if you wanted.)

➤ Add the following code to the bottom of **LocationsViewController.swift**, outside of the class implementation:

```swift
// MARK:- NSFetchedResultsController Delegate Extension
extension LocationsViewController:
        NSFetchedResultsControllerDelegate {

  func controllerWillChangeContent(_ controller:
        NSFetchedResultsController<NSFetchRequestResult>) {
    print("*** controllerWillChangeContent")
    tableView.beginUpdates()
  }

  func controller(_ controller:
        NSFetchedResultsController<NSFetchRequestResult>,
        didChange anObject: Any, at indexPath: IndexPath?,
        for type: NSFetchedResultsChangeType,
        newIndexPath: IndexPath?) {

    switch type {
    case .insert:
      print("*** NSFetchedResultsChangeInsert (object)")
      tableView.insertRows(at: [newIndexPath!], with: .fade)
```

```
  case .delete:
    print("*** NSFetchedResultsChangeDelete (object)")
    tableView.deleteRows(at: [indexPath!], with: .fade)

  case .update:
    print("*** NSFetchedResultsChangeUpdate (object)")
    if let cell = tableView.cellForRow(at: indexPath!)
                                  as? LocationCell {
      let location = controller.object(at: indexPath!)
                    as! Location
      cell.configure(for: location)
    }

  case .move:
    print("*** NSFetchedResultsChangeMove (object)")
    tableView.deleteRows(at: [indexPath!], with: .fade)
    tableView.insertRows(at: [newIndexPath!], with: .fade)
  }
}

func controller(_ controller:
        NSFetchedResultsController<NSFetchRequestResult>,
        didChange sectionInfo: NSFetchedResultsSectionInfo,
        atSectionIndex sectionIndex: Int,
        for type: NSFetchedResultsChangeType) {
  switch type {
  case .insert:
    print("*** NSFetchedResultsChangeInsert (section)")
    tableView.insertSections(IndexSet(integer: sectionIndex),
                                        with: .fade)
  case .delete:
    print("*** NSFetchedResultsChangeDelete (section)")
    tableView.deleteSections(IndexSet(integer: sectionIndex),
                                        with: .fade)
  case .update:
    print("*** NSFetchedResultsChangeUpdate (section)")
  case .move:
    print("*** NSFetchedResultsChangeMove (section)")
  }
}

func controllerDidChangeContent(_ controller:
        NSFetchedResultsController<NSFetchRequestResult>) {
  print("*** controllerDidChangeContent")
  tableView.endUpdates()
}
}
```

Yowza, that's a lot of code. Don't let this freak you out! This is the standard way of implementing these delegate methods.

For many apps, this exact code will suffice and you can simply copy it over. Look it over for a few minutes to see if this code makes sense to you. You've made it this far, so I'm sure it won't be too hard.

NSFetchedResultsController will invoke these methods to let you know that certain objects were inserted, removed, or just updated. In response, you call the corresponding methods on the UITableView to insert, remove or update rows. That's all there is to it.

I put print() statements in these methods so you can follow along in the Console as to what is happening. Also note that you're using the switch statement here. A series of if's would have worked just as well but switch reads better.

➤ Run the app. Edit an existing location and press the Done button.

The debug area now shows:

```
*** controllerWillChangeContent
*** NSFetchedResultsChangeUpdate (object)
*** controllerDidChangeContent
```

NSFetchedResultsController noticed that an existing object was updated and, through updating the table, called your cell.configure(for:) method to redraw the contents of the cell. By the time the Edit Location screen disappears from sight, the table view is updated and your change is visible.

This also works for adding new locations.

➤ Tag a new location and press the Done button.

The debug area says:

```
*** controllerWillChangeContent
*** NSFetchedResultsChangeInsert (object)
*** controllerDidChangeContent
```

This time it's an "insert" notification. The delegate methods tells the table view to do insertRows(at:with:) in response and the new Location object is inserted in the table.

That's how easy it is. You make a new NSFetchedResultsController object with a fetch request and implement the delegate methods.

The fetched results controller keeps an eye on any changes that you make to the data store and notifies its delegate in response.

It doesn't matter where in the app you make these changes, they can happen on any screen. When that screen saves the changes to the managed object context, the fetched results controller picks up on it right away.

"It's not a bug, it's an undocumented feature"

There is a nasty bug with Core Data that still appears to be present in iOS 11. Here is how you can reproduce it:

1. Quit the app.

2. Run the app again and tag a new location.

3. Switch to the Locations tab.

You'd expect the new location to appear in the Locations tab, but it doesn't.

It's even possible that the app crashes as soon as you switch tabs. The error message is:

```
CoreData: FATAL ERROR: The persistent cache of section
information does not match the current configuration. You have
illegally mutated the NSFetchedResultsController's fetch
request, its predicate, or its sort descriptor without either
disabling caching or using +deleteCacheWithName:
```

We did no such thing! Interestingly, this problem does not occur when you switch to the Locations tab before you tag the new location.

There are two possible fixes:

1 - You can delete the cache of the NSFetchedResultsController. To do this, add the following line to viewDidLoad() before the call to performFetch():

```
NSFetchedResultsController<Location>.deleteCache(withName:
  "Locations")
```

This isn't a great solution as it negates the whole point of having a cache.

2 - You can force the LocationsViewController to load its view immediately when the app starts up. Without this, it delays loading the view until you switch tabs, causing Core Data to get confused. To apply this fix, add the following to application(_:didFinishLaunchingWithOptions:), immediately below the line that sets controller2.managedObjectContext:

```
let _ = controller2.view
```

If this problem also affects you, then implement one of the above solutions (my suggestion is #2). Then throw away DataModel.sqlite and run the app again. Verify that the bug no longer occurs.

iOS is pretty great but unfortunately it's not free of bugs (what software is?). If you encounter what you perceive to be a bug in one of the iOS frameworks, then report it at bugreport.apple.com. Feel free to report this Core Data bug as practice. :-)

Delete locations

Everyone makes mistakes. So, it's likely that users will want to delete locations from their list at some point. This is a very easy feature to add: you just have to remove the Location object from the data store and the NSFetchedResultsController will make sure it gets dropped from the table (again, through its delegate methods).

➤ Add the following method to **LocationsViewController.swift** (under the table view delegate section):

```
override func tableView(_ tableView: UITableView,
            commit editingStyle: UITableViewCellEditingStyle,
            forRowAt indexPath: IndexPath) {
  if editingStyle == .delete {
    let location = fetchedResultsController.object(at:
                                        indexPath)
    managedObjectContext.delete(location)
    do {
      try managedObjectContext.save()
    } catch {
      fatalCoreDataError(error)
    }
  }
}
```

You've seen tableView(_:commit:forRowAt:) before. It's part of the table view's data source protocol. As soon as you implement this method in your view controller, it enables swipe-to-delete.

This method gets the Location object from the selected row and then tells the context to delete that object. This will trigger the NSFetchedResultsController to send a notification to the delegate, which then removes the corresponding row from the table. That's all you need to do!

➤ Run the app and remove a location using swipe-to-delete. The Location object is dropped from the database and its row disappears from the screen with a brief animation.

Swipe to delete rows from the table

Many apps have an Edit button in the navigation bar that triggers a mode that also lets you delete (and sometimes move) rows. This is extremely easy to add.

➤ Add the following line to viewDidLoad() in **LocationsViewController.swift**:

```
navigationItem.rightBarButtonItem = editButtonItem
```

That's all there is to it. Every view controller has a built-in Edit button that can be accessed through the editButtonItem property. Tapping that button puts the table in editing mode:

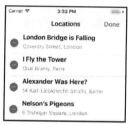

The table view in edit mode

➤ Run the app and verify that you can now also delete rows by pressing the Edit button.

Pretty sweet, huh? There's more cool stuff that NSFetchedResultsController makes really easy, such as splitting up the rows into sections.

Table view sections

The Location objects have a category field. It would be nice to group the locations by category in the table. The table view supports organizing rows into sections and each of these sections can have its own header.

Putting your rows into sections is a lot of work if you're doing it by hand, but NSFetchedResultsController practically gives you section support for free.

➤ Change the creation of the sort descriptors in the fetchedResultsController initialization block:

```
lazy var fetchedResultsController: . . . = {
  . . .
    let sort1 = NSSortDescriptor(key: "category", ascending: true)
    let sort2 = NSSortDescriptor(key: "date", ascending: true)
    fetchRequest.sortDescriptors = [sort1, sort2]
  . . .
```

Instead of one sort descriptor object, you now have two. First you sort the Location objects by category and inside each of the category groups you sort by date.

➤ Also change the initialization of the NSFetchedResultsController object:

```
let fetchedResultsController = NSFetchedResultsController(
    fetchRequest: fetchRequest,
    managedObjectContext: self.managedObjectContext,
    sectionNameKeyPath: "category",          // change this
    cacheName: "Locations")
```

The only difference here is that the sectionNameKeyPath parameter is set to "category", which means the fetched results controller will group the search results based on the value of the category attribute.

You're not done yet. The table view's data source also has methods for sections. So far you've only used the methods for rows, but now that you're adding sections to the table you need to implement a few additional methods.

➤ Add the following methods to the table view delegate section:

```
override func numberOfSections(in tableView: UITableView)
              -> Int {
  return fetchedResultsController.sections!.count
}

override func tableView(_ tableView: UITableView,
    titleForHeaderInSection section: Int) -> String? {
  let sectionInfo = fetchedResultsController.sections![section]
  return sectionInfo.name
}
```

Because you let NSFetchedResultsController do all the work already, the implementation of these methods is very simple. You ask the fetcher object for a list of the sections, which is an array of NSFetchedResultsSectionInfo objects, and then look inside that array to find out how many sections there are and what their names are.

Exercise. Why do you need to write sections! with an exclamation point?

Answer: the sections property is an optional, so it needs to be unwrapped before you can use it. Here you know for sure that sections will never be nil – after all, you just told NSFetchedResultsController to group the search results based on the value of their "category" field – so you can safely force unwrap it using the exclamation mark. Are you starting to get the hang of these optionals already?

➤ Run the app. Play with the categories on the Locations tab and notice how the table view automatically updates. All thanks to `NSFetchedResultsController`!

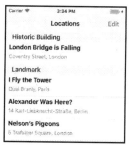

The locations are now grouped in sections

You can find the project files for this chapter under **28 – Locations Tab** in the Source Code folder.

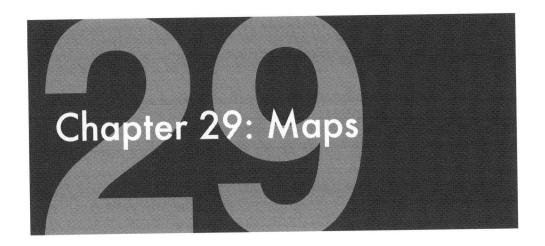

Chapter 29: Maps

Showing the locations in a table view is useful, but not very visually appealing. Given that the iOS SDK comes with an awesome map view control, it would be a shame not to use it :]

In this chapter, you will add a third tab to the app that will look like this when you are finished:

The completed Map screen

This is what you'll do in this chapter:

• **Add a mp view:** Learn how to add a map view to your app and get it to show the current user location or pins for a given set of locations.

- **Make your own pins:** Learn to create custom pins to display information about points on a map.

Add a map view

First visit: the storyboard.

➤ From the Objects Library, drag a **View Controller** on to the canvas.

➤ Control-drag from the Tab Bar Controller to this new View Controller to add it to the tabs (choose **Relationship segue – view controllers**).

➤ The new view controller now has a **Tab Bar Item**. Change its title to **Map** (via the Attributes inspector).

➤ Drag a **Map Kit View** into the view controller. Make it cover the entire area of the screen, so that the lower part of the map view sits under the tab bar. (The size of the Map View should be 320 × 568 points.)

➤ In the **Size inspector**, change the autoresizing settings for the Map View to:

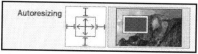

The autoresizing settings for the Map View

➤ In the **Attributes inspector** for the Map View, enable **Shows: User Location**. That will put a blue dot on the map at the user's current coordinates.

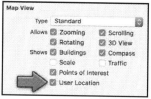

Enable show user location for the Map View

➤ Select the new view controller and select **Editor** → **Embed In** → **Navigation Controller**. This wraps your view controller in a navigation controller, and makes the new navigation controller the view controller displayed by the Tab Bar Controller.

➤ Change the view controller's (not the new navigation controller, but its root view controller) Navigation Item title to **Map**.

➤ Drag a **Bar Button Item** into the left-hand slot of the navigation bar and set the title to **Locations**. Drag another into the right-hand slot and set its title to **User**. Later on you'll use nice icons for these buttons, but for now these labels will do.

This part of the storyboard should look like this:

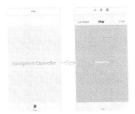

The design of the Map screen

In older versions of Xcode, the app would compile without any problems at this point, but would crash when you switched to the Map tab. This does not appear to be the case with the latest version of Xcode, but if you do run into this issue, here's what you need to do:

➤ Go to the **Project Settings** screen and select the **Capabilities** tab. Scroll down to where it says **Maps** and toggle the switch to ON.

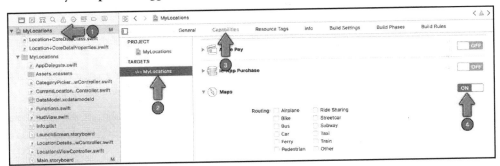

Enabling the app to use maps

➤ Run the app. Choose a location in the Simulator's Debug menu and switch to the Map. The screen should look something like this – the blue dot shows the current location:

The map shows the user's location

Sometimes, the map might show a different location than the current user location and you might not see the blue dot. If that happens, you can pan the map by clicking the mouse and dragging it across the Simulator window. Also, to zoom in or out, hold down the Alt/Option key while dragging the mouse.

Zoom in

Next, you're going to show the user's location in a little more detail because that blue dot could be almost anywhere in California!

➤ Add a new source file to the project and name it **MapViewController**.

➤ Replace the contents of **MapViewController.swift** with the following:

```swift
import UIKit
import MapKit
import CoreData

class MapViewController: UIViewController {
  @IBOutlet weak var mapView: MKMapView!

  var managedObjectContext: NSManagedObjectContext!

  // MARK:- Actions
  @IBAction func showUser() {
    let region = MKCoordinateRegionMakeWithDistance(
                  mapView.userLocation.coordinate, 1000, 1000)
    mapView.setRegion(mapView.regionThatFits(region),
                  animated: true)
  }

  @IBAction func showLocations() {
```

```
    }
}

extension MapViewController: MKMapViewDelegate {
}
```

This is a standard view controller, and not one of the specialized types like a table view controller. It has an outlet for the map view and two action methods that will be connected to the buttons in the navigation bar. The view controller is also the delegate of the map view, courtesy of the extension.

➤ In the storyboard, select the Map scene (the one with the view controller, not the one with the navigation controller) and in the **Identity inspector** set its **Class** to **MapViewController**.

➤ Connect the Locations button to the showLocations action and the User button to the showUser action. (In case you forgot how, Control-drag from the button to the yellow circle for the view controller.)

➤ Connect the Map View with the mapView outlet (Control-drag from the view controller to the Map View), and its delegate with the view controller (Control-drag the other way around).

Currently the view controller only implements the showUser() action method. When you press the **User** button, it zooms in the map to a region that is 1000 by 1000 meters (a little more than half a mile in both directions) around the user's position.

Try it out:

Pressing the User button zooms in to the user's location

Show pins for locations

The other button, Locations, is going to show the region that contains all the user's saved locations. But first you have to fetch those locations from the data store.

Even though this screen doesn't have a table view, you could still use an NSFetchedResultsController object to handle all the fetching and automatic change detection. But this time, I want to make it hard on you, so you're going to do the fetching by hand.

➤ Add a new array to **MapViewController.swift**:

```
var locations = [Location]()
```

➤ Also add this new method:

```
// MARK:- Private methods
func updateLocations() {
  mapView.removeAnnotations(locations)

  let entity = Location.entity()

  let fetchRequest = NSFetchRequest<Location>()
  fetchRequest.entity = entity

  locations = try! managedObjectContext.fetch(fetchRequest)
  mapView.addAnnotations(locations)
}
```

The fetch request is nothing new, except this time you're not sorting the Location objects. The order of the Location objects in the array doesn't really matter to the map view, only their latitude and longitude coordinates.

You've already seen how to handle errors with a do-try-catch block. But if you're certain that a particular method call will never fail, you can dispense with the do and catch and just write try! with an exclamation point. As with other things in Swift that have exclamation points, if it turns out that you were wrong, the app will crash without mercy. But in this case there isn't much that can go wrong. So, you can choose to live a little more dangerously.

Once you've obtained the Location objects, you call mapView.addAnnotations() to add a pin for each location on the map.

The idea is that updateLocations() will be executed every time there is a change in the data store. How you'll do that is of later concern, but the point is that when this happens, the locations array may already exist and may contain Location objects. If so, you first remove the pins for these old objects with removeAnnotations().

Xcode says the lines with `mapView.addAnnotations()` and `removeAnnotations()` have errors. This is to be expected and you'll fix it in a minute.

➤ First, add the `viewDidLoad()` method:

```
override func viewDidLoad() {
  super.viewDidLoad()
  updateLocations()
}
```

This fetches the `Location` objects and shows them on the map when the view loads. Nothing special here.

Before this class can use the `managedObjectContext`, you have to give it a reference to that object first. As before, that happens in `AppDelegate`.

➤ In **AppDelegate.swift**, extend `application(_:didFinishLaunchingWithOptions:)` to pass the context object to the `MapViewController` as well. This goes inside the `if let` statement:

```
// Third tab
navController = tabViewControllers[2] as! UINavigationController
let controller3 = navController.viewControllers.first
                    as! MapViewController
controller3.managedObjectContext = managedObjectContext
```

You're not quite done yet. In `updateLocations()` you told the map view to add the `Location` objects as annotations (an annotation is a pin on the map). But `MKMapView` expects an array of `MKAnnotation` objects, not your own `Location` class.

Luckily, `MKAnnotation` is a protocol. So, you can turn the `Location` objects into map annotations by making the class conform to that protocol.

➤ Change the `class` line from **Location+CoreDataClass.swift** to:

```
public class Location: NSManagedObject, MKAnnotation {
```

Just because `Location` is an object that is managed by Core Data doesn't mean you can't add your own stuff to it. It's still an object!

> **Exercise.** Xcode now says "Use of undeclared type MKAnnotation". Why is that?

Answer: You still need to `import MapKit`. Add that line at the top of the file.

> **Exercise.** Xcode still gives a compiler error when you try to build the project. What is wrong now?

Answer: You said `Location` conforms to the `MKAnnotation` protocol - you have to provide all the required features from that protocol in the `Location` class.

The `MKAnnotation` protocol requires the class to implement three properties: `coordinate`, `title`, and `subtitle`.

It obviously needs to know the coordinate in order to place the pin in the correct place on the map. The title and subtitle are used to display additional information about the location for each pin.

➤ Add the following code to **Location+CoreDataClass.swift**:

```
public var coordinate: CLLocationCoordinate2D {
  return CLLocationCoordinate2DMake(latitude, longitude)
}

public var title: String? {
  if locationDescription.isEmpty {
    return "(No Description)"
  } else {
    return locationDescription
  }
}

public var subtitle: String? {
  return category
}
```

Do you notice anything special here? All three items are instance variables (because of `var`), but they also have a block of source code associated with them.

These variables are **read-only computed properties**. That means they don't actually store a value in a memory location. Whenever you access the `coordinate`, `title`, or `subtitle` variables, they perform the logic from their code blocks. That's why they are *computed* properties: they compute something.

These properties are read-only because they only return a value – you can't assign them a new value using the assignment operator.

The following is OK because it reads the value of the property:

```
let s = location.title
```

But you cannot do this:

```
location.title = "Time for a change"
```

The only way the `title` property can change is if the `locationDescription` value changes. You could also have written this as a method:

```
func title() -> String? {
    if locationDescription.isEmpty {
        return "(No Description)"
    } else {
        return locationDescription
    }
}
```

This is equivalent to using the computed property. Whether to use a method or a computed property is often a matter of taste and you'll see both ways used throughout the iOS frameworks.

(By the way, it is also possible to make *read-write* computed properties that *can* be changed, but the `MKAnnotation` protocol doesn't use those.)

One more thing that you might have noticed about the variables above is the fact that they all have a `public` attribute. You've never used a `public` attribute for variables before. So why here?

That's because the `MKAnnotation` protocol delcares all three properties as `public`. You have to match the protocol declaration exactly and so your properties must have the `public` attribute as well. If you don't, Xcode will start whining :] Try removing the `public` attribute from one variable and see what happens ...

➤ Run the app and switch to the Map screen. It should now show pins for all the saved locations. Below each pin you should see the value of the `title` property from the `MKAnnotation` protocol.

The map shows pins for the saved locations

If you tap on a pin, the category for the location, which comes from the `subtitle` property, would be add below the title while the pin itself would scale up to indicate that it is currently selected.

> **Note:** So far, all the protocols you've seen were used for making delegates. But that's not the case here - `Location` is not a delegate of anything.
>
> The `MKAnnotation` protocol simply lets you pretend that `Location` is an annotation that can be placed on a map view. You can use this trick with any object you want; as long as the object implements the `MKAnnotation` protocol, it can be shown on a map.
>
> Protocols let objects wear different hats.

Show a region

Tapping the User button makes the map zoom to the user's current coordinates, but the same thing doesn't happen yet for the Locations button and the location pins.

By looking at the highest and lowest values for the latitude and longitude of all the `Location` objects, you can calculate a region and then tell the map view to zoom to that region.

➤ In **MapViewController.swift**, add the following new method:

```
func region(for annotations: [MKAnnotation]) ->
    MKCoordinateRegion {
  let region: MKCoordinateRegion

  switch annotations.count {
  case 0:
    region = MKCoordinateRegionMakeWithDistance(
          mapView.userLocation.coordinate, 1000, 1000)

  case 1:
    let annotation = annotations[annotations.count - 1]
    region = MKCoordinateRegionMakeWithDistance(
          annotation.coordinate, 1000, 1000)

  default:
    var topLeft = CLLocationCoordinate2D(latitude: -90,
                                       longitude: 180)
    var bottomRight = CLLocationCoordinate2D(latitude: 90,
                                       longitude: -180)

    for annotation in annotations {
      topLeft.latitude = max(topLeft.latitude,
              annotation.coordinate.latitude)
      topLeft.longitude = min(topLeft.longitude,
              annotation.coordinate.longitude)
      bottomRight.latitude = min(bottomRight.latitude,
                      annotation.coordinate.latitude)
      bottomRight.longitude = max(bottomRight.longitude,
                      annotation.coordinate.longitude)
    }

    let center = CLLocationCoordinate2D(
      latitude: topLeft.latitude -
              (topLeft.latitude - bottomRight.latitude) / 2,
      longitude: topLeft.longitude -
              (topLeft.longitude - bottomRight.longitude) / 2)

    let extraSpace = 1.1
    let span = MKCoordinateSpan(
      latitudeDelta: abs(topLeft.latitude -
                    bottomRight.latitude) * extraSpace,
      longitudeDelta: abs(topLeft.longitude -
                    bottomRight.longitude) * extraSpace)

    region = MKCoordinateRegion(center: center, span: span)
  }

  return mapView.regionThatFits(region)
}
```

region(for:) has three situations to handle. It uses a switch statement to look at the number of annotations and then chooses the corresponding case:

1. There are no annotations. You center the map on the user's current position.

2. There is only one annotation. You center the map on that one annotation.

3. There are two or more annotations. You calculate the extent of their reach and add a little padding. See if you can make sense of those calculations. The max() function looks at two values and returns the larger of the two; min() returns the smaller; abs() always makes a number positive (absolute value).

Note that this method does not use Location objects for anything. It assumes that all the objects in the array conform to the MKAnnotation protocol and it only looks at that part of the objects. As far as region(for:) is concerned, what it deals with are annotations. It just so happens that these annotations are represented by your Location objects.

That is the power of using protocols. It also allows you to use this method in any app that uses Map Kit, without modifications. Pretty neat.

➤ Change the showLocations() action method to:

```
@IBAction func showLocations() {
   let theRegion = region(for: locations)
   mapView.setRegion(theRegion, animated: true)
}
```

This calls region(for:) to calculate a reasonable region that fits all the Location objects and then sets that region on the map view.

➤ Finally, change viewDidLoad():

```
override func viewDidLoad() {
   . . .
   if !locations.isEmpty {
     showLocations()
   }
}
```

It's a good idea to show the user's locations the first time you switch to the Map tab. So viewDidLoad() calls showLocations() if the user has any saved locations.

➤ Run the app and switch to the Map tab, the map view should be zoomed in on your saved locations - because you have the code in viewDidLoad, remember? (This only works well if the locations aren't too far apart, of course.)

The map view zooms in to fit all your saved locations

Make your own pins

You made the `MapViewController` conform to the `MKMapViewDelegate` protocol, but so far, you haven't done anything with that.

This delegate is useful for creating your own annotation views. Currently, a default pin is displayed with a title below it, but you can change this to anything you like.

Create custom annotations

➤ Add the following code to the extension at the bottom of **MapViewController.swift**:

```
func mapView(_ mapView: MKMapView,
    viewFor annotation: MKAnnotation) ->
  MKAnnotationView? {
  // 1
  guard annotation is Location else {
    return nil
  }
  // 2
  let identifier = "Location"
  var annotationView = mapView.dequeueReusableAnnotationView(
                              withIdentifier: identifier)

  if annotationView == nil {
    let pinView = MKPinAnnotationView(annotation: annotation,
                              reuseIdentifier: identifier)
```

```
   // 3
   pinView.isEnabled = true
   pinView.canShowCallout = true
   pinView.animatesDrop = false
   pinView.pinTintColor = UIColor(red: 0.32, green: 0.82,
                                  blue: 0.4, alpha: 1)

   // 4
   let rightButton = UIButton(type: .detailDisclosure)
   rightButton.addTarget(self,
                 action: #selector(showLocationDetails),
                   for: .touchUpInside)
   pinView.rightCalloutAccessoryView = rightButton

   annotationView = pinView
 }

 if let annotationView = annotationView {
   annotationView.annotation = annotation

   // 5
   let button = annotationView.rightCalloutAccessoryView
                 as! UIButton
   if let index = locations.index(of: annotation
                                  as! Location) {
     button.tag = index
   }
 }
}

 return annotationView
}
```

This is very similar to what a table view data source does in `cellForRowAt`, except that you're not dealing with table view cells here but with `MKAnnotationView` objects. This is what happens step-by-step :

1. Because `MKAnnotation` is a protocol, there may be other objects apart from the `Location` object that want to be annotations on the map. An example is the blue dot that represents the user's current location.

    You should leave such annotations alone. So, you use the special `is` type check operator to determine whether the annotation is really a `Location` object. If it isn't, you return `nil` to signal that you're not making an annotation for this other kind of object. The `guard` statement you're using here works like an `if`: it only continues if the condition – `annotation is Location` – is true.

2. This is similar to creating a table view cell. You ask the map view to re-use an annotation view object. If it cannot find a recyclable annotation view, then you create a new one.

Note that you're not limited to using MKPinAnnotationView for your annotations. This is the standard annotation view class, but you can also create your own MKAnnotationView subclass and make it look like anything you want. Pins are only one option.

3. This sets some properties to configure the look and feel of the annotation view. Previously the pins were red, but you make them green here.

4. This is where it gets interesting. You create a new UIButton object that looks like a detail disclosure button - ⓘ. You use the target-action pattern to hook up the button's "Touch Up Inside" event with a new method showLocationDetails(), and add the button to the annotation view's accessory view.

5. Once the annotation view is constructed and configured, you obtain a reference to that detail disclosure button again and set its tag to the index of the Location object in the locations array. That way, you can find the Location object later in showLocationDetails() when the button is pressed.

➤ Add the showLocationDetails() method but leave it empty for now. Put it in the main class, not the extension.

```
@objc func showLocationDetails(_ sender: UIButton) {
}
```

Because you've told the button its #selector is showLocationDetails, the app won't compile unless you add at least an empty version of this method.

This method takes one parameter, sender, that refers to the control that sent the action message. In this case, the sender will be the ⓘ button. That's why the type of the sender parameter is UIButton.

➤ Run the app. The pins don't look the same as the standard pins from before, and are green.

There's no title below each pin, but there's a callout when you tap a pin, and the callout has a custom button.

If the pins don't change, then make sure you connected the view controller as the delegate of the map view in the storyboard.

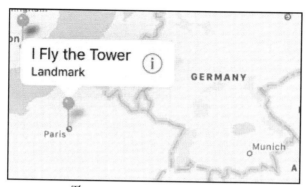

The annotations use your own view

Guard

In the map view delegate method, you wrote the following:

```
guard annotation is Location else {
   return nil
}
```

The `guard` statement lets you try something. If the result is `nil` or `false`, the code from the `else` block is performed.

If everything works like it's supposed to, the code simply skips the `else` block and continues.

You could also have written it as follows:

```
if annotation is Location {
   // do all the other things
   . . .
} else {
   return nil
}
```

This uses the familiar `if` statement. But notice how the code that handles the situation when `annotation` is *not* a `Location` is now all the way at the bottom of the method. If you have several of these `if` statements, your code ends up looking like this:

```
if condition1 {
   if condition2 {
      if condition3 {
      . . .
      } else {
         return nil  // condition3 is false
      }
   } else {
```

```
        return nil     // condition2 is false
    }
} else {
    return nil        // condition1 is false
}
```

This kind of structure is known as the "Pyramid of Doom". There's nothing wrong with it per se, but it can make the program flow hard to decipher. With guard you can write this as:

```
guard condition1 else {
    return nil              // condition1 is false
}
guard condition2 else {
    return nil              // condition2 is false
}
guard condition3 else {
    return nil              // condition3 is false
}
. . .
```

Now all the conditions are checked first and any errors or unexpected situations are handled straight away. Many programmers find this easier to read.

Add annotation actions

Tapping a pin on the map now brings up a callout with a blue ⓘ button. What should this button do? Show the Edit Location screen, of course!

➤ Open the storyboard. Find the Map View Controller, and **Control-drag** from the yellow cirlce at the top to the Tag Location scene, which is the Location Details View Controller.

Make this a new **Show** segue named **EditLocation**.

Tip: If making this connection gives you problems because the storyboard won't fit on your screen, then try Control-dragging from (or to) the Document Outline. You can also zoom out to show more of the storyboard.

The storyboard should now look be looking quite busy.

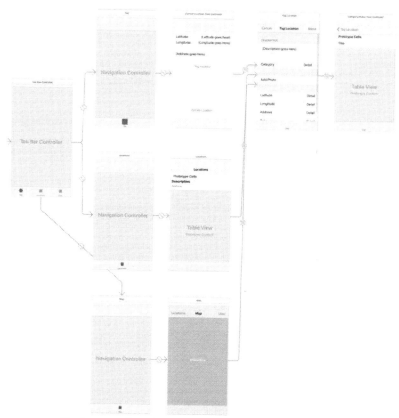

The Location Details screen is connected to all three screens

I had to zoom out the Storyboard in order to make the screen capture. Not sure if you can see very clearly at this level, but you should see that there are now three segues going to the Tag Location scene.

➤ Back in **MapViewController.swift**, change showLocationDetails(_:) to trigger the segue:

```
func showLocationDetails(sender: UIButton) {
  performSegue(withIdentifier: "EditLocation", sender: sender)
}
```

Because the segue isn't connected to any particular control in the view controller, you have to perform the segue manually. You pass along the button object as the sender, so you can read its tag property later.

➤ Add the `prepare(for:sender:)` method:

```
// MARK:- Navigation
override func prepare(for segue: UIStoryboardSegue,
                        sender: Any?) {
  if segue.identifier == "EditLocation" {
    let controller = segue.destination
                     as! LocationDetailsViewController
    controller.managedObjectContext = managedObjectContext

    let button = sender as! UIButton
    let location = locations[button.tag]
    controller.locationToEdit = location
  }
}
```

This is very similar to what you did in the Locations screen, except that now you get the `Location` object to edit from the `locations` array, using the `tag` property of the `sender` button as the index in that array.

➤ Run the app, tap on a pin and edit the location.

It works, except ... the annotation's callout doesn't change until you tap the pin again. Likewise, changes on the other screens, such as adding or deleting a location, have no effect on the map.

This is the same problem you had earlier with the Locations screen. Because the list of `Location` objects is only fetched once in `viewDidLoad()`, any changes that happen afterwards are overlooked.

Live-updating annotations

The way you're going to fix this for the Map screen is by using notifications. Recall that you have already put `NotificationCenter` to use for dealing with Core Data save errors.

As it happens, Core Data also sends out a bunch of notifications when changes are made to the data store. You can subscribe to these notifications and update the map view when you receive them.

➤ In **MapViewController.swift**, change the `managedObjectContext` property declaration to:

```
var managedObjectContext: NSManagedObjectContext! {
  didSet {
    NotificationCenter.default.addObserver(forName:
      Notification.Name.NSManagedObjectContextObjectsDidChange,
      object: managedObjectContext,
```

```
      queue: OperationQueue.main) { notification in
      if self.isViewLoaded {
        self.updateLocations()
      }
    }
  }
}
```

This is another example of a property observer put to good use.

As soon as `managedObjectContext` is given a value – which happens in `AppDelegate` during app startup – the `didSet` block tells the `NotificationCenter` to add an observer for the `NSManagedObjectContextObjectsDidChange` notification.

This notification (with the very long name) is sent out by the `managedObjectContext` whenever the data store changes. In response you would like the following closure to be called. For clarity, here's what happens in the closure:

```
if self.isViewLoaded {
  self.updateLocations()
}
```

This couldn't be simpler: you just call `updateLocations()` to fetch all the `Location` objects again. This throws away all the old pins and it makes new pins for all the newly fetched `Location` objects. Granted, it's not a very efficient method if there are hundreds of annotation objects, but for now it gets the job done.

> **Note:** You use `isViewLoaded` to make sure `updateLocations()` only gets called when the map view is loaded. Because this screen sits in a tab, the view from `MapViewController` does not actually get loaded from the storyboard until the user switches to the Map tab.
>
> So the view may not be loaded yet when the user tags a new location. In that case, it makes no sense to call `updateLocations()` – it could even crash the app since the `MKMapView` object doesn't exist at that point!

➤ Run the app. First go to the Map screen to see your existing location pins. Then tag a new location. The map should have added a new pin for it, although you may have to press the Locations bar button to make the new pin appear if it's outside the visible range.

Have another look at that closure. The `notification` in bit is the parameter for the closure. Like functions and methods, closures can take parameters.

Because this particular closure gets called by `NotificationCenter`, you're given a `Notification` object in the `notification` parameter. Since you're not using this `notification` object anywhere in the closure, you could also write it like this:

```
{ _ in
  . . .
}
```

You've already seen the _ underscore used in a few places in the code. This symbol is called the **wildcard** and you can use it whenever a name is expected but you don't really care about it.

Here, the _ tells Swift you're not interested in the closure's parameter. It also helps to reduce visual clutter in the source code; it's obvious at a glance that this parameter – whatever it may be – isn't being used in the closure.

So whenever you see the _ used in Swift source code it just means, "there's something here but the programmer has chosen to ignore it".

Exercise. The `Notification` object has a `userInfo` dictionary. From that dictionary it is possible to figure out which objects were inserted/deleted/updated. For example, use the following `print()`s to examine this dictionary:

```
if let dictionary = notification.userInfo {
  print(dictionary["inserted"])
  print(dictionary["deleted"])
  print(dictionary["updated"])
}
```

This will print out an (optional) array of `Location` objects or `nil` if there were no changes. Your mission, should you choose to accept it: try to make the reloading of the locations more efficient by only inserting or deleting the items that have changed. Good luck! (If you are stuck, you can find the solutions from other readers on the raywenderlich.com forums.)

That's it for the Map screen.

You can find the project files for this chapter under **29 – Maps** in the Source Code folder.

Chapter 30: Image Picker

Your Tag Locations screen is mostly feature complete, except that is for the ability to add a photo for a location. Time to fix that!

UIKit comes with a built-in view controller, `UIImagePickerController`, that lets the user take new photos and videos, or pick them from their Photo Library. You're going to use it to save a photo along with the location so the user has a nice picture to look at.

This is what your screen will look like when you're done:

A photo in the Tag Location screen

In this chapter, you will do the following:

- **Add an image picker:** Add an image picker to your app to allow you to take photos with the camera or to select existing images from your photo library.

- **Show the image:** Show the picked image in a table view cell.

- **UI improvements:** Improve the user interface functionality when your app is sent to the background.

- **Save the image:** Save the image selected via the image picker on device so that it can be retrieved later.

- **Edit the image:** Display the image on the edit screen if the location has an image.

- **Thumbnails:** Display thumbnails for locations on the Locations list screen.

Add an image picker

Just as you need to ask the user for permission before you can get GPS information from the device, you need to ask for permission to access the user's photo library.

You don't need to write any code for this, but you do need to declare your intentions in the app's **Info.plist**. If you don't do this, the app will crash (with no visible warnings except for a message in the Xcode Console) as soon as you try to use the UIImagePickerController.

Info.plist changes

➤ Open **Info.plist** and add a new row (either use the plus (+) button on existing rows, or right-click and select **Add Row**, or use the **Editor → Add Item** menu option).

For the key, use **NSPhotoLibraryUsageDescription**, or choose **Privacy - Photo Library Usage Description** from the dropdown list.

For the value, type: **Add photos to your locations.**

Key	Type	Value
▼ Information Property List	Dictionary	(16 items)
Privacy - Photo Library Usage Description	String	Add photos to your locations.
Privacy - Location When In Use Usage Description	String	This app lets you keep track of interesting places. It needs

Adding a usage description in Info.plist

➤ Also add the key **NSCameraUsageDescription** (or choose **Privacy - Camera Usage Description**) and give it the same description.

Now when the app opens the photo picker or the camera for the first time, iOS will tell the user what the app intends to use the photos for, using the description you just added to Info.plist.

Use camera to add image

➤ In **LocationDetailsViewController.swift**, add the following extension to the end of the source file:

```swift
extension LocationDetailsViewController:
    UIImagePickerControllerDelegate,
    UINavigationControllerDelegate {

  func takePhotoWithCamera() {
    let imagePicker = UIImagePickerController()
    imagePicker.sourceType = .camera
    imagePicker.delegate = self
    imagePicker.allowsEditing = true
    present(imagePicker, animated: true, completion: nil)
  }
}
```

The `UIImagePickerController` is a view controller like any other, but it is built into UIKit and it takes care of the entire process of taking new photos or picking them from the user's photo library.

All you need to do is create a `UIImagePickerController` instance, set its properties to configure the picker, set its `delegate`, and then present it. When the user closes the image picker screen, the delegate methods will let you know the result of the operation.

That's exactly how you've been designing your own view controllers. (Except that you don't need to add the `UIImagePickerController` to the storyboard.)

Note: You're doing this in an extension because it allows you to group all the photo-picking related functionality together.

If you wanted to, you could put these methods in the main class body. That would work fine too, but view controllers tend to become very big with many methods that all do different things.

As a way to preserve your sanity, it's nice to extract conceptually related methods — such as everything that has to do with picking photos — and place them together in their own extension.

You could even move each of these extensions to their own source file, for example "LocationDetailsViewController+PhotoPicking.swift", but personally, I find having less files to manage to be a good thing :]

➤ Add the following methods to the extension:

```
// MARK:- Image Picker Delegates
func imagePickerController(_ picker: UIImagePickerController,
        didFinishPickingMediaWithInfo info: [String : Any]) {
  dismiss(animated: true, completion: nil)
}

func imagePickerControllerDidCancel(_ picker:
                    UIImagePickerController) {
  dismiss(animated: true, completion: nil)
}
```

Currently these delegate methods simply remove the image picker from the screen. Soon, you'll take the image the user picked and add it to the Location object, but for now, you just want to make sure the image picker shows up.

Note that the view controller (in this case the extension) must conform to both UIImagePickerControllerDelegate and UINavigationControllerDelegate for this to work, but you don't have to implement any of the UINavigationControllerDelegate methods.

➤ Now change tableView(_:didSelectRowAt:) in the class as follows:

```
override func tableView(_ tableView: UITableView,
            didSelectRowAt indexPath: IndexPath) {
  if indexPath.section == 0 && indexPath.row == 0 {
    . . .
  } else if indexPath.section == 1 && indexPath.row == 0 {
    takePhotoWithCamera()
  }
}
```

Add Photo is the first row in the second section. When it's tapped, you call the takePhotoWithCamera() method that you just added.

➤ Run the app, tag a new location or edit an existing one, and tap **Add Photo**.

If you're running the app in the Simulator, bam! It crashes. The error message is this:

```
*** Terminating app due to uncaught exception
'NSInvalidArgumentException', reason: 'Source type 1 not
available'
```

The culprit for the crash is the line:

```
imagePicker.sourceType = .camera
```

Not all devices have a camera, and the Simulator does not. If you try to use the
UIImagePickerController with a sourceType that is not supported by the device or
the Simulator, the app crashes.

If you run the app on your device – and if it has a camera (which it probably does if it's a
recent model) – then you should see something like this:

The camera interface

That is very similar to what you see when you take pictures using the iPhone's Camera
app. (*MyLocations* doesn't let you record video, but you can certainly enable this feature
in your own apps.)

Use photo library to add image

You can still test the image picker on the Simulator, but instead of using the camera, you
have to use the photo library.

➤ Add another method to the extension:

```
func choosePhotoFromLibrary() {
   let imagePicker = UIImagePickerController()
   imagePicker.sourceType = .photoLibrary
   imagePicker.delegate = self
   imagePicker.allowsEditing = true
   present(imagePicker, animated: true, completion: nil)
}
```

This method does essentially the same thing as takePhotoWithCamera, except now you
set the sourceType to .photoLibrary.

➤ Change didSelectRowAt to call choosePhotoFromLibrary() instead of
takePhotoWithCamera().

➤ Run the app in the Simulator and tap **Add Photo**.

First, you need to give *MyLocations* permission to access the photo library:

The user needs to allow the app access to the photo library

If you tap Don't Allow, the photo picker screen remains empty. (You can undo this choice in the Settings app, under **Privacy → Photos**.)

➤ Choose **OK** to allow the app to use the photo library.

At this point you should generally see a handful of stock images, but on older Xcode versions it was possible that you would not see any images at all.

➤ If you don't see any images for some reason, stop the app and click on the built-in **Photos** app in the Simulator. This should display a handful of sample photos. Run the app again and try picking a photo. You may or may not see these sample photos now. If not, you'll have to add your own.

There are several ways you can add new photos to the Simulator. You can go into **Safari** (on the Simulator) and search the internet for an image. Then press down on the image until a menu appears and choose Save Image:

Adding images to the Simulator

Instead of surfing the internet for images, you can also simply drop an image file on to the Simulator window. This adds the picture to your library in the Photos app.

Finally, you can use the Terminal and the `simctl` command. Type the following, all on one line (the last part, `~/Desktop/MyPhoto.JPG`, should be replaced with an actual path to an image you want to add):

```
/Applications/Xcode.app/Contents/Developer/usr/bin/simctl
addphoto booted ~/Desktop/MyPhoto.JPG
```

The `simctl` tool can be used to manage your Simulators (type `simctl help` for a list of options). The command `addphoto booted` adds the specified image to the active Simulator's photo library.

➤ Run the app again. Now you should be able to choose a photo from the Photo Library:

The photos in the library

➤ Choose one of the photos. The screen now changes to:

The user can tweak the photo

This happens because you set the image picker's `allowsEditing` property to `true`. With this setting enabled, the user can do some quick editing on the photo before making their final choice. (In the Simulator you can hold down Alt/Option while dragging to rotate and zoom the photo.)

So, there are two types of image pickers you can use: the camera and the Photo Library. But the camera won't work everywhere. It's a bit limiting to restrict the app to just picking photos from the library, though.

You'll have to make the app a little smarter and allow the user to choose the camera when it is present.

Choose between camera and photo library

First, you check whether the camera is available. When it is, you show an **action sheet** to let the user choose between the camera and the Photo Library.

➤ Add the following methods to **LocationDetailsViewController.swift**, in the photo extension:

```swift
func pickPhoto() {
  if UIImagePickerController.isSourceTypeAvailable(.camera) {
    showPhotoMenu()
  } else {
    choosePhotoFromLibrary()
  }
}

func showPhotoMenu() {
  let alert = UIAlertController(title: nil, message: nil,
                    preferredStyle: .actionSheet)

  let actCancel = UIAlertAction(title: "Cancel", style: .cancel,
                    handler: nil)
  alert.addAction(actCancel)

  let actPhoto = UIAlertAction(title: "Take Photo",
                    style: .default, handler: nil)
  alert.addAction(actPhoto)

  let actLibrary = UIAlertAction(title: "Choose From Library",
                    style: .default, handler: nil)
  alert.addAction(actLibrary)

  present(alert, animated: true, completion: nil)
}
```

You use `UIImagePickerController`'s `isSourceTypeAvailable()` method to check whether there's a camera present. If not, you call `choosePhotoFromLibrary()` as that is the only option then. But when the device does have a camera, you show a `UIAlertController` on the screen.

Unlike the alert controllers you've used before, this one has the `.actionSheet` style. An action sheet works very much like an alert view, except that it slides in from the bottom of the screen and offers the user one of several choices.

➤ In `didSelectRowAt`, change the call to `choosePhotoFromLibrary()` to `pickPhoto()` instead. This is the last time you'll change this line, honest.

➤ Run the app on your device to see the action sheet in action:

The action sheet that lets you choose between camera and photo library

Tapping any of the buttons in the action sheet simply dismisses the action sheet but doesn't do anything else yet.

By the way, if you want to test this action sheet in the Simulator, then you can fake the availability of the camera by writing the following in `pickPhoto()`:

```
if true || UIImagePickerController.isSourceTypeAvailable(
                                              .camera) {
```

That will always show the action sheet because the condition is now always true.

The choices in the action sheet are provided by `UIAlertAction` objects. The `handler:` parameter determines what happens when you press the corresponding button in the action sheet.

Right now the handlers for all three choices – Take Photo, Choose From Library, Cancel – are `nil`, so nothing will happen.

➤ Change these lines to the following:

```
let actPhoto = UIAlertAction(title: "Take Photo",
      style: .default, handler: { _ in
        self.takePhotoWithCamera()
      })
```

```
let actLibrary = UIAlertAction(title: "Choose From Library",
      style: .default, handler: { _ in
        self.choosePhotoFromLibrary()
      })
```

This gives `handler:` a closure that calls the corresponding method from the extension. You use the _ wildcard to ignore the parameter that is passed to this closure (which is a reference to the `UIAlertAction` itself).

➤ Run the app make sure the buttons from the action sheet work properly.

There may be a small delay between pressing any of these buttons before the image picker appears, but that's because it's a big component and iOS needs a few seconds to load it up.

Notice that the Add Photo cell remains selected (dark gray background) when you cancel the action sheet. That doesn't look so good.

➤ In `tableView(_:didSelectRowAt)`, add the following line before the call to `pickPhoto()`:

```
tableView.deselectRow(at: indexPath, animated: true)
```

This first deselects the Add Photo row. Try it out, it looks better this way. The cell background quickly fades from gray back to white as the action sheet slides into the screen.

By the way, if you still have the Core Data debug output enabled, then you should see a whole bunch of output in the Xcode Console when the image picker is active. Apparently the `UIImagePickerController` uses Core Data as well!

Show the image

Now that the user can pick a photo, you should display it somewhere (otherwise, what's the point?). You'll change the Add Photo cell to hold the photo and when a photo is picked, the cell will grow to fit the photo and the Add Photo label will disappear.

➤ Add two new outlets to the class in **LocationDetailsViewController.swift**:

```
@IBOutlet weak var imageView: UIImageView!
@IBOutlet weak var addPhotoLabel: UILabel!
```

➤ In the storyboard, drag an Image View into the Add Photo cell. It doesn't really matter how big it is or where you put it. You'll programmatically move it to the proper place later. (This is the reason you made this a custom cell way back when, so you could add this image view to it.)

Adding an Image View to the Add Photo cell

➤ Connect the Image View to the view controller's `imageView` outlet. Also connect the Add Photo label to the `addPhotoLabel` outlet.

➤ Select the Image View. In the **Attributes inspector**, check its **Hidden** attribute (in the Drawing section). This makes the image view initially invisible, until you have a photo to give it.

Now that you have an image view, let's make it display something.

➤ Add a new instance variable to **LocationDetailsViewController.swift**:

```
var image: UIImage?
```

If no photo is picked yet, `image` will be `nil`, so the variable has to be an optional.

➤ Add a new method to the class:

```
func show(image: UIImage) {
  imageView.image = image
  imageView.isHidden = false
  imageView.frame = CGRect(x: 10, y: 10, width: 260,
                                      height: 260)

  addPhotoLabel.isHidden = true
}
```

This puts the image from the parameter into the image view, makes the image view visible, and gives it the proper dimensions. It also hides the Add Photo label because you don't want it to overlap the image view.

➤ Change the `imagePickerController(_:didFinishPickingMediaWithInfo:)` method from the photo picking extension to the following:

```
func imagePickerController(_ picker: UIImagePickerController,
    didFinishPickingMediaWithInfo info: [String : Any]) {

  image = info[UIImagePickerControllerEditedImage] as? UIImage
```

```
    if let theImage = image {
        show(image: theImage)
    }

    dismiss(animated: true, completion: nil)
}
```

This is the method that gets called when the user has selected a photo in the image picker.

You can tell by the notation [String : Any] that the info parameter is a dictionary. Whenever you see [A : B] you're dealing with a dictionary that has keys of type "A" and values of type "B".

The info dictionary contains data describing the image that the user picked. You use the UIImagePickerControllerEditedImage key to retrieve a UIImage object that contains the final image after the user moved and/or scaled it. (You can also get the original image if you wish, using a different key.)

Once you have the photo, you store it in the image instance variable so you can use it later.

Dictionaries always return optionals, because there is a theoretical possibility that the key you asked for – UIImagePickerControllerEditedImage in this case – doesn't actually exist in the dictionary.

Since the image instance variable is an optional, you simply assign the value from the dictionary.

If info[UIImagePickerControllerEditedImage] is nil, then image will be nil too. You do need to cast the value from the meaningless Any to UIImage using the as? operator. In this case you need to use the optional cast, as? instead of as!, because image is an optional instance variable.

Once you have the image and it is not nil, the call to show(image:) puts it in the Add Photo cell.

Exercise. See if you can rewrite the above logic to use a didSet property observer on the image instance variable. If you succeed, then placing the photo into image will automatically update the UIImageView, without needing to call show(image:).

➤ Run the app and choose a photo. Whoops, it looks like you have a small problem here:

The photo gets cut off

(It's also possible that the photo overlaps the rows below it. In any case, it doesn't look good...)

The `show(image:)` method made the image view 260-by-260 points tall, but the table view cell doesn't automatically resize to fit that image view. You'll have to add some logic to the `heightForRowAt` table view method to make the table view cell resize.

Resize table view cell to show image

➤ Change the `tableView(_:heightForRowAt:)` method:

```
override func tableView(_ tableView: UITableView,
          heightForRowAt indexPath: IndexPath) -> CGFloat {
  if indexPath.section == 0 && indexPath.row == 0 {
    return 88

  } else if indexPath.section == 1 {  // this else if is new
    if imageView.isHidden {
      return 44
    } else {
      return 280
    }

  } else if indexPath.section == 2 && indexPath.row == 2 {
    . . .
```

If there is no image, then the height for the Add Photo cell is 44 points just like a regular cell. But if there is an image, it's a lot higher: 280 points. That is 260 points for the image view plus 10 points margin on the top and bottom.

➤ Add the following line to `imagePickerController(_Pdidfinishpickingmediawithinfo:)`, just before you dismiss the view controller:

```
tableView.reloadData()
```

This refreshes the table view and sets the photo row to the proper height.

➤ Try it out. The cell now resizes and is big enough for the whole photo. The image does appear to be stretched out a little, though.

The photo is stretched out a bit

The image view is square but most photos won't be. By default, an image view will stretch the image to fit the entire content area. That's probably not what you want for this app.

Set image to display correctly

➤ Go to the storyboard and select the Image View (it may be hard to see on account of it being hidden, but you can still find it in the Document Outline). In the **Attributes inspector**, set its **Content Mode** to **Aspect Fit**.

Changing the image view's content mode

This will keep the image's aspect ratio intact as it is resized to fit within the image view. Play a bit with the other content modes to see what they do. (Aspect Fill is similar to Aspect Fit, except that it tries to fill up the entire view.)

The aspect ratio of the photo is kept intact

That looks better, but there are now larger margins at the top and bottom of the image.

> **Exercise.** Make the height of the photo table view cell dynamic, depending on the aspect ratio of the image. This is a tough one! You can keep the width of the image view at 260 points. This should correspond to the width of the UIImage object. You get the aspect ratio by doing `image.size.width / image.size.height`. With this ratio you can calculate what the height of the image view and the cell should be. Good luck! You can find solutions from other readers at
> forums.raywenderlich.com

Refactor the code

By the way, notice how the `if` statements in `tableView(_:heightForRowAt:)` all look at the index-path's section and/or row?

```
if indexPath.section == 0 && indexPath.row == 0 {
  . . .
} else if indexPath.section == 1 {
  . . .
} else if indexPath.section == 2 && indexPath.row == 2 {
  . . .
} else {
  . . .
}
```

Whenever you see `if – else if – else if – else` where the conditions all check the same thing, it's a good opportunity to use a `switch` statement instead.

➤ Change the `tableView(_:heightForRowAt:)` method to:

```
override func tableView(_ tableView: UITableView,
          heightForRowAt indexPath: IndexPath) -> CGFloat {

  switch (indexPath.section, indexPath.row) {
    case (0, 0):
      return 88

    case (1, _):
      return imageView.isHidden ? 44 : 280

    case (2, 2):
      addressLabel.frame.size = CGSize(
                width: view.bounds.size.width - 115,
              height: 10000)
      addressLabel.sizeToFit()
      addressLabel.frame.origin.x = view.bounds.size.width -
```

```
                                      addressLabel.frame.size.width - 15
            return addressLabel.frame.size.height + 20

        default:
            return 44
        }
    }
```

The logic inside each of the sections is the same as before, but now the different cases are easier to distinguish:

```
switch (indexPath.section, indexPath.row) {
    case (0, 0):
    case (1, _):
    case (2, 2):
    default:
}
```

This switch statement puts indexPath.section and indexPath.row into a **tuple**, and then uses *pattern matching* to look for the different cases:

- case (0, 0) corresponds to section 0, row 0.

- case (1, _) corresponds to section 1, any row. The _ is the wildcard again, which means any value for indexPath.row is accepted here.

- case (2, 2) corresponds to section 2, row 2.

- The default case is for any other rows in sections 0 and 2.

Using switch is very common in Swift because it makes large blocks of if — else if statements much easier to read.

> **Note:** A tuple is nothing more than a list of values inside ( ) parentheses. For example, (10, 3.14, "Hello") is a tuple with three elements.
>
> Tuples have various uses, such as allowing a method to return more than one value (simply put the different values into a tuple and return that). They are also very convenient in switch statements.

There was another change. The following lines have changed from this,

```
if imageView.isHidden {
    return 44
} else {
    return 280
}
```

into this:

```
return imageView.hidden ? 44 : 280
```

You've seen the the ternary conditional operator in action before, so you know that it works like an `if` − `else` statement compressed into a single line, right? Using `?` `:` is often simpler than writing it out as `if` − `else`.

But, be careful: there tmust be a space between `imageView.isHidden` and `?`, or else Swift thinks `isHidden` is an optional that you're trying to unwrap, which results in an error. This is a case where the same symbol, `?`, can mean more than one thing.

UI improvements

The user can take a photo, or pick one, now but the app doesn't save it yet to the data store. Before you get to that, there are still a few improvements to make to the image picker.

Apple recommends that apps remove any alert or action sheet from the screen when the user presses the Home button to move the app to the background.

The user may return to the app hours or days later and they will have forgotten what they were going to do. The presence of the alert or action sheet is confusing and the user might think, "What's that thing doing here?!"

To prevent this from happening, you'll make the Tag Location screen a little more attentive. When the app goes to the background, it will dismiss the action sheet if that is currently showing. You'll do the same for the image picker.

Handle background mode

You saw in the *Checklists* app that the `AppDelegate` is notified by the operating system, when the app is about to go to the background, through its `applicationDidEnterBackground(_:)` method.

View controllers don't have such a method, but fortunately, iOS sends out "going to the background" notifications through `NotificationCenter` that you can configure the view controller to listen to.

Earlier you used the notification center to observe notifications from Core Data. This time you'll listen for the `UIApplicationDidEnterBackground` notification.

➤ In **LocationDetailsViewController.swift**, add a new method:

```swift
func listenForBackgroundNotification() {
  NotificationCenter.default.addObserver(forName:
      Notification.Name.UIApplicationDidEnterBackground,
      object: nil, queue: OperationQueue.main) { _ in

    if self.presentedViewController != nil {
      self.dismiss(animated: false, completion: nil)
    }

    self.descriptionTextView.resignFirstResponder()
  }
}
```

This adds an observer for the UIApplicationDidEnterBackground notification. When this notification is received, NotificationCenter will call the closure.

(Notice that you're using the "trailing" closure syntax here; the closure is not a parameter to addObserver(forName, ...) but immediately follows the method call.)

If there is an active image picker or action sheet, you dismiss it. You also hide the keyboard if the text view is active.

The image picker and action sheet are both presented as modal view controllers that appear above everything else. If such a modal view controller is active, UIViewController's presentedViewController property has a reference to that modal view controller.

So, if presentedViewController is not nil you call dismiss() to close the modal screen. (By the way, this has no effect on the category picker; that does not use a modal segue but a push segue.)

➤ Call the listenForBackgroundNotification() method from within viewDidLoad().

➤ Try it out. Open the image picker (or the action sheet if you're on a device that has a camera) and exit to the home screen to put the app to sleep.

Then tap the app's icon to activate the app again. You should now be back on the Tag Location screen (or Edit Location screen if you opted to edit an existing one). The image picker (or action sheet) has automatically closed.

That seems to work, cool!

Remove notification observers

There's one more thing to do. You should tell the `NotificationCenter` to stop sending these background notifications when the Tag/Edit Location screen closes. You don't want `NotificationCenter` to send notifications to an object that no longer exists, that's just asking for trouble! The `deinit` method is a good place to tear this down.

➤ First, add a new instance variable:

```
var observer: Any!
```

This will hold a reference to the observer, which is necessary to unregister it later.

The type of this variable is `Any!`, meaning that you don't really care what sort of object this is.

➤ In `listenForBackgroundNotification()`, change the first line so that it stores the return value of the call to `addObserver()` into this new instance variable:

```
func listenForBackgroundNotification() {
    observer = NotificationCenter.default.addObserver(forName: . .
  .
```

➤ Finally, add the `deinit` method:

```
deinit {
    print("*** deinit \(self)")
    NotificationCenter.default.removeObserver(observer)
}
```

You're also adding a `print()` here so you can see some proof that the view controller really does get destroyed when you close the Tag/Edit Location screen.

➤ Run the app, edit an existing location, and tap Done to close the screen.

I don't know about you, but I don't see the *** `deinit` message anywhere in the Xcode Console.

Guess what? The `LocationDetailsViewController` doesn't get destroyed for some reason. That means the app is leaking memory... Of course, this was all a big setup on my part so I can tell you about closures and capturing.

Remember that in closures you always have to specify `self` when you want to access an instance variable or call a method? That is because closures capture any variables that are used inside the closure.

When it captures a variable, the closure simply stores a reference to that variable. This allows it to use the variable at some later point when the closure is actually performed.

Why is this important? If the code inside the closure uses a local variable, the method that created this variable may no longer be active by the time the closure is performed. After all, when a method ends all locals are destroyed. But when such a local is captured by a closure, it stays alive until the closure is also done with it.

Because the closure needs to keep the objects from those captured variables alive in the time between capturing and actually performing the closure, it stores a *strong* reference to those objects. In other words, capturing means the closure becomes a shared owner of the captured objects.

What may not be immediately obvious is that `self` is also one of those variables and therefore gets captured by the closure. Sneaky! That's why Swift requires you to explicitly write out `self` inside closures, so you won't forget this value is being captured.

In the context of `LocationDetailsViewController`, `self` referrs to the view controller itself. So, as the closure captures `self`, it creates a strong reference to the `LocationDetailsViewController` object, and the closure becomes a co-owner of this view controller. I bet you didn't expect that!

Remember, as long as an object has owners, it is kept alive. So this closure is keeping the view controller alive, even after you closed it!

This is known as an **ownership cycle**, because the view controller itself has a strong reference back to the closure through the `observer` variable.

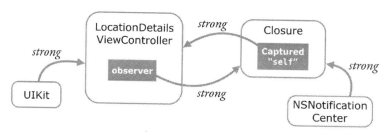

The relationship between the view controller and the closure

(In case you're wondering, the view controller's other owner is UIKit. The observer is also being kept alive by `NotificationCenter`.)

This sounds like a classic catch-22 problem! Fortunately, there is a way to break the ownership cycle. You can give the closure a **capture list**. (What's *that* you ask? All will be explained soon!)

➤ Change `listenForBackgroundNotification()` to the following:

```
func listenForBackgroundNotification() {
  observer = NotificationCenter.default.addObserver(
    forName: Notification.Name.UIApplicationDidEnterBackground,
```

```
    object: nil, queue: OperationQueue.main) { [weak self] _ in

    if let weakSelf = self {
        if weakSelf.presentedViewController != nil {
            weakSelf.dismiss(animated: false, completion: nil)
        }
        weakSelf.descriptionTextView.resignFirstResponder()
    }
  }
}
```

There are a couple of new things here. Let's look at the first part of the closure:

```
{ [weak self] _ in
  . . .
}
```

The [weak self] bit is the capture list for the closure. It tells the closure that the variable self will still be captured, but as a weak reference. As a result, the closure no longer keeps the view controller alive.

Weak references are allowed to become nil, which means the captured self is now an optional inside the closure. You need to unwrap it with if let before you can send messages to the view controller.

Other than that, the closure still does the exact same things as before.

➤ Try it out. Open the Tag/Edit Location screen and close it again. You should now see the print() from deinit in the Xcode Console.

That means the view controller gets destroyed properly and the notification observer is removed from NotificationCenter. Good riddance!

Exercise. What happens if you remove the call to removeObserver() from deinit? Hint: add print(self) inside the closure.

Answer: Because the observer is not removed, it stays alive and active. The next time you put the app in the background, even if you're not on the Tag/Edit Location screen, the closure from this "old" observer is called again, but self is now nil (the object that it captured no longer exists).

This may seem innocuous, but it's a serious bug. Every time the user opens and closes the Tag/Edit Location screen, you end up with a new observer that stays in memory forever. The if let prevents the app from crashing on a nil dereference of self as you go to the background, but over time the leftover observers will eat up all available memory.

That's why it's always a good idea to clean up after yourself. Use `print()`'s to make sure your objects really get deallocated! (Xcode also comes with Instruments, a handy tool that you can use to detect such issues.)

Save the image

The ability to pick photos is rather useless if the app doesn't also save them. So, that's what you'll do here.

It is possible to store images in the Core Data store as "blobs" (**B**inary **L**arge **OB**jects), but that is not recommended. Large blocks of data are better off stored as regular files in the app's Documents directory.

> **Note:** Core Data has an "Allows external storage" feature that is designed to make this process completely transparent for the developer. In theory, you can put data of any size into your entities and Core Data automatically decides whether to put the data into the SQLite database or store it as an external file.
>
> Unfortunately, this feature doesn't work very well in practice. Last time I checked, it just had too many bugs to be useful. So, until this part of Core Data becomes rock solid, we'll be doing it by hand.

When the image picker gives you a `UIImage` object for a photo, that image only lives in the iPhone's working memory.

The image may also be stored as a file somewhere if the user picked it from the photo library, but that's not the case if they just snapped a new picture. Besides, the user may have resized or cropped the image.

So you have to save that `UIImage` to a file of your own if you want to keep it. The photos in *MyLocations* will be saved in JPEG format.

You need a way to associate that JPEG file with your `Location` object. The obvious solution is to store the filename in the `Location` object. You won't store the entire filename, just an ID, which is a positive number. The image file itself will be named **Photo-XXX.jpg**, where XXX is the numeric ID.

Data model changes

➤ Open the Data Model editor. Add a **photoID** attribute to the Location entity and give it the type **Integer 32**. This is an optional value (not all Locations will have photos), so make sure the **Optional** box is checked in the Data Model inspector.

➤ Add a property for this new attribute to **Location+CoreDataProperties.swift**:

```
@NSManaged public var photoID: NSNumber?
```

Remember that for an object that is managed by Core Data, you have to declare the property as @NSManaged.

You may be wondering why you're declaring the type of photoID as NSNumber and not as Int (or more precisely Int32). Remember that Core Data is an Objective-C framework, so you're limited by the possibilities of that language. NSNumber is how number objects are handled in Objective-C.

For various reasons, you can't represent an Int value as an optional in Objective-C. Instead, you'll use the NSNumber class. Swift will automatically convert between Int values and this NSNumber, so it's no big deal.

You'll now add some other properties to the Location object to make working with photos a little easier.

➤ Add the hasPhoto computed property to **Location+CoreDataClass.swift**:

```
var hasPhoto: Bool {
  return photoID != nil
}
```

This determines whether the Location object has a photo associated with it or not. Swift's optionals make this easy.

➤ Also add the photoURL property:

```
var photoURL: URL {
  assert(photoID != nil, "No photo ID set")
  let filename = "Photo-\(photoID!.intValue).jpg"
  return applicationDocumentsDirectory.appendingPathComponent(
                                              filename)
}
```

This property computes the full URL for the JPEG file for the photo. Note that iOS uses URLs to refer to files, even those saved on the local device.

You'll save these JPEG files in the app's Documents directory. To get the URL to that directory, you use the global variable `applicationDocumentsDirectory` that you added to Functions.swift earlier.

Notice the use of `assert()` to make sure the `photoID` is not `nil`. An **assertion** is a special debugging tool that is used to check that your code always does something valid. If not, the app will crash with a helpful error message. You'll see more of this later when we talk about finding bugs – and squashing them.

Assertions are a form of defensive programming. Most of the crashes you've seen so far were actually caused by assertions in UIKit. They allow the app to crash in a controlled manner. Without these assertions, programming mistakes could crash the app at random moments, making it very hard to find out what went wrong.

If the app were to ask a `Location` object for its `photoURL` without having given it a valid `photoID` earlier, the app will crash with the message "No photo ID set". If so, there is a bug in the code somewhere because this is not supposed to happen. Internal consistency checks like this can be very useful.

Assertions are usually enabled only while you're developing and testing your app and disabled when you upload the final build of your app to the App Store. By then, there should be no more bugs in your app (or so you would hope!). It's a good idea to use `assert()` in strategic places to catch yourself making programming errors.

➤ Add a `photoImage` property:

```
var photoImage: UIImage? {
  return UIImage(contentsOfFile: photoURL.path)
}
```

This returns a `UIImage` object by loading the image file. You'll need this later to show the photos for existing `Location` objects.

Note that this property has the optional type `UIImage?` – that's because loading the image may fail if the file is damaged or removed. Of course, that *shouldn't* happen, but no doubt you've heard of Murphy's Law… As I've repeatedly said, it's good to get into the habit of defensive programming.

There is one more thing to add, a `nextPhotoID()` method. This is a class method, meaning that you don't need to have a `Location` instance to call it. You can call this method anytime from anywhere.

➤ Add the method:

```
class func nextPhotoID() -> Int {
  let userDefaults = UserDefaults.standard
  let currentID = userDefaults.integer(forKey: "PhotoID") + 1
```

```
    userDefaults.set(currentID, forKey: "PhotoID")
    userDefaults.synchronize()
    return currentID
}
```

You need to have some way to generate a unique ID for each `Location` object. All
`NSManagedObjects` have an `objectID` method, but that returns something unreadable
such as:

```
<x-coredata://C26CC559-959C-49F6-BEF0-F221D6F3F04A/Location/p1>
```

You can't really use that in a filename. So instead, you're going to put a simple integer in
`UserDefaults` and update it every time the app asks for a new ID. (This is similar to
what you did in the last app to make `ChecklistItem` IDs for use with local
notifications.)

It may seem a little silly to use `UserDefaults` for this when you're already using Core
Data as the data store, but with `UserDefaults`, the `nextPhotoID()` method is only five
lines. You've seen how verbose the code is for fetching something from Core Data and
then saving it again. This is just as easy. (As an exercise, you could try to implement these
IDs using Core Data.)

That's itfor `Location`. Now you have to save the image and fill in the `Location` object's
`photoID` field. This happens in the Location Details View Controller's `done()` action.

Save the image to a file

➤ In **LocationDetailsViewController.swift**, in the `done()` method, add the following in
between where you set the properties of the `Location` object and where you save the
managed object context:

```
// Save image
if let image = image {
  // 1
  if !location.hasPhoto {
    location.photoID = Location.nextPhotoID() as NSNumber
  }
  // 2
  if let data = UIImageJPEGRepresentation(image, 0.5) {
    // 3
    do {
      try data.write(to: location.photoURL, options: .atomic)
    } catch {
      print("Error writing file: \(error)")
    }
  }
}
```

This code is only performed if image is not nil, in other words, when the user has picked a photo.

1. You need to get a new ID and assign it to the Location's photoID property, but only if you're adding a photo to a Location that didn't already have one. If a photo existed, you simply keep the same ID and overwrite the existing JPEG file.

2. The UIImageJPEGRepresentation() function converts the UIImage to JPEG format and returns a Data object. Data is an object that represents a blob of binary data, usually the contents of a file.

3. You save the Data object to the path given by the photoURL property. (Also notice the use of a do-try-catch block again.)

➤ Run the app, tag a location, choose a photo, and press Done to exit the screen. Now the photo you picked should be saved in the app's Documents directory as a regular JPEG file.

The photo is saved in the app's Documents folder

> **Note:** The first time you run the app after adding a new attribute to the data model (photoID), the NSPersistentContainer performs a migration of the data store behind the scenes to make sure the data store is in sync again with the data model. If this doesn't work for you for some reason, then remove the old DataModel.sqlite file from the Library/Application Support folder and try again (or simply reset the Simulator or remove the app from your test device).

➤ Tag another location and add a photo to it. Hmm… if you look into the app's Documents directory, this seems to have overwritten the previous photo.

> **Exercise.** Try to debug this one on your own. What is going wrong here? This is a tough one!

Answer: When you create a new `Location` object, its `photoID` property gets a default value of 0. That means each `Location` initially has a `photoID` of 0. That should really be `nil`, which means "no photo".

➤ In **LocationDetailsViewController.swift**, add the following line near the top of `done()`:

```
@IBAction func done() {
    . . .
    if let temp = locationToEdit {
        . . .
    } else {
        . . .
        location.photoID = nil          // add this
    }
    . . .
```

You now set the `photoID` of a new `Location` object to `nil` so that the `hasPhoto` property correctly recognizes that these `Locations` as not having a photo yet.

➤ Run the app again and tag multiple locations with photos. Verify that now each photo is saved individually.

Verify photoID in SQLite

If you have Liya or another SQLite inspection tool, you can verify that each Location object has been given a unique photoID value (in the ZPHOTOID column):

The Location objects with unique photoId values in Liya

Edit the image

So far, all the changes you've made were for the Tag Location screen and adding new locations. Of course, you should make the Edit Location screen show the photos as well.

The change to `LocationDetailsViewController` is quite simple.

➤ Change `viewDidLoad()` in **LocationDetailsViewController.swift** to:

```
override func viewDidLoad() {
  super.viewDidLoad()

  if let location = locationToEdit {
    title = "Edit Location"
    // New code block
    if location.hasPhoto {
      if let theImage = location.photoImage {
        show(image: theImage)
      }
    }
    // End of new code
  }
  . . .
```

If the `Location` that you're editing has a photo, this calls `show(image:)` to display it in the photo cell.

Recall that the `photoImage` property returns an optional, `UIImage?`, so you use `if let` to unwrap it. This is another bit of defensive programming.

Sure, if `hasPhoto` is `true` there should always be a valid image file present. But it's possible to imagine a scenario where there isn't – the JPEG file could have been erased or corrupted – even though that "should" never happen. (I'm sure you've had your own share of computer gremlins eating important files.)

Note also what you **don't** do here: the `Location`'s image is *not* assigned to the `image` instance variable. If the user doesn't change the photo, then you don't need to write it out to a file again – it's already in that file and doing perfectly fine, thank you.

If you were to put the photo in the `image` variable, then `done()` would overwrite that existing file with the exact same data, which is a little silly. Therefore, the `image` instance variable will only be set when the user picks a new photo.

➤ Run the app and take a peek at the existing locations from the Locations or Map tabs. The Edit Location screen should now show the photos for the locations you're editing.

➤ Verify that you can also change the photo and that the JPEG file in the app's Documents directory gets overwritten when you press the Done button.

There's another editing operation the user can perform on a location: deletion. What happens to the image file when a location is deleted? At the moment nothing. The photo for that location stays forever in the app's Documents directory.

Clean up on location deletion

Let's add some code to remove the photo file, if it exists, when a `Location` object is deleted.

➤ First add a new method to **Location+CoreDataClass.swift**:

```
func removePhotoFile() {
  if hasPhoto {
    do {
      try FileManager.default.removeItem(at: photoURL)
    } catch {
      print("Error removing file: \(error)")
    }
  }
}
```

This code snippet can be used to remove any file or folder. The `FileManager` class has all kinds of useful methods for dealing with the file system.

➤ Deleting locations happens in **LocationsViewController.swift**. Add the following line to `tableView(_:commit:forRowAt:)`:

```
override func tableView(_ tableView: UITableView,
             commit editingStyle:
UITableViewCellEditingStyle,
             forRowAt indexPath: IndexPath) {
  if editingStyle == .delete {
    let location = fetchedResultsController.object(at:
                                          indexPath)

    location.removePhotoFile()                 // add this line
    managedObjectContext.delete(location)
    . . .
```

The new line calls `removePhotoFile()` on the `Location` object just before it is deleted from the Core Data context.

➤ Try it out. Add a new location and give it a photo. You should see the JPEG file in the Documents directory.

From the Locations screen, delete the location you just added and look in the Documents directory to make sure the JPEG file truly is a goner.

Thumbnails

Now that locations can have photos, it's a good idea to show thumbnails for these photos in the Locations tab. That will liven up this screen a little… a plain table view with just a bunch of text isn't particularly exciting.

Storyboard changes

➤ Go to the storyboard editor. In the prototype cell for the **Locations** scene, move the two labels to X = 76. Make them 230 points wide.

➤ Drag a new **Image View** into the cell. Place it at the top-left corner of the cell. Give it the following position: X = 16, Y = 2. Make it 52 by 52 points big.

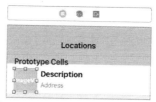

The table view cell has an image view

➤ Connect the image view to a new `UIImageView` outlet on `LocationCell`, named **photoImageView**.

> **Exercise.** Make this connection with the Assistant editor. Tip: you should connect the image view to the cell, not to the view controller.

Now you can put any image into the table view cell simply by passing it to the `LocationCell`'s `photoImageView` property.

Code changes

➤ Go to **LocationCell.swift** and add the following method:

```swift
func thumbnail(for location: Location) -> UIImage {
  if location.hasPhoto, let image = location.photoImage {
    return image
  }
  return UIImage()
}
```

This returns either the image from the `Location` or an empty placeholder image.

You should read this if statement as, "if the location has a photo, and I can unwrap `location.photoImage`, then return the unwrapped image."

You have previously seen the && ("logical and") used to combine two conditions, but you cannot write the above like this:

```
if location.hasPhoto && let image = location.photoImage
```

The && only works if both conditions are booleans, but here you're unwrapping an optional as well. In that case you must combine the two conditions with a comma.

➤ Call this new method from the end of `configure(for:)`:

```
photoImageView.image = thumbnail(for: location)
```

➤ Try it out. The Locations tab should now look something like this:

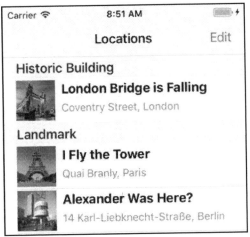

Images in the Locations table view

You've got thumbnails, all right!

But look closely and you'll see that the images are a little squashed again. That's because you didn't set the Aspect Fit content mode on the image view – but there's a bigger problem here. Literally.

These photos are potentially huge (2592 by 1936 pixels or more), even though the image view is only 52 pixels square. To make them fit, the image view needs to scale down the images by a lot (which is also why they look a little "gritty").

What if you have tens or even hundreds of locations? That is going to require a ton of memory and processing speed just to display these tiny thumbnails. A better solution is to scale down the images before you put them into the table view cell.

And what better way to do that than to use an extension?

Extensions

So far you've used extensions on your view controllers to group related functionality together, such as delegate methods. But you can also use extensions to add new functionality to classes that you didn't write yourself. That includes classes such as `UIImage` from the iOS frameworks. If you ever catch yourself thinking, "Gee, I wish object X had such-or-so method", then you can probably add that method by using an extension.

Suppose you want `String` to have a method for adding random words to a string. You could add the `addRandomWord()` method to `String` as follows.

First you create a new source file, for example **String+RandomWord.swift**:

```swift
import Foundation

extension String {
  func addRandomWord() -> String {
    let words = ["rabbit", "banana", "boat"]
    let value = arc4random_uniform(UInt32(words.count))
    let word = words[Int(value)]
    return self + word
  }
}
```

You can now call `addRandomWord()` on any `String` value in your code:

```swift
let someString = "Hello, "
let result = someString.addRandomWord()
print("The queen says: \(result)")
```

Extensions are pretty cool because they make it simple to add new functionality into an existing class. In other programming languages you would have to make a subclass and put your new methods in there, but extensions are often a cleaner solution.

Besides new methods, you can also add new computed properties, but you can't add regular instance variables. You can also use extensions on types that don't even allow inheritance, such as `struct`s and enums.

Thumbnails via UIImage extension

You are going to add an extension to `UIImage` that lets you resize the image. You'll use it as follows:

```swift
return image.resized(withBounds: CGSize(width: 52, height: 52))
```

The `resized(withBounds:)` method is new. The "bounds" is the size of the rectangle (or square in this case) that encloses the image. If the image itself is not square, then the resized image may actually be smaller than the bounds.

Let's write the extension.

➤ Add a new file to the project and choose the **Swift File** template. Name the file **UIImage+Resize.swift**.

➤ Replace the contents of this new file with:

```swift
import UIKit

extension UIImage {
    func resized(withBounds bounds: CGSize) -> UIImage {
        let horizontalRatio = bounds.width / size.width
        let verticalRatio = bounds.height / size.height
        let ratio = min(horizontalRatio, verticalRatio)
        let newSize = CGSize(width: size.width * ratio,
                             height: size.height * ratio)

        UIGraphicsBeginImageContextWithOptions(newSize, true, 0)
        draw(in: CGRect(origin: CGPoint.zero, size: newSize))
        let newImage = UIGraphicsGetImageFromCurrentImageContext()
        UIGraphicsEndImageContext()

        return newImage!
    }
}
```

This method first calculates how big the image should be in order to fit inside the bounds rectangle. It uses the "aspect fit" approach to keep the aspect ratio intact.

Then it creates a new image context and draws the image into that. We haven't really dealt with graphics contexts before, but they are an important concept in Core Graphics (it has nothing to do with the managed object context from Core Data, even though they both use the term "context").

Let's put this extension to work.

➤ Switch to **LocationCell.swift**. Update the `thumbnail(for:)` method:

```swift
func thumbnail(for location: Location) -> UIImage {
    if location.hasPhoto, let image = location.photoImage {
        return image.resized(withBounds: CGSize(width: 52,
                                                height: 52))
    }
    return UIImage()
}
```

➤ Run the app. The thumbnails should look like this:

London Bridge is Falling
Coventry Street, London

The photos are shrunk to the size of the thumbnails

The images are a little blurry and they still seem to be stretched out. This is because the content mode on the image view is still wrong.

Previously it shrunk the big photos to 52 by 52 points, but now the thumbnails may actually be smaller than 52 points (unless the photo was perfectly square) and they get scaled up to fill the entire image view rectangle.

➤ Go to the storyboard and set the **Content Mode** of the image view to **Center**.

➤ Run the app again and now the photos look A-OK:

London Bridge is Falling
Coventry Street, London

The thumbnails now have the correct aspect ratio

Exercise. Change the resizing function in the `UIImage` extension to resize using the "Aspect Fill" rules instead of the "Aspect Fit" rules. Both keep the aspect ratio intact but Aspect Fit keeps the entire image visible while Aspect Fill fills up the entire rectangle and may cut off parts of the sides. In other words, Aspect Fit scales to the longest side but Aspect Fill scales to the shortest side.

Aspect Fit
Keeps the entire image
but adds empty border

Aspect Fill
Fills up the whole frame
but cuts off sides

Aspect Fit vs. Aspect Fill

Handling low-memory situations

The `UIImagePickerController` is very memory-hungry. Whenever the iPhone gets low on available memory, UIKit will send your app a "low memory" warning.

When that happens you should reclaim as much memory as possible, or iOS might be forced to terminate the app. And that's something to avoid – users generally don't like apps that suddenly quit on them!

Chances are that your app gets one or more low-memory warnings while the image picker is open, especially when you run it on a device that has other apps suspended in the background. Photos take up a lot of space – especially when your camera is 5 or more megapixels – so it's no wonder that memory fills up quickly.

You can respond to memory warnings by overriding the `didReceiveMemoryWarning()` method in your view controllers to free up any memory you no longer need. This is often done for things that can easily be recalculated or recreated later, such as thumbnails or other cached objects.

UIKit is already pretty smart about low memory situations and it will do everything it can to release memory, including the thumbnail images of rows that are not (or no longer) visible in your table view.

For *MyLocations* there's not much that you need to do to free up additional memory, you can rely on UIKit to automatically take care of it. But in your own apps you might want to take extra measures, depending on the sort of cached data that you have.

By the way, on the Simulator you can trigger a low memory warning using the **Debug →
Simulate Memory Warning** menu item. It's smart to test your apps under low memory conditions, because they are likely to encounter such situations out in the wild once they're running on user devices.

Great! That concludes all the functionality for this app. Now it's time to fine-tune its looks.

You can find the project files for this chapter under **30 – Image Picker** in the Source Code folder.

Chapter 31: Polishing the App

Apps with appealing visuals sell better than ugly ones. Usually I don't wait with the special sauce until the end of a project, but for these apps it's clearer if you first get all the functionality in before you improve the looks. Now that the app works as it should, let's make it look good!

You're going to go from this:

To this:

The main screen gets the biggest makeover, but you'll also tweak the others a little.

You'll do the following in this chapter:

- **Convert placemarks to strings:** Refactor the code to display placemarks as text values so that the code is centralized and easier to use.

- **Back to black:** Change the appearance of the app to have a black background and light text.

- **The map screen:** Update the map screen to have icons for the action buttons instead of tet.

- **Fix the table views:** Update all the table views in the app to have black backgrounds with white text.

- **Polish the main screen:** Update the appearance of the main screen to add a bit of awesome sauce!

- **Make some noise:** Add a sound effect to the app.

- **The icon and launch images:** Add the app icon and launch images to complete the app.

Convert placemarks to strings

Let's begin by improving the code. I'm not really happy with the way the reverse geocoded street address gets converted from a CLPlacemark object into a string. It works, but the code is unwieldy and repetitive.

There are three places where this happens:

- CurrentLocationViewController, the main screen.

- LocationDetailsViewController, the Tag/Edit Location screen.

- LocationsViewController, the list of saved locations.

Let's start with the main screen. **CurrentLocationViewController.swift** has a method named string(from:) where this conversion happens. It's supposed to return a string that looks like this:

```
subThoroughfare thoroughfare
locality administrativeArea postalCode
```

This string goes into a UILabel that has room for two lines, so you use the \n character sequence to create a line-break between the thoroughfare and locality.

The problem is that any of these properties may be `nil`. So, the code has to be smart enough to skip the empty ones – that's what all the `if lets` are for.

What I don't like is that there's a lot of repetition going on in this method. You can refactor this.

Exercise. Try to make this method simpler by moving the common logic into a new method.

Answer: Here is how I did it. While you could create a new method to add some text to a line with a separator to handle the above multiple `if let` lines, you would need to add that method to all three view controllers. Of course, you could add the method to the Functions.swift file to centralize the method too...

But better still, what if you created a new `String` extension since this functionality is for adding some text to an existing string? Sounds like a plan?

➤ Add a new file to the project using the **Swift File** template. Name it **String+AddText**.

➤ Replace the contents of **String+AddText.swift** with:

```
extension String {
  mutating func add(text: String?,
    separatedBy separator: String) {
    if let text = text {
      if !isEmpty {
        self += separator
      }
      self += text
    }
  }
}
```

Most of the code should be pretty self-explanatory. You ask the string to add some text to itself, and if the string is currently not empty, you add the specified separator first before adding the new text.

Mutating

Notice the `mutating` keyword. You haven't seen this before. Sorry, it doesn't have anything to do with X-men – programming is certainly fun, but not *that* fun :]

When a method changes the value of a struct, it must be marked as mutating. Recall that String is a struct, which is a value type, and therefore cannot be modified when declared with let.

The mutating keyword tells Swift that add(text:separatedBy:) can only be used on strings that are made with var, but not on strings made with let.

If you try to modify self in a method on a struct that is not marked as mutating, Swift considers this an error.

You don't need to use the mutating keyword on methods inside a class because classes are reference types and can always be mutated, even if they are declared with let.

➤ Switch over to **CurrentLocationViewController.swift** and replace string(from:) with the following:

```
func string(from placemark: CLPlacemark) -> String {
  var line1 = ""
  line1.add(text: placemark.subThoroughfare, separatedBy: "")
  line1.add(text: placemark.thoroughfare, separatedBy: " ")

  var line2 = ""
  line2.add(text: placemark.locality, separatedBy: "")
  line2.add(text: placemark.administrativeArea,
      separatedBy: " ")
  line2.add(text: placemark.postalCode, separatedBy: " ")

  line1.add(text: line2, separatedBy: "\n")
  return line1
}
```

That looks a lot cleaner. The logic that decides whether or not to add a CLPlacemark property to the string now lives in your new String extension, so you no longer need all those if let statements. You also use add(text:separatedBy:) to add line2 to line1 with a newline character in between.

➤ Run the app to see if it works.

There's still a small thing you can do to improve the new add(text:separatedBy:) method. Remember default parameter values? You can use them here.

➤ In **String+AddText.swift**, change the line that defines the method to:

```
mutating func add(text: String?,
                  separatedBy separator: String = "") {
```

Now, instead of:

```
line1.add(text: placemark.subThoroughfare, separatedBy: "")
```

You can write:

```
line1.add(text: placemark.subThoroughfare)
```

The default value for `separator` is an empty string. If the `separatedBy` parameter is left out, `separator` will be set to `""`.

➤ Make these changes in **CurrentLocationViewController.swift**:

```
func string(from placemark: CLPlacemark) -> String {
    . . .
    line1.add(text: placemark.subThoroughfare)
    . . .
    line2.add(text: placemark.locality)
    . . .
```

Where the separator is the empty string, you leave out the `separatedBy: ""` part of the method call. (Note that the other instances of `add(text:separatedBy:)` in the method don't have empty strings as the separator but instead, have a space.)

Now you have a pretty clean solution that you can re-use in the other two view controllers.

➤ In **LocationDetailsViewController.swift**, replace the `string(from:)` code with:

```
func string(from placemark: CLPlacemark) -> String {
    var line = ""
    line.add(text: placemark.subThoroughfare)
    line.add(text: placemark.thoroughfare, separatedBy: " ")
    line.add(text: placemark.locality, separatedBy: ", ")
    line.add(text: placemark.administrativeArea,
        separatedBy: ", ")
    line.add(text: placemark.postalCode, separatedBy: " ")
    line.add(text: placemark.country, separatedBy: ", ")
    return line
}
```

It's slightly different from how the main screen does it. There are no newline characters and some of the elements are separated by commas instead of just spaces. Newlines aren't necessary here because the label will word-wrap.

The final place where placemarks are shown is `LocationsViewController`. However, this class doesn't have a `string(from:)` method. Instead, the logic for formatting the address lives in `LocationCell`.

➤ Go to **LocationCell.swift**. Change the relevant part of `configure(for:)`:

```
func configure(for location: Location) {
  . . .
  if let placemark = location.placemark {
    var text = ""
    text.add(text: placemark.subThoroughfare)
    text.add(text: placemark.thoroughfare, separatedBy: " ")
    text.add(text: placemark.locality, separatedBy: ", ")
    addressLabel.text = text
  } else {
    . . .
```

You only show the street and the city, so the conversion is simpler.

And that's it for placemarks.

Back to black

Right now the app looks like a typical standard iOS app: lots of white, gray tab bar, blue tint color. Let's go for a radically different look and paint the whole thing black.

➤ Open the storyboard and go to the **Current Location View Controller**. Select the top-level view and change its **Background Color** to **Black Color**.

➤ Select all the labels (probably easiest from the Document Outline since they are now invisible) and set their **Color** to **White Color**.

➤ Change the **Font** of the (**Latitude/Longitude goes here**) labels to **System Bold 17**.

➤ Select the two buttons and change their **Font** to **System Bold 20**, to make them slightly larger. You may need to resize their frames to make the text fit (remember, ⌘= is the magic keyboard shortcut).

➤ In the **File inspector**, change **Global Tint** to the color **Red: 255, Green: 238, Blue: 136**. That makes the buttons and other interactive elements yellow, which stands out nicely against the black background.

➤ Select the Get My Location button and change its **Text Color** to **White Color**. This provides some contrast between the two buttons.

The storyboard should look like this:

The new yellow-on-black design

When you run the app, there are two obvious problems:

1. The status bar text has become invisible (it is black text on a black background)

2. The grey tab bar sticks out like a sore thumb (also, the yellow tint color doesn't get applied to the tab bar icons)

To fix this, you can use the `UIAppearance` API. This is a set of methods that lets you customize the look of the standard UIKit controls.

Use UIAppearance

When customizing the UI, you can customize your app on a per-control basis, or you can use the "appearance proxy" to change the look of all of the controls of a particular type at once. That's what you're going to do here.

➤ Add the following method to **AppDelegate.swift**:

```swift
func customizeAppearance() {
  UINavigationBar.appearance().barTintColor = UIColor.black
  UINavigationBar.appearance().titleTextAttributes = [
    NSAttributedStringKey.foregroundColor:
    UIColor.white ]

  UITabBar.appearance().barTintColor = UIColor.black

  let tintColor = UIColor(red: 255/255.0, green: 238/255.0,
                          blue: 136/255.0, alpha: 1.0)
  UITabBar.appearance().tintColor = tintColor
}
```

This changes the "bar tint" or background color of all navigation bars and tab bars in the app to black in one fell swoop. It also sets the color of the navigation bar's title label to white and applies the tint color to the tab bar.

➤ Call this method from the top of application(_:didFinishLaunchingWithOptions:):

```
func application(_ application: UIApplication,
               didFinishLaunchingWithOptions . . .) -> Bool {
   customizeAppearance()
   . . .
}
```

This looks better already.

The tab bar is now nearly black and has yellow icons

On the Locations and Map screens you can clearly see that the bars now have a dark tint:

The navigation and tab bars appear in a dark color

Keep in mind that the bar tint is not the true background color. The bars are still translucent, which is why they appear as a medium gray rather than pure black.

Tab bar icons

The icons in the tab bar could also do with some improvement. The Xcode Tabbed Application template put a bunch of cruft in the app that you're no longer using - let's get rid of it.

➤ Remove the **SecondViewController.swift** file from the project.

➤ Remove the **first** and **second** images from the asset catalog (Assets.xcassets).

Tab bar images should be basic grayscale images of up to 30 × 30 points (that is 60 × 60 pixels for Retina and 90 × 90 pixels for Retina HD). You don't have to tint the images; iOS will automatically draw them in the proper color.

➤ The resources for this **tutorial** include an **Images** directory. Add the files from this folder to the asset catalog.

➤ Go to the storyboard. Select the **Tab Bar Item** of the navigation controller embedding the Current Location screen. In the **Attributes inspector**, under **Image** choose **Tag**. This is the name of one of the images you've just added.

Choosing an image for a Tab Bar Item

➤ For the Tab Bar Item of the navigation controller attached to the Locations screen, choose the **Locations** image.

➤ For the Tab Bar Item of the navigation controller embedding the Map View Controller, choose the **Map** image.

Now the tab bar looks a lot more appealing:

The tab bar with proper icons

The status bar

The status bar is currently invisible on the Tag screen and appears as black text on dark gray on the other two screens. It would look better if the status bar text was white instead.

To do this, you need to override the `preferredStatusBarStyle` property in your view controllers and make it return the value `.lightContent`.

The simplest way to make the status bar white for all your view controllers in the entire app is to replace the `UITabBarController` with your own subclass.

➤ Add a new source file to the project and name it **MyTabBarController.swift**.

➤ Replace the contents of **MyTabBarController.swift** with:

```swift
import UIKit

class MyTabBarController: UITabBarController {
  override var preferredStatusBarStyle: UIStatusBarStyle {
    return .lightContent
  }

  override var childViewControllerForStatusBarStyle:
              UIViewController? {
    return nil
  }
}
```

By returning `nil` from `childViewControllerForStatusBarStyle`, the tab bar controller will look at its own `preferredStatusBarStyle` property instead of those from the other view controllers.

➤ In the storyboard, select the Tab Bar Controller and in the **Identity inspector** change its **Class** to **MyTabBarController**. This tells the storyboard that it should now create an instance of your subclass when the app starts up.

That's right, you can replace standard UIKit components with your own subclasses!

Subclassing lets you change what the built-in UIKit objects do – that's the power of object-oriented programming. But don't get carried away and alter their behavior *too* much - before you know it, your app ends up with an identity crisis!

`MyTabBarController` still does everything that the standard `UITabBarController` does. You only override `preferredStatusBarStyle` to change the status bar color.

You can plug this `MyTabBarController` class into any app that uses a tab bar controller, and from then on, all its view controllers will have a white status bar.

Now the status bar is white everywhere:

The status bar is visible again

Well, almost everywhere... When you open the photo picker, the status bar fades to black again. Subclasses to the rescue again!

➤ Add a new file to the project and name it **MyImagePickerController.swift**. (Getting a sense of déjà vu?)

➤ Replace the contents of **MyImagePickerController.swift** with:

```swift
import UIKit

class MyImagePickerController: UIImagePickerController {
  override var preferredStatusBarStyle: UIStatusBarStyle {
    return .lightContent
  }
}
```

Now, instead of instantiating the standard `UIImagePickerController` to pick a photo, you should use this new subclass.

➤ Go to **LocationDetailsViewController.swift**. In `takePhotoWithCamera()` and `choosePhotoFromLibrary()`, change the line that creates the image picker to:

```swift
let imagePicker = MyImagePickerController()
```

This is allowed because `MyImagePickerController` is a subclass of the standard `UIImagePickerController` - it has the same properties and methods. As far as UIKit is concerned, the two are interchangeable. So, you can use your subclass anywhere you'd use `UIImagePickerController`.

While you're at it, the photo picker still uses the standard blue tint color. That makes its navigation bar buttons hard to read. The fix is simple: set the tint color on the Image Picker Controller just before you present it.

➤ Add the following line to the two methods:

```swift
imagePicker.view.tintColor = view.tintColor
```

Now the Cancel button appears in yellow instead of blue.

The photo picker with the new colors

There is one more thing to change. When the app starts up, iOS looks in the Info.plist file to determine whether it should show a status bar while the app launches, and if so, what color that status bar should be.

Right now, it's set to Default, which is the black status bar.

➤ Just to be thorough, go to the **Project Settings** screen. In the **General** tab, under **Deployment Info** is a **Status Bar Style** option. Change this to **Light**.

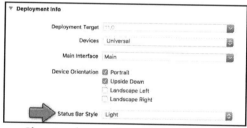

Changing the status bar style for app startup

And now the status bar really is white everywhere!

The map screen

The Map screen currently has a somewhat busy navigation bar with three pieces of text in it: the title and the two buttons.

The bar button items have text labels

The design advice that Apple gives is to prefer text to icons because icons tend to be harder to understand. The disadvantage of using text is that it makes your navigation bar more crowded.

There are two possible solutions:

1. Remove the title. If the purpose of the screen is obvious, which it is in this case, then the title "Map" is superfluous. You might as well remove it.

2. Keep the title but replace the button labels with icons.

For this app, you'll choose the second option.

➤ Go to the Map scene in the storyboard and select the **Locations** bar button item. In the **Attributes inspector**, under **Image** choose **Pin**. This will remove the text from the button.

➤ For the User bar button item, choose the **User** image.

The Map screen now looks like this:

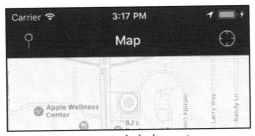

Map screen with the button icons

Notice that the dot for the user's current location is drawn in the yellow tint color (it was a blue dot before).

The ⓘ button on the map annotations also appears in yellow, making it hard to see on the white callout. Fortunately, you can override the tint color on a per-view basis. There's no rule that says the tint color has to be the same everywhere!

➤ In **MapViewController.swift**, in the method `mapView(_:viewFor:)`, add this below the line that sets `pinView.pinTintColor`:

```
pinView.tintColor = UIColor(white: 0.0, alpha: 0.5)
```

This sets the annotation's tint color to half-opaque black:

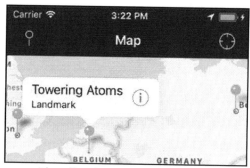

The callout button is now easier to see

Fix the table views

The app is starting to shape up but there are still some details to take care of. The table views, for example, are still very white.

Unfortunately, what UIAppearance can do for table views is very limited. So, you'll have to customize each of the table views individually.

This can be done either via code, or via storyboard. Personally, I prefer to make UI changes as much as possible via storyboards since then I can see the actual changes such as color, spacing, font etc. and be sure how a change affects the rest of the UI. So, let's do these changes via storyboards as much as possible.

Storyboard changes for the Locations scene

➤ Open the storyboard and select the table view for the Locations scene. Set **Table View - Separator** color to **white with 20% Opacity**, **Scroll View - Indicators** to **white**, and **View - Background** to **black**.

Table view color changes

This makes the table view itself black but does not alter the cells.

➤ Select the prototype cell in the table view and set its **View - Background** to **black**.

➤ Next, select the Description label in the cell and set its **Label - Color** and **Label - Highlighted** color to **white**.

➤ Select the Address label and set its **Label - Color** and **Label - Highlighted** color to **white with 40% Opacity**.

➤ Run the app. That's starting to look pretty good already:

The table view cells are now white-on-black

That's as far as we can get with customization via storyboard. But there are a couple of small issues still.

Code changes for the Locations view

The first, when you tap a cell it still lights up in a bright color, which is a little jarring. It would look better if the selection color was more subdued.

Unfortunately, there is no "selectionColor" property on `UITableViewCell`, but you can give it a different view to display when it is selected via a `UITableViewCell`'s `selectedBackgroundView` property.

➤ In **LocationCell.swift**, replace `awakeFromNib()` with the following:

```
override func awakeFromNib() {
  super.awakeFromNib()
  let selection = UIView(frame: CGRect.zero)
  selection.backgroundColor = UIColor(white: 1.0, alpha: 0.2)
  selectedBackgroundView = selection
}
```

Every object that comes from a storyboard has the `awakeFromNib()` method. This method is invoked when UIKit loads the object from the storyboard. It's the ideal place to customize its looks.

Here, you create a new `UIView` filled with a dark gray color. This new view is placed on top of the cell's background when the user taps on the cell. It will look like this:

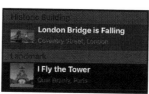

The selected cell has a subtly different background color

The second issue is that the section headers are on the heavy side. There is no easy way to customize the existing headers, but you can replace them with a view of your own.

➤ Go to **LocationsViewController.swift** and add the following table view delegate method:

```swift
override func tableView(_ tableView: UITableView,
      viewForHeaderInSection section: Int) -> UIView? {

  let labelRect = CGRect(x: 15,
                         y: tableView.sectionHeaderHeight - 14,
                         width: 300, height: 14)
  let label = UILabel(frame: labelRect)
  label.font = UIFont.boldSystemFont(ofSize: 11)

  label.text = tableView.dataSource!.tableView!(
               tableView, titleForHeaderInSection: section)

  label.textColor = UIColor(white: 1.0, alpha: 0.4)
  label.backgroundColor = UIColor.clear

  let separatorRect = CGRect(
        x: 15, y: tableView.sectionHeaderHeight - 0.5,
        width: tableView.bounds.size.width - 15, height: 0.5)
  let separator = UIView(frame: separatorRect)
  separator.backgroundColor = tableView.separatorColor

  let viewRect = CGRect(x: 0, y: 0,
                        width: tableView.bounds.size.width,
                        height: tableView.sectionHeaderHeight)
  let view = UIView(frame: viewRect)
  view.backgroundColor = UIColor(white: 0, alpha: 0.85)
  view.addSubview(label)
  view.addSubview(separator)
  return view
}
```

This method gets called once for each section in the table view. Here, you create a label for the section name, a 1-pixel high view that functions as a separator line, and a container view to hold these two subviews.

It looks like this:

The section headers now draw much less attention to themselves

If the section header has now completely disappeared on you, then add the following line to viewDidLoad():

```
tableView.sectionHeaderHeight = 28
```

This fixes a bug in Xcode that sets the section header height to -1 if you leave it at its default value of 28 in Interface Builder.

Note: Did you notice anything special about the following line?

```
label.text = tableView.dataSource!.tableView!(tableView,
titleForHeaderInSection: section)
```

This asks the table view's data source for the text to put in the header. The dataSource property is an optional so you're using ! to unwrap it. But that's not the only ! in this line…

You're calling the tableView(_:titleForHeaderInSection:) method on the table view's data source, which is of course the LocationsViewController itself.

But this method is an optional method – not all data sources need to implement it. Because of that you have to *unwrap the method* with the exclamation mark in order to use it. Unwrapping methods… does it get any crazier than that?

By the way, you can also write this as:

```
label.text = self.tableView(tableView, titleForHeaderInSection:
section)
```

> Here you use `self` to directly access that method on `LocationsViewController`. Both ways achieve exactly the same thing, since the view controller happens to be the table view's data source.

Another small improvement you can make is to always put the section headers in uppercase.

➤ Change `tableView(_:titleForHeaderInSection:)` to:

```
override func tableView(_ tableView: UITableView,
    titleForHeaderInSection section: Int) -> String? {
  let sectionInfo = fetchedResultsController.sections![section]
  return sectionInfo.name.uppercased()
}
```

Now the section headers look even better:

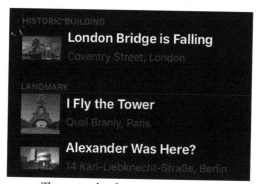

The section header text is in uppercase

Currently, if a location does not have a photo, there is a black gap where the thumbnail is supposed to be. That doesn't look very professional. It's better to show a placeholder image. You already added one to the asset catalog when you imported the Images folder.

➤ In **LocationCell.swift**'s `thumbnail(for:)`, replace the last line that returns an empty `UIImage` with:

```
return UIImage(named: "No Photo")!
```

Recall that `UIImage(named:)` is a failable initializer, so it returns an optional. Don't forget the exclamation point at the end to unwrap the optional.

Now locations without photos appear like so:

A location using the placeholder image

That makes it a lot clearer to the user that the photo is missing. (As opposed to, say, being a photo of a black hole.)

The placeholder image is round. That's the fashion for thumbnail images on iOS these days, and it's pretty easy to make the other thumbnails rounded too.

➤ Still in **LocationCell.swift**, add the following lines to the end of `awakeFromNib()`:

```
// Rounded corners for images
photoImageView.layer.cornerRadius =
                    photoImageView.bounds.size.width / 2
photoImageView.clipsToBounds = true
separatorInset = UIEdgeInsets(top: 0, left: 82, bottom: 0,
                                                right: 0)
```

This gives the image view rounded corners with a radius that is equal to half the width of the image, which makes it a perfect circle.

The `clipsToBounds` setting makes sure that the image view respects these rounded corners and does not draw outside them.

The `separatorInset` moves the separator lines between the cells a bit to the right so there are no lines between the thumbnail images.

The thumbnails are now circular

> **Note:** As you'll notice from the above image, the rounded thumbnails don't look very good if the original photo isn't square. You may want to change the Mode of the image view back to Aspect Fill or Scale to Fill so that the thumbnail always fills up the entire image view.

The labels in this screen have one final problem: they do not extend to cover the full width of larger screens - remember that there are screens wider than the 320 points you've been designing for.

The obvious solution is to set autoresizing on the labels so they automatically resize.

➤ Change the autoresizing settings of the Description and Address labels to:

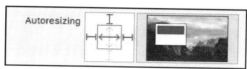

The autoresizing settings for the labels

Tip: To verify that the labels now take advantage of all the available screen space on larger screens, give them a non-transparent background color. I like bright purple!

➤ Add these lines to `awakeFromNib()` (in LocationCell.swift, of course) and run the app:

```
descriptionLabel.backgroundColor = UIColor.purple
addressLabel.backgroundColor = UIColor.purple
```

This is how it looks on an iPhone 8 Plus screen:

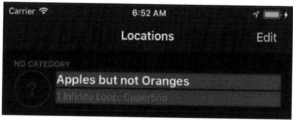

The labels resize to fit the iPhone 8 Plus

When you're done testing, don't forget to remove the lines that set the background color. It's useful as a debugging tool, but not particularly pretty to look at.

There are two other table views in the app and they get a similar treatment.

Table view changes for Tag Location screen

➤ Open the storyboard and select the table view for the Tag Location scene. Set **Table View - Separator** color to **white with 20% Opacity, Scroll View - Style** to **white**, and **View - Background** to **black**.

➤ Select all the static cells in the table view and set their **View - Background** to **black**.

➤ Select the Description text view and set its **Text View - Color** to white, and **View - Background** to **black**.

➤ Select the Add Photo label and set its **Label - Color** and **Label - Highlighted** color to white.

➤ Select the main label from all the cells with the Right Detail style and set their **Label - Color** and **Label - Highlighted** color to **white**.

➤ Select the detail label from all the cells with the Right Detail style and set their **Label - Color** and **Label - Highlighted** color to **white with 40% Opacity**.

➤ Select the Address label and set its **Label - Color** and **Label - Highlighted** color to white.

➤ Select the Address detail label and set its **Label - Color** and **Label - Highlighted** color to **white with 40% Opacity**.

That completes all the storyboard changes but there are a few code changes left.

Previously, you modified the cell's subclass to add the selection highlighting. However, you have static table view cells here and don't have a subclass to modify. Don't despair yet though, the table view delegate has a handy method that comes in useful here.

➤ Open **LocationDetailsViewController.swift** and add the following method:

```
override func tableView(_ tableView: UITableView,
                willDisplay cell: UITableViewCell,
              forRowAt indexPath: IndexPath) {
  let selection = UIView(frame: CGRect.zero)
  selection.backgroundColor = UIColor(white: 1.0, alpha: 0.2)
  cell.selectedBackgroundView = selection
}
```

The willDisplay delegate method is called just before a cell becomes visible. So, you can do some last-minute customizations on the cell and its contents in this method.

➤ Run the app. The Tag Location screen should now looks like this:

The Tag Location screen with styling applied

Table view changes for the Category Picker screen

The final table view is the category picker. There's nothing new here, the changes are basically the same as before.

➤ Open the storyboard and select the table view for the Category Picker view controller. Set **Table View - Separator** color to **white with 20% Opacity**, **Scroll View - Style** to **white**, and **View - Background** to **black**.

➤ Select the prototype cell in the table view and set its **View - Background** to **black**.

➤ Select the label in the prototype cell and set its **Label - Color** and **Label - Highlighted** color to **white**.

All that's left is to set the cell background for highlighted cells. Since there is no subclass for the cell, do I hear you saying that we should use the table view delegate's `willDisplay` method again? That certainly is an option ...

But rememember that we are dealing with a prototype cell here. That means that it already is being set up in code via `cellForRowAt`. So why not simply use the existing method to do the extra work? (Remember, there's often multiple ways to do the same thing.)

➤ Open **CategoryPickerViewController.swift** and add the following code to cellForRowAt, just before the return:

```
override func tableView(_ tableView: UITableView,
            cellForRowAt indexPath: IndexPath) ->
            UITableViewCell {
    . . .
    let selection = UIView(frame: CGRect.zero)
    selection.backgroundColor = UIColor(white: 1.0, alpha: 0.2)
    cell.selectedBackgroundView = selection
    // End new code
    return cell
}
```

Now the category picker is dressed in black as well. It's a bit of work to change the visuals of all these table views by hand, but it's worth it.

The category picker is lookin' sharp

Polish the main screen

I'm pretty happy with all the other screens, but the main screen needs a bit more work to be presentable.

Here's what you'll do:

- Show a logo when the app starts up. Normally such splash screens are bad for the user experience, but here I think we can get away with it.

- Make the logo disappear with an animation when the user taps Get My Location.

- While the app is fetching the coordinates, show an animated activity spinner to make it even clearer to the user that something is going on.

- Hide the Latitude: and Longitude: labels until the app has found coordinates.

You will first hide the text labels from the screen until the app actually has some coordinates to display. The only label that will be visible until then is the one at the top and it will say "Searching…" or give some kind of error message.

In order to do this, you must have outlets for the labels.

➤ Add the following properties to **CurrentLocationViewController.swift**:

```
@IBOutlet weak var latitudeTextLabel: UILabel!
@IBOutlet weak var longitudeTextLabel: UILabel!
```

You'll put the logic for updating these labels in a single place, updateLabels(), so that hiding and showing them is pretty straightforward.

➤ Change updateLabels() in **CurrentLocationViewController.swift**:

```
func updateLabels() {
  if let location = location {
    . . .
    latitudeTextLabel.isHidden = false
    longitudeTextLabel.isHidden = false
  } else {
    . . .
    latitudeTextLabel.isHidden = true
    longitudeTextLabel.isHidden = true
  }
}
```

➤ Connect the **Latitude:** and **Longitude:** labels in the storyboard to the latitudeTextLabel and longitudeTextLabel outlets.

➤ Run the app and verify that the **Latitude:** and **Longitude:** labels only appear when you have obtained GPS coordinates.

The first impression

The main screen looks decent and is completely functional, but it could do with more pizzazz. It lacks the "Wow!" factor. You want to impress users the first time they start your app, in order to keep them coming back. To pull this off, you'll add a logo and a cool animation.

When the user hasn't yet pressed the Get My Location button, there are no GPS coordinates and the Tag Location button is hidden. Instead of showing a completely blank upper panel, you can show a large version of the app's icon.

The welcome screen of MyLocations

When the user taps the Get My Location button, the icon rolls out of the screen (it's round so that kinda makes sense) while a panel with the GPS status will slide in.

This is pretty easy to program thanks to the power of Core Animation and it makes the app a whole lot more impressive for first-time users.

First, you need to move the labels into a new container subview.

➤ Open the storyboard and go to the **Current Location View Controller**. In the Document Outline, select the six labels and the Tag Location button. With these seven views selected, choose **Editor** → **Embed In** → **View** from the Xcode menu bar.

This creates a blank, white UIView and puts these labels and the button inside that new view.

➤ Change the **Background** color of this new container view to **Clear Color**, so that everything becomes visible again.

The layout of the screen hasn't changed; you have simply reorganized the view hierarchy so that you can easily manipulate and animate this group of views as a whole. Grouping views in a container view is a common technique for building complex layouts.

➤ To avoid problems on smaller screens, make sure that the Get My Location button sits higher up in the view hierarchy than the container view. If the button sits under another view you cannot tap it anymore.

Non-intuitively, in the Document Outline the button must sit below the container view. If it doesn't, drag to rearrange.

Get My Location must sit below the container view in the Document Outline

Note: When you drag the Get My Location button, make sure you're not dropping it into the container view. The view you just added and the Get My Location button should sit at the same level in the view hierarchy.

➤ Add the following outlet to **CurrentLocationViewController.swift**:

```
@IBOutlet weak var containerView: UIView!
```

➤ In the storyboard, connect the new container UIView to the containerView outlet.

Now on to the good stuff!

➤ Add the following instance variables to **CurrentLocationViewController.swift**:

```
var logoVisible = false

lazy var logoButton: UIButton = {
  let button = UIButton(type: .custom)
  button.setBackgroundImage(UIImage(named: "Logo"),
                            for: .normal)
  button.sizeToFit()
  button.addTarget(self, action: #selector(getLocation),
                   for: .touchUpInside)
  button.center.x = self.view.bounds.midX
  button.center.y = 220
  return button
}()
```

The logo image is actually a button, so that you can tap the logo to get started. The app will show this button when it starts up, and when it doesn't have anything better to display (for example, after you press Stop and there are no coordinates and no error). To orchestrate this, you'll use the boolean logoVisible.

The button is a "custom" type UIButton, meaning that it has no title text or other frills. It draws the **Logo.png** image and calls the getLocation() method when tapped.

This is another one of those lazily loaded properties; I did that because it's nice to keep all the initialization logic inline with the declaration of the property.

➤ Add the following method:

```
func showLogoView() {
  if !logoVisible {
    logoVisible = true
    containerView.isHidden = true
    view.addSubview(logoButton)
  }
}
```

This hides the container view so the labels disappear, and puts the `logoButton` object on the screen. This is the first time `logoButton` is accessed, so the lazy loading kicks in.

➤ In `updateLabels()`, change the line that says,

```
statusMessage = "Tap 'Get My Location' to Start"
```

into:

```
statusMessage = ""
showLogoView()
```

This new logic makes the logo appear when there are no coordinates or error messages to display. That's also the state at startup time, so when you run the app now, you should be greeted by the logo.

➤ Run the app to check it out.

When you tap the logo (or Get My Location), the logo should disappear and the panel with the labels ought to show up. That doesn't happen yet, so let's add some more code to do that.

➤ Add the following method:

```
func hideLogoView() {
  logoVisible = false
  containerView.isHidden = false
  logoButton.removeFromSuperview()
}
```

This is the counterpart to `showLogoView()`. For now, it simply removes the button with the logo and un-hides the container view with the GPS coordinates.

➤ Add the following to `getLocation()`, right after the authorization status checks:

```
if logoVisible {
  hideLogoView()
}
```

Before it starts the location manager, this first removes the logo from the screen if it was visible.

Currently, there is no animation code to be seen. When doing complicated layout stuff such as this, I always first want to make sure the basics work. If they do, you can make it look fancy with an animation afterwards.

➤ Run the app. You should see the screen with the logo. Press the Get My Location button and the logo is replaced by the coordinate labels.

Great! *Now* you can add the animation. The only method you have to change is hideLogoView().

➤ First, give CurrentLocationViewController the ability to handle animation events by making it the CAAnimationDelegate:

```
class CurrentLocationViewController: UIViewController,
          CLLocationManagerDelegate, CAAnimationDelegate {
```

➤ Then replace hideLogoView() with:

```
func hideLogoView() {
  if !logoVisible { return }

  logoVisible = false
  containerView.isHidden = false
  containerView.center.x = view.bounds.size.width * 2
  containerView.center.y = 40 +
    containerView.bounds.size.height / 2

  let centerX = view.bounds.midX

  let panelMover = CABasicAnimation(keyPath: "position")
  panelMover.isRemovedOnCompletion = false
  panelMover.fillMode = kCAFillModeForwards
  panelMover.duration = 0.6
  panelMover.fromValue = NSValue(cgPoint: containerView.center)
  panelMover.toValue = NSValue(cgPoint:
      CGPoint(x: centerX, y: containerView.center.y))
  panelMover.timingFunction = CAMediaTimingFunction(
            name: kCAMediaTimingFunctionEaseOut)
  panelMover.delegate = self
  containerView.layer.add(panelMover, forKey: "panelMover")

  let logoMover = CABasicAnimation(keyPath: "position")
  logoMover.isRemovedOnCompletion = false
  logoMover.fillMode = kCAFillModeForwards
  logoMover.duration = 0.5
  logoMover.fromValue = NSValue(cgPoint: logoButton.center)
  logoMover.toValue = NSValue(cgPoint:
```

```
          CGPoint(x: -centerX, y: logoButton.center.y))
   logoMover.timingFunction = CAMediaTimingFunction(
              name: kCAMediaTimingFunctionEaseIn)
   logoButton.layer.add(logoMover, forKey: "logoMover")

   let logoRotator = CABasicAnimation(keyPath:
                    "transform.rotation.z")
   logoRotator.isRemovedOnCompletion = false
   logoRotator.fillMode = kCAFillModeForwards
   logoRotator.duration = 0.5
   logoRotator.fromValue = 0.0
   logoRotator.toValue = -2 * Double.pi
   logoRotator.timingFunction = CAMediaTimingFunction(
              name: kCAMediaTimingFunctionEaseIn)
   logoButton.layer.add(logoRotator, forKey: "logoRotator")
 }
```

This creates three animations that are played at the same time:

1. The containerView is placed outside the screen (somewhere on the right) and moved to the center.

2. The logo image view slides out of the screen.

3. The logo image also rotates around its center, giving the impression that it's rolling away.

Because the "panelMover" animation takes longest, you set a delegate on it so that you will be notified when the entire animation is over.

➤ Now add the necessary CAAnimationDelegate method:

```
// MARK:- Animation Delegate Methods
func animationDidStop(_ anim: CAAnimation,
              finished flag: Bool) {
  containerView.layer.removeAllAnimations()
  containerView.center.x = view.bounds.size.width / 2
  containerView.center.y = 40 +
              containerView.bounds.size.height / 2
  logoButton.layer.removeAllAnimations()
  logoButton.removeFromSuperview()
}
```

This cleans up after the animations and removes the logo button, as you no longer need it.

➤ Run the app. Tap on Get My Location to make the logo disappear. I think the animation looks pretty cool.

Tip: To get the logo back so you can try again, first choose **Location → None** from the Simulator's **Debug** menu. Then tap Get My Location followed by Stop to make the logo reappear.

Apple says that good apps should "surprise and delight", and modest animations such as these really make your apps more interesting to use – as long as you don't overdo it!

Add an activity indicator

When the user taps the Get My Location button, you currently change the button's text to say Stop to indicate the change of state. You can make it even clearer to the user that something is going on by adding an animated activity "spinner".

It will look like this:

The animated activity spinner shows that the app is busy

UIKit comes with a standard control for this, `UIActivityIndicatorView`. You could add the spinner to the storyboard (and that's the way I generally prefer to do things). However, it's good to learn diffrent techniques and so you'll create the spinner in code this time.

The code to change the appearance of the Get My Location button sits in the `configureGetButton()` method. That's also a good place to show and hide the spinner.

➤ Replace `configureGetButton()` with the following:

```swift
func configureGetButton() {
  let spinnerTag = 1000

  if updatingLocation {
    getButton.setTitle("Stop", for: .normal)

    if view.viewWithTag(spinnerTag) == nil {
      let spinner = UIActivityIndicatorView(
            activityIndicatorStyle: .white)
      spinner.center = messageLabel.center
      spinner.center.y += spinner.bounds.size.height/2 + 15
      spinner.startAnimating()
      spinner.tag = spinnerTag
      containerView.addSubview(spinner)
    }
  } else {
    getButton.setTitle("Get My Location", for: .normal)
```

```
    if let spinner = view.viewWithTag(spinnerTag) {
      spinner.removeFromSuperview()
    }
  }
}
```

In addition to changing the button text to "Stop", you create a new instance of `UIActivityIndicatorView`. Then you do some calculations to position the spinner view below the message label at the top of the screen. The call to `addSubview()` actually adds the spinner to the container view and makes it visible.

To keep track of this spinner view, you give it a tag of 1000. You could use an instance variable but this is just as easy and it keeps everything local to the `configureGetButton()` method. It's nice to have everything in one place.

When it's time to revert the button to its old state, you call `removeFromSuperview()` to remove the activity indicator view from the screen.

And that's all you need to do.

➤ Run the app. There should now be a cool little animation while the app is busy talking to the GPS satellites.

Make some noise

Visual feedback is important, but you can't expect users to keep their eyes glued to the screen all the time, especially if an operation might take a few seconds or more.

Emitting an unobtrusive sound is a good way to alert the user that a task is complete. When your iPhone has sent an email, for example, you hear a soft "whoosh" sound.

You're going to add a sound effect to the app too, which is to be played when the first reverse geocoding successfully completes. That seems like a reasonable moment to alert the user that GPS and address information has been captured.

There are many ways to play sounds on iOS, but you're going to use one of the simplest: system sounds. The System Sound API is intended for short beeps and other notification sounds, which is exactly the type of sound that you want to play here.

➤ Add an import for AudioToolbox, the framework for playing system sounds, to the top of **CurrentLocationViewController.swift**:

```
import AudioToolbox
```

➤ Add a `soundID` instance variable:

```
var soundID: SystemSoundID = 0
```

Because writing just 0 would normally give you a variable of type Int, you explicitly mention the type that you want it to be: SystemSoundID. This is a numeric identifier – sometimes called a "handle" – that refers to a system sound object. 0 means no sound has been loaded yet.

➤ Add the following methods to the class:

```
// MARK:- Sound effects
func loadSoundEffect(_ name: String) {
  if let path = Bundle.main.path(forResource: name,
                                 ofType: nil) {
    let fileURL = URL(fileURLWithPath: path, isDirectory: false)
    let error = AudioServicesCreateSystemSoundID(
                    fileURL as CFURL, &soundID)
    if error != kAudioServicesNoError {
      print("Error code \(error) loading sound: \(path)")
    }
  }
}

func unloadSoundEffect() {
  AudioServicesDisposeSystemSoundID(soundID)
  soundID = 0
}

func playSoundEffect() {
  AudioServicesPlaySystemSound(soundID)
}
```

The loadSoundEffect() method loads the sound file and puts it into a new sound object. The specifics don't really matter, but you end up with a reference to that object in the soundID instance variable.

➤ Call loadSoundEffect() from viewDidLoad():

```
loadSoundEffect("Sound.caf")
```

➤ In locationManager(_:didUpdateLocations:), in the geocoder's completion closure, change the following code:

```
if error == nil, let p = placemarks, !p.isEmpty {
  // New code block
  if self.placemark == nil {
    print("FIRST TIME!")
    self.playSoundEffect()
  }
  // End new code
```

```
    self.placemark = p.last!
} else {
    . . .
```

The new `if` statement simply checks whether the `self.placemark` instance variable is `nil`, in which case this is the first time you've reverse geocoded an address. It then plays a sound using the `playSoundEffect()` method.

Of course, you shouldn't forget to add the actual sound effect to the project!

➤ Add the **Sound** folder from this app's Resources to the project. Make sure **Copy items if needed** is selected (click the Options button in the file open panel to reveal this option).

➤ Run the app and see if you can let it make some noise. The sound should only be played for the first address it finds – when you see the FIRST TIME! log message – even if more precise locations keep coming in afterwards.

Note: If you don't hear the sound on the Simulator, try the app on a device. Sometimes system sounds will not play on the simulators.

CAF audio files

The Sound folder contains a single file, **Sound.caf**. The **caf** extension stands for Core Audio Format, and it's the preferred file format for these kinds of short audio files on iOS.

If you want to use your own sound file but it is in a different format than CAF and your audio software can't save CAF files, then you can use the `afconvert` utility to convert the audio file. You need to run it from the Terminal:

```
$ /usr/bin/afconvert -f caff -d LEI16 Sound.wav Sound.caf
```

This converts the Sound.wav file into Sound.caf. You don't need to do this for the audio file from this app's Sound folder because that file is already in the correct format. But if you want to experiment with your own audio files, then knowing how to use `afconvert` might be useful. (By the way, iOS can play .wav files just fine, but .caf is more optimal.)

The icon and launch images

The Resources folder for this app contains an **Icon** folder with the app icons.

➤ Import the icon images into the asset catalog - you can simply drag them from Finder into the **AppIcon** group. It's best to drag them one-by-one into their respective slots (if you drag the whole set of icons into the group at once, Xcode can get confused).

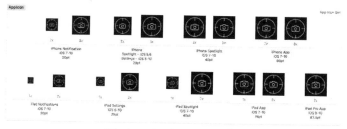

The icons in the asset catalog

The app currently also has a launch file, **LaunchScreen.storyboard**, that provides the splash image for when the app is still loading.

Instead of using a storyboard for the launch screen, you can also supply a set of images. Let's do that for this app.

➤ In the **Project Settings** screen, in the **General** tab, find the **App Icons and Launch Images** section. Click the **Use Asset Catalog** button next to **Launch Images Source**:

Using the asset catalog for launch images

Xcode now asks if you want to migrate the launch images. Click **Migrate**.

➤ Clear the **Launch Screen File** text field.

➤ Also remove **LaunchScreen.storyboard** from the project. It's also a good idea to delete the app from the Simulator, or even reset it, so that there is no trace of the old launch screen.

➤ Open **Assets.xcassets**. There is now a **LaunchImage** item in the list. Select it and go to the Attributes inspector. Under both **iOS 8.0 and Later** and **iOS 7.0 and Later,** put checkmark by **iPhone Portrait**:

Enabling the launch images for iPhone portrait

You should now have four slots for dropping the launch images into. (If you have any slots that say "Unassigned", then select and remove them by pressing the delete key.)

The Resources folder for this app contains a **Launch Images** folder. Let's take a look at one of those images, **Launch Image Retina 4.png**:

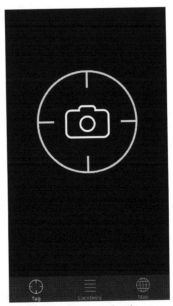

The launch image for this app

The launch image only has the tab bar and the logo button, but no status bar or any buttons. The reason it has no "Get My Location" button is that you don't want users to try and tap it while the app is still loading (it's not really a button!).

To make this launch image, I ran the app in the Simulator and chose **File** → **Save Screen Shot**. This puts a new PNG file on the Desktop. I then opened this image in Photoshop and blanked out any text and the status bar portion of the image. The iPhone will draw its own status bar on top anyway.

➤ Drag the files from the **Launch Images** folder into the asset catalog, one at a time. The slot for each image should be pretty obvious.

Done. That was easy. :-)

And with that, *MyLocations* is complete! Woohoo!

You can find the final project files for the app under **31 - Polishing the App** in the Source Code folder.

The end

Congrats on making it this far! It has been a long and winding road with a lot of theory to boot. I hop you learned a lot of useful stuff.

The final storyboard for *MyLocations* looks like this:

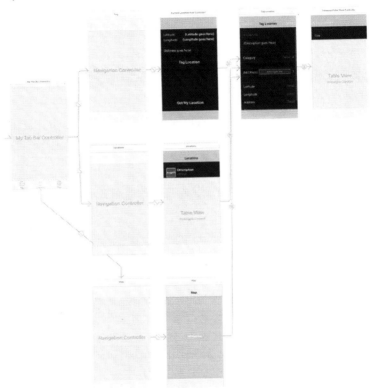

In this lesson you took a more detailed look at Swift, but there's still plenty to discover. To learn more about the Swift programming language, I recommend that you read the following books:

- **The Swift Programming Language** by Apple. This is a free download on the iBooks Store. If you don't want to read the whole thing, at least take the Swift tour. It's a great introduction to the language.

- **Swift Apprentice** by the raywenderlich.com tutorial Team. This is a book that teaches you everything you need to know about Swift, from beginning to advanced topics. This is a sister book to the iOS Appentice; the iOS Apprentice focuses more on making apps, while the Swift Apprentice focuses more on the Swift language itself:

- https://store.raywenderlich.com/products/swift-apprentice

There are several good Core Data beginner books on the market. Here are two recommendations:

- **Core Data by Tutorials** by the raywenderlich.com tutorial Team. One of the few Core Data books that is completely up-to-date with the lastest iOS and Swift versions. This book is for intermediate iOS developers who already know the basics of iOS and Swift development, but want to learn how to use Core Data to save data in their apps. https://store.raywenderlich.com/products/core-data-by-tutorials

- **Core Data Programming Guide** by Apple. If you want to get into the nitty gritty, then Apple's official guide is a must-read. You can learn a ton from this guide. apple.co/2wNgiRu

Credits for this tutorial:

- Sound effect based on a flute sample by elmomo, downloaded from The Freesound Project (freesound.org)

- Image resizing category is based on code by Trevor Harmon (bit.ly/2wNGRX3)

- HudView code is based on MBProgressHud by Matej Bukovinski (github.com/matej/MBProgressHUD)

Are you ready for the final app? Then continue on to the next chapter, where you'll make an app that communicates with a web service over the network!